Juvenile Delinquency

Juvenile Delinquency
Causes and Control
THIRD EDITION

ROBERT AGNEW

Emory University

New York   Oxford
OXFORD UNIVERSITY PRESS
2009

Oxford University Press, Inc., publishes works that further Oxford University's
objective of excellence in research, scholarship, and education.

Oxford   New York
Auckland   Cape Town   Dar es Salaam   Hong Kong   Karachi
Kuala Lumpur   Madrid   Melbourne   Mexico City   Nairobi
New Delhi   Shanghai   Taipei   Toronto

With offices in
Argentina   Austria   Brazil   Chile   Czech Republic   France   Greece
Guatemala   Hungary   Italy   Japan   Poland   Portugal   Singapore
South Korea   Switzerland   Thailand   Turkey   Ukraine   Vietnam

Copyright © 2009 by Oxford University Press, Inc.

Published by Oxford University Press, Inc.
198 Madison Avenue, New York, New York 10016
http://www.oup.com

Oxford is a registered trademark of Oxford University Press

Library of Congress Cataloging-in-Publication Data
Agnew, Robert, 1953–
    Juvenile delinquency: causes and control/Robert Agnew. —3rd ed.
        p. cm
    Includes bibliographical references and index.
    ISBN 978-0-19-537113-0 (alk. paper)
    1. Juvenile delinquency.   I. Title.
    HV9069.A55   2009
    364.36—dc22

                                                      2008022177

Printing number: 9 8 7 6 5 4 3 2

Printed in the United States of America
on acid-free paper

Contents

PART 2
The Causes of Delinquency: Theories 83

5 What Is a Theory and How Do We Test Theories? 87

6 Strain Theory: Does Strain or Stress Cause Delinquency? 104

10 The Life Course: How Do We Explain Different Patterns of Offending over the Course of a Lifetime?   162

11 Is Delinquency More Likely in Certain Types of Situations?   175

12 Group Differences in Delinquency: How Can We Explain Group Differences, Particularly Community Differences in Rates of Delinquency?   189

PART 3
The Causes of Delinquency: Research   209

18 Pulling It All Together: Is It Possible to Construct a General Theory of Delinquency? 292

PART 4
The Control and Prevention of Delinquency 309

An Important Message for Instructors

Criminologists often complain about the limited impact of criminology on public perceptions and crime control policy. I believe that a major reason for this limited impact lies with our introductory textbooks. Our texts are perhaps the major way in which we communicate with the larger community. Yet, with a few notable exceptions, they do not provide students with a clear sense of what causes delinquency and what can be done to control delinquency. Rather, our texts tend to overwhelm and confuse students. Students get lost in all the theories of delinquency that are presented; they have trouble drawing conclusions from the discussions of empirical research, since contradictory studies are often described, with little effort to sort between them; and they are not provided with a good overview of the most promising approaches to delinquency control and prevention. If we were to ask the readers of such texts why juveniles engage in delinquency or what should be done to control delinquency, I venture to say that most would respond with blank stares or jumbled answers.

This book is very different from most delinquency texts now on the market, and those differences are described next.

Shorter and More Focused

First, the book is shorter and more focused than current texts. The dominant texts attempt to cover all the major research on delinquency, and they are often 500 pages or more in length. This text does not attempt to cover all major areas in the field. Rather, it devotes serious attention to what I consider to be the three major questions in the field: What is the nature and extent of delinquency? What are the causes of delinquency? What strategies should we employ to control delinquency? Students reading this text should be able to give reasonable answers to these questions. I am not sure that this is the case with many current texts.

At the same time, you may feel that this text does not devote adequate attention to certain topics. But the shortness and relatively low cost of this text make it easy for you to cover whatever additional topics you like with supplemental readings. In fact, I encourage this approach. I believe that it is important for students to read articles and paperbacks that describe original research and discuss particular issues in detail. There are many wonderful articles and books on delinquency, like *Code of the Street* by Anderson (1999) and *The Saints and the Roughnecks* by Chambliss (1973). I think it would be unfortunate for students to take a delinquency course without being exposed to these materials. And I believe that this view is becoming more common, as reflected in the increased number of delinquency readers and "companion" texts being offered by publishers.

More Synthetic Approach to Delinquency Theory and Research

Second, this text differs from most current texts in that it employs a more "synthetic" approach to delinquency theory and research. Most texts spend a great deal of time describing delinquency theories and research but make little effort to synthesize such theory and research. For example, they describe (often superficially) the four or five different versions of strain theory that now dominate the literature. They also describe the research on each of these versions of strain theory, noting both supportive and nonsupportive studies. They do not, however, attempt to draw on this theory and research in order to develop an up-to-date, comprehensive version of strain theory. Students reading such texts get caught up in trying to memorize all the different versions of strain theory (and other theories) and the mixed evidence on these versions. They come away confused and overwhelmed. Unlike virtually all other texts, my text does not describe the different versions of all the major delinquency theories. Rather, I attempt to synthesize the best of the current delinquency theories into a set of four "generic" theories: a strain-based theory, a social learning theory, a control-based theory, and a labeling-based theory. Since these generic theories represent a synthesis of the best of current theory and research, my empirical assessments of them are somewhat more optimistic than those found in other textbooks. This synthetic approach also saves much space, since current texts devote much coverage to the different versions of the major delinquency theories as well as to the history of delinquency theories.

After presenting these four generic theories, I devote several chapters to the major research on the causes of delinquency, including the research on individual traits, family factors, school experiences, and delinquent peer groups and gangs. I make a special effort to state, in a clear, concise manner, the major conclusions that can be drawn from these different areas of research. At the same time, I make note of problems in the research, and I attempt to sort through contradictory studies where necessary. The final section of the book provides an overview of the police, juvenile courts, and juvenile corrections. It then discusses four general strategies for controlling delinquency: deterrence, incapacitation, prevention, and rehabilitation. I describe the evidence on the effectiveness of these strategies and discuss ways to increase their effectiveness. While I give examples of successful programs and policies in these areas, my major focus is on describing the general features of those programs and policies that appear most successful.

Many instructors may object to this synthetic approach, especially as it applies to delinquency theories. I do not explicitly discuss certain popular theories. The four theories I present, however, dominate the delinquency literature, and I believe that they capture the essential ideas of most other theories. In particular, my discussion of these four theories presents the major arguments associated with rational choice, routine activities, self-control, life-course, social disorganization, subcultural deviance, and certain aspects of conflict and feminist theories. To give a few examples, I describe how these theories explain patterns of offending over the life course, and in doing so I present the essential ideas from the leading theories of crime and the life course. I describe how these theories explain why crime is more likely in some situations than others, and in doing so I present the essential ideas of rational choice and routine activities theories. And I describe how these theories explain why some communities have higher rates of delinquency than others, and in doing so I present the essential ideas of social disorganization, subcultural deviance, and macro-strain theories. Like Bernard and Snipes (1996) and others, I believe that there are too many theories in criminology. I think that the essential ideas of most theories can be presented in terms of the four generic theories, making life much simpler for students and researchers and making criminology more useful for policy makers.

More Student (and Instructor) Friendly

Third, I have done several things to make this text more student (and instructor) friendly. Unlike most other texts, this book is organized around questions rather than topics. For example, instead of a section on "the sociodemographic correlates of delinquency," there is a section on "who is most likely to engage in delinquency?" Students find questions more interesting than topics; questions invite students to become more actively involved in the learning process, and questions better convey what the research process is about—answering questions that researchers feel are interesting and important (see Goldsmid and Wilson, 1980). The subheadings under each question essentially form a sentence outline of the book. Students, then, can gain a quick overview of each chapter and section before reading it, and they can easily review the major points of each chapter/section after reading it.

The book also has a common theme: using the four delinquency theories to understand the basic facts about delinquency, to interpret the research on the causes of delinquency, and to evaluate and develop policies for the control of delinquency. For example, I stress that much of the research on delinquency was inspired by the four theories discussed and that all of the research is interpretable in terms of these theories. To illustrate, the biopsychological research describes several traits that are conducive to crime, such as impulsivity and irritability. I stress that the effect of these traits on crime can be explained in terms of the four theories: Such traits increase strain, reduce concern for the costs of crime, make crime seem more rewarding, and increase the likelihood of negative labeling. This common theme helps students master the material, since the book comes across as an integrated whole rather than a series of discrete facts. Chapters build on one another (although they can also stand on their own), and certain points are reemphasized throughout the text.

The book is also written in a more informal, conversational style than that found in most texts. I believe this style makes the book more interesting and accessible to students. Further, the book is divided into 25 relatively short chapters, each focusing on a discrete topic, which makes it easier for instructors to assign readings. With other texts, instructors frequently end up assigning portions of a chapter (e.g., they assign the four and a half pages of a chapter that deal with strain theory). Students should also appreciate the fact that the chapters are shorter and generally more coherent than those found in many other texts.

Finally, each chapter contains several Teaching Aids, including student exercises or controversial cases for students to consider, questions designed to test students' knowledge of the chapter, a list of Key Terms, and questions designed to encourage independent thinking and foster discussion. Many of these Teaching Aids can form the basis for classroom activities and discussions. (Additional suggestions for class activities and lectures are contained in the *Instructor's Manual* that accompanies this text.)

Having said all this, I should note that this book does not contain a lot of pictures or tables and figures. These features are nice, but I avoid them for two reasons. First, I want to keep the cost of the book as low as possible. In my experience, students prefer a cheaper textbook to one with a lot of pictures. Second, many students ignore tables and figures, and many others are overwhelmed by them. Rather than presenting students with a lot of numbers, I prefer to stress the essential points that these numbers are designed to convey.

Promotes Active Learning

Fourth, my text attempts to promote active learning, especially the application of text materials. Most notably, students are provided with numerous examples of how one might use the major theories of delinquency to explain the basic facts about delinquency, to understand the research on the causes of delinquency, and to develop and evaluate programs and policies for controlling delinquency. Also, students are frequently asked to engage in such applications themselves. Students are also asked to apply the text materials to their own lives. In particular, I regularly pose questions for students throughout the text. And I do the same at the end of each chapter, in the sections titled "Teaching Aids." This emphasis on the application of text materials is crucial in my view: It dramatically increases the students' understanding of the materials, and the materials are of little use unless students develop the ability to apply them.

Further, the text not only describes what criminologists know about delinquency, it also gives students a sense of *how* criminologists know what they know, that is, how criminologists collect and analyze data. In particular, I spend much time discussing how criminologists measure delinquency, how they test theories—especially how they determine whether one variable causes another—and how they determine whether a program or policy is effective in controlling delinquency. Students, then, are not asked to accept the findings of criminology on faith. They are given a sense of what the research process is like. I frequently apply these materials, pointing to problems in research studies and discussing the need for further research in certain areas. Further, I ask the students to apply these materials.

I Appreciate Your Feedback

I am most interested in receiving your impressions of the text, including things that you like and do not like (e.g., topics that I should devote more coverage to, sections that are unclear or too "dry," statements that you disagree with, literature that I should have cited, etc.). I will consider your comments carefully when revising the text. Please e-mail me at bagnew@emory.edu or write to me at the Department of Sociology, Emory University, Atlanta, GA 30322.

An Overview of This Book

The media are regularly filled with reports about juvenile crime. As I was finishing my revisions on this book, there was a media report of three teenagers who set a homeless man on fire. According to the report, "[T]hree teenage boys approached [the homeless man] as he was lying on cardboard just outside the gates of the brown brick and cement church [in New York City]. One boy touched a lighter to [the man's pants], the police said, and another rifled his pockets. . . . [A]s he stood up, the flames on his legs traveled quickly up and engulfed his entire body. . . . He was listed in critical condition . . . with second- and third-degree burns on his face, chest, arms and abdomen, the police said, and had burns over roughly 75 percent of his body" (*New York Times*, 2007b). This case and other incidents have led people throughout the country to ask a number of fundamental questions about juvenile delinquency: How common is juvenile delinquency? Is it increasing? Who is most likely to commit delinquent acts? What are the causes of juvenile delinquency? What can be done to control or prevent delinquency? These are the questions addressed in this book.

The book has four sections. The four chapters in the first section focus on the *Nature and Extent of Delinquency*. These chapters deal with the "basic facts" about delinquency, such as: What is delinquency? How much delinquency is there? Is delinquency increasing? And who is most likely to commit delinquent acts?

The eight chapters in the second section focus on the major *theories* or explanations of the *Causes of Delinquency*. These chapters describe the four leading theories, or explanations, of delinquency. These theories are used to explain why some juveniles are more likely than others to engage in delinquency; why some offenders engage in crime at high rates over much of their lives while others limit their offending to the adolescent years; why delinquency is more likely in some situations than others; and why some groups have higher rates of delinquency than other groups.

The six chapters in the third section focus on the *research* dealing with the *Causes of Delinquency*. Much of this research was designed to test the theories described in the second section. This research examines the extent to which delinquency is caused by individual traits (e.g., low intelligence, low self-control), family factors (e.g., broken homes, poor supervision), school factors, delinquent peers and gang membership, and a range of other factors, such as the mass media, religion, drugs, and guns. The concluding chapter in this section draws on this research and the leading delinquency theories to present an integrated or general theory of delinquency. This theory is used to explain many of the basic facts about delinquency presented in the first section, such as the fact that some juveniles are more delinquent than others and that males are more delinquent than females.

The seven chapters in the final section focus on the *Control and Prevention of Delinquency*. These chapters describe what the police, juvenile courts, and juvenile correctional agencies do to control delinquency. In particular, they describe how these agencies operate, how effective they are, what they might do to be more effective, and the extent to which they discriminate against certain groups in their efforts to control delinquency. These chapters then describe four general strategies for controlling delinquency that involve all of these agencies as well as other groups: the "get-tough" strategies of deterrence and incapacitation, and the strategies of rehabilitation and prevention. These strategies address many of the causes of delinquency described in the second and third sections.

I should note that this book does more than simply describe the major research on juvenile delinquency. It also describes how this research was carried out. That is, it describes how criminologists do such things as estimate the extent of delinquency, determine whether some factor causes delinquency, and determine whether some program or policy is effective at reducing delinquency. This information will not only increase your understanding of the delinquency research but also better enable you to evaluate the statements you hear about delinquency (and other topics) from friends, family, the media, politicians, and others. Furthermore, this book encourages you to apply the delinquency research. It encourages you, for example, to use the leading theories of delinquency to explain the basic facts about delinquency and to evaluate programs for reducing delinquency. It also encourages you to apply the delinquency research to your own lives and to issues in the larger community.

I hope you find this book useful, and I am most interested in hearing any comments you might have about it—including suggestions for improving the next edition. You can e-mail me at bagnew@emory.edu or write to me at the Department of Sociology, Emory University, Atlanta, GA 30322.

Acknowledgments

I would like to thank several people for their help in preparing this book. They include Ron Akers and Gary Jensen, who encouraged me to write the book and provided much useful feedback. Claude Teweles, who gave me the time and freedom to write the type of book I wanted. Frank Cullen, a valued friend and colleague, who has taught me much about crime and its control. Everett K. Wilson, whose ideas about teaching have had a tremendous influence on this book. The students in my juvenile delinquency classes. Several additional individuals who provided valuable comments on all or portions of the book: Charles Amissah, Candice Batton, Thomas J. Bernard, Patricia Brennan, Scott Decker, Michael Dindinger, Finn-Aage Esbensen, Joseph R. Franco, Stephanie Funk, Hua-Lun Huang, Michele Hussong, Marvin Krohn, David Mackey, David L. Myers, Judge Robin Nash, Dean Rojek, Joseph Sanborn, Frank Scarpitti, Randall Shelden, Sandra S. Stone, Sherod Thaxton, Charles M. ViVona, and Richard A. Wright. And my wife, Mary, and children Willie and Jenny. Mary provided the support and encouragement necessary to write this book, while Willie and Jenny provided the inspiration.

The Nature
and Extent
of Delinquency

CHAPTER 1

What Is Delinquency and How Does It Differ from Adult Crime?

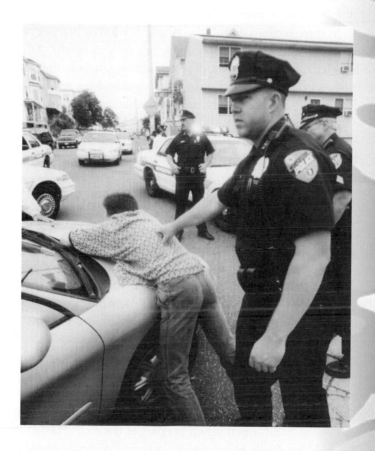

"What is delinquency?" is a relatively easy question to answer. *Juvenile delinquency* **refers to violations of the criminal law by minors.** In most states, a minor is anyone under the age of 18. In some states, however, minors are defined as anyone under the age of 17 or even 16. So if a minor commits an act that would be a crime when committed by an adult, that minor has engaged in "juvenile delinquency" and may be considered a "juvenile delinquent." This definition, while correct, might lead you to believe that the only way delinquency differs from adult crime is in terms of age. Delinquent acts are committed by minors while crimes are committed by adults.

But juvenile delinquency differs from adult crime in a number of major ways besides the age of the offender. In particular, we tend to view juvenile delinquents differently than adult criminals, and we tend to treat juvenile delinquents differently than adult criminals—with an important exception that I will note. When I say "we," I refer to both the general public and the juvenile justice system.

This chapter is in three sections. First, I describe how we view juvenile delinquents differently than adult criminals. Second, I describe how our different views of delinquents and adult criminals have led us to treat them differently. I note, however, that there has been a recent trend to view and treat juvenile offenders—especially older, serious offenders—like adult criminals. Finally, I discuss the "invention" of juvenile delinquency. People did not always view and treat juvenile delinquents differently than adult criminals. For most of history, in fact, juveniles who broke the law were viewed and treated very much like adults who broke the law. I briefly discuss some of the factors that led society to view and treat juvenile delinquents differently.

We View Juvenile Delinquents Differently than Adult Criminals

On the first day of my juvenile delinquency class I play a trick on my students. I pass out a description of a crime that has occurred: Someone walks into a bank, points a gun at a teller, and demands money. It is a toy gun, but the teller believes it is real and gives the bank robber several hundred dollars. The robber later spends most of the money on luxury items before being caught. I ask the students what the court should do to this robber. Unbeknownst to the students, the robber is described as a "7-year-old boy" in half the descriptions and a "32-year-old man" in the other half (the actual crime was committed by a 7-year-old boy).

After the students have considered the case for a few minutes, I ask for volunteers to tell me what they think should be done to the "bank robber." Some of the students describe what might be considered "mild" reactions on the part of the court: The robber should receive counseling, should be closely monitored for a period of time, should perform some community service, or the like. Other students describe what might be considered "tough" reactions on the part of the court; most commonly, they state that the robber should be locked up for several years. The students, of course, are confused by the responses of many of their classmates. Those with the 7-year-old robber wonder how some of their classmates could be so coldhearted as to recommend years of imprisonment, while those with the 32-year-old robber think some of their classmates are far too "soft" on crime.

I eventually tell the students that they are working with two different case studies and that this age discrepancy is the major reason for their different reactions. I then try to justify the trick I have played by telling the students that their different reactions to the 7- and

32-year-old robbers illustrate a very important point about juvenile delinquency: **We tend to view juvenile delinquents differently than adult criminals.**

If a juvenile breaks the law, we generally view that person as immature and in need of our guidance and help. There is no precise definition of *immaturity*, but notions of immaturity usually include one or more of the following: The individuals did not know that what they were doing was wrong; they did not appreciate the harm that their actions might cause; they could not control themselves; and they were easily led astray by others. (Data suggest that juveniles are more likely than adults to possess these traits, although there is no precise age at which individuals become "mature."[1] Rather, individuals mature in a gradual manner and at different rates—although juveniles are less mature on average than adults.)

This immaturity partly stems from a lack of experience. Older juveniles are no longer closely supervised by parents, and they must increasingly learn to make decisions on their own. They lack experience at decision making, however, and so it is not surprising that they sometimes show poor judgment in the choices they make (see Zimring, 2005). This immaturity also has biological roots. A colleague of mine at Emory recently coedited a book that focuses on the development of the adolescent brain (Walker and Romer, 2006). A central message of the book is that the "brain circuitry for pleasure and sensation develops rapidly during adolescence, while the brain circuitry responsible for behavioral control and inhibition lags behind" (Clark, 2007:6). As a consequence, adolescents have more trouble exercising self-control and resisting the influence of peers.

Given this view of juveniles as immature, most people tend to feel that juveniles do not deserve serious punishment. Rather, they need our help. So when a 7-year-old robs a bank, many students state that the major response of the court should be to provide that person with counseling. **But if an adult breaks the law, we generally view that person as someone who is responsible for his or her behavior and deserves to be punished.** So most students have no qualms about sending a 32-year-old who robbed a bank to prison for many years.

Many students take exception when I characterize juveniles in this way. They state that many juvenile offenders know exactly what they are doing and that these offenders should be punished just as severely as adults. They often describe some horrifying crime committed in the recent past by a juvenile, and they state that this juvenile surely deserves the most serious punishment the law can provide.

I realize that many people feel this way. Certain juvenile offenders—especially older juveniles who commit serious crimes—are not viewed as all that different from adult offenders. And the justice system is starting to treat these offenders like adult criminals. So when I say that we view juvenile delinquents differently than adult criminals, an important exception should be noted. We often view older, serious juvenile offenders like adult offenders. I will talk more about this exception shortly. Aside from this important exception, we still tend to view juvenile delinquents differently than adult criminals. I provide my students with a few additional examples to illustrate this point.

There is the case of a 6-year-old girl in Florida who got into a fight with her 7-year-old friend. The 6-year-old girl repeatedly hit her 7-year-old friend with a piece of wood, while an older boy held the 7-year-old's arms behind her back. The 7-year-old's nose was damaged and her dress was soaked with blood by the time she arrived home to her mother. Her mother, of course, was outraged and immediately called the police. For legal reasons that I will not describe, there was some discussion of trying the 6-year-old girl as an adult. If tried as an adult, she would face a maximum penalty of fifteen years in prison and a $10,000 fine. This story made the national news, and people were outraged that such a young girl might be so severely penalized. They felt that the 6-year-old did not know what she was doing and that she needed guidance and help much more than punishment. Imagine the reaction, however, if a 30-year-old woman had committed this crime. People would be demanding the severest of penalties.

To give another example, a 6-year-old boy in California was charged with savagely beating a month-old baby. He was accused of kicking, punching, and beating the sleeping baby with a stick, possibly causing permanent brain damage. The 6-year-old was said to have done this to seek revenge against the family of the baby for allegedly harassing him. I asked the students in my class how the court should respond to this boy. This is a savage crime, but the young age of the boy led many in the class to talk of his immaturity and to argue that he is in desperate need of guidance and help. Again, imagine the difference in reaction if a 30-year-old man were charged with this crime.

With the exception of older juveniles who commit serious crimes, we clearly tend to view juvenile delinquents differently than adult criminals. We view juvenile delinquents as immature and in need of guidance and help, while we view adult criminals as fully responsible for their behavior and deserving of punishment. To illustrate, one national poll found that only 21 percent of the public said that rehabilitation should be the most important sentencing goal for adults, but 50 percent said that it should be the most important sentencing goal for juveniles.[2]

We Treat Juvenile Delinquents Differently than Adult Criminals

The difference in the way we view juvenile and adult offenders has led us to treat juvenile delinquents differently than adult criminals (with an important exception, to be noted). In particular, we have created a special set of laws that apply just to juveniles in order to more closely regulate their lives. We have created a special court for juvenile offenders, a court that places more emphasis on rehabilitation and less on punishment than does adult criminal court. And we have created special correctional programs for juveniles, programs that also focus more on rehabilitation and less on punishment—at least in theory.[3]

Special Laws for Juveniles: Status Offenses

Juveniles are delinquent if they commit any act whose violation by an adult would be a crime—acts like homicide, assault, rape, robbery, burglary, and larceny. However, in most states juveniles can be arrested and referred to juvenile court for certain acts that are legal for adults. These acts are called *status offenses,* since they apply only to people with the status of juvenile.

The most common status offenses are running away from home, failure to attend school (truancy), refusing to obey parents (incorrigibility), drinking alcoholic beverages, violating curfew, and engaging in certain consensual sexual activities. These activities are illegal for juveniles in all or many areas, but they are legal for adults; for example, it is illegal for juveniles to stop attending school. They can be arrested and taken to juvenile court in most states if they do so. It is perfectly legal for you, however, to stop coming to class.

The state felt that it was necessary to regulate the lives of juveniles more closely than the lives of adults. Rather than intervening only when juveniles committed a crime, the state felt it necessary to intervene when juveniles gave indications that they might be heading down the "wrong path"—a path that might lead to crime. Status offense laws, then, are directly tied to the view of juveniles as immature and in need of guidance or direction.

These status offense laws were **taken quite seriously until the late 1960s and early 1970s.** Juveniles who committed status offenses were frequently arrested and referred to juvenile court. They were often formally processed by the court, and they could be "adjudicated," or judged, "delinquent" by juvenile courts in nearly every state. And status offenders were sometimes subject to severe punishments. In particular, about half the juveniles in correctional institutions were there for status offenses like running away and being incorrigible. Status offense laws were especially likely to be enforced against females. Females were (and are) more closely supervised than males, and their sexual behavior, in particular, is more closely regulated. Females who committed status offenses like disobeying parents, running away from home, drinking, and having sex were more likely than boys to be arrested, referred to the court, and sent to institutions for such offenses. There is some evidence that this is still the case today (see Chapter 22 for a fuller discussion).

Status offense laws **came under heavy criticism during the 1960s and 1970s.** They were **often vague.** What, for example, does it mean to be incorrigible? Virtually all juveniles disobey their parents at some point. Also, these laws **often subjected juveniles who had not committed any criminal acts to severe penalties,** such as confinement in an institution (where they were exposed to serious offenders and sometimes subject to physical and sexual assault). Further, there was evidence that **poor, minority, and female juveniles were more likely to be punished for such offenses.**

In response to such criticisms, most states developed "diversion" programs designed to divert status offenders from the juvenile court. Rather than being formally processed by the court, most status offenders were dealt with informally by the court or were referred to special programs outside the court. Status offenders who were processed by the juvenile court were **no longer classified as "delinquents" in most states.** Rather, they were classified as Children in Need of Supervision (CHINS), Persons in Need of Supervision (PINS), or similar labels. This new designation was partly designed to reduce the stigma of a delinquent label. The federal government passed a law in 1974 that **strongly encouraged states to stop placing status offenders in institutions.** And evidence suggests that this law was largely effective: There has been a dramatic decline in the number of status offenders confined in institutions. Finally, a few states went so far as to **decriminalize status offenses.** Status offenses could no longer result in arrest and referral to the juvenile court; rather, status offenses were dealt with by social service agencies.

Nevertheless, status offenses are **still illegal in almost all states.** Several hundred thousand status offenders are arrested each year, and tens of thousands are formally processed by the juvenile court (precise estimates are not available). As indicated in Chapter 21, some status offenders still get confined in institutions. So while status offenses are not treated as severely today as in the past, they are still taken seriously in many cases.

A Special Court for Juveniles: Juvenile Court

Every state has created special courts for juvenile offenders. *Juvenile court* differs from adult court in several fundamental ways, with the differences between the two courts reflecting our different views of juvenile delinquents and adult criminals. The differences between juvenile court and adult court have diminished in recent years, but they are still substantial.

First, the **goals of juvenile court are different from those of adult court.** Adult court determines whether individuals are guilty of committing specific crimes and then punishes them if they are. Juvenile court was set up **not to punish juveniles but rather to guide and help them.** The court was supposed to act in "the best interests" of juveniles, providing them with the guidance and help that their parents should have provided. The court, in fact, was supposed to play the role of "superparent," assisting children whose parents had failed them. Judge Julian Mack, who helped develop the first juvenile court in the United States, said that the juvenile court should treat delinquents like "a wise and merciful father handles his own child" and that the goal of the court is "not so much as to punish as to reform, not to degrade but to uplift, not to crush but to develop, [and] not to make [the delinquent] a criminal but a worthy citizen" (quoted in Singer, 2001:350). The goals of many juvenile courts have changed in recent years, with more courts coming to place an increased emphasis on punishing juveniles—especially older, serious offenders. Nevertheless, the juvenile court still places more emphasis on the goal of rehabilitation than does adult court. (This is not to say that the court always accomplishes or even tries to accomplish the goal of rehabilitation. As discussed later, there is often a large gap between goals and accomplishments.)

Second, the juvenile court **focuses more on the offender than on the offense.** Adult court focuses primarily on the offense(s) that the individual has committed. The punishment that individuals receive is based largely on their current and past offenses. Juvenile court is less concerned about punishing individuals for the specific offenses they have committed. Rather, it seeks to help juveniles. The court therefore focuses on the entire juvenile—not just the offense(s) that brought the juvenile to court. The court seeks to learn all it can about the juvenile, especially any personal, family, school, peer, or other problems the juvenile may have. And the actions that the court takes are supposed to address these problems—not simply respond to the juvenile's specific offense(s). Again, some changes are taking place in this area, with many juvenile courts putting more emphasis on the specific offenses that juveniles have committed and basing their response to juveniles largely on these offenses. Even so, there is still a substantial difference between juvenile and adult courts in this area.

Third, the juvenile court is **more informal and less adversarial than adult court.** Adult court provides accused individuals with numerous *due process rights* designed to protect them from being unfairly punished. These rights include the right to be represented by an attorney, the right to confront and cross-examine the witnesses against you, the right to proof beyond a reasonable doubt, and the right to a trial by jury. As a consequence of such rights, adult court is very formal and it is adversarial in nature—at least in theory. The prosecution and defense attorneys are pitted against one another, arguing their cases before a judge or jury. The juvenile court, however, initially provided juveniles with few due process rights. It was felt that such rights were unnecessary since the court sought to help rather than punish juveniles. Juveniles, then, did not need protection from unfair punishment. As a consequence, the juvenile court was more informal and less adversarial than adult court. Juveniles, for example, were not represented by attorneys. Often, the judge would simply talk with the juvenile—much like parents having a firm talk with their child. The judge might also question the police, witnesses, and others.

This informality has changed since the 1960s. In particular, a series of **Supreme Court decisions have granted juveniles most—although not all—of the due process rights available to adults.** The Supreme Court essentially argued that the juvenile court often fails to help the juveniles it processes and it often does punish them. They are sometimes confined in institutions, for example. They therefore deserve at least some of the due process protections available to adults. So juveniles now have such rights as the right to be represented by an attorney and to confront and cross-examine witnesses (see Chapter 21 for a fuller discussion). Juvenile court is now more formal and adversarial than it once was. But juveniles do not have all the rights available to adults; most notably, they lack the right to a trial by jury. Further, juveniles frequently waive their rights—sometimes with the encouragement of the juvenile court. In many courts, for example, less than half the juveniles are represented by an attorney. So while juvenile court has changed a great deal in recent decades, it is still less formal and adversarial than adult court—a difference that reflects the difference in goals between juvenile and adult court.

There are **still other differences between juvenile and adult court.** There are **differences in the terminology employed.** In juvenile court, the juvenile is not found "guilty" of a particular offense like robbery or burglary. The word "guilt" implies responsibility. Rather, the juvenile is *adjudicated* a "delinquent," regardless of the particular criminal offense(s) he or she committed. (In the case of status offenses, the juvenile is adjudicated a "Person in Need of Supervision" or whatever the label is for status offenders in that court.) Once adjudicated, the judge does not "sentence" the juvenile. A sentence implies punishment. Rather, the judge renders his or her *disposition.*

Juvenile court hearings are **usually closed to the public and the media to protect the juvenile from adverse publicity and stigma.** Likewise, juvenile court records are usually unavailable to the public and media. Further, juveniles are often able to "seal," or erase, their juvenile court records if they stay out of trouble for a certain period of time. These policies are beginning to change; the public and media are being given greater access to juvenile court hearings and records. Nevertheless, the privacy of juvenile offenders receives much more protection than that of adult offenders. Adult court hearings are open to the public, adult court records are available to the public, and adult court records remain for life except under certain very special circumstances. The juvenile court tends to view delinquent acts as the mistakes of immature children, and it wants to minimize the damage that might result from such mistakes. One way to do this is to protect the privacy of juvenile offenders and allow them to "erase" their records in certain cases.

There are also **differences in the sentences given out by juvenile and adult courts.** In particular, juvenile courts cannot impose the death penalty, and there are limits as to how long juvenile courts can confine juveniles. Most juvenile courts cannot confine juveniles beyond their 21st birthday. This age limit often angers people because it means that juveniles who commit serious crimes cannot be confined for more than a few years (unless they are transferred to adult court). This age limit, however, is beginning to change as a number of states make it possible for juvenile court judges to confine juveniles for longer periods (and make it easier to try certain juvenile offenders as adults). Nevertheless, the sentences given out by juvenile courts are generally milder than those imposed by adult courts. There are still other differences between juvenile and adult court, and excellent summaries can be found in Bernard (1992) and Snyder and Sickmund (2006).

Special Correctional Programs for Juveniles

Finally, the **view of juveniles as immature creatures in need of guidance and help has led us to develop special correctional programs for them.** Juvenile correctional institutions protect juveniles from contact with adult criminals, who might exploit and corrupt them. And these institutions are more concerned with rehabilitation than with punishment. Unfortunately, juvenile institutions often do not live up to their stated aim of rehabilitation. Again, there is often a large gap between goals and accomplishments. Nevertheless, juvenile institutions place more stress on the goal of rehabilitation than do adult institutions. Juvenile institutions are not called "prisons" rather, they are called *youth development centers* or *training schools* or similar names that reflect their supposed emphasis on rehabilitation. A range of community-based programs designed to rehabilitate juveniles has also been developed. This is not to say that there is no concern with the rehabilitation of adult offenders, but rather that rehabilitation is a greater concern in the juvenile justice system.

In sum, the general public and the justice system tend to view most juvenile delinquents differently than adult criminals and tend to treat them differently as a result. As noted, however, our view of delinquents—especially older, serious offenders—is changing. And related to this, our treatment of delinquents—especially older, serious offenders—is starting to resemble our treatment of adult criminals.

Older, Serious Juvenile Offenders as an Exception

I earlier provided several examples of juvenile offending—a 7-year-old boy who robbed a bank, a 6-year-old girl who assaulted someone, and a 6-year-old boy who seriously assaulted an infant—and I asked how you would respond to these crimes. My examples, however, were carefully chosen. They were designed to get you to think about the immaturity of juveniles and their need for guidance and help. Let me next provide you with two additional examples of juvenile offending.

A husband, wife, and their two young children were driving home one evening. They stopped at a convenience store in a crime-ridden neighborhood to buy a soda. The wife got out of the car to purchase the soda, while the husband and children remained in the car with the engine running and lights on. The parking lot adjacent to the store was a popular location for drug sellers. A 13-year-old known in the neighborhood as "Little B" approached the husband and told him to turn off his car lights (which were illuminating the drug market). The husband refused. Little B felt that he had been "disrespected" in front of the older drug dealers. He got a rifle that he had hidden nearby and fired two shots into the car. The husband was killed in front of his two children. According to witnesses, Little B exclaimed that "This is still New Jack City!" referring to a movie about violent drug gangs.

My second example occurred one month after two juveniles shot 13 other people to death at Columbine High School in Colorado. A 15-year-old juvenile entered the commons area at Heritage High School in Conyers, Georgia. The juvenile was carrying a 22-caliber sawed-off rifle, and he started shooting into a crowd of between 150 and 200 students. He hit six of the students, although none died. He ran out of the school. Two of his classmates chased him. He pulled out a .357 magnum handgun and fired at them but missed both. A letter was later found under the juvenile's bed. Part of it read:

> The one big question everybody is probably wondering is, Why? Well, for the sake of my brothers and sisters related to the Trenchcoat Mafia, that will have to remain a mystery to the public eye. I have been planning this for years, but I finally got pissed off enough to really do it (Stafford, 1999). (Note: The juveniles who killed thirteen others at Columbine High School were said to be part of a group known as the "Trenchcoat Mafia.")

These two juveniles elicited a different reaction from the community and juvenile justice system than the juvenile offenders described earlier. With isolated exceptions, there was little talk of their immaturity and the need to guide and help them. Little B, in fact, was described in the media and by politicians as a "thug" and an "evil" in the city, among other things. Most people were outraged at the horrible crime he had committed and demanded that he be severely punished. Little B was tried as an adult and sentenced to life in prison. He will be eligible for parole in 14 years. The second juvenile was also tried as an adult and is now serving a 20-year term in prison; he will be eligible for parole when he is 33 years old.

These case studies illustrate an important point about the changing nature of juvenile delinquency: **We are starting to view and treat older juveniles who commit serious crimes like adult offenders.** There was a dramatic increase in serious juvenile violence from the late 1980s to the mid-1990s. Further, many of the violent crimes committed by juveniles received massive publicity, like the shooting deaths that occurred at several schools throughout the United States. Many people came to feel that this violence was not the work of "immature" juveniles who needed guidance and direction but rather the work of "younger criminals" and "stone cold predators."[4] Also, many people came to feel that the juvenile court was not equipped to deal with such violence. In particular, they came to feel that such juveniles should be treated and punished like adults.[5] In a 2003 national survey, for example, 59 percent of respondents agreed that "juveniles between the ages of 14 and 17 who commit violent crimes should be treated the same as adults in the criminal justice system" (Pastore and Maguire, 2007).

As a consequence, there has been a major movement in recent years to punish more severely older juveniles who commit serious crimes. Part of this movement has focused on increasing the severity of the punishments administered by the juvenile court, but its major thrust has focused on making it easier to try older juveniles who commit serious crimes in adult court. These issues are discussed more fully in Chapter 23.[6] I simply want to emphasize the point that there is an important exception to my statement that we view and treat juvenile delinquents differently than adult criminals.

How Can We Explain the Invention of Juvenile Delinquency?

It may sound strange to speak of the *invention of juvenile delinquency*. I do not mean to imply that juveniles did not commit delinquent acts in the past. Juveniles have always committed those acts we now label as "delinquent" and "status" offenses. In fact, there is reason to believe that some of these acts, such as fighting, drinking alcohol, and engaging in sex, were much more common at certain points in the past than they are today (see Empey et al., 1999).

When I speak of the invention of juvenile delinquency, I refer to the special way that we view and treat juvenile delinquents. As discussed in the preceding pages, we tend to view delinquents as immature and in need of guidance and help. And we tend to treat juvenile offenders differently: They are subject to a special set of laws that apply only to juveniles, they are sent to a special court, and they are placed in special correctional programs. Compared to adult criminals, we place much more emphasis on their rehabilitation and much less on their punishment. **We have not, however, always viewed and treated juvenile delinquents differently than adult criminals.**

Juvenile offenders were viewed and treated very much like adult offenders until the 1800s. There were no separate correctional facilities for juveniles in this country until the early to mid-1800s. The first juvenile court did not appear until 1899, and it was not until 1945 that all states had juvenile courts. Many status offense laws are also of recent origin. Laws requiring school attendance, for example, did not emerge until the late 1800s and early 1900s in most places. Even the word "delinquent" was not used until the 1800s. So the special way that we view and treat juvenile delinquents is relatively new, having emerged in the last 100 to 200 years. As one of the first juvenile court judges stated, prior to the 1900s:

> No matter how young, . . . children [who committed crimes] were indicted, prosecuted, and confined as criminals, in prison, just the same as were adults. . . . The State kept these little ones in police cells and jails among the worst men and women to be found in the vilest parts of the city and town." (quoted in Zimring, 2005:35)

Criminologists have recently tried to explain the invention of juvenile delinquency—that is, why society and the law started to view and treat juvenile delinquents differently than adult criminals over the last 100 to 200 years. Space prevents me from providing a full answer to this question, but I will describe the key features of the answer that has emerged from the research.[7]

Changing Conception of Children

Part of the answer has to do with our changing conception of children. Children past the age of 6 or 7 were not viewed much differently than adults until a few hundred years ago. The fact that children were viewed as adults is reflected in paintings from the 1600s and earlier, where the children have adult features and are dressed and posed like adults. The children, in fact, look like miniature adults. Children were also treated like adults: They lived and slept in large rooms with adults, drank alcohol, engaged in sexual behavior (willingly and unwillingly), began work at an early age, and were subject to severe punishments if they misbehaved. In fact, children were routinely subjected to treatment that would be classified as abusive today. Children who broke the law were treated very much like adults who broke the law. They were tried in the same courts and given the same punishments, including the death penalty and confinement in the same institutions as adults. Very young children, however, were usually exempted from state punishments, and older children sometimes received lighter punishments than adults.

However, **people's view of children began to change in the 1500s and 1600s.** Children began to be seen as different from adults—as immature and dependent on adults for guidance and protection. There are a variety of reasons for this change. The decline in the death rate of children is viewed as a major factor. Prior to this time, perhaps as many as two-thirds of all children died before the age of 20. Partly as a consequence, parents did not form strong attachments to their young children—it was emotionally risky to do so, since their children would likely die. Very young children were viewed with indifference, while older children were viewed as adults. The decline in the death rate, however, made it easier for parents to form close attachments to their children. As they formed such attachments, they were more inclined to view children as different from adults—as less developed and more in need of their special care and protection. Another factor contributing to this new view of children was the extension of education to broader segments of the population. Several factors increased the need for a formal education, including the increase in industry and trade and the invention of the printing press and subsequent spread of printed materials. Formal education also highlighted the immaturity and dependence of children because it widened the gap between what children knew and what adults knew. Still other factors can be listed, but the central point is that the new view of children paved the way for the invention of juvenile delinquency. **As people came to view children differently than adults, they were more inclined to view and treat juvenile offenders differently than adult offenders.**

Major Social Changes, Especially the Growth of Urban Slums

The new view of children, however, was not the only factor that led to the invention of juvenile delinquency. Also important were the major social changes that occurred in the United States during the 1800s and early 1900s (and in many other countries at the same or somewhat different times). The United States underwent a radical transformation during this time, moving from a largely rural to a largely urban society. Further, the urban areas that developed were populated by a large number of poor people, including many recent immigrants to the United States, and these areas were plagued by a range of problems, including crime. Before describing how these changes contributed to the invention of juvenile delinquency, let me first provide some more information on the nature of these changes.

At the end of the 1700s the United States was largely a rural society. In 1790, only 5.1 percent of the population lived in urban areas. There were only a few cities with populations over 2,500. By 1920, over 50 percent of the population lived in urban areas. Many cities experienced a tremendous increase in population over a very short period of time. Chicago, for example, had a population of 5,000 in 1840. By 1890, it had a population of 1 million. This rapid growth in urban populations was largely due to the industrial revolution. Technological advances were improving farming techniques, so fewer people were necessary to work the land. Many rural residents then moved to the city, hoping to find work in the newly emerging industries. Likewise, many foreign residents came to the United States hoping to find work in those industries. In fact, it is estimated that in 1920 about half the residents of major urban areas were immigrants or the children of immigrants.

Many of these people were poor and they were not always able to find work, or at least work that paid a decent wage. As a result, **large slums began to appear. These slums suffered from a variety of problems:** poor housing, overcrowding, sanitation problems, health problems, and much crime and vice. **Many individuals became especially concerned about the children living in these slums.** These children often spent much time on the streets, frequently stealing things and committing other crimes to survive. Their families and neighborhood residents seemed unable to control them, and there was concern that they were being corrupted by the "unwholesome" environment in which they lived. There were individuals, however, who felt that there was hope for these children. They believed the children were not yet fully developed, and with the proper guidance from adults they might be diverted from a life of crime.

There are **two interpretations**, however, **about how this concern over poor children contributed to the invention of juvenile delinquency.** The first interpretation argues that **reformers were genuinely concerned about the plight of poor children growing up in the city.** These reformers were primarily middle-class women, many of them involved with charity or social welfare organizations. They felt that slum children needed protection from the evils of city life and should have more guidance and direction than they were receiving. So they lobbied to get special laws passed, laws that would more closely regulate the behavior of these children (e.g., status offense laws like those requiring school attendance). They also lobbied for the creation of a special court and special correctional facilities that would provide these children with the protection and guidance they needed. According to this view, then, the invention of juvenile delinquency sprang from the desire of middle-class reformers to help children, especially poor children in the city.

A second interpretation argues that **many upper-class people were disturbed by the large concentration of poor people—especially immigrants—in the city.** They were concerned that these people—frequently referred to as the "dangerous classes"—might become a disruptive force in society. The upper class wanted to ensure that these people did not threaten their privileged position, and one way they did this was by exercising greater control over the children of the poor. They lobbied for laws requiring these children to attend school so that they would be properly socialized. They lobbied for other laws designed to more closely regulate the children's behavior. The juvenile court was the institution designed to enforce these laws, even if it meant removing the children from their parents. And juvenile institutions were designed to teach these juveniles proper discipline and respect for authority. According to this view, the invention of juvenile delinquency is due to the desire of upper-class people to protect their privileged position in society.

Which interpretation is correct? A number of historians and criminologists have examined what is called the "child-saving movement." That is, they have examined individuals and groups who worked to pass status offense laws and create a separate juvenile court and juvenile correctional institutions. Each state and major city in the United States had its own group of *child savers.* Researchers have looked at whether the leaders of the child-saving movement were members of the middle or upper class. They have tried to examine the motives of the child savers on the basis of what they said and what they did. For example, do their statements indicate a genuine concern about the plight of children, or do they simply express a desire to control poor children and thereby protect "society"? Were these children helped and protected or simply subject to greater control? Studies have examined the child-saving movements in such cities as Chicago, Los Angeles, New York, and Memphis (see the sources cited in note 7). Different studies reach different conclusions about which interpretation is correct, and there is no clear resolution of the issue yet. Perhaps both interpretations have some merit, with the invention of delinquency being partly motivated by a genuine concern for poor children and partly by a desire to control such children because of their perceived threat. In any event, it is important to remember that we did not always view and treat juvenile delinquents differently than adult criminals. Juvenile delinquency is a social invention.

Summary

You now know what juvenile delinquency is. It refers to violations of the criminal law (and sometimes status offense laws) by minors. You also know that we tend to view and treat juvenile delinquents differently than adult criminals—although older juveniles who commit serious crimes are something of an exception. Now that you know what delinquency is, I next want to examine the extent of delinquency and the characteristics of delinquents. Before doing that, however, I must present information on how delinquency is measured—which is the topic of Chapter 2.

Teaching Aids

Controversial Cases

As indicated in this chapter, we have started to treat older juveniles who commit serious crimes more like adult offenders, trying these juveniles in adult courts and subjecting them to the same punishments as adults. Some individuals argue that we have gone too far in this effort, while others say that we have not gone far enough. In fact, some argue that we should abolish the juvenile court and try all juvenile offenders above a certain minimum age in adult court.[8] The two case studies that follow are designed to get you to think about the extent to which juvenile offenders should be treated like adult offenders.

Case 1. The juvenile death penalty. In early 2005, 20 states permitted the execution of individuals who committed their crimes when they were 16 or 17 years old. Over 70 such individuals were on death row at this time (see Sharp et al., 2007). Since 1973, 22 individuals who committed their crimes while juveniles have been executed. On March 1, 2005, the Supreme Court forbid the execution of individuals who committed their crimes before turning 18. An excerpt from the Supreme Court decision follows:

> Three general differences between juveniles under 18 and adults demonstrate that juvenile offenders cannot with reliability be classified among the worst offenders. First, as any parent knows and as the scientific and sociological studies . . . tend to confirm, "a lack of maturity and an undeveloped sense of responsibility are found in youth more often than in adults and are more understandable among the young. These qualities often result in impetuous and ill-considered actions and decisions."
>
> The second area of difference is that juveniles are more vulnerable or susceptible to negative influences and outside pressures, including peer pressure. The third broad difference is that the character of a juvenile is not as well formed as that of an adult. The personality traits of juveniles are more transitory, less fixed . . .
>
> These differences render suspect any conclusion that a juvenile falls among the worst offenders. Once the diminished culpability of juveniles is recognized, it is evident that the penological justifications for the death penalty apply to them with lesser force than to adults. . . . The age of 18 is the point where society draws the line for many purposes between childhood and adulthood. It is, we conclude, the age at which the line for death eligibility ought to rest. (from Greenhouse, 2005:A14)

Do you agree with the Supreme Court decision? (Note: Five of the nine Supreme Court justices voted to forbid the execution of juveniles, while four did not.) What is meant by the "diminished culpability of juveniles"? What might the "justifications" for the death penalty be? Do you think these justifications apply to juveniles with "less force"? For example, one justification for the death penalty is that it deters potential offenders from committing crimes. Do you think juveniles may be less subject to this deterrent effect than adults? If so,

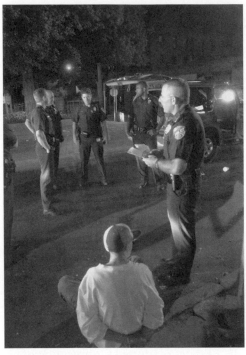

why? Can you imagine a case where the execution of a juvenile might be justified? Do you agree that 18 years of age is a good dividing line between juveniles and adults? If not, what would you propose?[9]

Case 2. The Lionel Tate Case. Lionel Tate was 12 years old when he killed a 6-year-old girl who was staying at his house. Lionel and the girl were watching TV while Lionel's mother, who was baby-sitting the girl, was asleep upstairs. Lionel, who weighed 166 pounds, picked up the 48-pound girl and, imitating some wrestling moves he had seen on TV, body slammed and stomped her. He fractured her skull and caused extensive internal damage. When he realized that the girl was no longer breathing, he ran to tell his mother—but it was too late to save the girl.

Lionel was arrested, tried as an adult, and sentenced to life in prison with no possibility of parole; he was perhaps the youngest person ever to receive such a sentence. The judge described Lionel's actions as "cold, callous and indescribably cruel," and said that "the acts of Lionel Tate were not the playful acts of a child. The acts of Lionel Tate were not the acts born out of immaturity." Attorney General John Ashcroft, commenting on the case, said that "I'm not one of those who thinks we should signal to young people, 'You have an interval during which you can do adult criminal activity and you don't get charged with the responsibility for it' " (*Atlanta Constitution*, March 13, 2001, 10A).

An editorial in the *Atlanta Constitution* took a different position. The editorial pointed out that Lionel had no prior record of violence and argued that his acts were very much the result of his immaturity. Therefore, according to the editorial, Lionel deserved a punishment that was much less severe. In particular, the editorial stated that:

> Children are not little adults, and no "adult-like" action changes that. Brain research shows that young people don't fully develop the physiological capacity to control impulses and foresee consequences until their late teens. They depend on adults to have the insight and wisdom to protect them from harm and to recognize their potential for growth, change and redemption. (March 13, 2001, 10A)

A court overturned Lionel's conviction in late 2003, stating that Lionel's mental competency should have been tested before his trial. Lionel and his mother then accepted a deal offered by prosecutors. In exchange for pleading guilty to second degree murder, Lionel received a sentence of three years in prison, one year of house arrest, and ten years' probation. He got credit for time served so had to serve only three additional months in prison before being released in early 2004.

Do you think Lionel Tate should have received his original sentence of life without parole? If not, do you think his new sentence of three years in prison is appropriate? Should Lionel have been tried as an adult or as a juvenile? Justify the positions you take.

TEST YOUR KNOWLEDGE OF THIS CHAPTER

1. What is juvenile delinquency?
2. Describe the major differences in the way we *view* juvenile offenders and adult offenders.
3. What does it mean to say that juveniles are "immature"?
4. Describe the major differences in the way we *treat* juvenile offenders and adult offenders. Discuss how these differences reflect our different *view* of juvenile and adult offenders.
5. What is a status offense? Name at least five status offenses. What is the rationale or reason for having status offenses?
6. What are the major criticisms against status offense laws?
7. How have states responded to these criticisms?
8. List the major ways in which juvenile court differs from adult court. Discuss the reasons for such differences.
9. Describe the ways in which juvenile courts are starting to become more like adult courts.
10. Describe how juvenile correctional institutions differ from those for adults.
11. Why are we starting to view and treat older juveniles who commit serious crimes like adult offenders?
12. What do I mean by "the invention of juvenile delinquency"?
13. How can we explain the invention of juvenile delinquency?
14. How has our view or conception of children changed over time? What are some of the reasons for this change?
15. Describe the major social changes that occurred in the United States during the 1800s and early 1900s and how they contributed to the invention of juvenile delinquency.
16. There are two interpretations of how concern over the poor children in slums contributed to the invention of juvenile delinquency. Describe these interpretations. Describe how we might determine which is correct.

THOUGHT AND DISCUSSION QUESTIONS

1. Do you think status offenses should be illegal? Defend your answer. If status offenses should *not* be illegal, how should we respond to them, if at all? (It may help to consider each status offense in turn. For example, should running away from home be illegal? If not, how should we respond to juveniles who run away?)
2. Do you think older juveniles who commit serious crimes should be treated like adult offenders? Defend your answer.

KEY TERMS

- Juvenile delinquency
- Immaturity
- Status offenses
- Juvenile court
- Due process rights
- Adjudicated
- Disposition
- Youth development centers and training schools
- Invention of juvenile delinquency
- Child savers

ENDNOTES

1. *See* Feld, 1999; Rutter et al., 1998; Scott, 2002; Steinberg and Cauffman, 2000; Zimring, 1998, 2005.

2. *See* Bishop, 2006; Cullen, 2006; Gerber and Engelhardt-Greer, 1996; Mears et al., 2007; Roberts, 2004; *also see* Bernard, 1992; Empey et al., 1999; Feld, 1999; Howell, 1997a; Moon et al., 2000; Roberts and Stalans, 1997; Triplett, 1996; Zimring, 1998.

3. *See* Bernard, 1992; Butts and Mitchell, 2000; Empey et al., 1999; Feld, 1998, 1999; Howell, 1997a, 2003a; Krisberg, 2005; Kupchik, 2006; Roberts, 2004; Rosenheim et al., 2002; Snyder and Sickmund, 2006; Zimring, 1998.

4. *See* Cullen, 2006; Howell, 2003a; Zimring, 1998.

5. *See* Cullen, 2006; Mears et al., 2007; Moon et al., 2000; Pastore and Maguire, 2007; Robert and Stalans, 1997; Roberts, 2004; Triplett, 1996; Zimring, 2005.

6. *Also see* Butts and Mitchell, 2000; Cullen, 2006; Feld, 1999; Howell, 2003a; Krisberg, 2005; Kupchik, 2006; Snyder and Sickmund, 2006; Zimring, 2005.

7. For excellent overviews of this topic, *see* Bernard, 1992; Empey et al., 1999; Feld, 1999; Howell, 1997a; *also see* Aries, 1962; DeMause, 1974; Finestone, 1976; Platt, 1969; Salerno, 1991; Schlossman, 1977; Shelden and Osborne, 1989; Sutton, 1988.

8. *See* Butts and Mitchell, 2000; Feld, 1999; Howell, 2003a; Jackson and Knepper, 2003.

9. For further information on juveniles and the death penalty, *see* Chapter 23 of this text; Bohm, 2003; Cothern, 2000; Feld, 1999:236–238; Howell, 2003a:37–39; Zimring, 2005.

CHAPTER 2

How Is Delinquency Measured?

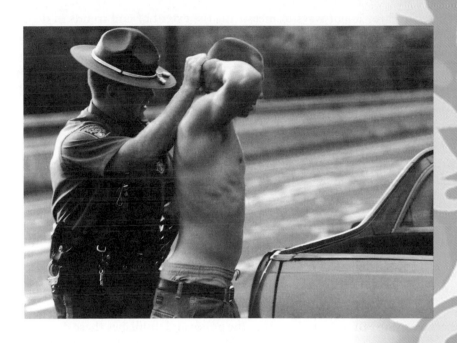

Now that you know what delinquency is, I want to answer two basic questions about it: How much delinquency is there in the United States, and is delinquency increasing? But before I can answer these questions (Chapter 3), I first have to discuss the different ways of measuring delinquency. As you will see, the way in which delinquency is measured often has a major impact on the conclusions we draw about the extent of delinquency and trends in delinquency. You might be groaning a bit right now, thinking, "Oh no, I don't want to read some technical discussion about how to measure delinquency!" But bear with me; this information is important. A lot of what you hear about the extent of delinquency and trends in delinquency is wrong or misleading. This section will help you understand why.

There are **three major ways of measuring the extent of and trends in delinquency:** (1) **"official" statistics** from the police, juvenile court, and juvenile correctional agencies; (2) **"self-report" data** from juveniles, with juveniles being asked about the offenses they have committed; and (3) **"victimization" data,** with people being asked whether they have been the victims of various crimes. This chapter describes each of these methods and their advantages and disadvantages.[1]

Official Statistics—Especially Arrest Data from the Police

Official statistics **include data from the police, the courts, and juvenile correctional agencies,** that is, data from those "official agencies" responsible for dealing with juvenile offenders. **The most commonly used official statistics are arrest data from the police.** Because only some of the juveniles arrested by the police are referred to juvenile court, and only some of the people referred to juvenile court are sent to juvenile correctional agencies, arrest data provide a more accurate indication of the extent of delinquency. I therefore focus on arrest data in this discussion (data from juvenile courts and correctional agencies are described in Chapter 21).

Each year the FBI collects data from the police and publishes these data in a volume called *Crime in the United States: The Uniform Crime Reports.* Copies are probably available in the reference department or government documents section of your library (copies are also available on the FBI's website at http://www.fbi.gov/). This volume is divided into several sections. The first section contains information on the number of *crimes known to the police.* As the name implies, these are crimes that the police know about, both crimes that have been reported to the police and crimes that the police have discovered on their own. The second section contains information on the number of *crimes that have been "cleared" or solved by arrest.* Contrary to the impression you might get from the media, most crimes are not cleared by arrest. In 2006, 20 percent of the crimes known to the police were cleared by arrest. The third section contains information on the **number of arrests** and the characteristics of the people who were arrested, including the most serious offense they were arrested for and their age, sex, and race. Note that the number of crimes cleared by arrest is not equal to the number of arrests. Sometimes multiple crimes might be cleared by a single arrest. For example, an individual may be arrested for several burglaries. And sometimes a single crime might be cleared by the arrest of many people. For example, several people may be arrested for a single burglary. Juveniles usually commit their crimes in groups, and it is often the case that several juveniles are arrested for a single crime.

Information on the extent of delinquency and trends in delinquency comes from the clearance and arrest data. These data (unlike the crimes known to the police data) contain information on the age of the offender. So they allow us to estimate such things as the number of crimes committed by juveniles, the number of arrests that involve juveniles, the most serious offense these juveniles were arrested for, and whether juvenile arrests are increasing or decreasing. Most media reports regarding the extent of and trends in delinquency are based on this clearance and arrest data.

The FBI Crime Reports focus on what are known as "Part I," or "Index," offenses and "Part II" offenses. The *Part I, or Index, offenses* are eight relatively serious violent and property crimes. They include *murder and nonnegligent manslaughter, forcible rape, robbery, aggravated assault, burglary, larceny-theft, motor vehicle theft, and arson.* The FBI reports both "crimes known to the police" and clearance/arrest data on these offenses. The top half of Table 2.1 provides a definition of each of these offenses. Read these definitions and then try to answer the following multiple-choice question:

Your roommate steals your TV from the living room of your apartment while you are attending class. Is this a:
a. burglary
b. larceny-theft
c. robbery
d. all of the above

The *Part II offenses* consist of 20 additional offenses as well as a category for "all other offenses." These offenses are listed in the bottom part of Table 2.1. Note that this list

TABLE 2.1	**Part I and Part II Offenses**

Part I or Index Offenses

1. **Criminal Homicide:** The willful (nonnegligent) killing of one human being by another. Deaths caused by negligence and justifiable homicides are excluded.
2. **Forcible rape:** The carnal knowledge of a female forcibly and against her will. Attempts to commit rape by force or threat of force are included. Statutory rapes (no force used and victim under age of consent) are excluded.
3. **Robbery:** The taking or attempting to take anything of value from the care, custody, or control of a person or persons by force or threat of force or violence and/or by putting the victim in fear.
4. **Aggravated assault:** An unlawful attack by one person upon another for the purpose of inflicting severe or aggravated bodily injury. This type of assault is usually accompanied by the use of a weapon or by means likely to produce death or great bodily harm. Simple assaults are excluded.
5. **Burglary:** The unlawful entry of a structure to commit a felony or a theft. Use of force to gain entry is not required.
6. **Larceny-theft:** The unlawful taking, carrying, leading, or riding away of property from the possession or constructive possession of another. It includes crimes like shoplifting, pocket picking, purse snatching, thefts from motor vehicles, thefts of motor vehicle parts and accessories, and bicycle thefts in which no force, violence, or fraud occurs. Embezzlement, con games, forgery, worthless checks, etc. are excluded.
7. **Motor vehicle theft:** The theft or attempted theft of a motor vehicle—includes automobiles, trucks, buses, motorcycles, motor scooters, snowmobiles, etc.
8. **Arson:** The willful or malicious burning or attempt to burn, with or without intent to defraud, a dwelling house, public building, motor vehicle or aircraft, personal property of another, etc.

Part II Offenses

Other assaults
Forgery and counterfeiting
Fraud
Embezzlement
Stolen property: buying, receiving, possessing
Vandalism
Weapons: carrying, possessing, etc.
Prostitution and commercialized vice
Sex offenses (except forcible rape and prostitution)
Drug abuse violations
Gambling
Offenses against family and children
Driving under the influence
Liquor laws
Drunkenness
Disorderly conduct
Vagrancy
All other offenses
Curfew and loitering law violations
Runaways

SOURCE: Federal Bureau of Investigation, 1998.

includes two status offenses: running away and curfew violation. Also, liquor law violations often involve the status offense of drinking under age. Arrests for all other status offenses are included in the "all other offenses" category. The FBI only reports arrest data for the Part II offenses.

The data from the FBI have several advantages. They are collected from police departments representing approximately 95 percent of the U.S. population. They have been collected since 1930, so they provide long-term information on trends in crime. And certain evidence suggests that the "crimes known to the police" data provide a moderately accurate measure of the extent of and trends in certain types of serious crime, particularly homicide and serious instances of certain other crimes like robbery, burglary, and motor vehicle theft (see Gove et al., 1985). But at the same time, the FBI data, particularly the arrest data, have a number of problems.

Problems with Arrest Data

Arrest data greatly underestimate the extent of most forms of delinquency, and they may sometimes provide misleading information about trends in delinquency. There are several reasons for this underestimation, including the following:

Most delinquent acts do not become known to the police. There are three reasons for this. **First,** the police usually find out about a crime when someone else—usually the crime victim—reports it to them. But surveys of crime victims indicate that only about 40 percent of all crime victimizations are reported to the police. Not surprisingly, serious crimes are more likely to be reported to the police than minor crimes. Serious crimes include those where a weapon is used, the victim is injured, and/or there is a significant financial loss. Crimes involving strangers are also more likely to be reported to the police. And crimes against adults are more likely to be reported to the police than crimes against juveniles (see Finkelhor and Ormond, 1999; Watkins, 2005). **Second,** many crimes do not have a "victim" in the usual sense of the word—that is, someone who feels that he or she has been injured. I am referring to crimes like drug use, gambling, and consensual sex. It is unlikely that the participants in these crimes will notify the police. And **third,** it is physically difficult for the police to detect most crimes on their own. Obviously they cannot detect crimes that occur in private, but they also have trouble detecting crimes that occur in public. The police in a patrol car may pass a given spot on their beat once or twice a day, if that much, so it is unlikely that they will come upon a crime in progress. The police therefore do not even know about the large majority of crimes that occur, especially the less serious crimes. As a result, even the "crimes known to the police" data greatly underestimate the extent of crime, with the exception of homicide and serious instances of a few other crimes.

Even when crimes become known to the police, the police do not catch the offender in most cases. As indicated in Chapter 20, the police are unlikely to catch the offender unless they discover the offender at the scene of the crime or someone can identify the offender to them; this is one reason why they are more likely to catch offenders who commit violent crimes than those who commit property crimes. Most violent crimes involve people who know one another, so the victim can often identify the offender (or the police have a good idea of who the offender might be). But for nonviolent crimes, which constitute the vast majority of crimes, the police usually do not catch the offender.

The police do not arrest most of the suspected offenders they catch. As you will learn in Chapter 20, the police have a lot of discretion over whether or not to arrest suspected offenders. They exercise that discretion by releasing most of the suspected offenders they encounter. **Several factors influence whether the police make an arrest;** the seriousness of the offense is most important. But other factors also have an impact. The attitude of the victim or complainant is quite important. Does the victim press for arrest? If so, the police will usually make an arrest. If the victim argues against arrest, the police will usually let the offender go. As discussed in Chapter 22, the characteristics of the offender—including race, class, and sex—often influence the likelihood of arrest. The characteristics of the police department may also be important. Some police departments encourage officers to informally resolve criminal matters, while others encourage officers to make arrests.[2] Also, police departments occasionally crack down on certain offenses, like drug crimes, prostitution, curfew violation, and truancy. The police are more likely to search for and arrest individuals committing such crimes during these crackdowns. For example, the transit police in the city of Atlanta recently instituted a crackdown against truancy, and as a result the number of juveniles apprehended for truancy increased by almost 200 percent over a two-year period.

Research has shown that only about 20 percent of the crimes known to the police are cleared by arrest. (The percentage varies by type of crime. In 2006, 61 percent of all murders and 54 percent of all aggravated or serious assaults were cleared by arrest, versus 13 percent of all burglaries and 14 percent of all motor vehicle thefts.)

Police data reported to the FBI are sometimes inaccurate. On top of all this, the police sometimes report inaccurate data to the FBI. Sometimes these inaccurate reports are the result of mistakes on the part of the police, and sometimes the police deliberately distort crime data in an effort to make themselves look good. One common way in which this distortion occurs is by *unfounding crime reports.* The police usually investigate crime reports by citizens to determine whether a crime has occurred and what type of crime has occurred, if any. If they feel that a crime has not occurred, they "unfound" the crime report. And that "crime" does not become part of the "crimes known to the police" data reported to the FBI. Some police departments have lowered their crime rates by unfounding a large percentage of the crimes reported to them. The police in my hometown of Atlanta were accused of wrongly unfounding a large number of crimes in 1996. An external audit found some support for this accusation. For example, Atlanta reported 392 rapes to the FBI in 1996. This represented an 11 percent decrease in rapes compared to 1995. The external audit, however, concluded that the Atlanta police wrongly unfounded 56 rapes in 1996. If these 56 rapes had been reported to the FBI along with the other rapes, the number of rapes in Atlanta would have increased 2 percent from 1995 (Martz, 1999).

Another common way in which the police distort crime data involves **reclassifying crimes** from more to less serious categories. For example, police officials may reclassify aggravated assaults as simple assaults or burglaries as larcenies. A report in the *New York Times* stated that about one quarter of the felonies or serious crimes recorded in a New York City precinct in 2002 were improperly downgraded to misdemeanors or minor crimes. As a result of this downgrading, the precinct reported a 7.4 percent drop in serious crime compared to 2001. But when the improperly downgraded crimes were reclassified as felonies, the precinct had a 15 percent increase in serious crime. According to the news report, precinct commanders in New York City were under much pressure to keep crime rates down, and some claim that this occasionally led certain officials to "shave numbers" (Rashbaum, 2003).

The FBI arrest data only report the most serious offense for which the person is arrested. For example, suppose a juvenile robs someone while under the influence of an illicit drug. The juvenile may be arrested for both robbery and drug abuse, but only the robbery arrest will be shown in the FBI data. The FBI data on drug abuse arrests only indicate the number of arrests for which drug abuse is the most serious charge. Many additional drug abuse arrests may have been made, but these arrests are not reported by the FBI because drug abuse is not the most serious charge. (Note: The new National Incident-Based Reporting System [NIBRS] will eventually provide more complete data on juvenile arrests, but not enough states are participating in the program at this time to permit generalizations to the United States as a whole [see Maxfield, 1999; Mosher et al., 2002].)

Summary

Arrest data, then, vastly underestimate the extent of delinquency. This underestimation is **especially true for minor delinquency,** which is less likely to become known to the police and is less likely to result in arrest. Further, **arrest data may provide misleading information on trends in delinquency.** Suppose, for example, that arrest data show an increase in juvenile delinquency over time. This increase could be due to a number of factors. Perhaps victims have become more likely to report crimes to the police (e.g., the percentage of violent crimes reported to the police increased from 43 percent in 1993 to 49 percent in 2002 (Rennison and Rand, 2003)). Perhaps complainants have become more likely to press for arrest (e.g., stores have become more likely to press for arrest in shoplifting cases). Perhaps police departments have become more likely to encourage officers to make arrests (e.g., some police departments are adopting "zero-tolerance" policing, where even minor violations of the law may result in arrest). Perhaps the police have cracked down on certain types of crime, like drug use or gun-related crimes. Perhaps the police are turning in more accurate crime reports (data suggest that crime reports have become more accurate in recent decades). Or perhaps juvenile delinquency really is increasing. It is sometimes the case that we cannot tell which factor or factors are responsible for a change in arrest rates.

Self-Report Data

Given the problems with arrest data, criminologists have tried to develop alternative ways to measure the extent of delinquency. The major alternative they have developed is *self-report data.* Self-report data are obtained by asking juveniles about the extent of their delinquency. Sometimes the juveniles are interviewed, and sometimes they fill out questionnaires. Most self-report surveys focus on delinquency committed during the previous year, to minimize problems with memory. In almost all cases, self-report surveys are anonymous or respondents are assured that their answers are confidential. A popular self-report measure of delinquency is shown in Table 2.2. Take a few minutes to answer the questions in this measure (although you should not record the answers in this book in case it gets lost or borrowed).

Self-report surveys of delinquency did not come into wide use until the 1960s, but they are now the major way that criminologists use to measure delinquency. The major advantage of self-report data is that they provide an estimate of all delinquency committed by

TABLE 2.2 A Popular Self-Report Measure of Delinquency

How many times in the last year have you:

1. Purposely damaged or destroyed property belonging to your *parents* or other *family members.*
2. Purposely damaged or destroyed property belonging to a *school.*
3. Purposely damaged or destroyed *other property* that did not belong to you (not counting family or school property).
4. Stolen (or tried to steal) a *motor vehicle,* such as a car or motorcycle.
5. Stolen (or tried to steal) something worth more than $50.
6. Knowingly bought, sold, or held stolen goods (or tried to do any of these things).
7. Thrown objects (such as rocks, snowballs, or bottles) at cars or people.
8. Run away from home.
9. Lied about your age to gain entrance or to purchase something (lied about your age to buy liquor or get into a movie).
10. Carried a hidden weapon other than a plain pocket knife.
11. Stolen (or tried to steal) things worth $5 or less.
12. Attacked someone with the idea of seriously hurting or killing him/her.
13. Been paid for having sexual relations with someone.
14. Had sexual intercourse with a person of the opposite sex other than your wife/husband.
15. Been involved in gang fights.
16. Sold marijuana or hashish ("pot," "grass," hash").
17. Cheated on school tests.
18. Hitchhiked where it was illegal to do so.
19. Stolen money or other things from your *parents or other members of your family.*
20. Hit (or threatened to hit) a *teacher* or other adult at school.
21. Hit (or threatened to hit) one of your *parents.*
22. Hit (or threatened to hit) other *students.*
23. Been loud, rowdy, or unruly in a public place (disorderly conduct).
24. Sold hard drugs, such as heroin, cocaine, and LSD.
25. Taken a vehicle for a ride (drive) without the owner's permission.
26. Bought or provided liquor for a minor.
27. Had (or tried to have) sexual relations with someone against their will.
28. Used force (strong-arm methods) to get money or things from other *students.*
29. Used force (strong-arm methods) to get money or things from a *teacher* or other adult at school.
30. Used force (strong-arm methods) to get money or things from *other people* (not student or teachers).
31. Avoided paying for such things as movies, bus or subway rides, and food.
32. Been drunk in a public place.
33. Stolen (or tried to steal) things worth between $5 and $50.
34. Stolen (or tried to steal) something at school, such as someone's coat from a classroom, locker, or cafeteria, or a book from a library.
35. Broken into a building or vehicle (or tried to break in) to steal something or just to look around.
36. Begged for money or things from strangers.
37. Skipped classes without an excuse.
38. Failed to return extra change that a cashier gave you by mistake.
39. Been suspended from school.
40. Made obscene telephone calls (calling someone and saying dirty things).

How often in the last year have you used:

41. Alcoholic beverages (beer, wine, and hard liquor).
42. Marijuana or hashish ("grass," "pot," "hash").
43. Hallucinogens ("LSD," "mescaline," "peyote," "acid").
44. Amphetamines ("uppers," "speed," "whites").
45. Barbiturates ("downers," "reds").
46. Heroin ("horse," "smack").
47. Cocaine ("coke").

SOURCE: Elliott and Ageton, 1980.

juveniles, regardless of whether that delinquency is known to the police or has resulted in arrest. As a consequence, self-report data indicate that delinquency is far more extensive than arrest data suggest. But before I continue my discussion of self-report data, let me address a question that I know is on your mind.

How Do We Know That Juveniles Are Telling the Truth?

Most people have the same reaction to self-report surveys: How do researchers know that juveniles are telling the truth? They are asking juveniles whether they have engaged in a range of illegal behaviors, some of which are strongly condemned and subject to severe punishment. It is reasonable to think that many juveniles will underreport their delinquency. Researchers have tried to estimate the accuracy of self-report data in several ways. None of these ways are perfect, but taken together they provide a rough estimate of the accuracy of self-report data (see Thornberry and Krohn, 2000, for an excellent overview of this issue).

1. **Official record comparisons.** Most commonly, researchers compare the self-reported delinquent acts of respondents with their police or court records. They determine whether respondents report the offenses for which they have been arrested or convicted.[3] The failure of respondents to report such offenses suggests that self-report data are inaccurate. Reporting such offenses suggests that self-report data *may* be accurate. It does not, of course, prove that self-report data are accurate. People may admit to offenses for which they have been arrested or convicted but fail to report other offenses.

2. **Comparisons with peer, family, or school reports.** Certain researchers have estimated the accuracy of self-reports by determining whether respondents report the delinquent acts that their friends, parents, and/or teachers attribute to them (e.g., Gold, 1966). If they do not, that suggests that self-report data are inaccurate. If they do, that suggests that self-report data may be accurate.

3. **Lie-detector tests.** Certain researchers have used lie-detector tests or the threat of lie-detector tests to estimate the accuracy of self-report data (e.g., Clark and Tift, 1966; Hindelang et al., 1981). For example, juveniles in one study were interviewed about the extent of their delinquency. They were then interviewed again, but this time they were told that their answers would be evaluated using a "psychological stress evaluator" that detects dishonest responses. They were then asked a variety of questions, including the same questions they had previously been asked about the extent of their delinquency. The researchers then determined whether the juveniles changed their answers in the second interview.

4. **Comparisons with drug tests.** Researchers have estimated the accuracy of self-reports of drug use by comparing such reports to estimates of drug use obtained from urine, saliva, or blood tests (e.g., Akers et al., 1983).

5. **Comparisons between groups known to differ in their level of delinquency.** Researchers have also estimated the accuracy of self-reports by comparing the self-reported delinquency of groups known to differ in their level of delinquency. For example, they have compared the self-reported delinquency of institutionalized delinquents to that of high school students (e.g., Short and Nye, 1958). If there is little difference in self-reported delinquency between these groups, that suggests that self-report data are inaccurate. If the institutionalized delinquents have a higher level of self-reported delinquency, that suggests that self-report data may be accurate.

Again, none of these methods is perfect, but taken together they allow researchers to form a rough estimate of the accuracy of self-report data. **Overall, they suggest that self-report data provide a moderately accurate estimate of the extent of delinquency.** Most juveniles are reasonably honest in their responses, although there is some underreporting (and even a little overreporting) of delinquency. Data suggest that this underreporting is greatest for serious offenses. That is, juveniles are more likely to conceal serious offenses than minor ones. And certain data suggest that black males are more likely to underreport the extent of their delinquency, although findings here are somewhat mixed.[4]

Problems with Many Self-Report Surveys

While self-report surveys appear to provide a moderately accurate estimate of the extent of delinquency, they do have some problems (see Thornberry and Krohn, 2000, for a full discussion). One problem is that there are **very few long-term, nationwide self-report surveys of delinquency.** While the federal government collects data from police departments on an annual basis, the government has no comparable program for the collection of self-report data. Most self-report surveys are administered by university professors (who may receive government funding for their research). Their surveys usually focus on the extent of self-reported delinquency in a single city or region at one point in time. Only a few national self-report surveys have been done. As a result, estimates of the extent of self-reported delinquency in the United States and trends in such delinquency are somewhat limited.

A second problem is that **many self-report surveys often underestimate the extent of serious delinquency.** One reason for this has already been indicated: Data suggest that respondents sometimes underreport serious delinquent acts. Three additional reasons for the underestimation of serious delinquency are described next. (Some of the more recent self-report surveys, however, have taken significant steps to obtain better estimates of serious delinquency. These steps are described in the following section.)

Many self-report surveys employ measures of delinquency that focus on minor offenses and employ vague response categories. The early self-report surveys and some recent self-report surveys employ questions identical or similar to the ones in Table 2.3. Take

---

TABLE 2.3   **An Early Self-Report Measure of Delinquency**

Have you ever:
1. Driven a car without a driver's license or permit?
   No _____
   Once or twice _____
   Several times _____
   Very often _____
2. Skipped school without a legitimate excuse?
   (Same response categories as above.)
3. Defied your parents' authority (to their face)?
4. Taken little things (worth less than $2) that did not belong to you?
5. Bought or drunk beer, wine, or liquor (include drinking at home)?
6. Purposely damaged or destroyed public or private property that did not belong to you?
7. Had sexual relations with a person of the opposite sex?

SOURCE: Nye, 1958.

a moment to examine these questions. You will immediately notice that the questions focus on minor forms of delinquency. There is a reason for this. Most self-report surveys, especially the early surveys, examine samples of only a few hundred juveniles. Serious delinquent acts, like serious assaults and rapes, are not common, so only a small number of juveniles will report such acts in a sample of a few hundred. As a consequence, there are too few instances of these acts to allow for any meaningful analyses. Many self-report researchers therefore focus on the more frequently occurring minor offenses.

Further, notice the response categories for each delinquency question ("no," "once or twice," "several times," "very often"). Respondents who commit an act 10 times will probably select "very often," but so will respondents who commit an act 100 times. The response categories do not distinguish offenders who commit an act a few times from those who commit an act scores or even hundreds of times. This lack of precision is a serious problem. Recent data indicate that there is a small group of high-rate offenders, each of whom commits hundreds of delinquent acts per year. These offenders account for a majority of all delinquent acts in some studies. But the response categories used in the survey shown in Table 2.3 do not provide an accurate count of the number of delinquent acts committed by these offenders. So not only do some self-report surveys focus on minor delinquency, they often provide an imprecise estimate of the extent of delinquency.

Juveniles often report trivial acts on self-report surveys—acts that would probably not be considered delinquent by law enforcement officials. Examples of trivial acts would be sipping a little wine at the dinner table with your parents' permission or playfully shoving one of your siblings. While juveniles might report these as underage drinking and minor assault, it is quite unlikely that law enforcement officials would see them as such. Trivial events are most likely to be reported in response to questions about minor delinquent acts. In one study, over 75 percent of the minor assault reports were classified by the researcher as trivial (Elliott et al., 1989:15). Trivial events, however, are sometimes reported when respondents are questioned about serious delinquent acts like aggravated assault.

Most self-report surveys tend to under sample the most serious delinquents. Self-report surveys are usually based on school or household samples. For example, a researcher might try to survey a sample of students from several schools in a city. Or a researcher might try to survey juveniles from a sample of households in a city. The researcher first selects the juveniles to survey and then tries to obtain their permission to conduct the interview or complete the questionnaire. It is usually necessary to obtain the permission of their parents or guardians as well.

These strategies have the advantage of reaching broad samples of juveniles—both those who have been arrested and those who have not. These strategies, however, tend to under sample the most serious delinquents, including those who commit the most offenses and those who commit very serious offenses. If you sample school students, you miss students who have dropped out of school, are suspended, or are truant. These students tend to be the more serious offenders. This under sampling is less of a problem if the researchers sample households, but even here they are likely to miss juveniles who live on the street or spend a lot of time on the street. Such juveniles tend to be more serious offenders (see Hagan and McCarthy, 1997a, 1997b). Furthermore, there is reason to believe that the more serious offenders (and their parents) are less likely to agree to participate in the survey (Brame and Piquero, 2003). In fact, it is often the case that 30 percent or more of the juveniles who are selected in the initial sample refuse to participate in the survey or cannot be reached. As a consequence, data suggest that most self-report surveys under sample serious delinquents (see Cernkovich et al., 1985).

In sum, there is reason to believe that **many self-report surveys underestimate the extent of serious delinquency.** This underestimation occurs because (1) serious offenses are more likely to be underreported, (2) measures of delinquency often focus on minor offenses and employ vague response categories, (3) respondents often report trivial acts, and (4) most self-report surveys tend to under sample serious offenders.

Several Recent Self-Report Surveys Have Made Much Progress in Overcoming the Preceding Problems

Criminologists have made much progress in overcoming the preceding problems in recent years. As a consequence, several recent self-report surveys provide much more accurate information about the extent of delinquency, including serious delinquency (see Thornberry and Krohn, 2000, 2003). Criminologists have overcome the preceding problems in several ways:

New methods of administering self-report surveys have been developed, methods **that appear to substantially reduce the amount of underreporting.** One of the most promising of these methods is the *Audio Computer-Assisted Self-Administered Interview.* This rather long name basically refers to a technique whereby juveniles are interviewed by a personal computer. The computer screen presents the juveniles with questions, including questions about the extent of their delinquency. They also hear these questions over a headset at the same time they are presented on the screen. The juveniles then respond to each question by striking the appropriate key on the computer. As Thornberry and Krohn (2000:62–63) point out, this approach has several advantages. Among other things, it overcomes the reading problems that sometimes arise when a respondent is asked to fill out a questionnaire. Also, "the respondent does not have to reveal potentially embarrassing behavior directly to another person," as happens in interviews (also see Turner et al., 1998).

Many recent self-report surveys also **employ better measures of delinquency.** In particular, they **obtain accurate counts of the number of delinquent acts committed.** Further, they **focus on both minor and serious offenses** (such surveys collect larger samples of juveniles, which allows them to examine the less frequently occurring serious offenses). The self-report delinquency measure in Table 2.2 is an example of a measure that focuses on both minor and serious delinquency and that tries to accurately measure the number of times delinquent acts have been committed. This measure was developed by Elliott and associates and has served as a model for measures in many recent self-report studies (see Elliott and Ageton, 1980).

Further, certain of these recent surveys **make an effort to eliminate trivial acts from their delinquency counts.** Researchers ask respondents a series of follow-up questions about the delinquent acts they report, which allows them to classify such acts as trivial or nontrivial. The trivial acts are then excluded from the estimates of delinquency.

Finally, certain of these surveys **make a special effort to include serious offenders in their samples.** For example, they over sample juveniles in neighborhoods that have high delinquency rates. Also, they screen juveniles before including them in the survey, making a special effort to detect and recruit serious offenders in their survey (see Thornberry et al., 1995; Thornberry and Krohn, 2003).

These recent self-report studies are *not* problem-free. For example, they still encounter some difficulty in recruiting the most serious offenders, and there may still be some under-reporting of delinquency. Nevertheless, these surveys represent a major improvement over earlier self-report surveys, and there is good reason to believe that they provide reasonably accurate estimates of the extent of delinquency—serious and minor—in most groups.

Victimization Data

The problems with police data have also motivated criminologists to develop another way of estimating the extent of crime and delinquency: *victimization data.* **Victimization data are obtained by asking people to report on their experiences as crime victims.** Several victimization surveys were conducted in the 1960s, and the federal government started compiling victimization data on an annual basis in the early 1970s through the adminis-tration of the *National Crime Victimization Survey.* Each year people ages 12 and older in approximately 50,000 households throughout the United States are asked about their experiences as crime victims. These households are selected so as to be representative of all households in the United States. Data from the National Crime Victimization Survey allow researchers to estimate the total amount of crime and delinquency in the United States. These victimization data are published annually in a report titled *Criminal Victimization in the United States* or, more recently, *Criminal Victimization* (see Rennison and Rand, 2003; also look for victimization data on the website of the Bureau of Justice Statistics: http://www.ojp.usdoj.gov/bjs/).

The respondents in the victimization survey are asked if they have been the victims of crime, including aggravated assault, simple assault, rape/sexual assault, robbery, burglary, motor vehicle theft, and larceny. (They are not, of course, asked if they have been the vic-tims of homicide.) If they reply that they have been the victim of one of these crimes, they are asked a number of questions about this victimization. For example, they are asked whether they reported the victimization to the police, and if not, why not. In 2006, only 42 percent of all victimizations were reported to the police; the most common reason for not reporting is that the victimization is a private or personal matter. Respondents are also asked if they saw the person(s) who victimized them. If so, they are asked about the age, sex, and race of this person(s), among other things. On the basis of their responses, re-searchers can estimate the number of victimizations committed by young people and trends in such victimization over time.

Like self-report data, victimization data provide information on both crimes that have come to the attention of the police and crimes that have not. They also provide much information on the experiences and characteristics of crime victims.

Problems with Victimization Data

There are, however, problems with using victimization data to estimate the extent of delinquency (see Cantor and Lynch, 2000, for an excellent overview).

1. Victimization data only focus on a few violent and property crimes committed against individuals ages 12 and older. They do not provide any information on crimes such as drug use and on status offenses. They do not provide any information on crimes committed against businesses—like shoplifting at department stores. And they do not provide any information on crimes committed against people less than 12 years of age.

2. **Certain groups with high rates of criminal victimization are under sampled, such as homeless people, transients, and institutionalized persons.**

3. **There is evidence that many crime victims do not report their victimizations to the interviewers.** There are a variety of reasons for this nonreporting, including memory loss and embarrassment. Data suggest that victimizations by family members, friends, and acquaintances are often not reported to the interviewer. There have been some attempts to increase reporting; for example, the wording of the survey has been changed to better prompt respondents to report certain kinds of victimization. To illustrate, respondents are now encouraged to report crimes by friends and family members with the following prompt:

People don't often think of incidents committed by someone they know. Did you have something stolen from you OR were you attacked or threatened by: (a) someone at work or school, (b) a neighbor or friend, (c) a relative or family member, or (d) any other person you've met or known?

Such prompts and other changes have substantially reduced the extent of underreporting, but there is reason to believe that much underreporting still occurs for certain crimes (see Cantor and Lynch, 2000; Mosher et al., 2002).

4. **The victim often does not see the offender and so cannot estimate the offender's age.** This is especially likely for property crimes. One study found that the victim only saw the offender in 6 percent of all burglaries and motor vehicle thefts and in 4 percent of all household larcenies (Hindelang, 1981). The victim, of course, does see the offender in most violent crimes. The victim, however, can only make a rough estimate of the offender's age. In particular, it is often hard to distinguish older juveniles from young adults.

For these reasons, victimization data are somewhat limited in the information they provide about the extent of and trends in delinquency. The discussion in Chapter 3 therefore draws primarily on arrest and self-report data. However, I will note certain relevant findings from victimization data. And I will also briefly discuss the extent to which juveniles are crime victims, as well as offenders.

Summary

There are three major ways to measure the extent of delinquency and trends in delinquency: arrest, self-report, and victimization data. Each has its advantages and disadvantages. With the exception of homicide, arrest data vastly underestimate the extent of delinquency and may provide misleading information on trends in delinquency. Arrest data are especially likely to provide misleading information on minor crimes, since these crimes are the least likely to be reported to the police and the least likely to result in arrest. Self-report data provide a better estimate of the extent of delinquency since they focus on all offenses, both those that have come to the attention of the police and those that have not. Many self-report surveys, however, tend to focus on minor offenses committed in the general population. Such surveys provide less accurate estimates of the extent of serious delinquency. Several recent self-report surveys, however, likely provide reasonably accurate estimates of both minor and serious delinquency. Victimization data also attempt to measure both crimes that have come to the attention of the police and those that have not. But victimization data suffer from several problems; most notably, they focus only on a small number of crimes, and victims usually have not seen the offenders who committed the crime—with the exception of violent crimes.

As you can tell, measuring delinquency is not a simple matter. It is easy to produce estimates of the extent of delinquency and trends in delinquency, and we are exposed to such estimates on a regular basis in the media. Most estimates, however, are problematic for the reasons indicated here. The situation is not as bad as it might appear, however. We can often use our knowledge of these data sources to judge which provides the best estimate of the extent of delinquency or trends in delinquency in a particular situation. And it is sometimes the case that the three data sources agree with one another. We can, of course, be more confident in the conclusions we draw when this is the case.

Teaching Aids

A Challenge

A criminologist is asked to estimate the extent of delinquency in City X. The criminologist decides to interview all of the high school students in the city, asking them the questions shown in Table 2.4. Eighty percent of the high school students and their parents agree to participate in the interviews (returning consent forms to the criminologist). The interviews are conducted during school hours on a certain day. Ninety percent of those who agreed to participate in the survey are in school that day and complete the interviews. Based on their responses to the questions in Table 2.4, the criminologist produces an estimate of the extent of delinquency in City X. Is this estimate accurate? If not, list all of the reasons why not. (These reasons are listed after the Key Terms for this chapter.)

Practical Advice: Three Things to Beware of When Others Discuss the Extent of and Trends in Delinquency (and a Challenge)

We often hear a lot about delinquency from family members, friends, the news media, and politicians. Unfortunately, a lot of the information that is presented is misleading or wrong. The following is a list of three things you should be wary of when others are discussing delinquency. These are not the only things you should be wary of, but they are also among the more common ways that misleading information is conveyed about the extent of and

---

TABLE 2.4   A Self-Report Measure of Delinquency

Respondents are asked whether they engaged in the following offenses in the prior year, with the response categories for each offense ranging from "never" to "five or more" times.

1. Taken something not belonging to you worth under $50.
2. Taken something not belonging to you worth over $50.
3. Got something by telling a person something bad would happen to them if you did not get what you wanted.
4. Got into a fight.
5. Used marijuana.
6. Consumed alcohol.
7. Skipped a day of school without a real excuse.

SOURCE: Adapted from Gold, 1966.

trends in delinquency. **Your challenge:** Draw on this chapter and the next three chapters to expand this list (also see Mosher et al., 2002).

1. **The sensational case.** The news media, politicians, and others will often focus on a sensational crime, such as a crime committed by a famous person, a gruesome crime, and/or a crime with many victims. There will be much discussion of this crime, and the impression will be given that this type of crime (or crime in general) is more extensive or is increasing faster than is actually the case. Perhaps the best recent example of this is school shootings. The media devoted major attention to school shootings in the 1990s and 2000s, often implicitly or explicitly suggesting that school violence was common and that it was increasing. But as indicated in Chapter 15, school violence, especially of a serious nature, is quite uncommon. Further, such violence has been decreasing. This is not, of course, to claim that all media reports focusing on sensational crimes are misleading. Rather, it is to suggest that you should be cautious in generalizing from one or a few crimes to crime more generally. If possible, examine what official, self-report, and victimization data say about the type of crime being discussed.

2. **The reliance on one data source.** Reports on crime are usually based on a single data source, often official statistics from the FBI's *Uniform Crime Reports.* But as indicated in this chapter, each data source has some major disadvantages (and advantages). We should therefore be cautious when we hear a report based on a single source. In particular, we should keep the advantages and disadvantages of that source in mind. We should also ask what other data sources say about the same issue. If the different data sources are in agreement, we can be more confident about the information presented. If the data sources disagree, we need to delve into the possible sources of this disagreement. Mosher et al. (2002:1–2) present a good example of this point. The FBI *Uniform Crime Reports* that were released in 2001 indicated that crime rates had increased for the first time in many years. The news media reported headlines such as "Decade-Long Crime Drop Ends," and commentators were trying to make sense of the increase. Two weeks later, data from the National Crime Victimization Survey were released, and they indicated that the crime rate had decreased by 15 percent. A subsequent headline read "Crime Is: Up? Down? Who Knows?"

3. **Percentage changes based on a small number of cases.** Others will sometimes report that there has been a large percentage increase or decrease in crime. So, for example, drawing on the *Emory Campus Annual Security Report,* someone might report that there was a 50 percent decrease in drug law arrests from 2004 to 2005. This might lead you to think that drug abuse had become much less common on the Emory campus in the space of a year. In fact, the number of drug law arrests decreased from three in 2004 to two in 2005. When you are dealing with a small number of cases, a small change in raw numbers can produce a large change in percentages. This, in turn, can convey a misleading impression about trends in crime. It's quite unlikely that there was actually a 50 percent decrease in drug abuse on the Emory campus from 2004 to 2005. So be sure to look at the raw numbers involved when you hear others talk about what percentage crime increased or decreased. (Note: This illustration also shows the dangers of relying on one data source. Arrest data are clearly a poor way to estimate the extent of or changes in drug use in this case. Most drug abuse incidents do not result in arrest, and the number of drug arrests may be influenced by many factors in addition to the actual extent of drug abuse. Can you list several such factors?)

TEST YOUR KNOWLEDGE OF THIS CHAPTER

1. What are the three major ways of estimating the extent of and trends in delinquency?

2. Why is it important to know something about these methods, including their advantages and disadvantages?

3. What are "official statistics"? Why are arrest data the main source of official data on the extent of and trends in delinquency?

4. What are the major types of information you would find in the FBI's report on *Crime in the United States: The Uniform Crime Reports*?

5. List the eight Part I or Index offenses. List any four Part II offenses.

6. Why is it that the number of crimes "cleared" by the arrest of juveniles usually does not equal the number of arrests that involve juveniles?

7. What are the major advantages and disadvantages of arrest data? Why do arrest data vastly underestimate the extent of delinquency?

8. How have researchers tried to estimate the accuracy of self-reports of delinquency (i.e., estimate whether juveniles are telling the truth on self-report surveys)? What conclusions do researchers draw about the accuracy of self-report surveys?

9. Many self-report surveys suffer from a number of problems that cause them to underestimate the extent of serious delinquency. What are these problems?

10. How have researchers tried to overcome these problems?

11. What are the major advantages and problems with victimization data?

THOUGHT AND DISCUSSION QUESTIONS

1. City X experienced a 30 percent increase in the juvenile *arrest* rate. List all of the possible reasons for this increase *other than a real increase in the rate of delinquency* (e.g., the arrest rate may have increased because crime victims have become more likely to report crimes to the police).

2. I state that none of the methods for estimating the accuracy of self-reports is perfect. Is it possible to develop a method that would precisely estimate the accuracy of self-reports of delinquency? If not, why not?

3. Describe how you might best estimate the extent of delinquency or crime on your campus (indicate the method or methods of data collection you would use and the steps you would take in employing these methods).

KEY TERMS

- Official statistics
- *Crime in the United States: The Uniform Crime Reports*
- Crimes known to the police
- Crimes cleared by arrest
- Part I, or Index, offenses
- Homicide, rape, robbery, aggravated assault, burglary, larceny-theft, motor vehicle theft, and arson
- Part II offenses
- Unfounding crime reports
- Self-report data
- Audio Computer-Assisted Self-Administered Interview
- Victimization data
- National Crime Victimization Survey

ANSWERS TO THE CHALLENGE

The criminologist would not produce an accurate estimate of the extent of delinquency in City X because:

1. Only high school students were interviewed, so the delinquency of juveniles not in high school (e.g., high school dropouts, junior high students) is *not* estimated.

2. Twenty percent of the high school students did not agree to participate in the survey, so their delinquency is not estimated. The more serious delinquents may be more likely to be in this missing group.

3. Ten percent of the students who agreed to participate in the survey were not present on the day of the interviews, perhaps because they were truant or cutting class, so their delinquency is not estimated. Again, the more serious delinquents may be more likely to be in this missing group.

4. Many juveniles may underreport their level of offending, especially serious offending, since a face-to-face interview is used (versus a technique like the Audio Computer-Assisted Self-Administered Interview method).

5. The measure of delinquency in Table 2.4 tends to focus on minor offenses and employs vague response categories.

6. No effort was made to distinguish trivial from nontrivial acts and eliminate the trivial acts from the delinquency count.

ENDNOTES

1. For fuller discussions, *see* Bernard, 1999; Cantor and Lynch, 2000; Cernkovich et al., 1985; Elliott, 1982; Elliott and Ageton, 1980; Elliott et al., 1989; Farrington et al., 1996; Gove et al., 1985; Hindelang et al., 1979, 1981; Huizinga and Elliott, 1986; Jackson, 1990; Maxfield, 1999; Mosher et al., 2002; O'Brien, 2000; Reiss and Roth, 1993; Rutter et al., 1998; Thornberry and Krohn, 2000, 2003; Weis, 1986; Wells and Rankin, 1995.

2. *See* Smith, 1984; Wilson, 1976; *also see* Chappel et al., 2006.

3. *See* Farrington et al., 1996; Hindelang et al., 1981; Huizinga and Elliott, 1986; Paschall et al., 2001; Thornberry and Krohn, 2000.

4. *See* Farrington et al., 1996; Hindelang et al., 1981; Huizinga and Elliott, 1986; Mosher et al., 2002; Thornberry and Krohn, 2000; Weis, 1986.

CHAPTER 3

How Much Delinquency Is There and Is Delinquency Increasing?

This chapter focuses on the two simple questions asked in the title: How much delinquency is there in the United States? Is delinquency increasing? Simple questions, however, often have complex answers. This complexity can be frustrating at times, but you will have a much fuller understanding of the extent of and trends in delinquency after reading this chapter. I first focus on the extent of delinquency in the United States, presenting estimates from arrest, self-report, and victimization data. I then focus on trends in delinquency, again presenting estimates from arrest, self-report, and victimization data. These data sources do not always agree with one another, but I think there are some conclusions that we can safely draw about the extent of and trends in delinquency. One such conclusion is that there has been a dramatic decrease in serious delinquency in recent years, and I end this chapter by discussing some possible reasons for this decrease.

I should warn you that any discussion in this area is going to contain a lot of numbers. I try to keep the numbers to a minimum, and I encourage you to focus on the central points that are being made and to avoid getting caught up in the specific numbers. Many of the numbers that follow come from the *Sourcebook of Criminal Justice Statistics* (see http://www.albany.edu/sourcebook/). The *Sourcebook* publishes a wide range of data on crime from the FBI, self-report surveys, the National Crime Victimization Survey, and other sources. It is a great place to look if you ever want to know anything about the extent of crime, trends in crime, the characteristics of delinquents, or a range of other topics.

How Much Delinquency Is There?

How Many Juveniles Are Arrested and What Are They Arrested For?

As you know, arrest data vastly underestimate the extent of delinquency. Most delinquent acts do not come to the attention of the police, and acts that do come to the attention of the police usually do not result in arrest. This is especially true for minor crimes. Nevertheless, many juveniles are arrested each year (see FBI, 2007; Snyder and Sickmund, 2006).

Table 3.1 shows the estimated number of juvenile arrests in 2006 broken down by type of crime. The top part of the table focuses on Part I or Index crimes, while the bottom part focuses on Part II crimes. Overall, there were about 2.2 million juvenile arrests. That number does not mean that 2.2 million different juveniles were arrested. Many juveniles were arrested more than once.

About 513,000 of these arrests were for Part I crimes. Note that arrests for property crimes are much more common than arrests for violent crimes. In fact, well over half of all Part I arrests are for larceny-theft. Larceny-theft, in fact, is the crime with the highest number of arrests. About 1.7 million arrests were for Part II offenses, with the most arrests being for "other assaults," disorderly conduct, drug abuse violations, liquor law violations, curfew violations, vandalism, and running away.

Overall, note that the number of arrests tends to be higher for minor crimes than for serious crimes. For example, 1,321 juveniles were arrested for homicide and 3,464 were arrested for forcible rape. About 284,000 were arrested for larceny-theft, however.

These data, while useful, may be a little difficult to interpret. One way to help interpret them is to look at *arrest rates.* Arrest rates show the number of juvenile arrests per 100,000 juveniles ages 10 to 17 in the population (very few juveniles under age 10 are ar-

TABLE 3.1	Estimated Number of Juvenile Arrests, 2006

Total	**2,239,966**
Part I Offenses	
Murder and nonnegligent manslaughter	1,321
Forcible rape	3,464
Robbery	36,007
Aggravated assault	61,229
Burglary	84,226
Larceny-theft	283,526
Motor vehicle theft	34,936
Arson	8,108
Part II Offenses	
Other assaults	250,486
Forgery and counterfeiting	3,548
Fraud	7,815
Embezzlement	1,431
Stolen property (buying, receiving, possessing)	21,518
Vandalism	118,619
Weapons (carrying, possessing, etc.)	47,822
Prostitution and commercialized vice	1,668
Sex offenses (except forcible rape and prostitution)	15,841
Drug abuse violations	197,952
Gambling	2,238
Offenses against the family and children	5,003
Driving under the influence	19,655
Liquor law violations	141,251
Drunkenness	16,629
Disorderly Conduct	211,219
Vagrancy	5,159
All other offenses (except traffic)	385,359
Suspicion	437
Curfew and loitering	157,793
Runaways	115,716

SOURCE: Federal Bureau of Investigation, 2007.

rested). Arrest rates are useful because they give us an idea of the probability that a juvenile will be arrested. The overall juvenile arrest rate was about 6,665 per 100,000 juveniles. In other words, there were about 6,665 juvenile arrests for every 100,000 juveniles ages 10 to 17 in the population (or about 6.7 arrests per 100 juveniles). The arrest rate for Part I violent crimes was about 304 per 100,000 juveniles (or about 0.3 arrests per 100 juveniles). The arrest rate for Part I property crimes was about 1,222 per 100,000 juveniles (or about 1.2 arrests per 100 juveniles).

I want to add a note of caution: The fact that there were 2.2 million juvenile arrests does not mean that juveniles committed 2.2 million crimes. I earlier stated that juveniles usually commit their crimes in groups. As a consequence, several juveniles are often arrested for a single crime. For example, several juveniles might be arrested for a single act of vandalism. To estimate the number of crimes committed by juveniles, it is best to look at the number of crimes cleared by the arrest of juveniles. *Clearance data* allow us to estimate the number of Part I crimes committed by juveniles (clearance data are not reported for Part II crimes). While about 513,000 juveniles were arrested in 2006 for Part I crimes, only about 387,000 Part I crimes were cleared by the arrest of juveniles.

You know that arrest data vastly underestimate the extent of delinquency. Self-report data, discussed in the following section, provide a more accurate estimate of the extent of delinquency.

How Much Self-Reported Delinquency Is There?

I have the students in my juvenile delinquency course fill out a short survey on the first day of class. Among other things, the survey asks whether they have ever committed any of 14 different delinquent acts as juveniles. Some of these acts are status offenses, like running away and truancy. Some are minor crimes, like petty larceny and trespassing. And some are more serious crimes, like burglary and robbery. The students are always shocked by the results. I typically find that anywhere from 90 to 100 percent of the students have committed at least one of the delinquent acts. And it is often the case that about half the class has committed at least 7 of the 14 delinquent acts. Keep in mind that these are largely upper-middle-class students who have done quite well in school. A high percentage of them will go on to become doctors, lawyers, and business managers. (Look at the self-report survey in Table 2.2 again; how many of the delinquent acts have you committed?) Self-report surveys typically find that 90 percent or more of all juveniles have engaged in at least some forms of delinquency—usually minor delinquency but often a few instances of more serious delinquency as well.

I do not, however, want you to think that I am picking on juveniles. Two criminologists conducted a self-report survey of crime among criminologists (Robinson and Zaitzow, 1999). They describe their motivation for doing such a survey by stating, "We were in an airplane on our way back from a recent American Society of Criminology meeting [and] we overheard from the seats directly in front of us two criminologists discussing what they had taken (i.e., stolen) from the conference hotel." They began to wonder just how common crime was among criminologists. So they surveyed 522 criminologists from throughout the United States, most of whom had doctoral degrees and half of whom were faculty members at colleges and universities. The large majority of these criminologists had engaged in one or more crimes at some point in their lives. For example, 55 percent had committed theft, 22 percent had committed burglary, 60 percent had used illicit drugs, and 25 percent had physically attacked another person. Self-report data, then, indicate that delinquency (and crime) are common, even among students like yourselves and the faculty who teach you. Keep this in mind when we are examining topics like the causes of delinquency. To some extent, we are examining your (and my) behavior.

As indicated earlier, not many self-report surveys have been administered to juveniles throughout the United States. But a few such surveys exist. The most recent is the 2006 Monitoring the Future survey (see the *Sourcebook of Criminal Justice Statistics* at the website identified earlier). **The Monitoring the Future survey is administered to a sample of about 2,500 high school seniors throughout the United States each year.** While the survey provides national data on the extent of self-reported delinquency, it does have certain problems. It focuses on high school seniors, thereby missing dropouts and students who were suspended or truant when the survey was administered. As indicated earlier, such juveniles are more likely to be serious offenders. It does not examine many delinquent offenses, especially serious offenses like homicide and rape. And it employs vague response categories. In particular, it uses the response category "five or more times," so that researchers cannot distinguish someone who committed an act 5 times from someone who committed the same act 100 times. Nevertheless, the data in Table 3.2 provide you with an idea of the extent of delinquency in this group.

Note that certain forms of delinquency are quite common, particularly status offenses and minor forms of delinquency. For example, the large majority of high school seniors have drunk alcohol and have argued or fought with their parents in the past year (the status offense of "incorrigibility"). And a substantial percentage of students have engaged in petty theft and fighting. More serious forms of delinquency are less frequent but not uncommon. For example, about 11 percent of high school seniors reported that they "hurt someone badly enough to need bandages or a doctor" in 2006.

The best self-report survey conducted on a national level is the National Youth Survey (see Elliott et al., 1985). This survey was administered to a sample of 1,725 adolescents ages 11 through 17 throughout the United States in 1977. These adolescents were asked about the extent of their delinquency in 1976. The same group of adolescents was surveyed several additional times through the 1990s, but they, of course, turned from adolescents into adults as the surveys progressed. Elliott and his associates looked at a total of 47 delinquent acts, including status offenses, minor crimes, and serious crimes (see Table 2.2 for a list of these acts). They took care to precisely measure the number of times each act was committed, avoiding the use of vague response categories. They found that the average number of delinquent acts committed by a juvenile in 1976 was 52 (there is reason to believe this number is similar today, as indicated by the trend data in the next section). So while FBI data indicate that there are 6.7 arrests per 100 juveniles, self-report data indicate that there are at least 5,200 self-reports of delinquency per 100 juveniles (52×100). And while arrest data indicate that there were 2.2 million juvenile arrests in 2006, self-report data suggest that the 34 million juveniles between ages 10 and 17 in the United States engaged in hundreds of millions of delinquent acts in 2006.

Again, self-report data indicate that most of these delinquent acts are status offenses and minor crimes. More serious crimes are less frequent, although they are not uncommon, particularly in certain subgroups. For example, Elliott (1994) found that 36 percent of 17-year-old African American males and 25 percent of 17-year-old white males committed at least one serious act of violence over the course of a year. Serious acts of violence include aggravated assaults, robberies, and rapes; all involve some injury or the use of a weapon.

The large discrepancy between arrest data and self-report data highlights the fact that **most delinquent acts do not come to the attention of the police or result in arrest.** Dunford and Elliott (1984) used the National Youth Survey to explore the relationship between self-reported delinquency and arrest data. They classified youth according to the number of delinquent acts they self-reported in a two-year period and then examined the percentage of youth in each group who had been arrested at least once during the same two-year period. They found that the probability of arrest was quite low, even among youths who had committed a large number of offenses. For example, only 7 percent of the youths who self-reported between 101 and 200 delinquent acts were arrested. Only 19 percent of the youths who self-reported over 200 delinquent acts were arrested. Overall, the probability that a youth will be arrested for a given delinquent act is well under

| TABLE 3.2 | The Extent of Self-Reported Delinquency Among High School Seniors, 2006 | | | | |

During the last 12 months how often have you:	Not at All (%)	Once (%)	Twice (%)	Three or Four times (%)	Five or more times (%)	Rate (no. of acts per 100 juveniles)
1. Argued or had a fight with either of your parents?	11.8	10.5	14.1	25.6	38.0	318.3
2. Hit an instructor or supervisor?	97.1	1.3	.8	.3	.4	6.0
3. Gotten into a serious fight in school or at work?	88.2	7.2	2.4	1.3	1.0	21.6
4. Taken part in a fight where a bunch of your friends were against another group?	82.1	9.6	4.8	1.7	1.8	33.2
5. Hurt someone badly enough to need bandages or a doctor?	88.8	6.4	2.1	1.4	1.2	21.5
6. Used a knife or gun or some other thing (like a club) to get something from a person?	96.4	1.7	1.1	.3	.6	8.6
7. Taken something not belonging to you worth under $50?	72.3	12.5	6.3	3.7	5.2	64.1
8. Taken something not belonging to you worth over $50?	89.5	5.5	1.8	1.1	2.0	23.0
9. Taken something from a store without paying for it?	74.3	10.7	5.7	4.0	5.3	62.6
10. Taken a car that didn't belong to someone in your family without permission of the owner?	94.7	3.1	1.1	.5	.6	10.1
11. Taken part of a car without permission of the owner?	95.6	2.5	.9	.4	.5	8.2
12. Gone into some house or building when you weren't supposed to be there?	75.0	11.8	7.2	3.1	2.8	51.1
13. Set fire to someone's property on purpose?	96.9	1.5	.9	.4	.4	6.7
14. Damaged school property on purpose?	88.0	5.9	3.6	1.2	1.3	23.8
15. Damaged property at work on purpose?	94.4	2.7	1.3	.6	.9	11.9
16. Used alcohol at least once in 2006?	—	—	66.7	—	—	—
17. Used marijuana at least once in 2006?	—	—	7.1	—	—	—

SOURCE: Monitoring the Future survey, as reported in the *Sourcebook of Criminal Justice Statistics* (http://www.albany.edu/sourcebook/).

1 percent. The probability of arrest is low even for those who commit serious offenses. For example, Elliott (1995) estimated that the probability of arrest for a serious violent offense (aggravated assault, rape, robbery) is about 2 in 100 (also see Farrington et al., 2007).

What can we **conclude** about the extent of delinquency according to self-report data? Delinquency is far more common than arrest data suggest. Most juveniles engage in delinquency. They generally commit status offenses and minor crimes, but serious crimes are not uncommon.

How Many Juveniles Are Victimized and How Many Victimizations Are Committed by Juveniles?

Victimization data provide another alternative to arrest data. As indicated earlier, victimization data tell us a lot about crime victims. Such data have somewhat less to say about the number of victimizations committed by juveniles, largely because crime victims usually do not see the person who victimized them. Nevertheless, victimization data do provide some information about the number of violent crimes committed by juveniles.

Table 3.3 shows the number of victimizations experienced by U.S. residents ages 12 or older in 2005, as estimated by the National Crime Victimization Survey. About 23 million victimizations were reported in 2005, including 5.2 million violent victimizations and 18.2 million property victimizations. That amounts to about 2.1 violent victimizations for every 100 people age 12 or older and 15.4 property victimizations for every 100 households. As you can see, people are most often the victims of larceny-theft. Victimization data, like arrest and self-report data, indicate that property crimes are more common than violent crimes, and minor crimes are more common than serious crimes.

Who is most likely to be victimized? Who do you think is most likely to be victimized by crime: young or old, male or female, white or African American, Hispanic or non-Hispanic, poor or rich?

Young people have higher rates of victimization than older people for violent crimes (data for property crimes are reported for households rather than for individuals). Rates of

TABLE 3.3	Number and Rate of Victimizations, 2005	
	Number	**Rate**
All crimes	23,440,720	
Rape/sexual assault	191,670	0.8
Robbery	624,850	2.6
Aggravated assault	1,052,260	4.3
Simple assault	3,304,930	13.5
Personal theft*	227,070	0.9
Household burglary	3,456,220	29.5
Motor vehicle theft	978,120	8.4
Theft	13,365,590	116.2

SOURCE: U.S. Department of Justice, Office of Justice Programs, Bureau of Justice Statistics, *Criminal Victimization in the United States, 2005: Statistical Tables* (http://www.ojp.usdoj.gov/bjs/pub/pdf/cvus05.pdf).

Note: Rate of victimization is per 1,000 persons age 12 or older, or per 1,000 households.

*Personal theft includes pocket picking, purse snatching, and attempted purse snatching.

victimization are highest for those between 20 and 24 years old followed closely by 12- to 19-year-olds. Rates of victimization generally decline with age and are lowest among those 65 or older. To illustrate, almost 5 out of every 100 people ages 20 to 24 were the victims of violence in 2005, a rate about 17 times higher than those ages 65 and over. As dramatic as this difference is, there are data suggesting that the National Crime Victimization Survey substantially underestimates the extent of victimization against young people. Data from other surveys suggest that at least 50 of every 100 adolescents are the victims of violence each year and that more than 25 of every 100 are the victims of theft (Finkelhor et al., 2005; *Sourcebook of Criminal Justice Statistics*).

Males have higher rates of victimization than females for violent crimes, with the exception of rape/sexual assault. About 2.6 of every 100 males were the victims of violence in 2005, versus about 1.7 of every 100 females. Females, however, were about 12 times more likely than males to be the victims of rape/sexual assault. About 1.8 rapes, attempted rapes, or sexual assaults per 1,000 females were reported in 2005. These estimates, however, should be viewed with much caution. Data suggest that the National Crime Victimization Survey substantially underestimates the amount of rape and other violence against women. In particular, some data suggest that 15 to 20 percent of all females will be the victims of a completed or attempted rape at some point in their lives, with at least half of these rapes occurring before the age of 18 (Tjaden and Thoennes, 2006; also see Fisher and Cullen, 2000). In a single year, more than 300,000 women and 90,000 men are raped. Most of the rapes and other violence against women are committed by "intimate partners" (current and former spouses, cohabiting partners, and dates or boyfriends). As indicated by Gove et al. (1985), intimate partner violence is much less likely to be reported in the National Crime Victimization Survey than is violence committed by strangers.

African Americans are somewhat more likely than whites to be victims of violence, with the exception of simple assault. About 2.7 of every 100 African Americans were victims of violence in 2002, versus about 2.0 of every 100 whites. **Hispanics** are somewhat more likely to be the victims of violence than non-Hispanics. ("Hispanics" are defined as persons of Spanish-speaking origin; they may identify themselves as white, African American, or members of other racial groups.)

People with lower incomes are generally more likely to be victims of violence. About 4.1 of every 100 people in households with incomes of less than $7,500 were victims of violence, versus about 1.7 of every 100 people in households with incomes of $75,000 or more. **The relationship between household income and property crime is mixed.** About 5.5 of every 100 households with incomes lower than $7,500 were burglarized, versus 2.4 of every 100 households with incomes of at least $75,000. Households with higher incomes, however, were slightly more likely to experience larceny-theft.

In sum, the victims of violence tend to be young, male (except for rape/sexual assault), African American (except for simple assault), and poor. The relationship between household income and property crime is mixed.

How many victimizations are committed by juveniles? What do victimization data tell us about the number of crimes committed by juveniles? As indicated, crime victims are asked whether they saw the person(s) who victimized them. They rarely see the offender(s) in property crimes like larceny and burglary, but they almost always see the offender in violent crimes like assault, rape, and robbery. If victims saw the offender(s), they are asked to estimate the offender's age. The information that victimization data provide about the extent of juvenile delinquency, therefore, is largely limited to violent crimes (although see Hindelang, 1981, regarding property crime). Data from 2005 indicate that juveniles ages 12 to 17 committed about 437,000 serious violent crimes (rape/sexual assault, robbery, and aggravated assault), or about 1.8 serious violent crimes per 100 juveniles ages 12 to 17 (Federal Interagency Forum on Child and Family Statistics, 2007). These estimates exceed by several times those provided by FBI arrest and clearance data (e.g., 100,700 juveniles under age 18 were **arrested** for these crimes in 2006). So victimization data show that violent crime among juveniles is far more extensive than arrest data indicate, although not as extensive as indicated by self-report data.

Summary

You have been presented with a lot of numbers and may be feeling a little overwhelmed right now. Again, try not to get too caught up in all the numbers. Focus on the basic points being made by these numbers. These points include the following:

1. Arrest, self-report, and victimization data provide different estimates of the extent of delinquency in the United States. Arrest data provide the lowest estimates, and self-report data provide the highest. You should be able to explain why this is the case, drawing on the discussion of the advantages and disadvantages of each type of data.

2. Self-report data probably provide the most accurate estimate of the extent of delinquency. At least 90 percent of all adolescents engage in delinquency at some point, and, on average, each juvenile commits about 52 delinquent acts per year.

3. All three data sources indicate that minor offenses are more common than serious offenses and that property crime is more common than violent crime, although minor or simple assault is common.

Is Juvenile Delinquency Increasing?

As Bernard (1992) points out, most people think that juvenile delinquency is worse now than in the past. In fact, they often think of the past as the "good old days," a time when it was safe to walk the streets and juveniles almost never committed serious crimes like murder and rape. It is easy to understand why people feel this way. The media regularly report on the horrible crimes committed by juveniles. But what do the data show? Is delinquency increasing, decreasing, or staying the same? Once more, we must examine arrest, self-report, and victimization data. As you will see, they sometimes disagree with one another regarding trends in delinquency. Nevertheless, an examination of these data sources will allow us to draw some tentative conclusions about trends in delinquency. My focus is on **trends in delinquency since the early 1980s.**

Are Juvenile Arrests Increasing?

When examining trends in juvenile arrests, it is best to look at **arrest rates** rather than the number of arrests. Arrest rates are usually presented as the number of arrests per 100,000 juveniles ages 10 to 17 in the population. Arrest rates have the advantage of controlling for changes in the size of the juvenile population. If there is an increase in the number of juveniles, the number of juvenile arrests will likely increase because there are more juveniles to be arrested. This will occur even if the typical juvenile is no more or less delinquent than before. For example, there was a dramatic increase in the number of juvenile arrests during the 1960s and early 1970s. But part of this increase was because there were more juveniles to be arrested. As a result of the post–World War II baby boom, the number of juveniles between 10 and 17 years of age increased from about 25 million in 1960 to over 33 million in 1975. The arrest **rate** is not influenced by changes in the size of the juvenile population, since it shows the number of arrests per 100,000 juveniles. Changes in the arrest rate, then, provide a better indication of whether juveniles are becoming more or less delinquent.

The two graphs in Figure 3.1 show changes in the juvenile arrest rate for Part I violent crimes (homicide, aggravated assault, robbery, rape) and Part I property crimes (burglary, larceny, motor vehicle theft). Take a moment to look at these graphs.

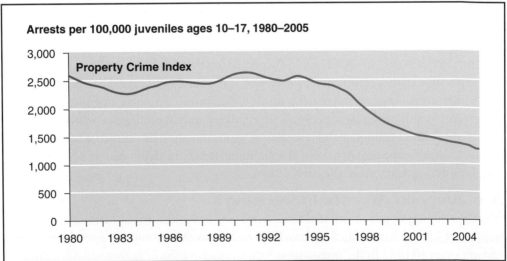

FIGURE 3.1 Trends in the Juvenile Arrest Rate for Part 1 Violent and Property Crimes

SOURCE: *Office of Juvenile Justice and Delinquency Prevention Statistical Briefing Book*, 2007.

These graphs suggest the following:

Property crime. The rate of property crime was reasonably stable from the early 1980s to 1994, with perhaps a modest increase in rates during the late 1980s and early 1990s. The rate has been declining since the mid-1990s, dropping from over 2,500 arrests per 100,000 juveniles in 1994 to less than 1,300 arrests per 100,000 juveniles in 2005. The rate of juvenile property crime is now at its lowest level since the 1960s. (The trends for particular types of property crime sometimes differ from the overall trend shown in Figure 3.1. The rate of burglary has been declining since the early 1980s. In fact, the 2005 burglary rate is about one-third of the 1980 rate. The rate of motor vehicle theft increased markedly from 1983 to 1989 but has been declining since 1991.)

Violent crime. The rate of violent crime arrests was reasonably stable from 1980 to 1988. It then increased by more than 60 percent between 1988 and 1994. This increase did much to draw attention to the juvenile crime problem, with the media running numerous stories about juvenile violence during this time. Violent crime arrests then declined from 1994 through the early 2000s. Violent crime rates have increased somewhat since 2004 but still remain well below their levels in the early to mid-1990s. This very recent increase has led to some discussion over whether the dramatic drop in violence since the mid-1990s has come to an end (see Butts and Snyder, 2007; Zimring, 2007). (With some moderate variations, this pattern tends to hold for most for most violent crimes.)

Trends in murder rates. I want to draw special attention to the crime of murder, since trends in the arrest rate for murder have been the subject of much discussion in the media and in the criminology literature.[1] The juvenile arrest rate for murder more than doubled between 1987 and 1993. This increase was especially dramatic because the arrest rate for murder among those over 25 declined during this period. Further, the increase in the juvenile arrest rate for murder was entirely due to an increase in gun-related murders. The juvenile arrest rate for nongun murders was stable (see Blumstein, 2006; Blumstein and Rosenfeld, 1998; Snyder, 2001).

There has been much discussion about **why the juvenile arrest rate for gun-related murders increased so dramatically during the late 1980s and early 1990s.** Among other things, some evidence suggests that the increase was due to the spread of crack cocaine during the mid- to late 1980s. Juveniles became heavily involved in the crack trade, and they often armed themselves for protection (you cannot call the police for protection if you are a crack dealer). So guns became more common among certain juveniles. This led other juveniles to feel that they had to carry guns for protection. The end result was that guns spread throughout the juvenile population, and disputes that used to be settled with fists or knives came to be settled with bullets (Blumstein and Rosenfeld, 1998; Blumstein and Wallman, 2006; Cork, 1999).

The increase in juvenile homicides (and serious violence more generally) has also been linked to certain social changes which led to an increase in gangs (see Braga, 2003; Greenwood, 2002). These changes include a decline in manufacturing jobs, especially in inner-city neighborhoods; an increase in single-parent families; and tensions involving recent immigrants to the United States (see Chapter 16 for further discussion). Such changes likely contributed to the dramatic growth in gangs during the 1980s and early to mid-1990s (Walter Miller, 2001). As discussed in Chapter 16, gang members are more likely than nonmembers to possess and use guns.

The juvenile arrest rate for murder declined sharply from 1994 to 2004, with the decline more than erasing the previous increase in arrest rates for murder. There has also been much discussion about the reasons for this decline and the more general decline in violent and property crimes—a topic that I address shortly. The juvenile murder rate has been increasing since 2004 but is still well below its levels in the early to mid-1990s. To illustrate, the rate peaked in 1993, with 14.4 juveniles per 100,000 being arrested for murder. The juvenile murder rate in 2006 was 3.9 per 100,000, less than one-third of the 1993 rate.

Overall, arrest data suggest the following about trends in delinquency since the early 1980s: (1) rates of property crime were fairly stable from the early 1980s to 1994, with perhaps a modest increase in the late 1980s and early 1990s, then rates declined sharply after 1994; (2) rates of violent crime were stable through the late 1980s, increased sharply from 1988 to 1994, then declined sharply until 2004, and have increased since 2004. I have focused on Part I crimes. I should note that trends in Part II crimes are somewhat varied, although arrests for most such crimes have declined in recent years. Perhaps the most striking trends in arrests for Part II crimes involve drug abuse and curfew/loitering violations. There was a dramatic increase in the arrest rates for drug abuse and curfew/loitering violations in the mid-1990s—followed by decreases in the arrest rates for these crimes in the later 1990s and early 2000s. (There is good reason to believe that much of the increase in curfew/loitering arrests reflects changes in the law and police practices. Many cities, for example, responded to the increase in juvenile violence by instituting curfews for juveniles or more strictly enforcing existing curfew laws.)

Is Self-Reported Delinquency Increasing?

The Monitoring the Future survey described earlier provides information on trends in self-reported delinquency. Again, these data focus on high school seniors. They do not contain information on certain serious crimes, like murder and rape. Rather, they tend to focus on minor offenses or minor instances of more serious offenses (for reasons indicated in Chapter 2). Also, their use of the response category "5 or more times" means that they underestimate the extent of delinquency. Nevertheless, these data provide some indication of trends in delinquency—especially minor delinquency—among high school seniors throughout the United States.[2]

The graph in Figure 3.2 shows trends in the rate of self-reported property crime and violent crime from 1980 to 2006. In particular, it shows the number of property and violent crimes reported each year per 100 high school seniors. I focus on four property crimes: larceny under $50, larceny over $50, shoplifting, and auto theft (there is no good measure of burglary in the survey). And I focus on three violent crimes: serious assault, group fights, and robbery. Take a moment to examine the graph in Figure 3.2. Focus on long-term trends, rather than short-term or year-to-year fluctuations in the delinquency rate. These short-term fluctuations may be due to chance, but substantial changes in the crime rate that last for several years likely reflect real changes.[3]

Property crime. The rate of property crime was generally stable during the early to mid-1980s, increased by a modest amount during the late 1980s and 1990s, then declined by a modest amount during the 2000s. To illustrate, the average rate of property crime each year from 1980 to 1986 was 159.6 property crimes per 100 high school seniors. The average rate of property crime per year from 1987 to 2002 was 188.2 property crimes per 100

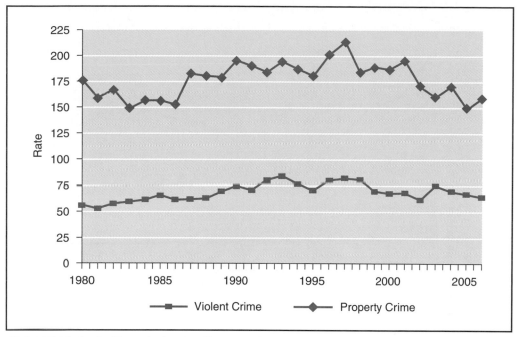

FIGURE 3.2 Trends in the Rate of Self-Reported Delinquency of High School Seniors (Rate = Number of Acts per 100 Seniors)

SOURCE: Monitoring the Future survey, as reported in the *Sourcebook of Criminal Justice Statistics*.

seniors. The average rate from 2003 to 2006 was 159.7 per 100 seniors. These data are somewhat at odds with arrest data. While arrest data also show a modest increase in rates of property crime during the late 1980s, arrest data show a sharp decline in rates of property crime since the mid-1990s.

Violent crime. It is more difficult to discern clear patterns in the rate of self-reported violence. Rates of violence were fairly stable during much of the 1980s but then increased somewhat during the late 1980s and 1990s. To illustrate, the average rate of violence each year from 1980 to 1988 was 59.6 violent acts per 100 high school seniors. The average rate of violence each year from 1989 to 1998 was 76.3 violent acts per 100 seniors. There perhaps has been a slight decrease in the rate of violence since 1998, with the average rate of violence from 1999 to 2006 being 67.4 acts per 100 seniors. These data are also somewhat at odds with arrest data. Arrest data show a larger increase in violence in the late 1980s. Also, arrest data show a larger decline in violence, beginning in the mid-1990s.

Drug use. Figure 3.3 shows trends in drug use using data from the Monitoring the Future study of high school seniors. In particular, Figure 3.3 shows the percentage of high school seniors who used an illicit drug in the last 30 days. Illicit drugs include marijuana, LSD and other hallucinogens, crack and other cocaine, heroin and other narcotics, amphetamines, barbiturates, and tranquilizers (not under a doctor's orders). As can be seen, there was a dramatic decrease in illicit drug use from the early 1980s to 1992. Illicit drug use then increased a good deal during the 1990s, with the percentage of high school seniors reporting illicit drug use almost doubling. This increase attracted much attention in the media

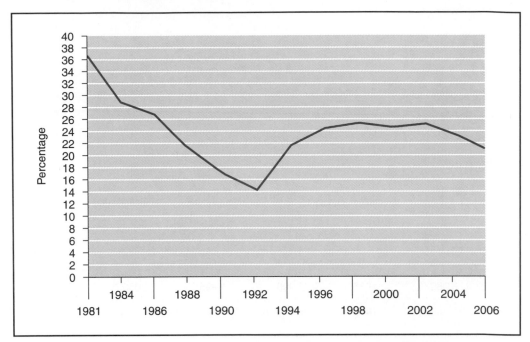

FIGURE 3.3 Percentage of High School Seniors Using Illicit Drugs in the Last 30 Days

SOURCE: Monitoring the Future survey, as reported in the Federal Interagency Forum on Child and Family Statistics, 2007.

and was a major issue in the 1996 presidential campaign. A major antidrug initiative was launched by the federal government in response to this increase (see Office of National Drug Control Policy, 1999, 2007). And illicit drug use has in fact been decreasing since the early 2000s. (Note: Other data on illicit drug use, including data on younger juveniles, largely confirm these trends; see Federal Interagency Forum on Child and Family Statistics, 2007; and http://oas.samhsa.gov/NSDUHLatest.htm. I should note, however, that trends in the use of particular drugs sometimes differ from the general trends in illicit drug use just described.)

In sum, self-report data suggest the following about trends in delinquency: (1) the rate of property crime was generally stable during the early to mid-1980s, increased by a modest amount during the late 1980s and 1990s, then declined by a modest amount during the 2000s; (2) the rate of violent crime was stable during much of the 1980s, increased during the late 1980s and generally remained high during much of the 1990s, then decreased slightly since 1998; and (3) the rate of illicit drug use decreased during the 1980s and early 1990s, increased during the 1990s, then decreased since the early 2000s.

Are Victimizations Committed by Juveniles Increasing?

We can use the National Crime Victimization Survey to estimate the rate of violent crime victimizations committed by juveniles ages 12 through 17. Data indicate that this rate was moderately stable during much of the 1980s, increased during the late 1980s and early 1990s, declined dramatically from 1993 to 2002, and has started to increase in recent years. These trends are illustrated in Figure 3.4, with this graph focusing on aggravated assaults, robberies, rapes, and homicides committed by juveniles ages 12 to 17 (the homicide data are from police reports).

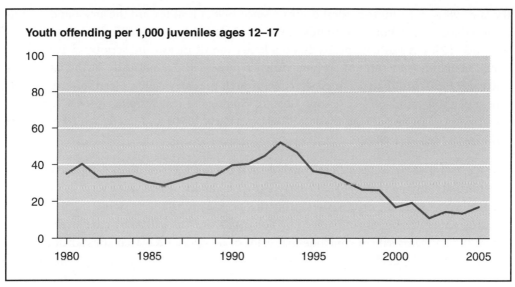

Youth offending per 1,000 juveniles ages 12–17

FIGURE 3.4 Trends in the Rate of Violent Victimizations Committed by Juveniles Ages 12–17

SOURCE: Federal Interagency Forum on Child and Family Statistics, 2007.

So victimization data, like arrest data, indicate that the violent crime rate for juveniles was reasonably stable during the early to mid-1980s, increased in the late 1980s and early 1990s, declined sharply through the early 2000s, and has started to increase in recent years. Unfortunately, victimization data on trends in property crime by juveniles are largely lacking.

Summary

We began with a simple question: Is juvenile delinquency increasing? But, as you can see, the answer is anything but simple. The answer varies somewhat by type of crime and by data source. Nevertheless, there are some general conclusions we can draw:

Property crime. Arrest and self-report data disagree somewhat regarding trends in property crime. Both arrest and self-report data suggest that rates of property crime were fairly stable during much of the 1980s, with a modest increase during the late 1980s. But arrest data show that rates of property crime have declined sharply since the mid-1990s, while self-report data only show a modest decline during the 2000s. One possible explanation for this difference is that arrest data are biased toward serious crimes and the more serious instances of less serious crimes, while self-report data are biased toward minor crimes. In particular, the Monitoring the Future survey does not measure the crime of burglary, it likely picks up large numbers of trivial property crimes, and it under samples those juveniles most likely to engage in serious property crime. So we might **tentatively** conclude that there has been **a decline in serious property crime since the mid-1990s, but only a modest decline in minor property crime since the early 2000s.**

Violent crime. Arrest and victimization data indicate that rates of juvenile violence were generally stable in the early to mid-1980s, increased substantially in the late 1980s and early 1990s, decreased substantially from the mid-1990s to early 2000s, and increased since 2003 or 2004. Self-report data, however, show a more modest increase in violence during the late 1980s and a more modest decrease since 1998. I lean toward the arrest and victimization data when it comes to trends in serious violence. For reasons indicated earlier, arrest and victimization data probably do a better job of measuring serious violence. So I would conclude that **rates of serious violence increased dramatically in the late 1980s and early 1990s but then declined sharply through the early 2000s.** I lean toward the self-report data for trends in less serious violence. So **rates of less serious violence increased by a modest amount during the late 1980s and early 1990s and decreased by a modest amount in the late 1990s.**

Drug crime. It seems safe to conclude that **overall rates of illicit drug use declined substantially during the 1980s and early 1990s.** All major self-report data indicate such a decline. Arrest rates for drug abuse during this period are relatively stable, but arrest rates for drug abuse are heavily influenced by police practices as well as by true levels of drug abuse. It also seems safe to conclude that **rates of drug use increased substantially from about 1992 to the early 2000s.** Both self-report and arrest data are in agreement here. **Rates of illicit drug use have been declining since the early 2000s,** with this decline evident in both self-report and arrest data.

How Can We Explain the Dramatic Decline in Serious Crime Since the Mid-1990s?

As indicated, there is good reason to believe that there has been a dramatic decline in the rates of serious violent and property crime from the mid-1990s to at least the early 2000s. It is, of course, important to determine why this decline has occurred. Doing so may help us better predict future trends in crime and may even help us influence those trends. For example, if we determine that certain police practices contributed to the decline, we might make an effort to continue or increase the use of such practices.

Unfortunately, **it is often difficult to determine whether particular factors contributed to the decline.** Researchers need to demonstrate that a particular factor changed around the time that crime rates declined and that there is good reason to believe that this change affected crime rates. But this is not always possible. Nevertheless, there is some reason to believe that **several factors may have contributed to the decline in juvenile crime rates.**[4]

Two such factors are the **decline in crack use** and in the **turf disputes between crack dealers.** As indicated earlier, the increase in crack use in the 1980s likely contributed to the increase in serious juvenile violence during this time. Juveniles became heavily involved in the crack trade; they armed themselves for protection, given the dangers involved; other juveniles responded by arming themselves; and, as a consequence, disputes that used to be settled with fists came to be settled with guns. Crack use, however, began to decline in the 1990s, partly because attitudes toward crack became more negative as people became aware of the devastating effects of this drug. Also, competition between crack dealers decreased as dealers established their territories. As a consequence, juvenile involvement in the crack trade declined, and the trade itself became less violent. This, in turn, contributed to a decrease in gun carrying and use among juveniles.

The decline in crime rates was also probably influenced by **improvements in the economy** during the 1990s. Among other things, the percentage of children living in poverty fell sharply from 1993 through the early 2000s, especially for African American children (Federal Interagency Forum on Child and Family Statistics, 2007). Reductions in poverty contribute to **better parenting practices and improved school performance,** which in turn contribute to lower delinquency (see Bellair and Roscigno, 2000; Chapters 14 and 15 in this text). Also, unemployment declined to the point that **teenagers with few skills and a limited education were able to get jobs.** Data suggest that employment reduces crime, especially when illegal opportunities to make money—like selling crack—are on the decline (see Allan and Steffensmeier, 1989; Grogger, 2006; Zimring, 2006). Further, improvements in the economy likely contributed to the **decline in gangs** that began in the mid-1990s, with this decline also contributing to the reduction in crime rates (see Chapter 16).

Improvements in police practices may have also contributed to the decline in crime rates, although the data here are less clear-cut. Many cities adopted new methods of policing. Evidence suggests that certain of these methods are effective at reducing crime. These include efforts to crack down on particular types of crime such as drug selling and gun carrying, to crack down on gangs, and to crack down on locations with high rates of crime. These methods also include certain types of "community policing," such as problem-oriented policing where the police attempt to address the underlying problems that contribute to crime. (These methods and the evidence on their effectiveness are described in Chapter 20.) However, we lack good data on the extent to which these methods were adopted by police departments across the country. Also, many cities experienced substantial reductions in crime even though they did not adopt such methods to any significant degree (see Conklin, 2003; Eck and Maguire, 2006; Zimring, 2007). Even so, some criminologists feel that new methods of policing helped contribute to the reduction in crime rates.

Further, **the increased use of prevention and rehabilitation programs** during the 1990s may have contributed to the decline. These programs include efforts to help troubled families, to help children do better in school, to provide mentors for at-risk and delinquent children, to mediate gang disputes, and to provide teenagers with organized recreational activities (see Chapter 24 for a discussion of rehabilitation and prevention programs). However, we lack good data on the extent to which effective rehabilitation and prevention programs were employed during the 1990s.

Finally, **the higher rate at which juvenile offenders were incarcerated** in the 1990s may have contributed to the decline. Confining more juvenile offenders may prevent crime in two ways: the confined juveniles are unable to commit crimes on the street, and their confinement may deter others from crime. It is estimated that increased rates of confinement accounted for about one-fourth of the reduction in **adult** crime during the 1990s (see Blumstein and Wallman, 2006; Conklin, 2006; Zimring, 2006). But the rate at which juveniles were confined increased at a much slower pace than the rate at which adults were confined, so **increased rates of confinement probably account for only a small portion of the decrease in juvenile crime rates** (see Chapter 23).

In sum, several factors likely contributed to the decline in rates of serious offending that began in the mid-1990s. Whether this decline continues likely depends on such things as trends in the economy and the extent to which the United States makes use of effective crime control strategies, including new methods of policing (see Chapter 20), better methods of sanctioning juvenile offenders (see Chapter 23), and effective methods of rehabilitating offenders and preventing delinquency (see Chapter 24). All of these things are important because they impact the causes of delinquency, described in Chapters 6 through 18.

Teaching Aids

Exercise: The Extent of and Trends in Campus Crime

Colleges and universities are required to collect data on the extent of crime on campus and make that data available to the public. I would like you to obtain data on the extent of crime on your campus during the previous two years (you can probably obtain such data by visiting the office or website of your campus police or security force). Then do the following:

1. Figure out what data are being reported. In particular, what crimes are listed and what types of data are available on each crime (e.g., number of crimes known to the police, number of arrests)?

2. Look at the number of crimes listed for each type of crime. Do you think these numbers provide an accurate indication of the extent of crime on your campus (e.g., the extent of liquor law violations, drug offenses, sexual assaults)? If not, list all the reasons why such data may underestimate the extent of campus crime.

3. Determine whether the number of crimes increased, decreased, or stayed the same over the previous two years. In particular, calculate the percentage change in the number of crimes. Do this for each type of crime. (For example, you might find that the number of liquor law violations increased 50 percent from 2006 to 2007.) Do you think these data provide a good indication of the true amount of change in the extent of crime? If not, list all of the reasons why not.

4. How might you go about better determining the extent of crime on campus and trends in crime? (Note: See Fisher et al., 1998, for an example of a victimization survey conducted on 12 college campuses. They found that more than 33 percent of the students they surveyed had been the victims of crime during the academic year. Furthermore, "the main predictor of violent victimization was a lifestyle that included high levels of partying on campus and the recreational use of drugs" [Fisher et al., 1998:671; also see Hart, 2003].)

TEST YOUR KNOWLEDGE OF THIS CHAPTER

1. What general conclusions can we draw about the extent and nature of delinquency from arrest data (e.g., how widespread is delinquency, what types of crime are most common)?

2. What is the "arrest rate"?

3. What do clearance data show?

4. Why is the number of juveniles arrested greater than the number of crimes cleared by the arrest of juveniles?

5. What general conclusions can we draw about the extent and nature of delinquency from self-report data?

6. Why are estimates of the extent of delinquency based on self-report data so much larger than those based on arrest data?

7. Who is most likely to be victimized?

8. Why is it that victimization data provide so little information about the characteristics of people who commit property crimes?

9. Why do I argue that we should examine arrest rates when investigating trends in delinquency?

10. Drawing on arrest data, describe the major trends in property and violent crimes since the early 1980s.

11. Describe the major trends in arrest rates for murder. How have criminologists explained the sharp increase in arrest rates for murder in the late 1980s and early 1990s?

12. Drawing on self-report data, describe trends in violent crime, property crime, and illicit drug use since the early 1980s.

13. Drawing on victimization data, describe trends in violent crime since the early 1980s.

14. Drawing on all data sources, I draw general conclusions about trends in property crime, violent crime, and illicit drug use since the early 1980s. What are they?

15. Describe those factors that may have contributed to the large decline in serious crime rates in the 1990s. Briefly note any problems in the evidence linking these factors to the decline in crime rates (e.g., indicate that we lack good data on the extent to which effective rehabilitation and prevention programs were employed in the 1990s).

THOUGHT AND DISCUSSION QUESTIONS

1. Self-report data suggest that 90 percent or more of all adolescents engage in delinquency at some point. Why do you think delinquency is so common among adolescents? How might we explain the fact that a small portion of adolescents—10 percent or less—manage to refrain from delinquency? (See Chapter 10; Agnew, 2003a; and Moffitt, 1993, for discussions of these issues.)

2. Despite the sharp decline in serious crime during the 1990s and early 2000s, many people believe that delinquency increased during this time. How might we explain this?

3. Give an example of a situation where the juvenile arrest rate remains the same, but the number of crimes committed by juveniles increases. (Hint: The number of persons under age 18 will increase by over 10 million in the next 20 years.)

4. Data suggest that while rates of serious delinquency declined sharply during the 1990s, rates of minor delinquency did not. How might we explain this difference in trends?

5. Do you think rates of serious delinquency will decline any further? Justify your response.

6. Why do you think rates of illicit drug use have declined since the late 1990s?

KEY TERMS

- Arrest rates
- Clearance data

ENDNOTES

1. For examples, *see* Blumstein, 1995; Blumstein and Rosenfeld, 1998; Blumstein and Wallman, 2006; Braga, 2003; Cook and Laub, 1998; Cork, 1999; Fox and Zawitz, 1999; National Institute of Justice, 1998a; Ousey and Lee, 2004; Messner et al., 2005; Zimring, 1998, 2007.

2. *See* Browning and Huizinga, 1999; Huizinga et al., 2003; McCord et al., 2001; and Steffensmeier et al., 2005, for additional self-report data on trends in delinquency.

3. Jensen and Rojek (1998), McCord et al. (2001), and Osgood et al. (1989) have conducted similar analyses using earlier data from the Monitoring the Future survey.

4. *See* the discussions in Blumstein, 2002; Blumstein and Rosenfeld, 1998; Blumstein and Wallman, 2006; Conklin, 2003; LaFree, 1999; Ousey and Augustine, 2001; Ousey and Lee, 2004, 2007; Messner et al., 2005; Steffensmeier and Harer, 1999; Zimring, 2007.

CHAPTER 4

Who Is Most Likely to Engage in Delinquency?

Suppose that you encountered a group of people, some young and some old, some male and some female, some white and some African American, and some lower class and some middle class. Further, suppose that you wanted to divide this group in two: criminals on the one side and noncriminals (or less serious criminals) on the other. What characteristic would best allow you to do this: age, gender, race, or social class?

If you are like many people, you probably think that race and class do the best job of distinguishing criminals from noncriminals. This view is often fostered by the media, which tend to portray crime as a problem that is concentrated in poor African American communities. But in fact, age and gender do a far better job of distinguishing criminals from noncriminals. In particular, adolescent males have crime rates that far exceed those of other groups. Of course, not all adolescent males engage in crime. While age and sex are strongly related to crime, the relationship is far from perfect. Nevertheless, age and sex are more strongly related to crime than class and race.

This chapter examines the *sociodemographic characteristics* **of delinquents.** I focus on the relationship between delinquency and social class, race/ethnicity, gender, and age. (Social class is usually measured in terms of the occupational prestige, education, and/or income of the juvenile's parents.) Once more, you will find that simple questions often have complex answers. This is especially the case when I ask whether lower-class juveniles are more delinquent than middle-class juveniles and whether African Americans are more delinquent than whites. Also, you will find that arrest, self-report, and victimization data sometimes disagree about the characteristics of delinquents. I think that there are nevertheless a number of conclusions that can safely be drawn about the characteristics of delinquents, and I think that you will find some of these conclusions rather surprising, because I suspect that they will challenge your view of the typical juvenile delinquent.

Is Social Class Related to Delinquency?

Before I talk about social class in my juvenile delinquency course, I tell the students about a trait known as "tolerance of ambiguity." Some individuals have a low tolerance of ambiguity. That is, they have a strong need for definite, clear-cut answers. When they take a course, they want to be told what is right and what is wrong—no "ifs, ands, or buts." They get very uneasy, even upset, if they are told that the studies in an area contradict one another or that the relationship between certain factors depends on other factors. I mention this trait to you for a good reason: I want to warn you in advance. If you have a low tolerance of ambiguity, you might get a little uneasy with the following discussion on the relationship between social class and delinquency.

Most people assume that lower-class juveniles are more delinquent than middle-class juveniles. A large number of studies have tried to determine whether this is true, but these studies often contradict one another. In fact, you can find studies that support just about any position you like. Many studies find that lower-class juveniles are more delinquent than middle-class juveniles. Many studies find that lower-class and middle-class juveniles engage in about the same amount of delinquency. And a few studies even find that middle-class juveniles are more delinquent than lower-class juveniles. The conclusions that criminologists draw about the relationship between social class and delinquency reflect these studies. Some prominent criminologists argue that there is little or no relationship between class and delinquency, while others argue that lower-class juveniles are more likely to engage in at least some types of delinquency. So we ask a simple question: Are lower-class juveniles more delinquent than middle-class juveniles? But the answer is anything but simple.[1]

I want to help you make sense of the contradictory research on this topic. The best way to do that is by providing you with a historic overview of the research on the relationship between class and delinquency. At the end of this overview, I'll draw two general conclusions about the relationship between class and delinquency, one well supported by the data and the other more tentative.

Early Studies Based on Arrest Data

Until the 1960s, the main way of measuring delinquency was through the use of arrest data or police reports. Criminologists asked whether lower-class juveniles were more likely to be arrested or come in contact with the police than higher-class juveniles. The FBI does not provide any information on the social class of arrested individuals. But researchers compared the juvenile arrest rates of lower- and higher-class communities. And, less commonly, they compared the arrest records of lower- and higher-class juveniles.

Virtually every study found that lower-class communities had much higher arrest rates than higher-class communities (see the discussion on communities in Chapter 12). Also, most studies found that lower-class juveniles were more likely to be arrested or have police reports than middle-class juveniles (see especially Braithwaite, 1981). One of the best studies in this area looked at all juveniles who were born in Philadelphia in 1958 and who lived in Philadelphia from the ages of 10 through 17—a total of 27,160 juveniles. It was found that 42 percent of the lower-class males had a police record, as compared to 24 percent of the higher-class males (Tracy, 1990).

On the basis of these studies, criminologists came to the conclusion that social class was strongly associated with delinquency. In fact, criminology textbooks from the 1960s and before often state that one of the most important and best-supported facts about delinquency is that it is concentrated in the lower classes. This belief led criminologists to construct a number of theories to explain why delinquency was concentrated in the lower classes. And billions of dollars were spent on the War on Poverty in the 1960s and early 1970s, partly on the assumption that poverty was a major cause of crime and delinquency. Criminologists, however, experienced a major shock in the 1960s.

Early Self-Report Studies

Self-report surveys of delinquency came into wide use during the 1960s, and most of these surveys found **little or no relationship between social class and delinquency.** This result challenged a fundamental belief of most criminologists, as well as of policy makers and people in the general public. (Victimization data cannot be used to examine the relationship between social class and delinquency, since crime victims are not asked to estimate the class of the people who victimized them.)

The finding that lower- and middle-class adolescents are equally delinquent seems to challenge our personal experiences. Lower-class neighborhoods, for example, seem unsafe to us, while middle-class neighborhoods seem quite safe. This finding also seems to challenge common sense. It is easy to think of reasons why lower-class adolescents should be more delinquent than middle-class adolescents, but difficult to think of reasons why lower- and middle-class adolescents should be equally delinquent. Nevertheless, numerous self-report studies during the 1960s and 1970s found little or no relationship between class and delinquency. Further, some evidence suggested that the relationship between social class and arrest rates was becoming weaker over time (Tittle et al., 1978). As a consequence, many criminologists came to feel that class was unrelated to delinquency. A major review article published in 1978, in fact, was titled "The Myth of Social Class and Criminality" (Tittle et al., 1978).

If class is unrelated to delinquency, **how can one account for the findings from arrest data?** It was said that arrest data were biased. Only a small number of delinquent offenses were reported to the police and, of those, only a small number resulted in arrest. It was claimed that offenses committed by lower-class juveniles were more likely to come to the attention of the police and were more likely to result in arrest. (Chapter 22 discusses the evidence on police discrimination against lower-class juveniles.)

Likewise, if class is unrelated to delinquency, **how can one account for the perception that lower-class juveniles are more delinquent?** A fascinating study by Chambliss (1973) suggests why perceptions regarding the relationship between social class and delinquency may be wrong. Chambliss examined two groups of adolescent males in a high school: the "Saints" and the "Roughnecks." The middle-class Saints were well liked and respected by their teachers and members of the community. In fact, the Saints included some of the top students in the school. The lower-class Roughnecks were disliked and seen as delinquents by their teachers and community residents. Chambliss, however, discovered that the two groups were about equally delinquent. Why, then, were they perceived so differently? Chambliss lists three reasons. **First,** the delinquency of the Saints was less visible. The Saints went to great lengths to hide their delinquency; for example, their greater access to cars allowed them to commit many of their delinquent acts in remote locations. **Second,** the Saints had a better demeanor: They were respectful and apologetic when caught doing something wrong. The Roughnecks, however, were often hostile. As a consequence, people tended to assume that the Saints were basically "good kids" who would occasionally "sow their wild oats," while the Roughnecks were "troublemakers." **Finally,** people were simply biased in favor of the Saints and against the Roughnecks, this bias reflecting their beliefs about what lower-class and middle-class people are like. This bias, in turn, influenced their perceptions of the two groups—what they noticed and how they interpreted what they noticed.

Finally, if class is unrelated to delinquency, **how can we account for all the good reasons linking class to delinquency?** A recent study presents data indicating that while higher-class juveniles are less likely to engage in delinquency for some reasons, they are more likely to engage in delinquency for other reasons (Wright et al., 1999a). For example, higher-class juveniles are less likely to engage in delinquency because they have less need for money. But higher-class juveniles are more likely to engage in delinquency because they have greater "social power"; that is, they are better able to avoid detection and are better able to resist the efforts of others—teachers and police, for example—to punish them. These effects tend to cancel one another out, so one finds that social class has little relationship to delinquency.

By the late 1970s many criminologists were stating that there was little or no relationship between social class and delinquency. Several criminologists, however, challenged this conclusion.

Criticisms of the Early Self-Report Studies

Some criminologists said that the early self-report studies suffered from several problems and that these problems account for their failure to find any relationship between social class and delinquency.[2]

First, the early self-report studies **focused on minor delinquent acts.** That is, they used measures that focus on status offenses and minor delinquent acts like petty theft and simple assault. Many of these studies, for example, employed the measure of delinquency shown in Table 2.3 (p. 28). Or if the studies did consider serious acts, these acts were not examined separately. Rather, the researchers created general scales that measured the extent to which adolescents engage in both minor and serious delinquency. The more frequently occurring minor offenses have a much greater influence on counts of delinquency than the less frequently occurring serious offenses (see Elliott and Huizinga, 1983:153–154). The early self-report studies, then, do not tell us anything about the relationship between class and serious delinquency. They simply suggest that class is unrelated to minor delinquency. It may be that class is related to serious delinquency. In this area, some criminologists note that arrest data contain a higher portion of serious offenses than self-report data. This may be why arrests are typically related to social class, while self-reports of delinquency are not.

Second, the early self-report studies **often used delinquency measures with truncated response categories, like "5 or more times."** So someone who commits an act 5 times is included in the same category as someone who commits the act 100 times. Again, this is a serious problem because there is a small group of high-rate offenders who commit an enormous number of delinquent acts. The early self-report surveys, however, did not accurately measure the delinquency of these high-rate offenders. These high-rate offenders, committing scores or even hundreds of delinquent acts, are not distinguished from juveniles committing only a few delinquent acts. It may be that the lower class has more high-rate offenders than the middle class. And if the delinquency of these high-rate offenders was accurately measured, one might well find that the lower class engages in more delinquency than the middle class.

Third, the early self-report studies **often employed problematic measures of social class.** Most notably, they **failed to examine very poor juveniles.** Many of the early self-report studies examined only a few hundred juveniles from one or a few schools; there are not enough very poor juveniles in these studies to examine separately. In other cases, researchers failed to distinguish the very poor juveniles from other groups. For example, the very poor are combined with the working class. It may be that delinquency is higher among the very poor, but that there is no difference in delinquency between the working and middle classes. So it is important to examine the very poor separately, and criminologists have started to experiment with different methods for better identifying the very poor. For example, they focus on juveniles whose parents receive welfare benefits (see Brownfield, 1986; Farnworth et al., 1994). Also, the early self-report studies **failed to measure the duration of poverty** or the length of time that juveniles have been poor. Many juveniles experience short periods of poverty, while others live in poverty for long periods. We would expect long-term or persistent poverty to have a stronger effect on delinquency (see Farnworth et al., 1994; Jarjoura et al., 2002).

The Later Self-Report Studies

Several criminologists have conducted self-report studies that attempt to correct for some or all of the problems discussed in the preceding section. Perhaps the most prominent of these studies are the analyses of the National Youth Survey (NYS) conducted by Elliott and associates (Elliott and Ageton, 1980; Elliott and Huizinga, 1983). The NYS was described earlier. It examines both minor and serious delinquency. It accurately measures the number of delinquent acts that juveniles commit. And Elliott and associates distinguish lower-class juveniles from both working- and middle-class juveniles (although they do not measure the duration of poverty). What do their analyses of the NYS data reveal about the relationship between social class and delinquency? Their major findings are as follows:

1. **There are few or no class differences in most types of minor delinquency.** Table 4.1 reports the average number of delinquent acts committed by lower-, working-, and middle-class juveniles for several types of delinquency. Note that the averages are quite similar for the minor types of delinquency.

2. **The lower class is more likely to engage in serious delinquency.** As indicated in Table 4.1, the average number of violent crimes committed by a lower-class juvenile is about four times as high as the average number committed by a middle-class juvenile. The average number of property crimes committed by a lower-class juvenile is about twice as high as the average number committed by a middle-class juvenile.

3. **The reason that lower-class juveniles have a higher average rate of serious delinquency is that there are more high-rate offenders in the lower class.** For example, 2.8 percent of the lower-class juveniles commit more than 55 serious violent acts per year, whereas only 0.8 percent of the middle-class juveniles commit more than 55 violent acts per year. This point is very important. The lower class has a higher average rate of serious crime not because the typical lower-class juvenile is more involved in serious crime than the typical working- or middle-class juvenile. Most lower-class juveniles commit very few serious crimes. Rather, most of the serious crimes are committed by a small group of high-rate offenders. These high-rate offenders make up only a very small proportion of the lower class, but these high-rate offenders are two to three times more common in the lower class than in the middle class. And that is why the average rate of serious crime is higher in the lower class.

| TABLE 4.1 | Average Number of Self-Reported Delinquent Acts Committed by Lower-, Working-, and Middle-Class Juveniles in 1976 |

	Violent Crimes	Property Crimes	Public Disorder Crimes	Status Offenses
Lower class	12	14	14	14
Working class	8	9	16	14
Middle class	3	7	14	16

SOURCE: Elliott and Ageton, 1980.

Note: Violent crimes include sexual assault, aggravated assault, simple assault, and robbery. Property crimes include vandalism, burglary, auto theft, larceny, stolen goods, fraud, and joyriding. Public disorder crimes include carrying a concealed weapon, hitchhiking, disorderly conduct, drunkenness, panhandling, making obscene phone calls, and marijuana use. Status offenses include runaway, sexual intercourse, alcohol use, and truancy.

There have been several attempts to replicate the findings of Elliott and associates. That is, other researchers have examined serious delinquency separately from minor delinquency, have accurately measured the extent of delinquency, and/or have focused on the very poor. Not all of these attempts at replication have reached the same conclusions as Elliott and associates. Certain studies, in particular, have found that social class is unrelated to both serious and minor delinquency (e.g., Weis, 1987). Other studies, however, tend to support the work of Elliott and associates, although some of these studies find that social class has only a moderate association with serious delinquency.[3] In addition, two studies have examined the effect of persistent poverty on delinquency (Farnworth et al., 1994; Jarjoura et al., 2002). These studies have found that the length of time a juvenile lives in poverty does make a difference, with **those juveniles experiencing persistent poverty being more likely to engage in delinquency.**

Taken as a whole, I believe that the previous studies provide some support for the critiques of the early self-report surveys. They demonstrate that it is important to examine serious delinquency separately from minor delinquency; to accurately count the number of delinquent acts that are committed; pay special attention to the very poor; and examine the duration of poverty. When these steps are taken, researchers tend to find a relationship between class and serious delinquency. At the same time, most find little or no relationship between class and minor delinquency.

Summary

You can see why there is still some confusion in the field about the relationship between social class and delinquency. Again, we began with a simple question, but the answer turns out to be quite complex. Nevertheless, I believe that there are some general conclusions that can be drawn about the relationship between social class and delinquency.

1. **There is good reason to believe that social class is largely unrelated to minor delinquency.** The large majority of self-report studies come to this conclusion. Arrest data tend to focus on more serious delinquency, so they are of limited relevance here.

2. **It is likely that social class is moderately related to serious delinquency, with lower-class juveniles having higher average rates of such delinquency.** The average rates of serious delinquency may be higher in the lower class because there are more high-rate offenders in the lower class—not because the typical lower-class juvenile is more delinquent than the typical working- or middle-class juvenile. Most of the better self-report studies suggest a relationship between class and serious delinquency, as do most studies based on arrest data. Further, there is little doubt that lower-class communities have higher rates of serious crime. As Braithwaite (1981:37) points out, "It is hardly plausible that one can totally explain away the higher risks of being mugged and raped in lower-class areas as a consequence of the activities of middle-class people who come into the area to perpetrate such acts."

Are Race and Ethnicity Related to Delinquency?

As with social class, the data on race and ethnicity and delinquency are somewhat contradictory, but there are some conclusions that criminologists can more or less safely draw.[4] My focus is on African Americans and whites because most data deal with these groups. Unfortunately, we lack extensive data on other race and ethnic groups, including Latinos,

Asians and Pacific Islanders, and American Indians. And there are often problems with the data we do have. For example, studies often fail to distinguish between the major Latino groups in the United States, such as Mexican Americans, Puerto Ricans, and Cuban Americans. While these groups have much in common, they also differ in important ways. To illustrate, Puerto Ricans are United States citizens, while many Mexican immigrants struggle with citizenship-related problems (see Cintron, 2006). Whenever possible, however, I note what the data say regarding the delinquency of racial and ethnic groups other than whites and African Americans.

I first describe what arrest, self-report, and victimization data have to say about the relationship between race/ethnicity and delinquency. I then draw two general conclusions about the relationship. And I finish by discussing whether the relationship between race and serious delinquency is explained by race-related differences in social class.

Arrest Data

The racial composition of the juvenile population in 2006 was 76 percent white, 15 percent African American, 5 percent Asian or Pacific Islander, 1 percent American Indian, and 3 percent other or mixed races. Latinos are an ethnic group, and most Latinos classify themselves as white. Mexican Americans constitute the largest share of Latinos, followed by Puerto Ricans and Cuban Americans. About 20 percent of the juvenile population was Latino in 2006, but the FBI does not report arrest data on Latinos and non-Latinos. Several individual studies, however, suggest that Latinos have higher arrest rates than non-Latinos for at least certain crimes—with Latino rates often falling between African American and white rates (Hawkins et al., 1998; Riedel, 2003).

Arrest data indicate that African Americans are disproportionately involved in delinquency. African Americans accounted for 30 percent of all juvenile arrests in 2006, whites accounted for 67 percent, Asians and Pacific Islanders accounted for 1.4 percent, and American Indians accounted for 1 percent (the percentage for American Indians should be interpreted cautiously, since arrests by tribal police and federal agencies are not recorded in the FBI arrest data). African Americans were especially likely to be arrested for more serious violent offenses, accounting for 59 percent of murder arrests, 34 percent of rape arrests, 67 percent of robbery arrests, and 42 percent of aggravated assault arrests. African Americans were less likely to be arrested for property crimes, although they were still disproportionally arrested for such crimes. For example, they accounted for 30 percent of all larceny-theft arrests.

It is important to note that race differences in arrest rates have declined in recent years. In 1980, the juvenile arrest rate for Part I violent crimes was 6.3 times higher for African Americans than for whites. In 2006, it was 4.8 times higher.

Criticisms of Arrest Data

Arrest data suggest that African Americans are more likely to engage in most forms of delinquency, especially serious violence, but arrest data, as you know, have a number of problems. Only a small percentage of the crimes that are committed come to the attention of the police, and only a small percentage of these crimes result in arrest. Perhaps crimes committed by African Americans are more likely to come to the attention of the police and result in arrest. The data in this area are somewhat complex, but they suggest that African Americans who commit a given offense are often more likely to be arrested than whites who commit the same offense (see Chapter 22 for a full discussion). As a consequence, it is important to examine the relationship between race and delinquency using self-report and victimization data. These data sources have the advantage of measuring delinquent acts that do and do not result in arrest.

Self-Report Data

There are certain dangers in using self-report data to study the relationship between race and delinquency. As indicated in Chapter 2, **some** evidence suggests that African American males may be more likely than other groups to underreport their delinquency in self-report surveys. Nevertheless, it is instructive to examine what self-report data say about the relationship between race and delinquency.

Most early self-report surveys find that there is little or no relationship between race and delinquency. African Americans and whites are about equally delinquent. As you know, however, the early self-report surveys suffer from a number of problems: a focus on minor offenses, the use of truncated response categories, and the under sampling of serious offenders.

Later self-report surveys that correct for these problems find a more complex relationship between race and delinquency, a relationship similar to that found for social class and delinquency. These studies include the National Youth Survey, described earlier, and studies in Seattle, Denver, Rochester, and Pittsburgh.[5] The results of these studies may be summarized as follows:

1. **African Americans and whites report similar levels of minor delinquency.**

2. **African Americans are more likely to engage in serious delinquency, although not to the extent reported in arrest data.** For example, Elliott et al.'s (1989) analysis of the 1976 National Youth Survey found that African Americans had a rate of serious assault about two and one-half times higher than the white rate. Arrest data, however, suggested that the African American rate for serious assault was about five times higher than the white rate.

3. **The average rate of serious crime among African Americans is higher because there are more high-rate offenders among African Americans** (see Elliott and Ageton, 1980). This point requires emphasis: African Americans have a higher rate of serious crime not because the typical African American is more criminal than the typical white. Most African Americans commit no or very few serious crimes. Rather, most serious crimes are committed by a small group of high-rate offenders. These high-rate offenders make up only a small proportion of African American juveniles, but they are about twice as common among African Americans as among whites.

Asian Americans, Latinos, and Native Americans. While most self-report data focus on whites and African Americans, limited self-report data suggest the following: Asian Americans have the lowest rates of offending, followed by whites, Latinos, and African Americans, with Native Americans having the highest offending rates. Some self-report studies suggest that Latino and African American juveniles have similar rates of offending, while others suggest that Latinos have lower rates of offending than African Americans.[6]

Does immigration increase delinquency? Self-report and arrest data might lead you to conclude that immigration increases crime, since most immigrants to the United States are now Latinos. You would not be alone in this belief: most U.S. residents believe that immigration increases crime (Martinez and Lee, 2000; Press, 2006). Research, however, suggests that recent immigrants to the United States have lower rates of crime than U.S. natives.[7] This is especially the case when the immigrants live in communities with a high proportion of other immigrants. (Findings, however, vary somewhat by immigrant group and the city being examined.) Researchers have explained the lower crime rate of immigrants in several ways. Among other things, recent immigrants tend to have strong family ties, strong social ties to their neighbors, and high rates of employment, although often in blue-collar jobs.

Related to this, there is evidence that first-generation immigrants (those who are foreign born) have lower crime rates than second-generation immigrants (those whose parents are foreign born). Second-generation immigrants, in turn, have lower crime rates than third-generation immigrants. Sampson et al. (2005), for example, found that first-generation immigrants in Chicago had self-reported rates of violence about half those of third-generation immigrants. Given these data, it may be more accurate to say that residence in the United States increases the crime rate of immigrants than it is to say that immigration increases the crime rate of the United States.

Victimization Data

There are no victimization data on the relationship between social class and delinquency, but such data have been collected for race. Crime victims are asked to identify the race of the person or persons who victimized them. Such data are limited, however, since victims usually see the offender only in violent crimes. Nevertheless, victimization data suggest that African Americans are disproportionately involved in violent crime. In particular, data from 1998 indicate that African American juveniles had rates of serious violent offending 2.4 times higher than whites (Lynch, 2002).[8] This race difference, however, was not as large as that revealed by arrest data. In 1998, African American juveniles had an arrest rate for serious violent crime that was 3.9 times as high as white juveniles. Like arrest data, victimization data indicate that race differences in offending have declined over time. African American juveniles had rates of serious violent offending that were 6.1 times as large as white rates in 1992 but only 2.4 times as large in 1998.

Data also indicate that African American juveniles are more likely than white juveniles to be the **victims** of serious violence (Rennison, 2001). African American juveniles, for example, are about five times as likely as white juveniles to be the victims of homicide. Criminologists know that most crimes are **intraracial:** African Americans tend to victimize other African Americans and whites tend to victimize other whites. The fact that African Americans have higher victimization rates for serious violence suggests that they have higher offending rates as well.

Is Race Related to Delinquency?

I think we can safely draw the following conclusions about race and delinquency:

1. **There is little or no relationship between race and minor delinquency.** Self-report surveys consistently find little relationship between race and minor delinquency. Arrest and victimization data are less relevant here, since they tend to focus on more serious delinquency.

2. **African Americans are more likely than whites to engage in serious delinquency, especially serious violence.** The relationship between race and serious delinquency, however, is probably not as strong as suggested by arrest data. Arrest data, victimization data,

and most of the better self-report surveys indicate that African Americans are more in-volved in serious delinquency, although self-report and victimization data suggest that ar-rest data exaggerate the involvement of African Americans in such delinquency. **The greater involvement of African Americans in serious delinquency may reflect the fact that there are more high-rate offenders among African Americans.**

3. **Race differences in serious delinquency have declined in recent years.**

Are Race Differences in Serious Delinquency Explained by Social Class?

Given the history of discrimination in this country, it should come as no surprise that race and social class are related. African Americans are more likely to be members of the lower class than whites (although most African Americans are **not** members of the lower class). As discussed, lower-class individuals are more likely to engage in serious delinquency than higher-class individuals. So it is reasonable to ask whether African Americans are more likely to engage in serious delinquency because they are more likely to be in the lower class.

Researchers have examined this issue by comparing the delinquency of lower-class African Americans to that of lower-class whites and by comparing the delinquency of middle-class African Americans to that of middle-class whites. Class is usually measured in terms of family income, parents' occupational prestige, and/or parents' education. If social class explained the higher rate of serious delinquency among African Americans, we would expect that lower-class African Americans and whites would have similar levels of serious delinquency. Likewise, we would expect that middle-class African Americans and whites would have similar levels of delinquency.

The data suggest that social class explains some but not all of the association between race and serious delinquency. For example, comparisons find that lower-class African Americans are still more likely to engage in serious delinquency than lower-class whites, but race differences in delinquency are reduced somewhat when the researchers take account of class.

Researchers, however, have recently pointed out that the life circumstances of poor African Americans are often quite different from those of poor whites. Most notably, poor African Americans are much more likely than poor whites to live in disadvantaged communities; that is, communities where a high percentage of the other people are poor and a low percentage are advantaged (hold well-paid, high-status jobs and have good edu-cations). As Sampson and Bean (2006:12) state, "Whereas less than 10 percent of poor whites typically live in extreme poverty areas, almost half of poor blacks live in such areas." These high-poverty neighborhoods suffer from a range of problems, such as an absence of jobs, a high percentage of single-parent families, inferior schools, and few conventional role models. As Sampson and Lauritsen (1997:338) state, "Even given the same objective socio-economic status, African Americans and whites face vastly different environments in which to live, work, and raise their children." African Americans are more likely to live in high-poverty areas for several reasons, including the effects of past and present discrimination in housing and jobs. So it is misleading to simply compare poor African Americans to poor whites. One must also take account of the type of community in which they live.[9]

A few studies have attempted to take account of community context. That is, they have attempted to compare African Americans and whites who live in high-poverty communi-ties, as well as African Americans and whites who live in higher-class communities. Such comparisons are difficult to make, since it is hard to find more than a few whites who live in high-poverty communities. But limited data suggest that race differences in delinquency are substantially reduced when researchers take account of the types of communities in which African Americans and whites live.[10] More research is needed in this area, but we may tentatively conclude that **much—perhaps all—of the race difference in serious delinquency is explained by the fact that African Americans are more likely to be poor and to live in high-poverty communities,** which suffer from a host of problems that are conducive to delinquency (see Chapter 12 for a discussion of such communities).

Is Age Related to Delinquency?

The data on social class, race, and delinquency are complex and frustrating. The data on the relationship between age and delinquency, however, are fairly straightforward. Arrest, self-report, and victimization data generally agree with one another in this area.[11]

Crime rates are highest for people in mid- to late adolescence. The graphs in Figure 4.1 show the relationship between age and the 2001 arrest rates for Part I property crimes and Part I violent crimes. Arrest rates for property crime peak in mid- to late adolescence and then decline rapidly. A 16-year-old, for example, is about three times more likely to be arrested for a property crime than a 26-year-old. Arrest rates for violent crime peak in late adolescence and early adulthood and then decline somewhat more slowly. A 19-year-old, for example, is almost twice as likely to be arrested for a violent crime as a 29-year-old. These data should be interpreted somewhat cautiously. Some evidence suggests that juvenile offenders may be more likely to be arrested than adult offenders, perhaps because juvenile offenders do not plan their crimes as carefully or are more conspicuous because they tend to commit their crimes in groups (see Snyder, 1999). As a result, these data may exaggerate the juvenile contribution to crime. Also, it should be noted that the relative involvement of juveniles in crime has declined somewhat from a high point reached in the mid-1990s. Juveniles accounted for 18.7 percent of all Part I violent crime arrests in 1995 versus 16.5 percent in 2006, and juveniles accounted for 34.7 percent of all property crime arrests in 1995 versus 26.3 percent in 2006.

Nevertheless, self-report and victimization data tend to show similar patterns. **Rates for property crime tend to peak in mid-adolescence and decline rapidly thereafter. Rates for violent crime peak somewhat later, in late adolescence/early adulthood, and decline more slowly.** Although not illustrated in a graph, rates of illicit drug use tend to peak in the late teens and early 20s, but the peak varies somewhat by type of drug (e.g., inhalant use peaks in the early to mid-teens). There is little doubt, then, that most crimes reach a peak during mid- to late adolescence.

Crime rates may peak during adolescence because there are a fixed number of criminals who increase their rate of offending during adolescence. Or they may peak because there is an increase in the number of criminals during adolescence; that is, new criminals appear. What do the data show? Do criminals start committing more crimes during adolescence, or is there an increase in the number of criminals during adolescence? The data tend to support both explanations. The peak in crime rates during adolescence is partly due to the fact that many juveniles start committing crimes when they become adolescents. Most of these juveniles then stop committing crimes when they become adults, or at least they substantially reduce their level of offending. Also, there is some evidence that offenders commit more crimes during their adolescent years—although not all studies show this.

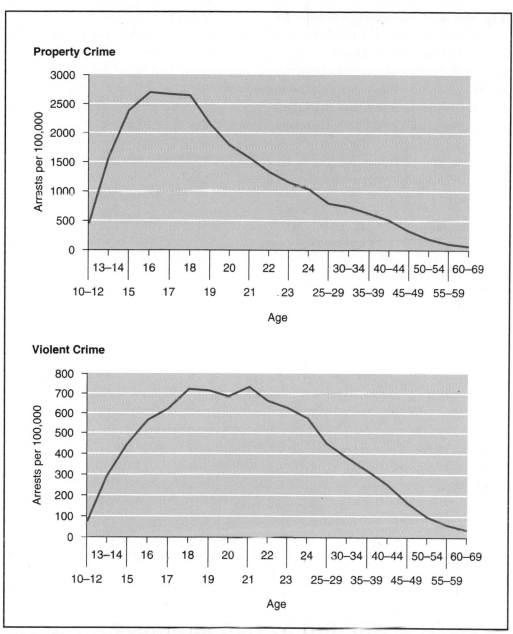

FIGURE 4.1 Relationship Between Age and Arrest Rates for Property and Violent Crime, 2001.

SOURCE: *Office of Juvenile Justice and Delinquency Prevention Statistical Briefing Book,* 2003.

Criminologists have recently devoted much attention to explaining these patterns, and you should ask yourself the following questions:

1. Why do so many juveniles start committing criminal acts when they become adolescents?

2. Why do most of these adolescent offenders stop committing criminal acts when they become adults?

3. Why do offenders commit more crimes during adolescence?

(I address these questions in Chapter 10.)

I should note that the relationship between age and crime is somewhat different for females and for African Americans. Female offending, especially violence, tends to peak at a slightly earlier age than male offending. And African Americans are less likely than whites to stop offending when they become adults. Elliott (1994), for example, used data from the National Youth Survey to study African Americans and whites who had committed serious violent crimes as juveniles. He found that the African Americans were almost twice as likely as the whites to continue committing such offenses in their 20s. Elliott and others explain this finding by arguing that African Americans have more difficulty obtaining decent work when they enter adulthood. In the words of Steffensmeier and Allan (1995:103):

> In the inner cities of this nation, where the labor market for young adults is dominated by marginal jobs with low hours, low pay, high turnover, and limited benefits and opportunities for advancement, the other goals of conventional life—marriage, family, community involvement—are more difficult to attain, and the proportion of the population still attracted to illegitimate alternatives will be greater.

A note on out-of-control toddlers. When I state that crime peaks in mid- to late adolescence, you should not take this to mean that toddlers and children are relatively well behaved. The peak in adolescent crime refers to property crimes such as larceny and burglary, status offenses such as running away and truancy, and more serious violent crimes such as aggravated assault and robbery. Lahey and Waldman (2005) refer to these as "developmentally-late conduct problems." Several recent studies show that toddlers and children regularly engage in other types of misbehavior, especially minor forms of aggression (e.g., hitting, kicking, biting).[12] In describing one study in this area, Lahey and Waldman (2005:18) state that "nearly half of all toddlers hit, kick, intentionally break things, take other children's toys, state untruths, and resist the authority of adults from the time they can walk and talk." These "developmentally-early conduct problems" appear to peak at ages 2–4 for most individuals and then decline sharply by preadolescence. Individuals with the highest levels of developmentally early conduct problems, however, are more likely to have the highest levels of developmentally late conduct problems. That is, the out-of-control toddlers are more likely to become adolescent offenders. This relationship, however, is far from perfect and is more true of boys than girls.

Is Gender Related to Delinquency?

The data on the relationship between gender and delinquency are also fairly straightforward.

Arrest, self-report, and victimization data (where applicable) agree on the following facts about gender and delinquency: Males have a higher rate of delinquency than females. Gender differences in delinquency are greatest for serious violent and property crimes. They are lowest for minor crimes and status offenses, with males and females having similar rates of involvement in certain minor crimes and status offenses. Males have higher rates of delinquency because there are more male than female delinquents and because male delinquents commit more offenses than female delinquents. In particular, there are more male than female high-rate offenders. I elaborate on some of these points later. I also point to a key area where arrest and self-report data disagree.[13]

Arrest Data

Arrest ratios. Overall, there were about 2.5 male juveniles arrested for every female juvenile arrested in 2006. The ratio of male to female arrests is highest for serious violent and property crimes. For example, males are about 18 times more likely to be arrested for murder, 10 times more likely to be arrested for robbery, and 8 times more likely to be arrested for burglary. Sex ratios are lowest for minor crimes and status offenses. For example, males are about 1.4 times as likely to be arrested for larceny-theft and 2 times as likely for simple assault. Females are more likely than males to be arrested for only two offenses: prostitution and running away (57 percent of runaway arrests are females). (I discuss the higher female arrest rate for running away in Chapter 22, when examining gender discrimination in the juvenile justice system.)

What crimes are males and females arrested for? Males generally commit more crimes than females, but do males commit different types of crime than females? The preceding discussion might lead you to believe that males commit serious crimes, whereas females commit less serious crimes. This belief is not correct. Consider the four crimes for which male and female juveniles are most frequently arrested. For males, 18 percent of all arrests are for "all other offenses" (including status offenses like incorrigibility and truancy); 11 percent are for larceny-theft; 10 percent are for simple assaults; and 10 percent are for drug abuse violations. For females, 18 percent of all arrests are for larceny-theft; 16 percent are for "all other offenses"; 13 percent are for simple assaults; and 11 percent are for disorderly conduct. **Thus, both males and females are most often arrested for minor crimes.** Further, males and females are arrested for many of the same minor crimes—larceny-theft, "all other offenses," and simple assault.

At the same time, there are some differences in the types of crimes for which males and females are arrested. **A greater portion of all male arrests are for serious crimes** (although such crimes constitute only a small portion of all male arrests). About 5.3 percent of all male arrests are for serious violent crimes, versus 2.8 percent of all female arrests. And about 6.5 percent of all male arrests are for the serious property crimes of burglary and motor vehicle theft, versus 2.4 percent of all females arrests. **By contrast, a greater portion of all female arrests are for larceny-theft (most often shoplifting) and status offenses.** About 18 percent of all female arrests are for the status offenses of running away and curfew violation, versus 10 percent of all male arrests. Further, some data suggest that a large portion of the female arrests for "all other offenses" involve the status offense of incorrigibility (Chesney-Lind and Shelden, 2004:11).

Trends in male and female delinquency. Even though males are generally more likely to be arrested than females, the proportion of all arrests accounted for by females has been increasing over time. In 1980, females accounted for 18 percent of all juvenile arrests for Part I offenses. Today, females account for 29 percent of all Part I arrests. This increase has occurred for both violent and property crimes. Arrest rates generally **increased faster for females** than males from the mid-1980s to the mid-1990s. Then arrest rates **declined more slowly for females** than males from the mid-1990s. As a result of these trends, the gender gap in arrest rates is much lower than it once was. In 1980, male juveniles were 8.3 times more likely to be arrested for violent crimes than female juveniles. By 2003, males were only 4.2 times more likely to be arrested for violent crimes. In 1980, male juveniles were 4 times more likely to be arrested for property crimes than females. By 2003, males were only 2 times more likely to be arrested for property crimes.

Self-Report Data

Like arrest data, self-report data reveal that males have higher rates of delinquency than females, with gender differences in delinquency being greatest for serious crimes and lowest for minor crimes and status offenses. Self-report data also indicate that while males generally commit more delinquent acts than females, females commit a broad range of delinquent acts. Females, for example, steal, fight, and use drugs—they just do so less frequently than males. There is, however, one key area in which self-report data are at odds with arrest data.

Self-report surveys do not indicate that the proportion of all offenses committed by females is increasing.[14] The limited self-report data we have on trends in delinquency suggest that the gender ratio in delinquency has been fairly stable since the late 1960s. This has led some researchers to question the accuracy of arrest data; they claim that the increase in female arrests may reflect changes in police practices or the behavior of those who report crimes to the police. In particular, Steffensmeier et al. (2005) make a rather convincing argument that this is the case, at least with respect to violent crime.

Trends in female violence. Steffensmeier et al. (2005) point out that the proportion of violent crime arrests accounted for by female juveniles has increased a good deal since 1980. This is especially true for the crime of assault. For example, girls accounted for 21 percent of simple assault arrests in 1980 versus 34 percent in 2006. Steffensmeier et al. note that such arrest data have led some researchers and people in the news media to conclude that girls really are becoming more violent. This alleged increase in female violence is frequently explained by arguing that in the past, girls were taught to be submissive and weak, while now they are taught to be assertive and strong. It is said that this change in socialization practices is reflected in many recent movies and video games, such as *Kill Bill* and *Tomb Raiders*, where the lead character is a female who engages in much violence.

Steffensmeier et al., however, also examine gender trends in violence using two self-report surveys and victimization data. These alternative data sources do not indicate that the percentage of violent crimes committed by females has increased since 1980. Rather, the percentage has stayed about the same. Steffensmeier et al. believe that the self-report and victimization data are the more accurate, and that the share of violence committed by females has not really increased. How, then, do we explain the increase shown in arrest data? Steffensmeier et al. offer several explanations, all involving changes in police practices since 1980.

They claim that the police have become more likely to make arrests for those types of violence in which females most often engage. In particular, the police have become more likely to make arrests for minor violence. While males are much more likely to engage in serious violence than females, rates of minor violence are more similar for males and females. The increased likelihood of arrest for minor violence therefore raises the percentage of violent crime arrests accounted for by females. Also, Steffensmeier et al. claim that the police have become more likely to make arrests in cases involving domestic or family violence. While males are much more likely than females to commit violent acts against strangers and acquaintances, rates of family violence are more similar for males and females. So, again, this change in policy increases the percentages of violent crime arrests accounted for by females.

Further, Steffensmeier et al. argue that the police have become more likely to "charge up" minor forms of violence. So a violent act that might have resulted in a charge of simple or minor assault in the past now results in a charge of aggravated or serious assault. Finally, Steffensmeier et al. argue that the police have become less tolerant of female offenders. In the past, the police were more likely to deal with female violent offenders in an informal manner or to charge them with status offenses, such as incorrigibility. Today, they are more likely to charge such offenders with violent crimes.

Steffensmeier et al. discuss the factors that have led to these changes in police practices. These factors include the rise of "zero-tolerance" policies, which encourage the police to make arrests even in the case of minor crimes (see Chapter 20). They include the increased social concern with domestic violence, with many police departments implementing mandatory arrest policies in this area. And they include the feminist movement, which has contributed to the more similar treatment of male and female offenders. Their central point, however, is that the increase in the percentage of violence crime arrests involving females reflects a change in police practices rather than a real increase in female violence.

Summary

Overall, the following conclusions can be drawn about the relationship between gender and delinquency:

1. **There is little doubt that males generally have higher rates of delinquency than females, with gender differences in delinquency being greatest for serious violent and property crimes.** Males have higher rates of delinquency because there are more male than female offenders and because male offenders commit more offenses on average than female offenders.

2. **While males commit more offenses than females, females commit a broad range of offenses.** Contrary to certain stereotypical views, female offending is not limited to a few sex-related offenses. Females, like males, fight, steal, use drugs, and engage in other delinquent acts. They just do so less than males. **At the same time, a relatively greater proportion of all male offenses involve serious crimes, and a relatively greater proportion of all female offenses involve larceny-theft and status offenses.**

3. **Arrest data suggest that gender differences in delinquency have become smaller since 1980, but self-report and victimization data do not show this.** Some evidence suggests that the increase in the percentage of arrests involving females reflects a change in police practices rather than a real increase in female delinquency.

Are There Different Types of Delinquents?

We have been talking about delinquents and nondelinquents, with an occasional reference to high-rate and serious offenders. As you might imagine, though, dividing juveniles into delinquents and nondelinquents is a bit simplistic. There are many types of delinquents. As mentioned earlier, for example, delinquents differ greatly in their frequency of delinquency. Some delinquents commit only a few offenses each year, while others commit hundreds—thus, we have low-rate and high-rate delinquent offenders.

Criminologists are now devoting much attention to the identification of different types of delinquents. As you will see, this is an important task. The factors that cause juveniles to become one type of delinquent may differ from those that cause them to become another type. For example, the factors that cause juveniles to become low-rate offenders may differ from those that cause them to become high-rate offenders. Also, the existence of different types of delinquents has important implications for society's efforts to control delinquency. For example, we may want to focus our control efforts on high-rate offenders, since they commit so many delinquent acts. Further, high-rate offenders may require different types of intervention programs than low-rate offenders.

This section briefly reviews the research on the different types of delinquents. While criminologists still have much to learn in this area, some generally accepted conclusions can be drawn about the types of delinquent offenders.[15]

An Overview of the Research on the Different Types of Delinquents

Researchers try to classify delinquents into different types on the basis of such things as their frequency of offending, the types of offenses they commit, and when they start and stop offending. The major research in these areas is reviewed next.

How many offenses do juveniles commit? Both arrest and self-report data indicate that juveniles vary a great deal in the frequency of their delinquency. Self-report surveys typically find the following: A small percentage of juveniles—10 percent or less in most studies—refrain from delinquency. A much larger percentage of juveniles—a majority in all studies—commit a small to moderate number of delinquent offenses each year. And a small percentage of juveniles commit an enormous number of offenses each year. The relative size of this high-rate group depends on the cutoff point that is used, but it is usually about 5 to 15 percent of all juveniles.

For example, Dunford and Elliott (1984) examined the frequency of offending using self-report data from the National Youth Survey. They found that about 11 percent of the juveniles did not report any delinquent acts over a two-year period. About 34 percent reported 1 to 10 delinquent acts during this period. About 41 percent reported 11 to 100 acts. About 8 percent reported 101 to 200 delinquent acts (1 to 2 delinquent acts per week). And about 6.5 percent reported 201 or more delinquent acts (at least 2 delinquent acts per week).

In some studies, the high-rate offenders account for a majority of all delinquent offenses and for the large majority of serious delinquent offenses. For example, a major study in Philadelphia found that 7.5 percent of the juvenile males accounted for 61 percent of all juvenile arrests, including 61 percent of the homicide arrests, 65 percent of the aggravated assault arrests, 76 percent of the forcible rape arrests, and 73 percent of the robbery arrests (Tracy et al., 1990). Clearly, then, at a minimum, one can distinguish high-rate offenders from lower-rate offenders.

What types of offenses do juveniles commit? Criminologists once assumed that juveniles specialized in particular types of crimes. For example, it was argued that some juveniles specialized in property crimes like larceny and burglary, others specialized in violent crimes, and still others specialized in drug use and sales (e.g., Cloward and Ohlin, 1960). Recent data suggest that there is some specialization in juvenile offending—but not nearly as much as previously believed. Most juveniles who commit more than a few offenses tend to commit a variety of offenses. There is, however, some specialization against this backdrop of diversity. One of the most recent and best studies in this area found that some juvenile offenders are more likely than others to engage in violence—although these "violent offenders" also commit other types of crime (Osgood and Schreck, 2007). It is possible that further research will find that some offenders are also more likely than others to engage in such crimes as drug use and theft. Juvenile offenders, then, tend to commit a range of offenses—although they may favor some offenses more than others. (Note: Adult offenders are more likely to specialize in particular types of crime than juvenile offenders.)

If we move beyond particular types of crime, data suggest that some offenders commit primarily minor offenses, while others commit a mixture of minor and serious offenses. (It is rare for an offender to commit only serious offenses; individuals who commit serious offenses usually commit minor offenses as well.) In particular, the large majority of juvenile offenders commit a range of minor offenses, plus the occasional serious offense. A much smaller percentage of juvenile offenders commit a range of both minor and serious offenses. Even though most offenders commit a variety of offenses, it is possible to distinguish between offenders who commit primarily minor crimes and those who commit both minor and serious crimes. And several researchers have distinguished minor from serious offenders. An analysis of data from the 1976 National Youth Survey found that about 8.6 percent of the juveniles could be classified as "serious" offenders, meaning that they had committed at least three Part I or serious offenses during 1976. These serious offenders accounted for more than three-fourths of all the Part I offenses, and they also committed a large number of minor crimes and status offenses. Most of the remaining juveniles committed a small to moderate number of minor crimes and status offenses (Dunford and Elliott, 1984; Elliott et al., 1989).

When do juveniles start to commit delinquent acts and when do they stop? Studies in this area find much variation among offenders. Some offenders start committing delinquent acts in childhood, while others wait until late adolescence. And some offenders stop committing crimes in adolescence, while others continue to offend well into the adult years. The most common pattern is for offenders to start committing crimes in late childhood to mid-adolescence and to stop committing crimes in late adolescence. Individuals who follow this pattern have been described as *adolescent-limited offenders,* since their offending is largely limited to their adolescent years (see Moffitt, 1993, 1997). These adolescent-limited offenders are partly responsible for the fact that rates of offending peak during mid- to late adolescence (see the discussion on age and crime).

There is a much smaller group of offenders who begin to engage in delinquent or "antisocial" behavior as young children. They lie, steal, cheat, and engage in aggressive behavior at an early age; their parents and others commonly describe them as "troublesome" or "difficult." Studies suggest that these individuals are more likely to offend at high rates, to commit serious offenses, and to continue offending as adults than juveniles who start committing delinquent acts at a later age. In fact, the "early onset" of delinquency is one of the best predictors of the frequency, seriousness, and duration of offending. I should note, however, that the early onset of delinquency does not guarantee that a person will have problems later in life. For example, only about half of the juveniles with an early onset of delinquency become adult offenders. Nevertheless, there is a small group of individuals who offend from early childhood well into adulthood. These individuals have been referred to as *chronic offenders,* and they may be distinguished from the adolescent-limited offenders.

Are there any patterns to juvenile offending over the life course? Juveniles vary a good deal in the frequency of their offending, the seriousness of their offending, and the ages at which they start and stop offending. Despite this variation, there are certain common patterns in juvenile offending over the life course.

First, studies suggest that there is a general tendency to move from less serious to more serious offending. For example, minor delinquency like petty theft and status offending tends to precede more serious delinquency like burglary and aggravated assault. And alcohol use tends to precede marijuana use, which tends to precede hard drug use. Most juveniles, of course, do not advance all the way from minor to serious offending. Most remain at the level of minor offending. But those who engage in serious offending usually begin their careers with minor offending.

Second, studies suggest that there is a general tendency for the frequency of offending to increase during early to mid-adolescence and to decrease during late adolescence and adulthood. This behavior pattern is especially true for adolescent-limited offenders. It is less true for chronic offenders, but recent data suggest that even chronic offenders increase their level of offending somewhat during adolescence (see D'Unger et al., 1998).

What Are the Different Types of Delinquents?

As indicated, juvenile offenders differ in terms of the frequency of their offending, the seriousness of their offending, and the ages at which they start and stop offending. Researchers have drawn on these differences to describe the major types of delinquent offenders. Some descriptions focus on the frequency of offending, distinguishing low-rate from high-rate offenders. Some focus on the seriousness of offending, distinguishing minor from serious offenders (or serious violent offenders). Some focus on the duration of offending, distinguishing adolescent-limited from chronic offenders. And some descriptions focus on two of the previous dimensions—the frequency and duration of offending, for example (D'Unger et al., 1998; also see Loeber et al., 1991). It is probably best, however, to classify offenders using all three dimensions. Although these dimensions are related to one another (e.g., high-rate offenders are more likely to be serious offenders), the relationship is not perfect (e.g., certain high-rate offenders commit only minor crimes).

Some researchers are beginning to classify offenders using all three dimensions. At one extreme, we have **high-rate, serious, chronic offenders.** Data suggest that only a small percentage of juveniles fall into this group: perhaps 5 percent or so of the juvenile population. Nevertheless, this small group is an important one, given the enormous amount of crime, especially serious crime, they commit. Data suggest that members of this group are more likely to be male, poor, and African American (although race may be important because of its correlation with individual- and community-level social class). At the other extreme, we have **low-rate, minor, adolescent-limited offenders.** Between these two extremes there are several groups. It is unclear what percentage of juveniles fall into each of these groups. The answer depends, in part, on the type of data used (arrest versus self-report) and the definitions employed for high-rate, chronic, and serious offending. For example, how many delinquent acts must juveniles commit each year before they rate classification as high-rate offenders?

In any event, it is important to keep in mind that there are different types of delinquent offenders. These types will come up again when I discuss the causes of crime. Some evidence suggests that the causes of high-rate, serious, chronic offending differ somewhat from the causes of less extreme types of offending. These types will also come up when I discuss strategies to control delinquency. In particular, there has been a major movement to crack down on the more extreme types of delinquents, especially those who commit serious crimes.

Summary

We can draw the following major conclusions about the characteristics of delinquents:

1. Males have higher rates of delinquency, especially serious delinquency, than females. There are more male offenders, and male offenders offend at higher rates than female offenders.

2. Rates of delinquency peak in mid- to late adolescence and decline rapidly thereafter. This peak and decline occurs largely because there is an increase in the number of offenders during adolescence, but data also suggest that rates of offending increase during adolescence as well.

3. Lower-class juveniles are more likely to engage in serious delinquency than higher-class juveniles. This difference exists because there are more high-rate offenders in the lower class. There is little or no relationship between class and minor delinquency.

4. African Americans are more likely to engage in serious delinquency, especially violent delinquency, than whites. Again, data suggest that this difference occurs because there are more high-rate offenders among African Americans. There is little or no relationship between race and minor delinquency.

5. Juveniles differ a great deal in the frequency, seriousness, and duration of their offending.

The next section of the book focuses on the causes of delinquency. I will try to explain the basic facts about delinquency presented in this chapter and Chapter 3. Most notably, I will try to explain why some juveniles commit more delinquent acts, commit more serious delinquent acts, and offend for longer periods than other juveniles. I will also try to explain why certain groups have higher rates of delinquency than other groups. Why, for example, are males more delinquent than females?

Teaching Aids

Exercise 1: Perceptions of Race and Crime

One of the central points made in this chapter is that the perceptions many people have of juvenile delinquents are mistaken. In particular, many people think that class and race are the factors that best distinguish delinquents from nondelinquents, when in fact age and gender do a much better job of differentiating delinquents from nondelinquents. As indicated in this chapter, class and race are largely unrelated to minor delinquency. They are related to serious delinquency but not as strongly as gender and age. For example, African American juveniles have an arrest rate for Part I violent crimes that is 3.6 times higher than that for whites, while male juveniles have an arrest rate that is almost 5 times higher than that for females. Further, lower-class juveniles and African Americans have higher rates of serious crime not because the typical lower-class or African American juvenile is involved in serious crime but because high-rate offenders are more common among the lower-class and African Americans. Such offenders, however, constitute a very small percentage of all lower-class and African American juveniles.

Nevertheless, many people still view African Americans and poor people as strongly involved in delinquency. One recent study provides an excellent illustration of this point; it focuses on the factors that influence perceptions of neighborhood crime rates (Quillian and Pager, 2001). This study examined people living in a variety of neighborhoods in three cities: Chicago, Seattle, and Baltimore. These people were asked to estimate the level of crime in their neighborhood (e.g., "How much crime would you say there is in your own immediate neighborhood?"). The researchers then examined the factors that influenced perceptions of neighborhood crime levels. They found that one of the strongest factors was the percentage of young African American men in the neighborhood (the percentage of poor people in the neighborhood also had an effect). People living in neighborhoods with a higher percentage of young African American men were much more likely to say that crime was a problem, *even after* the researchers took account of the neighborhood's actual level of crime (measured by crimes known to the police and victimization data), the economic characteristics of the neighborhood, the physical appearance of the neighborhood (as rated by trained staff), neighborhood problems (e.g., teenagers hanging out on the street, noise), the age, sex, education, income, and personal victimization experiences of the respondents, and other factors. These findings held for both white and African American residents, although whites were more likely than African Americans to associate young African American men with crime.

The researchers summarized their study by stating that their "results suggest that the strong mental association between race and crime has a powerful influence on perceptions of neighborhood crime levels, *beyond any actual association between race and crime*" (Quillian and Pager, 2001:746; emphasis added).

1. What accounts for the perception among many people that race is strongly associated with crime?
2. What can be done to counter this perception?

Exercise 2: Why Do Asian Americans Have Lower Crime Rates?

Both arrest and self-report data indicate that Asian Americans have much lower crime rates than other race and ethnic groups. Why might this be the case? In responding to this question, be sure to consider such things as community characteristics, socioeconomic status, family factors, school factors, peer factors, and values and beliefs. (For excellent examples of research on this question, see Jang, 2002, and McNulty and Bellair, 2003; for an overview of research in this area, see Unnithan, 2006. Also, it is important to note that Asian Americans comprise many different groups, and these groups sometimes differ from one another in their backgrounds and current circumstances. Jang [2002] divides Asian Americans into four regional groups: Far Eastern (e.g., Chinese, Japanese, and Korean), East Asian [e.g., Filipinos], Southeast Asian [e.g., Vietnamese, Laotian, Cambodian, Thai], and South Asian [e.g., Indian, Pakistani].)

Exercise 3: Explaining the Association Between Gender and Crime

I present several basic facts about the characteristics of delinquents in this chapter. One of the key facts is that males are more likely to engage in delinquency than females, especially serious violent and property crime. I suspect that this is true of the males and females in your class (you might verify this with a self-report survey of the students in your class). I discuss the relationship between gender and delinquency at several points in this text, with an extended discussion in Chapter 18. For now, I would like you to try to answer the following questions:

1. Why do you think males have higher rates of delinquency than females?
2. Do you think that the causes of delinquency among males are the same as those among females?
3. Do you think the gender difference in levels of delinquency will ever become smaller?

TEST YOUR KNOWLEDGE OF THIS CHAPTER

1. What do I mean by the "sociodemographic characteristics" of juveniles?
2. How is social class usually measured?
3. Describe the relationship between social class and delinquency according to arrest data.
4. Describe the relationship between social class and delinquency according to the early self-report studies. How did researchers explain the difference in findings between the early self-report studies and studies using arrest data? How did researchers account for the perception that lower-class juveniles are more delinquent? How did researchers account for all of the good reasons linking class to delinquency?
5. Describe the major criticisms of early self-report studies.
6. Describe the major findings of later self-report studies.
7. Describe the relationship between social class and delinquency according to victimization data (hint: this might be a trick question).
8. Provide a summary of the relationship between social class and delinquency.

9. Describe the relationship between race, ethnicity, and delinquency according to arrest data. Why might arrest data provide a biased view of this relationship?

10. Describe the relationship between race, ethnicity, and delinquency according to self-report data. Be sure to distinguish between the early and later self-report studies. Also, note any similarities and differences between the findings from self-report and arrest data.

11. Describe the relationship between race and delinquency according to victimization data, noting any similarities and differences between the findings from victimization and arrest data.

12. What do I mean when I ask whether the relationship between race and delinquency can be explained by social class? What do the data in this area indicate? Why is it important to consider both an individual's social class and the class composition of the community in which the individual lives?

13. Provide a summary of the relationship between race, ethnicity, and delinquency.

14. Describe the relationship between immigration and delinquency.

15. Describe the relationship between age and delinquency (be sure to distinguish between property and violent crimes). Describe how the relationship between age and delinquency differs somewhat for females and African Americans.

16. Describe the relationship between gender and crime (be sure to distinguish between serious and less serious crimes).

17. Describe trends in female violence according to arrest , self-report, and victimization data. How can we account for differences between these data sources?

18. Describe what the research says regarding differences between juveniles in (a) the number of delinquent acts committed, (b) the types of delinquent acts committed, and (c) when they start and stop committing criminal acts.

19. Describe the two major patterns of juvenile offending over the life course.

20. What are the major types of juvenile offenders?

THOUGHT AND DISCUSSION QUESTIONS

1. Arrest data, early self-report studies, later self-report studies, and victimization data occasionally disagree regarding the characteristics of delinquents (e.g., whether African Americans have higher rates of delinquency, whether rates of male and female delinquency are becoming more similar). Point to an area of disagreement and discuss how one might decide which data source(s) is more accurate or how one might reach a compromise position between the data sources. (Note: You will need to consider the advantages and disadvantages of each data source, as discussed in this chapter and in Chapters 2 and 3.)

2. Reread the discussion about the Saints and Roughnecks (in the section on social class and delinquency). Were there similar groups in your high school? Do you think that our perceptions of upper- and lower-class delinquency are biased for the three reasons indicated by Chambliss (1973)?

3. Can you think of any reasons why middle- and upper-class juveniles might be more likely to engage in delinquency than lower-class juveniles (see Wright et al., 1999a)?

4. Why do you think rates of serious delinquency among whites and African Americans have become more similar in recent years?

5. Pick a race or ethnic group other than African Americans and whites. Find whatever information you can about levels of delinquency in this group and about the ways in which the life circumstances of this group (e.g., level of poverty, family relations, discrimination experienced) may have influenced levels of delinquency. (You might begin by looking at certain of the sources in note 4 and at indexes to journal articles and reports, like *Sociological Abstracts*, *Criminal Justice Abstracts*, and the *National Criminal Justice Reference Service Abstracts Database* (http://abstractsdb.ncjrs.org).

6. Why do you think so many juveniles start committing criminal acts when they become adolescents? And why do most of these adolescent offenders stop committing criminal acts when they become adults? (Note: Chapter 10 addresses these questions.)

7. A distinction was made between "high-rate, chronic, serious offenders" and "low-rate, adolescent-limited, minor offenders." Do you think the causes of delinquency differ between these two groups of offenders? (Note: Chapter 10 addresses this issue.)

KEY TERMS

- Sociodemographic characteristics
- Adolescent-limited offenders
- Chronic offenders

ENDNOTES

1. For selected studies and overviews of the research in this area, *see* Bjerk, 2007; Braithwaite, 1981; Elliott and Ageton, 1980; Elliott and Huizinga, 1983; Farnworth et al., 1994; Hagan, 1992; Harris and Shaw, 2000; Heimer, 1997; Hindelang et al., 1979, 1981; Jarjoura et al., 2002; Tittle and Meier, 1990; Tittle et al., 1978; Wright et al., 1999a.

2. *See* Bjerk, 2007; Brownfield, 1986; Elliott and Ageton, 1980; Farnworth et al., 1994; Hagan, 1992; Hindelang et al., 1979, 1981; Jarjoura et al., 2002; Thornberry and Farnworth, 1982.

3. *See* Bjerk, 2007; Brownfield, 1986; Farnworth et al., 1994; Jarjoura et al., 2002; Loeber, Farrington, Stouthamer-Loeber, Moffitt, and Caspi, 1998.

4. For selected studies and overviews of the research on race/ethnicity, and delinquency, *see* Cintron, 2006; Elliott and Ageton, 1980; Elliott et al., 1989; French, 2006; Hagan and Peterson, 1995; Harris and Shaw, 2000; Hawkins, Laub, and Lauritsen, 1998; Hindelang, 1978; Hindelang et al., 1981; Huizinga and Elliott, 1987; Kaufman, 2005; Lauritsen, 2005; Lauritsen and Sampson, 1998; McCluskey, 2002; McNulty et al., 2003; McNulty and Bellair, 2003; Mears and Bhati, 2006; Morenoff, 2005; Sampson and Lauritsen, 1997; Sampson et al., 2005; Traver et al., 2002; Velez et al., 2003; Walker et al., 2004.

5. *See* Elliott and Ageton, 1980; Elliott et al., 1989; Farrington et al., 1996, 2003; Hindelang et al., 1981; Huizinga and Elliott, 1987; Kaufman, 2005; Kelley et al., 1997; Lauritsen, 2005; Liberman, 2007; McNulty et al., 2005; Morenoff, 2005; Office of Juvenile Justice and Delinquency Prevention, 1999a; Peeples and Loeber, 1994.

6. *See* French, 2006; Hawkins et al., 1998; Jang, 2002; Kaufman, 2005; Lauritsen, 2005; McNulty and Bellair, 2003; Morris et al., 2007; Sampson et al., 2005; Smith and Krohn, 1995.

7. *See* Martinez and Lee, 2000; Martinez and Nielsen, 2006; Morenoff, 2005; Nielsen et al., 2005; Press, 2006; Sampson and Bean, 2006; Sampson et al., 2005; Velez, 2006.

ENDNOTES (continued)

8. *See* Snyder and Sickmund, 1999:192; *also see* Hindelang, 1981; Lauritsen, 2005; Liberman, 2007; Tonry, 1995.

9. For a fuller discussion of these issues, *see* Chapter 12 in this text and Crutchfield et al., 2006; Hawkins, Laub, and Lauritsen, 1998; Lauritsen and Sampson, 1998; Mears and Bhati, 2006; Sampson and Bean, 2006; Sampson and Lauritsen, 1997; Sampson and Wilson, 1995; Sampson et al., 2005; Velez et al., 2003.

10. *See* Peeples and Loeber, 1994; *also see* Bellair and McNulty, 2005; Crutchfield et al., 2006; Johnson and Chanhatasilpa, 2003; Kaufman, 2005; Krivo and Peterson, 1996; Liberman, 2007; McNulty and Bellair, 2003; Sampson, 1985, 1987; Sampson and Bean, 2006; Sampson et al., 2005; Velez et al., 2003.

11. For overviews and selected studies, *see* Bushway et al., 2003; Cook and Laub, 1998; Elliott, 1994; Elliott et al., 1989; Farrington, 1986, 1994, 2005; Farrington et al., 2003; Greenberg, 1977, 1985; Hirschi and Gottfredson, 1983; Huizinga, 1995; Kelley et al., 1997; Le Blanc and Loeber, 1998; Moffitt, 2006; Osgood et al., 1989; Piquero et al., 2003; 1989; Rowe and Tittle, 1977; Sampson and Laub, 1993b; Snyder, 2003; Snyder and Sickmund, 1999; Steffensmeier and Allan, 1995, 2000; Steffensmeier et al., 1989; Warr, 1993; Zimring, 2005.

12. *See* Broidy et al., 2003; Lahey and Waldman, 2005; Nagin and Tremblay, 2005; for information on "child delinquents," *see* Loeber et al., 2003.

13. For overviews and selected studies on gender and delinquency, *see* Canter, 1982; Chesney-Lind, 2001; Chesney-Lind and Shelden, 2004; Daly, 1998; Elliott et al., 1989; Federal Bureau of Investigation, 2003; Hindelang et al., 1981; Jensen and Rojek, 1998; Kelley et al., 1997; Poe-Yamagata and Butts, 1996; Steffensmeier, 1993; Steffensmeier and Allan, 1996, 2000.

14. *See* Canter, 1982; Chesney-Lind and Shelden, 2004; Huizinga et al., 2003; Steffensmeier, 1993; and trend data from the Monitoring the Future survey as reported in the *Sourcebook of Criminal Justice Statistics; also see* Jensen and Rojek, 1998.

15. For overviews and selected studies in this area, *see* Bushway et al., 2007; Caspi and Moffitt, 1995; Chung et al., 2002; Cohen and Villa, 1996; Deane et al., 2005; Dunford and Elliott, 1984; D'Unger et al., 1998, 2002; Elliott et al., 1989; Farrington, 1986, 1994, 2005; Hawkins, 2003; Howell, 1997a, 2003a; Howell, Krisberg, and Jones, 1995; Huizinga, 1995, 2003; Kelley et al., 1997; Le Blanc and Loeber, 1998; Loeber et al., 2003; Loeber, Farrington, and Waschbusch, 1998; Moffitt, 1997, 2006; Osgood and Schreck, 2007; Piquero, 2000, 2003; Piquero et al., 1999; Piquero and Mazerolle, 2001; Sampson and Laub, 1993a; Sullivan et al., 2006; Thornberry et al., 1995; Tolan and Gorman-Smith, 1998; Visher, 2000.

PART 2

The Causes of Delinquency
Theories

The next eight chapters focus on what is probably the most frequently asked question about delinquency: What causes it? In particular, these chapters present the leading theories or explanations of delinquency. There are numerous theories of delinquency, especially if we count the different versions of more general theories.[1] For example, there are several major versions of strain theory (Agnew, 1992; Berkowitz, 1993; Cloward and Ohlin, 1960: Cohen, 1955; Colvin, 2000; Elliott et al., 1979; Greenberg, 1977; Merton, 1938). As a consequence, most introductory texts in delinquency end up describing 20 or more different delinquency theories. And, not surprisingly, many of these theories are superficially described; there is simply not enough space to adequately describe them all. Based on my experience, this approach typically overwhelms and confuses students. Students struggle to keep track of all the different theories, the evidence on these theories, and the relationship between these theories. I take a different approach in this text.

I attempt to "synthesize" the best of the current delinquency theories into a smaller set of "generic" theories, theories that I believe represent our best answers to the question, What causes delinquency? Four major generic theories are presented in Chapters 6 through 9: **strain theory, social learning theory, control theory,** and **labeling theory.** These theories are used to explain **why some individuals are more likely than others to engage in delinquency.** They do so by arguing that some individuals develop traits and are in social environments that create a predisposition for delinquency.

Theories of delinquency, however, attempt to explain more than individual differences in offending (see Tittle, 2000). Theories also try to explain **patterns of offending over the course of the individual's life.** For example, they try to explain why some individuals offend at high rates for much of their lives, while others limit their offending largely to the adolescent years. Chapter 10 addresses this issue, drawing heavily on the four theories presented in Chapters 6 through 9. Further, theories try to explain **why individuals are more likely to engage in delinquency in some types of situations than others.** For example, they try to explain why individuals are more likely to engage in delinquency when they are involved in unstructured, unsupervised activities with peers. Chapter 11 addresses this issue, again drawing heavily on the theories presented in earlier chapters. Finally, theories try to explain **why some groups have higher rates of delinquency than other groups.** Chapter 12 addresses this issue, with a focus on explaining why some communities have higher rates of delinquency than other communities. Once again, I draw heavily on the theories presented in earlier chapters. I address other group differences in delinquency, including age and gender differences, later in the book—especially in Chapter 18.

But before I describe the theories of the causes of delinquency, I describe what a theory is and how we test theories in Chapter 5.

ENDNOTE

1. For recent overviews, see Akers and Sellers, 2004; Cullen and Agnew, 2006; Cullen et al., 2006; Shoemaker, 2004; Vold et al., 2001.

What Is a Theory and How Do We Test Theories?

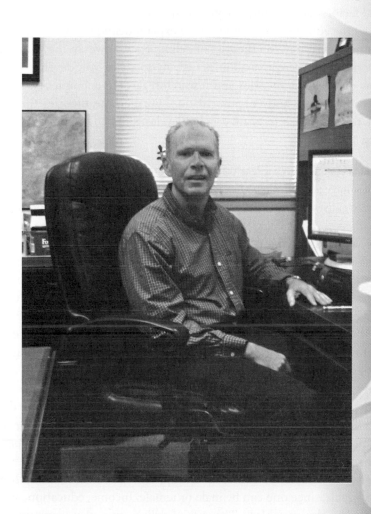

The leading theories or explanations of delinquency are presented in chapters 6–12. But before presenting these theories, I need to address three basic questions in this chapter: (1) What is a theory? (2) Why is it important to study theories of delinquency? And (3) How do we go about testing theories or testing ideas derived from them? In particular, how do we determine whether some factor causes delinquency?

What Is a Theory?

A *theory* **is an attempt to explain something or describe the causes of something.** Most of you probably already have theories of delinquency in mind. You may believe, for example, that poverty causes delinquency or that poor parental supervision causes delinquency (or that several factors cause delinquency). The delinquency theories that we will examine simply represent the efforts of criminologists to explain delinquency.

When criminologists develop theories of delinquency, however, they draw not only on their own experiences and creative abilities (as you do, when you develop your theories). They also draw on previous theories and research regarding delinquency. Their theories, then, are based on a large body of information. Further, the theories they develop are tested, and the results of such tests are used to develop still better theories or explanations of delinquency.

What Are the Basic Parts of a Theory?

Theories usually have several parts. Let us take the following simple theory as an illustration: Child abuse causes delinquency. Abuse makes children angry, and they often take this anger out on others through delinquency.

First, this theory lists what it is that we want to explain. In our case, we want to explain **juvenile delinquency.** In particular, we want to explain why some juveniles are more delinquent than others. As indicated in the introduction to Part II of this book, the delinquency theories we will examine attempt to explain (1) why some individuals are more likely than others to engage in delinquency, (2) patterns of offending over the course of the individual's life, (3) why delinquency is more likely in some types of situations than others, and (4) why some groups have higher rates of delinquency than other groups. These theories typically focus on a wide range of delinquent acts, including violent acts, property crimes, drug offenses, and status offenses.

Second, the theory lists what we believe to be the cause of juvenile delinquency: child abuse. In the language of social research, child abuse is our *independent variable* and juvenile delinquency is our *dependent variable.* Delinquency is said to depend on child abuse. Most theories of delinquency are more complicated than our simple theory and list several independent variables or causes of delinquency. (**A variable is anything that can vary.** Sex is a variable, since one can be male or female. Income, education, and beliefs regarding violence are also variables.) Theories of delinquency also sometimes discuss the relationship between these independent variables. For example, they argue that income influences beliefs regarding violence.

Third, the theory explains why the independent variable causes delinquency. In particular, we claim that child abuse causes delinquency because it angers the child, who then strikes out at others. You can probably think of other reasons why child abuse might cause delinquency. Child abuse, for example, may teach children that violence is an appropriate way to deal with one's problems. Or child abuse may reduce the child's respect and affection for parents, thereby making it difficult for parents to properly raise their children. **The leading theories of delinquency often share many of the same independent variables;** these theories are most **sharply distinguished from one another in terms of their description of why these independent variables cause crime** (see Agnew, 1995a).

Many delinquency theories also have a fourth part. In the preceding example, we claim that child abuse causes delinquency. Studies provide some support for this theory: Abused children are somewhat more likely than nonabused children to engage in delinquency (see Chapter 14). But not all abused children have high rates of delinquency. Child abuse increases the likelihood of delinquency, but it does not result in delinquency in all cases. Many theories try to specify the conditions under which a variable like child abuse is most likely to cause delinquency.

The simple theory we stated did not do this. We might, however, argue that child abuse is most likely to cause delinquency when the child is also having problems at school (Zingraff et al., 1994). **Certain theories list those factors that influence the likelihood that their independent variables will cause delinquency.** Such factors are sometimes called *conditioning variables,* since they specify the conditions under which the independent variables are most likely to cause delinquency (see Cullen, 1984, for an extended discussion of conditioning variables in crime theory).

You now know the basic parts of a theory, and I'll make reference to them in the descriptions of the delinquency theories presented in subsequent chapters.

Why Is It Important to Study Theories of Delinquency?

It is important to study theories for several reasons. First, **these theories help explain the "basic facts" about delinquency that were discussed in previous chapters.** In particular, they help explain why certain individuals are more likely to engage in delinquency than others; why individuals are more likely to engage in crime at certain points in their life, like adolescence; and why some groups have higher rates of delinquency than others. For example, they help explain why males are more delinquent than females.

Second, **most of the research on the causes of delinquency is guided by these theories or can be interpreted in terms of them.** These theories are basically "educated guesses" about why juveniles engage in delinquency. Most of the research conducted by criminologists—like surveys and field studies—represents an attempt to test and extend these theories. Chapters 13 through 18 describe this research.

Third, **these theories can help society prevent and control delinquency.** These theories point to the major causes of delinquency, and prevention and control programs are more likely to be successful to the extent that they target these causes. Chapters 20 through 25 describe a number of successful programs that are based on or compatible with these theories.

Finally, **these theories can help us better understand our own behavior and the behavior of those around us.** As discussed in Chapter 3, most of us have committed at least minor delinquent acts. Most of us know individuals who have committed delinquent acts. And most of us live in communities where delinquency is a problem.

How Do We Test Theories of Delinquency (or Determine Whether Some Factor Causes Delinquency)?

As indicated, theories are basically educated guesses about what causes delinquency. That is, they describe factors that may cause delinquency. It is therefore important that we test theories to determine if they are true. But how do we go about determining if some factor really does cause delinquency? For example, how do we determine whether child abuse causes delinquency? This question is relevant not only to the causes of delinquency, but also to all areas where causal statements are made. It is relevant to many of the other courses you are taking and to your daily lives. You are constantly exposed to causal statements like the following: mass media violence causes crime, secondhand smoke causes cancer, and certain human activities cause global warming. The discussion that follows will not only help you better understand the research on the causes of delinquency, but it will help you better judge the accuracy of these sorts of claims.

The Scientific Method

Suppose you believe that child abuse causes delinquency. That is your theory of delinquency. You may have good reason to believe that this theory is correct. It may be supported by your personal experiences; perhaps you know someone who was abused and that individual turned out to be delinquent. The theory may make much sense to you; you can think of many good reasons why abuse might lead to delinquency. The theory may be held by other people whom you respect. It is, nevertheless, still important to test the theory. Personal experiences do not provide a sufficient basis for judging the accuracy of our theory. Even though you may know an abused individual who turned out to be delinquent, that does not prove that abuse causes delinquency. It may be that abused and nonabused individuals are equally likely to engage in delinquency; you just happen to know one of the abused individuals who engages in delinquency. It is dangerous to generalize from this one individual to all abused individuals. Also, the fact that this theory makes sense to you or is supported by others does not mean that it is correct. Many people, for example, believe that low self-esteem is a major cause of delinquency, and this belief makes much sense to them. The data, however, suggest that self-esteem has little or no effect on delinquency (Blackburn, 1993; Jang and Thornberry, 1998).

How, then, do we determine whether our theory that abuse causes delinquency is correct? We test our theory against data gathered from juveniles. Social and behavioral scientists have developed a number of guidelines for us to follow in this process: guidelines for collecting and analyzing data. These guidelines form the core of the *scientific method,* and they describe the steps that we should follow in order to provide an accurate test of our theories. A brief overview of these guidelines is provided next (see Babbie, 2006; Champion, 2005, for fuller discussions).

Carefully Define Your Independent and Dependent Variables

The first step in testing our theory involves carefully defining our independent and dependent variables (remember, the independent variable is what causes the dependent variable). For our theory, we must carefully define what we mean by abuse and delinquency. For example, does abuse constitute only physical aggression, or does it also include such things as inappropriate sexual contact, verbal harassment, and physical neglect (e.g., the failure to provide adequate food, clothing, medical care, and shelter)? Suppose we decide to limit our definition of abuse to physical aggression. What constitutes such aggression? If a parent softly spanks her or his child for a misdeed, is that aggression? If not, what is the dividing line between physical contact that is abusive and contact that is not abusive? As you can see, it is sometimes difficult to carefully define variables. Nevertheless, it is important: We cannot test our theory that abuse causes delinquency unless we can precisely define abuse and delinquency. For the purposes of our example, let us define abuse as any deliberate act of physical violence against the child (see English, 1998, for a discussion of efforts to define child abuse).

In evaluating any piece of research, you should **carefully examine the definitions of all variables: Are these variables precisely defined and do the definitions seem reasonable?** For example, you might criticize the definition of abuse that I just presented. This definition excludes acts that many people would define as abusive, such as verbal abuse, physical neglect, and certain forms of sexual behavior. Further, it includes certain acts that many people would not define as abusive, such as spanking.

Decide How to Gather Data to Test Your Belief or Theory

Second, you must decide how you will gather data to test your belief or theory. Criminologists gather data from juveniles in three major ways. As you will see, each method has certain advantages and disadvantages.

Surveys. The most common way is by surveying juveniles. Surveys **involve asking people questions.** We **either interview them or have them fill out questionnaires.** For our theory, we might ask a sample of juveniles how many times their parents deliberately hit them in the last year and how many times they have engaged in certain delinquent acts in the last year. We would then have data on the extent of their abuse and delinquency. We could use this data to begin to explore whether abuse causes delinquency. In particular, we could determine whether abused juveniles are more likely to engage in delinquency than nonabused juveniles.

Surveys have the advantage of allowing us to study a large number of juveniles. Further, if we select these juveniles carefully, we can ensure that they are similar to or representative of all juveniles. As a consequence, we can generalize from our survey to all juveniles. For example, suppose we find that child abuse causes delinquency in the sample of juveniles we survey. Since these juveniles are representative of all juveniles, we have some basis for concluding that child abuse causes delinquency among all juveniles. At the same time, surveys do have certain disadvantages. Most notably, there is the danger that some juveniles may not provide accurate answers to our questions. They may forget some of the things that they have done or that others have done to them. Also, they may lie to us in an effort to make themselves look good.

Experiments. Criminologists also collect data by doing experiments on juveniles. In an experiment, **you do something to a group of people and then observe the consequences.** For example, you show them a violent video and then observe whether they act in a more aggressive manner.

As discussed in Chapter 19, properly conducted experiments are a good way to determine if something causes something else. Many laboratory experiments, however, have been criticized as artificial. Conditions in the lab may not adequately reflect conditions in the real world, so when someone behaves a certain way in the lab, it does not necessarily mean that he or she will behave the same way in the outside, or "real," world. For example, a laboratory experiment may reveal that juveniles often respond to violent cartoons by hitting an inflated doll in a playroom. This behavior, however, does not necessarily mean that they respond to violent cartoons in the real world by hitting other people. Further, ethical considerations often prevent social scientists from doing experiments on the causes of delinquency. For example, we would not want to abuse a group of juveniles and then determine whether they become more delinquent. Likewise, we would not want to create conditions of poverty, broken homes, or poor grades to study such alleged causes of delinquency. Such ethical considerations are why experiments are used less often than surveys when studying the causes of delinquency. Experiments are more often used to determine whether programs are successful at reducing or preventing delinquency, and we will discuss them further in Chapter 19. Nevertheless, experiments are sometimes used to study the causes of delinquency. For example, numerous experiments have investigated the impact of media violence on juveniles. Juveniles are exposed to media violence (e.g., a clip from a violent TV show), and researchers then observe the consequences of this exposure on their behavior (e.g., are they more aggressive to a toy clown in the playroom?).

Field studies. Finally, criminologists collect data by studying juveniles, including delinquents, in the "field." That is, **criminologists sometimes go out into the community and study juveniles firsthand** in an effort to determine the causes of delinquency. Such study usually **involves a combination of observation and intensive interviewing** (see Lofland and Lofland, 1995, for an excellent overview). Criminologists, for example, may spend time observing the behavior of gang members in a particular community. What do they do each day? How do they get along with one another, with family members, with school officials, and others? What do they talk about? Criminologists may also conduct intensive interviews with these gang members. Intensive interviews differ from the interviews associated with surveys. Survey interviews are usually highly structured: respondents are asked to answer a set of predetermined questions, and each question usually has a list of predetermined answers from which they must choose. For example, the survey interviewer may ask: "How many of your friends have been arrested?" and respondents must select their answer from a list that includes "all," "most," "some," or "none." *Intensive interviews* are much less structured. The interviewer usually has a list of topics to explore, but there are few predetermined questions, and respondents can answer each question in their own words. Intensive interviews have been described as "guided conversations." Field studies, then, involve a combination of "looking, listening, and asking" (Lofland and Lofland, 1995:70).

Field studies provide a much more detailed picture of social life than is provided by surveys and experiments. Researchers directly observe juveniles over an extended period of time and have long conversations with them. As a consequence, they get a fuller picture of the circumstances in which juveniles live and the factors that influence their behavior. Also, since the researcher directly observes juveniles, field studies are less affected by the fact that juveniles are sometimes unable or unwilling to provide accurate answers to survey questions.

At the same time, field studies have certain limitations. It is difficult for a criminologist to observe and intensely interview more than a small number of juveniles. As a consequence, we need to be much more cautious about generalizing from a particular field study to all juveniles. A field study, for example, may find that the members of a particular gang are heavily involved in selling drugs. But since only one of the many thousands of gangs in the United States was studied, there is some danger in concluding that all or most gangs are heavily involved in selling drugs. The results of a field study, however, can be verified with additional field studies of different gangs and sometimes with surveys. There are also limits to what can be observed. Most families, for example, would probably be reluctant to have a researcher in their home observing them. Further, the presence of the researcher might change the behavior being observed. Parents might be reluctant to abuse their kids, and juveniles might be reluctant to commit delinquent acts if there is an observer present. Finally, the researchers' biases may influence what researchers observe and how they interpret what they observe.

Despite these limitations, field studies have provided criminologists with important information about the causes of delinquency—information that would have been difficult or impossible to obtain with surveys and experiments. Field studies, in particular, have played a key role in helping us understand the role of gangs and community characteristics in causing delinquency.[1] I describe the findings from a number of field studies throughout this book.

Each method of collecting data, then, has its own special set of advantages and disadvantages. Ideally, researchers should study the causes of delinquency using all three methods when feasible and ethical.

Develop Measures of Your Independent and Dependent Variables

Since most research on the causes of delinquency employs surveys, I **will focus on survey research** for the remainder of this discussion. Once you have decided to conduct a survey, you need to decide how you will measure your variables. That is, you need to **decide what questions you will ask the juveniles in your sample** to measure variables like child abuse and delinquency. You want to make sure that your questions reflect the definitions you have developed. At the same time, you want to make sure that your questions will be properly understood by your respondents, many of whom may be young and of limited intellectual ability. In some cases, it is an easy matter to develop questions. For example, if you want to measure a variable like age, you can simply ask juveniles, "How old are you?" In other cases, it is much more difficult to develop good questions. For example, how do you measure a variable like "low self-control" (defined in Chapter 13)? This variable has several components, including impulsivity and a preference for risky activities. Researchers have measured low self-control by asking respondents whether they agree with a series of questions, such as "I often act on the spur of the moment without stopping to think," and "Sometimes I will take a risk just for the fun of it" (see Grasmick et al., 1993). Responses to these questions are then used to develop an overall measure of low self-control.

Textbooks on social research, like Babbie (2006) and Champion (2005), provide guidelines for researchers to follow in developing good measures. In evaluating a piece of research, you should **ask yourself whether there are any potential problems with the measures employed.** As you may recall from earlier chapters, one major issue in delinquency research involves the way delinquency is measured. Many researchers measure delinquency using arrest data. Arrest data, however, suffer from several problems, including the fact that they overlook the vast majority of delinquent acts, which do not come to the attention of the police. As a consequence, most criminologists studying the causes of delinquency now rely on self-report measures of delinquency. Such measures are not problem-free, but if properly constructed they are generally thought to provide a better indicator of delinquency. Researchers, however, place greatest confidence in findings that hold for both self-report and arrest measures. We can be more confident, for example, that child abuse really does cause delinquency if it affects both self-reported delinquency and arrests. Fortunately, the research based on arrest data and the research based on comparable self-report measures have generally produced similar results about the causes of delinquency, although there are some exceptions.

Select a Sample of Juveniles to Survey

There are about 34 million juveniles between the ages of 10 and 17 in the United States. But it is not necessary to survey all of them. **If researchers carefully select a *sample* of one or two thousand juveniles, they can accurately generalize from this sample to all juveniles in the United States.** If the researchers find, for example, that abused juveniles are more delinquent than nonabused juveniles in this sample, they can be reasonably confident that they would find the same thing if they surveyed all 34 million juveniles ages 10 to 17 in the United States. Researchers must, however, carefully select their sample so that it is *representative* of all juveniles in the United States. What do I mean by "representative"? I mean that the characteristics of the juveniles in our sample should be similar to those of all juveniles in the United States. The two groups should be proportionately similar in terms of delinquency and all the potential causes of delinquency—including variables like class, race, sex, and age. How do we ensure that our sample is similar to or representative of all juveniles? The best way to do this is to collect a *random sample.*

A random sample is collected such that each juvenile in the population has an equal chance of being selected. For example, imagine that we put the names of all juveniles in the United States in an enormous hat. We then thoroughly mixed the names up and had a blindfolded person pull out 2,000 names. We would have a random sample, and we could be reasonably sure that the juveniles in this sample were similar to or representative of all juveniles in the United States. Researchers do not collect random samples in quite this manner; rather, they have developed more sophisticated techniques for randomly sampling juveniles from a population (see Babbie, 2006; Champion, 2005). Unfortunately, it is often difficult for researchers to collect random samples of juveniles—even random samples of juveniles from a single city. There is no list containing the names of every juvenile in the United States (or in cities or states within the United States). Even if there were such a list, it is often hard to locate certain juveniles, and if you do locate them, they may refuse to participate in your survey.

As a consequence, most studies of delinquency are based on samples that are not quite representative of all juveniles or that are of questionable representativeness. For example, researchers commonly collect random samples of students from high schools (e.g., they select every 20th student on the rolls from all the high schools in a city or from a random sample of high schools in the United States). As indicated earlier, however, many juveniles have dropped out of school, are suspended, or are absent from school the day the survey is administered. This is especially likely to be true of lower-class juveniles and serious delinquents. Also, many students refuse to participate in the survey, or their parents refuse to allow them to participate. So the final sample of students is not representative of all juveniles. As a consequence, criminologists have to be cautious when generalizing from their sample to all juveniles. In fact, some researchers have claimed that the use of unrepresentative samples—including school samples—has led scientists to draw some inaccurate conclusions about the causes of delinquency (e.g., Bernard, 1984; Hagan and McCarthy, 1997a, 1997b). The extent to which the sample is unrepresentative obviously depends on the particular survey, and some of the more recent surveys on juvenile delinquency have gone to great lengths to select more representative samples of juveniles. In particular, they have made a special effort to make sure that serious delinquents are included in the sample (see Thornberry et al., 1995; Thornberry and Krohn, 2003). In any event, when you are evaluating a piece of survey research, you should **ask whether the sample is representative of the population from which it is drawn. And if it is not representative, how might that affect the results?** (Good researchers will usually address these issues in their research reports.)

Analyze the Data You Have Collected

Once researchers have developed their measures and selected their sample, they administer the survey. Most delinquency surveys today contain hundreds of questions (remember, it may take several questions to measure a single variable) and are administered to as many as 1,000 or more juveniles. Researchers enter all the data they have collected into a computer and then analyze this data using certain statistical techniques. Before researchers can conclude that some independent variable like child abuse causes delinquency, **they must demonstrate four things: The independent variable is associated with delinquency; the association is not due to chance; the association is not due to third variables; and the independent variable precedes delinquency in time.** These are the four conditions for making causal statements. Let me describe each of them in turn (see Hirschi and Selvin, 1967, for a fuller discussion).

Association. Before we can say that our independent variable causes delinquency, we must first demonstrate that our independent variable is associated, or correlated, with delinquency. For example, before we can say that child abuse causes delinquency, we must demonstrate that abused juveniles are higher in delinquency. This requirement makes sense. If child abuse causes delinquency, then we would expect abused juveniles to be more delinquent than nonabused juveniles. (This is an example of a *positive association:* A high score on our independent variable is associated with a higher level of delinquency. This positive association is illustrated in Figure 5.1A; as the level of abuse increases, the level of delinquency also increases.) To give another example, suppose we argue that school grades cause delinquency: Those with higher grades have more to lose by engaging in delinquency and should therefore be lower in delinquency. If this argument is correct, school grades should be associated with delinquency: Those with high grades should be less delinquent than those with low grades. (This is an example of a *negative association:* A high score on our independent variable is associated with a lower level of delinquency. This negative association is illustrated in Figure 5.1B; as grades increase, the level of delinquency decreases.)

It is important to emphasize that **most associations are far from perfect.** Do not expect to find that all abused juveniles are delinquent and that all nonabused juveniles are not delinquent. Instead, you might find that 30 percent of all abused juveniles are high in delinquency compared to 17 percent of all nonabused juveniles. Delinquency is caused by a large number of variables, most of which have small to moderate associations with delinquency. So when you read that low grades or broken homes are associated with delinquency, you should not assume that all or even most juveniles with low grades or from broken homes are delinquent (or that all juveniles with high grades or from intact homes are nondelinquent). What you can safely assume is that juveniles with low grades and juveniles from broken homes are somewhat more likely to engage in delinquency than juveniles with high grades and juveniles from intact homes.

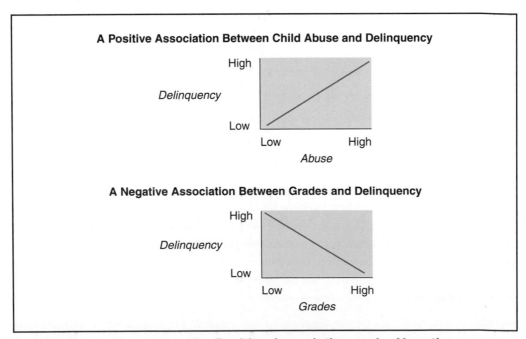

FIGURE 5.1 Examples of a Positive Association and a Negative Association

Most of the statistics employed by researchers summarize the association between the independent and dependent variables. These statistics usually tell the researcher how much delinquency increases or decreases when the independent variable increases by a certain amount. For example, they might tell the researcher that juveniles commit an average of five fewer delinquent acts every time school grades increase by one unit (from D to C, C to B, etc.). See Babbie (2006), and Champion (2005) for an overview of such statistics.

Association not due to chance. Suppose we find that child abuse and delinquency are associated, with abused juveniles being more delinquent than nonabused juveniles. Does that mean that child abuse causes delinquency?

It does not. The association may be due to chance. For example, suppose you randomly sample 10 students from your school. You find that 40 percent of the blue-eyed students in your sample are delinquent, whereas only 20 percent of the brown-eyed students are. So there is an association between eye color and delinquency. But this association may be due to chance. If you surveyed **all** the students at your school, you might find that eye color is unrelated to delinquency (e.g., 30 percent of the blue-eyed students are delinquent and 30 percent of the brown-eyed students are delinquent). But, by chance, your sample of 10 happened to include too many blue-eyed delinquents and too few brown-eyed delinquents. The fact that two variables are associated does not prove that one causes the other; the association may be due to chance.

The likelihood that a given association is due to chance becomes smaller as the sample size increases. Larger samples generally produce more accurate results, although increases in sample size beyond 2,000 or so juveniles only produce small increases in accuracy (see Babbie, 2006, for a discussion of factors affecting the accuracy of sample results, including sample size). Also, if you have collected a random sample, you can estimate the probability that any association you find is due to chance. For example, you can say that the probability that the association between child abuse and delinquency is due to chance is less than 1 in 20 (5 percent) or less than 1 in 100 (1 percent). Researchers state that such associations are **"statistically significant."**

Association not due to third variables. Now suppose that we have demonstrated that child abuse and delinquency are associated and that it is unlikely that this association is due to chance. Can we now say that child abuse causes delinquency? I'm afraid the answer is still no. The association between child abuse and delinquency may be caused by a third variable that is causally prior to both of the original variables.

Let me provide an example from actual research. Criminologists have found that there is an association between IQ and delinquency: People with low IQs are higher in delinquency. Further, it is quite unlikely that this association is due to chance. Does that mean that low IQ causes delinquency? Many criminologists argue that it does not. They claim that the association between IQ and delinquency is not due to the fact that low IQ causes delinquency. Rather, it is due to the fact that both IQ and delinquency are caused by the same third variable. In particular, they claim that the third variable, social class, affects both IQ and delinquency (see Figure 5.2). Lower-class people have lower IQs and are higher in delinquency. That is why low IQ is associated with high delinquency—not because low IQ causes delinquency but because both IQ and delinquency are caused by the same third variable, social class. (Try to think of another example where the association between two variables may be caused by a third variable. Hint: A popular example involves

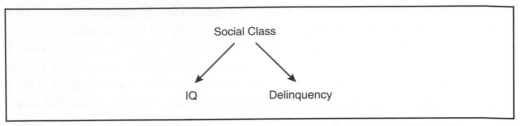

FIGURE 5.2 Some Claim That Social Class Affects Both IQ and Delinquency

the following three variables: number of storks in an area, area birthrate, and urban/rural location—see Babbie, 2006.)

Before we can argue that the independent variable in our theory causes delinquency, we must also demonstrate that the association between our independent variable and delinquency is not caused by a third variable. How do we do this? Let us continue with the example. Again, many criminologists argue that people with low IQs are more likely to be delinquent because they are more likely to be lower class, not because they have low IQs. Likewise, they argue that people with high IQs are less likely to be delinquent because they are more likely to be higher class, not because they have high IQs. If these arguments are correct, the association between IQ and delinquency should disappear if we examine just lower-class people. That is, IQ should be unrelated to delinquency in a sample of lower-class people: Lower-class people with low IQs should be about as delinquent as lower-class people with high IQs. Likewise, the association should disappear if we examine just higher-class people: Higher-class people with low IQs should be about as delinquent as higher-class people with high IQs. If IQ is no longer associated with delinquency when we examine lower-class people separately from higher-class people, that finding suggests that the original association between IQ and delinquency is caused by social class and we can no longer claim that IQ causes delinquency.

What if the association does not disappear? What if we find that lower-class people with low IQs are more delinquent than lower-class people with high IQs, and that higher-class people with low IQs are more delinquent than higher-class people with high IQs? This finding means that the association between IQ and delinquency is not caused by the third variable of social class. And, in fact, that is what researchers have found: IQ is still associated with delinquency even when the analysis is limited to lower-class people only or to higher-class people only (e.g., Hirschi and Hindelang, 1977).

Researchers, then, determine whether the association between an independent variable and delinquency is caused by a third variable by *"controlling" for the third variable, or "holding it constant."* We examined the association between IQ and delinquency separately for each category of social class—lower and higher. If the association disappears, that suggests that it was caused by our third variable. (I realize that these arguments may be difficult for some of you to follow. I encourage you to consult with your classmates and to try to come up with examples of your own; also see the discussion in Hirschi and Selvin, 1967:73–87.)

When you are evaluating a piece of research, you should **ask yourself whether any of the reported associations might be caused by a third variable.** Is there some causally prior third variable that might account for the association between the independent variable and delinquency? Are there any third variables, for example, that might account for the association between child abuse and delinquency? Most researchers will try to anticipate third variables that might account for the associations they report and then control for them. This is not always done, however.

Correct *causal order*. Suppose you find that child abuse is associated with delinquency, the association is not due to chance, and it appears that it is not caused by a third variable. Can you now state that child abuse causes delinquency? If not, why not?

It may be that the association between child abuse and delinquency exists because delinquency causes child abuse. Juveniles who commit delinquent acts may upset their parents, and the upset parents may react by striking their children. Much recent data, in fact, suggest that the behavior of juveniles often has a large effect on how others treat them, including how their parents treat them. Children who are difficult to raise, for example, are more likely to be rejected and elicit negative reactions from their parents (see Rutter et al., 1998:171–174).

Before we can say that child abuse causes delinquency, we must demonstrate that the abuse preceded the delinquency in time. That is, the abuse came first and the delinquency followed. This is usually accomplished by conducting a ***longitudinal survey.*** We survey the same group of juveniles over time. For example, during our initial survey we ask a sample of juveniles about the extent of their delinquency and whether their parents hit them. Then we survey the same group of juveniles one year later, once again asking them about the extent of their delinquency. These two surveys allow us to determine whether abused juveniles engage in more **subsequent** delinquency than nonabused juveniles.

It is difficult to do longitudinal surveys of this type, since it is often hard to keep track of a large group of juveniles over time. Much research on the causes of delinquency suffers from the fact that it is not longitudinal in nature (such research is said to be ***cross-sectional,*** since it looks at juveniles at one cross section in time). Nevertheless, several excellent longitudinal surveys of delinquency have been conducted or are now in progress (e.g., Elliott et al., 1985; Thornberry and Krohn, 2003; Thornberry et al., 1995). One interesting finding to emerge from these studies is that variables sometimes have a ***reciprocal effect*** on one another. For example, research suggests that associating with delinquent peers and delinquency are reciprocally related. Associating with delinquent peers causes delinquency, and delinquency causes a juvenile to associate with delinquent peers (see Chapters 16 and 18).

Summary

Determining whether your beliefs or theories about the causes of delinquency are correct is not an easy matter. There are a number of guidelines that should be followed when collecting and analyzing data, but it is often difficult to follow them all, and sometimes the research on the causes of delinquency is suspect as a result. Perhaps a variable is not well defined or measured. Perhaps an unrepresentative sample is employed. Perhaps there is a failure to control for relevant third variables. Perhaps the research is not longitudinal in nature. Given these problems, criminologists sometimes need to be cautious when making causal statements. I will try to indicate when that is the case in the discussions that follow. At the same time, there are some areas in which they can make causal statements with some confidence. Certain areas have been well researched, and a range of studies have come to similar conclusions. Criminologists do not like to place too much faith in a single study. But if a number of different studies agree—especially well-conducted studies that use different measures and samples—we are more confident in our conclusions.

Teaching Aids

Some Challenges

The data that follow are not real, and answers to the challenges are given after the Key Terms.

1. Someone decides to sample 100 students at your college or university. They set up a table in front of the main dining hall during dinner. They then ask passing students to fill out their survey until 100 students have responded. Do these 100 responders constitute a *random sample* of the students at your school? If not, why not? How would you collect a random sample of students at your school?

2. A researcher finds that 90 percent of all delinquent boys played violent video games before they became delinquents. Does this prove that playing video games causes delinquency among boys? If not, why not?

3. A researcher finds that 50 percent of all spanked juveniles are delinquent compared to 30 percent of all nonspanked juveniles. Does this prove that spanking causes delinquency? If not, why not?

4. After analyzing data from many years, a researcher finds that delinquency is much more common during a full moon. Does this prove that a full moon causes delinquency? If not, why not? (Note: This is a rather tough challenge.)

TEST YOUR KNOWLEDGE OF THIS CHAPTER

1. What is a theory? What are the basic parts of a theory?

2. Why is it important to study theories of delinquency?

3. What is meant by the "scientific method"?

4. List and briefly describe the major steps in testing a theory (or determining whether some factor causes delinquency).

5. List and briefly describe the three major methods of gathering data to test theories. Describe the advantages and disadvantages of each method.

6. How do the "intensive interviews" that are part of field studies differ from the interviews that are part of surveys?

7. What is a random sample? Why is it important to collect random samples? Related to this, what is a "representative" sample?

8. Many researchers who study delinquency try to collect random samples of students in high schools. Do such surveys result in a "representative" sample of juveniles? If not, why not?

9. When analyzing their data, researchers must satisfy four conditions before they can conclude that some factor or variable causes delinquency. What are these four conditions?

10. What do researchers mean when they state that two variables are "associated"? Give an example of a positive association and a negative association. What is meant by the statement that "most associations are far from perfect"?

11. What do researchers mean when they state that an association is probably due to chance?

12. When researchers say than an association is "statistically significant," what do they mean?

13. What do researchers mean when they state that they have "controlled for" a third variable or "held it constant"?

14. What is a "longitudinal survey"? Why is it important to conduct longitudinal surveys?

15. What is a "reciprocal effect"? Give a plausible example of a reciprocal effect.

THOUGHT AND DISCUSSION QUESTIONS

1. Develop a simple theory of delinquency other than those discussed in this chapter. Identify the independent variable(s), dependent variable, and explanation of why the independent variable(s) causes the dependent variable in your theory. Describe a plausible "conditioning variable" for your theory.

2. Describe how you would ideally test the simple theory of delinquency you developed in question 1.

3. Give an example of how you would determine whether some factor causes delinquency by doing an experiment. Give an example of how you might examine some possible cause(s) of delinquency by doing a field study.

4. Draw a "two-variable table." At the left side of this table will be your dependent variable, "delinquency," and it will have two categories: "low" and "high." At the top of your table will be your independent variable, and it will also have two categories: "low" and "high" (or two other categories of your choice, like "yes" and "no" or "male" and "female"). Fill in the table with percentages that indicate a strong association between your independent variable and dependent variable. Then fill in the table with percentages that indicate no association between your independent variable and dependent variable. Remember that percentages must always add up to 100; also, percentage in the direction of your independent variable, since you are comparing one category of your independent variable to the other (e.g., you are comparing the percentage of males who are high in delinquency to the percentage of females who are high in delinquency).

5. Give a plausible example of an association that is due to a third variable. Create a diagram like that shown in Figure 5.2 to illustrate your example.

6. How would you go about determining whether the association you just described is, in fact, due to the third variable you list?

7. Can we ever "truly" determine (with 100 percent confidence) that some factor causes delinquency? Justify your response.

KEY TERMS

- Theory
- Independent variable
- Dependent variable
- Conditioning variable
- Scientific method

- Surveys
- Experiments
- Field studies
- Intensive interviews
- Sample

- Representative samples
- Random sample
- Association
- Positive association
- Negative association

KEY TERMS (continued)

- Association not due to chance
- Association not due to third variables
- "Controlling" for the third variable, or "holding it constant"
- Causal order
- Longitudinal survey
- Cross-sectional survey
- Reciprocal effect

Answers to the Challenges

1. The sample of 100 responders is probably not a random sample of students. It is probably the case that some students are less likely to pass by the dining hall during dinner than other students; for example, those who live off campus or in fraternities or sororities are probably less likely to pass by the dining hall during dinner. Also, some of the students who do pass by the dining hall are probably less likely to fill out the survey than others; for example, those who are busy or have little interest in the topic of the survey may be less likely to fill out the survey. So it is *not* the case that each student on campus has an equal chance of being in the sample. Rather than being representative of all students, the sample of 100 responders is likely biased toward students who live on campus, are not in fraternities or sororities, have more free time, care about the topic of the survey, and so on. You might collect a random sample of the students in your school by obtaining an up-to-date list of students, then selecting every 10th student on that list (if there are 1,000 students in your school and you want a sample of 100) or using a table of random numbers to select 100 students from the list (see Babbie, 2000).

2. The researcher cannot safely conclude that playing video games causes delinquency among boys. The main reason for this is that the data do *not* demonstrate an *association* between playing violent video games and delinquency. Most adolescent boys play violent video games at some time. As a consequence, it is likely the case that most delinquent boys *and most nondelinquent boys* have played violent video games (e.g., 90 percent of all nondelinquent boys may have played violent video games). To demonstrate that playing violent video games causes delinquency among boys, we must *determine whether boys who play violent video games are more likely to engage in delinquency than boys who do not play violent video games (and, of course, we must do so by using a random or representative sample of boys and good measures)*. If we find an association between playing violent video games and delinquency, we must then try to demonstrate that the association is not due to chance and that the association is not caused by a third variable (e.g., maybe poor parental supervision leads to violent video game playing on the one hand and delinquency on the other). Since the example states that the delinquents played violent video games *before* they became delinquent, causal order is not a problem.

3. These data demonstrate that there is an association between spanking and delinquency, with spanked juveniles being more likely to engage in delinquency (I'm assuming that the researcher has a representative sample of juveniles and good measures of spanking and delinquency). But these data do *not* prove that spanking *causes* delinquency. The association may be due to chance. The association may be caused by a third variable (e.g., parental criminality may be such a variable; criminal parents may be more likely to spank and more likely to cause their children to engage in delinquency, perhaps because they are poor role models). And the association may be due to the fact that the delinquency of the child causes the parent to engage in spanking rather than spanking causing delinquency.

4. These data demonstrate an association between a phase of the moon and delinquency (delinquency is more common during a full moon). It is unlikely this association is due to chance if the researcher analyzed data from many years. It is hard to think of a third variable that causes a full moon on the one hand and delinquency on the other (e-mail me if you come up with a good candidate). And it is quite unlikely that delinquency causes a full moon. So these data do strongly suggest that a full moon causes delinquency. These data, of course, are not real; but an astute student in one of my classes nevertheless came up with the following explanation about how a full moon might cause delinquency. Since it is lighter outside when the moon is full, people are more likely to go outside at night. And this creates more opportunities for delinquency (among other things, delinquency is more likely when juveniles are associating with one another in the absence of authority figures).

ENDNOTE

1. For examples, *see* Anderson, 1990, 1999; Campbell, 1984; Decker and Van Winkle, 1996; Hagedorn, 1988; Jody Miller, 2001; Moore, 1991; Padilla, 1992; Sullivan, 1989.

CHAPTER 6

Strain Theory

Does Strain or Stress Cause Delinquency?

ccording to *strain theory*, **when juveniles experience strain or stress, they become upset, and they sometimes engage in delinquency as a result.** They may engage in delinquency to reduce or escape from the strain they are experiencing. For example, they may engage in violence to end harassment from peers; they may steal to reduce their money problems; or they may run away from home to escape abusive parents. They may also perform delinquent acts to seek revenge against those who have "wronged" them. And they may engage in illicit drug use in an effort to feel better.

Many of the delinquent acts that you may have committed or come close to committing can probably be explained using strain theory. You experienced some type of *strain* or stress; most probably, someone did something to you that you did not like. Perhaps someone insulted you or did not give you something you wanted. You became angry and frustrated as a result, and you thought about or actually committed some delinquent act. In this area, studies indicate that a large number of violent acts start off with one person insulting another or otherwise doing something that the other person does not like.[1]

There are several versions of strain theory, the most prominent being those of Merton (1938, 1968), Cohen (1955), Cloward and Ohlin (1960), Greenberg (1977), Elliott et al. (1979), Agnew (1992), Berkowitz (1993), and Colvin (2000). Each version basically tries to do two things: **describe the major types of strain that lead to delinquency and describe the conditions under which strain is most likely to lead to delinquency.** All strain theorists recognize that strain usually does not lead to delinquency. As a consequence, such theorists describe those "conditioning variables" that influence the likelihood that strain will result in delinquency. Rather than describe each version of strain theory, I will present a generic version that incorporates the central arguments of the major strain theories, although this generic theory draws most heavily on Agnew's (1992, 2006a, 2006b) general strain theory.

What Are the Major Types of Strain?

Researchers often measure strain by presenting juveniles with lists of strainful events and conditions and asking them which events/conditions they have experienced.[2] Certain of these lists contain over 200 items, including things like parents divorcing, parents arguing or fighting, a close friend dying or becoming seriously ill, not being selected for a much-wanted extracurricular activity, disagreements with teachers, disagreements with friends, breaking up with a romantic partner, and money problems. Theorists have tried to categorize these types of strain in various ways and to list the types of strain that are most strongly related to delinquency. Two general categories of strain have been linked to delinquency: the failure to achieve your goals and the loss of positive stimuli/presentation of negative stimuli.

The Failure to Achieve Your Goals

All strain theorists argue that a major type of strain is the failure to achieve your goals. And several theorists argue that the inability of adolescents to achieve certain goals contributes to much delinquency. These goals include money, status/respect, thrills/excitement, and autonomy from adults.

Money. Certain strain theorists argue that money is the central goal in the United States (see especially Merton, 1968; Cloward and Ohlin, 1960). All people, poor as well as rich, are encouraged to work hard so that they might make a lot of money. Further, money is necessary to buy many of the things people want, including the necessities of life and all those luxury items to which most people are regularly exposed. Money is said to be important for adolescents as well as for adults, since adolescents need money for such things as clothing, social activities, automobiles, and drugs (see Greenberg, 1977). Many adolescents, however, are not able to obtain the money they need through legal channels, such as parents and work. This inability is especially true of poor adolescents, but it may also be true of many middle-class adolescents. As a consequence, such adolescents experience strain and may attempt to get money through illegal channels, such as theft, selling drugs, and prostitution. Studies provide some support for this argument.

Several field studies have found that criminals and delinquents often report that they engage in income-generating crime because they want money but cannot easily get it any other way.[3] In particular, researchers have asked individuals like burglars, robbers, shoplifters, drug addicts, and prostitutes why they engage in crime. Perhaps the most common response is that they have a **desperate need for money,** and crime is the only way or the easiest way for them to get it. It is important to note, however, that they usually do not need money for necessities like food and shelter; rather, they need it for things like partying, gambling, and drugs. Nevertheless, in their view they desperately need cash.

The fact that some delinquents report monetary strain, however, does not prove that such strain is a cause of delinquency. Many individuals who experience monetary strain do not engage in delinquency. Many of you, for example, have probably been in situations where you wanted more money than you had, yet you did not engage in crime. Criminologists must demonstrate that people who are high in monetary strain are more likely to engage in delinquency than people low in such strain (see the discussion of "association" in Chapter 5). Surprisingly, only a few studies have tried to do this, and most suffer from serious problems.[4] Some data, however, suggest that crime is more common among people who are dissatisfied with their monetary situation; such dissatisfaction is higher among lower-class people and people who state that they want "a lot of money."[5] So there is limited support for the idea that monetary strain is related to delinquency. More research is needed in this area, however.

Status/respect. Closely related to the desire for money is the desire for status and respect (see Cohen, 1955). People want to be positively regarded by others and want to be treated respectfully, which at a minimum involves being treated in a just or fair manner (see Agnew, 1992). Data suggest that anger is often the result of disrespectful or unjust treatment (Agnew, 1992, 2006a). Although people have a general desire for status and respect, the desire for "masculine status" is said to be especially relevant to delinquency.[6]

There are class and race differences in views about what it means to be a "man," although most such views emphasize traits like independence, dominance, toughness, competitiveness, and heterosexuality (see Messerschmidt, 1993; Oliver, 1994). Most male juveniles experience difficulties in their desire to be viewed and treated as a man, particularly given the emphasis of the school system on docility and submission (see Greenberg, 1977; Messerschmidt, 1993). Certain juveniles, however, experience special difficulties in this area, especially lower-class and minority group members.[7] **Such juveniles may attempt to "accomplish masculinity" through delinquency.** They may engage in delinquent acts to demonstrate that they possess traits like toughness, dominance, and independence. And they may attempt to coerce others into giving them the respect they believe they deserve as "real men." In this connection, they may adopt a tough demeanor, respond to even minor shows of disrespect with violence, and occasionally assault and rob others in an effort to establish a tough reputation. There have been no large-scale tests of this idea, although several field studies provide support for it.[8]

For example, Oliver (1994) conducted intensive interviews with 41 lower-class African American males about their participation in violent events. He discovered, like other researchers, that many of these events were precipitated by what were seen as challenges to one's masculinity. He asked one of his respondents, "Why do you think so many fights among black males are centered around manhood?" and received the following reply:

> "I believe with us, the black man, that our manhood is very important to us. That's about the only thing we have to hold on to—besides our families—is our manhood. And when that's threatened, it's time to fight. 'I'm going to show you I'm not a punk,' 'I'm going to show you I'm not a faggot'—you know, that sort of thing. I've seen fights where words were exchanged for at least ten, fifteen minutes and they just stood there and exchanged words with one another, and one guy told the other guy, 'Look, just leave me alone,' and the other guy just kept on you know, 'Fuck you punk,' and the other guy was getting tired of the exchange of words, being called punk, faggot, sissy, so forth, that he just went ahead and punched the guy, and a fight occurred." (Oliver, 1994:90)

There is reason to believe that concern with one's manhood or masculine status is not limited to African American males, although African American males and lower-class males may have more trouble "accomplishing masculinity" though legal channels—as a result of the discrimination and limited opportunities they encounter (see Messerschmidt, 1993). In any event, the previous quote makes clear how threats to one's masculine status sometimes lead to crime.

Thrills/excitement. Some individuals have a strong desire to engage in thrilling or exciting activities. These individuals are sometimes referred to as "sensation seekers" (see White et al., 1985). They gain much pleasure from engaging in risky, even life-threatening activities. As argued in Chapter 13, there is some reason to believe that this desire for thrills/excitement is in part biologically based. In any event, many individuals discover that they have trouble satisfying this desire through legal channels. This may be especially true of juveniles, who are confined in school for much of the day and prevented from engaging in a range of risky behaviors by adults. Such juveniles, then, may attempt to satisfy their desire for thrills/excitement through delinquent acts, like aggression, theft, and drug use. Several studies provide support for this argument. Criminals and delinquents often state that they engage in illegal acts "for the thrill of it" or because of the "rush" they get from it. Further, juveniles with a strong need for thrills and excitement are more likely to engage in delinquency.[9]

To illustrate, Katz (1988) asked the students in his criminology classes to report on their shoplifting experiences. He discovered that many of the shoplifting incidents committed by these largely upper-middle-class students were motivated not by material need, but rather seemed to be motivated by a desire for thrills or excitement—as suggested by the following quotes:

> "Once outside the door I thought Wow! I pulled it off, I faced danger and I pulled it off. I was smiling and I felt at that moment like there was nothing I couldn't do." (Katz, 1988:64)

"The experience was almost orgasmic for me. There was a build up of tension as I contemplated the danger of the forbidden act, then a rush of excitement at the moment of committing the crime, and finally a delicious sense of release." (Katz, 1988:71)

Autonomy from adults. Several researchers have argued that a major goal of most adolescents is to achieve autonomy from adults.[10] Autonomy may be defined as freedom from the control of others. Adolescents come to desire autonomy as they physically and socially mature. Adults, however, often deny adolescents the autonomy they desire. Although adolescents have more autonomy than children, their behavior is still subject to much control; a broad range of behaviors are prohibited or restricted. Most notably, adolescents find their desire for autonomy frustrated in the school system with its extensive regulations and emphasis on authoritarian styles of teaching (see Greenberg, 1977). Parents may also continue to restrict the freedom of adolescents. The denial of autonomy may lead to delinquency for several reasons: Delinquency may be a means of asserting autonomy (e.g., sexual intercourse or disorderly behavior), achieving autonomy (e.g., stealing money to gain financial independence from parents), or venting frustration against those who deny autonomy.

Some data support these arguments. Adolescents often demand greater autonomy from parents and teachers, and they frequently clash with these individuals over issues involving autonomy. Such issues include doing chores, clothing, appearance, schoolwork, interpersonal relations, and rules for such things as bedtime and curfew (see Agnew, 1997). Agnew (1984) examined the relationship between the need for autonomy and delinquency and found that adolescents with a strong need for autonomy were angrier and more frustrated and, partly as a consequence, more likely to engage in delinquency than other adolescents (also see Piquero and Brezina, 2001).

Strain, then, may result from the failure to achieve one's goals. I have listed four goals that are said to be important to most adolescents: money, status/respect, thrills/excitement, and autonomy from adults. Strain may also result from the failure to achieve other goals, and any test of strain theory should attempt to determine what goals the people being examined consider important. For example, one goal that many college students consider important is good grades. And many college students experience strain when they find that they are unable to achieve this goal through legitimate channels—like studying. I have the students in my juvenile delinquency course fill out a survey on the first day of class; among other things, I ask them what grade they would ideally like to get in my class and what grade they realistically expect to get. Not surprisingly, almost all the students state that they would ideally like to get an A (sometimes one or two students with more modest ambitions state that they would like a B). Such ideal goals have something of the utopian in them and probably are not taken seriously by many students. I find, however, that roughly 70 percent of the students state that they realistically expect to get an A. The percentage of students who actually end up getting an A, however, is usually between 25 and 30 percent. Many students thus experience strain, and although I have not tested this idea, I suspect that some of these students respond to such strain with deviance, such as cheating on exams or excessive alcohol use.

Loss of Positive Stimuli/Presentation of Negative Stimuli

The types of strain just described all involve what might be called "nonevents." The juvenile wants or expects something—like money or autonomy—but does not get it. The second major category of strain involves negative events or conditions. Juveniles lose something they value (*loss of positive stimuli*) or are *presented with noxious or negative stimuli.* For example, the juvenile may break up with a boyfriend or girlfriend, someone may take something from the juvenile, or someone may insult or physically assault the juvenile. In short, people treat the juvenile in a negative manner—in a way that she or he does not like. Such negative treatment may upset or anger the juvenile and, as indicated earlier, delinquency may be the result.

Several studies have asked juveniles about the types of events that anger or upset them (see Agnew, 1997, for an overview). The answers inevitably focus on interpersonal problems, typically interpersonal problems with parents, siblings, teachers, friends, and romantic partners. Juveniles report that they became angry or upset because these others insulted them, physically assaulted them, disciplined or sanctioned them when they did not deserve it, pressured them, overburdened them, got into conflicts with them, or rejected them. Studies have found that many of these negative events and conditions increase the likelihood of delinquency. This is especially true of those events and conditions that are likely to be viewed as unjust and serious in nature.

In particular, **delinquency has been linked to the following types of negative treatment** (see especially Agnew, 2001a, 2001b, 2006a):

1. **Parental rejection.** Parents who reject their children show little interest in them, provide little support and affection to them, and often display hostility toward them (see Chapter 14).

2. **Parental supervision and discipline that is very strict, erratic, excessive given the infraction, and/or harsh (use of humiliation, insults, threats, screaming, and/or physical punishments)** (see Chapter 14).

3. **Child abuse and neglect.** See Chapter 14.

4. **Negative school experiences.** These include low grades, poor relations with teachers (e.g., teachers treat the juvenile unfairly, belittle or humiliate the juvenile), and the experience of school as boring and a waste of time (see Chapter 15).

5. **Abusive peer relations.** These include insults and ridicule, gossip, threats, attempts to coerce, and physical assaults.[11]

6. **Criminal victimization.** Much recent data suggest that being the victim of a crime, especially a violent crime, substantially increases the likelihood of offending.[12]

7. **Homelessness.** Youths living on the street encounter a broad range of strains or stresses, like the inability to obtain food and shelter, frequent conflicts with others, and criminal victimization (Hagan and McCarthy, 1997a; Hoyt et al., 1999).

8. **Experiences with prejudice and discrimination based on ascribed characteristics like gender and race/ethnicity.**[13]

A study by Wilkinson (2002) illustrates certain of these strains, especially abusive peer relations and criminal victimization. The study involved intensive interviews with 125 adolescent males who had recently committed violent acts. The interviews suggested that these acts were usually prompted by strains like the following:

- a range of abusive behaviors that made the respondent feel "dissed, challenged, or played," with such behaviors including insults, bumps, "grilling" (staring at the respondent in a way seen as inappropriate), and threats;

- competition over girls, including advances on "one's girl" by another man;
- physical attacks;
- material attacks, including the theft or attempted theft of one's possessions; and
- disputes centered around the drug trade, including attempted robberies, turf disputes, and disputes over the price, quantity, or quality of the drugs being sold.

Jody Miller's (2001) field study of female gang members in St. Louis and Columbus indicates that these sorts of strains are not limited to males. For example, Miller (2001:116) states:

> Young women acknowledged that male-female relationships were often a source of strife between and among gang members. Most often, they described the source of conflict as two girls fighting over a particular boy. . . . Tonya recalled when "this girl named Patricia threatened a girl named Dana 'cause she tried to take her dude.' " . . . Alecia said members of her gang, the 2-1s, often fought with female members of the 2-2s because young women in both groups competed for the attention of male members of 2-2.

What Impact Does Strain Have on the Juvenile?

Strainful events and conditions make juveniles feel bad—angry, frustrated, depressed, anxious, and the like. These negative feelings, in turn, create pressure for corrective action. That is, juveniles want to do something to alleviate their bad feelings. And delinquency is one possible response. The emotions of anger and frustration are said to be especially conducive to a delinquent response, since they energize the individual for action, create a desire for revenge, and lower inhibitions. And certain studies indicate that strain affects delinquency partly because it increases the adolescent's level of anger/frustration.[14]

It is important to emphasize, however, that there are **several possible ways to cope with strain and the negative emotions associated with strain. Only some of these coping strategies involve delinquency.**

Adolescents may cope by **cognitively reinterpreting the strain they experience so as to minimize its impact.** Agnew (1992) lists three major *cognitive coping* strategies, summarized in these phrases: "It's not that important." "It's not that bad." "I deserve it." Imagine, for example, an individual who is unable to achieve his monetary goals. This individual may minimize the failure to obtain enough money by claiming that money is not that important, perhaps claiming that other goals, such as having good friends, are more important. Or this individual may come to exaggerate the amount of money he has, claiming that he really has enough money to satisfy his needs. Or this individual may state that he is to blame for his lack of money. This may not reduce feelings of depression, but it is likely to reduce anger at others. All these cognitive coping strategies reduce the likelihood that individuals will react to strain with delinquency.

Adolescents may also employ *behavioral coping* strategies, **attempting to act in ways that reduce the strain they are experiencing. Certain of these strategies may involve nondelinquent behavior.** Adolescents, for example, may get a job to earn money; they may avoid the peers who harass them; or they may negotiate with the teachers who frustrate them. **Other behavioral strategies for reducing strain, as indicated earlier, involve delinquency** (e.g., stealing money or attacking the peers who harass you).

Finally, adolescents may engage in *emotional coping.* Rather than trying to reduce their strain or cognitively reinterpret it, they act directly on the negative emotions that result from strain. They may attempt to reduce their negative emotions through **nondelinquent strategies** like exercise, deep breathing, listening to music, or other relaxation techniques. Or they may employ **delinquent strategies,** such as the use of illegal drugs.

The existence of these different coping strategies, some involving delinquency and some not, raises a major question for strain theorists.

Why Are Some Juveniles More Likely to Cope with Strain Through Delinquency?

Strain theorists have argued that several factors influence whether or not people will respond to strain with delinquency (see Agnew, 1992, 2001b, 2006a, 2006b; Agnew et al., 2001).

Strain is more likely to lead to delinquency when it involves areas of life that the individual considers important. For example, challenges to masculinity are more likely to result in delinquency among individuals who attach great importance to their masculine identity. Likewise, threats to autonomy are more likely to lead to delinquency among individuals who strongly desire autonomy. If strain affects a central area of a person's life, it will be more difficult to ignore it or define it away using the cognitive strategies described in the preceding section.

Strain is more likely to lead to delinquency among individuals with poor *coping skills* and resources. Some individuals are better able to legally cope with strain than others. For example, they have the verbal skills to negotiate with peers and adults, or they have a high level of "self-efficacy," believing that they have the ability to solve their problems. A variety of factors influence an individual's ability to legally cope, including financial resources, intelligence, problem-solving skills, interpersonal skills, and self-efficacy. Individuals who lack these skills and resources, however, may find that delinquency is the only way they can cope with their strain.

Strain is more likely to lead to delinquency among individuals with few *conventional social supports.* Family, friends, and others often help us cope with our strain, providing advice, direct assistance, and emotional support. Individuals who lack such supports are more likely to find themselves in a situation where delinquency is their only means of coping (see Cullen, 1994).

Strain is more likely to lead to delinquency when the costs of delinquent coping are low and the benefits are high. In particular, delinquent coping is more likely when the juvenile has little to lose from delinquency, does not believe that delinquency is wrong in her particular case, and is in a situation where the likelihood of getting caught and sanctioned in a meaningful manner is low. Delinquent coping is also more likely when the juvenile believes that delinquency will result in certain benefits, like the reduction of her strain (see Brezina, 2000). As a simple illustration, strain theory would predict that people are more likely to respond to monetary strain with theft if they encounter an open cash register and no one is around.

Finally, strain is more likely to lead to delinquency among individuals who are disposed to delinquency. The individual's disposition to engage in delinquency is influenced by a number of factors (see Agnew, 1992, 2001a). Among other things, individuals are more disposed to respond to their strain with delinquency if they were reinforced for delinquent responses in the past, if they have been exposed to models who have responded to similar strains with delinquency, and if they believe that delinquency is a desirable or justifiable response in their situation. Individuals are also more disposed to respond to strain with delinquency if they possess certain personality traits, like irritability and low self-control (see Chapter 13). Individuals with these traits are easily upset and have trouble controlling themselves.

A variety of factors, then, may influence whether individuals respond to strain with delinquency. Research on whether these factors do in fact condition the effect of strain on delinquency has produced mixed results. Some studies find that the sorts of factors just listed increase the likelihood that individuals will respond to strain with delinquency, while other studies do not. Part of the reason for these mixed results is that it is difficult to detect conditioning effects in survey research (see Mazerolle and Maahs, 2000). Nevertheless, **certain recent research suggests that at least some of the preceding factors influence the likelihood that individuals will respond to strain with delinquency.**[15] For example, Mazerolle and Maahs (2000) found that strain was more likely to lead to delinquency when juveniles associated with delinquent peers and had weak moral beliefs (did not strongly condemn delinquency). And Agnew et al. (2001) found that strain was more likely to lead to delinquency among individuals who were irritable and low in self-control.

Summary

At core, strain theory is rather simple: Strain makes people upset, and they **may** respond with delinquency. As you can see, however, this rather simple idea has been the subject of much elaboration. In particular, there has been much discussion of the major types of strain that contribute to delinquency and the factors that condition the effect of strain on delinquency. The data provide some support for strain theory, suggesting that the inability to achieve certain goals and the experience of certain negative events increase the likelihood of delinquency. The research on those factors predicted to condition the effect of strain on delinquency has been more mixed, but recent data suggest that at least some of these factors increase the likelihood that juveniles will respond to strain with delinquency.

Teaching Aids

Case Studies

Cases involving juvenile violence are regularly in the news. News reports frequently indicate that the perpetrators of such violence have often been the victims of peer abuse, an assertion supported by surveys and field studies of violent juveniles (e.g., Lockwood, 1997; Wilkinson, 2002, 2003). Recently, I read a newspaper account about three teenagers who "were arrested while carrying an arsenal of machetes, guns, and ammunition after, the police said, they had tried to hijack a car on a quiet residential street. Prosecutors said they had a list of three middle school students they planned to kill" and that they then planned to "use all 2,000 rounds of ammunition they were carrying to kill other town residents at random." The article focused on one of the teenagers who had been arrested, reporting that he "was often teased." Some of his classmates said that the teasing stemmed from the fact that "he usually wore the same clothes—a ragged T-shirt and tight sweatpants—and walked with stooped shoulders and an awkward gait" (Kocieniewski, 2003:A21). Such teasing, of course, does not justify the mass slaughter that the teenagers were allegedly planning. Other cases, however, cause one to wonder about the extent to which the strain or abuse suffered by certain juvenile offenders should be taken into account when sanctioning them. A few such cases follow. What is your reaction to them? In particular, to what extent do you think we should take account of the strain suffered by juvenile offenders when deciding how to respond to them?

Case 1. My local newspaper recently ran a major story about child prostitutes, many of whom are arrested, placed in youth detention centers while awaiting court processing, and sometimes sanctioned by being sent to juvenile institutions. (Note: See the discussion of gender and delinquency in Chapter 18.) Two brief selections from the newspaper story follow:

> One girl sings in the church choir and dreams of becoming a judge. Another lives on pizza, plays basketball and enjoys the Dixie Chicks. A third spends her free time at the mall and watching cartoons. They're typical teenagers in many respects. They're also prostitutes. . . . The reason young people become prostitutes varies, but common themes run throughout. Although some are boys, the majority in Atlanta are girls. Many come from homes where they were sexually abused or abandoned to raise themselves by drug-addicted parents. They're running away from bad situations. . . . Like any child, most are craving love and affection. Many girls find that in a pimp. . . . Often they [the pimps] flatter them, buy them a new dress, a new hairdo. . . . Many pimps give the girls a place to stay. Then they start training them. . . . [Each] girl becomes isolated and dependent on her pimp. . . . [T]hey are also subjected to violence. At least two-thirds of the prostituted children report being physically or sexually assaulted by customers and pimps. . . .

> In 1997, police found a 12-year-old prostitute naked on the streets, her body riddled with crack cocaine and alcohol. "She was smelly and stinky, and she had this dead, vacant look in her eyes. . . ." She had allegedly had sex with 10 men. Eventually, [authorities] found a residential treatment program for the child, but the girl ran away. "She called the pimp, and he came and got her." Less than two months later an officer. . . . found the child with "a known pimp." A man in his 40s had flagged down the officer, saying the child had stolen his handgun and jewelry. He told the officer the child was a runaway who had been living with him. The child was arrested. The man was not. (Hansen, 2001:A1,9,10)

Case 2. A guest editorial in my local newspaper discussed the reasons for some of the incidents of school violence that periodically make the headlines. Selections from this editorial follow:

> The media keep asking "Why?" They have been told, but they refuse to hear. They bring out experts. "It's the guns. The video games, movies, and CDs!" they say. But those people who have the privilege of being asked to give their opinions to a national audience are probably the same ones who had the privilege of growing up popular. Those of us who didn't can understand. . . . I remember once as a freshman, the varsity jocks hung me up on a coat hook in the locker room. The coach thought it was funny. There were no repercussions for their actions. As a 5 foot 2 sophomore, a football player didn't like something I said to him, and the result was my trip to the hospital for a fractured clavicle. The police weren't even called. . . . To this day, when I hear of these horrible shootings, I know right away the answer to the question, "Why?" When a person has so much power over you that they feel that they can do anything

to you and get away with it, no matter whom you turn to . . . what are you supposed to do? You can't leave. You can't walk away. You have only one option: Remove the menace yourself. As rational adults, we can argue that there are always options. The confused teenager does not see that. . . . When I was a teenager, I got a gun. I had it in my pants at a movie theater when I saw one of my regular tormentors. By the grace of God, this guy wasn't in the mood to confront me that night. . . . Later that night . . . I realized what could have happened. . . . That kid is lucky to be alive. If he had died, he would have had himself to blame as much as me. (Honohan, 2001) (Note: See the discussion of antibullying programs in Chapter 24.)

TEST YOUR KNOWLEDGE OF THIS CHAPTER

1. Describe the essential arguments of strain theory in a few sentences, including the reasons why strain increases the likelihood of delinquency.

2. Each version of strain theory tries to do two things. What are they?

3. What are the two major types of strain?

4. The failure to achieve four goals is said to contribute to much delinquency. What are these goals?

5. List four of the negative events or conditions that contribute to delinquency.

6. Describe the major ways in which individuals cope with strain and the negative emotions associated with strain.

7. What factors increase the likelihood that juveniles will cope with strain through delinquency?

THOUGHT AND DISCUSSION QUESTIONS

1. How might strain theory explain forms of deviance like cheating and excessive drinking on college campuses?

2. Develop a set of survey questions that measure the key independent and conditioning variables in the explanations for cheating and excessive drinking that you developed in question 1.

3. How might strain theory explain the fact that males have higher rates of delinquency than females? (Note: See Broidy and Agnew, 1997.)

4. What recommendations based on strain theory would you make for reducing crime? (Note: See Agnew, 2001a.)

KEY TERMS

- Strain theory
- Strain
- Loss of positive stimuli and presentation of negative stimuli
- Cognitive coping
- Behavioral coping
- Emotional coping
- Coping skills
- Conventional social supports

ENDNOTES

1. *See* Felson, 1993; Felson and Steadman, 1983; Lockwood, 1997; Luckenbill, 1977; Oliver, 1994; Wilkinson, 2002, 2003.

2. *See* Agnew, 2006a; Compas, 1987; Kohn and Milrose, 1993; Williams and Uchiyama, 1989.

3. *See* Agnew, 2006c; Anderson, 1990; Jankowsi, 1995; MacLeod, 1995; Padilla, 1992; Sullivan, 1989; Wright and Decker, 1997.

4. *See* Agnew, 1994a, 1995b; Agnew et al., 1996; Burton and Cullen, 1992.

5. *See* Agnew, 1994a:423–426, 2006a; Agnew et al., 1996; Baron, 2004, 2007; Burton and Dunaway, 1994; Wright et al., 1999a.

6. *See* Agnew, 1997, 2006a; Anderson, 1994, 1999; Greenberg, 1977; Majors and Billson, 1992; Messerschmidt, 1993; Oliver, 1994.

7. *See* Agnew, 2006a; Anderson, 1994, 1999; Greenberg, 1977; Majors and Billson, 1992; Messer-schmidt, 1993.

8. *See* Anderson, 1994, 1997, 1999; Fagan, 1998; Majors and Billson, 1992; Messerschmidt, 1993; Oliver, 1994.

9. *See* Agnew, 2006a; White et al., 1985; Wood et al., 1993, 1997.

10. *See* Agnew, 1997; Greenberg, 1977; Moffitt, 1993, 1997.

11. *See* Agnew, 2006a; Colvin, 2000; De Coster and Kort-Bulter, 2006; Lockwood, 1997; Rusby et al., 2005; Wallace et al., 2005; Wilkinson, 2002.

12. *See* Agnew, 2002, 2006a, 2006b; Carter and Evans, 2006; Eitle and Turner, 2002; Kaufman, 2005; Shaffer and Ruback, 2002; Spano et al., 2006.

13. *See* Agnew, 2006a, 2006b; Eitle, 2002; Katz, 2000; McCord and Ensminger, 2003; Simons et al., 2003.

14. *See* Agnew, 1985a, 1992, 1997, 2001a, 2006a, 2006b; Agnew and Brezina, 1997; Agnew and White, 1992; Aseltine et al., 2000; Baron and Hartnagel, 1997; Brezina, 1998; Broidy, 2001; Capowich et al., 2001; Carter and Evans, 2006; Hagan and McCarthy, 1997a; Hay, 2003; Hoffmann and Cerbone, 1999; Hoffmann and Miller, 1998; Jang and Johnson, 2003; Landau, 1998; Mazerolle and Piquero, 1997, 1998; Mazerolle et al., 2003; Paternoster and Mazerolle, 1994; Piquero and Sealock, 2000, 2004.

15. *See* Agnew, 2001a, 2006a, 2006b; Agnew and White, 1992; Aseltine et al., 2000; Baron, 2004, 2007; Baron and Hartnagel, 2002; Capowich et al., 2001; Carter and Evans, 2006; Hoffmann and Cerbone, 1999; Hoffmann and Miller, 1998; Hoffmann and Su, 1997; Jang and Johnson, 2003; Johnson and Kercher, 2007; Mazerolle and Piquero, 1997; Paternoster and Mazerolle, 1994.

CHAPTER 7

Social Learning Theory

Do Individuals Learn to Be
Delinquent from Others?

ocial learning theory **says that juveniles learn to engage in delinquency from others.** These others reinforce juveniles for delinquency, teach them beliefs that are favorable to delinquency, and expose them to delinquent models. As a consequence, the juveniles come to view delinquency as something that is desirable or at least justifiable in certain situations. The primary version of social learning theory in criminology is that of Akers, and the description that follows draws heavily on his work (Akers, 1985, 1998; Akers and Jensen, 2003, 2006; Akers and Sellers, 2004; also see Bandura, 1973, 1986; Patterson et al., 1992). Akers' theory, in turn, represents a reformulation and elaboration of Sutherland's differential association theory (see Matsueda, 1988; Sutherland et al., 1992).

Juveniles Learn to Engage in Delinquency from Others

According to social learning theory, juveniles learn to engage in delinquent behavior in the same way they learn to engage in conforming behavior: through association with or exposure to others. Primary or intimate groups like the family and peer group have an especially large impact on what juveniles learn. This is not surprising, since juveniles usually spend a lot of time with family members and friends and are quite close to them. Juveniles also learn how to behave from people in their school, religious community, neighborhood, and other settings. Further, juveniles do not have to be in direct contact with others to learn from them; for example, they may learn from observing people in the media or interacting with others over the Internet.

Whether juveniles learn to conform or engage in delinquency depends primarily on the nature of the people they associate with. If they associate with others who engage in delinquency/crime and hold beliefs favorable to delinquency, they are likely to learn to engage in delinquency. In this area, data indicate that juveniles are much more likely to engage in delinquency if intimate others like their friends, parents, and siblings engage in delinquency/crime. In fact, having delinquent friends is perhaps the strongest predictor of subsequent delinquency, other than prior delinquency (see Chapter 16 for a fuller discussion).[1]

The fact that associating with delinquent others increases the likelihood of delinquency provides strong support for social learning theory, but it does not prove that the theory is correct. Associating with delinquent others may increase delinquency for reasons related to strain or other theories (see Agnew, 1995a; Warr, 2002). For example, juveniles who associate with delinquent peers may be more likely to engage in delinquency because they are higher in strain; delinquent peers are more likely to abuse one another and get into conflicts with outsiders (see Colvin, 2000:72–81; Chapter 16). In order to prove that social learning theory is correct, we must demonstrate that juveniles **learn** to engage in delinquency from delinquent others.

Much of social learning theory involves a description of the mechanisms by which juveniles learn to engage in delinquency from others. According to the theory, juveniles learn to engage in delinquency when others (1) differentially reinforce their delinquent behavior, (2) teach them beliefs favorable to delinquency, and (3) provide delinquent models for them to imitate. I describe each of these learning mechanisms next and examine what the research says about their role in fostering delinquency.

The Differential Reinforcement of Delinquency

Other individuals may teach us to engage in delinquency through the reinforcements and punishments they provide for our behavior. **We are more likely to engage in delinquency when others have reinforced our delinquency in the past and we anticipate that they will continue to reinforce our delinquency.** Let me illustrate this point with a simple example. When Jody Miller (2001) asked certain of the female gang members in her study why they sometimes sell drugs, they told her that they do it for the money (a major reinforcer). In the words of one gang member:

> They just sell it [drugs] to get them some money 'cause they need some. Whatever they need they'll make the money and then probably won't sell drugs no more until they need something else. And then they'll just go buy them some drugs and sell it and that's it. (Miller, 2001:145)

So these gang members sell drugs because doing so has been reinforced in the past with money and they anticipate that drug selling will continue to be reinforced with money. Social learning theory, however, has taken this simple idea—that we are more likely to engage in delinquency when it is reinforced—and elaborated on it in several important ways.

The Frequency, Amount, and Relative Probability of Reinforcement

Social learning theory argues that reinforcement is not an all-or-nothing matter. In particular, if we want to best predict delinquency, we need to examine the *frequency* with which it is reinforced, the *amount* of reinforcement received or expected, and the *relative probability of reinforcement.* Delinquent behavior is more likely to occur when it (1) is frequently reinforced and infrequently punished; (2) results or is expected to result in large amounts of reinforcement (e.g., a lot of money, social approval, or pleasure) and little punishment; and (3) is more likely to be reinforced than alternative behaviors.

These three factors—the frequency, amount, and relative probability of reinforcement/punishment—are easy to understand if you think of a concrete example. Let's begin with the frequency of reinforcement and punishment. This simply means that juveniles are more likely to commit a delinquent act like fighting if they are frequently reinforced and seldom punished for fighting. Juveniles who win most of their fights and receive praise from their friends are more likely to fight than juveniles who lose most of their fights and are ridiculed. We tend to repeat behaviors that are reinforced and avoid those that are punished. As for the amount of reinforcement and punishment, juveniles who receive or expect to receive a lot of reinforcement and little punishment for fighting are more likely to fight than juveniles who receive little reinforcement and much punishment. The relative probability of reinforcement refers to the likelihood that delinquent acts will be reinforced relative to other behaviors. For example, juveniles who get into conflicts with others might resolve these conflicts through fighting or through negotiation. They are more likely to choose fighting if fighting is more likely to result in reinforcement than negotiation. The term *differential reinforcement* means simply that different behaviors have different probabilities of being reinforced. We are more likely to engage in behaviors with the highest probabilities of reinforcement. I encourage you to think of additional examples involving the frequency, amount, and relative probability of reinforcement/punishment.

Positive and Negative Reinforcement

Reinforcement may be positive or negative. **In** *positive reinforcement,* **the behavior results in something good—some positive consequence.** This consequence may be in the form of money, the pleasurable feelings associated with drug use, attention from parents, approval from friends, or an increase in social status. For example, suppose you shoplift a video game with your friends. Your friends congratulate you for the theft and you spend the afternoon playing the game with them. The approval of your friends and the pleasure you get from playing the game function as positive reinforcers for your shoplifting. **In** *negative reinforcement,* **a behavior results in the removal of something bad—a punisher is removed or avoided.** For example, suppose your friends have been calling you a coward because you refuse to use drugs with them. You eventually take drugs with them, after which time they stop calling you a coward. Your drug use has been negatively reinforced.

Punishment

Reinforcement increases the likelihood that a behavior will be repeated, and **punishment reduces the likelihood that a behavior will be repeated.** Like reinforcement, punishment may be either positive or negative. *Positive punishment* **involves the presentation of something bad.** For example, you engage in a delinquent act and your parents spank you or verbally reprimand you. *Negative punishment* **involves the removal of something good.** For example, your parents punish your delinquency by reducing your allowance or prohibiting you from watching your favorite TV show.

The Sources of Reinforcement and Punishment

Our behavior is reinforced and punished primarily by family members, friends, teachers, neighborhood residents, and others, although family members and friends are the major sources of reinforcement and punishment for juveniles. The key role that **other people** play in reinforcing and punishing our behavior is the major reason that social learning theory is called "social learning" theory.

Social learning theory, however, also recognizes that individuals may engage in *self-reinforcement* **and punishment.** Individuals usually adopt or internalize standards for their behavior from others—parents, for example. They may then evaluate their own behavior using these standards, praising themselves when they meet these standards and criticizing themselves when they do not (see Akers, 1998: 72–75; Bandura, 1973:207–221, 1986:335–389).

Finally, social learning theory recognizes that some delinquent acts may be *intrinsically reinforcing* **or punishing.** Perhaps the best example is drug use; individuals sometimes experience a "high" or pleasurable feeling from drug use that is intrinsically reinforcing (or reinforcing in and of itself, independent of the reactions of others). There is also evidence that some individuals experience a range of delinquent acts as intrinsically reinforcing. This is said to be especially true of "sensation seekers," who often receive a "rush" or "thrill" from the delinquent acts they commit. For example, Wood et al. (1997) asked a sample of prison inmates about "the types of feelings a person may get when committing different crimes," and they found that many of the inmates said that such feelings included positive emotions like being "on a high or rush," "pumped up," "on top of the world," and "happy/excited" (college undergraduates were much less likely than the inmates to list such positive emotions). These intrinsic reinforcers are sometimes referred to as **nonsocial** reinforcers, since it is assumed that they are not derived from others. It has been argued, however, that individuals are sometimes taught to experience delinquent acts as "intrinsically reinforcing." Becker (1953:239), for example, argues that "marijuana-produced sensations are not automatically or necessarily pleasurable." Rather, individuals must be taught to interpret the effects of marijuana as pleasurable (see Brezina and Piquero, 2003, for an excellent discussion of this issue).

In any event, social learning theory argues that the major sources of reinforcement and punishment for us are other people, especially intimate others like family members and friends.

Some Individuals Are More Likely to Be Reinforced for Delinquency than Others

According to social learning theory, some individuals are more likely to be reinforced for delinquency than others. **Sometimes this reinforcement is deliberate.** For example, the parents of aggressive children often deliberately encourage and reinforce aggressive behavior outside the home (Anderson, 1994; Bandura, 1973). Anderson (1994:86) states that some families in inner-city communities tell their children that they should respond to provocations with aggression. Furthermore,

> Many parents actually impose sanctions if a child is not sufficiently aggressive. For example, if a child loses a fight and comes home upset, the parent might respond, "Don't you come in here crying that somebody beat you up; you better get back out there and whup his ass. I didn't raise no punks! Get back out there and whup his ass. If you don't whup his ass, I'll whup your ass when you come home." Thus the child obtains reinforcement for being tough and showing nerve.

At other times, the reinforcement for delinquency is less deliberate (see Patterson et al., 1989; Patterson et al., 1992). Two common scenarios will illustrate what I mean. First, a mother repeatedly asks her son to clean up his room. The son ignores her. The mother eventually starts to yell at and threaten her son. The son yells back at his mother and then slams the door to his room and locks it. The mother, exasperated with her son's behavior, leaves. Without intending to do so, the mother has just negatively reinforced her son's belligerent behavior. Second, a father takes his daughter to the supermarket. The daughter says she wants a candy bar at the checkout line, but the father refuses. The daughter repeatedly asks for the candy bar, but the father continues to refuse. Eventually, the daughter is screaming for the candy bar and attempting to hit her father. Everyone is now watching and the embarrassed father gives his daughter the candy bar. The daughter stops screaming and eats the bar. In this instance, the father has positively reinforced his daughter's screaming and hitting by giving her a candy bar. Also, the daughter has negatively reinforced the father for giving in to her demand (she stopped screaming after she got the candy bar).

Not only are some individuals **more likely** to be reinforced for delinquency, but some are also **less likely to be reinforced for conventional behavior.** Many parents, for example, often ignore or otherwise fail to reinforce the conventional behavior of their children (Patterson et al., 1989; Patterson et al., 1992). For example, they ignore a child who brings home good grades or displays good manners at a social function, rather than praising him or her. **In some cases, conventional behaviors may even be punished.** For example, behaviors like studying or cooperating with teachers are punished in certain peer groups. And "inmates" in juvenile institutions often reinforce behaviors like fighting and punish behaviors like cooperating with the staff.

According to social learning theory, individuals in these types of environments—where delinquency is more likely to reinforced and conventional behavior is more likely to be ignored or punished—should be higher in delinquency. Again, we tend to repeat behaviors that are reinforced and avoid those that are punished.

Intermittent Reinforcement

Delinquents, of course, are rarely reinforced for every delinquent act they commit. Only some of their delinquent acts are reinforced. For example, it may be the case that only every third or fourth delinquent act, on average, results in significant reinforcement. This type of schedule is referred to as an *intermittent schedule of reinforcement* (as opposed to a *continuous schedule of reinforcement,* in which every act is reinforced). Such intermittent schedules, however, are usually sufficient to maintain a behavior. (For example, witness the behavior of slot machine players: They continue to pour money into the machine even though they are only occasionally reinforced.) In fact, behaviors that are reinforced on an intermittent schedule are more difficult to eliminate than those reinforced on a continuous schedule. As Bandura states, "Behavior that has been reinforced on a thin unpredictable schedule is exceedingly difficult to extinguish because one's efforts are sustained by the belief that the actions will eventually prove successful" (1973:186).

Discriminative Stimuli

Juveniles usually find that their delinquency is more likely to be reinforced in some situations than in others. For example, smoking marijuana with your friends may result in much reinforcement, including the approval and companionship of your friends. Smoking marijuana in front of your parents, however, may result in far more punishment than reinforcement. Individuals soon learn to distinguish between situations in which delinquency is likely to be reinforced and those in which it is likely to be punished. They do so based on *discriminative stimuli,* such as the presence of friends or parents. Juveniles, of course, are most likely to commit delinquent acts in situations where the probability of reinforcement is highest.

Research on the Reinforcement and Punishment of Delinquency

Numerous studies have examined the effect of reinforcement and punishment on delinquency and aggression.[2] **Experimental studies** have focused on the effects of reinforcing or punishing aggressive behavior. For example, children might be rewarded with praise or with marbles for hitting a toy clown. These experiments usually indicate that such reinforcement or punishment has a strong effect on subsequent aggression (which might be measured by how often the child continues to hit the toy clown). Other experimental studies have examined the punishments applied by the police and juvenile justice agencies. As discussed in Chapters 20 and 23, such punishments reduce delinquency *when they are properly applied.* That is, such punishments are effective when individuals are properly monitored and consistently sanctioned for rule violations in an appropriate manner.

   Surveys and field studies have examined the impact of reinforcement and punishment on various types of delinquency. As indicated in Chapters 14 and 15, these studies indicate that delinquency is less likely when parents and teachers closely monitor the behavior of juveniles and consistently punish them for rule violations. And as discussed in Chapter 23, surveys indicate that individuals are less likely to engage in delinquency when they believe that the likelihood of arrest is high and the likelihood of reinforcement is low (also see Matsueda et al., 2006). Akers and his colleagues conducted one of the best surveys examining the effects of reinforcements and punishments.[3] They asked a sample of adolescents about the punishments and reinforcements they received (or expected to receive) from their parents and friends for using drugs. They obtained a range of responses. Some adolescents, for example, reported that their friends encouraged their drug use, while others said that their friends threatened to turn them in to the authorities. They also asked adolescents about the effects that drugs had on them (or, in the case of nonusers, the effects that they expected drugs to have). The responses ranged from mostly good effects to mostly bad effects. Akers and his colleagues found that drug use was higher among those respondents who said they were usually reinforced and seldom punished for such use.

Studies, then, suggest that reinforcements and punishments have an important effect on behavior. Further, studies suggest that reinforcements and punishments help explain why associating with delinquent others—such as delinquent friends—increases the likelihood of delinquency. Delinquent others lead us into delinquency partly because they are more likely to reinforce our delinquency and less likely to punish it. It is important to note, however, that reinforcements and punishments do not fully explain the effect of delinquent friends on delinquency (see Akers, 1999; Krohn, 1999). Delinquent friends increase the likelihood of delinquency for other reasons as well (more on this later).

Beliefs Favorable to Delinquency

Other individuals may not only reinforce our delinquency, they may also teach us beliefs favorable to delinquency. Most individuals, of course, are taught that delinquency is bad or wrong. They eventually accept or "internalize" this belief, and they are less likely to engage in delinquency as a result. For example, suppose I were to ask you why you do not burglarize houses or rob people. You would probably reply that burglary and robbery are wrong. This value is what you have been taught all your life—by parents, friends, and others—and you have come to believe it. Some individuals, however, learn beliefs that are favorable to delinquency, and they are more likely to engage in delinquency as a result.

When I speak of "beliefs favorable to delinquency," **I do not mean that some people believe that serious delinquent acts like burglary and robbery are generally good or acceptable.** Few people, including delinquents, generally approve of serious delinquent acts.[4] Surveys and interviews with juveniles suggest that **beliefs favoring delinquency fall into three categories,** and data suggest that **each type of belief increases the likelihood of delinquency.**[5]

Generally Approve of Minor Delinquency

Some juveniles generally approve of certain minor forms of delinquency, such as sexual intercourse between consenting adolescents; certain forms of gambling, truancy, and curfew violations; and certain forms of alcohol and "soft" drug use. For example, a nationwide survey of high school seniors in 2002 found that 30.8 percent believed that using marijuana should be "entirely legal" (see the *Sourcebook of Criminal Justice Statistics* at http://www.albany.edu/sourcebook/). Presumably, these seniors generally approve of marijuana use. The federal government and other organizations are trying to counter this belief in the hopes of reducing drug use. In particular, the White House Office of National Drug Control Policy sponsors a National Youth Anti-Drug Media Campaign (see http://www .mediacampaign.org). The campaign, working in partnership with other organizations, produces antidrug publications and places antidrug ads in a variety of media outlets— including TV, radio, newspapers, magazines, and the Internet. One ad, for example, states that "kids who regularly smoke marijuana" experience a "decreased ability to learn; impaired judgment about driving or sex; symptoms of depression, even thoughts of suicide; breathing problems; greater exposure to cancerous chemicals than from tobacco; [and an] increased likelihood of using even more dangerous drugs" (http://www.mediacampaign .org/mg/print/ad_joints.html). (See Earlywine, 2002, for a discussion of the research on the effects of marijuana use; see Orwin et al., 2006, for an evaluation of the effectiveness of the National Youth Anti-Drug Media Campaign.)

Conditionally Approve of Delinquency, Including Some Serious Delinquency

Some juveniles conditionally approve of, justify, or excuse certain forms of delinquency, including some serious delinquent acts. These juveniles believe that delinquency is generally wrong but that some delinquent acts are excusable, justifiable, or even desirable in certain conditions. Many juveniles, for example, will state that violence is generally wrong but that it is justified if you have been insulted or provoked in some way. This idea is at the heart of Anderson's (1999) work on the **"code of the street."** Anderson argues that many individuals in disadvantaged communities are unable to achieve respect or status through conventional channels, such as getting a good education and then a prestigious job. Some of these individuals cope by trying to achieve respect by adopting a tough demeanor and responding to disrespectful treatment with violence. Many such individuals come to believe that violence is justified or even desirable when others treat them in a disrespectful manner. One recent study (Stewart and Simons, 2006) measured the extent to which individuals have adopted the code of the street by asking them to indicate how much they agreed with statements such as the following:

> When someone disrespects you, it is important that you use physical force or aggression to teach him or her not to disrespect you.

> If someone uses violence against you, it is important that you use violence against him or her to get even.

> People do not respect a person who is afraid to fight physically for his or her rights.

Researchers have found that many juveniles agree with such statements and that such juveniles are more likely to engage in violence.[6]

Sykes and Matza (1957) argue that **the excuses and justifications employed by juveniles assume five basic forms,** each of which specifies the conditions in which crime is justified/excused.

1. *Denial of responsibility:* Delinquents claim that delinquency is excusable when a person is not responsible for his or her behavior (e.g., "I was drunk and didn't know what I was doing" or "My parents abused me and I can't help myself").

2. *Denial of injury:* Delinquents claim that delinquency is excusable when no one is harmed by it (e.g., "Insurance will cover the loss" or "I was just borrowing the car").

3. *Denial of the victim:* Delinquents claim that delinquency is justifiable when the victim deserves it (e.g., "The store owner is dishonest" or "She started it by insulting me"). This justification is closely related to the code of the street, which claims that violence is justified when others treat you in a disrespectful manner.

4. *Condemnation of the condemners:* Delinquents claim that delinquency is justifiable or excusable when those who condemn them also engage in questionable behavior (e.g., "All the cops and politicians are crooked" or "My parents drink and that's just as bad as using marijuana").

5. *Appeal to higher loyalties:* Delinquents claim that delinquency is justifiable when it serves some higher purpose ("I did it to help my friends" or "to protect my turf").

Other researchers have listed additional justifications and excuses.[7] Not all juveniles accept such justifications/excuses, but those who do are more likely to engage in delinquency.[8]

Many of us employ such justifications/excuses when we engage in deviant acts, minor or otherwise. Suppose, for example, you wake up one morning and do not feel like going to class. You may believe that cutting class is generally bad, but you tell yourself that in your case it is justified because you are not feeling well (a form of "denial of responsibility"). What other sorts of justifications/excuses do students employ for cutting class and for other forms of deviance like cheating on exams (see Agnew and Peters, 1985; McCabe, 1992)? Do these justifications/excuses fall into the categories described by Sykes and Matza, or are additional categories necessary?

General Values Conducive to Delinquency

Some juveniles hold certain general values that are conducive to delinquency. These values do not explicitly approve of or justify delinquency, but they make delinquency appear a more attractive alternative than might otherwise be the case. Theorists have listed three general sets of values in this area. The first is **an attraction to "excitement," "thrills," or "kicks."** The desire for excitement can be satisfied through legitimate as well as illegitimate means, but criminal activities hold a special appeal, since they have the added element of danger—of "experimenting with the forbidden." Individuals who value excitement, then, are more likely to find crime an attractive alternative in a given situation. The second value involves **a disdain for hard work and a desire for quick, easy success.** Many delinquents, for example, are said to have "grandiose dreams of quick success." Crime, of course, would have an obvious appeal to those who place a low value on hard work and a high value on money and pleasure. Finally, delinquents are said to place **a high value on toughness—on being "macho."** Macho includes being physically strong, being able to defend yourself, not letting others "push you around," and showing bravery in the face of physical threat. Such individuals will clearly view delinquent activities like fighting in a more favorable light than people without those values.

Where Do the Beliefs Favorable to Delinquency Come From?

Juveniles learn the beliefs favorable to delinquency from others, including family members, friends, community residents, and the media. Data suggest that delinquent friends are an especially important source of such beliefs.[9] **Also, juveniles often come to adopt such beliefs after engaging in delinquency.**[10] In particular, juveniles who engage in delinquency—for whatever reason—often find it advantageous to adopt such beliefs. Such beliefs allow them to neutralize whatever guilt they might feel and to reduce the likelihood of punishment by others (which is why young children often try to convince their parents that the victims of their delinquency deserved it). Once such beliefs are adopted, however, they make further delinquency more likely, since they define delinquency in a favorable light or at least allow a juvenile to justify or excuse delinquent behavior.

These beliefs also help explain why associating with delinquent others like friends increases the likelihood of delinquency. Delinquent friends teach the juvenile beliefs favorable to delinquency, and these beliefs in turn increase the likelihood of delinquency. Beliefs, however, do not fully explain the effect of delinquent friends on delinquency (see Akers, 1999; Krohn, 1999). Also, it is important to note that factors other than association with delinquent peers influence the adoption of beliefs favorable to delinquency. Most notably, the experience of certain strains appears to increase the likelihood that individuals will adopt such beliefs. As indicated, individuals who cannot achieve respect through legal channels may come to believe that violence is sometimes an acceptable method for achieving respect. Also, individuals in high-crime communities with poor police protection may come to believe that violence is justified if one is threatened or provoked (Brezina et al., 2004; Stewart and Simons, 2006). Further, researchers have argued that individuals who cannot achieve monetary success through legal channels may come to believe that theft, drug selling, and prostitution are sometimes justified (Agnew, 2006a; Cloward and Ohlin, 1960).

The Imitation of Delinquent Models

People's behavior is not only a function of their beliefs and the reinforcements and punishments they receive, but also of the behavior of those around them. In particular, people often imitate or model the behavior of others, especially when they have reason to believe that such imitation will result in reinforcement. It is perhaps for this reason that we are most likely to imitate a model when we "like or respect the model, see the model receive reinforcement, see the model give off signs of pleasure, or are in an environment where imitating the model's performance is reinforced" (Baldwin and Baldwin, 1981:187).

I should note that some people may inadvertently model delinquent or aggressive behavior for juveniles, just as they inadvertently reinforce delinquency/aggression. Parents, for example, may punish aggression in their children by spanking or beating them, or parents who smoke or drink may warn their children about the dangers of drug use. In each case, the parents are modeling the type of behavior they wish to stop in their child.[11]

I should also note that we do not have to be in direct contact with the models we imitate. In fact, a good deal of research has focused on the extent to which juveniles model the aggressive behavior of those in the media, especially television. The media often show glamorous characters engaging in frequent and extreme forms of violence. Such characters often receive much reinforcement and little punishment for their aggression. As Bandura (1973:101) states, "The modern child has witnessed innumerable stabbings, shootings, stompings, stranglings, muggings and less blatant but equally destructive forms of cruelty before [he/she] has reached kindergarten age." The negative impact of media violence is discussed in Chapter 17.

Data from a wide range of studies demonstrate the importance of imitation (see Akers, 1998; Akers and Sellers, 2004; Bandura, 1973, 1986). A large number of **experimental studies** have exposed individuals to aggressive models and then observed the impact of such exposure on the subjects' behavior. Such studies typically demonstrate an increase in aggression. Likewise, several **survey studies** have examined the effect of imitation on delinquency. One study, for example, examined the effect of imitation on "courtship violence" (the use of physical violence against dating partners; Sellers et al., 2003). Imitation was measured by asking respondents whether they had "*actually seen* any of the following role models use physical actions (hitting, slapping, etc.) against a spouse or partner: (1) father or stepfather, (2) mother or stepmother, (3) siblings, (4) other relatives, (5) friends, (6) actors on TV/movies, and (7) others" (Sellers et al., 2003:116). The researchers found that those who had witnessed more physical violence were more likely to engage in courtship violence themselves. Likewise, **field studies** reveal the importance of imitation. Consider, for example, this quote from a juvenile delinquent in a public housing project in Boston:

> We were all brought up, all we seen is our older brothers and that gettin' into trouble and goin' to jail and all that shit. . . . We seen many fucking drugs, all the drinking. They fucking go; that group's gone. The next group came. It's our brothers that are a little older, y'know, twenty something years old. They started doing crime. And when you're young, you look up to people. You have a person, everybody has a person they look up to. And he's doing this, he's drinking, he's doing that, he's doing drugs, he's ripping off people. Y'know, he's making good fucking money, and it looks like he's doing good, y'know? So bang. Now it's our turn. We're here. What we gonna do when all we seen is fuckin' drugs, alcohol, fighting, this and that, no one going to school? (MacLeod, 1995:117)

Individuals who are exposed to delinquent models, then, are more likely to engage in delinquency themselves. Furthermore, imitation helps explain the effect of associating with delinquent others on delinquency, although it only explains part of the effect (see Akers, 1999; Krohn, 1999).

Summary

Social learning theory has much support. Data indicate that people in our environment have a strong impact on whether we become delinquent and that this impact is partly explained by the effect these people have on our beliefs regarding delinquency, the reinforcements and punishments we receive, and the models we are exposed to. Social learning theory and control theory, described in Chapter 8, are the leading explanations of delinquency (Ellis and Walsh, 1999).

Teaching Aids

Controversial Cases

The basic ideas behind social learning theory are straightforward: individuals are more likely to engage in delinquency when others reinforce their delinquency, teach them beliefs favorable to delinquency, and model delinquency for them. And, based on this, you might think that most people would agree that we should *not* reinforce delinquency, teach beliefs favorable to delinquency, and model delinquency. But, as the four case studies that follow illustrate, things are sometimes not quite so simple.

Case 1. To spank or not to spank. Most people in the United States believe that "it is sometimes necessary to discipline a child with a good hard spanking" (Straus, 1994). And most parents spank their children at some point. Many who do so claim that the practice is justified by the well-known biblical injunction: Spare the rod and spoil the child. There has been a fair amount of research on the relationship between spanking and delinquency (e.g., Farrington et al., 2003; Simons et al., 2007; Straus, 1994). Most such research suggests that spanking may increase the likelihood of delinquency somewhat (at least among whites; it does not appear to have this effect among African Americans). Part of the reason for the effect of spanking on delinquency is explained in terms of social learning theory: Parents who spank provide their child with a violent model and teach them that violence is sometimes an appropriate way to deal with one's problems. What do you think? Should parents spank their children?

Case 2. To lock up or not to lock up. We often respond to juvenile offenders, especially serious offenders, by confining them in institutions. In theory, such institutions are supposed to rehabilitate the youths who are sent there. In practice, things are sometimes rather different. One recent newspaper article on juvenile detention centers in my home state of Georgia began as follows:

> One thing the two childhood friends knew: They had to have a good plan to survive inside the gray concrete walls of the Metropolitan Regional Youth Detention Center. Kelsey Richardson, a sixth grader at Brown Middle School, tried to be macho, squinting his eyes and feigning a bravado much larger than his wispy physique. Dratez Wilcox, 5-foot-5 and 125 pounds but the larger of the two, took the "keep quiet, blend in" approach. The 13-year-old boys didn't want to be "ratpacked"—jumped and beaten by groups of boys—for pointless reasons: not handing over their snacks or accidentally sitting in someone's chair in the TV lounge. Both boys are among dozens of former teenage inmates who painted life inside the state's largest juvenile detention facility as a state-sanctioned "Lord of the Flies," where children survive by using their fists or the filed-down shanks of pens, wire or paper clips, or, as a last resort, by feigning attempts of suicide so they'll be moved to a more secure cell and constantly monitored. . . . By all accounts, many of the youths . . . are unruly and violent, and trying to keep them under control is a stressful, taxing job. They threaten guards, teachers and nurses and often make good their promises with physical violence (Dyer, 2000:A10).

Social learning theorists sometimes argue that correctional institutions are little more than "schools for crime." They segregate juvenile delinquents from conventional others and confine them with other juvenile delinquents, who often reinforce their delinquency, model delinquency, and foster beliefs favorable to delinquency. What are your thoughts? In particular, do you feel we should try to reduce the number of juvenile offenders who are sent to institutions? Do you feel we should modify juvenile institutions? If so, how? (See Chapter 21 for a discussion of juvenile institutions.)

Case 3. Growing up in an urban war zone. Earlier I said that some parents deliberately encourage their children to engage in violent acts, sometimes reinforcing them for violence and punishing them when they fail to resort to violence. There are several reasons for this, one of which is described by Geoffrey Canada (1995:6), who has worked with poor families in New York and Boston.

> I have counseled so many children who've said they acted violently because their parents told them to. Parents often give instructions similar to those my mother gave my brother: fight back or I will beat you when you get home. Many times children as young as six and seven would bring weapons to school, or pick up bottles, bricks, or

whatever was at hand. When asked about their violent behavior they'd often say their parents told them to "get something and bash his head in." The children were telling the truth. In the more than twenty years I have spent counseling, teaching, and running programs for poor, inner-city children, I have seen a steady stream of parents who have given their children these instructions. The parents, inevitably single women raising children in the midst of an urban war zone, come with similar stories of children being victimized again and again. Institutions do nothing to protect the child. The child coming home scared, scarred, looking to them for protection that they could not provide. The parents feeling as if they had no alternative. Accept it, this is a violent world, so teach them to cope by acting more violently than the others.

What would you do if you were a single parent raising a child in an "urban war zone," the child was being regularly victimized, and school officials and the police seemed unable to stop it? (See the discussion of antibullying programs in Chapter 24, as well as the answers that Geoffrey Canada provides in his book.)

Case 4. Social learning theory and binge drinking on college campuses. Binge drinking has been called the foremost public health problem on college campuses. Binge drinking is usually defined as the consumption of five or more drinks in one sitting. (A drink equals a 12-ounce beer or wine cooler, a 6- to 8-ounce glass of wine, or a shot of hard liquor.) Surveys suggest that more than 40 percent of college students have engaged in binge drinking at least once in the last two weeks (Durkin et al., 2005). As Durkin et al. (2005:256) state, binge drinkers are more likely to experience negative consequences such as "blackouts, hangovers, missing class, falling behind in their studies, doing something they later regretted, arguing with friends, getting involved in physical fights, and getting into trouble with the police." Further, binge drinking has negative consequences for others on campus, including "being verbally insulted or abused, being physically assaulted, having one's property damaged, experiencing unwelcome sexual advances, and having sleep or study disturbed because of the conduct of intoxicated students" (Durkin et al., 2005:257).

How would social learning theory explain binge drinking? In particular, why are some students more likely than others to engage in binge drinking according to social learning theory? Test your explanation by (1) developing a set of questions to measure binge drinking and your key independent variables, (2) having the students in your class answer these questions (by filling out an anonymous questionnaire), and (3) determining if your independent variables are associated with binge drinking. For example, you might ask students what proportion of their best friends on campus binge drink (or drink five or more drinks in a sitting). Then you can determine whether the students with a high proportion of binge drinking friends are more likely to binge drink themselves. If you like, you can compare your study to that of Durkin et al. (2005), who used social learning theory to explain binge drinking among students at four colleges.

Discuss the results with your classmates. Address questions such as the following: Does it matter who you associate with? How do individuals select their friends? How do individuals form their beliefs regarding alcohol and binge drinking? (And, related to this, why do individuals have different beliefs in this area?) Are students regularly exposed to others who binge drink? What factors influence whether students imitate the behavior of these other binge drinkers?

TEST YOUR KNOWLEDGE OF THIS CHAPTER

1. Describe the essential arguments of social learning theory in a few sentences.

2. Next to prior delinquency, what is probably the best predictor of subsequent delinquency?

3. Individuals who associate with delinquent others, like delinquent friends, are much more likely to engage in delinquency. I stated that this fact strongly supports social learning theory but does not prove that the theory is correct. Why do I make this statement?

4. What are the three major mechanisms by which individuals learn to be delinquent from others?

5. Define and then give examples involving the frequency, amount, and relative probability of reinforcement and punishment.

6. Define and give examples of positive and negative reinforcement. Do the same for positive and negative punishment.

7. List the three major sources of reinforcement and punishment. Which source of reinforcement is most important according to social learning theory?

8. Define and give an example of intermittent reinforcement. Do the same for discriminative stimuli.

9. What are the three major types of "beliefs favorable to delinquency"? Give two examples of each type (e.g., list two "general values conducive to delinquency").

10. List and give an example of each of the five justifications or excuses for delinquency developed by Sykes and Matza.

11. Where do "beliefs favorable to delinquency" come from?

12. What factors influence whether we imitate the delinquent behavior of others?

13. Give an example of how a parent might *unintentionally or inadvertently* reinforce delinquent or aggressive behavior. Give an example of how a parent might inadvertently model delinquent or aggressive behavior.

14. Describe the evidence in favor of social learning theory (evidence dealing with the effects of associating with delinquent others, reinforcements, beliefs, and imitation on delinquency).

THOUGHT AND DISCUSSION QUESTIONS

1. How might social learning theory explain a form of deviance like cheating on exams?

2. Develop a set of survey questions that measure the independent variables in the explanation for cheating you developed in question 1.

3. Describe how you might test social learning theory, or a portion of it, by doing an experiment and by doing a field study.

4. Much data indicate that there is a strong association between having delinquent friends and engaging in delinquency. Does this association demonstrate that having delinquent friends *causes* delinquency? If not, why? (See Chapter 16 for a fuller discussion of this question.)

5. Strain theory draws on social learning theory to some extent in explaining delinquency. Describe how.

6. What recommendations would a social learning theorist make for reducing delinquency (describe things that should and should *not* be done to reduce delinquency)?

KEY TERMS

- Social learning theory
- Frequency, amount, and relative probability of reinforcement
- Differential reinforcement of delinquency

- Positive and negative reinforcement
- Positive and negative punishment
- Self-reinforcement
- Intrinsically reinforcing
- Intermittent and continuous reinforcement

- Discriminative stimuli
- Denial of responsibility
- Denial of injury
- Denial of the victim
- Condemnation of the condemners
- Appeal to higher loyalties

ENDNOTES

1. *See* Akers, 1998; Akers and Jensen, 2006; Aseltine, 1995; Chapple, 2005; Elliott et al., 1985; Elliott and Menard, 1996; Gordon et al., 2004; Gorman and White, 1995; Haynie, 2001, 2002; Haynie and McHugh, 2003; Haynie and Osgood, 2005; Haynie and Payne, 2006; Huizinga et al., 2003; Thornberry et al., 2003a, 2003b, 2003c; Warr, 2002; Weerman and Smeenk, 2005.

2. For overviews, *see* Akers, 1985, 1998; Akers and Sellers, 2004; Bandura, 1973; Matsueda et al., 2006; Patterson et al., 1992; Rebellon, 2006; Rebellon and Manasse, 2004; Warr, 2002.

3. *See* Akers et al., 1979; *also see* Akers, 1998; Krohn et al., 1985; Patterson et al., 1992; Thornberry et al., 1994.

4. *See* Matza, 1964; Short and Strodtbeck, 1965; Agnew, 1994a.

5. *See* Agnew, 1994b, 1995b; Akers, 1998; Akers et al., 1979; Heimer, 1997; Markowitz and Felson, 1998; Maruna and Copes, 2005; Stewart and Simons, 2006; Thornberry et al., 1994; Zhang, Loeber, and Stouthamer-Loeber, 1997.

6. Agnew, 1994b; Brezina et al., 2004; Decker et al., 1997; Sheley and Wright, 1995; Stewart and Simons, 2006.

7. *See* Bandura, 1990; Conklin, 1992; Maruna and Copes, 2005; Minor, 1981.

8. *See* especially Matza and Sykes, 1961; *also see* Agnew, 1995b; Curtis, 1974; England, 1960; Maruna and Copes, 2005; Miller, 1958; Stewart and Simons, 2006; Vaz, 1967.

9. *See* Agnew, 1995b; Akers, 1998; Brezina et al., 2004; Heimer, 1997; Matsueda and Heimer, 1987; Stewart and Simons, 2006; Thornberry et al., 1994, 1998; Warr and Stafford, 1991.

10. *See* Agnew, 1995b; Brezina et al., 2004; Heimer, 1997; Thornberry et al., 1994; Zhang, Loeber, and Stouthamer-Loeber, 1997.

11. *See* Bandura, 1986; Heimer, 1997; Patterson et al., 1992.

CHAPTER 8

Control Theory
Do Weak Controls Result in Delinquency?

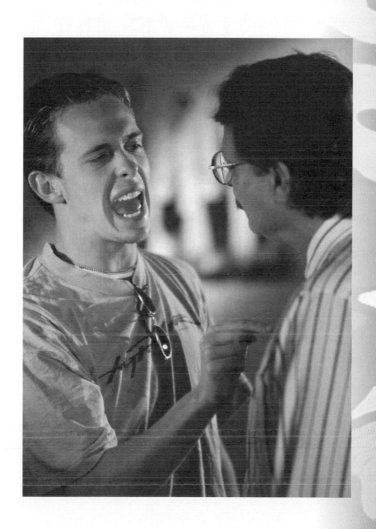

S train and social learning theorists ask: "Why do juveniles engage in delinquency?" They then focus on the factors that push or entice juveniles into committing delinquent acts. **Control theorists,** in contrast, **begin with the question "Why do juveniles conform?"** Unlike strain and social learning theorists, control theorists take the existence of delinquency for granted. They argue that all people have needs and desires that are more easily satisfied through delinquency than through legal channels. For example, it is much easier to steal money than to work for it. So in the eyes of control theorists, **delinquency requires no special explanation; it is usually the most expedient way for people to get what they want.** These theorists argue that rather than explaining why people engage in delinquency, we need to explain why they do not.

This argument may strike you as odd. Most of us take conformity for granted and feel that delinquency is in need of explanation. If you observe the behavior of very young children, however, you begin to appreciate the argument of control theorists. When these children want something, they simply take it, whether it belongs to them or not. When they get angry, they often hit and shove others. And when their verbal skills are sufficiently developed, they often lie and deceive others. Their behavior, however, usually does not impress us as odd; they are simply trying to satisfy their needs and desires in the most direct, expedient way possible. Control theorists ask why most older juveniles and adults do not do the same.

Why Do Juveniles Conform (and Sometimes Deviate)?

According to control theorists, **people do not engage in delinquency because of the controls or restraints to which they are subject.** While strain and social learning theory focus on the factors that push or entice the individual into delinquency, control theory focuses on the factors that restrain the individual from engaging in delinquency. These restraints might be portrayed as a wall holding the individual back from delinquency, as shown in Figure 8.1.

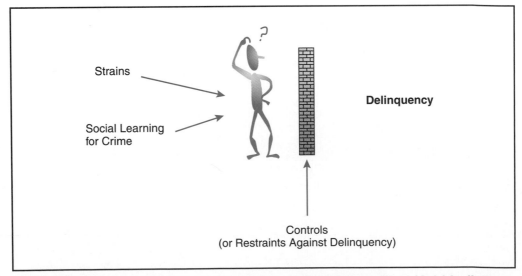

FIGURE 8.1 Control Theory Focuses on the Factors That Hold Individuals Back from Delinquency

Let me provide some examples of these controls or restraints. Each year I ask the students in my juvenile delinquency class the following question: **"Why are you not a delinquent?"** (or, in some cases, "Why are you a delinquent?"). Students then write their responses on a sheet of paper. Here are some examples of the most common types of responses: "I know the difference between what's right and wrong." "My parents raised me to respect the laws and follow them." "I was disciplined by my parents." "It's at odds with my belief in right and wrong, which comes from my religion." "I feel too guilty when I do something wrong." "Because I am afraid of getting caught." "My family would be greatly disappointed." "My parents would disown me." "My parents would kill me." "I'm worried about what my friends would think or say." "The consequences could somehow affect my college career and my other career goals." "I have many plans for the future and delinquency may hinder or destroy my future." "It would look bad on my resume." "I have more to lose than to gain from being delinquent." "I can control my anger instead of resorting to violence when I am in a conflict."

These responses nicely illustrate many of the controls or restraints that prevent people from engaging in delinquency (at least frequent or serious delinquency). We do not engage in delinquency because we believe it is wrong and because we fear that we will be caught and sanctioned in some way. We might get arrested, hurt people we care about, jeopardize our education and future career, and so on. Our beliefs and fear of sanctions, then, act as controls or restraints on our behavior: They help explain our conformity.

Control theory argues that **people differ in their level of control, or in the restraints they face to delinquency. Some individuals are high in control;** for example, they believe that delinquency is very wrong and that they would be heavily sanctioned if they committed a delinquent act. They would upset their beloved parents, their friends would leave them, they would lose their scholarship to college, they would ruin their chances of getting into law school, and so on. According to control theory, such individuals should be less likely than others to engage in delinquency.

Other individuals, however, are low in control; for example, they believe that delinquency is only a little bit wrong and that they would not be heavily sanctioned if they committed a delinquent act. They do not care what their parents think about them, their friends would not leave them, they have no scholarship to lose, and they have no plans for going to law school. According to control theory, such individuals should be more likely to engage in delinquency. Nothing is holding them back from delinquency, and so they are free to pursue their wants and desires in the most expedient way possible, which often involves delinquency. So if they see something they want, they may steal it. If someone upsets them, they may hit the person.

How Is Control Theory Similar to and Different from Social Learning Theory?

If you have been following this discussion closely, you may have noticed that there is some overlap between control theory and social learning theory. Social learning theory not only has a lot to say about the factors that cause delinquency, it also has a lot to say about the factors that prevent delinquency. In this area, both control theory and social learning theory argue that delinquency is less likely when it is sanctioned or punished and when conformity is reinforced. Individuals may be sanctioned by others, like parents and school officials, and they may sanction themselves if they believe that delinquency is wrong. Both theories, then, focus on the extent to which delinquency is prevented through sanctions. There is, however, a crucial difference between the theories.

Social learning theory also focuses on the extent to which delinquency is motivated through modeling, beliefs, and reinforcement. Some individuals are said to have a relatively strong motivation for delinquency because they have been exposed to delinquent models, have learned beliefs favorable to delinquency, and have been reinforced for delinquency. Social learning theory, then, is broader than control theory since it focuses on both the factors that prevent delinquency and the factors that motivate it. Theorists like Akers (1985) and Conger (1976) have argued that social learning theory is a more powerful theory as a result and that it is capable of incorporating control theory.

Control theorists, however, argue that it is not important to examine the motivation for delinquency. They claim that the motivation for delinquency is more or less equally strong for everyone: that we all have unfulfilled wants and desires that would more easily be satisfied through delinquency. **Delinquency is said to be largely a function of differences in the level of control.** As the leading control theorist has stated:

> Control theories assume that the potential for asocial conduct is present in everyone, that we would all commit delinquent acts were we not somehow prevented from doing so. The important differences between delinquents and non-delinquents are not differences in motivation; they are, rather, differences in the extent to which natural motives are controlled.[1]

What Are the Major Types of Control (or Restraints to Delinquency)?

Control theories basically describe the major types of control or the major restraints to delinquency. The leading control theories are those of Hirschi (1969) and Gottfredson and Hirschi (1990). Major versions of control theory have also been developed by Reiss (1951), Toby (1957), Nye (1958), Reckless (1961), Matza (1964), Briar and Piliavin (1965), Kornhauser (1978), and Sampson and Laub (1993a). Rather than describing the different types of control in all of these theories, I will present a generic version of control theory that draws from them.

This generic theory lists four major types of control, with certain types having two or more components. The first type is *direct control,* which refers to the efforts of others to directly control the juvenile's behavior by (1) setting rules for the juvenile, (2) monitoring the juvenile's behavior, (3) sanctioning the juvenile for rule violations and delinquency, and (4) reinforcing the juvenile for conventional behavior. The second type of control or restraint is the juvenile's **stake in conformity,** which refers to things that the juvenile might lose by engaging in delinquency. Juveniles with a lot to lose should be less likely to engage in delinquency. Stake in conformity is a function of the juvenile's (1) emotional attachment to conventional others and (2) actual or anticipated investment in conventional activities (like getting an education). The third type of control is **belief,** which refers to the juvenile's beliefs regarding delinquency. Juveniles who believe that delinquency is wrong should be less likely to engage in delinquency. The fourth type is **self-control,** which refers to the juvenile's ability to exercise self-restraint. Self-control is usually indexed by several personality traits, such as impulsivity or the tendency to act without thinking about the consequences of one's behavior. Control is highest, then, when others try to control the juvenile's behavior, when the juvenile has a lot to lose by engaging in delinquency, when the juvenile believes that delinquency is wrong, and when the juvenile has the ability to exercise self-restraint.

Direct Control

When most people think of control, they think of **direct control: someone watching over the juvenile and sanctioning him or her for deviance.** Much direct control is exercised by the justice system—the police, courts, and correctional agencies. The police try to watch juveniles and arrest suspected offenders, while the courts and correctional agencies sanction offenders. A fair bit of research has examined the extent to which these "official" efforts to exercise direct control are effective. That is, do the sanctions administered by the justice system control or "deter" delinquency? This research is discussed in some detail in Chapters 21 and 23, as part of a larger discussion of the juvenile justice system. Direct control, however, is not only exercised by the justice system. It is also exercised by parents, school officials, neighborhood residents, and others. In fact, these "unofficial" efforts to exercise direct control are far more common and influential than the efforts of official agencies like the police and courts. Parents are the major source of direct control. Given their long-standing and intimate relationship with the juvenile, parents are in a much better position to detect and sanction delinquency in their children than are representatives of the justice system.

Direct control has four components: setting rules, monitoring behavior, sanctioning deviance/delinquency, and reinforcing conventional behavior.

Setting rules. Direct control is enhanced to the extent that parents and others provide the juvenile with clearly defined rules that prohibit delinquent behavior and that limit the opportunities and temptations for delinquency. These rules may specify whom the juvenile associates with; for example, parents may forbid or strongly discourage their children from associating with juveniles who seem prone to delinquency. The rules may specify where the juvenile can and cannot go; for example, some parents may forbid their children from spending time in unsupervised locations, such as the street. The rules may specify the activities in which juveniles can and cannot engage; for example, some parents may forbid their children from attending unsupervised parties. The rules may specify what the juvenile can and cannot have; for example, parents may limit the spending money of their children or refuse to allow them to dress in a certain way. These rules may also specify time restrictions for the juvenile; for example, parents frequently impose curfews on their children.

A full-page newspaper advertisement from the "Partnership for a Drug-Free America" highlights the importance of setting rules (*New York Times*, May 16, 2003: A22). The ad aims to tell parents "how to keep your kids free of drugs." And in large, bold print, the ad states "Rule #4. Set the Rules." The ad goes on: "Kids need to know exactly what the rules are. The rules have to be clear, consistent, reasonable. And enforced. Every kid will try to find out exactly how far he or she can go. And drugs are no place for trial and error. To learn more about what kinds of rules to set and how to enforce them, call for a parent's handbook." (For further information, see http://www.drugfree.org.)

Monitoring. Direct control involves more than just setting rules. It also involves monitoring juveniles' behavior to ensure that they comply with the rules and do not engage in delinquency. Monitoring may be direct or indirect. In *direct monitoring,* the juvenile is under the direct surveillance of a parent or other conventional "authority figure." In *indirect monitoring,* the parent or authority figure does not directly observe the juvenile but makes an effort to keep tabs on what the juvenile is doing. The parent, for example, may ask the juvenile where he or she is going, may periodically phone him or her, may ask others about the juvenile's behavior, or the like. Juveniles obviously differ in the extent to which their behavior is monitored. In some cases, a parent meets the juvenile when he or she arrives home from school and the juvenile is seldom out of the sight of adults. In other cases, the juvenile's parents are seldom at home, or the juvenile spends much time on the street or in other locations where monitoring by conventional adults is minimal.

Elijah Anderson (1999) conducted a field study of residents in a poor, inner-city community in Philadelphia. He found that most parents in this community tried to monitor their children's behavior, but those parents who were part of what Anderson called "street-oriented families" were a prominent exception. In the words of Anderson (1999:69):

> At an early age, often even before they start school and without much adult supervision, children from street-oriented families gravitate to the streets, where they must be ready to "hang," to socialize competitively with peers. These children have a great deal of latitude and are allowed to rip and run up and down the streets. They often come home from school, put their books down, and go right back out the door. On school nights many eight- and nine-year olds remain out until nine or ten o'clock (teenagers may come home whenever they want to).

Setting rules and monitoring behavior should restrain delinquency: The rules prohibit delinquency and limit the temptations and opportunities for delinquency, while monitoring increases the likelihood that rule violations/delinquency will be detected. Several studies have examined the relationship between setting rules, monitoring, and delinquency, with most such studies focusing on parents.[2] These studies tend to find that higher levels of rule setting/monitoring are associated with moderately lower levels of delinquency, although certain data suggest that overly strict parents may be ineffective or that they may even increase delinquency (perhaps for reasons related to strain theory).

Sanctioning delinquency. Parents and others may closely supervise the child—setting rules and monitoring behavior—but they may fail to effectively sanction delinquency/deviance when it occurs. Direct control, then, is enhanced to the extent that delinquency/deviance is effectively sanctioned. What do I mean by "effectively sanctioned"? Effective sanctions are consistently applied. Studies indicate that the failure to punish and the inconsistent use of punishment contribute to delinquency. Effective punishments are also fairly applied; that is, the child is punished only when he or she deserves it and the punishment fits the offense (e.g., the child is not severely punished for trivial infractions). Further, effective punishments are not overly harsh. Data suggest that punishments using physical violence and verbal abuse are not effective; in fact, they tend to increase delinquency.[3] Such punishments may create "fear and resentment" in the child and "break the bonds of respect" between parent and child (Sampson and Laub, 1993a:68, 73). Many researchers recommend punishments like verbally condemning the act and explaining why it is wrong, time out, withdrawal of privileges, and requiring the juvenile to perform certain tasks (e.g., Patterson and Gullion, 1977; Straus, 1994).[4]

Reinforcing conventional behavior. Parents and others not only should sanction delinquency but also should reinforce conventional behaviors that compete with or provide alternatives to the delinquency. For example, suppose your child frequently resorts to violence when he or she gets into disputes with others. You should not only punish your child for such violence, you should also teach the child how to resolve disputes through verbal means, and you should reinforce the child when he or she does so.

Stake in Conformity

The efforts of others to directly control juveniles' behavior are a major restraint to delinquency. These efforts, however, are more effective with some juveniles than with others. For example, all juveniles are subject to more or less the same direct controls at school: the same rules, the same monitoring, and the same sanctions if they deviate. Yet some juveniles are very responsive to these controls, while others commit deviant acts on a regular basis. There are several reasons for this difference, but one fundamental reason is that some juveniles have more to lose by engaging in deviance. These juveniles have what has been called a strong *stake in conformity,* and they do not want to jeopardize that stake by engaging in deviance/delinquency (see Toby, 1957). For example, imagine two students: one has an A average and dreams of going to Harvard, and the other has a D average and dreams of dropping out of school. Who do you think is going to be more responsive to the threat of school sanctions?

An individual's stake in conformity—what a person stands to lose by engaging in delinquency—functions as another major restraint to delinquency. Those with a lot to lose will be more fearful of being caught and sanctioned and so will be less likely to engage in delinquency. A stake in conformity has two components: (1) emotional attachment to conventional others and (2) the actual or anticipated investment in conventional society.

Emotional attachment to conventional others. If we have a strong emotional attachment to conventional others, like parents and teachers, we have more to lose by engaging in delinquency. Our delinquency may upset people we care about, cause them to think badly of us, and possibly disrupt our relationship with them. For example, many of the students in my juvenile delinquency class report that they do not engage in delinquency because they do not want to hurt their parents or cause their parents to think badly of them. People's emotional bond to conventional others, then, is one major component of their "stake in conformity."

Studies generally confirm the importance of this bond.[5] Individuals who report that they love and respect their parents and other conventional figures are usually lower in delinquency. Individuals who do not care about their parents or others have less to lose by engaging in delinquency and so are more "free" to act on their desires. The association between emotional attachment and delinquency, however, is usually small to moderate in size. And I should note that an attachment to **delinquent** others does not reduce delinquency, since delinquency is not likely to jeopardize the relationship with these others. Attachment to delinquent others often increases delinquency, as one would expect from social learning theory.[6]

Actual or anticipated investment in conventional activities. A second major component of a person's stake in conformity is her or his investment in conventional society. Most people have put a lot of time and energy into conventional activities, like "getting an education, building up a business, [and] acquiring a reputation for virtue" (Hirschi, 1969:20). And they have been rewarded for their efforts in the form of good grades, material possessions, a good reputation, and the like. Juveniles may also expect their efforts to reap certain rewards in the future; for example, they may anticipate getting into college or professional school, obtaining a good job, and living in a nice house. In short, they have a large investment—both actual and anticipated—in conventional society. They do not want to jeopardize that investment by engaging in delinquency. Once again, they have too much to lose. Studies usually indicate that delinquency is moderately lower among juveniles who like school, are doing well in school, and have high educational and occupational expectations.[7]

As an illustration of someone with a low investment in conventional activities, consider this quote from a juvenile offender in MacLeod's (1995:124) study of youth in a Boston public housing project:

> I didn't really care to try in school. . . . You ain't got a chance of getting a good job, even with a high school diploma. You gotta go on to college, get your Masters and shit like that to get a good paying job that you can live comfortably on. So if you're not planning on going to college, I think it's a waste of time.

The youth who made this quote ended up dropping out of school and getting a job, only to be laid off a short time later. As MacLeod pointed out, he was "out of school, out of work, and out of money"; furthermore, he did "not have much to which he could look forward."

Belief

Imagine that you had the opportunity to steal something that you wanted but could not afford. Imagine further that you were certain that you would not be caught and sanctioned. Would you do it? Some of you will say yes; the absence of direct controls and the feeling that you have nothing to lose are enough to result in your delinquency. Others, however, will say no. A major reason for this is that you have come to believe that delinquency is wrong. This belief functions as a major restraint against delinquency. It is an important restraint, since we all sometimes find ourselves in situations where we are tempted to engage in crime and the probability of external sanction is low.

The extent to which people believe that delinquency is wrong is at least partly a function of their level of direct control and their stake in conformity. Did their parents provide them with a clear set of rules that condemned delinquency? Did their parents monitor their behavior and punish delinquency? Such actions serve to teach children that delinquency is wrong. Were the children strongly attached to their parents? Such attachment increases the likelihood that the children will adopt parental beliefs. Finally, do they have a large investment in conventional society? People are more likely to accept conventional beliefs when it is to their advantage to do so.

So individuals who are low in direct control and have a low stake in conformity are less likely to believe that delinquency is wrong. Such individuals often have an *amoral orientation to delinquency:* They believe that delinquency is neither good nor bad. As a consequence, their beliefs do not restrain them from engaging in delinquency. Their beliefs do not propel or push them into delinquency; they do not believe that delinquency is good. Their amoral beliefs simply free them to pursue their needs and desires in the most expedient way. Unlike social learning theorists, most control theorists argue that few people define delinquency as good or acceptable. Rather than being taught that delinquency is good, control theorists argue that some juveniles are simply not taught that delinquency is bad.

Studies suggest that juveniles do differ in the extent to which they condemn delinquency. Most juveniles define delinquent acts, especially serious acts, as generally wrong. A significant minority of juveniles, however, have a somewhat amoral view of delinquent acts. For example, a national sample of adolescents was asked, "How wrong is it for someone your age to hit or threaten to hit someone without any reason?" Seven percent of the respondents replied "a little bit wrong," while 93 percent said "wrong" or "very wrong." Individuals with amoral beliefs are somewhat more likely to engage in delinquency.[8] (Studies, however, also suggest that many juveniles do have beliefs favorable to delinquency, as described in the chapter on social learning theory.)

Self-Control

Several types of control have been listed, including direct control, stake in conformity, and beliefs regarding delinquency. Some individuals, however, are less responsive to these controls than others. These individuals **have trouble restraining themselves from acting on their immediate desires.** For example, if someone provokes them, they are more likely to get into a fight. Or if someone offers them drugs at a party, they are more likely to accept. They do not stop to consider the negative consequences of their behavior. Rather, they simply focus on the immediate, short-term benefits or pleasures of the delinquent act. In the words of Gottfredson and Hirschi (1990:87), they are more "vulnerable to the temptations of the moment." Such individuals are said to be low in *self-control.*

Self-control is usually indexed by several personality traits, including impulsivity, a strong preference for immediate over-delayed rewards, a preference for risky activities, high activity levels, and little ambition or motivation (see Grasmick et al., 1993; Piquero, 2008).[9] Many of these traits are discussed in Chapter 10. And such traits have been measured with survey items like the following (from Grasmick et al., 1993; respondents are asked to agree or disagree with each item):

1. I act on the spur of the moment without stopping to think.
2. I do things that bring me pleasure here and now.
3. I find it exciting to do things for which I might get in trouble.
4. I take risks just for the fun of it.
5. I feel better when I am on the move than when I am sitting and thinking.
6. I try to avoid projects that I know will be difficult.

There has been a great deal of research on self-control since the early to mid-1990s. This research has established that self-control is an important cause of delinquency—likely one of the most important causes.[10] (The other types of control that I've listed, however, also affect delinquency—even after we take account of levels of self-control.[11]) The fact that self-control has a large effect on delinquency has recently stimulated much research on those factors that affect one's level of self-control.

Why Is it that some individuals are low in self-control? Gottfredson and Hirschi (1990) argue that low self-control is our natural state; that is, individuals initially lack the ability to restrain themselves from acting on their immediate desires. People must be taught to exercise self-control. Gottfredson and Hirschi go on to argue that parents play the central role in this process. In particular, self-control is most likely to re-sult when parents have a strong emotional bond to their children, establish clear rules for behavior, closely monitor their children, and consistently sanction them for rule violations (i.e., exercise direct control over them). As a result of such factors, most children eventu-ally learn to exercise some self-restraint over their behavior. Some parents, however, fail to teach their children to exercise self-control. Data provide some support for these argu-ments, suggesting that factors like parental attachment, monitoring, and discipline have an important effect on the development of self-control.[12]

Recent research, however, suggests that other factors also influence the development of self-control. In particular, studies suggest that teachers, peers, and neighbors may also help juveniles develop self-control.[13] Further, research suggests that at least some of the traits that make up self-control have a biological basis (Chapter 13; Cauffman et al., 2005; Wright and Beaver, 2005). Many of these traits, for example, have a strong genetic basis—with individuals inheriting a predisposition for these traits from their parents.

Is it possible to alter one's level of self-control? Certain criminol-ogists argue that one's level of self-control is established early in life, before age 10, and is relatively stable thereafter (Gottfredson and Hirschi, 1990). Studies do find that the trait of self-control is somewhat stable, such that people who are low in self-control at one point in time tend to be low at a later point in time. Self-control, however, is far from perfectly stable. Some people experience increases or decreases in self-control during the adolescent years and beyond. These increases and decreases are caused by changes in those factors found to affect self-control, such as parenting practices, school factors, and the nature of one's peers.[14] This is an important finding, with implications for controlling delinquency (see Chapter 24).

Summary

Control theory asks why people conform rather than why they deviate. And it says we con-form because of the controls or restraints placed on our behavior. In particular, conformity is most likely when others attempt to directly control our behavior, when we have a large stake in conformity, when we believe that delinquency is wrong, and when we are able to control our own behavior. Conversely, delinquency is most likely when these forms of con-trol are low or absent. In such cases, individuals are free to satisfy their needs and desires in the most expedient way—which is often through delinquent acts. The data are generally supportive of control theory, and as indicated earlier, control and social learning theories are the leading explanations of delinquency.

Teaching Aids

Controversial Issue: The Nature of Human Nature

Control theorists hold a particular view of human nature. They believe that people "natu-rally" pursue their self-interest, seeking to maximize their pleasure and minimize their pain. This pursuit of self-interest is what explains crime, since criminal acts like theft and violence are often the easiest or most expedient way for people to get what they want. It is easier to steal money, for example, than it is to work for it. Crime, then, requires no special explanation. In particular, people do not need to be taught to engage in crime, nor are strains necessary to push them into crime. Rather, all people sometimes experience situations where crime is the most expedient way to satisfy their needs and desires. The only thing that prevents them from engaging in crime is the controls or restraints they face. This view is well expressed by one of the leading control theorists:

> Control theories all assume that all people are alike in that they tend to pursue self-interest—they seek pleasure and try to avoid harm. Because most criminal and deviant acts satisfy human needs and desires, control theories assume constant motivation for deviance. They further assume that individuals will engage in deviance if some form of restraint is not present. (Gottfredson, 2006:79)

Data presented in Chapter 4 suggest that there may be some basis for this view. Describing recent research on young children, Lahey and Waldman (2005:18) state that "nearly half of all toddlers hit, kick, intentionally break things, take other children's toys, state untruths, and resist the authority of adults from the time they can walk and talk."

Some scholars, however, have challenged this view of human nature. Frans De Waal, in particular, attacks the view that "morality is a thin crust underneath which boil human passions that are invariably antisocial, amoral, and egoistic" (De Waal, 2003:8). He claims that people are "naturally" social, inclined to cooperate with one another. This inclination is said to be evolutionarily based. Cooperation makes it easier to secure food and protect oneself against predators. Those individuals who are inclined to cooperate with others, then, are more likely to survive and pass their genes on to others. Further, De Waal argues that, with time, this inclination leads people to assist others even when there is no direct benefit in doing so.

> All species that rely on cooperation—from elephants to wolves and people—show group loyalty and helping tendencies. These tendencies evolved in the context of a close-knit social life in which they benefited relatives and companions able to repay the favor. The impulse to help was therefore never totally without survival value to the ones showing the impulse. But . . . the impulse became divorced from the consequences that shaped its evolution. This permitted its expression even when payoffs were unlikely, such as when strangers were beneficiaries. (2003:12)

De Waal draws on animal research to support his arguments about our "natural" tendency to cooperate with and help others, even when it is not in our self-interest to do so. For example, he notes that "rhesus monkeys refuse to pull a chain that delivers food to themselves if doing so shocks a companion. One monkey stopped pulling for five days, and another for twelve days after witnessing shock-delivery to a companion. These monkeys were literally starving themselves to avoid inflicting pain upon another" (2003: 17–18).

Which view of human nature do you think is more accurate: (1) humans as self-interested creatures who seek to maximize their pleasure and minimize their pain, or (2) humans as social creatures who show some concern for one another? How might we test or evaluate the accuracy of these views? Might both views have some merit? If the second view is more accurate, does that mean that control theories have little to say about the explanation of crime? If the first view is more accurate, does that invalidate strain and social learning theories?

Controversial Methods for Increasing Direct Control

Parents are the major source of control over their children, but unfortunately, many parents fail to exercise adequate control. For example, they fail to exercise sufficient direct control over their children. A number of programs have been developed to deal with this fact;

some try to get parents to exercise more control, and some try to increase the control exercised by other groups, such as schools and communities. Most of these programs, like parent training programs and after-school recreational programs, arouse little controversy (descriptions of these programs are provided in Chapter 24). Certain of these programs, however, have aroused a good deal of controversy. One example is drug testing in schools, designed to improve the monitoring of student behavior. (The U.S. Supreme Court has ruled that such testing is constitutional for those in athletic programs and other extracurricular activities.) Another example is curfews, also designed to increase direct control over juveniles. (The effectiveness of drug testing and curfews in controlling delinquency is discussed in Howell, 2003a.) Yet another example is suggested in the following selection from a guest editorial in the *New York Times,* written by a lieutenant in the New York City Police Department (McHugh, 2003).

Parental Guidance Required

Early Sunday morning, I got an emergency radio call on my portable radio . . . asking for assistance at the Skate Key, a South Bronx roller rink. . . . When I arrived at the scene, there was a great deal of confusion: people screaming, blood-soaked sidewalks, teenagers crying in pain. Four people had been stabbed . . . and five police officers had been injured trying to stem the violence. . . . As I watched the young teenagers leaving the club early Sunday morning, it was easy to figure out the missing element: parents. Sadly, I saw only half a dozen or so parents or guardians waiting for the hundreds of teenagers at the club. . . . How many parents even knew their children were at the club or whom they were "hanging" with? . . . If an employer may be held liable in civil court for the criminal act of an employee by failing to provide adequate supervision, shouldn't a progressive society require . . . that a parent or guardian be held at least partly liable for such offenses committed by their children? Of course, parents can't know everything their children are doing or be with them at all times. But when they know their children are going to a place with a history of criminal activity (like the Skate Key rink) there ought to be some consequence for letting them go there unsupervised. To me, knowingly permitting a teenage child to attend a club with a history of violence is negligent parenting. . . . If you're a mother or father, it should be you there watching your teenagers, not me frisking them for weapons.

Some jurisdictions have passed parental liability laws, making parents liable for the criminal behavior of their children in certain circumstances—like those where parents fail to provide adequate supervision. Efforts to enforce such laws have not fared well in the court system. Even so, do you think parents should be held responsible for the delinquent acts of their children in certain circumstances? If so, under what sorts of circumstances? What should be done to the "offending" parents?

TEST YOUR KNOWLEDGE OF THIS CHAPTER

1. Describe the essential arguments of control theory in a few sentences.
2. Rather than focusing on the causes of delinquency, control theorists focus on the causes of conformity. Why?
3. Describe the similarities and differences between control theory and social learning theory.
4. What are the major types of control or restraints to delinquency?

5. Describe the major components of direct control.

6. What are the characteristics of *effective* sanctions?

7. Describe the two components of "stake in conformity" and indicate why they reduce delinquency.

8. Give two examples of each of the components of stake in conformity.

9. What is meant by one's "anticipated investment in conventional society"?

10. What is meant by belief?

11. Unlike social learning theorists, control theorists do *not* argue that juveniles are taught beliefs favorable to delinquency. What do control theorists argue regarding beliefs?

12. List or briefly describe three of the personality traits that make up low self-control.

13. Why are some individuals low in self-control, and is it possible to alter one's level of self-control?

THOUGHT AND DISCUSSION QUESTIONS

1. Do you think that the justice system (police, courts, correctional agencies) does a good job of exercising direct control (setting rules, effectively monitoring behavior, effectively sanctioning deviance)? Explain your answer. (See Chapter 23 for a full discussion.)

2. How might control theory explain forms of deviance like cheating on exams and excessive drinking?

3. Develop survey questions to measure the independent variables in your explanation of cheating and drinking.

4. Describe, in detail, a high school student who is low in self-control (e.g., describe his or her relationship with parents, grades, and beliefs regarding delinquency).

5. What recommendations might a control theorist be making for reducing delinquency?

KEY TERMS

- Control theory
- Direct control
- Direct and indirect monitoring
- Stake in conformity
- Amoral orientation to delinquency
- Self-control

ENDNOTES

1. *See* Hirschi, 1977:329; *also see* Agnew, 1993; Britt and Gottfredson, 2003; Goode, 2008; Gottfredson, 2006; Kornhauser, 1978:46–50; Paternoster and Bachman, 2001.

2. *See* Browning and Huizinga, 1999; Burton et al., 1995; Costello and Vowell, 1999; Farrington, 1996a; Hagan, 1989; Hawkins, Herrenkohl, Farrington, Brewer, Catalano, and Harachi, 1998; Huizinga et al., 2003; Loeber, Farrington, Stouthamer-Loeber, and Van Kammen, 1998; Loeber and Stouthamer-Loeber, 1986; Nye, 1958; Patterson et al., 1992; Sampson and Laub, 1993a; Snyder and Patterson, 1987; Thornberry et al., 2003a; Wells and Rankin, 1988; Wright and Wright, 1995.

ENDNOTES (continued)

3. *See* Agnew, 1983; Loeber and Stouthamer-Loeber, 1986; Nye, 1958; Patterson et al., 1992; Sampson and Laub, 1993a; Snyder and Patterson, 1987; Straus, 1994; Wells and Rankin, 1988; Wright and Wright, 1995.

4. For additional information on the factors influencing the effectiveness of punishment, *see* Bandura, 1973:222–227; Quay, 1983; and Snyder and Patterson, 1987; *also see* Patterson and Gullion, 1977, for a child training manual.

5. *See* Costello and Vowell, 1999; Hirschi, 1969; Jang, 1999; Loeber and Stouthamer-Loeber, 1986; Longshore et al., 2005; Rankin and Kern, 1994; Sampson and Laub, 1993a; Stewart, 2003; Wright et al., 1999b; Wright and Wright, 1995; *also see* Kempf-Leonard, 1993, for an overview.

6. *See* Agnew, 1991b; Akers, 1998; Conger, 1976; Felson and Staff, 2006; Jensen and Brownfield, 1983.

7. *See* Chappel et al., 2005; Costello and Vowell, 1999; Hawkins and Lishner, 1987; Hirschi, 1969; Jang, 1999; Kempf, 1993; Maguin and Loeber, 1996; Matsueda et al., 2006; Sampson and Laub, 1993a; Stewart, 2003; Thornberry et al., 2003a; Wright et al., 1999b.

8. *See* Chappel et al., 2005; Hirschi, 1969; Kornhauser, 1978; Longshore et al., 2005; Stewart, 2003.

9. This conception of low self-control differs somewhat from that of Gottfredson and Hirschi (1990); most notably, Gottfredson and Hirschi view the trait of irritability as a component of low self-control, while I view irritability as part of a separate personality dimension. See Chapter 13 for further discussion.

10. *See* Burt et al., 2006; Burton et al., 1998: Cauffman et al., 2005; Evans et al., 1997; Goode, 2008; Grasmick et al., 1993; Hirshi, 2004; LaGrange and Silverman, 1999; Le Blanc, 1993; Longshore, 1998; Matsueda et al., 2005; Piquero and Boufford, 2007; Piquero and Tibbetts, 1996; Polakowski, 1994; Pratt and Cullen, 2000; Wood et al., 1993; Wright et al., 1999b.

11. *See* De Li, 2004; Longshore et al., 2005; Piquero and Bouffard, 2007; Tittle et al., 2004; Wright et al., 1999.

12. *See* Burt et al., 2006; Cullen et al., 2008; Gottfredson, 2006; Hay, 2001; Pratt et al., 2004; Unnever et al., 2003; Wright and Beaver, 2005.

13. *See* Burt et al., 2006; Cullen et al., 2008; Pratt et al., 2004; Wright et al., 1999.

14. *See* Burt et al., 2006; Hay and Forrest, 2006; Longshore et al., 2005; Winfree et al., 2006; Wright et al., 1999.

CHAPTER 9

Labeling Theory
Does the Reaction to Delinquency Lead to Further Delinquency?

S train, social learning, and control theories focus on the characteristics of juveniles and their environment. These theories describe how such characteristics lead juveniles to engage in delinquency. *Labeling theory* **focuses on the reaction to delinquency: both the** *official reaction* **by the justice system and the** *informal reaction* **by parents, peers, teachers, and others.** Labeling theory describes how the reaction to delinquency sometimes leads offenders to engage in further delinquency.

In particular, **labeling theorists argue that individuals who are labeled "delinquent" are often viewed as "bad" or "evil" people.** And this view **leads others to reject them and treat them in a harsh manner.** This "harsh/rejecting" response **increases the likelihood of further delinquency** because the juveniles subjected to this response:

1. Experience a reduction in control, partly because conventional others do not want to associate with them and they have trouble obtaining a stake in society.

2. Experience an increase in strain, since they have more trouble achieving their goals and others treat them in a harsh manner.

3. Experience an increase in the social learning for crime, because they are forced to associate with delinquent others (since conventional others reject them).

4. Come to view themselves as the type of people who commit delinquent acts, because that is how others view and treat them.

As is apparent, labeling theory draws heavily on strain, social learning, and control theories. And, to a large extent, labeling theory may be viewed as an elaboration or extension of these theories. But, again, labeling theory is distinguished by the fact that it focuses on how others react to the juvenile's delinquency and the impact of this reaction on the juvenile. Labeling theory, then, does not try to explain the juvenile's initial acts of delinquency, the acts that result in labeling. Rather, the theory tries to explain why some juvenile offenders are more likely than others to continue engaging in delinquency and perhaps move on to more serious delinquency (see Chapter 10 for additional explanations of why some individuals continue to engage in delinquency). This difference between labeling and other theories is illustrated in Figure 9.1.

This chapter begins by providing a brief overview of labeling theory, noting that the theory addresses several questions about the reaction to delinquency. I then present a generic version of labeling theory that draws from the leading versions of labeling theory, including those of Tannenbaum (1938), Lemert (1951, 1972), Becker (1963), Matza (1969), Paternoster and Iovanni (1989), Matsueda (1992), Heimer and Matsueda, (1994), Sampson and Laub (1997), and especially Braithwaite (1989, 2002) and Sherman (1993, 2000). This generic theory describes the different ways in which others react to delinquency, with a focus on the harsh/rejecting reaction. It describes why the harsh/rejecting reaction increases the likelihood of further delinquency. It discusses why some juvenile offenders are more likely than others to experience this reaction. And it argues that the effect of the harsh/rejecting reaction on delinquency is conditioned by the characteristics of juvenile offenders. That is, it argues that some juvenile offenders are more likely than others to respond to the harsh/rejecting reaction with further delinquency. The chapter concludes with a discussion of the evidence on labeling theory.

It is important to examine labeling theory not only because it helps us explain why some juvenile offenders continue to offend but also because it has had and continues to have a major impact on the juvenile justice system. In particular, labeling theory explicitly

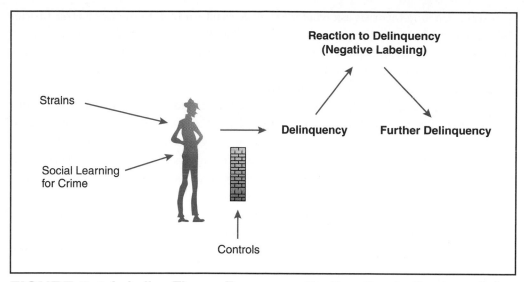

FIGURE 9.1 Labeling Theory Focuses on the Reaction to the Juvenile's Delinquency and Argues That This Reaction Sometimes Leads to Further Delinquency

addresses the issue of how we should (and should not) react to delinquency. Labeling theory is the primary inspiration behind the "restorative justice" approach to delinquency, which is having a major impact on the juvenile justice system in certain areas. This approach, described briefly in this chapter and more fully in Chapter 23, involves an alternative way of reacting to delinquency—one that is designed to reduce the likelihood of further delinquency.

Background on Labeling Theory

Labeling theorists ask five major questions about the reaction to delinquency.

First, labeling theorists ask **why certain acts are defined as delinquent or status offenses.** For example, why is using marijuana generally defined as a delinquent offense (see Becker, 1963)? Why are behaviors like skipping school and drinking alcohol defined as status offenses? I do not address this question in this chapter, although this question was addressed to some extent in Chapter 1, where I discussed the invention of juvenile delinquency. As part of that discussion, I examined the development of status offense laws. I presented a common argument made by labeling theorists: Powerful groups in our society have a large impact over what behaviors are and are not defined as illegal. These groups generally act in their own self-interest, so they work to get those behaviors that they find threatening or morally objectionable defined as illegal (see Jensen and Rojek, 1998; Paternoster and Bachman, 2001). As indicated in Chapter 1, for example, there is some evidence that upper-class individuals in the late 1800s and early 1900s felt threatened by the many poor children hanging out on the street, sometimes engaging in crime. As a result, they lobbied for the passage of status offense laws, like those requiring that juveniles attend school or be home by a certain hour.

Second, labeling theorists ask **how others react to delinquency.** They describe several major ways of reacting, including the harsh or rejecting reaction described earlier. This reaction is said to be especially common in the United States (Braithwaite, 1989).

Third, labeling theorists ask **what impact the reaction to delinquency has on further delinquency.** Most attention has focused on the harsh/rejecting reaction, since this reaction is said to increase the likelihood of further delinquency. Labeling theorists, then, make a rather provocative argument: The way in which we often react to delinquency in the United States has the effect of increasing delinquency.

Fourth, labeling theorists ask **why some juvenile offenders are more likely than others to experience the harsh/rejecting reaction.** Part of the answer has to do with the nature of a juvenile's delinquency. Juveniles engaging in more frequent and serious delinquency are more likely to experience the harsh or rejecting reaction. But the likelihood of experiencing this reaction is also influenced by factors beyond the juvenile's delinquency, such as the juvenile's race or ethnicity, social class, and gender.

Fifth, labeling theorists ask **whether some juvenile offenders are more likely than others to respond to the harsh/rejecting reaction with further delinquency.**

The answers that labeling theorists have provided to questions 2 through 5 are presented next.

How Do Others React to the Juvenile's Delinquency?

The police, courts, parents, school officials, and others may react to a juvenile's delinquency in several ways. Labeling theorists focus on three major types of reaction: Some may react in a harsh or rejecting manner, others may fail to respond to the juvenile's delinquency, and still others may condemn the juvenile's delinquency but accept the juvenile.

Harsh/Rejecting Reaction

The *harsh/rejecting reaction* is said to increase the likelihood of further delinquency. This reaction has two essential features. First, juveniles are labeled "delinquents," and this label **leads others to view them as "bad" or "evil" or "dangerous" people.** That is, others do not just view the juvenile's **behavior** as bad, they also view the **juvenile** as bad.

Second, this view of juveniles as bad **leads others to reject the juveniles and treat them in a harsh manner.** Others do not want to associate with or help the juveniles because they dislike and/or are fearful of them. Others treat the juveniles harshly; that is, they treat the juveniles in ways that are disrespectful, unfair, excessively punitive, and/or abusive (see especially Sherman, 1993).

Many labeling theorists focus on **the ways in which official agencies, like the police and courts, react to delinquency (or suspected delinquency).** It is said that these agencies often view juvenile offenders as bad or dangerous people and treat them in a harsh manner. To illustrate, a juvenile in a community with a gang problem described his relations with the police as follows:

> I wasn't a gangbanger. I used to hang out with them; they are my friends. The police started messing with me. They would pull me into their car and harass me. I kept telling them I was not a banger. But they don't believe anything we tell them. They asked me questions and this and other friends, guys from the hood who are gang-bangers, and since I wouldn't tell them what they wanted to hear, they would say things like, "Yes, you are one of those hoodlums from this street. We've been watching you for a long time, and now we got you, and you're going to pay."
>
> One day I was with my girlfriend and my friend and his girl—it was like the four of us. So we were walking by the neighborhood. . . . The police saw us and pulled us

over to a corner. They went through their shit—you know, "Who you be?" "Where are the other boys?" So, we didn't say nothing. They got really pissed and, in front of our girls, told us to kneel down and sing "Jingle Bells." So, there we are singing "jingle bells, jingle bells, jingle bells" for these pricks. . . . I wanted to kill them fuckers. How are you supposed to feel when they do that to you for no reason and then in front of your girl? And there's a lot of shit like that that goes on all the time. (Quoted in Padilla, 1992:83)

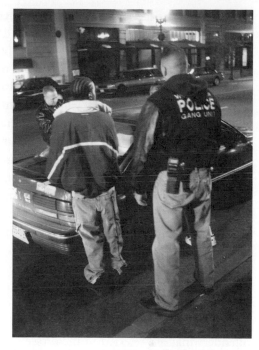

This juvenile did end up becoming a gang member, and he said he did so partly because of the way the police viewed and treated him. According to labeling theorists, being treated in a harsh or rejecting manner by the official agencies like the police often has this type of negative effect. Official agencies have much power over suspected offenders, and their actions can have a major effect on them. Further, the actions of official agencies may lead others to view juveniles as bad and treat them in a harsh or rejecting manner. Being arrested by the police, for example, may lead parents, teachers, and community residents to view and treat the juvenile as a "bad" person.

Recently, labeling theorists have come to focus on **the "informal" reactions to delinquency by parents, teachers, and others.** Many labeling theorists argue that these informal reactions are just as important, if not more important, than official reactions. These informal reactions are more common than official reactions; for example, most offenders do not have encounters with the police that often, but they may have encounters with their parents every day. And these informal reactions often involve intimate others that the juvenile cares about (see Paternoster and Bachman, 2001; Triplett and Jarjoura, 1994).

Data from surveys and field studies suggest that parents, peers, teachers, and others may also view juvenile offenders as bad and treat them in a harsh or rejecting manner. Parents may become overly strict with their delinquent children or reject them, perhaps "throwing" them out of the house. Other parents in the community may tell their children to avoid the juvenile offenders. Teachers and other school officials may harshly sanction offenders and segregate them in special classes or schools for "troublemakers," and employers may refuse to hire offenders.

To illustrate, a juvenile offender described his experience and that of his friends in elementary school by stating that "the teachers would put it in our heads, you know . . . 'You guys are the troublemakers,' and 'You guys are too loud,' and 'You're too this, and you just don't want to listen, and you just want to sit in your chairs and lay there' " (Padilla, 1992:71). This offender was put in a special class for the "learning disabled," a class that he said was for "the bad ones." And he was treated in a harsh manner by his teachers; for example, he was regularly blamed for delinquent acts that came to the attention of school authorities.

Failure to Respond to the Juvenile's Delinquency

A second way of reacting to the juvenile's delinquency involves the failure to respond to the delinquency. That is, others may do little or nothing in response to the juvenile's delinquency. In most cases, this is because **others never find out about the delinquency.** As indicated in Chapter 20, the police fail to detect the large share of delinquency that occurs. The same is probably true of parents and others. One recent study, for example, reported that about one in five teenagers has sex before age 15 (a status offense in most states). The study went on to report that only about one-third of the parents of sexually active 14-year-olds knew that their children were having sex (Lewin, 2003). Another study found that 39 percent of mothers and 62 percent of fathers of active gang members did not know their children were gang members. (Most of the gang members did not live with their fathers [Decker and Van Winkle, 1996:236].) So the failure to respond to delinquency is due largely to the fact that others are unaware of the juvenile's delinquency.

But even if the juvenile's delinquency is detected, **it may be ignored or subject to only a mild sanction.** For example, the police do not arrest most of the suspected juvenile offenders they encounter but instead release them, often with a warning (see Chapter 20). And juvenile courts do not formally process almost half of the suspected juvenile offenders that are referred to them (see Chapter 21). There are a number of reasons for this. Police and/or court officials may feel that the juvenile offender is basically a "good kid" who doesn't deserve to be sanctioned, they may lack good evidence to arrest or formally sanction, or they may be overwhelmed with more serious cases. Likewise, we know that some parents fail to sanction the delinquent behavior of their children, even when detected. The parents may also believe that their children are basically good kids who do not deserve serious sanctions. Or they may be overwhelmed by their children's behavior and have given up trying to discipline them. For example, one gang member who described his parents' reaction to his gang membership said, "My parents just say fuck it. He ain't going to listen. He going to do what he wants to do" (Decker and Van Winkle, 1996:244).

Some labeling theorists **argue that failure to respond to the juvenile's delinquency is a good strategy.** In particular, they claim that most juveniles engage in delinquency at one point or another, but this delinquency tends to be occasional and minor, and most juveniles "grow out of it" if left alone. According to these theorists, efforts to control the juvenile's delinquency run the risk of labeling the juvenile a "bad kid" and making matters worse. Ignoring the juvenile's delinquency avoids all of the negative effects associated with the harsh/rejecting reaction. Certain labeling theorists, then, advocate a policy of *radical nonintervention,* claiming that the best way to reduce delinquency is to do as little as possible about it.[1]

Labeling theorists, in particular, have argued that the police should handle cases informally whenever possible rather than arresting juveniles. Juvenile court officials should divert juveniles from the court whenever possible, either outright releasing them or placing them in programs outside the court system. If court officials do formally process and sanction offenders, the offenders should be placed in community-based programs rather than institutions whenever possible. Finally, status offenses and many minor delinquent acts, like marijuana use, should be legalized or at least decriminalized (e.g., treated as violations of civil rather than criminal law, that is, treated like "speeding" violations). Many of these recommendations were partly implemented by the juvenile justice system during the 1960s and 1970s, when labeling theory was at the height of its popularity (see Akers and Sellers, 2004; Matsueda, 2001; Chapter 21).

Increasingly, however, labeling theorists are **moving away from the position that ignoring delinquency is a good strategy.** While ignoring delinquency may avoid the negative effects associated with the harsh/rejecting reaction, it may nevertheless increase delinquency by reducing direct control. It may also reduce the likelihood that juveniles condemn delinquency and develop self-control, since these traits often result from direct control. Rather than ignoring delinquency, labeling theorists are starting to advocate a third type of reaction to delinquency.

"Condemn the Delinquency but Accept the Juvenile" Reaction

Many contemporary labeling theorists now argue that **the juvenile's delinquency should be condemned but in a way that is accepting of the juvenile** (recall the saying: "Condemn the sin, but love the sinner"). In particular, others should sanction the juvenile for his or her delinquency, emphasizing that the delinquency is morally wrong. The sanctions, however, should not be overly harsh. Further, the juvenile should not be rejected; rather, conventional others, like parents and teachers, should maintain close ties to the juvenile, even as the sanctions are being administered (see especially Braithwaite, 1989, 2002). The best way to appreciate this reaction is with an example.

Imagine that parents find out that their child has vandalized a local store. The parents explain to the child why they **disapprove of this act.** Among other things, they describe the harm that the act caused to the store owner and others in the community. If they are successful, the child will feel some shame and guilt for the act. The parents, however, **do not condemn the child.** For example, they do not tell the child, "You're no good" or "You're a rotten kid." The parents also sanction the child but in a way that is not overly harsh. Perhaps they require the child to apologize to the store owner, repair the damage or pay for the repairs, and do some community service (as opposed to beating the child, forcing the child out of the house, or trying to have the child "locked up"). And the parents continue to express their love and support for the child, forgiving the child once the sanctions have been administered (as opposed to rejecting the child).

Hay (2001b) measured this type of reaction by asking juveniles questions like the following:

1. When your parents are reacting to a rule violation they consider important, how much importance do they place on:
   a) Convincing you that what you did was immoral or unfair.
   b) Making you feel guilty or ashamed for what you did.
   c) Having you make up for your actions by apologizing or helping to erase any harm that was done.
2. Do your parents see you as a good person even when they are upset with you?
3. Do your parents treat you with respect when they are disciplining you?

4. How likely is it that your parents would tell you that you are a "bad kid" when disciplining you?

5. How likely is it that your parents would tell you that they forgive you after disciplining you?

Labeling theorists argue that this *"condemn the delinquency but accept the juvenile" reaction* does not have the negative effects associated with the harsh/rejecting reaction. In particular, it does not reduce control, since the juvenile maintains close ties to conventional others. It does not increase strain, since the juvenile is not treated in a harsh or rejecting manner. It does not foster the social learning of delinquency, since the juvenile is not driven to associate with delinquent others. And it does not lead the juvenile to view him- or herself as a bad person, since the parents and others condemn the juvenile's behavior rather than the juvenile. Further, this type of reaction does not have the negative consequences that result from ignoring delinquency, since the juvenile is sanctioned. This sanction imposes direct control on the juvenile and helps the juvenile learn to condemn delinquency, since parents and others try to convince the juvenile that his or her delinquency is morally wrong.

It is easy to understand how people like parents might go about condemning the juvenile's delinquency but accepting the juvenile. But how might official agencies like the police and courts react in this manner? According to labeling theorists like Braithwaite (1989, 2002) and Sherman (2000), the police and/or courts should respond to most juvenile offenders using the *restorative justice approach.* This approach focuses on making offenders aware of the harm they have caused and having them repair that harm. But it does so in a way that does not condemn the offender, is not overly harsh, and maintains or restores the offender's ties to conventional society.

The core part of the *restorative justice* approach involves a *conference* between the offender, the victim, family members of the offender and victim, and selected community representatives. This conference takes the place of a court hearing. The first part of the conference examines the harm caused by the offender's delinquency. Among other things, the victim tells the offender about the harm she or he has suffered and asks questions of the offender (e.g., "Why did you do it?" "Why did you pick me?"). The focus is on making the offender appreciate the harm caused by his or her behavior, not on condemning the offender. In fact, the victim and others often come to realize that the offender is a troubled juvenile, not a "monster" or "evil" person. In the second part of the conference, everyone—including the offender—develops a plan to repair the harm. The plan often involves an apology to the victim, restitution to the victim, and community service. Harsh sanctions like incarceration are avoided. The offender is forgiven once the harm is repaired, and efforts are made to maintain or restore the offender's ties to conventional society. For example, efforts may be made to help the offender with school or employment problems. This approach is discussed further in Chapter 23 (also see Bazemore, 2000; Braithwaite, 2002). Preliminary data on its effectiveness are encouraging, suggesting that it is often more effective at reducing offending than approaches that are more harsh or rejecting in orientation.

Summary

The essential point of labeling theorists is that others often respond to delinquency in ways that increase the likelihood of further delinquency, with labeling theorists focusing on the harsh/rejecting reaction to delinquency.

Why Does the Harsh/Rejecting Reaction Lead to Further Delinquency?

The harsh/rejecting reaction tends to reduce control, increase strain, foster the social learning of crime, and lead juveniles to view themselves as the type of people who engage in delinquent acts. I elaborate on each of these points in the following sections.

Reduces Control

Conventional others view the juvenile offender as a bad or evil person, and as a consequence, they avoid the offender or treat him or her in a harsh manner. This **reduces direct control,** since others, like parents and teachers, avoid the juvenile or employ overly harsh methods of discipline. It **reduces the juvenile's stake in conformity,** since emotional ties between the juvenile and others like parents and teachers are weakened.[2] Also, the juvenile's investment in conventional society is weakened. Being labeled a delinquent, for example, disrupts relations with school authorities and jeopardizes one's future educational and occupational plans.[3] To illustrate, a recent study by Sweeten (2006) examined the effect of arrest and court appearance on the likelihood of dropping out of high school. Sweeten examined a national sample of adolescents and took account of a range of "third variables," including school grades, achievement test scores, educational expectations, poverty status, and self-reported delinquency. Sweeten found that "first-time arrest during high school nearly doubles the odds of dropout, while a court appearance nearly quadruples the odds of dropout" (2006:473; also see Bernburg and Krohn, 2003, for similar results). Further, **the juvenile's beliefs may be weakened as well.** Juveniles are less likely to condemn delinquency if they are subject to weak direct controls and have a small stake in conformity. Finally, the experience of being viewed and treated as a bad person may weaken their resolve to exercise self-control.

Increases Strain

Others treat the juvenile in a harsh manner, thereby increasing levels of strain (Sampson and Laub, 1997; Stewart, Simons, Conger, and Scaramella, 2002). In particular, others may make it **more difficult for the juvenile to achieve his or her goals.** Employers, for example, may refuse to hire the juvenile (the blockage of money goals). The juvenile may be more closely monitored by parents, teachers, and police (the blockage of autonomy goals), and the juvenile may be treated in a disrespectful manner by these others (the blockage of status goals). Also, **the juvenile may experience the loss of positive stimuli and presentation of negative stimuli.** Conventional peers may avoid the juvenile. The juvenile may then associate with delinquent peers, where the likelihood of abuse is higher. Parents, teachers, and justice officials may employ harsh methods of control. Further, the experience of such harsh treatment may **increase the juvenile's level of irritability,** which in turn increases the juvenile's sensitivity to strains and likelihood of responding to strains in an aggressive manner (see Chapter 13).

Increases the Social Learning of Delinquency

Conventional others often try to avoid the juvenile, so the juvenile is more likely to associate with delinquent others as a result (Adams and Evans, 1996; Heimer and Matsueda, 1994; Johnson et al., 2004). To illustrate, Bernburg et al. (2006) examined whether contact with the juvenile justice system (e.g., arrest, court involvement) influenced the likelihood that juveniles would subsequently associate with delinquent peers or join gangs. They took account of a range of "third variables" in their analysis, including self-reported delinquency, prior levels of delinquent peer association, and prior gang membership. Bernberg et al. (2006:77) found that "youths who experience juvenile justice intervention are significantly more likely to be members of gangs during the successive period relative to [comparable youths] who have no intervention experience. . . . Juvenile justice intervention increases the odds of gang membership by a factor of 5.2." Likewise, they found that juvenile justice intervention increases the likelihood of associating with delinquent peers. This, of course, increases the likelihood that juveniles will be differentially reinforced for delinquency, exposed to delinquent models, and taught beliefs favorable to delinquency. Further, labeled juveniles are more likely to develop beliefs favorable to delinquency as they seek to rationalize or justify their behavior to themselves and others.

Creates a Delinquent Self-Concept

Labeling theory is derived from a perspective in sociology known as **symbolic interactionism.** A central tenet of this perspective is that our *self-concept*—the way in which we view ourselves—is a function of how others view and treat us (see Matsueda, 2001). Suppose, for example, that others view and treat you as an intelligent person (e.g., teachers give you good grades, your parents tell you how smart you are, your peers eagerly solicit your opinion on important issues). Eventually, you will come to view yourself as intelligent. Further, you will act on the basis of this self-concept; that is, you will act like an intelligent person. For example, you may participate frequently in class, regularly voice your opinions to others, and plan on obtaining an advanced education.

The same logic applies if others view and treat you as a bad person. **You may come to view yourself as a bad person and act accordingly** (Adams et al., 2003; Heimer and Matsueda, 1994; Matsueda, 1992). This does not happen immediately. It is not the case that someone calls you a delinquent or a bad kid, and you suddenly alter your self-concept. It happens gradually, if at all. Some juveniles are able to maintain a positive self-concept even in the face of harsh or rejecting treatment by others (see Rogers and Buffalo, 1974). Others alter their self-concept and behavior. As one juvenile offender stated, "If the teachers and everyone else thought we were bad, we started to show that we were. So, we started doing a lot of bad things" (Padilla, 1992:74).

What Determines Whether Juveniles Experience the Harsh/Rejecting Reaction?

Only some of the juveniles who engage in delinquency are subject to the harsh/rejecting reaction described earlier. What determines whether juveniles experience this reaction from others?

The most important factor is **whether juveniles engage in delinquency that becomes known to others, especially frequent and/or serious delinquency.** I should note that delinquency is not an absolute requirement for a harsh or rejecting response from others. Occasionally, juveniles are falsely accused of delinquent behavior and subject to a harsh or rejecting response. A number of prominent cases involving falsely accused criminals have been in the news recently, and a number of these falsely accused individuals have been sentenced to death. In fact, about 125 people on death row have been exonerated since 1976. In most cases, however, the harsh/rejecting reaction is stimulated by actual delinquency.

As indicated in Chapter 1, this harsh/rejecting reaction is especially common with serious offenders. The justice system and many people in the general public have increasingly come to view serious offenders as bad people who pose a major threat to our society and deserve harsh sanctions. One recent book on crime by several prominent authors, for example, stated:

> America is now home to thickening ranks of juvenile "superpredators"—radically impulsive, brutally remorseless youngsters, including ever more preteenage boys, who murder, assault, rob, burglarize, deal deadly drugs, join gun-toting gangs, and create serious communal disorders. (Bennett et al., 1996:27)

The justice system has started to punish many of these offenders, especially the older ones, more harshly in an effort to isolate them from conventional society (by confining them in institutions) and to make them suffer for their misdeeds.

Other factors influencing whether juveniles experience the harsh/rejecting reaction include **the sociodemographic characteristics of the juvenile (and the juvenile's parents).** In particular, lower-class juveniles, the members of certain minority groups, and older juveniles are said to be more likely to experience the harsh/rejecting reaction. Such juveniles are less able to resist the efforts of others to treat them in a harsh or rejecting manner and/or they fit the stereotype of a delinquent. In particular, lower-class juveniles (and their parents) are more likely to lack the financial resources, connections, reputation, and negotiating skills to convince others to ignore the delinquency or treat it in a mild manner. Furthermore, lower-class juveniles, the members of certain minority groups, and older juveniles fit the stereotype of serious delinquents or "superpredators" (see the discussion of race in Chapter 4). I discuss these issues in Chapter 22 when I examine discrimination by the juvenile justice system. For now, I note that the evidence suggests that poor individuals and members of certain minority groups are sometimes treated more harshly than others by juvenile justice officials, even after we take account of their level of delinquency.

The situation with respect to **gender** is more complex. Males fit the stereotype of a serious delinquent, and some data suggest that males are more likely than females to be arrested and severely sanctioned for serious offenses. However, things are different when it comes to status offenses, especially status offenses that involve sexual behavior or the possibility of sexual behavior, like running away. Females are more likely than males to be arrested and severely sanctioned for such offenses. This reflects a double standard regarding sexual behavior. Female juveniles who engage in sexual behavior are more likely to be

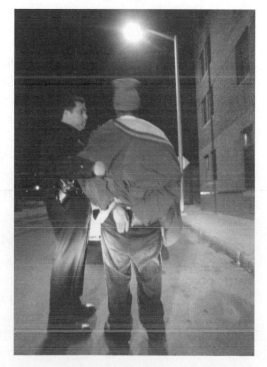

viewed as "bad," subject to efforts to control their behavior, and treated in a harsh manner (see Chapter 22; Bartusch and Matsueda, 1996:150; Chesney-Lind and Shelden, 2004).

Finally, **juveniles who are low in control and who associate with delinquent others** are more likely to experience the harsh/rejecting reaction. Such juveniles fit the stereotype of a delinquent or "bad person"; in particular, they do not get along with their parents and teachers, they do poorly at school, they have amoral beliefs or beliefs favoring delinquency, and they belong to delinquent peer groups or gangs. Also, such juveniles are less able to resist the efforts of others to treat them in a harsh or rejecting manner. They lack close ties to conventional others who might assist them, they have poor reputations, and they have poor problem-solving skills. Finally, such juveniles tend to associate with others who are more likely to treat them in a harsh or rejecting manner. Among other things, such juveniles are more likely to have parents and teachers who dislike them or are weakly attached to them—which increases the likelihood of harsh treatment.[4]

So juveniles are most likely to experience the harsh/rejecting reaction when they engage in delinquency that becomes known to conventional others, especially frequent and serious delinquency; when they are poor, members of certain minority groups, and older; and when they are low in control and associate with delinquent peers. Such juveniles fit the stereotype of a delinquent or bad person, they (or their parents) are less able to resist the efforts of others to treat them in a harsh or rejecting manner; and/or they are more likely to associate with others who respond in a harsh or rejecting manner.

Certain of these points are illustrated in Chambliss' (1973) classic study of the Saints and the Roughnecks, described in Chapter 4. As you may recall, the middle-class Saints were liked and respected by members of the community and were viewed as "good boys who just went in for an occasional prank." The lower-class Roughnecks were viewed as "tough, young criminals who were headed for trouble," and they were "constantly in trouble with the police and community." The two groups, however, were about equally delinquent. Chambliss argued that the Saints and Roughnecks were viewed and treated so differently for three reasons. The Saints were better able to hide their delinquency from others, partly because their access to cars allowed them to commit their delinquent acts in out-of-the-way places. The Roughnecks' delinquency, by contrast, was often committed in the center of town, where it was highly visible. The Saints were better able to resist the efforts of others to treat them in a harsh or rejecting manner. For example, the Saints were polite and apologetic when confronted by suspicious police officers and teachers, and this deflected harsh treatment. The Roughnecks, however, reacted with hostility and disdain when confronted by others, and this encouraged harsh treatment. Finally, the middle-class, high-achieving Saints did not fit the stereotype of serious delinquents, while the lower-class Roughnecks did.

Are Some Juveniles More Likely than Others to Respond to the Harsh/Rejecting Reaction with Further Delinquency?

Imagine a group of juvenile offenders who are being treated in a harsh or rejecting manner. According to some labeling theorists, certain of these offenders are more likely than others to respond to this treatment with further delinquency.[5] In particular, a delinquent response is most likely among offenders who are **low in control, believe that delinquency is a desirable or justifiable response, and are high in strain.**

You can appreciate why such offenders are more likely to respond with delinquency if you think back to our discussion of strain theory in Chapter 6. The harsh or rejecting treatment received by these offenders is a type of strain; that is, people treat the offenders in a negative manner. As indicated in Chapter 6, juveniles are more likely to respond to strain with delinquency if they are low in control. Among other things, they lack the resources to respond in a nondelinquent manner, they have less to lose through delinquency, and they give less thought to the consequences of their behavior. Likewise, they are more likely to respond to strain with delinquency if they believe that delinquency is a desirable or justifiable response (because they have been reinforced for delinquency or anticipate reinforcement, have been taught beliefs favorable to delinquency, and have been exposed to delinquent models). Finally, they are more likely to respond to strain with delinquency if they are experiencing other strains. These other strains reduce their ability to cope in a legal manner, since individuals experiencing several strains are easily overwhelmed. And these other strains make them irritable, which increases their sensitivity to negative treatment.

Consider, for example, two students who are treated in a harsh or rejecting manner by a teacher. One student is closely monitored by parents, has good grades, believes that delinquency is wrong, associates with conventional peers, and is generally treated well by others. The other student is poorly monitored by parents, is flunking out of school, believes that one should respond to disrespectful treatment with violence, associates with delinquent peers who often reinforce violence, and is experiencing many other strains. It is clear that the second student is more likely to respond to the harsh or rejecting treatment with violence, for all of the reasons indicated in the preceding paragraph.

Some juvenile offenders, then, are more likely than others to respond to harsh or rejecting treatment with delinquency. Unfortunately, those juvenile offenders most likely to respond to harsh or rejecting treatment with delinquency are also the juveniles most likely to be treated in a harsh or rejecting manner.

The Evidence on Labeling Theory

The generic labeling theory that I have just presented reflects recent developments in the field, especially the work of Braithwaite (1989, 2002) and Sherman (1993, 2000). And it has not yet been well tested. In particular, the **ideal test** of the theory would involve the examination of three groups of comparable offenders, the first of whom received the harsh/rejecting reaction, the second of whom received the "failure to respond to delinquency" reaction, and the third of whom received the "condemn the delinquency but accept the juvenile" reaction. If labeling theory is correct, those who received the harsh/rejecting reaction should be much more likely to engage in further delinquency than those who received the "condemn the delinquency but accept the juvenile" reaction and perhaps somewhat more likely to engage in delinquency than those who received the "failure to respond to delinquency" reaction. Further, a full test of labeling theory should determine whether the factors that I described condition the effect of the harsh/rejecting reaction on delinquency.

Most tests of labeling theory fall far short of this ideal.[6] Let me illustrate this with an example. Perhaps the major way that researchers have tested labeling theory is by **comparing arrested delinquents to comparable delinquents who have not been arrested.** These tests assume that the arrested delinquents are more likely to have experienced the harsh/

rejecting reaction. Therefore, the arrested delinquents should be more likely to engage in subsequent delinquency. Most such tests find that the arrested delinquents do have higher levels of subsequent delinquency, but not all tests find this.[7] Such tests, however, suffer from certain major problems.

First, while **arrested juveniles may be somewhat more likely to experience the harsh/reacting reaction, many arrested juveniles do not experience this reaction.** In particular, many arrested juveniles are treated in a respectful manner by the police and courts, experience only mild sanctions, and have few problems with others—like parents and teachers.[8] Further, some arrested juveniles are placed in programs that increase their level of control, reduce their strain, and/or foster the social learning of conventional behavior.

Second, **we cannot assume that the nonarrested juveniles experience the "condemn the delinquency but accept the juvenile" reaction.** Most of the nonarrested juveniles have probably had their delinquency ignored, which increases the likelihood of further delinquency. And some of the nonarrested juveniles have probably experienced the harsh/rejecting reaction. While these juveniles have not been arrested, their parents and others may have labeled them as "bad" and treated them in a harsh or rejecting manner. So, determining whether arrested juveniles have higher rates of subsequent delinquency than nonarrested juveniles is not a good way to test labeling theory.

To properly test labeling theory, **we must develop better measures of the three major ways of reacting to delinquency.**[9] A few studies have tried to do this, although their measures are still far from perfect. For example, Paternoster, Brame, Bachman, and Sherman (1997) examined how the police treated adults arrested for domestic violence. Some were treated in a respectful manner; the police took the time to listen to them, did not handcuff them in front of their spouses or partners, and did not use force. Others were treated in a more disrespectful manner, one that had elements of the harsh/rejecting reaction. The researchers found that those treated in a disrespectful manner were more likely to reoffend, even after taking account of prior levels of violence. Another set of studies examined the way in which parents viewed their children. Some parents viewed their children in a negative light, stating that their children often "get into trouble" or "break rules." And this negative view increased the likelihood that their children would engage in subsequent delinquency, even after taking account of a range of "third variables" like prior delinquency of the children. This negative view increased the likelihood of delinquency for many of the reasons listed earlier; most notably, it increased the likelihood that the children would form a delinquent self-concept and associate with other delinquents.[10]

More research is needed on labeling theory, however, particularly research that better measures the different reactions to delinquency, that better examines why the harsh/rejecting reaction may increase the likelihood of delinquency, and that explores the factors that may condition the effect of the harsh/rejecting reaction on delinquency (see Sherman, 1993, 2000). Such research is especially important given the fact that labeling theory is having an important impact on how we respond to delinquency, particularly as reflected in the restorative justice approach.

Summary

Labeling theory focuses on the reaction to delinquency. It is said that the way in which official agencies and others react to delinquency may increase the likelihood of further delinquency. Labeling theorists examine three major types of reaction, devoting most of their attention to the harsh/rejecting reaction in which offenders are viewed as bad, rejected by conventional others, and treated in a harsh manner. This reaction is said to increase the likelihood of further delinquency by reducing control, increasing strain, fostering association with delinquent peers, and leading the offender to form a delinquent self-concept. Certain types of juvenile offenders are said to be more likely than others to experience this reaction and to respond to it with further delinquency. The "condemn the delinquency but accept the juvenile" reaction, by contrast, is said to reduce subsequent offending. This reaction avoids the negative effects of the harsh/rejecting reaction, imposes direct control, and fosters the development of internal control. Labeling theory has not yet been well tested, but a few recent studies provide tentative support for the theory.

Teaching Aids

Controversial Issue: Is It Sometimes Best to Ignore Delinquency?

Some labeling theorists argue that the best way to control delinquency is to do as little as possible about it—a policy of "radical nonintervention." Such theorists contend that efforts to control delinquency, including many efforts to treat or rehabilitate delinquents, often make matters worse, because such efforts portray delinquents as different from nondelinquents and as a problem. Therefore, such efforts carry a high risk of labeling delinquents as "bad" and prompting the harsh/rejecting reaction. The policy of radical nonintervention involves tolerating much behavior that we now define as delinquent, dramatically limiting the role of the juvenile justice system and carefully structuring interventions so that they do not label or stigmatize juveniles as "bad." Schur (1973:154–155) describes this policy as follows:

> Radical nonintervention implies policies that accommodate society to the widest possible diversity of behaviors and attitudes, rather than forcing as many individuals as possible to "adjust" to supposedly common societal standards. This does not mean that anything goes, that all behavior is socially acceptable. But traditional delinquency policy has proscribed youthful behavior well beyond what is required to maintain a smooth-running society or to protect others from youthful depredations.
>
> Thus, the basic injunction for public policy becomes: *leave kids alone whenever possible.* This effort partly involves mechanisms to divert children away from the courts but it goes further to opposing various kinds of intervention by diverse social control and socializing agencies. . . . [P]olicies [should] favor collective action programs instead of those that single out specific individuals, and voluntary programs instead of compulsory ones.

To what extent do you agree with the policy of radical nonintervention? In particular, do you feel that the justice system and others (e.g., parents, school officials) sometimes go "too far" in trying to control delinquency and thereby make matters worse? If so, do you think they should sometimes ignore acts now defined as delinquent or status offenses? Or do you think they should respond in other ways, like those embodied in the restorative justice approach? Justify your responses.

TEST YOUR KNOWLEDGE OF THIS CHAPTER

1. Describe the essential arguments of labeling theory in a few sentences.
2. How is labeling theory different from and similar to the other major theories of delinquency?
3. Does labeling theory try to explain all delinquency?
4. What major questions do labeling theorists ask about the reaction of others to delinquency?
5. List and briefly describe the three major types of reaction to delinquency examined by labeling theorists. Indicate whether each type of reaction should increase or decrease the likelihood of subsequent offending. Explain why the reaction should have this effect.
6. What is meant by official and informal reactions to delinquency?
7. Why do some labeling theorists argue that the failure to respond to the individual's delinquency is a good strategy? What specific recommendations do such labeling theorists make for controlling delinquency (e.g., recommendations regarding the police, courts, and laws)?
8. How do juvenile justice agencies implement the restorative justice approach to delinquency? How does this approach reflect the "condemn the delinquency but accept the juvenile" reaction?
9. Why does the harsh/rejecting reaction increase the likelihood of subsequent delinquency?
10. What is the individual's self-concept? According to symbolic interactionism, how is the self-concept formed? How is the self-concept relevant to labeling theory?
11. What factors influence whether juveniles experience the harsh/rejecting reaction? Why do these factors influence the likelihood of experiencing the harsh/rejecting reaction?
12. What factors influence whether juveniles will respond to the harsh/rejecting reaction with further delinquency? Why do these factors influence the likelihood of a delinquent response?
13. Ideally, how should researchers go about testing labeling theory?
14. The major way in which labeling theory has been tested is by comparing the subsequent offending of arrested delinquents to that of comparable nonarrested delinquents. What are the major problems with this type of test?
15. Describe the evidence on labeling theory.

THOUGHT AND DISCUSSION QUESTIONS

1. How might labeling theory explain deviant behaviors like cheating on exams and excessive drinking?
2. Develop survey questions to measure the independent variables in your explanation of cheating and drinking in question 1.
3. Suppose you are a labeling theorist. What advice would you give to parents and teachers about responding to delinquency? What advice would you give to police and court officials about how to best control delinquency?

KEY TERMS

- Labeling theory
- Official reaction to delinquency
- Informal reaction to delinquency
- Harsh/rejecting reaction
- Radical nonintervention
- "Condemn the delinquency but accept the juvenile" reaction
- Restorative justice approach
- Restorative justice conference
- Self-concept

ENDNOTES

1. *See* Akers and Sellers, 2004; Matsueda, 2001; Schur, 1973.
2. *See* Ambert, 1997; Hay, 2001b; Sampson and Laub, 1997; Stewart et al., 2000; Stewart, Simons, Conger, and Scaramella, 2002.
3. *See* Bernburg and Krohn, 2003; De Li, 1999; Hagan, 1991; Sampson and Laub, 1997; Sweeten, 2006.
4. *See* Braithwaite, 1989; Hay, 2001b; Triplett and Jarjoura, 1994.
5. *See* Bernburg and Krohn, 2003; Bernburg et al., 2006; Hagan, 1991; Sampson and Laub, 1997; Sherman, 1993, 2000; Sweeten, 2006.
6. For overviews of the research on labeling theory, *see* Akers and Sellers, 2004; Jensen and Rojek, 1998; Paternoster and Iovanni, 1989; Sampson and Laub, 1997; Shoemaker, 2000.
7. *See* Chapter 23; Bernburg and Krohn, 2003; Bernburg et al., 2006; Farrington, 1977; Gold and Williams, 1969; Huizinga et al., 2003; Johnson et al., 2004; Palamera et al., 1986; Sampson and Laub, 1997; Smith and Brame, 1994; Stewart, Simons, Conger, and Scaramella, 2002.
8. *See* Jensen and Rojek, 1998; Paternoster and Iovanni, 1989; Sherman, 1993, 2000; Shoemaker, 2000.
9. For additional problems with tests of labeling theory, *see* Jensen and Rojek, 1998; Paternoster and Iovanni, 1989.
10. *See* Adams and Evans, 1996; Braithwaite et al., 2006; Hay, 2001b; Heimer and Matsueda, 1994; Matsueda, 1992; Sherman, 2000; Ward and Tittle, 1993; Zhang and Zhang, 2004.

CHAPTER 10

The Life Course

How Do We Explain Different Patterns of Offending over the Course of a Lifetime?

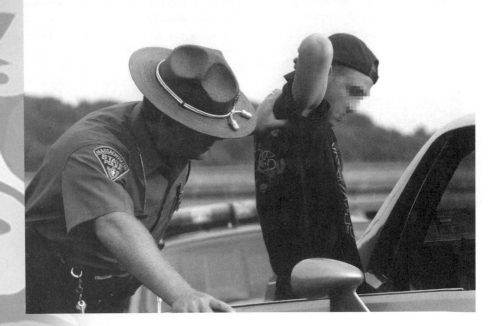

The theories of delinquency described in the last four chapters focus on explaining why some individuals engage in more delinquency than others. But there are also other facts about delinquency that are in need of explanation. Not only do some individuals commit more delinquency than others, but **individuals also exhibit different patterns of offending over the course of their lives.**[1] As I pointed out in Chapter 4, most individuals increase their level of offending when they enter adolescence and then reduce it when they enter adulthood. This is referred to as the *adolescence-limited* pattern of offending, since offenses are largely limited to the adolescent years. A smaller number of individuals, however, offend at high rates over much of their lives. Even though these *life-course persistent* offenders make up only 4 to 10 percent of the population, they are an important group—accounting for a large share of all delinquency, including perhaps a majority of all serious delinquency. This chapter seeks to explain patterns of offending over the life course, focusing on the adolescence-limited and life-course persistent patterns.

The first part of this chapter presents an integrated theory that explains why most individuals increase their offending during adolescence and then decrease it during adulthood. This theory draws heavily on the work of Agnew (1997, 2003a), Farrington (1986, 2006), M. Felson (2002), Greenberg (1977), Moffitt (1993, 2006), Osgood et al. (1996), Patterson et al. (1989), Raine (2002a), Sampson and Laub (1993a), Steffensmeier and Allan (1995, 2000), Thornberry and Krohn (2001), Walsh (2002), and Warr (2002), among others. This theory basically argues that **the biological and social changes associated with adolescence lead to an increase in strain, a reduction in control, and an increase in the social learning for crime.** This integrated theory, then, may be viewed as an elaboration of strain, control, and social learning theories.

The second part of this chapter presents an integrated theory that explains why a small percentage of individuals offend at high rates over much of their lives. This theory draws heavily on the work of Lahey and Waldman (2005), Moffitt (1993, 1997, 2006), Patterson et al. (1989), Sampson and Laub (1993a), and Thornberry and Krohn (2001, 2006). The theory argues that **certain biological and social factors cause some individuals to experience high levels of strain, low levels of control, and social learning for crime over much of their lives.** This integrated theory also represents an extension of strain, control, and social learning theories—as well as labeling theory.

Recent research has begun to identify other patterns of offending besides the adolescence-limited and life-course persistent patterns. Some individuals, for example, offend at low rates over much of their lives (e.g., Benson, 2002; Moffitt, 2006). And there is now some debate over how many different patterns of offending there are and how to best describe these patterns (see Nagin and Tremblay, 2005a, 2005b; Sampson and Laub, 2005). The adolescence-limited and life-course persistent patterns, however, are major patterns and most attention has focused on them.

Why Do Most Individuals Increase Their Levels of Offending During Adolescence?

The best self-report surveys suggest that 90 percent or more of all adolescents engage in delinquency. Typically, such adolescents commit a small to moderate number of minor offenses, like petty theft, minor acts of vandalism, fighting, drinking under age, marijuana use, sexual intercourse, truancy, and curfew violation. For example, one college student describes an adolescent shoplifting incident as follows:

> There we were, in the most lucrative department Mervyn's had to offer, two curious (but very mature) adolescent girls: the cosmetic and jewelry department. . . . We didn't enter the store planning to steal anything. In fact, I believe we had "given it up" a few weeks earlier; but once my eyes caught sight of the beautiful white and blue necklaces alongside the counter, a spark inside me was once again ignited. . . . Those exquisite puka necklaces were calling out to me, "Take me! Wear me! I can be yours!" All I needed to do was take them to make it a reality. (Quoted in Katz, 1988:54)

Wooden and Blazak (2001:49–57) describe some of the cliques that exist in four "typical," suburban, Southern California high schools. The members of certain of these cliques are involved to varying degrees in the types of delinquency characteristic of adolescence-limited offenders. For example,

> The Jocks [were] boys who actively participated in many of the sports on campus. They strutted around campus in their letter jackets. . . . Most were self-centered and egotistical. At parties jocks could be seen participating in beer-drinking contests and smoking marijuana. They had no problem finding dates. . . .

> The Tweakies were boys who had an extremely "laid back" attitude toward school. They often skipped class to go to the beach and consumed alcohol whenever they had the chance. Surfboards and girls were more important than school. . . .

> The Burners appeared to be stoned most of the time. This group included the rocker crowd, along with some punkers.

What is it about adolescence that causes most juveniles to engage in delinquency? Certain of the biological and social changes associated with adolescence lead to a reduction in control, an increase in the social learning for crime, and an increase in strain. I first describe these biological and social changes and then discuss how they impact control, social learning, and strain.

The Biological and Social Changes Associated with Adolescence

Certain of the changes associated with adolescence are biological in nature.[2] Perhaps the most visible of these changes is the increased physical and sexual maturation of adolescents. Adolescents come to resemble adults, and among other things, this leads adolescents to desire many of the privileges of adults—especially increased autonomy and sexual relations. Other of the biological changes associated with adolescence are less visible. Adolescent males experience increased levels of certain hormones, like testosterone. Some claim that this leads to an increase in irritability, so adolescents are quicker to take offense at slights and become angry. Also, some evidence suggests that a portion of the adolescent's brain—the prefrontal cortex—is not yet fully developed. The prefrontal cortex is involved in the control of emotions, among other things, so adolescents may be less able to exercise self-control than adults.

   Other of the changes associated with adolescence are social in nature. Adolescence is a period of transition from childhood to adulthood, a time when individuals prepare for adult family and work roles. Reflecting this fact, adolescents are given **some, but not all** of the privileges and responsibilities of adults. It is felt that these privileges and responsibilities will help adolescents prepare for adult roles but that adolescents are not able to handle all of the privileges and responsibilities of adulthood. Those privileges and responsibilities extended to adolescents include:

1. **More autonomy than children (but less than adults).** For example, parents relax the rules they impose on adolescents, allowing them more freedom to do such things as choose their friends, get involved in romantic relationships, and stay out late at night. State agencies allow adolescents above a certain age to drive automobiles.

2. **More material resources than children (but less than adults).** For example, parents give adolescents more spending money and access to cars. Adolescents are also allowed to earn money through after-school and summer jobs.

3. **Higher status than children (but less than adults).** Adolescents are no longer viewed and treated as "kids" or children, although they are not viewed and treated with as much respect as adults.

4. **More responsibility for managing their behavior and relations with others.** Parents and teachers hold adolescents more responsible for their behavior (although not as responsible as adults in most cases). Related to this, adolescents are more often expected to cope on their own when problems arise (but not to the same extent as adults).

5. **More responsibility for their educational and career goals.** Adolescents are expected to give serious thought to their educational and career goals and to devote more effort to the pursuit of these goals. **Related to this, school becomes more demanding.** There is more homework, teachers grade in a more rigorous manner, and there is heightened competition with other students.

The fact that adolescents have some but not all of the privileges and responsibilities of adults is reflected in the responses that a sample of college students gave when they were asked whether they thought they had reached adulthood. Almost two-thirds of the students chose the response category "in some respects yes, in some respects no" (Arnett, 1997). This fact is also reflected in the lyric from the Alice Cooper song "Eighteen": "I'm in the middle, without any plans, I'm a boy and I'm a man" (see Piquero and Brezina, 2001).

The biological changes and the limited privileges and responsibilities associated with adolescence lead to a **reduction in control,** an **increase in the social learning for crime,** and an **increase in strain.**

A Reduction in Control

Individuals experience a reduction in control as they move from childhood to adolescence. This is especially true of **direct control.** Parents grant adolescents more autonomy than children. In particular, parents relax the rules they impose on adolescents. Among other things, adolescents are given more freedom to leave home without parental supervision. As a consequence, adolescents spend much less time with their parents, which reduces direct monitoring. In fact, time spent with parents declines by almost half as juveniles move from childhood to adolescence (Larson et al., 1996). Likewise, teachers exercise less direct control over adolescents than children. Adolescents attend larger schools, are in larger classes, and are more likely to change classes several times a day. These facts reduce the extent to which teachers can effectively monitor behavior.

Adolescents may also **experience a reduction in their stake in conformity.** Their ties to parents and teachers sometimes suffer as they get into disputes with them over issues involving the privileges and responsibilities of adolescence. For example, adolescents and parents argue about things like curfews, appropriate dress, access to the family car, and the amount of time that should be spent on homework. Further, many adolescents experience a reduction in grades and satisfaction with school, reflecting the increased demands at school and the reduced support provided by school officials.

Finally, adolescents often **become less likely to condemn delinquency and exercise self-control.** The influence of parents on adolescent beliefs regarding delinquency is often reduced, since adolescents have weaker ties to parents and stronger ties to peers, who sometimes challenge parental beliefs. Also, the biological changes mentioned earlier often result in a reduction in self-control, with adolescents being less able to control their emotions.

Individuals, however, **experience an increase in control when they leave adolescence and enter adulthood.** Adults usually develop strong ties to their families and jobs, which increase their direct control and stake in conformity. Several studies suggest that such ties result in reductions in offending (see the reviews in Cernkovich and Giordano, 2001; Laub and Sampson, 2001). Further, data suggest that adults experience an increase in self-control. This occurs partly for biological reasons; hormonal surges subside and the prefrontal cortex of the brain becomes fully developed. Also, the increased ties of adults to family and work (and the reduced ties to peers) foster beliefs that condemn crime.

An Increase in the Social Learning for Crime

Social learning theory focuses on the extent to which juveniles associate with others who teach beliefs favorable to delinquency, model delinquency, and reinforce delinquency, with the theory arguing that delinquent peers are especially likely to engage in these activities. Data suggest that adolescents are much more likely than children and adults to associate with such peers. For example, one study based on a national sample of adolescents found the following: at age 11, approximately 9 of 10 respondents reported that none of their friends had used alcohol during the past year; at age 18, this figure had fallen to approximately 1 in 10 (Warr, 1993; also see Elliott and Menard, 1996). Similar, although less dramatic, figures were reported for other forms of delinquency. Further, adolescents spend more time with their peers, place more importance on peer activities, and are more loyal to their peers than are children and adults. A good part of the association between age and crime is explained by the increased association of adolescents with delinquent peers (see Warr, 2002).

But why are adolescents **more likely than children and adults to associate with delinquent peers?** Part of the answer has to do with the fact that adolescents have more freedom to associate with delinquent peers. Adolescents are subject to less direct control than children and adults. And they do not have the family and work responsibilities of adults. Further, adolescents have more exposure to delinquent peers, since they spend more time on the street and attend large, secondary schools populated by peers, including delinquent peers. Finally, adolescents are more attracted to delinquent peers. Adolescents are somewhat alienated from parents and teachers and are often drawn to delinquent peers because such peers possess many of the adult privileges they desire. Delinquent peers, in particular, usually drink, engage in sex, stay out late, have money, and demand to be treated with respect by others.

An Increase in Strain

Adolescents experience more strain than children and adults (see Agnew, 1997, 2003a; Greenberg, 1977). Adolescents are **more likely to have trouble achieving their goals.** In particular, adolescents come to desire many of the privileges of adults, like increased autonomy, money, and status. This desire partly stems from the fact that adolescents are physically mature and have certain adult responsibilities, which fosters the belief that they deserve adult privileges. Also, adolescents see that many of their peers, especially delinquent peers, have these privileges (see Agnew, 2003a; Moffitt, 1993).

At the same time, adolescents are often denied the money, autonomy, and status they desire. For example, parents limit their spending money and restrict their activities, and teachers and other adults sometimes treat them in a demeaning manner. As a consequence, adolescents become frustrated and may turn to delinquency. Delinquency may be a means of obtaining adult privileges (e.g., curfew violation, income-generating crimes), seeking revenge against those who deny adult privileges, or coping with the emotional problems that result from the denial of adult privileges (e.g., drinking to make oneself feel better). Children, by contrast, are not as interested in adult privileges as adolescents are. And adults are better able to obtain such privileges through legal channels. Adults, for example, are legally entitled to drink, stay out late, and engage in certain sexual activities. And adults are better able to obtain the money they need through work.

Adolescents are also **more likely to experience the loss of positive stimuli or presentation of negative stimuli.** In particular, adolescents live in a larger and less protected social world than children and adults live in, which increases the likelihood that they will be negatively treated by others. Adolescents leave elementary school and enter larger, more impersonal, and more diverse secondary schools. Partly as a consequence, they come to interact with a larger and more diverse group of peers, including delinquent peers. Much of their interaction with peers occurs away from adults, especially in the evenings and on weekends. This dramatic increase in the size of their social world is itself likely to be stressful, but it also increases the likelihood of negative treatment, since adolescents are interacting with many more people—often in unsupervised settings. As adolescents become adults, however, their social world begins to narrow again, and they have more control over the nature of this world (for example, they have some choice over where they live and work). Some data support the argument that adolescents experience more strains or stressors than children and adults (see Agnew, 1997, 2003a).

Finally, adolescents are **less able to legally cope with the strains they experience.** Adolescents have **fewer coping skills and resources** than adults. In particular, the biological conditions associated with adolescence make adolescents more sensitive to strains and more likely to react to them in a delinquent manner. Adolescents also have less experience at coping and fewer coping resources, like money and power, than adults. For example, due to their limited power, adolescents are "compelled to live with their family in a certain neighborhood; to go to a certain school; and, within limits, to interact with the same group of peers and neighbors" (Agnew, 1985a:156). If any of these contexts is aversive, there is often little that adolescents can do to legally cope. Adults, however, can divorce their partners, move to new neighborhoods, change jobs, and change their friends if they experience strain in any of these arenas. Adolescents have more coping skills and resources than children have, but children are usually under the protection of adults, who cope on their behalf. Further, adolescents are often **more disposed to delinquency.** They are more likely to associate with delinquent peers, for example, who provide delinquent models, teach beliefs favorable to delinquency, and reinforce delinquency. Adolescents, then, are more likely to cope with strain through delinquency than are children or adults.

Summary

The biological and social changes associated with adolescence lead to a reduction in control, especially direct control; an increase in the social learning for crime, as reflected in the marked increase in association with delinquent peers; an increase in strain; and an increase in the likelihood of coping with strain through delinquency. That is why most individuals increase their levels of offending during adolescence.

About 5 to 10 percent of adolescents are shielded from the effects described in this section and manage to refrain from delinquency. For example, they experience delayed puberty, they remain closely supervised by parents, and/or they avoid contact with delinquent peers. They may avoid contact with delinquent peers because they are shy and withdrawn, because they have strong ties to their parents and teachers, or because they are in settings where delinquent peer groups are less common—such as all-female schools (see Moffitt, 1993, 2006; Piquero et al., 2003, 2005).

Why Do a Small Percentage of Individuals Offend at High Rates over Much of Their Lives?

While most individuals tend to limit their offending to the adolescent years, about 4 to 10 percent of the population become "life-course persistent" offenders. Such individuals start offending at high rates early in life, they engage in both minor and serious crimes, and their offending often continues well into middle age.

One can get the flavor of these life-course persistent offenders by considering the case of a 10-year-old boy recently described in the *New York Times*. Even though this boy had not yet reached adolescence, it appears that he was already involved in much crime. According to the article:

> He caused trouble. But he was 10. How much trouble could he cause? He yanked out shrubs, or pounded them with his bat. He peeled the siding off neighbors' houses. He pelted dogs with rocks. He shoved classmates, and heckled them. . . . [Authorities] accused him of molesting and murdering 3-year-old Amir Beeks, after spiriting him from a library. Authorities said he beat Amir with a baseball bat . . . and left the 3-year-old to die inside a storm drain at the edge of his yard. . . . Because of his age, the suspect is not being publicly identified by the police. Those in Woodbridge [where the murder occurred] already know who he is. Many of his neighbors tell of having sampled his caustic nature. "Since I knew him, he's always been bad," said a 10-year-old who had been a classmate of the boy. . . . "No one wanted to play with him because he was so mean." He was the scourge of the neighborhood. Other children might annoy neighbors by trampling across their lawns. His neighbors said that he would yank out flowers or smack shrubs with his baseball bat. He would scrawl on fences. He would throw rocks at neighborhood pets. Any animal he saw would become a target. "Anything you could think of doing he was already into" [said a neighbor]. (Kleinfield, 2003)

It seems clear that this boy had gone far beyond the occasional, largely minor delinquency typical of adolescence-limited offenders. It is not clear whether he will continue to offend at a high rate throughout his life, but his early history of high-rate and serious offending is typical of most life-course persistent offenders.

What accounts for life-course persistent offending? Life-course persistent offenders differ from the adolescence-limited offenders in that they tend to suffer from a number of related problems early in life. Most notably, they have traits conducive to crime, like low self-control and irritability, and they experience poor parenting. These problems tend to persist over time and they contribute to additional problems later in life, like poor school performance, association with delinquent peers, employment problems, and marital problems. All of these problems result in a reduction in control, an increase in social learning for crime, and an increase in strain. That is why these individuals offend at high rates over much of their lives.

Traits Conducive to Crime

Life-course persistent offenders tend to have a number of personality traits conducive to crime. Most notably, they tend to be **irritable and low in self-control.** That is, they are quick to anger, and they have trouble restraining themselves from acting on their immediate impulses. In popular terms, they might be described as "mean" and "out of control." Although data are limited, the 10-year-old offender described in the *New York Times* article seems to fit this characterization.

Life-course persistent offenders **develop these traits early in life.** Certain **biological factors** increase the likelihood of developing these traits (see Chapter 13). In particular, these traits are inherited from parents to some degree, and they may also result from experiencing certain "biological harms," like birth complications and exposure to toxic substances like lead. **Poor parenting practices** also increase the likelihood of developing these traits. In particular, these traits are more likely to develop when parents fail to teach their children how to control their anger and exercise self-control. Parents, for example, may fail to effectively sanction children for angry outbursts and acting on immediate desires. Some of the neighbors of the 10-year-old boy described earlier said that the boy was poorly supervised by his blind father and that other family problems may have been present. The traits of irritability and low self-control are especially likely to develop when individuals with a biological predisposition for them experience poor parenting.

The traits of irritability and low self-control increase offending for reasons related to control, social learning, and strain theories. Individuals with these traits are, by definition, lower in self-control; that is, they have trouble restraining themselves from crime. These individuals are more likely to find crime rewarding, since they are often angry with others and they have a strong need for the immediate gratification of their desires. And these individuals are more easily upset by strains and disposed to respond to strain with crime. So, if provoked, they are more likely to become upset and respond in an aggressive manner.

Poor Parenting

Life-course persistent offenders also tend to experience poor parenting early in life. Their parents often reject them, fail to effectively supervise and discipline them, and treat them in a harsh or abusive manner. **There are several causes of this poor parenting** (see Chapter 14; Patterson et al., 1992). The parents themselves may be irritable and low in self-control, which increases the likelihood that they will neglect their children or respond to them in a harsh manner. The parents may be poor; data suggest that the stressors associated with poverty are a major cause of poor parenting. And the parents may have children who are irritable and low in self-control. These children are quite difficult to manage, and parents sometimes give up trying to discipline them or become so angry that they treat them in a harsh or abusive manner. (So poor parenting and irritability and low self-control are reciprocally related. Having kids who are irritable and low in self-control is a major cause of poor parenting, and poor parenting is a major cause of irritability and low self-control.)

Poor parenting also increases offending for reasons related to control, social learning, and strain theories. Juveniles who experience poor parenting are, by definition, subject to poor direct control by parents and weakly bonded to parents. Such juveniles also experience social learning for crime, since their abusive parents function as deviant models for them, sometimes teach them beliefs conducive to crime, and sometimes reinforce aggressive behavior. And such juveniles are high in strain, since their parents treat them in a harsh or abusive manner.

High Rates of Offending over the Life Course

Life-course persistent offenders, then, tend to start out as troubled individuals in troubled families. Their traits and family environment lead them to engage in high rates of deviance at an early age. They are aggressive, they lie, cheat, and steal, they are difficult to control, and they devote little effort to conventional pursuits like schoolwork.

Such individuals offend at high rates over the life course partly because **their traits and poor family experiences persist over time.** That is, individuals who are irritable and low in self-control as children tend to be irritable and low in self-control as adults. And individuals who experience poor parenting as children tend to have family problems as adolescents. This persistence partly stems from the fact that the causes of irritability/low self-control and poor parenting persist over time. For example, the biological factors that cause irritability and the poverty that causes poor parenting often persist over time. The persistence of these traits and parenting practices is also due to the fact that they have consequences that contribute to their continued existence. For example, irritability and low self-control contribute to poor parenting, which in turn contributes to further irritability and low self-control.

These traits and poor parenting experiences also contribute to high rates of offending over the life course because **they lead to school, peer, marital, and work problems.** Juveniles with these traits and experiences are more likely to dislike and perform poorly at school and work; they simply do not have the discipline and skills that are necessary to do well in these settings. Also, these juveniles are more likely to elicit negative reactions from others. Individuals with these traits and experiences are not pleasant people, and they often exasperate and irritate others. As a consequence, they are more likely to be avoided or treated in a negative manner by others. For example, school officials may place them in special tracks or schools for "problem" students. Conventional peers may reject them, causing them to associate with delinquent peers. Romantic partners may reject them or treat them harshly, and employers may refuse to hire them or may fire them. These additional problems also contribute to high rates of offending over the life course by reducing control, fostering the social learning of crime, and increasing strain. (These arguments, of course, are similar to those made by labeling theory, which argues that the individual's delinquency often elicits reactions from others that contribute to further delinquency.)

Summary

Life-course persistent offenders tend to experience poor parenting and develop traits conducive to delinquency early in life. These traits and poor parenting contribute to high rates of offending over the life course partly because they tend to persist over time and partly because they lead to additional problems with peers, school, romantic partners, and employers.

Unlike adolescence-limited offenders, life-course persistent offenders do not stop offending when they become adults, because their offending is **not** rooted in the biological and social changes associated with adolescence. Rather, it is rooted in ongoing problems that originate during the childhood years. Further, the family, school, and other problems experienced by life-course persistent offenders are more serious than those experienced by adolescence-limited offenders. This also makes it more difficult for life-course persistent offenders to escape from a life of crime.

These arguments have limited support. A few recent studies suggest that life-course persistent offenders are more likely than other individuals to have traits conducive to crime and to experience poor parenting early in life and that these early problems create additional problems over the life course—problems usually more severe than those experienced by the adolescence-limited offenders.[3]

But having said this, I should note that not all juveniles who experience poor parenting and irritability/low self-control early in life become life-course persistent offenders. While such juveniles have a much greater risk of becoming life-course persistent offenders, some manage to substantially reduce their levels of offending when they become adults. This usually occurs because they obtain decent jobs, get involved in good marriages, or have other life-changing experiences, like participation in the military or involvement in effective rehabilitation programs. It is not yet entirely clear why some of these individuals are able to turn their lives around in this manner while others are not, but this topic is starting to receive a good deal of attention by criminologists.[4]

Summary

The integrated theories in this chapter try to explain patterns of offending over the course of the individual's life. The first theory focuses on the "adolescence-limited" pattern of offending and the second on the "life-course persistent" pattern. Both of these theories represent extensions of strain, social learning, and control theories. The first theory argues that certain of the biological and social changes associated with adolescence lead to a reduction in control, an increase in the social learning for crime, and an increase in strain during adolescence. The second theory argues that certain biological and social factors lead some individuals to experience low levels of control, much social learning for crime, and high levels of strain over a good portion of their lives.

Teaching Aids

Controversial Issue: An Evolutionary Theory of Adolescence-Limited Offending

One of the first modern theories of crime and delinquency, that of Lombroso (1911), explained life-course persistent offending in terms of evolutionary theory. A large portion of the habitual offenders who committed serious crimes were said to be "genetic throwbacks," individuals who were not as evolved as other people. These genetic throwbacks were savages in the midst of modern society, and it was their savage or primitive nature that led them to engage in crime. Lombroso described certain of the physical characteristics of these individuals, like enormous jaws, flattened noses, arm span greater than the individual's height, and prehensile feet (feet capable of grabbing or picking up things). Individuals with such characteristics resemble the stereotypical "caveman."

Lombroso's theory was discredited when research revealed that most of the characteristics he listed failed to distinguish criminals from carefully matched samples of noncriminals. And evolutionary theories of crime—as well as biological theories of crime more generally—fell into decline for much of the 20th century. Also contributing to this decline was the fact that many people were disturbed by the racist elements of the early evolutionary theories (certain race and ethic groups were sometimes said to be biologically predisposed to crime). Many people were also disturbed by the policy implications of these theories. Certain of these theories, in particular, contributed to the eugenics movement, which sought to prevent certain categories of people from reproducing (for overviews, see Rafter, 1997; Vold et al., 1998).

Recently, however, evolutionary (and biological) theories of crime have experienced a revival. The new evolutionary and biological theories are much more sophisticated than the older theories. These new theories, however, still elicit some controversy. Evolutionary theories have been used to explain both life-course persistent and adolescence-limited offending.[5] As Ellis and Walsh (1997:232) point out, all such theories are based on a "simple but powerful idea: to the degree that a particular characteristic is prevalent in the population, it is likely to have contributed to the reproductive success of the individuals currently living."

One evolutionary theory of adolescence-limited offending argues that when males reach puberty they become involved in an effort to find a mate, protect that mate from rivals, and produce children. Males who are aggressive and attractive to females are more likely to be successful in this effort. As Rowe (2002:54) states, "The teenage boy needs to quickly establish his reputation [for aggression, among other things] and to acquire the material things that make him attractive to the opposite sex, which can be anything from a surfboard to a low-rider car." Aggressive and attractive males, then, are more likely to reproduce and thereby pass their genes on to their children. But once males find a mate and produce children, competition with other males becomes less critical. In fact, competition can be costly, threatening the physical well-being of males and reducing their ability to care for their children. Rather, males who provide material support and parenting help are more likely to have their children survive and do well, and these children then pass their genes on to still others. So, engaging in supportive behavior now provides a reproductive advantage.

According to this theory, then, the evolutionary process selects for males who are aggressive in adolescence (when seeking and protecting mates) and more supportive in adulthood (when raising children). Such males are most likely to have their genes passed on to others. This theory is said to explain such things as the increase in testosterone during adolescence and the decline during adulthood. And, more generally, it is said to explain why adolescents are generally more aggressive than children and adults (see Rowe, 1996, 2002).

This theory has not yet been fully tested, but certain data are said to be compatible with it. For example, Rowe (1996) states that the rapid increase in male testosterone levels during adolescence is correlated with both an increase in sexual activity and delinquency. And marriage is said to result in a decrease in testosterone levels. Can you think of additional ways in which we might test or explore the accuracy of this theory? If correct, does this theory mean that the social conditions associated with adolescence have little effect on adolescence-limited offending? How might evolutionary theory explain the fact that males are more likely to engage in most forms of crime than females (see Ellis and Walsh, 1997; Rowe, 1996)? What are the policy implications of evolutionary theories (see Raine, 1993; Rowe, 1996, 2002)? What is your overall reaction to such theories?

TEST YOUR KNOWLEDGE OF THIS CHAPTER

1. Describe the adolescence-limited and life-course persistent patterns of offending.
2. Briefly describe the integrated theories of adolescence-limited and life-course persistent offending presented in this chapter.
3. Why are adolescents granted some, but not all, of the privileges and responsibilities of adulthood? Describe some of the privileges and responsibilities granted to adolescents.
4. Describe how these privileges and/or responsibilities may reduce control, foster the social learning of crime, and increase strain.
5. Why do most adolescents reduce their level of offending when they become adults?
6. How do life-course persistent offenders differ from adolescence-limited offenders (in terms of traits and early life experiences)?
7. Why do the traits and family experiences of life-course persistent offenders tend to persist over time?
8. Describe how these traits and family experiences reduce control, foster the social learning of crime, and increase strain.
9. Why do these traits and family experiences lead to school, peer, marital, and work problems? Describe how arguments in this area are similar to those made by labeling theorists.
10. Adolescence-limited offenders reduce their level of offending when they become adults. Why don't life-course persistent offenders do the same?
11. Describe why some of the individuals who experience poor parenting and irritability/low self-control early in life do *not* become life-course persistent offenders.

THOUGHT AND DISCUSSION QUESTIONS

1. Is it possible to alter those biological and social changes associated with adolescence in ways that reduce offending? If so, how?
2. Can you think of additional reasons, beyond those presented in this chapter, why adolescents are more likely to engage in crime than children and adults?
3. Even though they are a small percentage of the population, life-course persistent offenders account for a large share of all delinquency, especially serious delinquency. How should we respond to them? For example, some argue that juvenile justice agencies should focus their resources on such offenders, attempting to identify them as early as possible, offer them treatment, and punish them severely if treatment is not effective. Do you agree?

KEY TERMS

- Adolescence-limited offending
- Life-course persistent offending

ENDNOTES

1. For overviews of the theories and research in this area, *see* Agnew, 2003a; Benson, 2002; Cullen and Agnew, 2003; Farrington, 2005, 2006; Le Blanc and Loeber, 1998; Moffitt, 1993, 1997, 2006; Nagin and Tremblay, 2005a; Piquero and Mazerolle, 2001; Sampson and Laub, 1993a; Smith, 2002; Thornberry, 1997; Tittle, 2000.

2. For overviews, *see* Benson, 2002:69–70; Raine, 2002a; Walsh, 2002.

3. *See* Agnew, 2005; Aguilar et al., 2000; Brame et al., 1999; Farrington, 2005; Fergusson et al., 2000; Lahey and Waldman, 2006; Moffitt and Harrington, 1996; Moffitt et al., 2001; Patterson et al., 1989; Patterson et al., 1998; Simons et al., 1994, 2002; Thornberry and Krohn, 2005; Thornberry et al., 2003a; Wiesner and Capaldi, 2003; Wright et al., 1999b.

4. *See* Giordano et al., 2002; Laub and Sampson, 2001; Laub et al., 2006; Shover, 1996; Simons et al., 2002.

5. For excellent overviews, *see* Cullen and Agnew, 2006; Ellis and Walsh, 1997; Raine, 1993; Rowe, 2002; Walsh, 2002.

CHAPTER 11

Is Delinquency More Likely in Certain Types of Situations?

The theories examined thus far focus on the factors that create a general *predisposition* or willingness to engage in delinquency. Such factors include high levels of strain, social learning for crime, low levels of control, and being labeled a delinquent (in some cases). Individuals who are predisposed to delinquency tend to commit more delinquent acts than others, as indicated in Chapters 6 through 9. And certain individuals tend to commit more delinquent acts at those times of their lives when their predisposition to delinquency is strongest, as indicated in Chapter 10. But **even the most predisposed individuals do not commit delinquent acts all of the time. In fact, they spend most of their time engaged in nondelinquent activities.** Decker and Van Winkle (1996:118–119) make this point in their field study of gang members:

> Gang members spend much of their time together being "normal" teenagers or young adults: hanging out at each others' homes, in parks, on street corners, at fast food joints, malls, skating rinks, bowling alleys, and youth clubs. When we asked subjects "What do you do the most with other gang members?" the dominant answer was "hang out" (or one of the many equivalents—"chill out," "playing," "hang," "fuck around"). . . . Nearly two-thirds of the responses involved fairly innocuous and non-criminal behaviors.

Whether predisposed individuals engage in delinquency depends heavily on the types of situations they encounter. The first part of this chapter draws on strain, control, and social learning theories to describe those situations most conducive to delinquency. The second part of the chapter discusses the factors that influence the likelihood that predisposed individuals will encounter such situations. The arguments made draw heavily on the work of Akers (1990), Birkbeck and LaFree (1993), Cohen and Felson (1979), Colvin (2000), Cornish and Clarke (1986), Marcus Felson (2002, 2006), Richard Felson (1993), Finkelor and Asdigian (1996), Kennedy and Forde (1999), Miethe and McCorkle (2001), Osgood et al. (1996), Sherman et al. (1989), Tedeschi and Felson (1994), and Wilcox et al. (2003).

Describing those situations most conducive to delinquency not only helps us predict when predisposed juveniles will engage in delinquency but also has important policy implications. In particular, it is sometimes difficult to reduce the individual's predisposition for delinquency. But it may still be possible to reduce the amount of delinquency the individual commits by **altering the situations he or she encounters.** For example, we know that delinquent acts are more likely to be committed in the hours immediately after school, when juveniles are more likely to be in situations where they are involved in unstructured, unsupervised activities with peers. We might, therefore, reduce delinquency by creating structured, after-school programs for juveniles (see Chapter 24).

What Types of Situations Are Most Conducive to Delinquency?

While the leading delinquency theories focus on the factors that predispose juveniles to delinquency, we can draw on these theories and certain other research to describe the types of situations most likely to result in delinquency. In particular, juveniles are most likely to engage in delinquency when they are in situations where (1) they are provoked or face other situational strains; (2) alcohol or drugs are being used, which increases the likelihood of delinquent coping; (3) the costs of delinquency are seen as low (i.e., control is low); and (4) the benefits of delinquency are seen as high (i.e., the anticipated reinforcement for delinquency is high).[1]

Strain Theory: Situational Strains

Strain theory argues that delinquency is most likely to occur in situations where individuals are subject to strain. Several types of situational strain have been described in the literature. The most common type is **provocations by others,** especially verbal and physical attacks that are perceived as deliberate. Several researchers state that such attacks are especially likely to provoke a violent response, particularly when males are attacked by other males.[2] Such attacks involve the presentation of negative stimuli, and they may also be seen as threats to one's status, especially on the part of certain males who view them as threats to their masculine status, or "manhood."

Using data from a national sample of adolescents, Agnew (1990a) found that over 60 percent of the juveniles engaging in assault said they did so because they were intentionally provoked in some way. Among other things, they said that they were insulted, annoyed, threatened, molested, or had their property damaged or taken. Being provoked or mistreated by others was also the main reason given for vandalism and running away. Provocations, however, were not a major cause of income-generating crimes, like theft.

A study by Lockwood (1997) also highlights the central role of provocations in producing violence. Lockwood interviewed 110 middle school and high school students from schools with high rates of violence. These students discussed 250 violent incidents in which they had been involved. About half of these incidents occurred at school; others occurred in public areas (e.g., sidewalks, streets, and parks) and homes. Most of these incidents involved acquaintances (58 percent); others involved friends (16 percent) and family members (15 percent). Only 11 percent involved strangers. The most common setting for a violent incident, then, was an encounter with an acquaintance at school. These violent incidents almost always began when one of the students did something that the other student did not like, that is, when one student provoked the other. The most common provocation was "offensive touching," such as pushing, grabbing, hitting, or throwing something. Other provocations included interfering with someone's possessions, refusing to do something when requested, saying something bad about someone to someone else, verbally teasing someone, and deliberately insulting someone. Such provocations typically led to an argument, the argument escalated and insults were exchanged, and violence was the result. Violence was performed to end the disliked behavior, seek revenge, and/or save face (also see Garofalo et al., 1987; Wilkinson, 2002).

It is important to stress that **many offenders are not the innocent victims of provocations by others.** Data suggest that many offenders mistreat others and, in doing so, elicit negative reactions from them (see Felson, R., 1993; Jensen and Brownfield, 1986). They then respond to these negative reactions with delinquency. A school bully, for example, may regularly "pick on" or harass another juvenile. When the harassed juvenile complains, the bully may respond with violence, claiming that he or she was "provoked." Many offenders behave in ways that call forth "provocations," or negative responses, from others.

When offenders are provoked, they may immediately attack the victim. As just suggested, however, the offender and victim more commonly engage in a series of verbal exchanges. The offender, for example, may demand that the victim apologize. The victim may refuse. The offender may then insult the victim. The victim, in turn, may reply with an insult. Neither the victim nor the offender is willing to back down, and violence eventually results. Audience members, if present, often contribute to the escalation of hostilities by encouraging violence.

Other types of situational strain have received less attention, although **data suggest that income-generating crimes are often produced by a desperate need for cash.** In particular, individuals are in situations where they believe they desperately need money, perhaps to purchase drugs, pay off gambling debts, finance their partying lifestyle or "high living," or survive on the street. Many engage in crimes like shoplifting, burglary, robbery, drug selling, and prostitution to get the money they need (e.g., Bennett and Wright, 1984; Wright and Decker, 1997). Still other situational strains involve **threats to autonomy** (e.g., parents or teachers prevent adolescents from engaging in a desired activity) and the **loss of positive stimuli** (e.g., romantic breakups, the murder of a friend).

There have been some **efforts to reduce crime by reducing situational strains.** For example, areas with lots of bars often have high rates of violence, especially when the bars close and the patrons pour out onto the streets. The inebriated patrons often get into confrontations with one another, and many of these confrontations are settled in a violent manner. Some jurisdictions have attempted to reduce the likelihood of such confrontations or provocations by staggering bar closing hours, so that not everyone pours out onto the street at the same time. To give another example, soccer violence in Britain has been reduced by separating rival fans in the stadium and taking steps to ensure that fans do not spend longs periods of time waiting around before or after the game.[3] (See Chapter 24 for additional information.)

Strain Theory: Situational Factors That Increase the Likelihood of Delinquent Coping

Predisposed individuals, then, are more likely to engage in delinquency when they are in strainful situations. But not all predisposed individuals respond to strainful situations with delinquency. Kennedy and Baron (1993), for example, found that this was the case with the punk rockers they examined in their field study. While these punk rockers were known for their violent behavior, Kennedy and Baron (1993:100) state:

> [We were] quite surprised at the amount of verbal abuse that [the punk rockers] absorbed without retaliatory measures. Passersby frequently made derogatory remarks about members' sexual preferences and "manliness." The members' appearance also made them the center of attention. Individuals passing by the group often stared and often made negative comments. This type of response was more noticeable when members were alone, away from the group, walking the downtown streets.

Kennedy and Baron go on to state that the punk rockers were more likely to retaliate in some situations than in others. For example, retaliation was more likely when the punk rockers were with one another and away from busy streets, where passersby might intervene.

More generally, a delinquent response to situational strain is most likely when **features of the situation increase the individual's sensitivity to strain, reduce the individual's ability to legally cope, reduce the perceived costs of delinquency, and increase the perceived benefits of delinquency.** In this area, the **use of alcohol and certain drugs like barbiturates** may increase the likelihood of a delinquent response by increasing the individual's sensitivity to provocations. Such drugs may also reduce the individual's ability to engage in legal coping, like negotiating with others. For example, one 17-year-old daily crack user stated:

> It doesn't seem to matter if you're on or off crack. . . . [Y]ou're crazy both times. If you're high, you think someone's goin' do something to you, or try an' take your stuff. If you're comin' down or waiting to make a buy or just get off, you seem to get pissed off easy. . . . A lot of people been cut just because somebody looked at them funny or said somethin' stupid. (Quoted in Inciardi et al., 1993:104).

Further, such drugs may reduce the individual's awareness of and concern with the costs of delinquency.[4] For example, one shoplifter stated:

> When I'm drunk or stoned, it's like I'm invisible. No, it's like I'm Superman. I ain't scared of nothing. Nobody can touch me. It seems like that's what always gets me in trouble. I'll just walk in and take something and walk out. (Quoted in Cromwell et al., 1999:65)

Other situational factors that increase the likelihood of delinquent coping are discussed in the following sections. They include the presence of attractive targets, the absence of capable guardians, and the presence of delinquent peers. These factors lead the juvenile to conclude that the costs of delinquent coping are low and the benefits are high. (Also see the discussion of guns in Chapter 17; some evidence suggests that the presence of guns in a situation increases the likelihood of delinquent coping.)

Social Learning and Control Theories: The Benefits and Costs of Delinquency

I treat social learning and control theories together here, since the arguments they make overlap to some extent. According to these theories, **crime is most likely in situations where the benefits of delinquency are seen as high and the costs as low.** The benefits of delinquency may be **tangible,** like money or property, and they may be **intangible,** like social approval from others and the thrills or excitement associated with the crime (see Katz, 1988). Agnew (1990a), for example, found that most of the juveniles who had stolen things said they did so because they needed to obtain a certain item or because it was fun or enjoyable. The costs of delinquency include the **likelihood of being caught** and punished, as well as the **"moral costs"** of committing the crime. That is, how bad or guilty would the juvenile feel if he or she committed a crime in that situation?

Few researchers argue that juveniles carefully consider all of the benefits and costs of delinquency in a particular situation. Most juveniles (and adults) are not that rational or thoughtful. Researchers argue, however, that most juveniles give at least some limited thought to the rewards and costs of delinquency. For example, juveniles in a particular situation may not pause and carefully calculate the probability that they will be caught and punished if they commit a delinquent act. At the same time, they usually do not commit delinquent acts when their parents are present or the police are nearby. Thus, they give some rough consideration to the costs (and benefits) of delinquency. For example, offenders are generally more likely to attack smaller or weaker targets than larger or stronger ones. This fact partly explains why males are more likely to engage in aggression than females (Felson, R., 1996). The amount of consideration given to costs and benefits varies by the characteristics of the juvenile. For example, some juveniles are very impulsive; they often commit crimes with little thought as to the consequences. Other juveniles, however, are more thoughtful (see Tibbetts and Gibson, 2002).

Several researchers have discussed the features of a situation that influence the individual's calculation of benefits and costs. In the language of social learning theory, we might describe these features as "discriminative stimuli" (see Chapter 7). They indicate the probability that a delinquent act will be reinforced or punished in a given situation. For example, imagine a predisposed offender who encounters a luxury car parked on a deserted street with the key in the ignition. The features of this situation are such that the predisposed offender is likely to conclude that the benefits of auto theft are high and the costs are low. But if the same offender encounters an old, beat-up car in a well-lit parking lot with an attendant, he or she will likely conclude that the benefits of auto theft are low and the potential costs are high. More generally, individuals are more likely to believe that the benefits of crime are high and the costs are low when attractive targets for crime are available, capable guardians are absent, and delinquent peers are present.

Attractive Targets

The benefits of delinquency are more likely to be seen as high and the costs as low in situations where an *attractive target* is present.[5] With respect to property, **attractive targets are (1) visible and accessible, (2) valuable, (3) easy to move and/or concealable, (4) enjoyable,** and **(5) unlikely to provoke guilt if stolen.** In particular, predisposed offenders must be able to see the target and gain access to it. The target must be valuable, like cash or jewelry. It must be easy to move, like a DVD player or automobile (which can be driven). Related to this, many attractive targets are also easily concealed in one's pocket or a bag, which makes shoplifting much easier. Items like refrigerators and washing machines are valuable but are seldom stolen because they are difficult to move and conceal. The ideal targets have a high value in proportion to their weight. Marcus Felson (1998), for example, reports that washing machines cost about $5 per pound, while other electronic goods cost much more per pound and so are more likely to be stolen. Further, attractive targets are enjoyable to the adolescents who take them. This is one reason why adolescents are more likely to steal such things as DVDs, liquor, cosmetics, and clothing (versus things such as vitamins and milk). Finally, the target should be unlikely to provoke guilt in the offender if stolen, perhaps because it belongs to someone who is disliked or the offender believes that insurance will cover the loss of the theft.

With respect to people, **attractive targets are (1) visible and accessible, (2) thought to possess valuable items like cash and jewelry, (3) unlikely to offer effective resistance,** and **(4) unlikely to provoke guilt if attacked.** Predisposed individuals may believe that others possess valuable items for a variety of reasons; for example, these others may display or "flash" lots of money, have just exited ATMs or check cashing establishments, wear expensive clothes or jewelry, or handle large sums of money in their occupation (e.g., drug dealers, prostitutes). The perceived likelihood that others will offer effective resistance depends on things such as their size, whether they are part of a group, and whether they are intoxicated. (See Tark and Kleck, 2004, for a recent study examining the ways victims offer resistance and the effectiveness of such resistance in preventing injury and property loss.) Also, some categories of people are seen as less likely to call the police (e.g., illegal immigrants, or those involved in illegal activities). Finally, certain targets are less likely to provoke guilt than others because offenders believe they deserve to be victimized (e.g., they provoked the offender or are rival gang members) or that they will not be seriously harmed by their victimization (e.g., their insurance will cover the loss). For example, the criminologists studying the punk rockers known for their violence stated:

> When asked about their targets, members informed the researcher that their targets or victims were "geeks." The term geek suggested a subcultural neutralization of the victim's humanity. Geeks were unworthy of respect or fear. They were lower on the cultural totem pole than any of the other groups that gathered downtown. A geek was unfit even to be a member of a rival group (Kennedy and Baron, 1993:102)

There have been efforts to reduce crime by **making targets less attractive.** Some of these efforts involve reducing the value of targets. The robbery of bus drivers, for example, was dramatically reduced when transit companies installed theft-proof change boxes on buses and required exact change (which reduced the amount of money that drivers carry). Other efforts employ certain "target-hardening" techniques that make targets less visible, less accessible, or more difficult to move. Antitheft devices on automobiles and burglar bars on windows are examples. Still other efforts increase the ability of targets to offer effective resistance. For example, individuals purchase guns (see Chapter 17), obtain large dogs, or take self-defense classes. Finally, there have been efforts to increase the moral costs of committing crimes against certain targets. For example, stores try to educate shoppers about the harm caused by shoplifting, and retailers in certain areas try to improve relations with community residents. (See Chapter 24 for more information.)

The Absence of Capable Guardians

The costs of delinquency are likely to be seen as low when there is no one around who might interfere with the crime. Individuals who might interfere are sometimes described as *capable guardians* (see Felson, 1994, 2002). The police often function as capable guardians, but it is more common for ordinary people to play this role. For example, the presence of people walking the street at night is often enough to prevent a robbery. The presence of neighbors during the day is often enough to prevent a burglary, and the presence of teachers in the school cafeteria is often enough to prevent fights. Offenders fear that guardians may directly intervene if they commit a crime or that they may indirectly intervene by calling the police. Capable guardians with strong ties to juveniles, like parents and respected teachers, are said to be especially effective at preventing crime, since juveniles are more responsive to them.

There have been efforts to reduce crime by **increasing the likelihood that others will intervene.** For example, convenience stores are frequently the target of robberies. Research suggests that the likelihood of robbery can be reduced by altering the staffing and layout of such stores. In particular, potential offenders are less likely to rob stores where two clerks rather than one are on duty, when the cashier is visibly stationed in the middle of the store rather than off to the side, and when the store is surrounded by businesses open in the evening. Potential offenders avoid such stores because one clerk may intervene on behalf of the other and because the offenders do not want to risk encountering or being noticed by others who might intervene. To give additional examples, parking lots with attendants have lower rates of auto theft than those without, and large households have lower rates of victimization than small households. (See Chapter 24 for more information.)

The Presence of Delinquent Peers

The presence of peers, especially delinquent peers, also influences the perceived costs and benefits of delinquency in a particular situation. **Peers often reduce the costs of delinquency** by preventing retaliation from others, by helping the juvenile commit delinquent acts, and by convincing the juvenile that such acts are justifiable or excusable (thereby reducing the moral costs of crime). The presence of delinquent peers **may also increase the anticipated benefits of delinquency,** since delinquent peers often reinforce delinquent acts. Kennedy and Baron (1993), for example, state that the punk rockers in their study were more likely to respond to provocations with violence when their friends were around partly because they anticipated that their friends would reward such a response. Given these arguments, it should perhaps come as no surprise that most delinquent acts occur in situations where peers are present (see Chapter 16).

Summary

Delinquency is most likely in situations where predisposed offenders are provoked or experience other situational strains, where situational factors like alcohol and drug use increase the likelihood of delinquent coping, where the perceived benefits of crime are seen as high, and where the perceived costs are seen as low. Benefits are most likely to be perceived as high and costs as low when attractive targets are available, capable guardians are absent, and delinquent peers are present.

These statements may seem straightforward, but they have led to a number of important, not-so-obvious conclusions about delinquency. In particular, researchers have argued that the level of delinquency is dependent not only on the number of predisposed offenders but also on such things as the frequency of provocations, the supply of attractive targets, the presence of capable guardians, and the presence of delinquent others. In this area, I briefly described several crime control programs that reduced levels of offending **not** by reducing the predisposition for delinquency but by doing such things as reducing the frequency of provocations, reducing the supply of attractive targets, and increasing the presence of capable guardians.

What Factors Influence the Likelihood That Predisposed Offenders Will Encounter Situations Conducive to Delinquency?

Sometimes individuals who are predisposed to delinquency **deliberately seek out situations that are conducive to delinquency.** They are more likely to do so for property crimes than for violent crimes. Predisposed offenders might actively search for good homes to burglarize or individuals to rob. Several studies, however, suggest that such searching behavior is not as wide-ranging as some people believe (see Bottoms and Wiles, 2002; Miethe and McCorkle, 2001). Individuals tend to search for targets in areas that are convenient and familiar to them, so they select targets near their homes, near the places they frequent (like school and recreational sites), and along the routes they frequently travel (like the routes to and from school and the mall). Selection of targets in these areas requires less effort on their part, and they feel less conspicuous and more secure in these areas, since they know them well. Offenders, however, usually do not commit property crimes too close to home because they might be recognized. Violent crimes, on the other hand, are frequently committed close to home or in the juvenile's home, since they often involve family members, friends, and acquaintances.

At other times, predisposed offenders **do not deliberately seek out situations that are conducive to crime.** Rather, they **encounter such situations during the course of their everyday, routine activities**—attending school, going to work, and hanging out with friends. For example, a juvenile might spot a tempting target for burglary while on the way to school or might encounter a good opportunity for shoplifting while hanging out with friends at the mall. Violent crimes are especially likely to emerge out of everyday activities. Such crimes are usually not planned but rather stem from the frictions of everyday life, such as disputes at school.

Certain factors influence the likelihood that individuals will find or encounter situations that are conducive to crime. Most prominent among these factors is the nature of the individual's routine, or everyday, activities (see especially Felson, M., 2002).

The Nature of the Individual's Routine Activities

The nature of individuals' *routine activities* refers to what they do each day, with whom they do it, when they do it, and where they do it. As argued next, certain types of routine activities increase the likelihood of being in situations conducive to crime.

What juveniles do and with whom they do it. Juveniles who spend a lot of time in **unstructured, unsupervised activities with peers,** especially delinquent peers, are more likely to encounter situations conducive to crime.[6] Unstructured activities include hanging out, riding around in a car, going to parties, and certain other recreational activities. Unsupervised activities are those where capable guardians, like parents and teachers, are absent. Individuals who spend a lot of time in unstructured, unsupervised activities with delinquent peers are more likely to be in situations where capable guardians are absent and delinquent peers are present. This lowers the perceived costs of delinquency and increases the perceived benefits. Also, such individuals are more likely to be in situations where they are provoked, since delinquent peers often provoke one another and get into conflicts with others.

When they do it. Crimes involving juveniles are more frequent on school days, and tend to occur before, during, and in the few hours after school (Gottfredson and Soule, 2005; Snyder and Sickmund, 2006). This temporal pattern is easily explained, since it is at these times that peers are most likely to be involved in activities with one another, often in unstructured, unsupervised settings (e.g., hanging out before or after school, interacting in school hallways or the cafeteria). It should be noted, however, that drug use displays a somewhat different temporal pattern. Drug use is less likely during school hours. While it might be easy to obtain and take drugs during school hours, the lingering effects of drug use might be detected by teachers. Drugs are more likely to be used after school and especially on weekends.

Where they do it. Public settings are generally more conducive to delinquency than private settings. In fact, each hour spent in public space is about 10 times more risky than each hour spent at home (Felson, M., 1994:39). Also, data suggest that certain locations are especially conducive to delinquency. Delinquency is most likely in settings that bring young people together in the absence of capable guardians. Such settings include the area around schools and the routes to and from school. As indicated, much crime occurs as juveniles are leaving school. When crime does occur in school, it is more likely to occur in hallways and restrooms than in classrooms, where teachers are typically present. Other locations, like bars, are also risky. Bars often bring together large numbers of young, intoxicated males.

Factors Influencing Routine Activities

Age and sex have an especially strong effect on routine activities. Adolescents are much more likely than other age groups to engage in unstructured, unsupervised activities with peers. This fact partly explains why crime rates peak in adolescence. Also, males are more likely than females to engage in unstructured, unsupervised activities with peers. This fact partly explains the gender difference in delinquency (see Osgood et al., 1996). Routine activities are also influenced by many of the factors that affect the juvenile's predisposition for delinquency, like the juvenile's **level of parental supervision, commitment to school,** and **level of self-control.** In particular, such factors increase the likelihood of engaging in routine activities that involve exposure to situations conducive to delinquency. For example, juveniles who are poorly supervised by parents are more likely to engage in unstructured, unsupervised activities with peers.

I should also note that **larger social and technological changes may influence the nature of routine activities and, in doing so, affect levels of delinquency.** For example, increases in parental work, single-parent families, and multicar households have led to a sharp decline in parental supervision since the 1950s. Parents are less likely to be home after school, they are less likely to engage in shared activities with their children, and they grant their children more freedom than in the past. Children today, for example, have fewer chores or duties around the house, later curfews, and greater access to automobiles. This decline in parental supervision, in turn, has led to a change in the routine activities of juveniles: Juveniles now spend more time with peers away from parents. This may partly explain the large increase in juvenile crime rates during the 1960s and early 1970s.

To give another example, technological advances have led to a dramatic increase in the number of lightweight, valuable products, like DVD players, VCRs, and computers. As a consequence, offenders are more likely to encounter attractive property targets during the course of their routine activities. Related to this, there has been a change in merchandising over the last few decades. Products are now more likely to be displayed on open shelves in large, high-volume stores with a limited number of clerks. The potential cost of shoplifting in such stores is much lower than in small stores, where goods are often kept behind the counter. These changes also may have contributed to increases in juvenile offending over the years. (For an excellent discussion of the impact of larger social and technological changes on routine activities and situations conducive to crime, see Marcus Felson, 1998. Felson argues that the recent decrease in crime partly reflects the fact that people are using cash less and credit or debit cards more.)

Summary

Individuals may deliberately seek out situations conducive to delinquency or they may encounter such situations during the course of their everyday, routine activities. Individuals who frequently engage in unstructured activities with peers in the absence of authority figures are especially likely to find themselves in situations conducive to delinquency. Adolescents, males, and those who are poorly supervised by their parents, among others, are more likely to fall into this category.

Summary

Delinquency is most likely to occur when predisposed juveniles encounter situations conducive to delinquency. The situations most conducive to delinquency are those where (1) juveniles are provoked or experience other situational strains, (2) factors like alcohol or drug use increase the likelihood of delinquent coping, (3) the perceived benefits of delinquency are high, and (4) the perceived costs are low. These factors interact in their effect on delinquency, that is, each factor conditions the effect of the other factors on delinquency. For example, provocations are more likely to lead to delinquency in situations where the costs of delinquency are low and the benefits are high.

Predisposed individuals may seek out situations conducive to delinquency. Also, predisposed individuals may encounter such situations during the course of their everyday or routine activities. Most notably, individuals who engage in unstructured, unsupervised activities with peers are especially likely to find themselves in situations with these four characteristics.

Teaching Aids

Applying the Research: Examining Your Own Routine Activities

1. The following exercise and most of the accompanying questions are taken from Felson (2002) and Felson and Gottfredson (1984). Answer each of the questions and then have someone who was a teenager in the 1950s or before (perhaps a parent or grandparent) answer these questions. How do the two sets of responses compare? (With your instructor's assistance, you might summarize the answers obtained by your classmates before comparing the two sets of responses.) How are these questions relevant to the explanation of delinquency? How might differences in the two sets of responses help explain increases in the rate of delinquency since the 1950s? (See Felson, 2002, Chapter 5, if you need assistance.)

    a. When you were 17, were you at home between 3 p.m. and 6 p.m. on weekdays always, most of the time, some of the time, or never?

    b. When you were at home between 3 p.m. and 6 p.m. on weekdays, was an adult there with you?

    c. On weekdays, did you have any regular household chores or duties to perform in the afternoon?

    d. Did all the members of your household usually eat the evening meal together on weekdays?

    e. When you were 17, were you at home between 9 p.m. and 12 p.m. on weekends always, most of the time, some of the time, or never?

    f. When you were 17, did your family own two or more automobiles?

2. The routine activities in which people engage not only influence the likelihood they will engage in crime but also influence the likelihood they will be crime victims (by influencing their exposure to predisposed offenders, how well guarded they or their property are, how attractive they or their property are as crime targets, and so on). For example, individuals who spend a lot of time out alone at night drinking in bars are more likely to be victimized. Such individuals are more

likely to encounter predisposed offenders, they are less likely to offer effective re-sistance (since they have been drinking), and they are less likely to have capable guardians come to their assistance.

Mustaine and Tewksbury (1998a) examined whether the routine activities of students in nine colleges and universities influenced the extent to which they were victims of minor theft (property worth less than $50) and major theft (property worth more than $50). The students were asked about a wide range of routine activities (what they do, when they do it, where they do it, whom they do it with). The following activities and individual and/or community characteristics were found to increase or decrease the likelihood of major theft:

- Threatened another with a gun (increases likelihood of major theft)
- Threatened another with no weapon (increases)
- Frequently eats out (increases)
- Neighborhood is too noisy (increases)
- Dog in residence (decreases)
- Installed extra locks (decreases)
- Belongs to many clubs and organizations (increases)
- Leaves home often for studying (increases)
- Lower social class (increases)
- Unemployed (increases)

The finding that people who engage in illegal activities are more likely to be the vic-tims of crime has also been reported in other studies. This is usually explained by arguing that such persons are more likely to associate with other criminals. Also, it may be that such persons are less likely to call the police if victimized, making them more attractive targets for crime. How would you explain the association between the other routine activities and characteristics listed here and the likelihood of being a victim of major theft? (See the dis-cussion in Mustaine and Tewksbury, 1998a, if you need assistance.)

TEST YOUR KNOWLEDGE OF THIS CHAPTER

1. What do I mean when I state that some individuals are "predisposed" to delin-quency? What major factors influence the individual's predisposition to delinquency?

2. Briefly describe those types of situations where predisposed individuals are most likely to engage in delinquency.

3. I state that it is possible to reduce juveniles' level of offending without affecting their predisposition to delinquency. Give three examples of how this might be done.

4. What types of situational strains increase the likelihood of delinquency? Give an ex-ample of a provocation likely to prompt a delinquent response.

5. What types of situational factors increase the likelihood that juveniles will cope with these strains in a delinquent manner? Why does the use of alcohol and certain other drugs increase the likelihood of delinquent coping?

6. What major factors affect the individual's perceptions of the costs and benefits of crime in a situation?

7. Do juveniles give careful thought to the costs and benefits of crime? If not, does that mean that costs and benefits are irrelevant?

8. Describe the major features of attractive property and person targets.

9. What is a capable guardian?

10. Describe how the presence of delinquent peers may affect the perceived costs and benefits of crime.

11. Give an example of efforts to reduce delinquency by (a) reducing situational strains, (b) reducing the attractiveness of property targets, (c) reducing the attractiveness of person targets, and (d) increasing the presence of capable guardians.

12. What is meant by routine activities?

13. Describe those routine activities that increase exposure to situations conducive to crime. Why does engaging in unstructured, unsupervised activities with delinquent peers increase exposure to situations conducive to crime?

14. Describe those factors that increase the likelihood one will engage in routine activities that increase exposure to situations conducive to crime.

THOUGHT AND DISCUSSION QUESTIONS

1. Describe those situational characteristics most conducive to cheating on exams and to minor theft on your college campus. How might such characteristics be altered to reduce cheating and theft?

2. Describe those routine activities that increase the likelihood that college students will be the victims of violence.

3. Are juveniles predisposed to delinquency more likely to encounter situations conducive to delinquency? Why (or why not)?

KEY TERMS

- Predisposition to delinquency
- Attractive targets
- Capable guardians
- Routine activities

ENDNOTES

1. For overviews and examples of the research in this area, *see* Agnew, 1990a, 2006; Akers, 1990; Birkbeck and LaFree, 1993; Bottoms and Wiles, 2002; Brantingham and Brantingham, 1984; Briar and Piliavin, 1965; Clarke and Cornish, 1985; Clarke and Eck, 2005; Cohen and Felson, 1979; Cohen et al., 1981; Colvin, 2000; Cornish and Clarke, 1986; Felson, M., 1987, 1994, 2002, 2006; Felson, R., 1993, 1997; Finkelor and Asdigian, 1996; Garofalo et al., 1987; Hindelang et al., 1978; Jensen and Brownfield, 1986; Kennedy and Baron, 1993; Kennedy and Forde, 1990, 1996, 1999; Massey et al., 1989; Matsueda et al., 2006; McCarthy, 1995; Miethe and McCorkle, 2001; Miethe and Meier, 1990, 1994; Mustaine and Tewksbury, 1998a; Osgood et al., 1996; Sampson and Wooldredge, 1987; Sherman et al., 1989; Tedeschi and Felson, 1994; Wilcox et al., 2003; Wilkinson, 2002.

2. *See* especially Athens, 2005; Colvin, 2000; Hughes and Short, 2005; Kennedy and Forde, 1999; Tedeschi and Felson, 1994; Wilkinson, 2002.

3. For further examples, *see* Clarke, 1992, 1995; Clarke and Eck, 2005; Eck, 2002; Felson, M., 2002, 2006; Geason and Wilson, 1989; Sherman et al., 1989.

ENDNOTES (continued)

4. *See* Assaad and Exum, 2002; Felson and Burchfield, 2004; White and Gorman, 2000; White et al., 2002.

5. *See* Clarke and Eck, 2005; Cohen and Felson, 1979; Felson, M., 2002, 2006; Finkelhor and Asdigian, 1996; Wilcox et al., 2003.

6. *See* Agnew and Petersen, 1989; Felson, R., 1997; Haynie and Osgood, 2005; Hundleby, 1987; Jensen and Brownfield, 1986; Lotz and Lee, 1999; Office of Juvenile Justice and Delinquency Prevention, 1999a; Osgood and Anderson, 2004; Osgood et al., 1996; Riley, 1987; Vazsonyi et al., 2002.

CHAPTER 12

Group Differences in Delinquency

How Can We Explain Group Differences, Particularly Community Differences in Rates of Delinquency?

We have so far examined how the leading theories of delinquency explain why some individuals engage in more delinquency than others, why individuals exhibit different patterns of offending over the life course, and why individuals are more likely to commit delinquent acts in some situations than in others. In this chapter we shift our focus from individuals to groups, and examine how the leading theories explain **why some groups have higher delinquency rates than others.** There are many groups we might examine, but this chapter focuses on communities, including neighborhoods and cities. The central question addressed is: **Why do some communities have higher rates of delinquency than others?**

The discussion in this chapter provides **a model for explaining group differences in delinquency rates.** As you will see, the major way such differences are explained is by arguing that group characteristics affect levels of strain, control, the social learning for crime, and labeling. (Chapter 18 draws on the leading theories, as well as the research inspired by these theories, to explain still other group differences in delinquency—including gender, age, class, and race and ethnic differences. My discussion of these group differences is delayed until Chapter 18, since it draws heavily on the research presented in Chapters 13 through 17.)

I begin this chapter by describing the characteristics of communities that have high rates of crime. I then describe how these characteristics reduce levels of control, increase the social learning for crime, and increase levels of strain—thereby accounting for the high rates of crime in these communities. I also draw on labeling theory, noting that high community crime rates often have consequences that increase the likelihood of further crime. The arguments draw heavily on the work of Agnew (1999), Akers (1998), Anderson (1999), Bernard (1990), Bursik and Grasmick (1993), Kornhauser (1978), Sampson and Groves (1989), Sampson and Raudenbush (1999), Sampson and Wilson (1995), Shaw and McKay (1942), and Sutherland et al. (1992).

This chapter completes my discussion of the leading theories of delinquency. I therefore conclude the chapter by providing a brief overview of strain, control, social learning, and labeling theories.

Why Are Crime Rates Higher in Some Communities than in Others?

There is little doubt that some communities have much higher crime rates than others. I am sure that many of you can think of neighborhoods in your hometowns that have relatively high crime rates or at least have reputations for having high crime rates. One neighborhood with a high crime rate was described in my hometown newspaper in an article titled "A Bad Way to Die."

Willie Arnold's first mistake that sweltering July night was to buy crack cocaine from a man he hardly knew on Beatie Avenue in Southwest Atlanta. His second mistake was to return to that street, known as one of the worst drug-infested neighborhoods in the city, to complain about the drugs he had bought. It was his last mistake. The gripe got Arnold killed, beaten and kicked to death in the front yard of a Beatie Avenue house as dozens of people watched and cheered the aggressors on. . . . The attack took about 35 minutes, as the men and women involved took breaks so they could ultimately beat on the victim some more. Even a couple of children, younger than 10 years of age, participated in the assault, kicking and punching Arnold a few times as he wailed and writhed on the grass. No one tried to stop the beating. No one dared. "If something bad happens around here, you keep quiet, you don't tell on your neighbors for fear of your life" [said a Beatie Avenue resident]. When the attack was over, not much remained of Arnold's head and torso but a bloody mass crushed into the weeds and gravel of an unkempt front lawn. (Longa, 1998)

It is also the case that some cities have higher crime rates than others. Each year the FBI publishes data on the crime rates of cities throughout the United States, and newspapers and TV stations often carry stories about the city with the highest crime rate (the "crime capital" of the United States) or the highest murder rate (the "murder capital"). Detroit had the highest homicide rate among large cities (500,000 plus) for the year 2006, with 47 homicides per 100,000 residents. (By contrast, New York City had 7 homicides per 100,000 residents.) You might look up the crime rate in your city and compare it to that of other cities (see the latest edition of the FBI *Uniform Crime Reports* at http://www.fbi .gov/ucr/ucr.html). (You should be aware, however, that the FBI data are not well suited for comparing crime rates in different cities—except for homicide rates and perhaps the rates of certain other serious crimes [see Gove et al., 1985]. Among other things, cities differ in the extent to which victims report crimes to the police and in police record-keeping practices.)

There has been much research on the characteristics of those neighborhoods and cities with high crime rates. Although the results of this research are sometimes contradictory, researchers now have a reasonably good idea what those characteristics are. Most of this research has focused on crimes committed by both adults and juveniles, but some data suggest that the conclusions that follow apply to juvenile delinquency alone.[1]

What Are the Characteristics of High-Crime Neighborhoods and Cities?

Generally speaking, urban communities have higher crime rates than suburban and rural communities, although the relationship between the degree of urbanization and crime is not as strong as many people think (Maguire and Pastore, 2003; Pratt and Cullen, 2005). Some urban communities have relatively low crime rates, while some rural communities have relatively high rates (Egan, 2002; Osgood and Chambers, 2000). Rather than the level of urbanization, the most important characteristics distinguishing high- from low-crime communities are the levels of economic deprivation, residential instability, family disruption in the community, and proximity to high crime/poor communities.[2]

Economic deprivation. The most distinguishing characteristic of high-crime communities is that they are economically deprived. Deprivation has been measured in a variety of ways, including the average or median family income level in an area, the percentage of families below the poverty line ($20,650 for a family of four in 2007), the percentage of adult males who are unemployed, the percentage of families that receive welfare, and the average or median educational level. These measures are highly correlated with one another, and they are often combined into more general measures of economic deprivation. Virtually all studies indicate that deprived cities and neighborhoods have more crime than other communities (see Land et al., 1990; Pratt and Cullen, 2005). For example, a study of neighborhoods in Columbus, Ohio, examined the relationship between the percentage of residents below the poverty line and neighborhood crime rates (based on crimes known to the police). Neighborhoods with extremely high levels of poverty (40 percent or more of the residents below the poverty line) had violent crime rates that were approximately five times as high as neighborhoods with low levels of poverty (5 percent or fewer below the poverty line). The difference in property crime rates was less extreme but still substantial (Krivo and Peterson, 1996).

I should note that several criminologists have argued that researchers should not only consider the extent to which community residents are poor, but also the extent to which they are **advantaged.** By advantaged, I refer to the extent to which community residents have high incomes, advanced educations, and/or prestigious jobs. Two communities may have identical levels of poverty (e.g., 25 percent of the residents are below the poverty line). One community, however, may be a "mixed-class" community and have a substantial number of residents who earn high salaries, have college degrees, and work in managerial and professional jobs. The other community may have few such advantaged residents; rather, most other residents may be just above the poverty line. Researchers argue that the advantaged residents may reduce levels of crime in the community for several reasons. For example, they may use their resources to secure better police protection, improve the quality of local schools, and limit the number of bars in the community. They may also act as role models and mentors for youth in the community. Certain data support these arguments, suggesting that the presence of advantaged residents in a community is associated with lower levels of crime—even after we take account of poverty levels (e.g., Kubrin and Weitzer, 2003; Sampson et al., 1999).

Residential instability. High-crime communities also tend to have high rates of *residential instability;* that is, **people frequently move into and out of the community.** Residential instability is often measured by the percentage of residents who lived in different houses five years ago and the percentage of housing units that are renter occupied. Residential instability is more common in poor communities. New immigrants to the city often locate in poor communities because they cannot afford to live elsewhere, so people are frequently moving into the community. And the residents of poor communities often move elsewhere as soon as they are able, so people are frequently moving out of the community. Some data suggest that residential instability is related to crime only in poor communities; that is, poor communities with high rates of instability have higher crime rates than poor communities with low rates of instability. Instability may be unrelated to crime rates in wealthier communities.

Family disruption. High-crime communities tend to have higher rates of family disruption. Disruption is usually measured by the percentage of families headed by females and/or the percentage of residents who are divorced or separated. Economic deprivation is a major cause of family disruption, since, among other things, it leads to a decline in the proportion of males who are able to support a family.[3] Nevertheless, data indicate that family disruption has an independent effect on community crime rates. In fact, certain data suggest that family disruption partly explains the effect of economic deprivation on community crime rates. That is, economic deprivation affects community crime rates partly through its effect on family disruption (Sampson, 1985, 1987).

Close proximity to high-crime/economically deprived communities. High-crime communities tend to be adjacent to other high-crime or economically deprived communities. Criminals often commit crimes in *nearby* communities, so areas that are close to high-crime communities tend to have higher crime rates for this reason. Also, areas that are close to economically deprived communities tend to have higher crime rates because these communities have fewer resources on which to draw—resources such as jobs and good schools. So if you live in a poor community, it is better to live in a poor community surrounded by wealthier communities, than in one surrounded by other poor communities. If you are surrounded by wealthier communities, you might have easier access to such things as decent jobs, good schools, and various social services.

Is race or ethnicity related to community crime rates? High-crime communities tend to have a higher percentage of African American and Latino residents. Data, however, suggest that **much or all of the association between race/ethnicity and community crime rates is due to third variables like economic deprivation, residential instability, family disruption, and proximity to high-crime communities.** For example, African Americans are more likely than whites to live in communities characterized by high rates of poverty, residential instability, family disruption, and proximity to high-crime communities. According to data from the 2000 census, 18.6 percent of poor African Americans versus 5.9 percent of poor whites lived in high-poverty neighborhoods (where 40 percent or more of the residents are below the poverty line) (Jargowsky, 2003). When we control for or take account of third variables like economic deprivation, the association between race or ethnicity and community crime rates is substantially reduced or eliminated in most studies.[4] So, for example, studies tend to find that very poor communities have similar rates of crime, regardless of whether they are populated by African Americans or whites.

Summary

Economic deprivation, residential instability, family disruption, and proximity to high crime/poor areas lead communities to develop high rates of crime. High-crime communities have a higher percentage of African Americans and Latinos because race/ethnicity is associated with factors like economic deprivation; the relationship between race/ethnicity and community crime rates is substantially reduced when we take account of these factors.

Are Communities with Characteristics Conducive to Crime Becoming More Common?

Most of the data we have on trends in community characteristics deal with economic deprivation. These data indicate that **the number of high-poverty neighborhoods and the number of people living in such neighborhoods increased dramatically from 1970 to 1990** (Jargowsky, 2003). In particular, the number of people living in such neighborhoods more than doubled, from less than 5 million in 1970 to 10.4 million in 1990. There are several reasons for this increase.[5]

1. **Working- and middle-class people moved out of mixed-income communities, leaving the poor behind.** This is **especially true of African American communities.** As late as the 1960s, many inner-city African American communities contained a mix of poor, working-class, and middle-class residents. Working- and middle-class African Americans were prevented from living in the suburbs by discriminatory housing policies. As these discriminatory practices declined, working- and middle-class African Americans started to move to the suburbs—which increased the concentration of poor African Americans in the inner city (Quillian, 1999).

2. **The government placed public housing projects in poor inner-city communities,** which further increased the concentration of poor people there. (As you may have noticed, there are few public housing projects in suburban areas.)

3. **The economic situation of poor people, especially those in the inner city, declined as a result of several major changes in the economy.** Most notably, **low-skill jobs paying a decent wage became scarcer.** There was a decline in the number of manufacturing jobs, partly due to technological changes and partly due to the movement of manufacturing jobs from the central city to suburban areas and overseas. For example, Philadelphia, Chicago, New York, and Detroit have lost more than half of their manufacturing jobs since the 1960s (Wilson, 1996). The wages in manufacturing jobs also became less competitive, owing to such factors as foreign competition, the increase in the size of the workforce, and the decline of unions. There was an increase in low-skill jobs in the service sector (e.g., sales, food service), but most of these jobs had low salaries and were located at a distance from inner-city communities. There was also an increase in high-skill jobs in the technology and information-processing areas, but these jobs were beyond the reach of most inner-city residents. Changes in the job market, then, made it much more difficult for unskilled workers—particularly those in inner-city communities—to earn an adequate living.

However, **the number of high-poverty neighborhoods and people living in such neighborhoods decreased from 1990 to 2000.** In particular, the number of people in very poor communities decreased by 24 percent during this time, with most of the decrease occurring in the South and Midwest (Jargowsky, 2003). The reasons for these changes are not entirely clear, but they likely include **the strong economy in the 1990s and federal housing policies that encouraged cities to replace public housing projects with mixed-income housing** (Atkin, 2003). For example, the percentage of children living below the poverty line decreased from 21 percent in 1990 to 16 percent in 2000 (for African Americans, the percentage decreased from 45 percent to 31 percent during these years). Unfortunately, it is uncertain whether the percentage of people living in high-poverty neighborhoods will continue to decline in the 2000s—especially given the recent slowdowns in the economy and the home mortgage crisis. For example, the percentage of children living below the poverty line increased from 16 percent in 2000 to 17 percent in 2006 (and from 31% to 33% for African Americans).

Why Are Deprived Communities Higher in Crime?

High-crime communities are high in crime for two fundamental reasons. First, crime-prone individuals may be attracted to these communities, or they may be more likely to live in them because they (or their families) cannot afford to live elsewhere. Second, the characteristics of high-crime communities may cause individuals to engage in crime. **High-crime communities, then, may both attract or select for crime-prone individuals and cause these individuals to engage in crime.** Data suggest that both explanations have some merit, although there is still some uncertainty about the size of the causal effect of communities on crime.[6] In this section, I examine the ways in which the characteristics of high-crime communities may cause crime.

Not surprisingly, researchers argue that the characteristics of high-crime neighborhoods cause crime for reasons related to strain, control, social learning, and labeling theories.

Deprived Communities Are Higher in Strain

Strain theorists argue that the residents of deprived communities are more likely to experience the types of strain described in Chapter 6: the failure to achieve positively valued goals, the loss of positive stimuli, and the presentation of negative stimuli. Also, the residents of such communities may be less able to cope with their strain through legitimate channels.[7]

Goal blockage. It is clear that the residents of such communities are less able to achieve the goal of economic success. In particular, the schools in such communities are generally inferior, and residents have less access to jobs in general and to stable, well-paying jobs in particular. Manufacturing and service-sector jobs (e.g., retail sales, restaurant workers) are often located at a distance from deprived communities, so they are less accessible, relatively few individuals in the community have job contacts or job information, and there are fewer individuals in the community to teach and model the skills and attitudes necessary for successful job performance. As a consequence, residents may be more likely to engage in theft, drug selling, prostitution, or other illicit income-generating activities. The frustration that results from goal blockage may result in violent behavior as well.

Related to this, residents in these communities are also less able to achieve social status, including "masculine status," through conventional means. One recent field study of crack dealers in a poor New York community, in fact, is titled "In Search of Respect" (Bourgois, 2003). As the author of this study states, "One message the crack dealers communicated clearly to me is that they are not driven solely by simple economic exigency. Like most humans on earth, in addition to material subsistence, they are also searching for dignity and fulfillment. In the Puerto Rican context this incorporates definitions of respeto [respect]" (2003:324). Unfortunately, the residents of deprived communities often have trouble achieving respect or status through legal channels, such as getting a good education and then a prestigious job. As a consequence, they may attempt to achieve this status through illegitimate means, or they may strike out at others in their frustration. These arguments have not received a good test, but much data are compatible with them (see Agnew, 1999; Kubrin and Weitzer, 2003; Messerschmidt, 1993).

Loss of positive stimuli/presentation of negative stimuli. The residents of high-crime communities are also subject to a range of other strains. In addition to economic hardships of various types, they are more likely to experience family disruption and the strains associated with such disruption, such as family conflict. They are more likely to experience problems at school, because they lack good preparation for school and attend inferior schools. They are more likely to get into interpersonal conflicts, because they often compete with others for scarce resources like money. As Anderson (1999:37) states, "Life in public often features an intense competition for scarce social goods in which 'winners' totally dominate 'losers.'" And, not surprisingly, they have higher rates of criminal victimization and child abuse.

A few studies have attempted to test these ideas.[8] Warner and Fowler (2003), for example, measured strain by asking neighborhood residents whether they or anyone in their household had "(1) received verbal threats or insults, (2) felt cheated by someone, [and] (3) been harassed by the police" (2003:514). They found that the residents of deprived communities were more likely to experience these types of strains and that these strains increased neighborhood levels of violence. To give another example, Kaufman (2005) found that the residents of deprived communities were more likely to witness and be the victims of violence. Witnessing or being victimized by violence, in turn, increased the residents' likelihood of engaging in violence.

Coping with strain. Finally, it has been argued that the residents of high-crime communities may be less able to cope with strain through legitimate channels. Among other things, they have fewer coping resources, like money and power. They are also less likely to receive assistance or support from others in their community (see the discussion of control theory in the next section). Furthermore, it has been argued that residents' continued experience with strain increases their underlying level of anger and their sensitivity to slights. That is, they develop what has been called a "short fuse."[9] Finally, they are subject to less control and are more likely to be predisposed to crime for reasons related to social learning theory (discussed later). All of these factors increase the likelihood that residents will respond to strain with crime (see Warner and Fowler, 2003, for a study in this area).

Deprived Communities Are Lower in Control

According to control theorists, **the characteristics of deprived communities reduce the ability and willingness of residents to exercise effective control** (see Chapter 8 for a description of control theory). This includes the ability and willingness of parents to control their children, of school officials to control students, and of community residents to control one another. In particular, the residents of high-crime communities **are less likely to exercise effective direct control.** For example, community residents are less likely to engage in activities like "taking note of and/or questioning strangers, watching over each other's property, assuming responsibility for supervision of general youth activities, and intervening in local disturbances" (Sampson, 1986a:27).

Wilkinson (2007) provides a nice illustration of this point. She interviewed several hundred "active violent offenders" in two very poor, high-crime communities in New York. Among other things, she asked these offenders what adults in their neighborhood do when they see juveniles engaging in various types of crime. One hundred percent of the offenders said that the adults in their neighborhoods "walk away or do nothing" when they see older juveniles fighting on the street, while 74.3 percent said adults walk away or do nothing when they see juveniles selling drugs. In describing how adults respond to drug sellers on the street, one offender stated that "half of them walk across the street and the other half they just walk right through them and act like they ain't even there. They try to ignore it. They don't want nothing to do with it." Another offender was asked why most adults ignore drug selling. He replied: "Cause they don't want no beef. You stick your nose in my mother fucking business, you getting popped . . . you'll be dead" (Wilkinson, 2007:205).

Communities where residents are willing to work together to exercise direct control over others are said to be high in *collective efficacy.* The extent of collective efficacy in a community has been measured in part by asking residents how much they trust and get along with one another. It is also measured by asking residents how likely their neighbors "could be counted on to take action if: (1) children were skipping school and hanging out on a street corner, (2) children were spray-painting graffiti on a local building, (3) children were showing disrespect toward an adult, (4) a fight broke out in front of their house, and (5) a fire station closest to home was threatened with a budget cut" (Sampson, 2006:153; also see Sampson et al., 1997; Simons et al., 2005).

The residents of deprived communities are also **less likely to provide juveniles with a stake in conformity,** which includes establishing close ties to juveniles and helping them succeed at school and work. And the residents are **less likely to socialize juveniles so that they condemn delinquency and develop self-control.** Elijah Anderson (1990) provides an excellent illustration of these points in his description of the Northton community. The Northton community was once a mixed-income African American community with a relatively low crime rate. Juveniles in the community often received assistance from many adults, including adults outside their family. These adults, referred to as *old heads,* would often function as surrogate fathers, providing guidance, encouragement, financial aid, and help in finding jobs. More generally, they served as conventional role models. As Anderson states, they "served the black community well as visible, concrete symbols of success and moral value, living examples of the fruits of hard work, perseverance, decency, and propriety" (Anderson, 1990:58). In recent years, however, the working- and middle-class residents of the community have moved to more affluent areas, so there are fewer old heads to assist youths. The old heads that remain have less influence, partly because decent-paying jobs in the inner city have become scarcer, making it difficult for the old heads to assist youths and undermining their lessons about the rewards of hard work and a conventional lifestyle. Partly as a consequence, crime rates have increased.

The residents of high-crime communities are less likely to engage in these types of control for at least three reasons.[10]

1. The residents of such communities have **trouble finding decent work.** As a result, they often struggle to deal with a range of economic and other problems, they are emotionally distressed, and they lack the skills and resources to legally cope with their own problems or assist others. These factors **undermine the ability of parents to exercise effective control over their children.** In particular, these factors often lead to the breakup of families and a host of family problems (see Chapter 14). Furthermore, these factors **undermine the efforts of community residents to exercise effective control over juveniles in the broader community.**

2. Community residents are **less likely to have ties to their neighbors and to care about their community.** They do not own their own homes, which lowers their investment in the community. They often hope to move to a more desirable community as soon as they are able, which also lowers their investment in the community. People are constantly moving into and out of their community, which makes it difficult for them to form ties with their neighbors. In fact, they may have trouble recognizing many of their neighbors. As you might imagine, these factors make residents reluctant to get involved in community affairs, including such risky activities as confronting delinquents in their neighborhood.

3. Residents are **less likely to support or form community organizations,** including educational, religious, and recreational organizations. This lack of participation is partly a consequence of their limited resources and their lower attachment to the community. Their failure to get involved in community organizations further reduces control, since these organizations often help supervise, assist, and guide youth. Such organizations also help ensure that outside agencies—like the police and city government—are more responsive to community needs. For example, these organizations may lobby for better schools and more police protection.

4. Community residents are **less likely to have a good working relationship with the police.**[11] The residents of deprived communities are more likely to hold negative attitudes toward the police. In Carr et al.'s (2007) study of three high-crime communities in Philadelphia, for example, over 60 percent of the young people expressed negative views of the police. These views at least partly stemmed from their negative experiences with the police. The police in deprived communities are more likely to use force against suspects and engage in misconduct. According to Carr et al. (2007:467), the young people in their study stated they had negative views of the police because they were "stopped for no good reason, . . . harassed or treated roughly, or . . . encountered dishonest or lackadaisical police." Also, the residents of deprived communities are more likely to view the police as ineffective. As Anderson (1999:321) states, based on his field study of a deprived Philadelphia community, the residents "believe the police are unlikely to come [if called] or, if they do come, may even harass the very people who called them." As a consequence of these views, the residents of deprived communities may be less likely to call the police when problems arise. In the Carr et al. (2007) study, less than 10 percent of the respondents said they would call the police if they saw a group of young people misbehaving (also see Warner, 2007). These views may also reduce the willingness of residents to intervene on their own, since they believe they cannot count on the police to support them if necessary. The result, then, is a reduction in direct control.

It should be noted that those theories that explain community crime rates in terms of control theory are called *social disorganization theories,* since they essentially argue that there has been a breakdown of control in the community, leaving the community disorganized.

Recent data provide some support for these arguments. Factors like economic deprivation, residential instability, and family disruption reduce the extent to which community residents engage in effective parenting, know and trust their neighbors, intervene in neighborhood problems, get involved in community organizations, and develop good relations with the police. These factors, in turn, directly influence crime rates or indirectly influence crime by allowing for the development of delinquent peer groups (discussed later).[12]

Deprived Communities Foster the Social Learning of Crime

Social learning theorists argue that economic deprivation, residential instability, and family disruption increase community crime rates because they lead to the development of delinquent groups—that foster the social learning of crime (see Akers, 1998; Sutherland et al., 1992). Related to this, learning theorists argue that the residents of deprived communities are more likely to develop beliefs favorable to delinquency, forming what have been called *delinquent or criminal subcultures.*

Delinquent groups. Delinquent groups include delinquent peer groups, gangs, drug-selling organizations, and prostitution rings. Such groups are said to be more common in deprived communities partly because **control is low** in such communities, so residents are less able to stop such groups from forming or operating. Also, such groups are more likely to form in these communities for reasons related to **strain theory.** Among other things, people in these communities are poor and often have little prospect for a better life. So illicit methods of making money, like selling drugs, theft, and prostitution, have more appeal.

As a consequence of such groups, juveniles in the community are provided with more opportunities to make money through delinquent channels. For example, opportunities to sell drugs are readily available. Juveniles are also more likely to be exposed to criminal models, like drug sellers on the street corner. And juveniles are more likely to become involved in delinquent groups, including delinquent peer groups and gangs. The members of such groups, of course, are more likely to model crime, teach beliefs conducive to crime, and reinforce crime.

Field studies and surveys provide some support for these arguments.[13] These studies, in particular, suggest that delinquent groups are more common in deprived neighborhoods and that they foster crime in the ways indicated earlier. For example, as Anderson (1999:29–30) states:

> In the impoverished inner-city neighborhood, the drug trade is everywhere, and it becomes ever more difficult to separate the drug culture from the experience of poverty. The neighborhood is sprinkled with crack dens located in abandoned buildings or in someone's home. On corner after corner, young men peddle drugs the way a newsboy peddles papers. . . . At times they sell drugs to passing motorists, who stop in broad daylight and hold up traffic during the transaction. . . . [S]mall children will occasionally be sitting in the back seat.

Beliefs favorable to delinquency. There is also some evidence suggesting that community characteristics like economic deprivation may lead some community residents—especially juveniles—to **develop beliefs favorable to delinquency.**[14] Such beliefs include a strong emphasis on toughness and the view that delinquency is justifiable or excusable under certain conditions (see Chapter 7). Juveniles with such beliefs are, of course, more likely to respond to a range of temptations and provocation with delinquency.

The origin of such beliefs may be partly explained using strain theory. Individuals who cannot obtain money through legitimate channels may attempt to obtain it through delinquent channels, such as theft and drug selling. In the process, they may come to justify or rationalize their delinquency. For example, they may claim that while theft in general is bad, it is justified or excusable if decent jobs are unavailable. Also, individuals who cannot obtain the more general goal of social status through legitimate channels may attempt to obtain it through violence. That is, they may attempt to coerce or intimidate others into treating them with respect. Among other things, these attempts may take the form of maintaining a tough demeanor, responding to even minor shows of disrespect with violence, and occasionally "campaigning for respect" by assaulting others (see especially Anderson, 1999). Such individuals may come to believe that violence is often justified and that it is important to be tough. Such "beliefs favorable to delinquency" may then spread through the community as these individuals interact with others. Finally, individuals who feel they cannot turn to the police for help may come to believe that they are justified in engaging in violence if provoked or insulted (see Kubrin and Weitzer, 2003).

A number of field studies and certain surveys suggest that **such beliefs are more common in deprived communities,** although it is important to stress that only a small percentage of the residents in such communities fully subscribe to them.[15] Even so, such beliefs can still have a large effect on community crime rates. As Anderson (1999) points out, many juveniles who do not subscribe to these beliefs must nevertheless act as if they do. Many juveniles, for example, may **not** place a strong emphasis on toughness, but they must act tough if they want to avoid being regularly victimized by others (especially those juveniles who do value toughness).

Community Crime Rates Reduce Control, Foster the Social Learning of Crime, and Increase Strain

To sum up, economic deprivation, residential instability, and family disruption increase community crime rates through their effects on control, social learning, and strain. These arguments are illustrated in Figure 12.1.

The community crime rate is the dependent variable in this figure. But research suggests that **the community crime rate may also function as an independent variable.**[16] Imagine a community in which the crime rate starts to rise. After a certain point, businesses and residents may begin to move out. Property values then start to fall, and poorer individuals begin to move into the community. A rise in community crime rates, then, may contribute to economic deprivation and residential instability, and through these effects, rising crime may indirectly lead to a reduction in control, an increase in the social learning for crime, and an increase in strain. Further, rising crime rates may directly affect levels of control, strain, and social learning. For example, rising crime rates may make residents fearful and thereby reduce the likelihood that they will exercise direct control

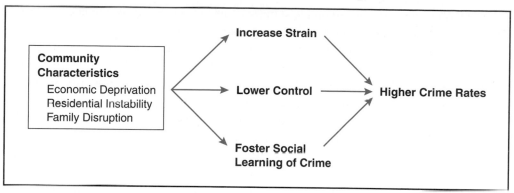

FIGURE 12.1 Community Characteristics Contribute to Higher Crime Rates Through Their Effects on Strain, Control, and Social Learning

over others in the community. Recall the quote near the beginning of this chapter: "If something bad happens around here, you keep quiet, you don't tell on your neighbors for fear of your life" (Longa, 1998). And rising crime rates directly increase the level of strain in the community, since being a crime victim and having close others victimized are major types of strain.

So **community crime rates are involved in a reciprocal relationship with community characteristics.** Community characteristics affect community crime rates, and community crime rates affect community characteristics. The latter effect is, of course, reminiscent of the arguments made by labeling theorists, who state that crime sometimes has consequences that increase the likelihood of further crime (also see Kubrin and Weitzer, 2003; Piquero et al., 2006).

Overview of the Leading Theories of Delinquency

This chapter concludes our discussion of the leading theories of delinquency. Four major theories were reviewed: strain theory, social learning theory, control theory, and labeling theory. These theories focus on explaining why some juveniles are more likely to engage in delinquency than others. But these theories have also been used to answer other major questions about delinquency: Why do individuals exhibit different patterns of offending over the life course? Why are individuals more likely to commit delinquent acts in some situations than in others? And, why do some groups have higher rates of delinquency than other groups? The best way to review these theories is to list their major independent variables and their explanations of why these independent variables cause delinquency.

Strain theory focuses on two major categories of strain: goal blockage and the loss of positive stimuli/presentation of negative stimuli. The experience of strain leads to negative emotions like anger and frustration, and individuals may turn to delinquency in an effort to cope with strain and these emotions. Delinquency may allow them to reduce or escape from their strain, seek revenge against those who have wronged them, or manage their negative emotions (e.g., through illicit drug use).

Social learning theory focuses on the extent to which individuals associate with others who reinforce delinquency, present beliefs favorable to delinquency, and model delinquent behavior. These activities lead individuals to believe that delinquency is a desirable or at least justifiable response in certain situations.

Control theory focuses on the extent to which individuals are subject to direct control, have a stake in conformity, believe crime is wrong, and are high in self-control. The absence of such controls frees individuals to satisfy their needs and desires in the most expedient way possible, which is often through delinquent acts.

Labeling theory focuses on the extent to which individuals are viewed and treated (labeled) as "bad" or "evil" by others. Such negative labeling leads to a reduction in control, an increase in strain, an increase in the social learning for crime, and a delinquent self-concept.

Each theory presents a different image of the delinquent. In strain theory, the delinquent is **angry and frustrated,** beset with a variety of problems or strains and unable to cope through legal channels. In social learning theory, the delinquent believes that **delinquency is a desirable or justifiable response** in her or his particular situation. In control theory, the delinquent is **unrestrained,** free to satisfy his or her needs and desires in the most expedient way possible. And in labeling theory, the delinquent is **branded as "bad,"** rejected and mistreated by conventional others.

All four theories have some support, with social learning and control theories dominating the literature. I should emphasize, however, that these theories continue to be tested and revised. They are not "engraved in stone." Rather, they are ongoing creations. In fact, strain, control, and labeling theories have been subject to major modifications in the recent past.

Each theory partly explains why individuals engage in delinquency. One theory may sometimes be more relevant to a particular individual or group than the other theories. For example, you may know a delinquent individual who appears to be high in control, low in strain, and low in labeling. This person's delinquency may best be explained in terms of social learning theory: Perhaps their delinquency is frequently reinforced and seldom punished; perhaps they accept certain beliefs that justify their delinquency; or perhaps they have had much exposure to delinquent models. Strain, control, and/or labeling theories, however, may provide the best explanation of delinquency for someone else. In most cases, all four theories probably have some relevance to the explanation of delinquency.

A complete explanation of delinquency, therefore, should draw on strain, social learning, control, and labeling theories. Given this fact, you might ask about the possibility of combining these theories into a more general theory of delinquency. Many criminologists have, in fact, tried to develop integrated theories of crime that combine all or some of these theories. I present one recent example of such an integration in Chapter 18, after I review the research inspired by these theories in Chapters 13 through 17.

Teaching Aids

Exercise: Increasing Community Control

I earlier described a study in which Wilkinson (2007) interviewed several hundred active, violent offenders in two very poor, high-crime New York City communities. She asked these offenders what they thought the adults in their neighborhoods would do if they witnessed various types of crime. She also asked these offenders how bystanders reacted to the violent events in which these offenders were involved (42 percent of these events involved guns). Here is what she found:

> In 31.4 percent of the events in which bystanders were present, they reportedly watched without intervening, in 19.9 percent of events they did nothing or ignored the conflict, in 14.1 percent they ran away or took cover for self-protection, in 12.8 percent of events they instigated or "amped up" the situation, in 9.0 percent they yelled to try to stop the violence, in 7.7 percent of events, they broke it up, and in 2.6 percent, they helped the respondent. Bystanders very rarely called the police or got involved by using violence. (Wilkinson, 2007:209)

It should be noted that these "bystanders" were distinct from the offender's associates. When the offender's associates were present, they most often helped the offender by engaging in violence themselves. The bystanders were also distinct from the opponent's associates.

How can we explain this lack of response to violence in these very poor, high-crime communities? Do you think the response would be very different in your community? If so, why do you think it would be different? What do you think can be done to increase the likelihood that bystanders will intervene in some manner to stop crimes (see Wilkinson, 2007)?

Exercise: Explaining Other Group Differences in Crime

This chapter draws on strain, social learning, control, and labeling theories to explain why some communities have higher crime rates than others. There are, of course, other group differences in delinquency rates that are in need of explanation. Drawing on strain, social learning, control, and labeling theories, **how would you explain the fact that males have higher rates of delinquency than females?**

The best way to answer this question is to outline or briefly describe the essential arguments of each theory. For example, list the major types of strain, the reasons why strain increases the likelihood of delinquency, and the factors that condition the effect of strain on delinquency. Then review each of the key points you have listed, asking whether it might shed light on the relationship between gender and delinquency. For example, is there reason to believe that males experience more strain than females or that males are more likely to experience those types of strain that are conducive to crime? Is there reason to believe that males are more likely to react to strain with negative emotions like anger? Is there reason to believe that males are more likely to respond to strain and negative emotions with crime (e.g., are males more likely to associate with delinquent peers, who increase the likelihood of a delinquent response to strain)?

Broidy and Agnew (1997) provide a nice illustration of how strain theory might be used to explain gender differences in crime (also see Piquero and Sealock, 2004). Chapter 18 uses all of the delinquency theories in this text, and the research inspired by these theories, to explain gender differences in delinquency—as well as age, class, and race/ethnic differences. But you should try completing this exercise before looking at Chapter 18. Applying the theories is important; it dramatically increases your understanding of the theories, and the theories are of little use to you unless you develop the ability to apply them.

TEST YOUR KNOWLEDGE OF THIS CHAPTER

1. How are group differences in crime rates usually explained?

2. What are the major characteristics distinguishing high-crime communities from low-crime communities? Describe one way in which each of these characteristics has been measured.

3. I argue that race and ethnicity are associated with community crime rates, but the association is largely, or perhaps entirely, due to third variables. Describe the argument I make in this area.

4. Why did the number of people living in high-poverty communities increase so much from 1970 to 1990? Why did the number decrease from 1990 to 2000?

5. I state that high-crime communities are high in crime for "two fundamental reasons." What are these reasons?

6. What do I mean when I state that the residents of high-crime communities are less likely to exercise control over other residents?

7. Why are the residents of high-crime communities less likely to exercise control? (Your answer should describe the three major ways in which economic deprivation, residential instability, and family disruption undermine control.)

8. What are the two major ways in which deprived communities foster the social learning of crime?

9. Why are delinquent groups and "beliefs favorable to delinquency" more common in such communities?

10. The residents of deprived communities are higher in strain than residents of other communities. List three specific strains that are more common in deprived communities.

11. Why are the residents of deprived communities more likely than those of other communities to cope with strain through delinquency?

12. I argue that not only do community characteristics affect crime rates but crime rates affect community characteristics. Describe the ways in which this occurs (i.e., how rising crime rates may affect community characteristics).

13. Briefly describe the major arguments of strain, social learning, control, and labeling theories. What four major questions about delinquency do these theories attempt to answer?

THOUGHT AND DISCUSSION QUESTIONS

1. Describe some of the ways in which the residents of your home community may have exercised control over other residents.

2. What types of government and other programs might be implemented to reduce community crime rates? (See Chapter 24.) What types of programs might inadvertently increase community crime rates?

3. How might you combine two or more of the leading delinquency theories into a more general or integrated theory of delinquency? (Note: Certain ways in which these theories might be combined or integrated have already been discussed. For example, this chapter states that high strain and low control lead to the formation

of delinquent groups, which are central to social learning theory. This particular idea is at the heart of the major integrated theory of delinquency developed by Elliott et al., 1979, 1985.)

KEY TERMS

- Residential instability
- Collective efficacy
- Old heads

- social disorganization theories

- Delinquent or criminal subcultures

ENDNOTES

1. *See* Bellair and McNulty, 2005; Bellair and Roscigno, 2000; Kaufman, 2005; Kornhauser, 1978; McNulty and Bellair, 2003; Ousey and Augustine, 2001; Sampson, 1997; Shaw and McKay, 1942.

2. For overviews of the research in this area, *see* Bursik and Grasmick, 1993, 1995; Byrne and Sampson, 1986; Haynie et al., 2006; Kubrin and Weitzer, 2003a; Kornhauser, 1978; Land et al., 1990; Mears and Bhati, 2006; Office of Juvenile Justice and Delinquency Prevention, 1999a; Pratt and Cullen, 2005; Sampson, 1997, 2002, 2006; Sampson and Lauritsen, 1993; Sampson and Wilson, 1995; Sampson et al., 2005; Silver and Miller, 2004; Simons et al., 2005; Stretesky et al., 2004; Taylor, 2001a; Thornberry et al., 2003b; Velez et al., 2003; White, G. 1999.

3. *See* Sampson, 1987; Shihadeh and Steffensmeier, 1994; Wilson, W., 1987.

4. *See* Bellair and McNulty, 2005; Crutchfield et al., 2006; Hawkins, Herrenkohl, Farrington, Brewer, Catalano, and Harachi, 1998; Johnson and Chanhatasilpa, 2003; Krivo and Peterson, 1996; McNulty and Bellair, 2003; McNulty and Holloway, 2000; Peeples and Loeber, 1994; Sampson, 1985, 1987, 2002; Sampson and Raudenbush, 1999; Sampson et al., 2005; Titterington and Damphouse, 2003; Velez, 2006; Velez et al., 2003.

5. For overviews, *see* Hagan, 1994; McNulty and Bellair, 2003; Sampson and Wilson, 1995; Simons et al., 2005; Velez et al., 2003; Wilson, W., 1987, 1996.

6. *See* Bursik and Grasmick, 1996; Elliott et al., 1996; Farrington, 1993a; Peeples and Loeber, 1994; Sampson et al., 1997.

7. *See* Agnew, 1999; Bernard, 1990; Hagan, 1994; Kaufman, 2005; Warner and Fowler, 2003.

8. *See* Piquero et al., 2006; McNulty and Bellair, 2003; Stewart and Simons, 2006.

9. *See* Agnew, 1999; Balkwell, 1990; Bernard, 1990.

10. *See* Bursik, 1988; Bursik and Grasmick, 1993, 1995; Kornhauser, 1978; Kubrin and Weitzer, 2003a; Sampson, 2002, 2006; Sampson and Groves, 1989; Sampson and Raudenbush, 1999; Sampson and Wilson, 1995; Sampson et al., 1997; Sampson et al., 2005; Simons et al., 2005; Taylor, 2001a.

11. *See* Carr et al., 2007; Kubrin and Weitzer, 2003; Silver and Miller, 2004; Warner, 2007.

12. Bellair, 1997, 2000; Bellair and McNulty, 2005; Bellair and Roscigno, 2000; Bellair et al., 2003; Elliott et al., 1996; Hay et al., 2005; Hoffmann, 2003; Kubrin and Weitzer, 2003a; Lee, 2000; Lowenkamp et al., 2003; Peterson et al., 2000; Pratt and Cullen, 2005; Pratt et al., 2004; Rosenfeld et al., 2001; Rountree and Warner, 1999; Sampson, 2002, 2006; Sampson and Groves, 1989; Sampson and Raudenbush, 1999; Sampson et al., 1997; Sampson et al., 2005; Silver and Miller, 2004; Simons et al., 1996; Simons et al., 2005; Stewart, Simons, and Conger, 2002; Velez, 2001; Warner, 2003; Wikstrom and Loeber, 2000.

13. *See* Anderson, 1994, 1999; Bourgois, 2003; Fagan, 1998; Kubrin and Weitzer, 2003a, 2003b; McNulty and Bellair, 2003; Pratt and Cullen, 2005; Sampson and Bartusch, 1999; Simons et al., 2005; Stewart et al., 2005; Veysey and Messner, 1999; Wilkinson, 2003; and Chapter 16.

14. *See* Anderson 1994, 1999; Bourgois, 2003; Brezina et al., 2004; Fagan, 1998; Kubrin and Weitzer, 2003a, 2003b; Majors and Billson, 1992; McNulty and Bellair, 2003; Oliver, 1994; Sampson and Bartusch, 1999; Stewart and Simons, 2006; Warner, 2003.

15. *See* note 14 above.

16. *See* Bellair, 2000; Liska and Warner, 1991; Liska et al., 1998; Sampson, 2002; Sampson and Raudenbush, 1999.

PART 3

The Causes of Delinquency
Research

Chapters 6 through 12 described the leading theories of delinquency. These theories have inspired much research on the causes of delinquency, with criminologists testing these theories or ideas derived from them. Criminologists have also conducted research on the causes of delinquency that was not directly inspired by these theories, but this research can nevertheless be interpreted in terms of these theories.

The next six chapters describe the major research on the causes of delinquency. Chapter 13 describes those individual traits that cause delinquency, with a focus on the traits of low intelligence, low self-control, and irritability. Chapters 14 through 17 then describe those features of the social environment that cause delinquency, with a focus on family, school, and peer environments. As you will see, the effect of individual traits and environmental factors on delinquency is readily explained in terms of strain, social learning, control, and/or labeling theories.

Chapter 18 attempts to "pull everything together" by presenting a general or integrated theory of delinquency. This theory lists the key causes of delinquency, describes why these causes increase delinquency, and discusses the relationship between these causes. The chapter then uses the integrated theory to explain certain basic facts about delinquency, such as why males are more delinquent than females.

But before I describe the research on the causes of delinquency, I want to highlight a few basic points about these causes.

First, **delinquency is caused by a good number of factors.** This may sound obvious, but it is common for politicians and people in the general public to blame delinquency on one or a few factors. For example, it is frequently claimed that delinquency is caused by mass media violence or a lack of religion. Not only do such claims ignore the many other causes of delinquency, but media violence and the lack of religion are not even among the most important causes of delinquency (see Chapter 17).

Second, **most factors have only small to moderate effects on delinquency, although a few factors have larger effects.** No factor, however, perfectly explains delinquency. So when I state that "factor X causes delinquency," you should **not** assume that all juveniles with factor X are delinquent and that all juveniles without factor X are nondelinquent. Factor X simply increases the probability that juveniles will engage in delinquency, perhaps by only a small amount. I try to provide some indication of the relative importance of the different causes of delinquency, although this is sometimes difficult because of a lack of good research (i.e., studies that examine large, representative samples of juveniles, employ good measures, examine a wide range of causes, and are longitudinal—see Chapter 5).

Third, **most of the causes of delinquency are related to one another.** For example, individuals with traits conducive to delinquency are more likely to be in environments conducive to delinquency. So, irritable juveniles are more likely to experience poor parenting (in part because they upset and overwhelm their parents). To give another example, juveniles who experience poor parenting are more likely to associate with delinquent peers and to belong to gangs. It is difficult to keep track of all the relationships between the causes of delinquency, but I will try to give you a rough sense of how these causes are related in the chapters that follow. And I provide a summary of such relationships in Chapter 18 when I present an integrated theory of delinquency.

Fourth, **not only are the causes of delinquency related to one another, they also sometimes condition the effect of one another on delinquency.** For example, many criminologists now argue that individual traits and the social environment condition the effect of one another on delinquency. So irritable individuals are more likely to engage in delinquency when they are in environments conducive to delinquency, such as abusive families and delinquent peer groups. There has not been much research on such conditioning effects, although the limited research that has been done is generally supportive of such effects. In particular, certain data suggest that delinquency is most likely among individuals who possess traits like irritability and low self-control *and* are in environments conducive to delinquency.

Keep these points in mind when you read the following chapters. While I often discuss the causes of delinquency in isolation from one another, there are **numerous causes, and they usually work together to produce delinquency.**

CHAPTER 13

Individual Traits
What Impact Do Individual Traits Have on Delinquency?

This chapter begins to describe the research on the causes of delinquency, focusing on those individual traits that increase the likelihood of delinquency. I first list the most important of these traits and describe why they increase delinquency, drawing on strain, social learning, control, and labeling theories. Then I discuss why some individuals are more likely than others to possess these traits.

Are Juveniles with Certain Traits More Likely to Engage in Delinquency?

Think back to some of the people you knew before college—not just your friends but others as well—and think about the ways these people differed from one another. They probably differed in terms of intelligence—some were smart and some were not so smart. Some were probably easygoing and friendly, while others were "touchy" or "irritable." Some liked excitement or adventure, even risky, dangerous activities, while others preferred safer activities. Some were impulsive, engaging in activities without much thought for the consequences, while others were more thoughtful and reflective. Some were socially skilled, getting along well with people, while others had problems in social relations. People often differ in the traits they possess. **By** *traits,* **I mean relatively stable ways of perceiving, thinking about, and behaving toward the environment and oneself** (see Blackburn, 1993). For example, if a person regularly acts without thinking, we say this person possesses the trait of impulsivity.

Research suggests that people with certain traits are more likely to engage in delin-quency. Such traits include low intelligence (IQ), learning disabilities (e.g., reading disabilities), attention deficit hyperactivity disorder (ADHD), impulsivity, risk seeking, the reduced ability to learn from punishment, irritability, insensitivity to others or low empathy, poor social skills, poor problem-solving skills, immature moral reasoning, amoral beliefs, and beliefs favorable to delinquency.[1]

Researchers are still trying to determine the relative importance of these traits in causing delinquency, although we have good evidence that certain of these traits have moderate to strong effects on delinquency. Researchers are also trying to determine how these traits are related to one another. We know that many of these traits are strongly correlated with one another; that is, they often appear together in juveniles. These clusters of related traits are sometimes called *super-traits.* One such super-trait was described in Chapter 8: low self-control. Low self-control comprises several more specific traits, including impulsivity, risk seeking, and a lack of ambition or motivation. There is still some debate, however, over how many super-traits there are and the composition of these traits.[2]

I focus on a few key traits in this chapter, traits whose effect on delinquency is reasonably well established. The first of these traits is *low verbal IQ.* The remaining traits are grouped together into the super-traits of *low self-control* and **irritability.** Recent data suggest that these super-traits play an especially important role in the explanation of delinquency, particularly high-rate, chronic offending (see Chapter 10).[3]

Low Verbal IQ

Much data suggest that **individuals with low IQ scores are more likely to engage in delinquency.**[4] This finding appears when criminologists use official and self-report measures of delinquency. It appears when researchers control for third variables like social class and race. For example, researchers find that IQ is associated with delinquency when they limit their analysis to whites only and to African Americans only. Also, this finding appears in longitudinal as well as cross-sectional studies. Data suggest that it is primarily a person's **verbal IQ** score that affects delinquency. (One's total IQ score is made up of two components: verbal and performance. The verbal IQ score reflects several subtests, measuring such things as general factual knowledge, vocabulary, memory, abstract thinking, and social comprehension and judgment. All these subtests are administered orally and require oral answers. The performance IQ score reflects several other subtests, which measure such things as attention to detail, visual puzzle solving, and maze completion. Manual rather than oral responses are required.) Individuals with low verbal scores have trouble expressing themselves, remembering information, and thinking abstractly.

How might we explain the effect of low verbal IQ on delinquency? A strain theorist would argue that low IQ leads to increased strain, making it more difficult for juveniles to achieve goals like educational success and increasing the likelihood of negative relations with teachers, peers, and others.[5] Low verbal IQ is also associated with problem-solving ability, so individuals with low verbal scores might be less able to cope with strain through legitimate channels (Moffitt, 1990). **Social learning theorists** argue that low verbal IQ **reduces** the likelihood that individuals will be reinforced for conventional behavior, like schoolwork, and thereby makes crime more appealing. **Control theorists** argue that low IQ leads to poor school performance and negative attitudes toward school, thereby weakening one's stake in conformity.[6] Also, low IQ may lead to offending because it reduces the individual's ability to foresee the consequences of offending and to exercise self-control.[7]

Low Self-Control

Low self-control is a super-trait consisting of several more specific traits.[8] Such traits include:

1. *Impulsivity,* or the tendency to act without considering the consequences of one's behavior. Impulsivity is sometimes measured with questions like "I often act on the spur of the moment without thinking" (agree or disagree). (Note: This question and the other questions used to illustrate the specific traits that make up low self-control and irritability are from Grasmick et al., 1993.)

2. A strong **preference for immediate versus delayed rewards,** even if the delayed rewards are larger. This trait is measured with questions like "I often do whatever brings me pleasure here and now, even at the cost of some distant goal."

3. *Risk seeking,* or a strong need for exciting, thrilling, and risky activities. This trait is measured with questions like "Sometimes I will take a risk just for the fun of it."

4. *Hyperactivity,* or high activity levels, restlessness, and a tendency to always be on the go. This trait is measured with questions like "I almost always feel better when I am on the move than when I am sitting and thinking."

5. **Low ambition, motivation, or perseverance.** Individuals with this trait do not finish tasks, have trouble making and carrying out plans, and are easily distracted or diverted. This trait is measured with questions like "When things get complicated, I tend to quit or withdraw."

6. **Amoral beliefs or beliefs favorable to delinquency.** Individuals believe that certain delinquent acts are neither bad nor good (amoral beliefs), they unconditionally approve of certain minor forms of delinquency, they believe more serious forms of delinquency are justifiable or excusable under certain conditions, and/or they hold values conducive to delinquency, like toughness. (Such beliefs are more fully described in Chapters 7 and 8.)

It may be difficult to keep all of these traits in mind, but try to imagine what people with these traits are like. Basically, they might be described as **"wild" or "out of control."**

How might we explain the effect of low self-control on delinquency? A **strain theorist** would argue that individuals low in self-control have more trouble achieving their goals through legitimate channels, especially given their low motivation. Further, such individuals are more likely to upset others, given that they are "out of control" and prone to risky behavior. These others might then respond with negative treatment, thereby increasing strain. Finally, individuals with low self-control are more likely to respond to strain with delinquency, given such things as their impulsivity, low motivation, and amoral beliefs or beliefs favorable to delinquency.

A **social learning theorist** would argue that individuals with low self-control are more attracted to the rewards associated with crime, since these rewards are typically immediate and easily achieved (e.g., it is much easier to steal money than to work for it). Further, they often find crime rewarding in and of itself, since crime typically involves risky behavior. Finally, they are more likely to view crime in a favorable light given their beliefs.

A **control theorist** would argue that individuals with low self-control are, by definition, less likely to be constrained by direct controls and by their stake in conformity. Being impulsive, they give less thought to the consequences of their crime. These individuals are also less likely to be constrained by their beliefs, since they hold amoral beliefs. Further, such individuals are less likely to develop a stake in conformity given their low ambition and their tendency to irritate conventional others like parents and teachers (which undermines their bonds to these individuals).

Finally, a **labeling theorist** would argue that such individuals are more likely to be labeled and treated as "bad" or "evil," with conventional others rejecting them or treating them in a negative manner. And this, in turn, increases their level of strain, reduces their control, fosters the social learning of crime (especially if they come to associate with delinquent peers), and leads to a delinquent self-concept.

Irritability

Irritability is also a super-trait consisting of several more specific traits.[9] Such traits include:

1. **A heightened sensitivity to stressors or strains.** Irritable individuals are more easily upset than others and display stronger emotional reactions when upset, including higher levels of anger. This trait is measured by questions like "I can get very upset when things don't go my way" and "My anger frequently gets the best of me."

2. **The tendency to attribute one's problems to the malicious behavior of others.** Irritable individuals believe others are "out to get them" and tend to blame others for their problems. For example, suppose someone bumps into an irritable person on the street; the irritable person would likely interpret this as a deliberate provocation, while others might simply view it as an accident.

3. **A tendency to be self-centered and to have little concern for the rights and feelings of others.** This trait is measured by questions like "I will try to get the things I want even when I know it's causing problems for other people" and "I am not very sympathetic to other people when they are having problems."

4. **An aggressive or antagonistic interactional style.** This trait includes a tendency to respond to conflicts physically.

Again, it may be difficult to keep all of these traits in mind. But if you imagine what someone with these traits is like, he or she might be described as **"mean" or "nasty" or "having a short fuse."**

It is easy to explain why this trait increases the likelihood of delinquency, especially if we draw on strain theory. Individuals with this trait are more likely to provoke negative reactions from others, thereby increasing their level of strain. They are more sensitive to strains, and they are more inclined to cope with strain through delinquency.

A **social learning theorist** would argue that irritable individuals are more likely to be rejected by conventional others and to associate with delinquent peers, who better tolerate their irritability (and sometimes reinforce it). Also, irritable individuals find crime more rewarding, given their tendency to blame others for their problems and their aggressive interactional style.

A **control theorist** would argue that irritable individuals are less responsive to direct controls, since their anger often "gets the best of them." Such individuals are also less likely to develop a stake in conformity; they frequently alienate conventional others like parents and teachers. Furthermore, such individuals are less likely to condemn crime.

A **labeling theorist** would argue that irritable individuals are more likely to be viewed and treated as "bad" people, with all of the negative effects I described.

Summary

Three major sets of traits increase the likelihood of delinquency: low verbal IQ and, especially, the super-traits of low self-control and irritability. The effect of these traits on delinquency is easily explained using strain, social learning, control, and labeling theories.

Having described these traits, I now turn to a rather important question: Why is it that some individuals are more likely than others to possess these traits?

Why Are Some Individuals More Likely than Others to Possess These Traits?

These traits are a function of biological factors and the social environment. I first discuss the ways in which biological factors may contribute to these traits, and then I examine the role of the social environment.

Biological Influences on Traits

Evidence suggests that **there may be a genetic component to crime** and that **crime may sometimes result from certain types of biological harm,** such as that caused by birth complications, head injury, and exposure to toxic substances such as lead. Researchers, however, do not claim that these factors lead directly to crime. For example, there is no gene for crime. Rather, it is usually claimed that **genetic factors and biological harms create a predisposition for crime** by influencing the likelihood that individuals will develop traits like those mentioned in the preceding section. Such factors are usually said to influence the development of these traits through their effect on the *central nervous system* (the brain and spinal cord) and the *autonomic nervous system* (which controls heart rate and gland secretions, among other things, and influences the emotional reaction to stimuli).

Genetic inheritance of crime.
Studies suggest that there is a genetic component to crime.[10] That is, crime is inherited to some extent. Researchers have tried to estimate the extent of genetic inheritance using several methods, most notably, *twin studies, adoption studies,* and *molecular genetic studies.* Twin studies compare identical twins to fraternal twins. Identical twins are genetically identical, while fraternal twins are about 50 percent genetically alike on those genes that vary among people (see Raine, 1993:54). It is assumed that twins, whether identical or fraternal, are exposed to the same environmental influences. If crime is genetically inherited, we would expect that identical twins would be more similar in criminal behavior than fraternal twins. Most studies indicate that this is the case. Twin studies, however, suffer from certain problems. Most notably, evidence suggests that identical twins are more likely to spend time together and share the same friends than are fraternal twins. These facts, rather than their identical genes, may explain their greater similarity in criminal behavior (see Rowe, 2002:19–21).

Adoption studies overcome these problems, although such studies are not problem-free. Adoption studies focus on children who were separated from their biological parents early in life. The traits of these children are compared to the traits of their biological parents. If a tendency to commit crime is inherited, there should be more crime among adopted children whose biological parents are criminals than among adopted children whose biological parents are not criminals. Most data suggest that this is the case. For example, one large study in Denmark found the following: When neither adopted nor biological parents were criminals, 13.5 percent of the adopted boys had criminal convictions; when adoptive parents were not criminals and the biological parents were, 20 percent of the adopted boys had criminal convictions (Raine, 1993).

Molecular genetic studies are a more recent development. Here researchers identify specific genes or DNA sequences (which carry genetic information) and try to determine the extent to which they are associated with criminal behavior (see Baker et al., 2006; Rutter et al., 2006). Researchers, in particular, examine individuals with varying DNA sequences to determine if those with certain sequences are more likely to engage in crime. In doing so, researchers try to take account of third variables that may affect the association between genes and crime.

Although the evidence suggests that the tendency to commit crime is inherited to some degree, it is difficult to precisely specify the extent to which the tendency is inherited. Genetic factors may be as important as environmental factors for some types of crimes and offenders. At the same time, certain cautions are in order. The extent to which crime is inherited may vary by type of crime (e.g., violent versus property) and type of offender. Evidence suggests that juvenile delinquency may be less heritable than adult crime, although genetic factors may play an influential role in the explanation of high-rate, chronic delinquency (Raine, 1993:73–76). Finally, both twin and adoption studies suggest that genetic inheritance only partly explains crime, and that environmental factors also play an important role in the explanation of crime. In particular, these studies suggest that crime is most likely when the individual possesses a biological predisposition for crime and is in an environment conducive to crime. For example, crime is most likely when the individual has both biological and adoptive parents who are criminals (see especially Rutter et al., 2006).

Biological harms and crime. Studies also suggest that experiencing certain *biological harms* increases the likelihood of crime. Such harms include: (1) the mother's poor health habits during pregnancy, including poor nutrition and alcohol and drug use; (2) certain types of delivery complications; (3) exposure to toxic substances such as lead; (4) certain dietary deficiencies; and (5) head injury.[11] The research in these areas often suffers from one or more of the problems listed in Chapter 5, such as the failure to control for relevant third variables or to conduct longitudinal studies. Nevertheless, the data as a whole suggest that certain types of biological harm may contribute to at least some crime.

The central and autonomic nervous systems. The mechanisms by which genetic inheritance and biological harm contribute to crime are not fully understood. Most researchers in the area, however, suggest that such factors contribute to crime through their effect on the central and autonomic nervous systems. A number of possible effects have been explored, the most popular of which include the following: Genetic factors and biological harm may contribute to **dysfunctions in the frontal lobe of the brain,** which is involved in abstract thinking, planning, the self-monitoring of behavior, and behavioral inhibition (Moffitt and Henry, 1989; Raine, 1993:105). These factors may also contribute to **dysfunctions in the left hemisphere of the brain;** such dysfunctions have been linked to low verbal IQ scores. These factors **may affect the autonomic nervous system,** with data suggesting that criminals are underaroused. That is, criminals show less emotional response to stimuli (they are "physiologically 'drowsy'" in the words of Bartol and Bartol, 1986:69). This underarousal is reflected in their lower than average skin conductance (i.e., criminals sweat less in response to stimuli), lower resting heart rate, and slower alpha brain waves. This underarousal may contribute to traits such as hyperactivity.

Researchers are now investigating the ways in which genetic inheritance and biological harms may affect the central and autonomic nervous systems. For example, recent data suggest some of these factors may result in reduced levels of *serotonin,* a neurotransmitter.[12] Neurotransmitters allow for communication between brain cells and so underlie all of our behavior, thoughts, perceptions, emotions, and the like. Reduced serotonin may lower one's level of inhibition, contributing to such traits as impulsivity.

Biological factors and traits conducive to crime. Genetic factors and certain types of biological harm, then, may increase the likelihood of crime through their effect on the central and autonomic nervous systems. There is still the question, however, of why **"dysfunctions" in the central and autonomic nervous systems** may lead to crime. The most commonly advanced theory is that such dysfunctions increase the likelihood that individuals will develop traits conducive to crime, such as low IQ, impulsivity, and irritability. There is some evidence for this line of argument.[13] In particular, there is good evidence of a genetic effect on IQ, low self-control, and irritability.[14] Related to this, molecular genetic studies are beginning to identify the specific genes related to traits like hyperactivity and impulsivity (see Baker et al., 2006; Fishbein, 2001; Rowe, 2002). There is also good evidence that many of the traits listed here are influenced by biological harms, such as birth complications and exposure to lead. Lead poisoning, for example, has been linked to such traits as hyperactivity (Denno, 1990).

Many of these traits have also been linked to dysfunctions in the central and auto-nomic nervous systems.[15] Dysfunctions in the frontal lobe of the brain may contribute to such traits as hyperactivity, the preference for immediate rewards, impulsivity, irritability, and insensitivity to others. Underarousal in the autonomic nervous system has been linked to traits such as hyperactivity and sensation seeking. It takes more to stimulate under-aroused individuals, which may cause them to become overly active and in greater need of thrills or excitement.

Environmental Influences on Traits

The traits discussed here are also a function of the individual's social environment, espe-cially the early family environment.[16] In particular, children are less likely to be irritable and low in self-control when **parents teach them** how to manage their anger and exercise self-control. Parents do this in a number of ways. For example, parents model **high** self-control; parents make clear that the impulsive, risky, and "lazy" behaviors associated with **low** self-control are not acceptable; and parents monitor their children's behavior, consis-tently sanctioning them when they exhibit low self-control and reinforcing them when they exercise high self-control (see Chapter 14 for a fuller discussion of effective parenting methods).

The **resources** possessed by parents also influence these traits. In particular, data sug-gest that a parent's **social class** has a strong effect on at least some of the individual traits listed here (e.g., Meich et al., 1999). At least part of this effect may stem from the impact of social class on parenting practices (see Chapter 14). Further, **social programs** that attempt to compensate for early family problems often lead to changes in these traits. For example, data indicate that children from deprived environments experience a boost in IQ when they are placed in programs that provide intellectual stimulation—such as certain types of preschool programs (Ramey and Ramey, 1995).

Traits, then, are a function of the social environment as well as of biological factors. It should be noted, however, that it is often difficult to separate out the effects of environ-mental and biological factors in a precise manner. Many types of biological harm are a function of the social environment (like one's social class). Lower-class individuals, for ex-ample, are more likely to be exposed to lead and to have poor prenatal care (Denno, 1990). At the same time, biological factors may shape one's social environment. Children with dysfunctions in their central and autonomic nervous systems, for example, may be more difficult for parents to raise. As a consequence, their parents may be more likely to ignore them or treat them in a harsh manner.

Further, **environmental and biological factors may condition the effect of one an-other on the traits discussed** (see the discussion of conditioning effects at the start of Chapter 5). For example, biological factors, like genetic inheritance or birth complications, may be more likely to produce these traits if the individual is in a poor family environment. A major new line of research, in fact, examines the extent to which environmental factors influence the "expression" of genes (see Rutter et al., 2006). Likewise, a poor family envi-ronment may be more likely to produce these traits if the individual has a genetic predis-position for such traits or has experienced certain types of biological harm. The most important point to remember, however, is that there is evidence suggesting that these traits are a function of both biological and environmental factors.[17]

Summary

Evidence suggests that juveniles with certain traits are more likely to engage in delinquency, especially high-rate, chronic offending. These traits include low verbal IQ and the super-traits of low self-control and irritability. The effect of these traits on delinquency is readily explained in terms of strain, social learning, control, and labeling theories. And, as just discussed, these traits are a function of both biological and environmental factors.

Teaching Aids

Controversial Issue: Should Delinquents Be Held Responsible for Their Behavior?

The following exercise is adapted from Raine (1993:309–312). Imagine a hypothetical juvenile named Joe with the following characteristics: Joe's mother is a drug addict, and his father is a life-course persistent offender. The mother suffered serious birth complications during Joe's delivery, probably due to her poor health habits during pregnancy, including her drug use. And Joe experienced a number of additional biological harms through adolescence, including head injuries from accidents and assaults. Joe, then, had a strong biological predisposition to develop those traits conducive to crime, like low self-control and irritability.

Joe grew up in a highly aversive environment. Joe never knew his father, who abandoned his mother when she became pregnant. Joe was rejected and abused by his drug-addicted mother and her boyfriends, was surrounded by siblings who regularly engaged in crime, and grew up in a deprived neighborhood with a high crime rate. Not surprisingly, Joe developed the traits of low self-control and irritability. Joe was rejected by conventional peers as a result and eventually joined a neighborhood gang. And Joe experienced numerous problems in school and eventually dropped out.

Joe was the subject of some pity and concern while a child. Social welfare agencies made an effort to respond to his poor home life and other problems, and Joe was placed in a series of foster homes—although he ran away from most of these homes. Joe, however, was shown little pity when he turned into an adolescent and started committing serious crimes. Joe was arrested on several occasions and spent some time in juvenile institutions—but such institutions provided few rehabilitative services. They did, however, provide much exposure to delinquent peers. At age 15, Joe held up a store with a gun, shooting the owner in the arm. Joe was arrested for armed robbery and aggravated assault, tried as an adult under a new "get tough" law, and sentenced to 20 years in prison.

While Joe is not real, elements of his life history are taken from real cases, and he resembles many life-course persistent offenders in the United States. So assume, for the sake of argument, that Joe is a real person. I have two questions for you: **Should we hold Joe responsible for his criminal behavior?** Related to this, **should Joe receive a 20-year sentence for his crimes?**

These questions involve a key issue regarding the causes of crime. Some individuals contend that crime is largely a matter of **free choice** and, as such, criminals deserve punishment, including serious punishment if they commit serious crimes. This is the underlying idea of the adult criminal justice system—although a very small percentage of offenders are able to escape punishment because they satisfy the legal criteria for mental illness. (Joe did not satisfy these criteria, since he knew what he was doing, knew his crime was considered wrong, and was not overcome by an "irresistible impulse" to commit the crime.) Other individuals, however, contend that crime is largely the result of **forces beyond the individual's control**—like biological factors and poor parenting. As such, criminals do not deserve serious punishment but rather are in need of help. (For an expanded discussion of these issues, see Agnew, 1995c; Wright and Brezina, 2001).

TEST YOUR KNOWLEDGE OF THIS CHAPTER

1. What is an "individual trait"?
2. List or briefly describe any five traits that appear to increase the likelihood of crime.
3. What is meant by a "super-trait"?
4. Describe the characteristics of someone with a low verbal IQ.
5. Drawing on the leading delinquency theories (strain, social learning, control, and labeling), describe why low verbal IQ increases the likelihood of delinquency.
6. Describe any three of the specific traits that make up low self-control. At a general level, describe what someone low in self-control is like.
7. Drawing on the leading delinquency theories, describe why low self-control increases the likelihood of delinquency.
8. Describe any three of the specific traits that make up irritability. At a general level, describe someone who is irritable.
9. Drawing on the leading delinquency theories, describe why irritability increases the likelihood of delinquency.
10. Describe the three major ways in which researchers have tried to determine whether crime is inherited.
11. Describe any three types of biological harm that may increase the likelihood of crime.
12. Genes and biological harms are said to influence the development of traits conducive to crime through their effects on the central nervous system (CNS) and autonomic nervous system (ANS). Describe any two of these effects on the CNS and/or ANS.
13. Describe one piece of evidence suggesting that dysfunctions in the CNS and/or ANS contribute to traits conducive to crime.
14. Traits conducive to crime are also a function of the early family environment. Describe those parenting practices that influence the level of self-control.
15. Why is it often difficult to precisely determine the extent to which crime is caused by biological or social factors?
16. What do I mean when I state that biological and environmental factors may condition the effect of one another on traits conducive to crime? Give an example of such a conditioning effect.

THOUGHT AND DISCUSSION QUESTIONS

1. Describe the ways in which individuals who are irritable and low in self-control may shape their social environment. Consider the reactions they might evoke from others in particular situations, how they might alter their ongoing relations with others such

as parents and school officials, and how they might "select themselves into" certain types of environments through their actions. (See Chapter 10.)

2. Do you think the juvenile's school and peer environments may influence his or her levels of self-control and irritability? If so, describe how.

3. Do you think there are gender differences in levels of self-control and irritability? If so, what might be the source of these differences? (See Chapter 18.)

4. Drawing on the arguments in this chapter, what policies or programs would you suggest to reduce delinquency? (Note: Some of these programs, like those designed to reduce exposure to the lead in old paint, might, at first glance, seem far removed from delinquency. See Chapter 24 for examples of programs designed to address the traits that cause delinquency and the biological and social factors that influence these traits.)

KEY TERMS

- Traits
- Super-traits
- Low verbal IQ
- Low self-control
- Impulsivity
- Risk seeking

- Hyperactivity
- Irritability
- Central nervous system
- Autonomic nervous system

- Twin studies
- Adoption studies
- Molecular genetic studies
- Biological harms
- Serotonin

ENDNOTES

1. For overviews, *see* Andrews and Bonta, 2003; Baron, 2003; Bennett et al., 2005; Blackburn, 1993; Caspi et al., 1994; Chapple, 2005; Dodge and Schwartz, 1997; Farrington, 1996b, 1998; Farrington and Welsh, 2007; Goode, 2008; Hollin, 2002; Lahey and Waldman, 2005; Little and Steinberg, 2006; Lynam and Miller, 2004; Miller and Lynam, 2001; Pratt and Cullen, 2000; Pratt et al., 2002; Matsueda et al., 2006; Piquero and Bouffard, 2007; Rutter et al., 1998.

2. *See* Arneklev et al., 1999; Caspi et al., 1994; Caspi et al., 2005; Farrington and Welsh, 2007; Lahey and Waldman, 2005; Lynam and Miller, 2004; Miller and Lynam, 2001; Piquero and Boufford, 2007; Wright et al., 1999b.

3. *See* Bartusch et al., 1997; Caspi et al., 2005; Colder and Stice, 1998; Farrington and Welsh, 2007; Lahey and Waldman, 2005; Lynam and Miller, 2004; McGloin et al., 2004; Miller and Lynam, 2001; Moffitt, 1993, 1997; Moffitt et al., 1994, 2001; Rutter et al., 1998.

4. *See* Bartusch et al., 1997; Bellair and McNulty, 2005; Blackburn, 1993; Denno, 1990; Farrington, 1996b, 1998; Farrington and Welsh, 2007; Hirschi and Hindelang, 1977; Lahey and Waldman, 2005; Loeber, Farrington, Stouthamer-Loeber, Moffitt, and Caspi, 1998; McGloin et al., 2004; Moffitt, 1990, 1997; Moffitt et al., 1994; Rutter et al., 1998; Wilson and Herrnstein, 1985.

5. *See* Bellair and McNulty, 2005; Loeber, Farrington, Stouthamer-Loeber, Moffitt, and Caspi, 1998; McGloin et al., 2004; Moffitt, 1990; Wilson and Herrnstein, 1985:171.

6. *See* Bellair and McNulty, 2005; Denno, 1990; Farrington and Welsh, 2007; Hirschi and Hindelang, 1977; McGloin et al., 2004; Rutter and Giller, 1983.

7. *See* Farrington, 1996b; Farrington and Welsh, 2007; McGloin et al., 2004; Moffitt, 1990; Wilson and Herrnstein, 1985.

8. *See* Arneklev et al., 1999; Gottfredson and Hirschi, 1990; Grasmick et al., 1993; Miller and Lynam, 2001; Moffitt et al., 2001; Pratt and Cullen, 2000; Pratt et al., 2001; Wright et al., 1999b.

9. *See* Agnew et al., 2002; Arneklev et al., 1999; Caspi et al., 1994; Caspi et al., 2005; Colder and Stice, 1998; Lahey and Waldman, 2005; Miller and Lynam, 2001; Moffitt et al., 2001; Wright et al., 1999b.

ENDNOTES (continued)

10. For excellent overviews, *see* Baker et al., 2006; Brennan et al., 1995; Carey and Goldman, 1997; Farrington 1998; Fishbein, 2001; Lahey and Waldman, 2005; Moffitt, 2006; Raine, 1993, 2002a; Rhee and Waldman, 2002; Rodgers et al., 2001; Rowe, 2002; Rutter et al., 1998; Rutter et al., 2006; Walsh, 2002.

11. *See* Brennan et al., 1995; Denno, 1990; Fishbein, 2001; Hawkins, Herrenkohl, Farrington, Brewer, Catalano, and Harachi, 1998; McGloin et al., 2006; Raine, 1993, 2002a, 2001b; Rutter et al., 1998; Tibbetts and Piquero, 1999.

12. *See* Baker et al., 2006; Berman et al., 1997; Fishbein, 2001; Moffitt et al., 1997.

13. *See* Baker et al., 2006; Bennett et al., 2005; Brennan et al., 1995; Cauffman et al., 2005; Denno, 1990; Farrington, 1996b, 1998; Farrington and Welsh, 2007; Fishbein, 2001; Gruber et al., 2005; Hollin, 1992; Moffitt, 1990; Raine, 1993, 2002a; Rowe, 2002; Rutter et al., 1998; Wilson and Herrnstein, 1985; Wright and Beaver, 2005.

14. *See* Baker et al., 2006; Caspi, 1998; Caspi et al., 2005; Lahey and Waldman, 2005; Plomin and Petrill, 1997; Rutter et al., 1998; Wright and Beaver, 2005.

15. *See* Baker et al., 2006; Bennett et al., 2005; Caufman et al., 2005; Gruber et al., 2005; Lykken, 1996; Moffitt, 1990; Moffitt and Henry, 1989; Raine, 1993, 2002a; Rowe, 2002; Wright and Beaver, 2005.

16. *See* Bartol and Bartol, 1986; Wright and Beaver, 2005; Blackburn, 1993; Caspi et al., 2005; Cullen et al., 2008; Gottfredson and Hirschi, 1990; Hay, 2001b; Hay and Forrest, 2006; Lahey and Waldman, 2005; Pratt et al., 2004; Pulkkinen, 1986; Unnever et al., 2003; Wilson and Herrnstein, 1985.

17. *See* Baker et al., 2006; Caspi et al., 2005; Lahey and Waldman, 2005; Ousey and Wilcox, 2007; Raine, 2002b; Raine et al., 1997; Rowe, 2002; Rutter and Silberg, 2002; Rutter et al., 1998; Rutter et al., 2006; Tibbetts and Piquero, 1999.

CHAPTER 14

The Family
What Impact Does the Family Have on Delinquency?

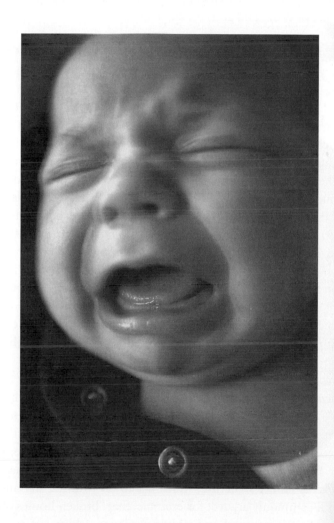

Chapter 13 stated that certain individual traits increase the likelihood of delinquency, especially high-rate, chronic delinquency. Delinquency is also caused by the individual's social environment. Individuals in certain types of environments are more likely to engage in delinquency—for reasons explained by strain, social learning, control, and labeling theories. These environments have a relatively large effect on individuals who possess traits conducive to delinquency, but they also lead many "normal" individuals to engage in delinquency.

This chapter begins to examine the effect of the social environment on delinquency. In particular, I ask what types of families increase the likelihood of delinquency. Chapter 15 examines the effect of school experiences and characteristics on delinquency. Subsequent chapters then focus on the effect of delinquent peer groups, gangs, religion, work, the mass media, and the presence of drugs and guns on delinquency.

The Effect of the Family on Delinquency

All major delinquency theories argue that the family plays a central role in determining whether juveniles engage in delinquency. **The family**—perhaps more than any other social group—**influences: (1) the juvenile's level of and reaction to strain, (2) whether the juvenile learns to conform or deviate, (3) the control to which the juvenile is subject,** and **(4) the extent to which the juvenile is subject to labeling.** The family sometimes has a **direct effect on delinquency,** and it sometimes has an **indirect effect** through its influence on such things as the juvenile's individual traits, school performance, and selection of friends. Many criminologists have gone so far as to claim that juvenile delinquency is largely a function of the juvenile's family experiences (e.g., Gottfredson and Hirschi, 1990; Patterson et al., 1989). Several states have even passed laws that hold parents responsible for the criminal behavior of their children in certain circumstances. These laws are seldom enforced, but a Michigan couple was recently fined $1,200 for not controlling their 16-year-old son. The son had been arrested for burglarizing several homes and having a four-foot marijuana plant in his bedroom. According to the verdict, the couple had failed to properly supervise their son after his earlier arrests for burglarizing churches and for attacking his father with a golf club (see Arthur, 2005; Brank et al., 2006; Murphy and Healy, 1999).

What does the research say about the influence of the family? Are family factors a major cause of delinquency? You've already been exposed to the family research in Chapters 6 through 9, where I discussed the evidence on strain, social learning, control theories, and labeling theories. Much of the research on the family has been directly guided by these theories. As a consequence, portions of the following discussion will sound familiar. The research on the family and delinquency has focused on **four major aspects of the family.** The first aspect is **family structure,** which has to do with the size and composition of the family; it is commonly argued, for example, that "broken homes" cause delinquency. The second aspect is **parental and sibling deviance,** which has to do with the extent to which parents and siblings engage in crime and deviant behavior. The third aspect is the **quality of family relationships,** which has to do with the emotional ties between family members and how well family members get along with one another. It is commonly argued, for example, that juveniles who love and respect their parents are less delinquent. The fourth aspect is **parental socialization,** which has to do with the extent to which parents teach their children to conform or to deviate. In particular, do parents provide clear rules, monitor behavior, sanction deviance, instruct and model conformity, reinforce conformity, and provide social support? I present here the major research findings in each of these four areas.

Family Structure

Are Juveniles from Broken Homes More Delinquent?

An "intact" home is typically defined as one in which both natural parents are present. *Broken homes* are defined as all other homes. Researchers sometimes distinguish between different types of broken homes, such as homes in which only the natural mother is present and homes in which there is a natural mother and a stepfather.

Many criminologists, politicians, and others argue that broken homes are a major cause of delinquency. The alleged impact of broken homes is usually explained in terms of the leading delinquency theories (see especially Rebellon, 2002). Juveniles in broken homes are said to be **under more strain,** partly because of the conflict associated with the breakup and partly because of the financial and other problems that often follow the breakup. Juveniles in broken homes are also said to be **subject to less control;** among other things, the breakup is said to disrupt the emotional bond between juveniles and their parents, reduce the ability of parents to exercise effective supervision, and have a negative impact on the juveniles' school performance. Further, it is said that juveniles in broken homes are **less exposed to conventional role models** and **more likely to fall prey to delinquent peers,** who encourage delinquent behavior. Finally, it is said that juveniles from broken homes are **more likely to be labeled delinquent.**

These arguments have taken on a special urgency in recent years, given the **large percentage of juveniles who now live in broken homes.** Thirty-three percent of all children under 18 lived in broken homes in 2006 (23 percent of all children lived with only their natural mothers, 5 percent lived with only their natural fathers, and 5 percent lived with neither of their natural parents; the percentage of children living with a natural parent and a stepparent was not estimated in this survey). About 24 percent of white, non-Hispanic children lived in broken homes, versus 34 percent of Hispanic children and 65 percent of African American children. The percentage of children living in broken homes has more than doubled since 1970, although the percentage has remained stable since the late 1990s for whites and Hispanics and has increased slightly for African Americans (from 62 to 65 percent). **Children in broken homes are more likely to suffer from a range of problems, most notably poverty.** In 2004, 10 percent of the children in married-couple families were living in poverty versus 37 percent of the children in mother-only families (see Federal Interagency Forum on Child and Family Statistics, 2007, or their website at http://www.childstats.gov). But are broken homes a major cause of delinquency?

The data on broken homes and delinquency are somewhat mixed.[1] Some studies find that juveniles from broken homes engage in about the same amount of delinquency as juveniles from intact homes, while other studies find that juveniles from broken homes are somewhat more likely to engage in delinquency. Studies based on official data, like arrest statistics, tend to find that broken homes are more strongly related to delinquency than studies based on self-report data. The reason for this difference may be that police and court officials are more likely to arrest and process juveniles from broken homes than similarly delinquent juveniles from intact homes. This may reflect a **labeling effect,** with officials being more likely to view and treat juveniles from broken homes as delinquents in need of intervention. In addition, broken homes generally have a stronger effect on status and minor offenses—especially family-related offenses like running away—than on serious offenses. **When one considers the data as a whole, the best conclusion is that broken homes have a small to moderate effect on delinquency.**

This conclusion is based on a simple comparison of broken homes and intact homes. You may wonder whether some types of broken homes have a bigger effect on delinquency than other types. For example, does it make a difference whether the home was broken by a divorce or separation versus the death of one of the parents? Since divorces and separations are often preceded by much conflict, we might expect that homes broken by divorce/separation would be more strongly related to delinquency. The data provide some support for this view, suggesting that **homes broken by divorce/separation have a stronger association with delinquency.**

You may also wonder whether delinquency is more likely in mother-only homes (the most common type of broken home), mother/stepfather homes (the next most common type), or father-only homes (rapidly becoming more common). A number of conflicting arguments have been made in this area. For example, some argue that homes with stepfathers should be lower in delinquency, since the stepfather provides an additional source of income and help with discipline. Others argue that homes with stepfathers should be higher in delinquency, since the stepfather may get into frequent conflicts with his stepchildren. Likewise, there are conflicting arguments about whether delinquency should be higher in mother-only versus father-only homes (see Demuth and Brown, 2004; Eitle, 2006). Further, some have argued that the relationship between family type and delinquency may depend on a number of factors, such as race/ethnicity and the sex of the child (see Eitle, 2006). Unfortunately, there has not been much research in these areas, and the research that has been done has produced mixed results. It is therefore **difficult to say at present whether delinquency is higher in single-mother, single-father, or mother/stepfather families.**

Overall, then, **broken homes have a small to moderate effect on delinquency.** Limited data suggest that this effect is at least partly due to the fact that broken homes have an effect on the quality of family relationships and parental socialization.[2] The fact that broken homes have only a small to moderate effect on delinquency may surprise you, but much data indicate that the structure of the family (e.g., broken versus intact) is much less important than the behavior and attitudes of family members. To paraphrase Van Voorhis et al. (1988), **what places a juvenile at risk for delinquency is not so much coming from a broken home as coming from a bad home.** While broken homes have an effect on the behavior and attitudes of family members, there are many broken homes with good relationships and many intact homes with poor relationships. A broken home with good relationships is less likely to result in delinquency than an intact home with bad relationships.

Does the Mother's Employment Outside the Home Increase Delinquency?

Until recently, it was the norm for fathers to work outside the home and for mothers to assume major responsibility for child care. In 1950, only 16 percent of all children had working mothers. There has been a dramatic increase in female labor force participation in recent years, however, and close to three-quarters of all mothers with dependent children work today (U.S. Bureau of Labor Statistics). As a consequence, some criminologists have asked whether the mother's employment outside the home increases delinquency. (Criminologists seldom ask whether the father's employment increases delinquency.) It has been argued that the mother's employment outside the home may increase the likelihood of delinquency for several reasons. Among other things, it may reduce maternal supervision of the child and weaken the emotional bond between the mother and child. Data, however, suggest that the mother's employment outside the home has little effect on these factors, and that **there is little or no relationship between delinquency and number of hours worked by the mother.**[3]

Does Placing Juveniles in Child-Care Facilities Increase the Likelihood of Delinquency?

Certain news reports have stated that placing juveniles in child-care facilities leads to an increase in behavioral problems, such as aggression (Gilbert, 2003). These reports probably inspired panic in many parents, especially given the fact that "in 2005, 61 percent of all children from birth through age 6 (not yet in kindergarten) received some sort of child care on a regular basis from persons other than their parents." That translates to about 12 million young children in child care. Most of these children (59 percent) were in child-care centers, with the rest receiving their child care from relatives or nonrelatives in a home setting (Federal Interagency Forum on Child and Family Statistics, 2007).

A major research project did find that children who spent more time in child-care centers were more likely to exhibit behavioral problems such as aggression later in life (Belsky et al., 2007). This finding obtained even after the researchers took account of a range of other factors, such as the parents' socioeconomic status and the quality of their parenting. It is important to note, however, that this finding only obtained for child care provided in centers—it was not true for home-based care provided by relatives or nonrelatives. Further, the effect of center-based child care on behavioral problems was modest in size. In addition, the researchers measured behavioral problems when the children were in the sixth grade. We do not know if the behavioral problems will continue into adolescence (the children are being followed over time). Finally, it is important to note that other researchers have found that participation in certain Head Start programs, which provide high-quality care for disadvantaged children, may reduce aggressive behavior (see Chapter 24).

Nevertheless, there is some indication that **time spent in child-care centers contributes to a modest increase in problem behaviors such as aggression.** It is not clear why this is the case, although the delinquency theories presented earlier provide some suggestions. For example, it may be that individuals who spend their early years in child-care centers are subject to less direct control and have weaker bonds to their caregivers. As a consequence, these individuals may be less likely to develop self-control and beliefs condemning aggression. Or it may be that individuals in child-care centers have more exposure to other aggressive children and are more often reinforced for aggression. More research is clearly needed in this important area.

Are Teenage Parents More Likely to Have Delinquent Children?

About 2.1 percent of all females ages 15 to 17 gave birth to a child in 2005 (for a total of about 133,000 births). The percentage of females ages 15–17 giving birth has declined by more than two-fifths since 1991, from 3.9 percent to 2.1 percent (Federal Interagency Forum on Child and Family Statistics, 2007). This decline partly reflects the fact that high school students have become less likely to have sex in recent years. In 2005, 47 percent of high school students reported having sex, down from 54 percent in 1991. Also, those students having sex are more likely to use condoms. In particular, 63 percent of those having sex during a three-month period in 2005 reported using condoms, versus 46 percent in 1991 (Federal Interagency Forum on Child and Family Statistics, 2007). These changes have been attributed to such things as educational campaigns and the HIV/AIDS epidemic (*New York Times,* 2007a).

Nevertheless, **teenage mothers** are still a cause for concern. A study compared mothers who gave birth at age 17 and under to mothers who had their first birth at ages 20 or 21 (which is two to three years younger than the average age at first birth). Even after background factors like race/ethnicity and class were controlled, it was found that the teenage mothers obtained less education, had larger families, were more likely to be single parents, were more likely to live in poverty, and were more likely to obtain welfare or public assistance. Further, the children of these teenage mothers were more likely to (1) be born prematurely and be of low birth weight (which increases the likelihood that they will develop traits like irritability and low self-control); (2) be physically abused, neglected, or abandoned; (3) be poorly supervised; (4) have trouble in school; and (5) become teenage mothers themselves (Maynard, 1997; Thornberry et al., 2003). Given such findings, one might expect that the children of teenage mothers would be more delinquent. The data tend to suggest that this is the case, although **the effect of teenage motherhood on delinquency is moderate in size.**[4]

Teenage fathers have not received as much research attention as teenage mothers, although recent data suggest that **delinquents are much more likely to become teenage fathers than nondelinquents.** Further, there is some indication that teenage fathers increase rather than decrease their level of delinquency after their child is born (Thornberry et al., 2000). While the impact of teenage fathers on the delinquency of their children has not been well studied, **there is good reason to expect that teenage fathers increase the likelihood of delinquency.** As Thornberry et al. (2000:7) state:

> Teen fathers are unlikely to be in a position to provide financial, emotional, or other parental support for their children, and in this regard can be considered poor role models. Their legacy to their children is likely to be one of socioeconomic disadvantage, poorer health, and poorer education, among other hardships.

Are Juveniles from Large Families More Delinquent?

Data suggest that **juveniles from large families are slightly more likely to engage in delinquency,** even after variables like class are controlled.[5] The reasons for the relationship between family size and delinquency are not entirely clear, but some evidence suggests that the following factors may play a role. Parental supervision is less adequate in large families. There are more children to supervise, and sometimes as a consequence child-rearing responsibilities are delegated to inexperienced siblings. Juveniles in large families are less attached to school and do less well in school. Strain or tension may be higher in large families, because of a number of factors: greater likelihood of overcrowding; the stretching of financial resources; and the competition among siblings for limited resources, such as material objects and attention or affection from parents. Finally, juveniles in large families are more likely to be exposed to delinquent siblings.

Parental and Sibling Crime/Deviance

Are Juveniles with Criminal or Deviant Parents and Siblings More Likely to Be Delinquent?

The research on parental criminality and delinquency is easy to summarize. **Juveniles with a criminal parent or parents are more likely to be delinquent.**[6] The likelihood is even greater if the parent has multiple convictions and if the convictions occurred after the juvenile was born. Also, juveniles with deviant parents (e.g., those with alcohol or drug problems or personality problems) are more likely to be delinquent. Having a criminal or deviant parent is a better predictor of delinquency than the family structure variables described earlier, but it is not as strongly related to delinquency as the family quality and socialization variables discussed next.

It is easy to think of reasons why parental criminality and deviance are associated with delinquency. One might draw on social learning theory and argue that criminal parents are more likely to model crime, to reinforce crime, and to teach values that favor crime. Limited data, however, suggest that this argument is too simplistic. Criminal parents seldom commit crimes with their children, and they usually disapprove of their children's crime.

Social learning theory, however, may still be of some relevance. While criminal parents may not model or directly encourage crime, they may model aggressive behavior and encourage their children to be tough and good fighters. Data also suggest that **control theory** at least partly explains the relationship between parental crime/deviance and delinquency (Sampson and Laub, 1993a). Criminal/deviant parents are less likely to establish a strong emotional bond with their children, properly supervise their children, or use effective disciplinary techniques. In particular, they are more likely to be erratic, threatening, and harsh or punitive in their discipline. Further, the children of criminal/deviant parents perform less well in school. **Strain theory** may shed some light on the relationship as well, since criminal/deviant parents may be more likely to engage in abusive behaviors and get into conflicts with one another and other family members. All of these effects reflect the fact that criminal/deviant parents are more likely to lack the skills and traits necessary to be effective parents and spouses.

In addition, parental crime and deviance may increase delinquency for reasons related to **labeling theory,** with the children of criminals being more likely to be viewed and treated as "bad." Finally, the effect of criminal/deviant parents on delinquency may be **partly genetic** (see McCord, 2001; Rowe and Farrington, 1997). That is, criminal/deviant parents may pass on a predisposition for traits conducive to delinquency (see Chapter 13).

Not only are juveniles with criminal parents more likely to be delinquent, but so are juveniles with **delinquent siblings.**[7] Since juveniles in the same family are exposed to similar family influences, it is not surprising that siblings tend to exhibit similar levels of delinquency. Data, however, suggest that this similarity is not simply a function of exposure to similar family influences. Delinquent siblings will often socialize one another in ways that increase the likelihood of crime; for example, they may provide models for delinquency, reinforce delinquency, and teach beliefs favorable to delinquency.

The Quality of Family Relationships

Family structure and parental/sibling crime affect delinquency largely through their effect on family relationships—how well family members get along and the extent to which the juvenile is socialized for conformity versus deviance. In this section and the next, I describe those family relationship variables related to delinquency. These variables tend to be more strongly related to delinquency than the family structure and parental/sibling crime variables just discussed. First, I consider the *quality of family relationships* and then parental socialization.

Are Juveniles With Warm or Close Relationships with Their Parents Less Delinquent?

Much data suggest that delinquency is lower among juveniles who have a close or warm relationship with their parents. This closeness or warmth involves several related dimensions.[8]

Parental rejection of or indifference to the juvenile. Delinquency is lower when parents love their children and express this love through their actions. Such parents talk with their children, engage in pleasurable activities with them, express interest in them, and provide them with comfort and support. Parents who do not do these things—who reject or ignore their children—are more likely to have delinquent children. In fact, **parental rejection is one of the strongest family correlates of delinquency.** If parents do not love their children and are unwilling to invest time and effort in them, parents are unlikely to earn their children's love or effectively socialize them.

Attachment of juvenile to parents. Delinquency is lower when juveniles have a strong emotional bond or attachment to their parents. Attachment to parents is usually measured by asking juveniles how much they love and respect their parents, care about them, identify with and want to be like them, feel close to them, or engage in intimate communication with them. Not surprisingly, attachment to parents is closely related to parental rejection of the juvenile, although parental attachment and parental rejection are distinct concepts (see Sampson and Laub, 1993a). Data suggest that **attachment to parents is associated with lower delinquency, although the association is often modest in size.** Attachment to mother and father have similar effects, although individuals who are attached to two parents are lower in delinquency than those attached to one (which partly explains why delinquency is higher among juveniles from single-parent homes; see Rankin and Kern, 1994).

Attachment may prevent delinquency for reasons related to control, social learning, and strain theories. Most notably, **attachment functions as a form of control.** Juveniles who are attached to their parents do not want to do anything to upset their parents. That is, they have a greater "stake in conformity." Further, juveniles who are attached to their parents will be more likely to model parental behavior, accept parental beliefs, and respond to parental sanctions. Among other things, this **reduces the likelihood that juveniles will fall under the influence of delinquent peers.** (It should be noted that while attachment to conventional parents reduces delinquency, attachment to criminal or deviant parents does not reduce delinquency and may even increase it; see Foshee and Bauman, 1992; Jensen and Brownfield, 1983.) Finally, **juveniles attached to their parents will likely find their home to be a less stressful place** (see Agnew et al., 2000).

Family conflict. Parental rejection and parental attachment are closely related to, but distinct from, family conflict. Juveniles may reject and be rejected by their parents, but family conflict may nevertheless be low. Family members, for example, may ignore one another or spend little time together. Data suggest that **delinquency is lower in families with little conflict.** This includes conflict between spouses and between parents and juveniles. Such conflict may assume a number of forms: frequent quarreling, expressions of disapproval, nagging, scolding, threatening, and the like. Family conflict, of course, may be caused by the delinquent or troublesome behavior of the juvenile. Data, however, suggest that conflict also has a causal effect on delinquency. It may weaken the emotional bond between parents and the juvenile, disrupt efforts to socialize the juvenile, expose the juvenile to aggressive models and beliefs, increase the likelihood of association with delinquent peers, and increase the level of strain to which the juvenile is subject.

Child abuse. The quality of family relationships may sometimes deteriorate to the point that the child is being abused. Researchers have examined the impact of several types of *child abuse* on delinquency, especially physical abuse, sexual abuse, and neglect (the failure to provide adequate food, shelter, medical care, affection/attention).[9] There were about 900,000 substantiated cases of abuse in 2005, representing a rate of 12.1 per 1,000 children. Seventeen percent of these cases involved physical abuse, 9 percent sexual abuse, 63 percent neglect, 7 percent emotional abuse, and 14 percent other types of abuse—like abandonment and parental drug addition (Note: Percentages do not add up to 100 because some children experienced more than one type of abuse; see the Child Welfare Information Gateway at http://childwelfare.gov.)

It is widely acknowledged that most cases of abuse are not detected by the authorities. Researchers have tried to estimate the full extent of abuse by surveying parents, juveniles, and community professionals such as doctors and school officials. One of the best surveys in this area focused on a nationally representative sample of 2,030 children ages 2 to

17 (Finkelhor et al., 2005). The researchers interviewed the children if they were 10 to 17 years old; otherwise they interviewed the caregiver most familiar with the children. Interviews were conducted between December 2002 and February 2003. According to this survey, more than 2 out of every 10 juveniles had been abused by family members during the previous year (a rate of 209 per 1,000). The most common form of abuse was psychological or emotional abuse, which includes name-calling and denigration (144 per 1,000). The rate of physical abuse was 56 per 1,000, or 12 per 1,000 if we focus on instances of physical abuse where the child showed evidence of physical harm (e.g., bruising). The rate of neglect was 29 per 1,000, and the rate of sexual abuse was about 2 per 1,000. (Note: Children are most likely to be sexually abused by acquaintances.)

Early studies on the relationship between child abuse and delinquency suffered from a number of methodological problems, such as the use of small, nonrepresentative samples, cross-sectional designs, and questionable measures of both abuse and delinquency. There is some indication that these studies may have exaggerated the effect of abuse on delinquency, leading many people to conclude that abuse is a very strong predictor of delinquency. More recent studies, however, have begun to overcome such problems. These studies suggest that **abuse increases the likelihood of delinquency by a moderate amount.**

The effect of abuse on delinquency is readily explained by the leading delinquency theories. Abuse is a major type of **strain,** and the child may turn to delinquency in an effort to end or reduce the abuse (e.g., running away from home, assaulting the abuser); seek revenge against the abuser or related targets; or manage the negative feelings that result from abuse (perhaps through drug use). A **social learning** theorist would argue that abuse increases the likelihood of delinquency, since it implicitly teaches the child that violence is an appropriate way to deal with problems. Abuse may also drive the child to run away from parents and increase the likelihood of association with delinquent peers (see Chapple et al., 2005). A **control** theorist would argue that abuse decreases all four types of control. Abused juveniles may avoid parents, reducing direct control. Abused juveniles may reduce their emotional bond to parents, reducing stake in conformity. Abused juveniles may also experience problems at school, further reducing stake in conformity (see Zingraff et al., 1994). And abuse may reduce the effectiveness of parents in transmitting antidelinquent beliefs and in instilling self-control. Finally, parents who abuse their child are implicitly or explicitly **labeling** the children as "bad." Brezina (1998) found evidence for many of these effects.

It is important to emphasize, however, that most abused individuals do not become serious delinquents. It appears that many children are able to escape at least some of the negative consequences of abuse. Researchers are now investigating this topic. For example, abuse is less likely to lead to delinquency among those who receive social support from others and do well in school.[10]

Parental Socialization

While it is important for parents to establish a warm or close relationship with their children, it is also important for them to **teach their children to engage in conventional behavior and avoid delinquency.** I have already discussed some of the steps parents must take in this area when I described social learning and control theories in Chapters 7 and 8. As a consequence, parts of this discussion will be familiar to you.

What Should Parents Do to Teach Their Children to Avoid Delinquency?

Provide clear rules for behavior. Parents must provide their children with a clear set of rules **that specify what behaviors are unacceptable and that restrict opportunities to engage in deviance.** Such rules, for example, may specify who the children can and cannot associate with, where they can and cannot go, and what time they should be home at night. As indicated in Chapter 8, such rules should not be overly strict. Overly strict rules may increase delinquency, perhaps for reasons related to strain theory.

Monitor the juvenile's behavior. Parents must monitor their children's behavior to ensure that they comply with the rules that the parents have set down. Monitoring may be **direct or indirect.** Direct monitoring involves the parents' direct observation of the juvenile. Indirect monitoring may involve talking to the juvenile on a regular basis about his or her activities, talking with the juvenile's teachers and others, and keeping track of what the juvenile is doing—including how well he or she does schoolwork and the character of the juvenile's friends. Patterson et al. (1992:63) state that the "parents of antisocial children have little information about where their children are, who they are with, what they are doing, or when they will be home."

Consistently sanction the juvenile for rule violations. Such sanctions should **not be too harsh or punitive.** In particular, some evidence suggests that parents' verbal abuse and physical punishment may increase their children's delinquency (see Chapter 8). Recommended types of sanctions include the loss of privileges, the imposition of chores, clear expressions of disapproval, reasoning, and—for younger children—time out.

These parental actions not only provide direct control over the juvenile, but they also increase the juvenile's level of internal control. They lead to the internalization of beliefs that condemn delinquency. When rule violations are consistently followed by sanctions, the juvenile soon becomes anxious or nervous at the thought of doing something wrong, which means that the rules have been "internalized," or the juvenile has developed a "conscience." These actions also cause the juvenile to develop some measure of self-control (see Chapter 8). Data indicate that delinquency is lower in families where parents take these actions; in fact, they are among the most important family variables.[11]

Employ effective techniques for resolving problems/crises. All families occasionally confront problems that threaten to disrupt members' relations with one another. It is important for family members to develop effective techniques for resolving these problems. Otherwise, such problems may interfere with the ability of parents to effectively socialize their children and may increase the level of strain or stress in family members. Families with delinquent children are more likely to employ poor problem-solving techniques: family members tend to blame one another when problems arise, they get angry and argue with one another, and they spend less time trying to define the problem and evaluate effective solutions.

The following model for effective problem solving has been suggested:

(1) The problem should be clearly stated in neutral terms; (2) the other person paraphrases to show that he or she has heard the problem correctly; (3) brainstorm a list

of possible solutions; (4) choose a solution through a process of negotiation (compromise), and write a contract that describes the terms of the agreement, the positive consequences for following the agreement, and the negative consequences for violating it. (Patterson et al., 1992:78)

Data on the relationship between delinquency and family problem-solving techniques is sparse, but limited data suggest a weak relationship (see Patterson et al., 1992).

Disciplinary styles. Data from Patterson and his associates suggest that the families of delinquent children frequently fall into one of **two types.** In the first type, **supervision and discipline are** *lax.* Parents do not define many objectionable acts as deviant, they do not closely monitor the juvenile, and they seldom punish deviant/delinquent acts.

In the second type, **parents frequently punish or threaten to punish, but such punishment is ineffective because it is inconsistently applied.** In particular, parents engage in what Patterson (1982) calls *nattering.* They are quick to condemn even the most trivial deviant acts, and they regularly nag, scold, lecture, and issue commands to the juvenile. Occasionally, they may "explode" and physically abuse the juvenile. On most occasions, however, the parents fail to back up their verbal reprimands with meaningful, nonviolent punishments. In the words of Patterson (1982:225), "They tend to natter, but they do not confront. They do not say, 'No.' They do not say, 'Stop that behavior here and now.' " So the parents complain a lot about the child's behavior, but the child is only occasionally punished for his or her misdeeds.

Often, a negative pattern of interaction develops between family members. Parents treat the child in an aversive way—for example, by threatening or scolding. The child responds by arguing or threatening. The situation escalates, with the parent and child threatening and insulting one another in a series of responses. Eventually, one of the family members—often a parent—backs down. The parent's backing down serves to negatively reinforce the juvenile's aversive behavior. In certain cases, the juvenile's aversive behavior may even be positively reinforced, often by attention from the parents. The juvenile's aggressive behavior, then, is inconsistently punished and frequently reinforced. The constant battles between family members have other negative effects. They reduce the emotional bonds between parent and child and the amount of time that family members spend interacting. This decrease in emotional bonds and interaction further reduces parents' control and makes it more difficult for them to effectively socialize the child. Antagonism between family members also creates a high level of strain and anger, which further increases the likelihood of aggression and delinquency.

What Should Parents Do to Teach Their Children to Engage in Conventional Behavior?

The socialization process has two sides. Parents not only need to teach their children to refrain from delinquency, they also need to teach them how to engage in conventional behavior. In particular, they **need to teach their children social, academic, and problem-solving skills.** Such skills are necessary if juveniles are to do well in school, become involved in conventional peer groups, and resolve any problems that arise with peers and others in a nondelinquent manner. The failure to teach such skills may result in school failure, rejection by conventional peers, and association with delinquent peers.[12]

Such skills are taught in several ways. Parents provide direct instruction (e.g., teaching children the alphabet, telling juveniles what they should do if they get into a dispute with a friend). Parents model these skills; for example, parents may model effective problem-solving skills when disputes arise between family members. Parents provide opportunities for juveniles to practice these skills; the parents should choose such opportunities so juveniles have a reasonable chance of successfully exhibiting the skill. And parents reinforce juveniles when they successfully employ these skills.

At the same time, juveniles often face problems or demands that they are not equipped to handle. In such cases, it is **important for parents to provide support and assistance.** Such support may assume several forms: emotional support, in which parents comfort or reassure the juvenile; informational support, in which parents provide advice on what to do or help clarify issues; and instrumental support, in which parents provide the juvenile with money, goods, or direct assistance. In some cases, parents may have to act on behalf of their children, functioning as their advocates (see especially Wright and Cullen, 2001).

The activities described in the preceding paragraphs are sometimes referred to as "positive parenting." There has not been much research on the relationship between these activities and delinquency, but limited data suggest that their absence is associated with delinquency. For example, data suggest that the parents of delinquent children are less likely to reinforce conventional behavior and provide social support.[13]

Summary

Most people believe that the family has a major impact on delinquency. The data suggest that they are right in this belief. Many people, however, are misinformed about what aspects of the family are most strongly related to delinquency. They believe, for example, that delinquency is caused by mothers who work or by parents who do not spank their children. The data suggest that these arguments are wrong.

We considered four sets of family variables: those having to do with family structure, parental and sibling crime, the quality of family relationships, and *parental socialization.* Certain variables, like mothers' employment, appear to have little or no effect on delinquency. Other variables have a small to moderate effect on delinquency, such as broken homes, placement in child care, teenage parents, and family size. Still other variables have a moderate effect on delinquency: parental and sibling crime, attachment of juvenile to parent, family conflict, and child abuse. The most important family variables are **parental rejection of the child** and **the nature of parental efforts to socialize the child against delinquency.** The effect of other variables, such as parental efforts to teach the child conforming behavior, are less clear.

Data suggest that our ability to explain delinquency is substantially improved when we consider several family variables together.[14] In particular, data suggest that delinquency is least likely when the quality of family relationships is good and parents attempt to socialize children against delinquency (they set clear rules, monitor behavior, and consistently sanction deviance). This style of parenting has sometimes been called *warm and authoritative* (or warm but firm). Parents have a warm or close relationship with their children, but at the same time they have clear rules, which they consistently enforce. **Delinquency is most common among the children of parents who employ warm and lax and cold and lax styles of parenting.**[15]

There is some evidence that family variables are more important during childhood and early adolescence than during mid- to late adolescence.[16] As children develop, they become more autonomous from parents and more subject to peer and community influences. Also, a person's predisposition to delinquency often forms early in life (Patterson et al., 1992:22–27). Once it is formed, the family may come to exercise less influence over the juvenile.

I explained the effect of family variables on delinquency using strain, social learning, control, and labeling theories. In most cases, the effect of a particular family variable can be explained using several of these theories. One can argue, for example, that child abuse increases juveniles' level of strain, reduces their level of control (e.g., attachment to parents), teaches them to engage in aggression (e.g., models aggression), and labels them as "bad". As you read the following chapters, you will notice that the impact of most variables on delinquency can usually be explained by most or all of the leading delinquency theories. I return to this point in Chapter 18, where I present a general or integrated theory of delinquency.

Why Do Some Parents Employ Poor Parenting Practices?

Several related explanations for poor parenting practices can be given. First, some parents **lack the traits necessary to be successful parents.** For example, parents may be irritable and low in self-control; as a consequence, they are quick to anger, employ harsh disciplinary techniques, and show little affection or concern for their children. This may partly explain why criminal parents are more likely to be poor parents, since criminal parents are more likely to have traits conducive to crime.[17]

Second, some parents **lack the knowledge to be effective parents.** Perhaps they never experienced good parenting when they were children, so they do not know how to be good parents themselves. In this area, Patterson (1986) found that the poor disciplinary practices of grandparents were associated with the antisocial behavior of both their children and grandchildren. Some evidence suggests that the grandparents failed to teach their children effective disciplinary techniques, and this partly accounts for the antisocial behavior of the grandchildren (Patterson et al., 1992; also see Thornberry et al., 2003). Also, family training programs that teach parents good parenting skills have shown signs of success. That is, parents enrolled in such programs are often able to reduce the delinquency of their children. (Chapter 24 contains more information on such programs.)

Third, some parents have **"difficult" children,** who possess traits like irritability and low self-control. Children with such traits can challenge even the best of parents. Such parents may come to dislike their children and may even stop trying to "parent" them in an effort to avoid conflict and gain some measure of peace. Data suggest that difficult children do have an adverse effect on parenting practices.[18] Further, since traits like irritability and low self-control are inherited to some extent, difficult children are more likely to have parents who are ill-equipped to care for them. The most demanding children, then, tend to be matched with the least able parents.

Fourth, many parents may experience **strains or stressors that make it difficult for them to employ good parenting practices.** In this area, poor parenting practices have been linked to low socioeconomic status, unemployment, residence in deprived communities, drug and alcohol use, divorce, teenage motherhood, large family size, and family violence.[19]

Also, an observational study revealed that mothers were more likely to engage in poor parenting practices on days when they experienced high stress (Patterson et al., 1989).

Many of these risk factors often converge, and poor parenting appears most likely when **unskilled parents facing numerous stressors attempt to raise difficult children.**

Teaching Aids

Exercise: Putting Your Knowledge to Use

Almost all parents have days when they wonder whether their child might turn out to be delinquent. Parents are often eager to know what they can do to prevent this. In fact, if any parents discover that you have had a course in juvenile delinquency, they might well ask you what they should do to prevent their children from becoming delinquent. (Or perhaps you are already a parent, or will be in the near future, and are wondering about the best way to raise your child.) **Draw on the materials in this chapter and put together a brief manual for parents on "How to Prevent Your Child from Becoming a Delinquent."**

The manual should list those things that parents should and should **not** do if they want to prevent their children from becoming delinquents. Further, the manual should provide examples of what parents should and should not do. For example, if you advise parents to avoid sanctions that are overly harsh or punitive, be sure to give examples of appropriate and inappropriate sanctions. Finally, be prepared to justify the advice you give by drawing on the leading delinquency theories. People are more likely to accept your advice if you present a good justification for it.

TEST YOUR KNOWLEDGE OF THIS CHAPTER

1. List and briefly describe the four major aspects of family life covered in this chapter. Which aspects of family life have the greatest effect on delinquency?

2. Briefly describe the relationship between delinquency and (a) broken homes, (b) the mother's employment outside the home, (c) child care, (d) teenage parenthood, and (e) family size. Explain the relationship between delinquency and any two of these factors using strain, control, social learning, and labeling theory (if applicable).

3. Describe recent trends in family life (regarding broken homes, teenage parenthood, and mother's employment), and discuss the possible impact of such trends on levels of delinquency.

4. Juveniles with criminal parents and siblings are more likely to engage in delinquency. Drawing on the leading delinquency theories, describe why this might be the case.

5. The quality of family relationships includes several dimensions. List these dimensions and briefly describe their relationship to delinquency.

6. Drawing on the leading delinquency theories, explain why child abuse increases the likelihood of delinquency.

7. What major steps must parents take in order to teach their child to avoid delinquency?

8. What are the two major disciplinary styles that increase the likelihood of delinquency?

9. What should parents do to teach their children to engage in conventional behavior?

TEST YOUR KNOWLEDGE OF THIS CHAPTER (continued)

10. Briefly describe the warm and authoritative style of parenting that is said to be most effective in preventing delinquency.

11. What are the major reasons why some parents employ poor parenting practices?

THOUGHT AND DISCUSSION QUESTIONS

1. Suppose you are a researcher investigating the effect of family factors on delinquency. Develop a survey with questions measuring the various dimensions of family life described in this chapter, with at least one question per dimension (e.g., at least one question measuring parental rejection, attachment of juveniles to parents, parental monitoring, and so on).

2. The effect of a given family factor on delinquency is often explained using several theories (e.g., the effect of child abuse on delinquency is explained using *all* of the leading delinquency theories). How might researchers go about determining which of these explanations is correct (or whether all are correct)? For example, how might researchers go about determining whether child abuse affects delinquency for reasons related to strain, control, social learning, and/or labeling theories? (See Agnew, 1995a; see Brezina, 1998, for an example.)

3. Drawing on the arguments in this chapter, recommend policies or programs to reduce delinquency (see Chapter 24 for a discussion of delinquency control and prevention programs focusing on the family).

KEY TERMS

- Broken homes
- Quality of family relationships
- Child abuse
- Lax and nattering disciplinary styles
- Parental socialization
- Warm but authoritative style of parenting

ENDNOTES

1. For overviews and selected studies on broken homes and delinquency, *see* Demuth and Brown, 2004; Eitle, 2006; Farrington, 1996a, 1996b, 2002a; Gove and Crutchfield, 1982; Henggeler, 1989; Hirschi, 1995; Hollin, 1992; Johnson, 1986; Loeber, Farrington, Stouthamer-Loeber, and Van Kammen, 1998; Loeber and Stouthamer-Loeber, 1986; Matsueda and Heimer, 1987; McNulty and Bellair, 2003; Nye, 1958; Rankin, 1983; Rankin and Wells, 1994; Rebellon, 2002; Rosen, 1985; Rutter et al., 1998; Sampson and Laub, 1993a; Simons et al., 1993; Thornberry et al., 2003a; Wells and Rankin, 1991; Wilson and Herrnstein, 1985; Wright and Wright, 1995.

2. *See* Demuth and Brown, 2004; Eitle, 2006; Farrington, 2002a; Jang and Smith, 1997; Matsueda and Heimer, 1987; Rankin and Kern, 1994; Rankin and Wells, 1994; Rebellon, 2002; Rutter et al., 1998; Sampson and Laub, 1993a; Simons et al., 2007; Snyder and Patterson, 1987; Van Voorhis et al., 1988.

3. *See* Farrington, 1995; Loeber and Stouthamer-Loeber, 1986; Vander Ven and Cullen, 2004; Vander Ven et. al., 2001; Wells and Rankin, 1988; Wright and Wright, 1995.

4. *See* Farrington and Welsh, 2007; Furstenberg et al., 1987; Grogger, 1997; Loeber, Farrington, Stouthamer-Loeber, and Van Kammen, 1998; Maynard and Garry, 1997; Moore et al., 1997; Pogarsky et al., 2003; Rutter et al., 1998.

5. *See* Farrington, 1995, 1996a, 2002a; Farrington and Welsh, 2007; Fischer, 1984; Hirschi, 1995; Hollin, 1992; Loeber and Stouthamer-Loeber, 1986; Patterson et al., 1992; Rutter et al., 1998; Sampson and Laub, 1993a; Tygart, 1991; Wells and Rankin, 1988.

6. For overviews and recent research in this area, *see* Canter, 1982; Farrington, 1995, 1996a, 1996b, 2002a; Farrington and Welsh, 2007; Henggeler, 1989; Loeber and Stouthamer-Loeber, 1986; Rowe and Farrington, 1997; Rutter and Giller, 1983; Sampson and Laub, 1993a; Snyder and Patterson, 1987; Wilson and Herrnstein, 1985; Wright and Wright, 1995; Wu and Kandel, 1995.

7. *See* Farrington, 1995; Haynie and McHugh, 2003; Hollin, 1992; Loeber and Stouthamer-Loeber, 1986; Rowe and Farrington, 1997; Rowe and Gulley, 1992; Stormshaker et al., 2004; *also see* Sampson and Laub, 1993a.

8. For overviews and recent studies in this area, *see* Burton et al., 1995; Canter, 1982; Cernkovich and Giordano, 1987; Conger et al., 1992, 1994; Farrington and Welsh, 2007; Fox and Benson, 2000; Gove and Crutchfield, 1982; Hay et al., 2006; Henggeler, 1989; Hollin, 1992; Jang and Smith, 1997; Loeber and Stouthamer-Loeber, 1986; Longshore et al., 2005; Matsueda and Heimer, 1987; McCord, 1991; McNulty and Bellair, 2003; Nye, 1958; Rankin and Kern, 1994; Rankin and Wells, 1990; Rosen, 1985; Sampson and Laub, 1993a; Simons et al., 2007; Snyder and Patterson, 1987; Thaxton and Agnew, 2004; Thornberry et al., 1998; Wells and Rankin, 1988; Wilson and Herrnstein, 1985; Wright and Wright, 1995.

9. For overviews and recent studies, *see* Chapple et al., 2005; Farrington, 2002a; Farrington and Welsh, 2007; Finkelhor and Hashima, 2001; Fox and Benson, 2000; Hirschi, 1995; Ireland et al., 2002; Rebellon and Van Gundy, 2005; Rutter et al., 1998; Siegel and Williams, 2002; Simons et al., 2007; Smith and Thornberry, 1995; Thornberry et al., 2003a; Wallace, 2005; Widom, 1989, 1997, 2001; Wilson and Herrnstein, 1985; Wright and Wright, 1995; Zingraff et al., 1993; Zingraff et al., 1994.

10. *See* note 9 above.

11. For overviews and selected studies, *see* Barnes et al., 2006; Burton et al., 1995; Cernkovich and Giordano, 1987; Conger et al., 1995; Cullen et al., 2008; Farrington, 1996a, b, 2002a; Farrington and Welsh, 2007; Fox and Benson, 2000; Gove and Crutchfield, 1982; Hay, 2001a; Hay et al., 2006; Henggeler, 1989; Hirschi, 1995; Hollin, 1992; Jang and Smith, 1997; Loeber, Farrington, Stouthamer-Loeber, and Van Kammen, 1998; Loeber and Stouthamer-Loeber, 1986; Matsueda and Heimer, 1987; McCord, 1991; Nye, 1958; Patterson, 1982; 1986; Patterson et al., 1989; Patterson et al., 1992; Rankin and Wells, 1990; Sampson and Laub, 1993a; Simons et al., 2007; Snyder and Patterson, 1987; Thornberry et al., 1998; Unnever et al., forthcoming; Wells and Rankin, 1988; Wright and Wright, 1995.

12. *See* Barnes et al., 2006; Patterson, 1982; Patterson et al., 1989; Patterson et al., 1992; Snyder and Patterson, 1987.

13. *See* Cullen's, 1994, discussion of social support and crime; Burt et al., 2006; Catalano and Hawkins, 1996; DuBow and Reid, 1994; Hay et al., 2006; Nye, 1958; Wright and Cullen, 2001; and the work of Patterson and associates cited earlier.

14. *See* Hay et al., 2006; Loeber and Stouthamer-Loeber, 1986; Snyder and Patterson, 1987; Wright and Wright, 1995.

15. For a fuller discussion, *see* Burt et al., 2006; Farrington and Welsh, 2007; Hay, 2001a; Hay and Forrest, 2006; Henggeler, 1989; Loeber and Stouthamer-Loeber, 1986; McCord, 1991; Simons et al., 2005; Snyder and Patterson, 1987; Stewart and Simons, 2006; Wilson and Herrnstein, 1985.

16. *See* Agnew, 1985b; Jang, 1999; Jang and Smith, 1997; Loeber and Stouthamer Loeber, 1986; Sampson and Laub, 1993a; Thornberry, 1987, 1996; Thornberry et al., 1991, 1998.

17. *See* Patterson et al., 1992; Rutter et al., 1998; Sampson and Laub, 1993a; Snyder and Patterson, 1987; Thornberry et al., 2003.

18. *See* Jang and Smith, 1997; Moffitt, 1997; Patterson, 1982; Rutter, 1985; Rutter et al., 1998; Sampson and Laub, 1993a; Thornberry and Krohn, 2005; Wilson and Herrnstein, 1985.

19. *See* Conger et al., 1992, 1994, 1995; Kaufman, 2005; Larzelere and Patterson, 1990; McNulty and Bellair, 2003; Moore et al., 1997; Patterson, 1982, 1986; Patterson et al., 1989; Patterson et al., 1992; Pratt et al., 2004; Rutter et al., 1998; Sampson and Laub, 1993a; Simons et al., 1993; Simons et al., 2005, 2007; Snyder and Patterson, 1987; Thornberry et al., 1998; Thornberry et al., 2003; Tygart, 1991.

CHAPTER 15

The School
What Impact Does the School Have on Delinquency?

chools may contribute to delinquency for reasons related to all of the major delinquency theories. Many juveniles do poorly in school and come to dislike or even hate school. School then becomes a source of strain for them, it exercises little control over them, and it provides a context for associating with other dissatisfied, often delinquent, juveniles. Further, school officials may view and treat many juveniles as "bad," particularly those who have trouble adjusting to school routines and are in tracks for "problem" students.

I first discuss those school experiences that may contribute to the juvenile's delinquency, including low grades, little involvement in school activities, poor relations with teachers, negative attitudes toward school, low educational and occupational goals, and dropping out of school. As indicated later, there is little dispute that these experiences are **associated** with delinquency. But there is some dispute over the extent to which these experiences **cause** delinquency. Some researchers argue that the association between these school experiences and delinquency is caused by third variables and by the causal effect of delinquency on school experiences. Others disagree, claiming that school experiences do have a causal effect on delinquency.

I then examine the extent to which school characteristics, like school size and disciplinary practices, influence levels of delinquency—particularly levels of in-school delinquency. I begin by discussing the amount of delinquency in schools, a topic that has attracted much attention in recent years as a result of several well-publicized school shootings. I then describe the characteristics of those schools with low levels of delinquency.

What School Experiences Contribute to Delinquency?

Delinquency is **associated** with a range of school experiences,[1] including:

   1. *Low academic performance.* Delinquents are more likely than nondelinquents to have lower grades and lower scores on tests measuring academic achievement, to be in special education classes or on noncollege tracks, and to be held back. One overview of the research in this area concluded that children with poor academic records (grades of F or D) were about twice as likely to engage in delinquency as children with good academic records (grades of C or above) (Maguin and Loeber, 1996).

   2. *Little school involvement.* Delinquents are less likely to participate in school activities; in particular, they spend less time on homework and are less involved in extracurricular activities (see Agnew and Petersen, 1989; Osgood et al., 1996).

   3. *Low attachment to school.* Delinquents are more likely to dislike school and to feel that school is irrelevant to them. For example, they are more likely to state that they do not like school, that they resent the restrictions at school, that school is boring and a waste of time, and that they would rather be elsewhere.

   4. *Poor relations with teachers.* Delinquents are more likely to report that they dislike their teachers and have unpleasant relations with them. For example, they are more likely to state that their teachers often lose their tempers, make negative comments, and talk down to students (see Agnew, 1985a).

   5. *Low educational/occupational goals.* Delinquents have lower educational and occupational goals. For example, they desire less education than nondelinquents and they expect to receive less education.

6. *Dropping out of school.* Delinquents are more likely to drop out of school.

7. *School misbehavior.* Finally, delinquents are more likely to violate school rules. In particular, they are more likely to cut classes, be truant from school, and violate other rules.

Jay MacLeod's study of a delinquent group (the "Hallway Hangers") in a Boston public housing project provides a nice illustration of the school experiences of delinquents. In the words of MacLeod (1995:77):

> The Hallway Hangers' attitudes toward the educational system can be summed up in Stoney's words: 'Fuck school. I hate fucking school.' Most of the Hallway Hangers have dropped out. While officially enrolled, most spent little time in school anyway, preferring the fun, companionship, and drugs at Pop's [a local hangout]. When in class, they generally were disruptive and undisciplined. None of the Hallway Hangers participated in any extracurricular activities. By their own accounts, they were high or drunk much of the time they spent in school . . . they all switched or were switched into different classes, some spiraling down through the array of alternative programs at amazing speed, landing in the last stop on the line. Some stayed there, most dropped out altogether.

Do School Experiences Cause Delinquency?

The association between the school experiences just described and delinquency is often modest in size, but few criminologists would dispute that such an association exists. What is in dispute, however, is the meaning of this association.[2] Some researchers suggest that school experiences have little causal effect on delinquency. The association between school experiences and delinquency is said to occur because **both school experiences and delinquency are caused by the same third variables,** in particular, by early family experiences and individual traits like low intelligence and low self-control. This argument has some support. Data suggest that early family experiences and individual traits have a causal effect on both school experiences and delinquency; there is also some evidence that when family experiences and traits are taken into account, the association between school experiences and delinquency is reduced and, in some studies, eliminated.[3] Further, some researchers argue that **delinquency may cause negative school experiences,** which would also help explain the associations just reported. The data also provide some support for this position.[4] So the association between school experiences and delinquency does not necessarily mean that school experiences cause delinquency. Rather, school experiences and delinquency may be caused by the same third variables, and delinquency may have a causal effect on school experiences.

Other researchers acknowledge the foregoing arguments but claim that **school experiences still have some causal effect on delinquency.** (You should test your knowledge of the leading delinquency theories by using them to explain why the school experiences listed above might cause delinquency.)[5] The debate over whether school experiences do have a causal effect on delinquency has important policy implications. If school experiences have a causal effect, then programs designed to improve school experiences should reduce delinquency. But if the association between school experiences and delinquency reflects third variables or the causal effect of delinquency on school experiences, such programs would have little effect. The resolution of this debate requires that researchers examine the effect of school experiences on later delinquency and take account of, or "control for," relevant third variables. Unfortunately, such research is scarce. As a consequence, the debate over whether school experiences have a causal effect on delinquency continues.[6]

My own reading of the data is that **school experiences have a modest causal effect on delinquency.** The effect is often demonstrated in longitudinal studies that control for at least some relevant third variables, such as social class, family characteristics, certain individual traits, and/or prior delinquency.[7] Further, programs designed to improve school experiences often reduce delinquency (see Chapter 24). The effect of school experiences on delinquency, however, is partly indirect. For example, placement in noncollege tracks affects delinquency partly through its impact on other variables, like association with delinquent peers (Colvin, 2000). Juveniles in noncollege tracks are more likely to be exposed to delinquent juveniles and form friendships with them. Also, the effect of school experiences on subsequent delinquency is sometimes conditioned by other variables. For example, dropping out of school seems to lead to an increase in delinquency for some individuals, like middle-class students, but not for other individuals, like lower-class students (Jarjoura, 1996).[8] But taken as a whole, I believe the data suggest that negative school experiences of the type listed earlier increase delinquency by a modest amount.

Why Do Some Juveniles Have Negative School Experiences?

Since school experiences may have a modest effect on delinquency, it is important to ask why some juveniles have negative school experiences. I have already mentioned certain potential factors. First, individuals with certain traits, like **low intelligence and low self-control**, are more likely to have negative school experiences. Such individuals have more trouble satisfying the academic demands of school and conforming to school requirements, such as remaining seated and attending to the teacher.[9]

Second, many of the family factors listed in Chapter 14 (such as **family size, parental criminality, parental rejection, and poor discipline**) affect school experiences.[10] Such factors reduce the likelihood that parents will equip their children with the skills and attitudes necessary to do well in school, that parents will effectively monitor their child's school activities, and that parents will assist their children with schoolwork (see Weishew and Peng, 1993).

Third, **associating with delinquent peers and gang members** negatively affects school experiences. Delinquent peers and gang members place little value on school activities and sometimes actively discourage adolescents from making an effort at school. Based on their field study of St. Louis gangs, Decker and Van Winkle (1996:190) state:

> Attending school, being on time, paying attention to teachers and other staff, getting passing grades—the daily routines and opportunities of our educational system—are not high priorities for most gang members. Truancy, tardiness, skipping classes, leaving school before the end of the day all appear to be popular responses to school discipline and rules. When asked what they did in school, few respondents identified classroom activities.

Fourth, **misbehavior and delinquency** affect school experiences. That is, data suggest that misbehavior has a causal effect on at least certain school experiences, like academic performance and relations with teachers. Children who misbehave are less attentive to the teacher and spend less time on school tasks, among other things.[11] Misbehavior may also lead to negative labeling by teachers and school officials, thereby contributing to poor relations with teachers and low attachment to school.

Finally, school experiences are affected by a range of background factors, including **social class, sex, race/ethnicity, residential mobility** (i.e., frequent moving), and **the type of community the juvenile lives in.**[12] In particular, juveniles from communities with high levels of poverty are more likely to have negative school experiences. The effect of these background factors on school experiences is partly indirect; that is, they affect school experiences through their effect on the juvenile's individual traits and behavior, family and other interpersonal experiences, and the type of school the juvenile attends. For example, juveniles from communities with high levels of poverty are more likely to attend inferior schools. And the effect of these factors is partly direct; for example, lower-class parents are less able to provide their children with the resources, skills, and attitudes necessary for school success.

Finally, as discussed next, **certain school characteristics** have an effect on school experiences and delinquency. That is to say, it does make a difference what type of school a child attends.

School Characteristics and Delinquency

Students in certain schools are much more likely to engage in delinquency, both within school and without, than students in other schools. The students in some schools, for example, have official rates of delinquency (e.g., court appearances per 100 students) more than 60 times greater than that of students in other schools (Farrington, 1996a). This section first discusses the extent of delinquency in schools and then focuses on those school characteristics that influence levels of school delinquency.

How Much Delinquency Occurs at School?

Crimes involving serious injury and major financial losses are rare in most schools, although **minor crimes are more common.** The Monitoring the Future survey interviews a nationally representative sample of high school seniors from the lower 48 states each year. These students are asked whether they have been the victims of various crimes at school (inside or outside school or on a school bus) during the previous 12 months. Results from the 2006 survey are reported in Table 15.1.

As can be seen, **serious violence was relatively rare;** 4.3 percent of the students were injured with a weapon (and most of these injuries were minor). **Less serious forms of violence were more common.** Close to one out of five students was threatened with injury (but not actually injured). Juveniles are about as likely to be the victims of violence at school as they are away from school, although **serious** violence is more likely to occur away from school (U.S. Department of Education and Office of Justice Programs, 2006). This is especially true of homicide. Although not reported in Table 15.1, 21 juveniles were murdered at school during the 2004–2005 school year. These homicides account for about 1 percent of all juvenile homicides during that time period. Juveniles were at least 50 times more likely to be murdered away from school than at school.

Theft is more common than violence at school. About 17 percent of the seniors reported that something worth more than $50 had been stolen from them at school, and about 28 percent reported that something worth under $50 had been stolen. About 21 percent of the seniors reported that someone had deliberately damaged their property (car, clothing, etc.) while they were at school. Juveniles are slightly more likely to be the victims of theft at school than away from school.

Data on trends in school crime are somewhat mixed, but they generally suggest that **most forms of school crime have been declining since the early to mid-1990s**—just as crime in the larger society has been declining (U.S. Department of Education and Office of Justice Programs, 2006).

So, overall, crimes involving serious injury and, to a lesser extent, serious theft are rare in most schools, although minor crimes are more common. As Gottfredson and Gottfredson (1985:167)

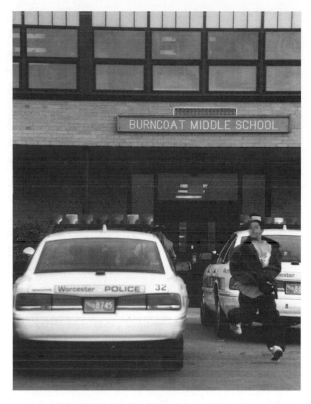

state, "Much of the 'victimization' that occurs in schools involves minor indignities: smart-ass remarks or gestures, one boy forcibly asking another for a quarter, a notebook lifted from someone's desk." Further, most types of school crime have been decreasing in recent years. These assertions regarding school crime are at odds with the impression of school violence conveyed by the mass media. The mass media have devoted extensive coverage to a series of school shootings in recent years, fostering the impression that schools are quite dangerous—even suburban schools populated by middle-class students. But this impression exaggerates the problem of school crime.

TABLE 15.1	Percentage of High School Seniors Reporting Various Victimization Experiences at School During the Previous 12 Months
Type of Victimization	**Number Experiencing Victimization (%)**
Violent Crime	
Injured with a weapon	4.3
Threatened with a weapon	11.0
Injured without a weapon	9.3
Threatened without a weapon	17.5
Property Crime	
Theft of something worth $50+	17.3
Theft of something worth <$50	28.2
Property damaged (vandalized)	20.5

SOURCE: Monitoring the Future survey, *Sourcebook of Criminal Justice Statistics* (http://www.albany.edu/sourcebook/).

At the same time, I do not want to minimize the problem of school crime. As we are painfully aware, serious acts of violence do happen. Certain schools, particularly schools in poor urban areas, do suffer from high rates of serious crime and violence. And the minor crime and violence that occurs in most schools can have a devastating impact on many of its victims, particularly those who are chronically victimized. In this area, recent attention has focused on the problem of bullying. This has occurred partly because recent surveys suggest that bullying is extensive and has a range of negative consequences (see later discussion). Also, many of the juveniles who shot others at their schools, like the two students who shot and killed 13 others at Columbine High School in Colorado, were said to be the victims of bullying (although this, of course, does not excuse their behavior).

Bullying has three dimensions: It involves behavior designed to harm or disturb others, it occurs on a repeated basis, and it involves a more powerful person or group attacking a less powerful one (Howell, 2003a:115). Estimates of the extent of bullying vary somewhat, but most estimates suggest that about 15 percent to 20 percent of students are subject to bullying each year (although see Berger, 2007, for the difficulties involved in measuring the extent of bullying).[13] And data suggest that the victims of bullying suffer a range of negative psychological and social consequences, including depression, a fear of going to school, trouble making friends, and—in some cases—delinquency (see Berger, 2007; Eisenbraun, 2007; Ericson, 2001; Smokowski and Kopasz, 2005). As described in Chapter 24, successful programs have been developed to reduce bullying.

How Can We Explain School Differences in Delinquency?

As indicated earlier, schools differ a good deal in the amount of delinquency they experience. Such differences are largely a function of **differences between the students who attend the schools and the communities in which the schools are located.** Delinquency rates are higher in schools that have a higher percentage of students who are less able, poor, male, and members of minority groups. Delinquency rates are also higher in schools that are located in urban communities with high rates of crime, poverty, unemployment, and female-headed households. However, when researchers take account of student and community characteristics, they find that **school characteristics do have a small to modest association with delinquency rates—especially rates of within-school delinquency.**

Several studies have focused on the association between school characteristics and in-school delinquency rates. One such study, for example, examined data from over 600 junior and senior public high schools in the United States (see Gottfredson and Gottfredson, 1985). Another examined data from a national sample of 1,051 schools that had eighth graders in 1988 (Weishew and Peng, 1993). These studies are not in full agreement with one another, and there is some evidence that the findings vary by grade level and by type of delinquency (e.g., theft versus violence, delinquency directed at teachers versus that directed at students). Nevertheless, there are some tentative conclusions that can be drawn about those school characteristics associated with in-school delinquency rates.[14]

The characteristics of low-delinquency or effective schools are similar to the characteristics of effective families—both tend to be *warm but firm.* In particular, there is some evidence that **rates of in-school delinquency tend to be somewhat lower in:**

1. *Small schools with good resources.* Delinquency tends to be lower in smaller schools and schools where the average teacher instructs a smaller number of different stu-

dents. It is also lower in schools where teachers are provided with the materials and equipment they need to teach. Drawing on the leading delinquency theories, why do you think school size and resources might be important (recall our discussion of family size and delinquency)?

2. *Schools with good discipline.* Delinquency is lower in schools where there are clear rules for behavior and these rules are consistently enforced in a fair manner. Schools with unclear or ambiguous rules have higher rates of delinquency, as do schools that fail to enforce their rules. This finding does not mean that schools should severely punish minor infractions. In fact, there is some evidence that overly punitive discipline contributes to higher rates of delinquency. Certain studies, for example, suggest that delinquency rates are higher in schools that use physical punishment and that make frequent use of punishment (note the parallels with the family research here). It is best to spot disruptive behavior early and deal with it in a firm but appropriate manner. In particular, there are techniques for responding to disruptive behavior that are not overly punitive and that do not disrupt teaching activities. This early but firm response may prevent more serious problems from developing; problems that may call forth frequent and punitive disciplinary responses.

3. *Schools that provide opportunities for student success and praise student accomplishments.* Delinquency tends to be lower in schools that actively involve students in the learning process and that increase the opportunities for students to succeed, including students who do not plan to attend college. Certain teaching techniques that help accomplish these goals are described in Chapter 24. Further, delinquency tends to be lower in schools where teachers praise student accomplishments. As indicated in the discussion of the family, it is important both to punish delinquency and to reinforce conventional behavior.

4. *Schools with high expectations for students.* Delinquency is lower in schools with high standards for success; that is, schools where the teachers have high expectations for their students and make rigorous but not unrealistic work demands on them.

5. *Schools with pleasant working conditions for students.* Delinquency is lower in schools where teachers and other school officials have positive attitudes toward students, allow students some say over school matters, provide support to students who are having problems, and create a pleasant physical space for students to work (e.g., cleaning up trash and graffiti, providing attractive decorations).

6. *Schools with good cooperation between the administration and teachers.* Delinquency is lower in schools where administrators and counselors keep teachers informed of disciplinary problems and support or assist teachers in their disciplinary efforts. This cooperation probably makes it easier for schools to develop and effectively enforce a clear set of rules.

7. *Schools with strong community involvement.* Delinquency is lower in schools with high levels of community involvement, especially parental involvement—with parents communicating regularly with teachers and school officials, assisting in the school, and having some say in how the school is run.

I should note that **private schools generally have lower rates of delinquency than public schools,** even after one takes account of differences between the students who attend private and public schools. Some evidence suggests that this difference arises because private and public schools differ on many of the characteristics just listed. Based on their extensive analysis of public and private schools, Coleman et al. (1982:102–103) state that "the Catholic schools are the strictest in discipline; the other private schools are somewhat less strict and appear to nurture the student to a greater degree (as evidenced by perceived teacher interest). The public schools, taken as a whole, are neither strict nor do they nurture the student. In addition, they are least often regarded by their students as fair in the exercise of discipline." Further, private schools are more academically demanding than public schools.

Taken as a whole, these data suggest that the schools with the lowest rates of delinquency are **firm** on the one hand; they have clear rules that are uniformly enforced and they are academically demanding. On the other hand, they are **"warm";** they treat students in a fair manner; teachers are interested in students, provide opportunities for success, and praise student accomplishments; school staff attempt to create a pleasant environment for the students; and parents are available to assist both students and school staff. It is easy to explain the effect of these school characteristics in terms of strain, social learning, control, and labeling theories. Schools with these characteristics should **create less strain.** They are more pleasant; students get along better with their teachers and presumably with other students (since student misbehavior is less tolerated). They are fairer. And students are more likely to achieve their success goals. The students in such schools are also **subject to greater control.** In particular, they are subject to more direct control, they are more likely to form an emotional attachment to teachers and an investment in conventional activities, and they may even be more likely to internalize beliefs condemning delinquency and develop some measure of self-control. Further, drawing on **social learning theory,** these schools are more likely to punish delinquency and reinforce conformity, teach conventional beliefs, and provide exposure to conventional models. Such schools may also be *less* likely to provide exposure to delinquent others, since the schools likely discourage the formation of delinquent peer groups. Finally, such schools should be **less likely to label** students as "bad."

Teaching Aids

Applying Theories and Research

The U.S. Department of Education and the Office of Juvenile Justice and Delinquency Prevention (part of the Department of Justice) published a document titled *Creating Safe and Drug Free Schools: An Action Guide* (1996; also available at http://www.ncjrs.org/pdffiles/safescho.pdf). The guide contains "action steps" for schools, students, parents, and community organizations and business groups. The following are some of the action steps that schools should take to reduce school crime. Examine each step and discuss the extent to which it is supported by the leading delinquency theories and the school research.

1. Ensure that students are engaged in schoolwork that is challenging, informative, and rewarding.

2. Establish, publish, publicize, and enforce policies that clearly define acceptable and unacceptable behavior. These policies should include zero tolerance for weapons, violence, gangs, and use or sale of alcohol and drugs.

3. Take immediate action on all reports of drug use or sales, threats, bullying, gang activity, or victimization. Anyone caught bringing a gun to school should be reported immediately to the appropriate law enforcement agency.

4. Create an environment that encourages parents and other adults to visit the school and participate in the school's activities. Develop a sense of community within the school.

5. Encourage staff to treat each other and students with respect and to act as good role models.

6. Involve youths in program and policy development.

7. Offer programs that teach peaceful, nonviolent methods for managing conflict to students and their families, as well as to staff.

What other steps would you recommend for reducing school crime? (See Chapter 24 for a discussion of school-based delinquency control and prevention programs.)

TEST YOUR KNOWLEDGE OF THIS CHAPTER

1. List those school experiences that are associated with delinquency.

2. Why do some criminologists argue that these school experiences do **not cause** delinquency? How should researchers go about testing these arguments?

3. Why do I argue that these school experiences have a modest causal effect on delinquency?

4. Why are some juveniles more likely than others to have negative school experiences?

5. Describe the extent of and trends in school crime. Why do I argue that the mass media exaggerate the problem of school crime?

6. What is bullying?

7. Why do some schools have more crime than other schools? List those school characteristics associated with lower levels of school crime. Describe the characteristics of "warm but firm" schools, which tend to have lower levels of school crime.

8. Why do private schools tend to have lower rates of school crime than public schools?

THOUGHT AND DISCUSSION QUESTIONS

1. Using those delinquency theories that are relevant, explain **why** any three of the major school **experiences** listed in this chapter increase the likelihood of delinquency.

2. Using those delinquency theories that are relevant, explain **why** any three of the school **characteristics** listed in this chapter reduce the likelihood of school crime.

3. Do you think there was a lot of crime in your high school (or a problem with bullying)? Drawing on this chapter and the major delinquency theories, discuss why there was or was not a lot of crime (or bullying) in your school. Can you think of any factors other than those listed in this chapter that might influence levels of school crime?

4. What recommendations would you make for reducing school crime, including violence and bullying (see the Endnotes section and Chapter 24 for further information).

KEY TERMS

- Bullying
- Warm but firm schools

ENDNOTES

1. For overviews and recent studies, *see* Agnew, 1985a; Bellair and McNulty, 2005; Cernkovich and Giordano, 1992; Chapple et al., 2005; Chung et al., 2002; Farrington and Welsh, 2007; Felson and Staff, 2006; Gottfredson, 2001; Hawkins and Lishner, 1987; Jang, 2002; Jarjoura and Triplett, 1997; Jenkins, 1997; Kaufman, 2005; Maguin and Loeber, 1996; McGloin et al., 2004; Sampson and Laub, 1993a; Stewart, 2003; Stewart and Simons, 2006; Thaxton and Agnew, 2004; Thornberry et al., 2003a; Wiatrowski and Anderson, 1987; Wiatrowski et al., 1981; Wiatrowski et al., 1982; Wilson and Herrnstein, 1985.

2. *See* Agnew, 2006; Gottfredson, 2001; Maguin and Loeber, 1996; McGloin et al., 2004; Thaxton and Agnew, 2004; Wilson and Herrnstein, 1985.

3. *See* Felson and Stott, 2006; Gottfredson, 2001; Krohn et al., 1995; Maguin and Loeber, 1996; Wiatrowski and Anderson, 1987; Wiatrowski et al., 1982; Wilson and Herrnstein, 1985:267.

4. *See* Hawkins and Lishner, 1987; Krohn et al., 1995; Sweeten, 2006; Thornberry, 1996; Thornberry et al., 2003a.

5. *See* Felson and Stott, 2006; Hawkins and Lishner, 1987; Maguin and Loeber, 1996; Wilson and Herrnstein, 1985.

6. *See* Felson and Stott, 2006; Jarjoura, 1993, 1996; Krohn et al., 1995; Maguin and Loeber, 1996; Wiatrowski et al., 1982.

7. *See* Bellair and McNulty, 2005; Chung et al., 2002; Loeber, Farrington, Stouthamer-Loeber, and Van Kammen, 1998; Maguin and Loeber, 1996; Matsueda et al., 2006; McGloin et al., 2004; Sampson and Laub, 1993a; Thornberry, 1996; Thornberry et al., 2003a; Wright et al., 1999b.

8. *See* research on the effect of dropping out of school on delinquency; *see* Krohn et al., 1995; Jarjoura, 1993, 1996.

9. *See* Bellair and McNulty, 2005; Gottfredson, 2001; Maguin and Loeber, 1996; McGloin et al., 2004; Sampson and Laub, 1993a; Wiatrowski et al., 1981; Wright et al., 2001.

10. *See* Jenkins, 1997; Patterson, 1986; Patterson et al., 1992; Sampson and Laub, 1993a.

11. *See* Bellair and McNulty, 2005; Hawkins and Lishner, 1987; Patterson, 1986; Patterson et al., 1989; Patterson et al., 1992; Thornberry, 1996; Thornberry et al., 2003a.

12. *See* Alexander, 1997; Bellair and McNulty, 2005; Gottfredson, 2001; Jenkins, 1997; Maguin and Loeber, 1996; McGloin et al., 2004; Payne et al., 2003; Sampson and Laub, 1993a; Wadsworth, 2000.

13. *See* U.S. Department of Education and Office of Justice Programs, 2006; Eisenbraun, 2007; Ericson, 2001; Howell, 2003a; Smokowski and Kopasz, 2005.

14. For overviews and recent studies, *see* Catalano and Hawkins, 1996; Coleman et al., 1982; Elliott et al., 1998; Farrington and Welsh, 2007; Gottfredson, 2001; Gottfredson and Gottfredson, 1985; Gottfredson et al., 2005; Hawkins and Lishner, 1987; Hellman and Beaton, 1986; Lawrence, 1998; Payne et al., 2003; Rutter et al., 1979; Rutter et al., 1998; Stewart, 2003; Weishew and Peng, 1993; Welsh, Greene, and Jenkins, 1999; Welsh et al., 2000; Wilson and Herrnstein, 1985; *also see* Alexander, 1997.

Billing Address:

Trisha Bergeron
12 Bridgham Street
Methuen, Ma 01844-1506
United States

SDTr4LsJGR

Shipping Address:

Trisha Bergeron
12 Bridgham Street
Methuen, Ma 01844-1506
United States

Returns Are Easy!
Visit http://www.amazon.com/returns to return any item -including gifts- in unopened or original
condition within 30 days for a full refund (other restrictions apply)

Your order of August 30, 2009 (Order ID:103 — 4971127 — 2079458)

Qty	Item	Item Price	Total
	IN THIS SHIPMENT		
1	Criminal Justice Student Writer's Manual, The (4th Edition... (** P-3-B40A4 **) 0132318768 : 0132318768 0132318768 Paperback	$36.70	$36.70
1	Ferri's Differential Diagnosis: A Practical Guide to the Different... (** P-3-B13F111 **) 0323040934 : 0323040934 0323040934 Turtleback	$17.46	$17.46
	8 Ball Chicks (** P-3-E14D154 **) 0385474326 : 0385474326 0385474326 Paperback	$10.85	$10.85
	My Bloody Life: The Making of a Latin King (Illinois) (** P-1-B4D146 **) 1556524277 : 1556524277 1556524277 Paperback	$11.53	$11.53
	Once a King, Always a King: The Unmaking of a Latin King (** P-2-C18E61 **) 1556525532 : 1556525532 1556525532 Paperback	$11.53	$11.53

Subtotal	$88.07
Shipping & Handling	$7.45
Order Total	$95.52
Paid via Visa	$95.52
Balance Due	$0.00

This shipment completes your order.

Have feedback on how we packaged your order? Tell us at www.amazon.com/packaging

3347 (5 of 5)

SDTr4LsJGR

amazon.com
and you're done.™

CHAPTER 16

Delinquent Peers and Gangs

What Impact Do Delinquent Peer Groups and Gangs Have on Delinquency?

As juveniles enter adolescence, the peer group comes to occupy a central—in many cases *the* central—place in their lives. Adolescents start spending much more time with their peers, they attach more importance to their peers, and they are more strongly influenced by their peers (Thornberry et al., 2003a; Warr, 2002). It is perhaps no surprise, then, that **most adolescents who commit delinquent offenses do so in the company of peers.** One study, based on a nationally representative sample of adolescents, found that 73 percent of all delinquent offenses were committed in a group. For example, 91 percent of all burglaries and alcohol violations were committed in a group, 79 percent of all drug violations, 71 percent of all assaults, 60 percent of all acts of vandalism, 49 percent of all acts of truancy, and 44 percent of all thefts (Warr, 1996). Other studies produce somewhat different percentages, but most show that a majority of all delinquent acts are committed with peers.

Based partly on such data, many criminologists argue that **associating with delinquent peers is a major cause of delinquency.** They most often draw on social learning theory when making this argument. As indicated in Chapter 7, delinquent peers are said to reinforce the adolescent's delinquency, model delinquent behavior, and present values conducive to delinquency. This chapter examines the impact of delinquent peers on delinquency. First, I focus on the impact of delinquent peers in general. Then I examine the impact of a particular type of delinquent peer group: the gang.

What Impact Do Delinquent Peers Have on Delinquency?

Is associating with delinquent peers an important cause of delinquency? Cross-sectional data indicate that juveniles with delinquent friends are much more likely to engage in delinquency. In fact, having delinquent friends is typically the strongest correlate of delinquency. But as you know, the fact that delinquent friends and delinquency are associated does not mean that having delinquent friends **causes** delinquency. Both of these variables may be caused by the same third variable(s). In particular, it has been argued that individual traits (e.g., low self-control), family problems, and negative school experiences cause delinquency on the one hand and association with delinquent peers on the other. It has also been argued that the association is due to the fact that delinquency causes one to associate with delinquent peers. Most people prefer to associate with people who are like them, so delinquents may choose to associate with fellow delinquents ("birds of a feather flock together"). Until recently, it was not clear **why** having delinquent peers was associated with delinquency.

Data now suggest that **the association between delinquent peers and delinquency is partly due to the causal effect of delinquent peers on delinquency.** Several longitudinal studies have found that associating with delinquent peers leads to an increase in subsequent delinquency, even when other variables are controlled. In fact, associating with delinquent peers is often the best predictor of subsequent delinquency (other than the juvenile's level of prior delinquency). At the same time, studies also indicate that the association is partly due to the fact that delinquent peers and delinquency are caused by the same third variables, such as negative family experiences. Further, delinquency has a causal effect on delinquent peers; that is, delinquent individuals are more likely to select fellow delinquents as friends.[1]

A study by Elliott and Menard (1996) sheds light on the relationship between delinquent peers and delinquency. Their data suggest that the progression from no delinquency to serious delinquency typically proceeds in the following manner: (1) juveniles associate with mildly delinquent peers before they engage in delinquency; (2) this peer association leads to minor delinquency; (3) this minor delinquency leads to association with more delinquent peers; (4) this association leads to more serious delinquency, and so on. Not all juveniles move as far as serious delinquency, and some juveniles do not complete these steps in the order shown. Some juveniles, for example, may engage in delinquency before associating with delinquent peers. Nevertheless, this pattern is the most common pattern of progression. It illustrates that delinquent peers and delinquent acts are **reciprocally related** to one another; each has a causal effect on the other.[2]

Under What Conditions Are Delinquent Peers Most Likely to Cause Delinquency?

Recent data suggest that the effect of delinquent peers on delinquency is not the same in all circumstances.[3] The effect of delinquent peers is greatest when **all of the adolescent's friends are delinquent** (versus only some of the adolescent's friends). It is greatest when the adolescent's friends form a **cohesive group;** that is, they all know and interact with one another. And it is greatest when these friends hold **beliefs conducive to delinquency, approve of the adolescent's delinquency, and pressure the adolescent to engage in delinquency.** The effect of delinquent peers may also be greater for certain types of offenses, like drug use. These conditional effects are easily explained by social learning and other theories. For example, social learning theory states that we are more likely to model someone's behavior if we are frequently exposed to her or his behavior and are infrequently exposed to competing behaviors.

It is also the case that the effect of delinquent peers on delinquency is influenced by factors other than the nature of one's peer associations. In particular, there is some evidence that association with delinquent peers is more likely to cause delinquency among those low in control. For example, delinquent peers are more likely to cause delinquency among those who are poorly supervised and weakly attached to their parents (see Barnes et al., 2006; Elliott et al.,1985). Related to this, delinquent peers are more likely to cause delinquency among males than females (Mears et al., 1998; Piquero et al., 2005). This may be the case because females are higher in control than males, including direct control, self-control, and the belief that delinquency is bad (see Chapter 18).

What Are Delinquent Peer Groups Like?

Only a small percentage of *delinquent peer groups* **are gangs.** The term "delinquent group," in fact, is somewhat misleading. Most delinquent groups are better described as friendship groups that occasionally engage in delinquency. This will become apparent as I comment on the types of delinquency committed by these groups, the size and composition of the groups, and the quality of relations between group members.

Types of delinquency. Most delinquent peer groups usually only engage in minor delinquency on an occasional basis, although a significant percentage of groups engage in more frequent and serious delinquency. Warr (1993), for example, found that by mid- to late adolescence, a majority of adolescents had close friends who engaged in minor forms of deviance such as marijuana and alcohol use, cheating, and petty theft. Less than 20 percent, however, had friends who engaged in serious offenses such as burglary, theft over $50, or selling hard drugs.[4]

Size and composition. The groups that engage in delinquency are usually small. The typical size is two to four juveniles, with the groups getting smaller in size as juveniles age. By mid- to late adolescence, the typical offending group consists of only two or three juveniles. (Adults, unlike juveniles, are most likely to commit their offenses alone.) These small groups are subsets of larger groups or cliques of youth (but usually not gangs). Juveniles seldom commit offenses with the same person(s) all the time; rather, they will usually commit offenses with different members of these larger groups or cliques. In this area, Warr (1996:16) states that "it is important to distinguish between *offending groups* (groups that actually commit delinquent acts) and *accomplice networks* (the pool of potential co-offenders available to the adolescent)." Warr found that the average size of accomplice networks was about seven, with the more delinquent youths having larger networks.

Group members are usually similar in terms of age and sex. Most delinquent groups are made up of males (see McCarthy et al., 2004). And membership in such groups peaks at ages 15 to 18. I should note that while males are most likely to offend with males and females are most likely to offend with females, female offenders are more likely to be a part of mixed-sex groups than are males.

One person in the group will usually suggest or instigate the offense (the "instigator"). Instigators are most often the same age as or a little older than the other group member(s), and they usually have a little more delinquent experience than the others. While the instigator is usually the same sex as the others in the group, females are more likely to report male instigators than males are to report female instigators (see Giordano, 1978; Warr, 1996). Most juveniles who have committed at least a few delinquent offenses report that they have played the role of both instigator and follower. They will often play the role of instigator with one set of friends and follower with another.

Quality of relations between group members. Some researchers have argued that the members of delinquent groups have poor relations with one another. One researcher describes these relations as "cold and brittle" (Hirschi, 1969). In particular, it is said that group members are not very attached to one another and that they frequently exploit one another. Other researchers, however, claim that the members of delinquent groups have great affection for and loyalty to one another. The latter image is often presented in films about gangs, the classic example being *West Side Story.*

Recent data suggest that the quality of peer relations varies a lot from delinquent group to delinquent group, but that overall, the **relations in delinquent groups are similar to those found in conventional groups** (see especially Agnew, 1991b; Giordano et al., 1986). One of the best studies in this area found that the members of delinquent groups spend as much time with one another as the members of conventional groups, have similar levels of caring and trust, are more likely to share private thoughts, are more influenced by one another, and find their friendships more rewarding in certain ways (Giordano et al., 1986). Reflecting these facts, the members of delinquent groups usually report that they are close friends or friends with one another (Warr, 1996). The members of delinquent groups, however, are also **more likely to report getting into conflicts with one another** than are the members of conventional groups (Giordano et al., 1986).

Romantic partners are also important. Most of the research on delinquent peers has focused on association with **friends.** Adolescents, however, also associate with romantic partners. And recent research suggests that individuals with delinquent romantic partners are more likely to engage in delinquency themselves. Haynie et al. (2005) examined a sample of adolescents in grades 7 through 12 in a diverse set of schools throughout the United States. These adolescents were asked, "In the past 18 months, have you had a special romantic relationship with someone?" Over half the respondents replied yes. About 90 percent of these respondents said they had only one romantic partner during this time. The average length of a romantic relationship was between 8 and 9 months, and the relationship involved a high level of romantic involvement (e.g., the romantic partners told each other that they loved one another). The researchers found that individuals with delinquent romantic partners were more likely to engage in delinquency themselves. This was true even after the researchers took account of a range of third variables, including the delinquency of the individual's friends. Friends' delinquency, however, had a stronger relationship to the individual's delinquency than did the romantic partner's delinquency. The researcher also examined whether the romantic partner's delinquency had a stronger effect on males or females. Since males often have more power in a relationship, they thought that the romantic partner's delinquency would have a greater effect on females. This was true when the researchers examined minor delinquency, but not true when they examined serious delinquency.

Why Are Individuals in Delinquent Groups More Likely to Engage in Delinquency?

As indicated, **social learning theory** is most often used to explain the effect of delinquent peers on a juvenile's delinquency. Data indicate that delinquent peers affect delinquency by reinforcing the juvenile's delinquency, providing delinquent models, and fostering beliefs that are conducive to delinquency. Warr (2002) provides an excellent discussion of some of these mechanisms. He states, for example, that juveniles in delinquent peer groups sometimes engage in delinquency because it increases their status or prestige with peers, with risky acts like delinquency often being admired in such groups. This, of course, is an example of the positive reinforcement of delinquency. Warr also states that juveniles in delinquent groups sometimes engage in delinquency because they fear they will be ridiculed if they do not. That is, they fear others in the group will do such things as laugh at them, tease them, call them derogatory names, or even reject them if they do not engage in delinquency on certain occasions. This is an example of the negative reinforcement of delinquency, with juveniles engaging in delinquency to avoid something bad. Further, Warr (2002:67) states that the juveniles in delinquent groups sometimes engage in delinquency because the group has developed its own "moral code that supplants that of the outside world, granting legitimacy to otherwise illegitimate conduct." Social learning theory, then, sheds much light on the reasons why individuals in delinquent peer groups are more likely to engage in delinquency.

At the same time, **most studies find that delinquent peers affect delinquency even after one takes account of reinforcement, modeling, and beliefs** (although the measures employed in such studies are often poor). And it has been argued that delinquent peers also increase the likelihood of delinquency for reasons related to control, strain, and labeling theories (see especially Agnew, 1995a; Warr, 2002).

Drawing on **control theory**, delinquent peers may reduce the juvenile's fear of direct controls, stake in conformity, and level of internal control. Being part of a delinquent peer group may reduce the fear of retaliation by others (a form of direct control), since there is strength in numbers. Also, witnessing one's friends engage in delinquency without sanction may reduce the fear of official or police sanctions (see Johnson, 1979; Meier et al., 1984). Further, delinquent friends may reduce the juvenile's bonds to conventional others and the amount of effort devoted to conventional activities, like schoolwork (see Decker and Van Winkle, 1996). The result is a lower stake in conformity. Finally, delinquent friends may weaken the juvenile's belief that delinquency is wrong or bad. This occurs partly because the friends often challenge the belief that delinquency is bad. For example, they tell the juvenile that smoking marijuana "is not so bad" (also see Warr, 2002).

Delinquent peers may also affect delinquency for reasons related to **strain theory** (see Agnew, 1995a). Delinquent peers experience more conflict with one another and with others in the community—with such conflict involving the presentation of negative stimuli (see Colvin, 2000; Giordano et al., 1986). And membership in delinquent peer groups may make it more difficult for juveniles to achieve certain of their goals **through legitimate channels,** including their monetary and status goals. Finally, the members of delinquent groups may be more likely to be **labeled** as delinquent by others. Although as Chambliss points out in his discussion of the Saints and Roughnecks, the members of certain delinquent peer groups are able to escape negative labeling (see Chapter 9). Still other explanations have been offered for the effect of delinquent peers on delinquency, although most are related to the leading delinquency theories.[5]

Why Are Some Juveniles More Likely than Others to Get Involved with Delinquent Peers?

It has been argued that juveniles with **the traits of irritability and low self-control are more likely to get involved with delinquent peers.** These traits increase the likelihood that juveniles will be rejected by conventional peers. And they increase the appeal of delinquent groups. Juveniles with a strong need for thrills and excitement (part of low self-control), for example, will probably be more attracted to the activities of delinquent groups. Limited data support these arguments, suggesting that traits like irritability and low self-control increase the likelihood of membership in delinquent groups.[6]

Most of the **family variables that promote delinquency also increase the likelihood of membership in delinquent peer groups.** Factors like large family size, parental criminality, parental rejection, low parental attachment, and poor parental supervision have all been shown to increase association with delinquent peers.[7] Likewise, certain data suggest that many of the **negative school experiences** described in Chapter 15 **increase the likelihood of association with delinquent peers.**[8] These family and school factors reduce the juvenile's level of control. Juveniles low in control are more likely to spend time on the "street," increasing their exposure to delinquent peers, and they have less to lose by associating with delinquent peers. These family and school factors also increase the juvenile's level of strain, which makes delinquent peer groups more appealing. Juveniles experiencing problems at school, for example, will probably be more attracted to certain of the activities of delinquent peers—like skipping school.

Further, **juveniles in deprived, inner-city communities are more likely to become involved with delinquent peers.** As indicated in Chapter 12, deprived communities are more likely to develop delinquent peer groups (also see Haynie et al., 2006). So juveniles in such communities will have greater exposure to such groups. Also, juveniles in such communities may be more attracted to delinquent peers, since associating with such peers may be seen as a way to cope with certain of the strains they face—like high levels of violence.

Finally, **delinquent behavior itself increases the likelihood of association with delinquent peers.** This effect may reflect the fact that delinquents prefer to associate with other delinquents. It may also reflect the fact that conventional peers are reluctant to associate with delinquents, compelling them to associate with one another.

What Impact Do Gangs Have on Delinquency?

While the most common type of delinquent peer group is the simple friendship group, several authors have pointed to additional types of delinquent or law-violating groups, with the street gang receiving the most attention. This section addresses several basic questions about street gangs: What is a *street gang*? How common are such gangs? What effect do gangs have on crime and delinquency? What are gangs like? And why do some individuals join gangs and some communities develop gangs?[9]

Before proceeding, however, it is important to emphasize that it is difficult to talk about gangs in general. **Gangs often differ greatly from one another.** Gangs in one city, for example, may be large, highly organized, and heavily involved in drug sales. Gangs in another city may be small, loosely organized, and have little or no involvement in drug sales. The gangs within a particular city may also differ from one another. These differences are related to a number of factors, including the race/ethnic and sex composition of the gangs and whether the gangs are newly formed or have a long history. For example, studies in certain cities report that Latino gangs are more concerned with issues of honor and protection of turf than other gangs. Perhaps because of this, they have higher rates of violence than other gangs. African American gangs are said to be more heavily involved in illegal methods of generating income, especially drug sales. Asian gangs are said to be less territorial, more highly organized, and more involved in property crimes like extortion and home invasions.[10] Certain other differences between gangs are described later.

What Is a Street Gang?

There is no generally agreed-upon definition of a street gang.[11] As will become apparent in the discussion that follows, this lack of a common definition has created a number of problems. For example, it is difficult to talk about the extent of gangs if there is no generally accepted definition of gangs. Two cities may have similar gang problems, but officials in one city may employ a narrow definition of gangs and claim they have few gangs, while officials in the other city may employ a broad definition and claim they have many.

The definition of gangs employed in this text is the one agreed to by a group of over 100 American and European gang researchers who held a series of meetings between 1997 and 2005 (see Klein and Maxson, 2006:4). A street gang is **"any durable, street-oriented youth group whose involvement in illegal activity is part of its group identity."** By "durable," the researchers mean that the group has existed for at least several months. By "street-oriented," they mean that the group spends much time in public settings such as the streets, parks, and malls. And by "group identity," they mean that group is viewed at least in part as one that engages in illegal activity. The dividing line between a delinquent peer group and a gang may sometimes be fuzzy, but gangs are distinguished by their stronger group identity and their relatively strong involvement in delinquency.

Certain researchers have offered more elaborate definitions of gangs. They state, for example, that gangs have territories or turfs they protect and that they have formal organizational structures (e.g., they have official positions like president, vice president, and war counselor). Many of the groups commonly thought of as gangs, however, are loosely organized at best and do not claim territories that they protect (Asian gangs, for example, often do not claim territories).

How Common Are Gangs?

Most estimates of the extent of gangs are obtained by surveying police and sometimes other officials in samples of cities around the United States (for an overview, see Curry and Decker, 2003). The estimates from these surveys should be regarded with caution. Not all jurisdictions are surveyed, many jurisdictions do not respond to the surveys, and police estimates of the number of gangs and gang members may be biased. Police departments employ different definitions of gangs. Further, many police departments deny that they have a gang problem, particularly in the initial stages of the problem (see Klein, 1995). Some police departments, however, may exaggerate their gang problem—perhaps to secure more funding (see Curry et al., 1996). Nevertheless, data suggest that gangs are widespread, present in all major cities (250,000+ population) and in many smaller areas in the United States.

The most comprehensive survey examining the extent of gangs is carried out by the National Youth Gang Center (http://www.iir.com/nygc)—an agency created by the U.S. Department of Justice. The 2004 survey of the Youth Gang Center was mailed to 2,554 police and sheriff's departments across the country, including departments in all major cities and suburban areas and a randomly selected sample of departments in small towns and rural areas (Egley and Ritz, 2006). Based on the 2,296 departments that responded to the survey, it was estimated that 80 percent of cities with populations of more than 50,000 had gangs, and a substantial minority of smaller areas had gangs (e.g., 40 percent of suburban counties and 12 percent of rural counties). Data, however, suggest that the gang problem is small in most areas, with fewer than 10 gangs and 500 gang members being reported (Klein, 1995). Data from the Youth Gang Center survey suggest that there were 24,000 gangs with 760,000 gang members in 2004.

Several self-report studies have examined the extent of gang membership. For the United States as a whole, these surveys suggest that about 2 percent of juveniles belong to gangs at any given time, and about 5 percent have belonged to a gang at some point in their lives (Klein and Maxson, 2006:21). Other self-report surveys have focused on the extent of gang membership in particular cities, such as Denver and Rochester. These surveys of urban youth suggest that about 5 to 15 percent of adolescents belong to gangs in a given year, and 8 to 30 percent of all adolescents belong to gangs at some point during adolescence.[12] So only a small portion of youths belong to gangs, even in urban areas known to have gang problems. Such youths, however, are responsible for much delinquency, especially serious delinquency, as indicated next.

Are Gangs Becoming More Common?

Data suggest that gangs became much more common from the 1970s to the mid-1990s. Estimates show a steady increase in the number of gangs, gang members, and cities with gang problems during this time (see Curry and Decker, 2003; Miller, W., 2001). For example, surveys suggest that the number of gang members in the United States increased from

55,000 in 1975 to almost 850,000 in the mid-1990s. These survey results must be inter-preted with caution, especially given that surveys in the 1990s became much more compre-hensive, interviewing officials in many more jurisdictions than the earlier surveys. Nevertheless, there seems little doubt that there was a **dramatic increase in gangs from the 1970s to the mid-1990s** (Curry and Decker, 2003; Miller, W., 2001).

Gang activity, however, declined somewhat from 1996 to 2002, especially in smaller areas. In particular, data from the National Youth Gang Center surveys indicate that the number of gang members decreased 14 percent from 1996 to 2002. Since 2002, there has been a slight increase in the number of gangs (National Youth Gang Center, 2007).

What Effect Do Gangs Have on Crime and Delinquency?

How much crime and delinquency is gang related? It is not possible at present to give a precise answer to this question. Most cities do not attempt to calculate the proportion of all crimes that are gang related. Cities that do attempt such calculations usually focus only on homicide and maybe a small number of other serious crimes. Further, these cities often employ different methods to determine if a crime is gang related. One city, for example, may classify a crime as gang related if the offender or victim is a known or suspected gang member. Another city, however, may classify a crime as gang related only if the motive for the crime is gang related (e.g., revenge against another gang, protection of turf).

Data, however, suggest that **a sizeable share of all crime, particularly serious crime, is gang related in certain cities.** In 2004, about half of all homicides in Los Angeles and Chicago—the two cities with the worst gang problems—were gang related (Egley and Ritz, 2006). Recent self-report studies also indicate that gang members account for a large share of crime, especially serious crime, in certain cities. In Denver, gang members made up 14 percent of all adolescents in high-crime communities, but they accounted for 79 percent of all serious violent crimes and 71 percent of all serious property crimes committed by adolescents (Huizinga et al., 1998). In Rochester, 30 percent of the juveniles belonged to a gang at some point during their high school career, but these juveniles accounted for 65 percent of all delinquent acts, including 86 percent of all serious delinquent acts, 69 per-cent of all violent acts, 68 percent of all property crimes, 70 percent of all drug sales, and 61 percent of all drug use (Thornberry and Burch, 1997). In Seattle, 15 percent of all juve-niles belonged to gangs, but these gang members committed 58 percent of all delinquent acts (Battin et al., 1998).

While we cannot precisely estimate the share of all delinquency committed by gang members in the United States, it is clear that **gang members commit a substantial share of all delinquency—perhaps the majority of all serious delinquency—in certain cities.** These data, along with other data reported later, indicate that gangs should be a central fo-cus of delinquency control and prevention efforts.

What types of crime do gang members commit? Gang members engage in a wide va-riety of criminal acts, both serious and minor. While gang members are disproportionately involved in all forms of crime, their disproportionate involvement is greatest for serious and violent offenses—including homicide. There are a number of reasons for this dispro-portionate involvement in serious crimes like homicide (discussed later), including the fact that gang members are more likely than other juveniles to own and carry guns, including automatic, high-powered guns.[13] The presence of guns often turns what would otherwise be an assault into a homicide (see Chapter 17).

Certain myths regarding gang crime should be addressed. First, some individuals have the impression that gang members spend most of their time engaged in crime. Although gang members do commit a lot of crime, **they spend the vast majority of their time simply hanging around**—talking and waiting for something to happen. Partying is perhaps their second most frequent activity. When gang members do engage in crime, they commit far more minor than serious crime, something that is true of delinquents in general.

Second, many commentators claim that street gangs control drug sales in the United States. Recent data suggest that this belief is mistaken. Many gang members do engage in drug sales—a majority in some studies. And gang members are more likely to engage in drug sales than nonmembers. But street gangs do not control drug sales (including crack sales) in the United States. **Most drug sales are not conducted by gang members,** and when gang members do sell drugs, they usually do so as individuals and on a sporadic basis. It is true that some street gangs have been become heavily involved in drug sales, especially in recent years. This involvement is more often true of African American gangs, many of whom have become involved in crack sales, but these street gangs by no means control drug sales in the United States.[14] (It should be noted that drug sales in a community may be controlled by **drug gangs.** Drug gangs, however, are distinct from street gangs. Drug gangs are smaller, made up of older members, better organized, and focused on drug sales. Drug gangs sometimes employ the members of street gangs; Klein, 1995.)

Third, many people believe that the victims of gang violence are frequently innocent bystanders. It is true that innocent bystanders are sometimes killed and wounded, but **the members of other gangs are far and away the most frequent targets of gang violence.** Most acts of gang violence involve acts of revenge or turf disputes.

Fourth, it should again be emphasized that **gangs are not all alike.** Among other things, they differ from one another in terms of the extent and nature of their crime. Based on a study of three communities, Fagan (1989) describes four types of gangs: (1) social gangs, whose members engage in high levels of alcohol and marijuana use but otherwise engage in little delinquency and other drug use; (2) party gangs, whose members engage in high rates of drug use and drug sales but otherwise engage in little delinquency (their drug sales help support their drug use); (3) serious delinquent gangs, whose members engage in a wide range of serious and minor delinquent acts but have little involvement in drug sales and serious drug use; and (4) "organization" gangs, whose members are heavily involved in delinquency, drug sales, and drug use. Other researchers have reported similar types of gangs (see Shelden et al., 2001; see Klein, 1998, for another recent typology of gangs).

Does gang membership cause delinquency? It is well established that gang members commit more delinquent acts, especially serious delinquent acts, than nonmembers. In fact, both official and self-report data suggest that gang members have rates of offending that are several times higher than nonmembers.[15] Further, recent data indicate that gang members also have much higher rates of delinquency than juveniles with delinquent friends.[16] This association, of course, does not mean that gang membership **causes** delinquency. The association may simply arise because delinquents are more likely to join gangs or because both gang membership and delinquency are caused by the same third variables. Recent data provide some support for these arguments: Delinquent individuals are more likely to join gangs than nondelinquent individuals, and both gang membership and delinquency are caused by many of the same third variables. At the same time, data indicate that individuals experience a dramatic increase in delinquency after they join a gang and a dramatic decrease after they leave the gang. Further, the higher offending rates of gang members appear to hold even when a range of third variables are taken into account.[17] These important data suggest that **there is something about the gang itself that leads to an increase in offending.**

As with peer groups, the effect of gangs on offending can be explained in terms of social learning, strain, control, and labeling theories. With respect to **social learning theory,** researchers report that gang members hold values conducive to delinquency, such as toughness, achieving quick success, and backing up fellow gang members. Gang members spend much time talking about their delinquent exploits and occasionally modeling delinquent behavior. And gang members frequently reinforce delinquent behavior and punish certain forms of conventional behavior. With respect to **strain theory,** gang members frequently get into conflicts with one another, the members of rival gangs, the police, and others. Such conflicts often lead to acts of retaliation or revenge (see Peterson et al., 2004). Further, gang membership makes it more difficult for individuals to achieve certain goals—like monetary success—through legitimate channels. This is because gang membership increases the likelihood that juveniles will do poorly in school, drop out of school, face employment problems, and become teenage parents (see Decker and Van Winkle, 1996; Thornberry et al., 2003b). With respect to **control theory,** gang members have less fear of being sanctioned by others (because there is "power in numbers"). And gang members have a lower stake in conformity, because the gang pulls members away from conventional others and institutions, like school and work. With respect to **labeling theory,** gang members are more likely to be viewed and treated as delinquents or "bad people."[18]

What Are the Characteristics of Gang Members?

Gang members tend to be **poor and live in lower-income, urban communities,** although gangs exist in some working-class and even middle-class areas.[19]

Gang members are **predominantly male.** The best data suggest that between 20 and 40 percent of gang members are female.[20] Self-report data show a greater percentage of female gang members than official estimates, which likely reflects the fact that the police are less likely to notice female gang members and keep official statistics on them. Some police departments, for example, have a policy of not counting females as gang members (Curry and Decker, 2003:111; Esbensen et al., 1999).

Most gang members are **young, typically teenagers.** Gang members tend to range in age from 12 to 30, with 14- to 15-year-olds having the highest rates of participation. There has been an increase in the number of younger and especially older gang members in recent years. More and more adults are maintaining their gang membership, with some gang members in their 40s and even 50s. In the past, juveniles would quit or drift out of the gang as they got jobs and formed families. There has, however, been a massive loss of manufacturing jobs in inner-city communities, and so it has become more difficult for the young adults in such communities to find decent work. As a consequence, many of these young adults elect to maintain their gang ties—particularly since the gang provides opportunities for obtaining money through illegal channels.

Most gang members **belong to minority groups.** According to one recent estimate based on a survey of law enforcement agencies, 34 percent of gang members are African American, 49 percent are Latino, 10 percent are white, and 6 percent are Asian (Egley and Ritz, 2004).[21] These numbers probably underestimate the percentage of white gang members because there is a tendency in law enforcement **not** to classify many white law-violating groups as street gangs. This includes groups such as Skinheads and Stoners (who emphasize heavy metal music, satanic themes, and drug use). Certain self-report studies have found the percentage of white gang members to be greater than 10 percent, although these studies still indicate that minorities are disproportionately involved in gangs (Esbensen and Osgood, 1997; Esbensen et al., 1999). There is also evidence that mixed-race gangs are becoming more common (Curry and Decker, 2003; National Youth Gang Center, 2003; Starbuck et al., 2004).

During the early 1900s, most gang members were white. They were often the children of recent immigrants to the United States—such as Italian, Polish, and Irish immigrants (see Thrasher, 1927, for a classic discussion of such gangs in Chicago). These ethnic groups were the ones that populated the poor inner-city communities, the communities in which gangs are most common. As these groups moved up the economic ladder, they were replaced by African Americans migrating from the rural South, Latinos from Mexico and other areas, and Asians. Unfortunately, it will be more difficult for today's inner-city residents to move up the economic ladder, given the recent losses in manufacturing jobs that pay a decent wage.

How Are Gangs Organized or Structured?

Gangs are often portrayed as highly organized groups. It is said that they have well-defined roles, such as president, vice president, war counselor, and treasurer; that they have well-defined goals and extensive rules that members are supposed to follow, with these goals and rules being specified in written constitutions or other documents; that they have hundreds or even thousands of members, with smaller gangs being organized into larger gang confederations; and that they are highly cohesive, with members expressing great loyalty to one another and to the larger group. It is true that some gangs are like this, particularly the older, larger gangs that exist in cities like Chicago and Los Angeles. Most gangs, however, do not fit this model.

Most gangs are **loosely organized** (see especially Klein, 1995; Klein and Maxson, 2006). They do not have well-defined roles. There is often a distinction between core members and fringe members, with the fringe members including "wannabes." Wannabes are individuals—often younger juveniles—who want to join or become more involved with the gang. Certain of the core members may function as leaders on occasion, but the leaders may shift from occasion to occasion and no one may claim to be the leader of the gang. The gang may also be divided into age groups (e.g., Pee Wees, Juniors, Seniors, Ancients), although this age division is becoming less common. In most gangs, however, members divide up into a number of informal cliques or subgroups—and crimes are often committed with the members of these cliques.

There are few well-defined goals or rules for members to follow, beyond the goals and rules that characterize many gang and nongang youth in inner-city communities (e.g., be tough, do not "squeal" or "rat" to authorities). The membership of a gang often changes a good deal over time; self-report studies indicate that most gang members belong to the gang less than a year. Most estimates of gang size are in the 25 to 250 range. The gang itself is not highly cohesive. Some researchers have noted that there is often more conflict between members of the same gang than between members of different gangs. Several observers, in fact, have pointed out that what binds gang members together is not so much their respect and affection for one another as it is their conflict with external groups like other gangs and the police.

What Are Female Gangs Like?

Females are found in **three types of gangs.** Most are in mixed-sex—gangs; that is, gangs involving both males and females. Many are in female gangs that are affiliated with male gangs (e.g., the Vice Queens are affiliated with the Vice Kings). And a much smaller number are in independent female gangs (see Maxson and Whitlock, 2002; Peterson et al., 2001).

The impression is sometimes given that female gang members are largely subservient to male members, with the female members being sexual objects to be used by the male members. Studies, however, suggest that female gang members exercise a good deal of control over their own affairs. And while both male and female gang members may engage in much sexual behavior, female gang members sanction indiscriminate sexual behavior. Further, female gang members engage in a wide range of delinquent acts, including aggressive acts. This is especially true of females in mixed-sex gangs that are predominantly male (see Peterson et al., 2001). Overall, however, **female gang members are not as delinquent as male gang members.**

Females join gangs for many of the same reasons that males join. They often have friends or relatives in the gang. And the gang is often seen as a solution to the problems they face. Many of these problems are shared with males, like class and race discrimination. Data, however, suggest that there are **two problems with special relevance to female gang members. First,** some data indicate that female gang members are more likely than male gang members to have experienced problems like **abuse at home.** Females may join the gang in an effort to cope with such problems: The gang makes it easier to escape from home life and may function as a surrogate family. In this area, some data suggest that females are more likely to join gangs in an effort to form close, family-like ties with their peers, while males are more likely to join because they are attracted to the "action" associated with the gang (see Esbensen et al., 1999). Jody Miller (2001:49–50) illustrates certain of these points in the following description of a female gang member, taken from her field study of female gangs in two cities:

> Brittany described a terrible violent family life. She lived in a household with extended family—twelve people in all—including her mother, grandmother, stepfather, and an adolescent uncle who was physically abusive. Her aunt's boyfriend had sexually assaulted her at the age of five, but family members didn't believe her. Although she didn't know her father, who was in jail, she had early memories of him physically abusing her mother. Moreover, she felt very disconnected and unloved by her family and also described being isolated at school: "I didn't have no friends, used to always get teased. . . . My grades started going down, I started getting real depressed, started skipping school, smoking weed after school and stuff." Brittany saw the gang as a means of finding love. She explained: "I felt that my family didn't care for me . . . that when I was on the streets I felt that I got more love than when I was in the house. So I felt that that's where my love was, on the streets, so that's where I stayed."

Second, females are more likely than males to join gangs in an effort to **partially escape from the gender oppression they encounter or anticipate encountering in the future.** Campbell (1990:172–173) describes the gender oppression that many lower-income females will likely encounter: (1) "a future of meaningless domestic labor with little possibility of educational or occupational escape," (2) "subordination to the man in the house," (3) "responsibility for children," and (4) "the social isolation of the housewife." According to Campbell (1990:172), the gang "represents for its members an idealized collective solution to the bleak future that awaits." That is, the gang represents a source of fun and excitement, although Campbell notes that gang members tend to exaggerate the positive side of gang life and minimize the negative.

This desire to escape from gender oppression does not mean that female gang members hold "liberated" views and that the gang is an effective solution to the problems they face. Female gang members often hold traditional gender role attitudes in many areas (although they are more accepting of the use of violence by females). As Chesney-Lind et al. state, "Girls' gang life is certainly not an expression of 'liberation,' but instead reflects the attempts of young women to cope with a bleak and harsh present as well as a dismal future" (1996:203). Furthermore, female gang members often find that they confront a range of problems when they join the gang, including physical and sexual abuse by the male gang members, many of whom hold sexist attitudes.[22]

Why Do Some Juveniles Join Gangs?

Juveniles give a variety of reasons for joining gangs. Some are **social in nature.** They have friends in the gang with whom they like to socialize. They see the gang as a source of fun and excitement (e.g., the gang holds a lot of parties and helps them meet romantic partners). They like the support, companionship, and sense of belonging they get from the gang. The gang is like a family for them. Some of the reasons relate to a **desire for a positive identity and status.** The gang makes them feel important, powerful, respected, and feared by others. Some of the reasons reflect a **desire for security or protection from others.** They believe the gang provides them with protection from rival gang members and others. (Note: This belief is mistaken. Individuals are more likely to be victimized after they join gangs [Peterson et al., 2004].) They may also believe that the gang provides protection for the neighborhood and that it is their duty or responsibility to join. Finally, individuals may join for reasons of **financial gain.** They believe that the gang will help them make money through activities like drug selling, robbery, and burglary. Individuals are forced to join gangs in some cases, but such forced entry is uncommon. Most individuals join gangs because they believe that it will benefit them in some way.

By the time juveniles decide to join the gang, they have usually been hanging around with gang members for a while. They typically go through an **initiation ceremony,** which may involve being "jumped in" or "beatin' in" by other gang members (that is, enduring a beating by other gang members). The initiation might also involve the commission of a crime or going on a "mission" against a rival gang (e.g., fighting or shooting a rival gang member).

As mentioned earlier, **most gang members leave the gang within a year.** There are a variety of reasons for leaving: witnessing the death or injury of a friend, being the direct victim of violence, being sent to a correctional institution, getting a job, having children, getting married, burnout from frequent arrests, or simply "maturing out" with age. The gang itself may also break up (see Decker and Lauritsen, 1996, for a discussion of leaving the gang). Contrary to certain accounts, most individuals are able to leave gangs without suffering serious reprisals from other gang members.

Applying the theories. At a deeper level, one can explain why individuals join gangs in terms of strain, social learning, and control theories. Individuals may join gangs in an effort to **cope with their strain.** In many cases, they may be unable to achieve their goals through legitimate channels. Most commonly, they cannot make enough money through legitimate work or obtain the respect they feel they deserve. The gang may be seen as a way to make money through illegitimate channels or to achieve status and respect (see Cloward and Ohlin, 1960; Cohen, 1955). Their strain may also result from the loss of positive stimuli or the presentation of negative stimuli. Juveniles, for example, may be neglected or abused by family members; the gang may allow them to escape from their family, and it may function as a surrogate family, albeit an imperfect one. Juveniles may be harassed by others in their school or community. The gang may be seen as a source of protection from such harassment. Juveniles may feel that their lives are rather dull or boring, and the gang may be seen as a source of excitement. In addition, the gang may be seen as a vehicle for rebelling or retaliating against individuals and groups who have mistreated the juvenile.

The experience of strain, however, does not guarantee that individuals will join a gang. Strained individuals are more likely to join gangs if they **have friends who are gang members and if they live in communities where gang members are respected and reinforced for gang membership.** In such cases, strained individuals will be exposed to attractive models who are gang members, will likely be exposed to beliefs favoring gang membership, and will likely conclude that gang membership has certain benefits for them.

Strained individuals with exposure to appealing gang members, however, may still not join gangs. Their parents or others may prevent them from doing so. And they may be concerned about the possible costs of gang membership. Among other things, gang membership may hurt their relations with parents and others, interfere with their schoolwork, and jeopardize their future career goals. Gang membership, then, is more likely when juveniles are **low in direct control (e.g., are not well supervised by parents) and have a low stake in conformity (e.g., they dislike their parents, are doing poorly in school, and have low aspirations for future success).**

If these arguments are correct, we would expect gang members to differ from nonmembers in a number of ways. Gang members should be more likely to possess traits that contribute to strain, low control, and a propensity to find delinquency reinforcing. Such traits include low intelligence, irritability, and low self-control. Gang members should be more likely to experience the types of strain described earlier. Gang members should be more likely to have had friends who were gang members before they joined the gang. Gang members should be more likely to experience the family problems described in Chapter 14, such as poor parental supervision, parental rejection, and abuse. And gang members should be more likely to experience the school problems described in Chapter 15, such as poor grades, low attachment to teachers, and dropping out.

Case studies of gang members provide some support for these arguments. Such studies usually report that juveniles join gangs partly because they are experiencing one or more types of strain, that juveniles knew gang members before they joined the gang, and that juveniles were low in at least certain types of control before they joined the gang. Some studies also suggest that gang members are likely to possess the individual traits listed in the preceding paragraph, although there is more disagreement about this point. These cases studies, however, suffer from certain problems. Most notably, they usually examine only a small number of gang members, and they seldom compare gang members to nongang members. It may be the case, for example, that nongang members in the community are just as high in strain and low in control as gang members.

A few studies have surveyed gang and nongang members in an effort to overcome these problems. Gang members are then compared to nonmembers in the same community. Sometimes a distinction is made between nonmembers who have engaged in certain types of delinquent offenses (nongang delinquents) and those who have not (nongang nondelinquents). These studies focus on some but not all the variables listed here (e.g., they often fail to measure certain types of strain and certain individual traits).

The results of these studies are generally supportive of the preceding arguments; **gang members usually differ from nondelinquents in the ways described.** Some studies, however, find only minimal differences between gang members and nongang delinquents. Part of the explanation for this similarity may be that many of the delinquents in the high-crime communities studied drift in and out of gangs. As a consequence, many of the nongang delinquents may be former gang members or may join gangs in the future. In any event, we may conclude that there is **some support for the strain, social learning, and control theory explanations of gang membership.**[23]

Why Do Some Communities Develop Gangs?

The same **deprived, inner-city communities** that have the highest rates of delinquency are also the **most likely to develop gangs** (see Klein and Maxson, 2006; Miller, Jody, 2001; Thornberry et al., 2003b). Not surprisingly, we can explain this in terms of the leading delinquency theories, especially control and strain theories.

As described in Chapter 12, **these deprived communities are lower in control;** residents are less likely to effectively supervise and sanction juveniles who engage in deviance, provide juveniles with a stake in conformity, and help juveniles develop strong internal controls. As a consequence, such juveniles frequently hang out on the street together and they have little to lose by engaging in crime. Further, **juveniles in these communities experience much strain.** They have trouble achieving their goals through legitimate channels, particularly their monetary and status goals. As indicated in Chapter 12, decent jobs are scarce in such communities. Further, juveniles in these communities are often treated in a negative manner by others, including family members, school officials, peers, and the police. These juveniles, then, experience a number of problems for which the gang might be seen as an effective solution.

The juveniles in deprived communities, then, are ripe for gang involvement (see Curry and Decker, 2003). Several reports suggest that **the triggering factor that turns these juveniles into gangs is conflict with others,** including conflict with other groups of youth, other gangs, and the police. Conflict with others is often an effective mechanism for uniting a group of people, and such conflict is often what turns the unorganized peer group into a gang. It has also been suggested that **many of these juveniles may form gangs in response to media portrayals of gang life** (more later).

How Can We Explain Trends in Gang Activity Since the 1970s?

There was a dramatic increase in the number of gangs and gang members from the 1970s to the mid 1990s. Further, gangs spread to many suburban communities, small towns, and even rural areas during this time. These changes have been explained in several ways.

As indicated in Chapter 12, **the number of high-poverty neighborhoods and the number of people living in such neighborhoods increased dramatically from the 1970s to the early 1990s.** This occurred for several reasons, including the loss of manufacturing jobs that paid a decent wage, the movement of middle and working-class African Americans from inner-city to suburban areas, and the concentration of public housing in inner-city communities. For reasons described in the last section, high-poverty communities are more likely to develop gangs. So as high-poverty communities become more common, gangs should become more common as well.

Gangs also spread to many working-class and even middle-class communities, including suburban communities and small towns. How might this be explained? The loss of manufacturing jobs, mentioned earlier, also had some effect on these communities. Many working- and lower-middle-class adolescents, especially those doing poorly in school, found themselves in a situation where their economic future was uncertain. They could no longer count on getting blue-collar jobs that paid decent wages. This reduced their stake in conformity and increased their level of strain, making them more amenable to gang involvement. Further, many suburban areas and small towns experienced large increases in population, particularly as urban residents left the city and immigrants settled in the United States. These population increases may have reduced levels of control (recall the discussion of residential instability in Chapter 12). These increases may have also **contributed to conflicts between youth groups.** (For an excellent illustration of these arguments, see the discussion of the rise of Skinhead groups among working- and lower-middle-class white youth in Blazak, 1999.)

Yet another factor contributing to the increase in gangs during this period may be the **increase in youth violence from the late 1980s to the mid-1990s,** an increase fueled by the crack trade (see Chapter 3). This increase in violence may have increased the appeal of gangs to many youths, with these youths viewing gangs as a way to protect themselves from the violence around them (see Rosenfeld et al., 1999).

It has also been argued that the **media and manufacturers contributed to the spread of gangs by introducing juveniles to gang culture,** including gang dress, talk, hand signals, graffiti, and behavior (see Klein, 1995). That is to say, the media and manufacturers provided juveniles with gang models to imitate. As Klein and associates (1995:110) point out:

> Baggy pants, Pendleton-style shirts, high-top shoes, ball caps worn backward or at angles, graffiti styles, words like "homey" and "hood" and other signs of affiliations have become part of the larger youth culture. In essence, commercial America has taught youthful America how to walk, talk, dress, and act "gangster-style."

Many juveniles, especially those experiencing the low control and strain described earlier, copied what they saw.[24]

It is sometimes claimed that the rapid growth in gangs was also the result of a plan on the part of certain gangs to increase their influence. Members of these gangs, it is said, deliberately moved to other cities with the intention of setting up gang chapters in these cities, thereby increasing their share of the drug trade and other illegal activities. It is easy to understand the basis of this belief, since the gangs in many cities adopted the names of well-known gangs or gang federations from other cities, such as the Bloods and Crips from Los Angeles or the People and Folks from Chicago. Data, however, suggest that **the spread of gangs was not the result of a deliberate plan by gang members from certain cities.** Most gangs were homegrown, although these gangs often adopted the names and symbols of well-known gangs in a copycat phenomenon. When members of gangs like the Bloods and Crips did move to a new city, it was usually because their families had decided to move, not because they were involved in a deliberate effort to spread gangs (see Howell, 1998a, and Klein, 1995, for a fuller discussion).

The decline in gangs from the mid-1990s to 2002 may also be explained in several ways. It may be partly due to the **strong economy** during this time and the **associated de-**

cline in high-poverty communities (see Chapter 12). It may be due to the **decline in youth violence during this time,** which possibly reduced the appeal of gangs as protective mechanisms. And it may be due to some of the **other factors** that contributed to the general decline in serious crime that began in the mid-1990s (see Chapter 3).

Summary

Delinquent peer groups and gangs are major causes of delinquency. It is true that delinquent individuals are more likely to associate with other delinquents and join gangs. It is also true that both delinquency and membership in delinquent groups are caused by many of the same third variables. At the same time, the data suggest that an individual's association with delinquent others, especially gang members, causes a substantial increase in the individual's delinquency. This increase was explained in terms of strain, social learning, control, and labeling theories.

Teaching Aids

Controversial Issue: What Is a Gang?

Bursik and Grasmick (1993) described a group allegedly involved in a gang rape in Philadelphia. The group was composed of older adolescents; it was recognized by others and recognized itself as a distinct group, with its own name and symbols; it was heavily involved in deviant and delinquent behavior; it had a reputation in the community as a deviant or troublesome group; it was cohesive and well organized; and it had a "turf" that it protected. According to Bursik and Grasmick:

> Women commonly reported that they had been harassed by members of the gang who hung around drinking beer on benches in the primary street in the area. Since these benches were situated in front of their clubhouse, the group made it clear that this was their "turf" to do with as they pleased. (1993:114)

Based on this description, most people would probably agree that this group was a gang. This group appears to satisfy the criteria of even the more restrictive definitions of gangs. This group, however, was a fraternity on the campus of a prestigious, upper-middle-class university in Philadelphia, and there is some evidence that others did not view this group as a gang. For example, the Gang Crimes Unit of the Philadelphia Police Department was not involved in the rape case against this group.

I do not mean to imply by this example that all fraternities are gangs. Clearly, they are not, although many colleges have at least one fraternity on campus that is heavily involved in deviant and illegal behaviors like drug and alcohol abuse, vandalism, and sexual violence. **Is it appropriate to classify these fraternities—or the fraternity in the example— as gangs?** Defend your position.

TEST YOUR KNOWLEDGE OF THIS CHAPTER

1. Having delinquent friends is typically the strongest correlate of delinquency, but this does not prove that delinquent friends cause delinquency. Why not?
2. Describe the evidence suggesting that delinquent friends cause delinquency.
3. Under what conditions are delinquent friends most likely to cause delinquency?

4. Describe the characteristics of a typical delinquent peer group (type and extent of delinquency, size and composition, age and sex, quality of relations between members).

5. How is an "offending group" different from an "accomplice network"?

6. Drawing on the major delinquency theories, explain why associating with delinquent peers increases the likelihood of delinquency.

7. Why are some juveniles more likely than others to associate with delinquent peers?

8. What impact do romantic partners have on delinquency. Is the impact stronger on males or females?

9. Describe the definition of gangs used in this book. How do gangs differ from delinquent peer groups?

10. How have researchers estimated the extent of gangs and gang membership? What major conclusions do they draw in this area?

11. Are gangs becoming more common? Describe trends in gangs and gang membership since the 1970s.

12. How much crime is gang related?

13. List any two "myths" about gangs and describe the evidence on these myths.

14. Drawing on the major delinquency theories, describe why gang membership increases the likelihood of delinquency.

15. Describe the characteristics of gang members (class, gender, age, race, ethnicity).

16. How would you respond to the statement that "gangs are highly organized"?

17. Females join gangs for many of the same reasons as males, although there are two reasons for joining that are more applicable to females than males. What are these reasons?

18. List any three of the major reasons that juveniles give for joining gangs.

19. Drawing on the leading delinquency theories, explain why some juveniles are more likely than others to join gangs.

20. Why are deprived, inner-city communities more likely to develop gangs?

21. How might we explain the major trends in gangs and gang membership since the 1970s?

THOUGHT AND DISCUSSION QUESTIONS

1. Did the delinquent peer groups in your high school or community fit the description provided in this chapter (size and composition, reasons for affecting delinquency, and so on)? Were there any gangs in your high school or home community? If so, to what extent did these gangs correspond to the descriptions presented in this chapter (characteristics of members, organization, extent of delinquency, reasons for joining, etc.)?

2. Why do you think street gangs lead to larger increases in delinquency than delinquent peer groups?

3. What policies or programs might we employ to address delinquent peer groups and gangs? (Note: Certain of these policies or programs might try to prevent delinquent

peer groups and gangs from forming; others might try to change the nature of these groups, making them more "prosocial" in focus; and others might try to increase the likelihood that individuals will avoid these groups or resist their negative influence. See Chapter 24 for a discussion of delinquency control and prevention programs focusing on delinquent peer groups and gangs.)

KEY TERMS

- Delinquent peer group
- Offending group
- Accomplice network
- Street gang

ENDNOTES

1. For overviews and recent studies on peers and delinquency, *see* Agnew, 1991b; Akers and Jensen, 2006; Barnes et al., 2006; Brame et al., 1999; Brezina et al., 2004; Chappel, 2005; Elliott and Menard, 1996; Elliott et al., 1985; Farrington and Welsh, 2007; Gifford-Smith et al., 2005; Gorman and White, 1995; Haynie, 2001, 2002; Haynie and Osgood, 2005; Haynie et al., 2006; Huizinga et al., 1998; Jang, 1999; Krohn et al., 1995; Matsueda and Anderson, 1998; Meier et al., 1984; Patterson and Dishion,1985; Patterson et al., 1992; Piquero et al., 2005; Pratt and Cullen, 2000; Reed and Rountree, 1997; Reiss, 1988; Rutter and Giller, 1983; Sampson and Laub, 1993a; Stewart and Simons, 2006; Thornberry, 1996; Thornberry et al., 1994, 2003a; Warr, 2002; Warr and Stafford, 1991; Wiesner and Capaldi, 2003; Wilson and Herrnstein, 1985; Zhang and Messner, 2000.

2. *Also see* Akers, 1998; Brezina et al., 2004; Matsueda and Anderson, 1998; Rutter et al., 1998; Thornberry, 1996; Thornberry et al., 1994, 2003a; Warr, 2002.

3. *See* Agnew, 1990a, 1991b, 1993; Elliott et al., 1985; Haynie, 2001, 2002; Piquero et al., 2005; Warr, 2002; Warr and Stafford, 1991; Weerman and Smeenk, 2005.

4. *Also see* Agnew, 1993; Elliott and Menard, 1996; Hagan, 1991.

5. *See* Agnew, 2006a; Akers and Jensen, 2006; Brezina et al., 2004; Briar and Piliavin, 1965; Gifford-Smith et al., 2005; Hughes and Short, 2005; Johnson et al., 1987; McCarthy et al., 2004; Rebellon, 2006; Short and Strodtbeck, 1965; Tittle et al., 1986; Warr, 2002.

6. *See* Chappel, 2005; Johnson, 1979; Patterson and Dishion, 1985; Thornberry, 1996; Thornberry et al., 1994; Wright et al., 1999b, 2001.

7. *See* Elliott et al., 1985; Jensen, 1972; Patterson and Dishion, 1985; Patterson et al., 1992; Sampson and Laub, 1993a; Warr, 2005.

8. *See* Elliott et al., 1985; Hawkins and Lishner, 1987; Johnson, 1979; Thornberry, 1987, 1996.

9. There have been several excellent ethnographies or case studies of specific gangs in recent years. Curry and Decker (2003) and Shelden et al. (2001) list and provide brief summaries of these studies. For recent overviews of the research on street gangs, *see* Curry and Decker, 2003; Decker and Van Winkle, 1996; Esbensen et al., 2004; Howell, 1995, 1998a, 2003a; Howell et al., 2002; Huff, 2002; Klein, 1995, 1998; Klein and Maxson, 2006; Knox, 2000; Miller et al., 2001; Moore and Hagedorn, 2001; National Youth Gang Center, 2003; Office of Juvenile Justice and Delinquency Prevention, 1999a; Shelden et al., 2001; Short, 1997; Spergel, 1995; Thornberry et al., 2003a,b.

10. *See* Freng and Winfree, 2004; Howell, 1998a; Klein, 1995; Klein and Maxson, 2006; Spergel, 1995.

11. For discussions of how to define gangs, *see* Bursik and Grasmick, 1993; Esbensen et al., 2001; Esbensen et al., 2004; Howell, 2003a:75–81; Klein and Maxson, 2006.

12. *See* Esbensen and Deschenes, 1998; Esbensen and Huizinga, 1993; Esbensen et al., 1993, 2001; Hill et al., 1999; Howell, 1995, 1997b; Klein and Maxson, 2006; Office of Juvenile Justice and Delinquency Prevention, 1999a; Spergel, 1995:31–32; Thornberry and Burch, 1997; Thornberry et al., 2003b.

ENDNOTES (continued)

13. *See* Bjerregaard and Lizotte, 1995; Curry and Decker, 2003; Howell, 1995, 1998a, 1999; Huff, 2002, 2004; Klein and Maxson, 2006; Lizotte et al., 1994.

14. *See* Curry and Decker, 2003; Howell, 1995, 1998a, 2003a; Howell and Gleason, 1999; Huff, 2002; Klein, 1995; Klein and Maxson, 2006; Klein et al., 1995; Maxson, 1995; Spergel, 1995.

15. *See* Bjerregaard and Smith, 1993; Curry and Decker, 2003; Esbensen and Huizinga, 1993; Esbensen et al., 2001; Fagan, 1990; Howell, 1995, 1997b, 2004; Huff, 1998, 2002, 2004; Huizinga et al., 2003; Klein and Maxson, 2006; Thornberry, 1998; Thornberry et al., 1993; Thornberry et al., 2003a, 2003b.

16. *See* Battin et al., 1998; Gatti et al., 2005; Gordon et al., 2004; Howell, 1998a; Huizinga, 1996; Huizinga et al., 2003; Klein and Maxson, 2006; Thornberry, 1998; Thornberry et al., 2003a, 2003b; Tita and Ridgeway, 2007.

17. *See* Esbensen et al., 1993; Gatti et al., 2005; Gordon et al., 2004; Huff, 1998; Thornberry, 1998; Thornberry et al., 1993, 2003a, 2003b.

18. *See* Brownfield and Sorenson, 2001; Decker and Van Winkle, 1996; Howell, 1998a; Klein and Maxson, 2006; Shelden et al., 2001; Short and Strodtbeck, 1965; Spergel, 1995.

19. *See* Curry and Decker, 2003; Klein and Maxson, 2006; Jody Miller, 2001; Thornberry et al., 2003b.

20. *See* Bjerregaard and Smith, 1993; Chesney-Lind et al., 1996; Curry and Decker, 2003; Esbensen and Deschenes, 1998; Esbensen and Osgood, 1997; Esbensen et al., 1993, 1999, 2001; Hill et al., 1999; Klein and Maxson, 2006; Jody Miller, 2001; Moore and Hagedorn, 2001; Shelden et al., 2001; Spergel, 1995; Thornberry et al., 2003a,b.

21. *See* Moore and Cook, 1999; also see Curry and Decker, 2003; Hill et al., 1999; Howell, 1997b; Klein and Maxson, 2006; Spergel, 1995; Thornberry et al., 2003b.

22. For a fuller discussion of female gang involvement, *see* Bowker and Klein, 1983; Campbell, 1990; Chesney-Lind and Shelden, 2004; Chesney-Lind et al., 1996; Curry, 1998; Curry and Decker, 2003; Esbensen and Deschenes, 1998; Esbensen et al., 1999; Fishman, 1995; Klein, 1995; Maxson and Whitlock, 2002; Miller and Brunson, 2004; Jody Miller, 2001; Moore and Hagedorn, 1996, 2001; Peterson et al., 2001; Shelden et al., 2001.

23. For examples and discussions of the research in this area, *see* Bjerregaard and Smith, 1993; Bowker and Klein, 1983; Brownfield et al., 1997; Curry and Decker, 2003; Esbensen and Deschenes, 1998; Esbensen et al., 1993, 2001; Esbensen et al., 2004; Fagan, 1990; Hill et al., 1999; Hill et al., 2004; Howell, 1998a, 2003a:89–91, 2004; Klein, 1995, 1998; Klein and Maxson, 2006; Klein et al., 1995; Miller et al., 2001; Shelden et al., 2001; Short, 1997; Spergel, 1995; Thornberry, 1998; Thornberry et al., 2003b; Vigil and Yun, 1996; Yoder et al., 2003.

24. For fuller discussions of these arguments, *see* Bursik and Grasmick, 1993; Fagan, 1996; Hagedorn, 1988; Jackson, 1991; Klein, 1995; Klein et al., 1995; Jody Miller, 2001; Shelden et al., 2001; Spergel, 1995.

CHAPTER 17

Other Social Influences

What Effects Do Religion, Work, the Mass Media, Drugs, and Guns Have on Delinquency?

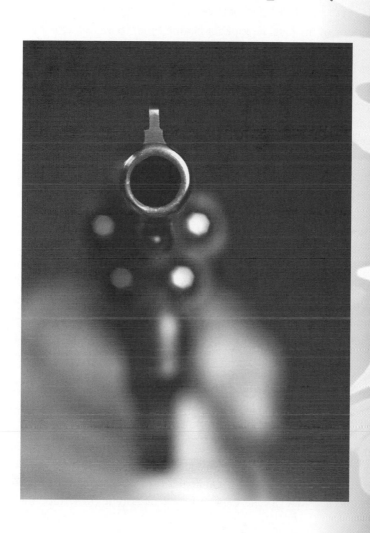

The family, school, and peer group constitute the major social environments for most adolescents. Adolescents spend most of their time in these environments and usually develop close relationships with the people in them. So it is not surprising that family members, peers, and sometimes school officials affect adolescents so strongly. But these are not the only influences on adolescents. Adolescents may also be influenced by their religion, their work experiences, the mass media, and their exposure to drugs and guns. This chapter examines these other influences. I address several questions that have been receiving a great deal of attention in the media lately: Does religion reduce delinquency? Does work prevent delinquency among juveniles attending school? Does mass media violence contribute to violent behavior? Do drugs increase delinquency? And does the possession of guns contribute to delinquency?

Does Religion Reduce Delinquency?

A letter to the editor of my local newspaper claimed that there was little mystery regarding the causes of crime and delinquency: "The answer is so simple. The answer is this: A lack of religion in these persons' lives has caused them to fail in our society." The letter writer went on to speculate that few delinquents attend church on a regular basis. Like this letter writer, many people believe that a lack of religion is a major cause of delinquency. In fact, many politicians and other people have claimed that the lack of religion is one of the major causes of crime and violence in our society—like the shooting deaths of 13 people at Columbine High School and other well-publicized incidents of school violence. Many politicians are now actively searching for ways to increase the role of religion in people's lives—ways like posting the Ten Commandments in public places such as courthouses and schools.

There are good reasons for believing that **religion has an effect on delinquency.**[1] Most notably, **religion may increase control.** Religion may increase direct control, since religious juveniles may come under the watchful eye of those in their religious community. And religion may instill a fear of supernatural sanction in juveniles—punishment by God. Religion may also increase one's stake in conformity; religious juveniles may develop good reputations and strong emotional bonds to others in their religious community. Further, religion may increase internal control, since religious juveniles may be more likely to learn beliefs that condemn delinquency and to be taught self-control. It is the effect of religion on internal control that is most commonly mentioned in discussions on the topic.

In terms of **social learning theory,** religion may increase the likelihood that juveniles are exposed to conventional models, are taught conventional beliefs, are punished for deviance, and are reinforced for conformity. Further, it has been suggested that religious participation **may reduce strain,** since religious communities may provide the juvenile with social support, and religious beliefs may divert attention from current problems to the rewards of the afterlife. Finally, religious participation may **reduce the likelihood of being labeled** a delinquent. What do the data indicate; does religion reduce the likelihood of delinquency?

The Evidence

There have been a moderate number of studies in this area. Religion is most commonly measured by asking respondents how frequently they attend religious services. Many studies also ask respondents what their religion or religious denomination is, how important religion is in their daily lives, and whether they hold certain religious beliefs (e.g., "Is there life after death?" "Will evil people suffer in hell?"). Most studies are cross-sectional, and many fail to control for potentially relevant third variables. Nevertheless, certain conclusions can be drawn from the data.

Most data indicate that **religious juveniles are somewhat less delinquent than nonreligious juveniles, especially when it comes to "victimless crimes" like alcohol and marijuana use.** Recent data, however, suggest that a good part of the association between religion and delinquency is caused by third variables, including variables like low self-control, parental attachment, parental supervision, and school attachment. But even after one takes account of these third variables, the data suggest that religion has a modest effect on delinquency, especially on victimless crimes like alcohol and marijuana use. **This effect is partly indirect.** For example, data suggest that religion affects delinquency partly through its effect on the peers with whom the juvenile associates. Religious individuals are less likely to associate with deviant peers.[2]

Why is it that religion affects victimless crimes more than serious crimes? The most commonly offered explanation is that serious crimes are condemned by both religious and nonreligious individuals and groups. Therefore, both religious and nonreligious juveniles are equally likely to refrain from such crimes. Victimless crimes, however, are condemned more strongly by religious groups, so we find that religious individuals are less likely to engage in such crimes.

I have been talking about religion in general up to this point. You might be wondering whether different religions or religious denominations have different effects on delinquency. The data in this area are mixed, although studies tend to indicate that **the members of more fundamentalist or conservative religious groups commit fewer victimless crimes.** Such groups include Baptists and Mormons (as opposed to more liberal religious groups like Unitarians and Presbyterians).

Researchers continue to study the effect of religion on delinquency. One major line of research argues that religion is more likely to affect delinquency in some circumstances than others. Most notably, some researchers argue that religion is more likely to reduce delinquency when adolescents are surrounded by other religious individuals. For example, the adolescent has religious parents, attends a school with a high percentage of religious students, and lives in a community where a high percentage of the population is religiously active. If religious individuals are surrounded by other religious people, they are more likely to form close bonds to these people and take account of religious considerations in their daily life. But if they are surrounded by people who are indifferent to religion, they are more likely to have conflicts with these others and to ignore or put aside religious considerations. Studies in this area have produced mixed results, but most find support for the argument that **religion is more likely to reduce delinquency when adolescents are surrounded by religious others.**[3]

In sum, religion appears to have a modest effect on delinquency, especially victimless crimes. The effect of religion is overshadowed by that of other groups, such as the family, peer group, and school.

Does Work Reduce Delinquency Among Juveniles Attending School?

The percentage of juveniles who work while attending school has increased dramatically since World War II. It is estimated that 90 percent of all students now hold jobs at some point, and 80 percent of all students work during the school year at some point. One study of high school students found that during the academic year, employed juniors worked an average of 18.6 hours per week and employed seniors worked an average of 23.5 hours per week. The world of work now occupies a central place in the lives of many adolescents—alongside the family, school, and peer group. It is therefore important to ask whether work has an effect on delinquency among juveniles attending school.[4]

There are **good reasons for expecting work to reduce delinquency,** most of them derived from the leading delinquency theories. Work **may reduce monetary strain,** since it provides adolescents with money for cars, clothing, socializing, and other things. (Data indicate that juveniles spend most of their wages on personal items and activities rather than giving their money to parents for family expenses or saving it for college.) Work **may increase control,** since adolescents in work settings are supervised by adults and their work provides them with a stake in conformity. Work may also increase the adolescent's acceptance of conventional moral values by increasing interaction with and attachment to adults who transmit such values. Work **may reduce the social learning of crime,** since adolescents who work have less time to interact with delinquent peers. Finally, limited data suggest that employment **often reduces crime among adults.**

It is therefore not surprising that most people believe work is beneficial for juveniles and reduces the likelihood of delinquency. One often hears, for example, that "work builds character and responsibility" (Williams et al., 1996). Several prominent national commissions during the 1970s and 1980s also argued that work benefits juveniles, and they recommended that society provide adolescents with more work experience (see Paternoster et al., 2006). Many delinquency-control programs followed this recommendation and provided juveniles with work. What do the data show about the effect of work on delinquency?

The Evidence

A number of studies from the mid-1980s to the early 2000s investigated the effect of work on delinquency.[5] These studies challenged the view just described and suggested that adolescents who worked while attending school were somewhat **more** likely to engage in delinquency. This was especially true of adolescents who worked more than 20 hours per week. As a result of such findings, a prominent research group recommended in 1998 that the federal government restrict the number of hours that high school students work during the school year. And efforts have been made to implement this recommendation (see Paternoster et al., 2006).

Researchers explained the higher delinquency among working adolescents in several ways. It was said that while work may reduce economic strain, it contributes to other types of strain. The working conditions associated with most adolescent jobs are rather poor, and the long hours worked by many adolescents—in combination with school, family, and social demands—can be stressful. In addition, it was said that the money from work makes it easier for adolescents to purchase drugs and alcohol and to engage in certain other illegal activities. (Data suggest that adolescents with more spending money are somewhat more likely to be delinquent.)[6] Further, it was said that work reduces certain types of control, since working adolescents spend less time with parents and have less time to devote to schoolwork. Finally, it was claimed that work does not reduce association with delinquent peers as much as originally thought, since adolescents often interact with delinquent peers at work (see Wright and Cullen, 2000).

The **most recent research, however, has challenged the view that work contributes to delinquency** (see especially Apel et al., 2007; Paternoster et al., 2003). According to this research, the studies mentioned earlier failed to properly take account of third variables that might influence the relationship between work and delinquency (see Chapter 5 for a discussion of "third variables"). In particular, certain of the factors that cause delinquency also increase the likelihood that adolescents will work long hours while in school. It is for this reason that work and delinquency are associated. Researchers, therefore, must adequately take account of or "control" for the factors that influence both work and delinquency. When this is done, evidence suggests that **work has little or no effect on delinquency for most adolescents.** Perhaps certain of the positive and negative effects of work listed earlier cancel one another out. **Work,** however, **leads to a reduction in delinquency among those with a strong predisposition for delinquency.** These are adolescents who have traits conducive to delinquency, such as low self-control; are experiencing problems at home and at school; and associate with delinquent peers. Work appears to be of some advantage to these adolescents, perhaps offering them somewhat more supervision and contact with conventional adults than they would otherwise have in their lives.

The preceding review highlights a key point made in Chapter 5. When evaluating research, it is important to keep the conditions for making causal statements in mind. At the same time, it is important to note that more research is needed in this area. As Chapter 5 also notes, it can be dangerous to form conclusions based on one or a few studies.

Does Mass Media Violence Cause Violence Among Juveniles?

Most research on media violence has focused on television and movies, although some research has examined violent video games, and a few studies have examined music with violent themes. I focus on TV and movie violence because of the massive presence of TV in our society and the abundant research in the area—although I briefly discuss violent video games and "violent music" as well.

TV and Movie Violence

About 98 percent of all households in the United States have TVs, and these TVs get watched a lot. They are on for an average of 28 hours a week in homes with children between 2 and 11, and 23 hours a week in homes with teenagers. Juveniles spend more time watching TV than they do in any other activity, except sleeping and attending school. Further, they see much violence on TV. If we focus on the three major television networks, there are about 5 to 6 acts of violence per hour on prime-time TV and about 20 to 25 acts per hour on Saturday morning children's programs. Cable TV contains more violence than the three major networks, and the availability of VCRs and DVD players has provided juveniles with the opportunity to watch unedited versions of violent movies. It is estimated that by the time children have finished elementary school, they have seen over 8,000 murders and 100,000 other acts of violence on TV. They have seen over 200,000 acts of violence by the time they leave high school.

Does this extensive exposure to TV and movie violence increase the likelihood that juveniles will engage in violent behavior? Most people believe that TV and movie violence is a major cause of violent behavior, and politicians often make statements to this effect. Further, the federal government has been actively involved in efforts to limit the amount and severity of TV violence or restrict access to violent programs. As a consequence of such efforts, there is now a ratings system that alerts viewers to the violence content of TV shows. Also, new TVs now contain V-chips, which allow parents to block violent shows.

What do the data show about the effect of TV and movie violence on juvenile violence?[7] There have been literally hundreds of studies in this area. We know that violent juveniles are more likely to watch violent TV shows. That does not, of course, mean that TV and movie violence causes juvenile violence. It might be that juvenile violence and watching violent TV shows are both caused by the same third variables, such as the individual traits or family variables mentioned in earlier chapters. It might also be that engaging in violence causes one to watch violent TV shows. Violent juveniles may simply prefer violent TV shows. There is, in fact, some evidence for these arguments. At the same time, most studies—not all—suggest that TV and movie violence does have a causal effect on violent behavior.

Hundreds of experiments have been conducted in this area. In most such experiments, one group of juveniles is exposed to media violence while a similar group of juveniles is not (these groups are similar on relevant third variables like individual traits and family variables). The experimenter then determines whether the juveniles exposed to the media violence engage in more subsequent aggression than the unexposed group (so causal order is not a problem). The experimenter, for example, determines whether the juveniles exposed to media violence are more likely to hit a doll in a playroom, press a button that allegedly harms another person, or play aggressively on the playground (e.g., hit, kick, and push others). Most experiments suggest that exposure to media violence does increase aggressive behavior—although the effect of media violence is often modest in studies that employ more realistic measures of aggression. Some individuals, however, claim that the experiments set up an artificial situation in which it is easy for juveniles to engage in aggression. The juveniles are often provided with a readily available opportunity to engage in aggression, and their aggression is rarely punished or condemned. As such, the results of these experiments may not apply to the real world.

In response to this criticism, researchers have conducted a number of **studies in the real world** that attempt to take account of relevant third variables and issues of causal order (see Chapter 5). One study, for example, determined whether childhood exposure to TV violence was related to violent behavior in adolescence and adulthood. This study controlled for several relevant third variables, such as social class, intelligence, and parenting practices. Another study examined the levels of juvenile violence in an isolated Canadian community before and after the introduction of TV. Still another study examined whether levels of violence increased after media coverage of violent events, like championship heavyweight prize fights. These studies are not perfect. Researchers often do not control for all potentially relevant third variables; sometimes it is impossible to do so (an excellent illustration of a flawed study in this area is provided by Jensen, 1998). Nevertheless, most—not all—studies in this area suggest that TV violence affects violent behavior.

Overall, the most reasonable conclusion to draw from the data is that **TV and movie violence has a modest effect on juvenile violence.** It does not appear to be the major cause of violence that some claim, but it is not an unimportant cause either. TV and movie violence is most likely to cause violent behavior when it is committed by attractive characters, when it is rewarded and not punished, when it is presented as justified, when the negative consequences of the violence are not shown, and when it is realistic. Unfortunately, much of the violence on TV is like this. For example, as the National Television Violence Study (1997:137) states: "Violence is typically sanitized on television. It is rarely punished in the immediate context in which it occurs and it rarely results in observable harm to the victims. In fact, violence is often funny on television." TV violence is also most likely to lead to violent behavior when the juvenile identifies with the aggressor and the juvenile is otherwise predisposed to engage in violence.

The effect of TV violence is **usually explained in terms of the leading delinquency theories.** Drawing on **social learning theory,** TV violence exposes juveniles to violent models. These models are often attractive characters, and their violence is frequently rewarded. As a consequence, juveniles may come to feel that violence is an appropriate response in certain situations. Drawing on **control theory,** TV violence may desensitize watchers to violence. That is, heavy exposure to TV violence may make violence seem less bad and reduce concern for the victims of violence. In effect, TV violence may reduce our level of internal control. And drawing on **strain theory,** TV violence may cause viewers to see the world as a more dangerous, violent place. They become more fearful and suspicious of others as a result, potentially increasing the likelihood of a violent response. Also, TV violence often arouses or excites individuals. And aroused individuals may be more likely to respond to certain strainful situations, like provocations by others, in an aggressive manner.

Violent Video Games

There has been less research on the effect of violent video games on violent behavior, although researchers are now devoting more attention to this topic. About 7 in 10 families with children have a video game system.[8] Data suggest that most adolescents play video games each week, with a substantial percentage playing three or more hours each week. Further, most adolescents prefer violent over nonviolent video games. Video game violence can be quite gruesome. For example, in *Grand Theft Auto,* "the player may be rewarded for having sex with a prostitute and kicking her to death to avoid payment. In *Mortal Combat,* a player earns extra points by ripping out the opponent's heart or decapitating him" (Weber et al., 2006:348). These examples highlight the fact that video game players are often **active participants** in the screen violence. They are encouraged to assume the identity of violent characters, they pull the trigger or press the button that results in violence, and they are often directly rewarded for their violence with points and additional playing time (as well as the approval of their friends if they are playing with others). This active involvement has led some to argue that video game violence may have a stronger effect on violent behavior than TV and movie violence (where individuals **passively observe** the screen violence).

A few **surveys** have examined the association between playing video games and aggression (or aggressive thoughts and feelings). Most, but not all, find that playing video games (or violent video games) is associated with aggression. This association, however, does not mean that violent video games cause aggression. The association may be due to third variables that cause both video game play and aggression. In this area, one study that took into account several third variables found that the association between violent video games and aggression disappeared. The association may also be due to the fact that aggression causes one to play violent video games. In particular, it is not unreasonable to suppose that aggressive people will be attracted to violent video games.

A number of **experiments** have examined the effect of violent video games on aggression. Typically, a researcher will have one group of juveniles play a violent video game and have another **similar group** of juveniles play a nonviolent video game (e.g., a sports game with a lot of action, but little violence). Then the experimenter will measure the aggressive behavior of the juveniles in each group **after they have finished playing the video games.** Most such studies (although not all) find that the juveniles who play the violent video games are more aggressive. These studies, however, measure only the short-term effect of violent video games. Further, the effect of violent video games on aggression is often small in such studies, especially when more realistic measures of aggression are employed.

More research is clearly needed in this area, particularly research that looks at the **long-term effects** of violent video games on aggression and research conducted in the real world. For example, surveys might examine whether individuals who play a lot of violent video games are more likely to engage in **subsequent** aggression, even after taking account of a range of **third variables** that might cause both violent video game playing and aggression. For now, the best conclusion seems to be that there is some evidence suggesting that **playing violent video games leads to a modest, short-term increase in aggression.**

Music with Violent Themes

A few studies have explored whether listening to music with violent themes, particularly heavy metal music and certain types of rap music, increases the likelihood of aggression (or aggressive thoughts and feelings). The results of these studies are mixed, although some suggest that there is an **association** between listening to "violent music" and aggression, and that listening to violent music increases aggressive **thoughts and feelings** (see Anderson et al., 2003a, 2003b; Kirsh, 2006; Singer et al., 1993). More research is needed in this area, however, before any conclusions can be drawn about the effect of violent music on aggression.

Summary

There is some reason to believe that mass media violence, particularly TV and movie violence and violent video games, may lead to a small to modest increase in violent behavior. Mass media violence, however, is **not** the major cause of violent behavior that many people claim.

Do Drugs Increase the Likelihood of Delinquency?

It is commonly argued that drug use and sales are a major cause of delinquency. And part of the motivation behind the current "war on drugs" is the belief that reducing drug use and sales will have a major impact on other types of delinquency. Drug use and sales are said to contribute to delinquency for at least four reasons.[9]

Reasons That Drugs May Affect Delinquency

The first reason has to do with the **pharmacological effect of certain drugs.** Drugs like alcohol, cocaine, amphetamines, and PCP are said to **weaken self-control and/or increase irritability**—if only temporarily. Also, withdrawal from drugs like heroin and crack may increase irritability and frustration. As a consequence of these effects, individuals under the influence of certain drugs may be (1) less aware of and concerned about the costs of crime, (2) more likely to become upset with others and respond to provocations in an aggressive manner, and (3) more likely to act in ways that upset or provoke others. Researchers, however, emphasize that not all drugs have this effect. Further, the impact of drugs is influenced by the individual and the social situation. For example, the effect of alcohol on aggression is strongest among individuals already predisposed to aggression.

Second, **juveniles may engage in crime in order to obtain money to purchase drugs,** especially individuals addicted to expensive drugs like heroin and cocaine. That is, drug use may lead to a particular type of strain—a desperate need for money. Individuals may then engage in a wide range of income-generating crimes, like larceny, burglary, robbery, prostitution, and drug sales. Some of these crimes, such as robbery, may result in violence. In one study of inner-city youth, about a quarter of the respondents who committed burglary said they did so in order to get money for drugs. About 36 percent of the youth who sold drugs and 19 percent who engaged in robbery said they committed these crimes to get money for drugs (Altschuler and Brounstein, 1991).

Third, **the drug trade contributes to crime.** Individuals who buy and sell drugs often carry large amounts of money and drugs, and they are generally reluctant to involve the police when disputes arise. As a consequence, crime is often the result. Drug sellers may employ violence against one another as they compete for turf or customers. Both drug sellers and customers are often attractive targets for robbers. And drug sellers and their customers often employ violence against one another when they get into disputes. These problems were especially severe during the early years of the crack trade, when many young, inexperienced dealers were competing against one another.

Fourth, some researchers argue that **drug use, especially chronic use, may increase the juvenile's predisposition to engage in delinquency by reducing the juvenile's bonds to family and school, lowering academic performance, and increasing the likelihood of association with delinquent peers.** Juveniles are frequently brought into contact with such peers when they buy and use drugs.[10]

It is also argued that drug use not only increases the likelihood that individuals will commit crimes but also increases the likelihood that they will be victims of crime. Among other things, drug users may be more likely to be victimized because they are less able to offer effective resistance and because their lifestyles sometimes place them in close contact with offenders. The former argument has been made with respect to rohypnol, or "roofies," the so-called date rape drug.[11]

The arguments set out in the preceding paragraphs play a central role in a **debate over whether drugs should be legalized.** Individuals who want to legalize drugs claim that drugs are expensive largely because they are illegal. Legalization will lower their cost and thereby reduce much income-generating crime. Further, legalization will also reduce crime associated with the illicit drug trade. Individuals opposed to legalization claim that drug use will increase if drugs are legalized. They point to several negative consequences of this increase, including increased crime arising from the pharmacological effects of drug use and the effects of drug use on such things as family bonds and school performance.[12]

The Evidence

What does the evidence suggest? Do drugs contribute to delinquency? **Individuals who commit crimes are frequently under the influence of drugs (including alcohol).** For example, a 2002 study of arrested male juveniles in five cities around the country found that 60 percent tested positive for drugs other than alcohol. Marijuana was by far the most common drug, followed by cocaine and methamphetamine.[13] Victimization data suggest that nearly 4 in 10 violent crimes involve the use of alcohol (Greenfeld, 1998).

Further, there is a **strong association between drugs and delinquency.** Juveniles who use drugs and especially those who sell drugs are much more likely to engage in crime. Some categories of drug users, like heroin addicts and heavy users of crack, engage in enormous amounts of crime. This does not, of course, mean that all drug users are delinquents or that all delinquents are drug users. For example, a self-report study found that a little more than half of the serious delinquents (those who admitted to three or more Part I crimes in the past three years) were also serious drug and/or alcohol users. About a third of the serious drug/alcohol users were serious delinquents.[14]

An association between drugs and delinquency, however, does not mean that drugs cause delinquency. Some researchers argue that drugs and delinquency are associated because both are caused by the same third variables. The data do indicate that drug use/sales and delinquency share many of the same causes, such as individual traits, family problems, school problems, and association with delinquent peers.[15] Also, some researchers argue that drugs and delinquency are associated because delinquency causes drug use and/or sales. Engaging in delinquency increases the likelihood that a person will be exposed to others who possess and use drugs, who reinforce drug use, and who hold values conducive to drug use. Data here indicate that delinquency typically precedes drug use. Also, some studies have found that prior delinquency increases the likelihood of subsequent drug use.[16]

At the same time, the evidence suggests that **drug use, especially serious drug use, does contribute to delinquency.** For example, although drug addicts typically engaged in crime before they became addicts, their level of crime increases during periods of high drug use and decreases during periods of low drug use. Also, longitudinal research suggests that drug use contributes to subsequent delinquency—even after selected third variables are controlled.[17] **The effect of drug use on delinquency, however, is not as large as many imagine or as the associational data suggest.** Much of the association between drugs and delinquency arises because both are caused by the same third variables and because delinquency has an effect on drug use.

Do Guns Increase the Likelihood of Delinquency?

Most criminologists agree that many juveniles own and carry guns and that there is reason to believe that guns contribute to serious violence. There is, however, a major debate over the extent to which guns contribute to crime/delinquency versus the extent to which they prevent crime and delinquency. Some researchers claim that guns prevent more crime and delinquency than they perpetuate. Let us examine the evidence in these areas.[18]

How Common Is Gun Ownership and Possession Among Juveniles?

There are between 200 and 250 million guns in the United States; a third of these are handguns. (Handguns are much more likely to be used in crimes than long guns like rifles and shotguns. For example, about 80 percent of all gun-related homicides are committed with handguns.) About 40 percent of all households in the United States have guns, with these gun-owning households each having an average of 4.5 guns. There is little doubt, then, that guns are common in the United States.

How common is it for juveniles to own or possess guns? It is illegal for juveniles to purchase guns, and, in most states, it is illegal for juveniles to possess handguns. Several studies have attempted to estimate the extent of gun ownership and possession among juveniles. These studies have focused on institutionalized delinquents, arrested delinquents, gang members, juveniles in high-crime inner-city areas, juveniles in urban areas, and juveniles throughout the country. The large majority of institutionalized delinquents—more than 90 percent in some studies—report having owned guns at some point in their lives (Harcourt, 2003:4). A 1995 survey of arrested male delinquents in seven cities found that 20 percent said they carried a gun all or most of the time—a percentage higher than that for arrested adults. For arrested gang members, the percentage was 31 percent. Five out of 10 of the arrested juveniles said they had been shot at; the figure for gang members was 8 out of 10 (Decker et al., 1997; Sickmund et al., 1997). Other studies have found that anywhere from a quarter to more than half of all gang members own guns, and even more have ready access to guns. A gang, for example, often has a stash of guns that members can use. A 1991 study of males in 10 inner-city high schools throughout the United States found that 22 percent owned guns, and 12 percent carried a gun all or most of the time (Sheley and Wright, 1995). A 1996 survey that interviewed a nationally representative sample of youth ages 12–16 found that about 10 percent carried a handgun in the last year.[19] And a 1995 nationally representative survey found that 10 percent of 15- to 17-year-olds carried a gun at least once in the last month (Cook and Ludwig, 2004). These percentages clearly indicate that gun ownership and possession is fairly common among certain categories of juveniles—particularly those involved in serious delinquency.

Several studies have asked juveniles why they own or carry guns. The most common reason given is "for protection." The juveniles most likely to own guns are heavily involved in crime, belong to gangs or delinquent peer groups, and live in dangerous, inner-city communities. Most have witnessed violent crimes and have been the victims of violence themselves. Their criminal activity puts them in situations where violence is a very real possibility, and they are surrounded by others who own and carry guns. It is no surprise, then, that they feel they need a gun for protection. Contrary to certain media accounts, juveniles are less likely to say that they own or carry a gun because it is a status symbol or because it makes you popular with peers—although some juveniles do say this. Some juveniles also say that they own guns **for sport or recreational purposes,** such as hunting and target shooting. Such juveniles differ from those who say that they own guns for protection. Among other things, they are much less likely to be involved in crime.

The **large majority of juveniles with guns get them illegally,** primarily from family members, friends, and street sources. In many communities, it is easy to purchase high-quality guns at prices well below retail. Also, the guns currently possessed by juveniles are more lethal than those owned in the past. Juveniles tend to own and carry high-quality, large-caliber, automatic or semiautomatic guns.

A few studies have examined the **factors associated with gun ownership.** Juveniles are more likely to own guns if they are male, their parents own guns, their peers own guns, they belong to gangs, they have been threatened or shot at with a gun, they **sell** drugs, or they engage in most other types of delinquency (although some data suggest that **using** drugs is not that strongly associated with owning or carrying a gun). The dramatic increase in gun-related juvenile homicide from the mid-1980s to the mid-1990s has been tied to the increased involvement of juveniles in drug selling and gangs during these years (see Chapter 3).

Do Guns Contribute to Delinquency?

It is commonly pointed out that **the United States has the highest rates of gun ownership and lethal violence in the industrialized world.** About 25 to 30 percent of United States households contain handguns. In most other industrialized nations, the rate of handgun ownership is 7 percent or lower (Messner and Rosenfeld, 2001). Further, the United States homicide rate is several times that of other industrialized countries. Differences in homicide rates are especially pronounced for gun-related homicides (about 70 percent of all homicides in the United States and 80 percent of all juvenile homicides are committed with guns). For example, during the early to mid-1990s, the gun-related homicide rate for children (ages 5–14) in the United States was about **17** times higher than the average rate in 15 other industrialized nations (the nongun homicide rate was only about **twice** as high in the United States) (Office of Juvenile Justice and Delinquency Prevention, 2000a).

In short, the United States has a lot of guns and a lot of gun-related crime. Most studies suggest that there is a **positive association between the rate of gun ownership and the rate of gun-related crime** in a country or community. That is, there is more gun-related crime in countries and communities where guns are more prevalent. It is important to note, however, that this association is far from perfect. There are certain communities and countries with high rates of gun ownership but low rates of gun-related crime (e.g., Switzerland). The rate of gun-related crime is likely dependent on both the availability of guns and the willingness of people to use them. Also, one recent study suggests that it is the availability of **illegal** guns that contributes to violent crime, not the availability of **legal** guns—although more research is needed on this topic (Stolzenberg and D'Alessio, 2000).

Studies also suggest that **juveniles who own or carry guns are much more likely to engage in most forms of delinquency.** This is most true of juveniles who own guns for protection. It is less true of juveniles who own guns for sport. For example, a study of juveniles in Rochester, New York, found that those who owned guns for protection were **23** times more likely to commit gun crimes than those who did not own guns. Those who owned guns for sport, however, were about 3 times more likely to commit gun crimes than the nongun owners.[20]

So most data suggest that **there is an association between guns and crime/ delinquency.** But as you know, this association does not prove that guns increase the likelihood of delinquency. The association may be explained in other ways. It may be that gun possession and delinquency are both caused by the same third variables, such as association with delinquent peers. There is some evidence for this position. It may also be that crime/delinquency causes gun ownership. People who live in high-crime countries or communities may purchase guns to protect themselves. Juveniles who engage in delinquency may likewise purchase guns for protection, since their delinquency is often associated with a risky lifestyle. There is also some evidence for this position.

At the same time, there is some data suggesting that **guns contribute to at least certain types of delinquency.** One study, for example, found that the increased availability of guns led to increases in the rate of homicide (Duggan, 2001). And a study of juveniles in Rochester, New York, found that illegal gun carriers committed about five times more serious, violent crime during those times they carried guns than during those times that they did not (see Lizotte et al., 2002).

Criminologists argue that **guns contribute to delinquency, especially serious violence, in several ways.** The most prominent argument is that guns increase the likelihood that certain crimes, such as assault and robbery, will result in serious injury or death. For example, it has been argued that the increased availability of guns played a key role in the dramatic increase in juvenile homicides from the late 1980s to the mid-1990s. As guns became more widespread throughout the community, disputes that used to be settled with fists or knives were more likely to be settled with guns. And serious injury and death were more likely to result. Data indicate that gun attacks are more likely to be fatal than attacks with knives, fists, or other weapons. One study, for example, found that attacks with guns were five times more likely to be fatal than attacks with knives. One might argue that gun attacks are more fatal because people who attack with a gun are more intent on killing their victims. Limited data, however, suggest that differences in the intent to kill do not fully explain the higher fatality rate of guns. Data, for example, suggest that most offenders who fire guns do not intend to kill their victims.[21] Guns, then, appear to increase the likelihood that crimes like assault and robbery will result in serious injury or death. (At the same time, it should be noted that assaults and robberies with guns have a **lower** likelihood of resulting in **less serious** injuries, partly because victims are less likely to resist.)

It has also been argued that the presence of guns increases the likelihood that certain predisposed adolescents will engage in crimes like assault and robbery. A gun may provide adolescents with the courage or the means to commit a crime they might otherwise avoid. Further, the presence of a gun may trigger an aggressive response in certain individuals— with the gun functioning as an "aggressive cue." Finally, as guns become more common, many adolescents may arm themselves for protection and become more likely to respond to conflicts with gun use. The evidence regarding these latter arguments, however, is less certain.[22]

On the basis of these data and arguments, one might conclude that there would be less delinquency, or at least less delinquency resulting in serious injury and death, if guns were not so widespread. The situation, however, is not so simple.

Do Guns Prevent More Crime than They Contribute To?

Some individuals acknowledge that guns may contribute to crime, but they claim that guns prevent more crime than they cause (you may have heard the expression that "a well-armed society is a polite society"). Many individuals buy guns for protection, and they may well use their guns to stop crimes from occurring or to subdue criminals. Likewise, many criminals may avoid victimizing people for fear they are armed. Many criminals, in fact, state that they have been scared off by armed victims or that they have avoided victimizing individuals because they thought these individuals were armed (Sheley and Wright, 1995). (It is unclear, however, whether these criminals then selected victims they thought were unarmed, thus displacing rather than preventing crime.)

Several studies have tried to determine whether guns prevent more crime than they cause. Data from the National Crime Victimization Survey indicate that guns are only used for self-defense purposes about 80,000 times a year. The same survey, however, indicates that guns are used to commit over 400,000 crimes each year. These data, then, suggest that guns contribute to more crime than they prevent. By contrast, other surveys indicate that guns are more likely to be used for self-defense purposes than they are to commit crimes. One survey, for example, estimates that guns are used for self-defense purposes at least 2.5 million times per year—far more than the 1 million gun-related crimes that occur each year (Kleck and Gertz, 1995). There is now a lively debate about the accuracy of these different surveys (see Hemenway and Miller, 2004; McDowall et al., 2000; also see Kovandzic and Marvell, 2003, on the effect of "right to carry" laws, which mandate that authorities allow qualified applicants to carry concealed handguns).

The outcome of this debate will allow society to better determine the net impact of guns on crime and delinquency. This debate also has important policy implications: If guns do prevent more crime than they cause, efforts to restrict or control gun ownership in the **general population** may not reduce crime. Even so, virtually everyone agrees that it is desirable to take guns away from criminals and delinquents and to at least restrict handgun possession by juveniles.[23] I will return to this point in Chapter 24, when strategies for reducing delinquency are discussed.

Summary

In sum, religion, work, the mass media, drugs, and guns do have an effect on delinquency—although in most cases this effect appears to be modest in size. Religion reduces delinquency, especially "victimless" crimes, by a small to modest amount. Work—especially long hours of work—by in-school juveniles who are predisposed to delinquency decreases delinquency by a modest amount. Mass media violence has a modest effect on violent behavior. Drug use and selling also appear to increase the likelihood of delinquency, although their effect on delinquency is not as large as is commonly portrayed. Finally, there is some evidence suggesting that the possession of guns increases the likelihood of serious violence, although there is now a debate over whether guns prevent more crime than they cause.

Teaching Aids

Controversial Issue: Should Marijuana Be Legalized?

Much of the discussion about how to control delinquency centers on religion, media violence, drugs, and guns (even though individual traits, family, school, and peer factors have larger impacts on delinquency). Such discussion often generates tremendous controversy. Should we expand the role of religion in public life (e.g., display the Ten Commandments in public places, allow school prayer, provide government funding to religious groups involved in social service activities)? And will doing so reduce problems like delinquency? Should the government exercise greater control over media violence? Should drugs be legalized, or should the war on drugs be expanded? Should we expand or restrict our efforts to control gun possession and use?

It is not possible to examine all of these issues in this book (although, see Chapter 24), so in this section I focus on an issue of some concern to many college students: **Should the use of marijuana be legalized?** Drawing on the arguments in this chapter, discuss what impact, if any, you think legalizing marijuana would have on crime and delinquency. What other impacts—positive and/or negative—might legalizing marijuana have? To stimulate your thinking, I present two selections. One is from an editorial by Asa Hutchinson, director of the Drug Enforcement Administration, who argues against the legalization of marijuana. The other is by David Boyum and Mark Kleiman, academics and policy consultants, who argue that legalizing marijuana would likely reduce crime. (For further information on the legalization debate, see the sources in note 12.)

In an editorial titled "Drug Legalization Doesn't Work," Asa Hutchinson (2002) argues:

> On a recent summer tour through south London, I saw the future of drug legalization. . . . [A] local police commander initiated a pilot program in which people caught possessing marijuana are warned rather than arrested. Often, they're just ignored. In news reports and my interviews, residents criticize the program for bringing more drug dealers, more petty criminals and more drug use . . . but Britain has announced that it will relax the country's marijuana laws. . . . What these legalization advocates do not talk about [is] . . . the sad misery of young people addicted to drugs. They ignore the serious problems that countries such as the Netherlands are experiencing. . . . The culture of drug use and acceptance in the Netherlands has played a role in that country's becoming the world's top producer of Ecstasy. It's interesting that, in a 2001 study, the British Home Office found that violent crime and property crime increased in the late 1990s in every wealthy country except the United States. No doubt effective drug enforcement had a part in declining crime in the United States. . . . Our approach—tough drug laws combined with effective education programs and compassionate treatment—is having success. . . . Overall drug use in the United States is down by more than a third since the late 1970s. . . . In fighting drugs, we do have new ideas: from drug courts to community coalitions; more investment in education to more effective treatment; from more drug testing in the workplace to drug counselors in schools. These are ideas that work. What doesn't work is legalization. . . . In 1975, Alaska's Supreme Court held that . . . an adult could possess marijuana for personal consumption at home. . . . A 1988 University of Alaska survey showed that the state's teenagers used marijuana at a rate more than twice the national average for this age group. . . . Alaska's residents voted in 1990 to recriminalize the possession of marijuana.

David Boyum and Mark Kleiman (2002:344), by contrast, argue that legalizing marijuana will reduce crime, although they acknowledge that legalization may have "noncrime costs," including "the almost inevitable increase . . . in the number of persons who become heavy, chronic marijuana users."

Making marijuana legally available to adults on more or less the same terms as alcohol would tend to reduce crime: certainly by greatly shrinking the illicit market and possibly reducing alcohol consumption via substitution. . . . [S]ince drinking seems to have a greater tendency to unleash aggression than does cannabis use, substituting cannabis for alcohol would tend to decrease violence. Insofar as some marijuana users are now committing income-producing crimes to pay for their habits, the price reduction that would follow legalization would also tend to reduce crime. . . . In addition, if marijuana is a "gateway" to other illicit drugs primarily because it is illicit, the legalization of marijuana, by breaking the link between marijuana users and illicit drug dealers, would be expected to somewhat reduce the number of cocaine and heroin users. . . . [T]he conditional probability that someone who smokes marijuana will go on to use cocaine is substantially, though not spectacularly, lower in the Netherlands where buying and selling small amounts of cannabis are effectively legal, than in the United States. . . . It is rather difficult to see any effects of marijuana legalization that would be crime-increasing, unless legalization for adults increased use by teenagers in ways that decreased either their prudence or their legitimate opportunities.

In reading the previous statements, you might consider how we might evaluate the accuracy of the competing claims that are made. Also, do you think the arguments regarding legalization would be different for other drugs, like cocaine? Further, are the only options in the drug debate complete prohibition and virtually free legal commerce (see Boyum and Kleiman, 2002)? Finally, should our current policies toward **alcohol** be altered, given the contribution that alcohol makes to crime and other social problems? (A recent study by the National Research Council and Institute of Medicine of the National Academies recommended higher taxes on alcohol and more limits on alcohol advertising, among other things, in an effort to reduce alcohol consumption, especially teen drinking.)

TEST YOUR KNOWLEDGE OF THIS CHAPTER

1. Drawing on the leading delinquency theories, why might we expect religious juveniles to be less delinquent?
2. Describe the major research findings regarding the effect of religion on delinquency. Why does religion have a larger effect on victimless crimes than on serious delinquency? Why does religion have a larger effect when the individual is surrounded by religious others?
3. Why might we expect work to reduce delinquency?
4. What does the research say about the effect of working while attending school on delinquency? How might we explain these results?
5. Violent juveniles are more likely to watch violent TV shows and movies. Does this mean that TV and movie violence causes violent behavior? If not, why not?
6. Describe a typical experiment examining the effect of TV and movie violence on aggression. Why have some people questioned such experiments?
7. Describe the major research findings regarding the effect of TV and movie violence on violent behavior.
8. Describe the major research findings on the effect of violent video games on aggression.

TEST YOUR KNOWLEDGE OF THIS CHAPTER (continued)

9. What are the four major ways in which drug use and sales are said to increase other forms of delinquency?

10. The strong association between drug use and sales and delinquency does not prove that drug use and sales cause other delinquency. Why not?

11. Describe the major research findings on the effect of drug use and sales on delinquency.

12. What reasons do juveniles give for possessing guns? Does the reason for gun possession have any effect on the relation between guns and delinquency?

13. What factors increase the likelihood that juveniles will possess guns?

14. Describe the major research findings on the effect of gun possession on delinquency. Why might gun possession increase the likelihood of certain types of delinquency?

15. Why do some people argue that guns prevent more crime than they contribute to?

THOUGHT AND DISCUSSION QUESTIONS

1. Politicians and others often focus on the lack of religion and mass media violence when discussing the causes of delinquency, even though data suggest that these factors have only a modest effect on delinquency. Why do you think politicians and others focus on religion and the media rather than more important causes of juvenile crime?

2. Do you think that recent efforts to restrict juveniles' access to media violence, like the V-chip and the ratings system for TV shows and video games, will be effective?

3. There is a major media campaign under way to reduce drug use, with antidrug ads appearing in such places as newspapers, magazines, and TV. Find or describe one such ad. What causes of delinquency does it attempt to address, if any? Do you think such ads are effective in reducing juvenile drug use?

ENDNOTES

1. For overviews and recent examples of the research on religion and delinquency, *see* Baier and Wright, 2001; Burkett and Warren, 1987; Cochran et al., 1994; Elifson et al., 1983; Evans et al., 1995; Evans et al., 1996; Jang and Johnson, 2001; Jensen and Rojek, 1998; Johnson, Jang, Larson, and Li, 2000; Johnson, Li, Larson, and McCullough, 2000; Johnson et al., 2001; Pearce and Haynie, 2004; Regnerus, 2003; Regnerus and Elder, 2003; Regnerus and Smith, 2005; Stark and Bainbridge, 1996; Tittle and Welch, 1983; Wallace et al., 2007.

2. For example, *see* Burkett and Warren, 1987; Evans et al., 1996; Johnson et al., 2001; Regnerus and Elder, 2003.

3. *See* Baier and Wright, 2001; Evans et al., 1995; Pearce and Haynie, 2004; Regnerus, 2003; Stark and Bainbridge, 1996; Tittle and Welch, 1983; Wallace et al., 2007.

4. For overviews and selected studies in this area, *see* Agnew, 1986; Cullen et al., 1997; Ploeger, 1997; Steinberg, 1996; Williams et al., 1996; Wright and Cullen, 2000; Wright et al., 1997.

5. *See* note 4 above.

6. *See* Agnew, 1990b; Cullen et. al., 1985; Wright et al., 2001.

7. For overviews of the research on TV and movie violence and violent behavior, *see* Anderson, 2007; Anderson and Bushman, 2001a, 2002; Anderson et al., 2003; Binder et al., 1997; Bloom, 2002; Browne and Hamilton-Giachritsis, 2005; Christensen and Wood, 2007; Donnerstein and Linz, 1995; Donnerstein et al., 1994; Freedman, 2002; Huesman and Kirwil, 2007; Kirsh, 2006; Levine, 1996; McCord et al., 2001; National Television Violence Study, 1997, 1998; U.S. Department of Health and Human Services, 2001.

8. For overviews of the research on violent video games and aggression, *see* Anderson, 2004; Anderson and Bushman, 2001b; Anderson et al., 2003; Anderson et al., 2007; Bensley and Van Eenwyk, 2001; Browne and Hamilton-Giachritsis, 2005; Dill and Dill, 1998; Griffiths, 1999; Kirsh, 2006; Sherry, 2001, 2007; Weber et al., 2006.

9. For overviews and examples of the recent research on drugs and delinquency, *see* Akers, 1992; Altschuler and Brounstein, 1991; Assaad and Exum, 2002; Boyum and Kleiman, 2002; Bureau of Justice Statistics, 1992; Chitwood et al., 1996; Crowe, 1998; Elliott et al., 1989; Fagan 1998; Gentry, 1995; Goldstein, 1985; Goode, 1993, 2008; Huizinga et al., 1989; Inciardi and McElrath, 1998; Kretschmar and Flannery, 2007; McBride and McCoy, 1993; Office of National Drug Control Policy, 1999; Ousey and Lee, 2007; Schroeder et al., 2007; Welte et al., 2001; White and Gorman, 2000; White and Hansell, 1996; White and Labouvie, 1994; White et al., 1987, 2002; Zhang, Wieczorek, and Welte, 1997.

10. *See* Crowe, 1998; Schroeder et al., 2007; Thornberry et al., 1998; Zhang, Wieczorek, and Welte, 1997.

11. *See* Saum, 1998; *also see* Crowe, 1998; Felson and Burchfield, 2004; Mustaine and Tewksbury, 1998b.

12. For a fuller discussion of these issues, *see* Boyum and Kleiman, 2002; Gentry, 1995; Goode, 1993; Inciardi and McElrath, 1998; Meier and Geis, 1997.

13. *See* Office of National Drug Control Policy, 2003; *also see* Altschuler and Brounstein, 1991; Elliott et al., 1989; National Institute of Justice, 2003; White et al., 2002.

14. *See* White et al., 1987; *also see* Akers, 1992; Elliott et al., 1989; Huizinga et al., 2003; NSDUH Report, 2006.

15. *See* Elliott et al., 1989; Neff and Waite, 2007; White and Gorman, 2000.

16. *See* Elliott et al., 1989; Goode, 2008; Huang et al., 2001; Huizinga et al., 1989, 2003; Kretschmar and Flannery, 2007; Messner et al., 2007; Schroeder et al., 2007; Welte et al., 2001.

17. *See* note 16 above.

18. For overviews and examples of recent research on guns and delinquency/crime, *see* Berkowitz, 1994; Bjerregaard and Lizotte, 1995; Blumstein, 1995; Cook, 1991; Cook and Ludwig, 1997, 2000, 2004; Cook et al., 2002; Decker et al., 1997; Duggan, 2001; Greenbaum, 1997; Harcourt, 2003; Kleck, 1997; Liberman, 2007; Lizotte and Sheppard, 2001; Lizotte et al., 1994, 2002; Ludwig and Cook, 2003; Office of Juvenile Justice and Delinquency Prevention, 1996; Reiss and Roth, 1993; Sheley and Wright, 1995, 1998; Thornberry et al., 2003a, 2003b; Walker, 1998; Wilcox et al., 2006; Wintemute, 2006; Wright, et al., 1992; Wright and Vail, 2000; Zawitz, 1995; Zimring, 2005, 2007; Zimring and Hawkins, 1997.

19. *See* Office of Juvenile Justice and Delinquency Prevention, 2000a; *also see* Sheley and Wright, 1998; Thornberry et al., 2003a.

20. *See* Lizotte and Sheppard, 2001; *also see* Sheley and Wright, 1995; Thornberry et al., 2003a; Wintemute, 2006.

21. *See* Berkowitz, 1994; Cook, Moore, and Braga, 2002; Kleck, 1997; Reiss and Roth, 1993; Wells and Horney, 2002; Zimring and Hawkins, 1997.

22. *See* Berkowitz, 1994; Blumstein, 1995; Cook and Ludwig, 2000; Kleck, 1997; Wells and Horney, 2002; Wilcox et al., 2006; Zimrig and Hawkins, 1997.

23. For discussions of gun control, *see* Cook and Ludwig, 1997, 1998, 2000; Cook et al., 2002; Harcourt, 2003; Kleck, 1997; Kleck and Gertz, 1995; Lott, 1998; Ludwig and Cook, 2003; McDowall and Wiersema, 1994; McDowall et al., 1991, 2000; Reiss and Roth, 1993; Sherman, 2001; Stolzenberg and D'Alession, 2000; Wintemute, 2006; Wright and Vail, 2000; Zimring, 2005, 2007; Zimring and Hawkins, 1997.

CHAPTER 18

Pulling It All Together

Is It Possible to Construct a General Theory of Delinquency?

Wе have now reviewed the major theories of delinquency (Chapters 6 through 12). We have also reviewed a large body of research that is derived from, or at least compatible with, these theories. This research focused on the individual traits and features of the social environment that cause delinquency, including family, school, and peer environments (Chapters 13 through 17).

You may feel somewhat overwhelmed by now. We have reviewed several theories and a lot of research based on these theories. You might wonder how everything fits together. In particular, you might wonder whether it is possible to pull all the theories and research together and construct an integrated or general theory of delinquency.

Several criminologists have tried to do this, and some of the integrated theories that they have produced are attracting a lot of attention.[1] Few criminologists, however, view these integrated theories as finished products. Rather, they are preliminary attempts to pull together the relevant theory and research on the causes of delinquency.

I present my own integrated or general theory of delinquency in this chapter in order to help you pull together the material in Chapters 6 through 17. This general theory draws heavily on the integrated theories developed by other criminologists, especially Thornberry's (1987) "interactional" theory of delinquency, as well as my own work (Agnew, 2005).

As you may recall from Chapters 5 through 12, theories try to explain several major facts about delinquency. Most notably, they **try to explain why some individuals engage in more delinquency than others.** This is the focus of the core part of my general theory. I then build on this core part to **explain patterns of offending over the life course and group differences in delinquency.** My theory does not attempt to explain why delinquency is more likely in certain types of situations, although it does take into account those factors that influence the juvenile's exposure to such situations. Doing so allows the theory to better explain delinquency: Some individuals and groups are more delinquent than others partly because they are more likely to be in situations conducive to delinquency.

Since my general theory attempts to pull together the material in Chapters 6 through 17, I begin this chapter by providing a brief overview of the key points in these chapters. Then I present the general theory in four stages.

1. I describe the **major direct causes of individual delinquency** and the reasons **why these causes affect delinquency.** These causes are grouped into *four clusters:* irritability/low self-control, poor parenting practices, negative school experiences, and association with delinquent peers or gang members. I argue that **the causes in each cluster affect delinquency for reasons related to all of the major delinquency theories.**

2. I describe **how these clusters are related to one another.** In particular, **these clusters have reciprocal effects on one another** (e.g., negative school experiences increase association with delinquent peers, which, in turn, increases negative school experiences).

3. I draw on labeling theory to argue that **delinquency often affects the clusters** (e.g., delinquency increases the likelihood of association with delinquent peers). I also argue that **prior delinquency often directly increases the likelihood of subsequent delinquency.**

4. I describe **the ways in which biological factors and the larger social environment affect the clusters,** with a focus on the effects of **gender/sex, age, parental social class, and community characteristics.** This discussion allows me to explain group differences in delinquency and patterns of offending over the life course.

It is important to stress that the general theory simplifies a complex reality. Among other things, it does not consider many of the less important causes of delinquency, like religion and media violence. The theory is designed to highlight the key causes of delinquency and describe the major ways in which these causes work together to affect delinquency.

The final section of the chapter provides an illustration of the general theory in action. The theory is used to explain one of the most important facts about delinquency: the fact **that males generally have higher rates of offending than females.** As indicated in Chapter 4, sex/gender and age are the strongest sociodemographic correlates of delinquency (age is discussed in Chapter 10 and briefly in this chapter).

A Brief Review of the Theories and Research on the Causes of Delinquency

Theories

The **major delinquency theories** devote most attention to explaining why some individuals engage in delinquency more than others. These theories describe the independent variables that cause delinquency and the reasons why these variables cause delinquency.

Strain theory argues that delinquency is caused by stressful events or conditions. The theory focuses on two major types of strain: the failure to achieve positively valued goals and the loss of positive stimuli or presentation of negative stimuli. The experience of strain leads to negative emotions, like anger and frustration, and juveniles may turn to delinquency in an effort to cope with strain and these emotions. Delinquency may allow juveniles to reduce or escape from their strain, seek revenge against those who have wronged them, or manage their negative emotions (e.g., through illicit drug use).

Social learning theory argues that delinquency is caused by associating with others who present beliefs favorable to delinquency, model delinquency, and reinforce delinquency. These activities lead individuals to conclude that delinquency is a desirable or at least justifiable response in certain situations.

Control theory argues that delinquency results from weak controls, including direct controls, stakes in conformity, beliefs regarding crime, and self-control. Weak controls free juveniles to satisfy their needs and desires in the most expedient way possible, which is often delinquency.

Labeling theory argues that individuals who are labeled "delinquent" are often rejected and treated in a harsh manner by others. This harsh/rejecting treatment increases the likelihood of further delinquency by increasing strain, reducing control, increasing the social learning for crime (since labeled individuals are forced to associate with other delinquents), and fostering a delinquent self-concept.

These theories have also been used to **explain patterns of offending over the life course,** especially the adolescence-limited and life-course persistent patterns of offending. Most individuals **increase their levels of offending during adolescence,** and they do so because the biological and social changes associated with adolescence lead to increases in strain, reductions in control, and increases in the social learning for crime. For example, the increased autonomy given to adolescents leads to a reduction in direct control and an increase in association with delinquent peers. A small percentage of individuals **offend at**

high rates over much of their lives. They do so because they experience poor parenting and develop the traits of irritability/low self-control early in life; these problems tend to persist over time and to contribute to school, peer, marital, and work problems later in life (partly for reasons related to labeling theory). As a consequence, such individuals experience high levels of strain, low control, and much social learning for crime over the greater part of their lives.

Further, these theories have been used to **describe those situations most conducive to delinquency.** In particular, delinquency is more likely in situations where the juvenile is provoked by others (a type of strain), with provocations like insults, threats, and attacks being especially conducive to delinquency. Delinquency is also more likely in situations where drugs and alcohol are being used, attractive targets are available, capable guardians are absent, and delinquent peers are present. Control is low in such situations, and the likelihood that crime will be reinforced is high. Juveniles who frequently engage in unstructured, unsupervised activities with peers are more likely to encounter these situations.

Finally, these theories have been used to **explain group differences in delinquency,** with Chapter 12 focusing on **community differences in delinquency.** Delinquency is highest in communities that are economically deprived, high in residential instability, and high in family disruption. Such communities are lower in control, higher in strain, and more likely to develop delinquent peer groups and gangs that foster the social learning of crime.

Research

The research derived from these theories focuses on a wide range of independent variables that may cause delinquency. These variables measure strain, the dimensions of control, factors associated with the social learning of crime, and/or labeling. Those factors that appear to have at least a small to moderate effect on delinquency include:

1. **Individual traits,** including low verbal IQ and, especially, the super-traits of irritability and low self-control. Evidence suggests that these traits are the product of biological and environmental factors, especially poor parenting.

2. **Family experiences,** including broken homes, long hours in child care, teenage parenthood, large families, criminal parents and siblings, parental rejection, low attachment to parents, family conflict, child abuse, poor parental supervision, poor family problem-solving techniques, and the lack of positive parenting.

3. **School experiences,** including low academic performance, low school involvement, low attachment to school, poor relations with teachers, low educational or occupational goals, and school misbehavior.

4. **School characteristics,** including large schools with poor resources, poor discipline, limited opportunities for student success, low expectations for students, unpleasant working conditions for students, poor cooperation between the administration and teachers, and little community involvement.

5. **Peer group and gang experiences,** including association with delinquent peers and, especially, gang membership.

6. **Religion, mass media, drugs, and guns,** including a lack of religion (mainly for victimless crimes), extensive exposure to media violence, drug selling and serious drug use, and gun possession, especially for protection (mainly for serious violence).

A General Theory of Delinquency

The Major Direct Causes of Individual Delinquency and the Reasons Why These Causes Affect Delinquency

The first thing that a general theory of delinquency should do is list those factors that have relatively large, direct effects on individual delinquency and explain why these factors affect delinquency. The major theories and the research on these theories provide guidance here.

The leading direct causes of delinquency are listed next. I describe these causes in concrete terms. So rather than stating that factors like the "presentation of negative stimuli" and "low direct control" cause delinquency, I state that factors like child abuse and poor parental supervision cause delinquency. These concrete descriptions are more meaningful to most people, although it should be kept in mind that factors like child abuse and poor supervision index, or measure, the more abstract causes described by the leading delinquency theories—like "presentation of negative stimuli" and "low direct control."

I group the leading causes into **four clusters: irritability/low self-control, poor parenting practices, negative school experiences,** and **peer delinquency.** These clusters reflect the four major domains of the juvenile's life: self (individual traits), family, school, and peers. The specific causes in each cluster generally have relatively strong associations with one another, so it is reasonable to group them together (see Agnew, 2005). Grouping these causes greatly simplifies the general theory, making it much easier to keep track of the causes and to describe how they work together to affect delinquency.

Finally, I describe why the causes in each cluster affect delinquency. The leading theories have much to say in this area, although there has not been much research on this topic. Nevertheless, the limited research that has been done tends to affirm one of the central points made in Chapters 13 through 17: Most causes affect delinquency for reasons related to most or all of the leading delinquency theories.[2] I reinforce this point later, arguing that **the causes in each cluster increase delinquency for reasons related to strain, control, social learning, and labeling theories.**

The **four clusters** of variables affecting individual delinquency are:

1. *Irritability/low self-control.* Recall that individuals with these super-traits are basically out of control and mean, nasty people. They are more likely to engage in delinquency because they are **low in internal control;** that is, they are less aware of and concerned about direct controls and jeopardizing their stake in conformity. They are **high in strain,** since they are more sensitive to strains, more likely to blame others for their strains, and more likely to provoke negative responses from others. They are also more disposed to cope with strain in a delinquent manner. They are more likely to **learn to engage in crime,** because they are less sensitive to the punishments for crime and more attracted to the rewards of crime—since crime often provides thrills and excitement and allows for the immediate gratification of one's desires. Finally, they are more likely to be **labeled as bad and treated in a harsh or rejecting manner.**

2. *Poor parenting practices.* Juveniles who experience poor parenting practices are rejected by their parents, dislike or hate their parents, frequently get into conflicts with their parents, are poorly supervised and disciplined by their parents, are abused by their parents, and/or receive little in the way of positive parenting. Other family factors, like living in a broken home or having criminal parents, are important largely because they affect these

dimensions of poor parenting (which refer to the quality of family relations and parental socialization).

Researchers can develop an overall measure of poor parenting practices by determining the extent to which juveniles experience each of the dimensions of poor parenting just listed. Scores on each of these dimensions can then be summed or averaged to create the overall measure. Juveniles who score high on this overall measure have high scores on each of the dimensions of poor parenting (e.g., they are strongly rejected by their parents, very poorly supervised, frequently abused, and so on). This overall measure should have a positive effect on delinquency, such that juveniles with high scores have higher levels of delinquency.

Poor parenting increases the likelihood of delinquency for reasons related to all of the leading theories. Individuals subject to poor parenting are **high in strain** (e.g., they are harshly disciplined, abused, and get into frequent conflicts with parents). They are more likely to cope with strain through delinquency, partly because their parents do not provide them with much social support or teach them legitimate coping skills (these are part of positive parenting). They are **low in direct control** (i.e., they are poorly supervised and disciplined) and have a **low stake in conformity** (i.e., they are weakly bonded to parents). They **learn to engage in aggressive behavior** from their parents, who often treat them harshly or abuse them. And their parents **label them as bad** and treat them in a harsh or rejecting manner.

3. *Negative school experiences.* Negative school experiences include low academic performance, low school involvement, including little time on homework, low attachment to school, poor relations with teachers, and low educational and occupational goals. Again, we can determine the extent to which juveniles experience each of these dimensions and use this information to develop an overall measure of negative school experiences.

Juveniles with negative school experiences are **high in strain.** For example, teachers give them low grades and otherwise treat them in a negative manner. They have a **low stake in conformity,** since they have low grades, little involvement in school, little attachment to school, and low goals. They are probably **low in direct control,** since they have little involvement in school activities. They are more likely to **learn to engage in crime.** In particular, they are more often in noncollege tracks, which increases their exposure to delinquent others. And they are more likely to be **labeled as bad** and treated accordingly.

4. *Association with delinquent peers or gang members (delinquent peer association for short).* Juveniles who score high on this cluster are part of a cohesive group of peers (including friends and siblings) who are heavily involved in delinquency. Further, these peers constitute a gang.

Delinquent peer association **increases strain,** since delinquent peers are more likely to get into conflicts with one another and others. Delinquent peer association **reduces direct control,** since delinquent peers reduce the fear of sanctions. Delinquent peer association **reduces stake in conformity** by reducing bonds to conventional others and efforts devoted to conventional pursuits, like schoolwork. Delinquent peer association strongly **fosters the social learning of crime,** since the juvenile is exposed to others who differentially reinforce crime, teach beliefs favorable to crime, and model crime. Delinquent peer association increases the likelihood of being **labeled as bad.** And delinquent peer association **increases the amount of time spent in unstructured, unsupervised activities with peers,** which in turn increases exposure to situations conducive to crime.

How These Clusters Are Related to One Another

A general theory should do more than list the major causes of delinquency and describe why they cause delinquency. It should also describe how these causes are related to one another.

The clusters have *reciprocal effects* on one another. Cluster X causes cluster Y **and** cluster Y causes cluster X. If you read Chapters 13 through 17 closely, you noticed that I argue that each cluster of variables is reciprocally related to the other clusters. For example, in Chapter 13, I argue that poor parenting practices contribute to traits like irritability and low self-control. Then in Chapter 14, I argue that irritability and low self-control contribute to poor parenting practices. Juveniles with these traits are difficult to raise, and their frustrated parents often become overly coercive or just give up trying to control their children. To give another example, in Chapter 16, I argue that negative school experiences increase delinquent peer association. People who do poorly in school are more likely to be exposed to delinquent peers (especially in noncollege tracks) and attracted to them. Then in Chapter 15, I argue that delinquent peer association increases the likelihood of negative school experiences, since delinquent peers often de-emphasize schoolwork. Similar arguments were made regarding the other combinations of clusters.

The reciprocal effects of the clusters on one another are shown in Figure 18.1. Such effects are also emphasized in Thornberry's (1987) integrated theory of delinquency. There has not been much research on reciprocal effects, but limited data provide some support for their existence.[3] More research is needed in this area, however, especially research on the relative size of such effects at different points in the individual's life (see Agnew, 2005; Thornberry, 1987). For example, there is reason to believe that irritability and low self-control have a relatively large effect on negative school experiences, since juveniles with these traits lack the motivation and ability to do well in school. Negative school experiences, however, may have a relatively small effect on irritability and low self-control, since these traits may be largely formed by the time juveniles begin school.

The reciprocal effects between the clusters shed important light on the causes of delinquency. We see that each cluster not only has a direct effect on delinquency but also has an indirect effect through the other clusters. For example, poor parenting directly affects delinquency and indirectly affects delinquency by contributing to irritability/low self-control, fostering negative school experiences and increasing delinquent peer associations.

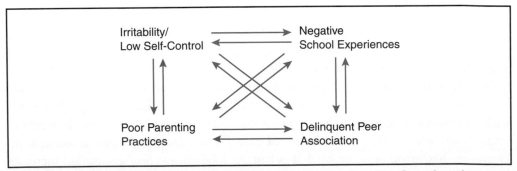

FIGURE 18.1 The Reciprocal Effects of the Clusters on One Another

Also we see that problems in one cluster tend to create problems in the other clusters. For example, problems at home tend to lead to problems at school. This point has important policy implications. Efforts to reduce problems in one cluster, like the school cluster, will be more effective to the extent that they take into account problems in other clusters, like the family cluster.

Delinquency Often Affects the Clusters, and Prior Delinquency Often Directly Increases the Likelihood of Subsequent Delinquency

I have usually treated delinquency as a dependent variable in this book. But, as indicated in the chapter on labeling theory, delinquency often affects its "causes." Engaging in delinquency may also **directly** increase the likelihood of further delinquency. These effects are illustrated in Figure 18.2. I describe these effects next and indicate when they are most likely to occur.

Delinquency often affects the clusters. Engaging in delinquency may foster traits like irritability and low self-control, disrupt relations with family members, lead to negative school experiences, and increase the likelihood of association with delinquent peers. But, as I emphasized in Chapter 9 on labeling theory, delinquency does not always have these effects. These effects are most likely when conventional others label delinquents as "bad" and treat them in a harsh or rejecting manner. Whether others treat delinquents in this manner is dependent on a number of factors, including the juvenile's prior standing on the four clusters.

Delinquents are most likely to be treated in a harsh or rejecting manner by conventional others when they are irritable/low in self-control, have family problems, have negative school experiences, and associate with delinquent peers. Among other things, such juveniles fit the stereotype of a bad person, they are less able to resist the efforts of others to treat them in a harsh or rejecting manner, and they are more likely to associate with others who will treat them in a harsh or rejecting manner, like parents and teachers who do not like them (see Chapter 9).

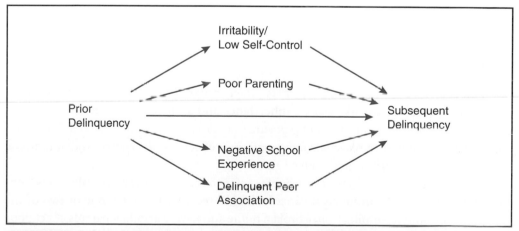

FIGURE 18.2 Delinquency Often Affects the Clusters, and Prior Delinquency Often Increases the Likelihood of Subsequent Delinquency

These arguments, then, suggest that **the effect of delinquency on the clusters is conditioned by the juvenile's prior standing on the clusters.** For example, engaging in delinquency is most likely to disrupt family relations among juveniles who are already having problems with family members. There has not been much research in this area.

Prior delinquency often directly increases the likelihood of subsequent delinquency. There are at least two reasons why engaging in delinquency **may** directly increase the likelihood of further delinquency. First, **delinquents often discover that their delinquency is not detected or sanctioned by conventional others.** This emboldens the delinquents, thereby increasing the likelihood of further delinquency. Second, **delinquents often find that their delinquency benefits them in certain ways** (i.e., their delinquency is reinforced). These benefits may include thrills or excitement, money, the pleasurable feelings that result from drug use, a reduction in strain (e.g., running away allows escape from abusive parents), and the social approval of others. It is often the case that these benefits are short-lived and that delinquency results in more harm than good over the long term. Nevertheless, these benefits are sufficient to motivate many delinquents to continue or even increase their delinquent offending.

Data provide some support for these arguments, with research suggesting that engaging in delinquency usually increases the likelihood of further delinquency, even after a host of third variables are controlled.[4]

Biological Factors and the Larger Social Environment Affect the Clusters

So far I have described the factors that have relatively large, direct effects on delinquency and how these factors work together to affect delinquency. This information sheds much light on why some individuals are more likely than others to engage in delinquency and is useful to those seeking to control delinquency (see Chapter 24). But there is one final issue that a general theory must address: **Why is it that some individuals are more likely than others to possess the traits of irritability and low self-control, experience poor parenting, have negative peer experiences, and associate with delinquent peers?** A general theory, then, must also describe the *background variables* that affect the major direct causes of delinquency. Doing so has the advantage of allowing the theory to explain patterns of offending over the life course and group differences in offending.

Two sets of background variables have substantial effects on irritability/low self-control, poor parenting, negative school experiences, and/or peer delinquency. (Certain of these background variables may also have small to moderate direct effects on delinquency.)

The first set of background variables affect irritability/low self-control, and they include biological factors like genetic inheritance and a range of biological harms, like poor prenatal care, head injuries, and exposure to toxic substances, such as lead. These factors affect irritability/low self-control through their effects on the central and autonomic nervous systems (described in Chapter 13).

The second set of background variables refer to features of the juvenile's social environment. Certain environmental variables have direct effects on just one or two of the clusters. For example, coming from a broken home and having criminal parents affect poor parenting practices, but these variables have little direct effect on the other clusters (although they have an indirect effect through their effect on poor parenting practices). Other environmental variables, however, affect all or most of the clusters. To keep the general theory simple, I focus on these variables. They include **the type of community in which one lives and one's position in the larger society, as reflected by one's gender, age, and parental social class.**

In particular, **those in deprived communities, males, adolescents, and lower-class individuals are higher in irritability/low self-control, poor parenting practices, negative school experiences, and delinquent peer associations.** As indicated in Chapters 13 through 17, these variables *directly affect* irritability/low self-control, poor parenting practices, negative school experiences, and delinquent peer association. Further, these variables *indirectly affect* the clusters, through their impact on or association with factors like coming from a broken home, having criminal parents, or attending an inferior school (e.g., juveniles in deprived communities are more likely to live in broken homes and attend inferior schools).

The reasons these variables affect the four clusters are described in Chapters 13 through 17. For example, Chapter 15 states that low parental social class increases the likelihood of negative school experiences, because lower-class parents are less likely to equip their children with the skills and attitudes necessary to do well in school. To give another example, Chapters 12 and 16 state that juveniles in deprived communities are more likely to join delinquent peer groups, because the low control and high strain in such communities foster the development of such groups and increase their appeal to juveniles. And to give a final example, Chapter 10 describes why adolescents are more likely than children and adults to be irritable and low in self-control, have family problems, have negative school experiences, and associate with delinquent peers.

I should note that **race/ethnicity is associated with the clusters.** However, evidence suggests that this association is largely due to the fact that **race and/or ethnicity is related to parental social class and community characteristics.** For reasons of past and present discrimination, members of certain races or ethnic groups, like African Americans, Latinos, and Native Americans, are more likely to be poor and live in deprived communities. That is the primary reason that race/ethnicity is often associated with the clusters. Once we take into account parental social class and community characteristics, the association between race/ethnicity and the clusters is substantially reduced. The association may not be eliminated entirely, which likely reflects the fact that race/ethnicity still affects how people treat one another—even after taking account of social class. African Americans, for example, encounter more racial discrimination than whites at all class levels (Hughes and Thomas, 1998).

I should also note that **it is possible to describe still other, larger social influences that directly and indirectly affect the clusters.** For example, does the economic system provide adults with decent work at a living wage? The lack of such work has far-ranging consequences that may affect the clusters. For example, the lack of decent work increases the economic strain faced by family members, which in turn contributes to poor parenting practices. Does the political system provide sufficient support to those experiencing economic, health, educational, and other problems? Again, the failure to provide such support has far-ranging consequences that affect the clusters. For example, the failure to provide adequate health care may increase the prevalence of biological harms, like birth complications, that contribute to irritability/low self-control. Does the cultural system place a strong emphasis on socializing boys to be aggressive? The impact of these and other larger social forces on crime is discussed in several excellent works.[5]

Explaining Patterns of Offending over the Life Course and Group Differences in Delinquency

Describing the effect of biological factors and the larger social environment on the direct causes allows the general theory to explain patterns of offending over the life course and group differences in delinquency.

As I indicated earlier, **the adolescence-limited pattern of offending is explained by the fact that the social and biological changes associated with adolescence affect the four clusters; adolescents are generally higher in irritability or low self-control, poor parenting practices, negative school experiences, and delinquent peer association.** This is why adolescents increase their levels of offending—with data suggesting that the increase in delinquent peer association during adolescence plays an especially important role in increased offending (Warr, 2002).

The life-course persistent pattern of offending reflects the fact that a small percentage of respondents develop the traits of irritability and low self-control and experience poor parenting early in life. As I indicated in Chapter 10, these problems tend to persist over time, and they create problems in other domains, like the school, peer, marital, and work domains. As a consequence, such individuals tend to offend at high rates over much of their lives. Whether individuals develop irritability/low self-control and experience poor parenting early in life are partly a function of biological factors. For example, do they have a genetic predisposition to develop these traits, did they experience poor prenatal care, or were they exposed to toxic substances like lead? It is also a function of their sex, parental social class, and the type of community in which they live. Males, lower-class individuals, and people in deprived communities are more likely to develop these traits and experience poor parenting. Such individuals are more likely to experience biological harms. For example, lower-class individuals are more likely to be exposed to toxic substances like lead (Denno, 1990). And males, lower-class individuals, and people in deprived communities are more likely to be socialized in ways that foster these traits. For example, the stresses associated with lower-class life and living in a deprived community foster poor parenting (see Chapter 14). Given these arguments, it should not be surprising that males, lower-class juveniles, and people living in deprived communities are more likely to be life-course persistent offenders.[6]

Group differences in delinquency are largely due to the fact that **members of some groups are more likely to score high on the clusters.** So the fact that group X has a higher rate of delinquency than group Y is due largely to the fact that the members of group X are more likely to be irritable and low in self-control, experience poor parenting, have negative school experiences, and associate with delinquent peers. However, this may not be the only reason that group X has a higher rate of delinquency. Certain group characteristics beyond those reflected in the four clusters may also have a direct effect on delinquency. For example, the level of direct control that neighborhood residents exercise over one another also helps explain why some communities have higher rates of delinquency than other communities (see Chapter 12). Nevertheless, the general theory predicts that **group differences in the four clusters largely account for group differences in delinquency.** This point is illustrated when I use the general theory to explain why males have higher rates of delinquency than females in the next section.

Using the General Theory to Explain Why Males Have Higher Rates of Delinquency than Females

As I discussed in Chapter 4, males are more likely than females to engage in most forms of delinquency, especially serious delinquency. According to the general theory, the major reason for this is that males are more likely to score high on the clusters—irritability/low self-control, poor parenting practices, negative school experiences, and delinquent peer association.[7]

Data suggest that **males are more likely than females to possess those traits that make up irritability and low self-control.**[8] Further, the fact that males are higher in irritability/low self-control appears to explain much of the gender difference in delinquency.[9] Gender differences in irritability/low self-control are likely due to both biological and environmental factors (see the biosocial model of gender differences in Udry, 2000).

The role of biological factors in explaining sex differences in irritability/low self-control and offending is suggested by several pieces of evidence: (1) sex-related differences in temperament have been noted at birth (e.g., newborn females are more likely to smile and cling to their mothers); (2) sex differences in physical aggression and crime emerge very early in life; and (3) historical and cross-cultural studies consistently find that males are more involved than females in most forms of physical aggression and crime (although the extent to which males are more involved varies over time and between societies). Further, evidence suggests that biological factors like genetic inheritance may have a strong impact on irritability/low self-control (Moffitt et al., 2001). The precise biological causes of sex differences in irritability/low self-control and offending, however, are unclear. The most commonly advanced explanation has to do with sex differences in the level of testosterone, a hormone that stimulates the development of masculine characteristics.[10] More research is needed in this area, however.

There is also reason to believe that **sex differences in traits and offending are partly due to environmental factors.** Males are treated differently than females from birth onward. In particular, males and females are socialized differently by family members and others. Among other things, females are more likely to be socialized to be submissive and dependent on others, empathetic with others, and supportive of others. Females are more often exposed to models that exhibit these behaviors, taught beliefs conducive to these behaviors, and reinforced for these behaviors. Males, by contrast, are more likely to be socialized to be aggressive and assertive, risk-taking, independent, and competitive with others. As a consequence of such differences in socialization, males may be more likely to possess many of the traits that make up irritability and low self-control, like risk seeking, little concern for the feelings and rights of others, and moral beliefs favorable to delinquency.

Gender differences with respect to the other clusters also help explain the fact that **males have higher rates of delinquency.** Among other things, it is argued that males: (1) are less closely supervised by family members; (2) are less strongly attached to family members; (3) are less attached to school; (4) spend less time on schoolwork; (5) do less well in school; and (6) are more likely to associate with delinquent peers.[11] These differences may partly reflect sex differences in irritability and low self-control. Males, for example, may be more likely to associate with delinquent peers because such peers are more attractive to them, given their greater irritability and lower self-control. These differences also reflect differences in the way males and females are viewed and treated. Females, for example, are more likely to be seen as submissive and weak, and therefore in need of greater supervision and protection. And females are under greater pressure to maintain their sexual virtue, which again fosters greater supervision and control over their lives.

Data regarding these gender differences in the clusters are somewhat mixed. Some studies, for example, find that males are less strongly bonded to family members, others find that males are more strongly bonded, and still others find that there are no gender differences in family bonding. Perhaps the most consistent findings deal with delinquent peer associations and parental supervision. Females are less likely to associate with delinquent peers and are more likely to be closely supervised by parents. Studies suggest that **gender differences in supervision and especially peer association explain a good portion of the gender difference in delinquency.**[12]

So gender differences in delinquency are due largely to gender differences in standing on the clusters, especially **gender differences in irritability/low self-control, delinquent peer association, and, to a lesser extent, parental supervision.** Some researchers also argue that certain of these clusters are more likely to affect delinquency among males than among females. For example, they argue that not only are males more likely than females to associate with delinquent peers, but delinquent peers are more likely to cause delinquency among males than females (Mears et al., 1998; Piquero et al., 2005). The data in this area are somewhat mixed, but most data suggest that the causes have similar effects on males and females with the exception of delinquent peers.[13]

The Special Role of Sexual Abuse in Explaining Serious Female Offending

There is, however, one particular cause that may have a larger effect on female offending than on male offending. It is important to single out this cause because it may play an especially important role in the explanation of serious female offending. Chesney-Lind (1989) argues that **abuse by family members, especially sexual abuse, plays a special role in the explanation of female delinquency.** While abuse may lead to delinquency among males, females are much more likely to be the victims of sexual abuse than males, and such abuse is said to have an especially devastating effect on females. Females, in particular, often respond to such abuse by running away from home, and they often find that they must turn to crime in order to survive on the street. Their age and runaway status rule out legitimate work as an option, so they engage in income-generating crimes like prostitution, drug selling, and petty theft. Life on the street, including involvement in activities like prostitution, leads to further abuse and exploitation. The police and juvenile courts often provide little assistance to these females. In fact, such females are frequently arrested and returned to their home environment, where they may suffer further abuse. Interviews with female offenders provide tentative support for this argument.[14]

An Overview of the General Theory of Delinquency

The general theory of delinquency makes several key arguments:

1. The major direct causes of delinquency can be grouped into four clusters: irritability/low self-control, poor parenting practices, negative school experiences, and delinquent peer association. These clusters affect delinquency by increasing strain, reducing control, increasing the social learning for crime, and increasing labeling.

2. These clusters have reciprocal effects on one another. For example, irritability/low self-control causes poor parenting, and poor parenting causes irritability/low self-control.

3. Engaging in delinquency often contributes to irritability/low self-control, poor parenting practices, negative school experiences, and delinquent peer association. Also, engaging in delinquency often directly increases the likelihood of further delinquency.

4. Biological factors and the larger social environment affect the clusters. In particular, males, adolescents, lower-class people, and the residents of deprived communities are more likely to be high in irritability/low self-control, poor parenting practices, negative school experiences, and delinquent peer association.

It is my hope that the general theory helps you keep track of the key points from previous chapters and see how this material fits together. Remember that the theory simplifies a complex reality, ignoring many of the less important causes of delinquency, among other things (see Agnew, 2005, for a more elaborate version of the general theory).

You now know quite a bit about the causes of delinquency. You can list most of the major causes of delinquency, you can describe the reasons why these causes increase delinquency, and you know something about how these causes work together to affect delinquency. As you will see in the final chapters of this book, that knowledge can go a long way toward reducing delinquency.

Teaching Aids

Exercise

Imagine that you are sitting at the dinner table with family or friends, engaged in casual conversation. Someone asks you what classes you are taking this term, and you mention that you are enrolled in a class studying juvenile delinquency. The mention of juvenile delinquency attracts much interest, and you are then asked, **"So what causes delinquency?"** Outline a 5- to 10-minute response to this question, a response that draws on the major points in this text and that will be meaningful to those at the dinner table. With your instructor's permission, several of the people in your class should share their responses with the class and solicit feedback.

TEST YOUR KNOWLEDGE OF THIS CHAPTER

1. Briefly describe how the major theories of delinquency explain why some juveniles are more likely to engage in delinquency than others (focus on strain, control, social learning, and labeling theories).

2. How do these theories explain patterns of offending over the life course? (Focus on the adolescence-limited and life-course persistent patterns, in particular.)

3. Drawing on these theories, describe the characteristics of those situations conducive to crime.

4. How do these theories explain group differences in delinquency, particularly community differences?

5. What should an integrated or general theory of delinquency do? (Hint: One thing it should do is describe the major direct causes of delinquency.)

6. Briefly describe the four clusters of variables that have a large, direct effect on delinquency.

7. Pick one of these clusters and describe **why** it increases the likelihood of delinquency, drawing on the major delinquency theories.

8. What do I mean when I state that a variable has a **direct** effect on delinquency? What do I mean when I state that a variable has an **indirect** effect on delinquency?

9. Describe how the four clusters are related to one another. Give an example of a reciprocal effect involving the clusters.

10. Why might engaging in delinquency contribute to irritability/low self-control, poor parenting practices, negative school experiences, and delinquent peer association? Why might engaging in delinquency directly increase the likelihood of further delinquency?

11. List the major background variables that affect the clusters. When discussing background variables of an environmental nature, why do I focus on community characteristics, age, gender, and parental social class? Why is it that I do **not** list race/ethnicity as one of the major causes of the clusters?

12. How does the general theory explain the adolescence-limited and life-course persistent patterns of offending?

13. How does the general theory explain group differences in rates of delinquency?

14. How does the general theory explain the fact that males have higher rates of offending than females? Be sure to identify the key factors accounting for gender differences in offending.

15. Most causes have similar effects on males and females, but one cause of delinquency is said to be especially relevant to females—and may help account for a significant portion of serious female offending. What is that cause, and how does it contribute to female offending?

THOUGHT AND DISCUSSION QUESTIONS

1. How would the general theory explain social class differences in delinquency?

2. Do you think that the general theory overlooks any relatively important causes of delinquency or relationships among the causes of delinquency?

3. How does the general theory incorporate the ideas of strain, social learning, control, and labeling theories?

KEY TERMS

- Four clusters
- Irritability/low self-control
- Poor parenting practices
- Negative school experiences
- Delinquent peer association
- Reciprocal effect
- Background variables
- Direct and indirect effects

ENDNOTES

1. For overviews and examples, *see* Agnew, 2005; Akers and Sellers, 2004; Bernard and Snipes, 1996; Braithwaite, 1989; Catalano and Hawkins, 1996; Colvin, 2000; Cullen and Agnew, 2003; Elliott et al., 1985; Farrington, 2006; Johnson, 1979; Lilly et al., 2002; Messner et al., 1989; Miethe and Meier, 1994; Pearson and Weiner, 1985; Robinson, 2004; Shoemaker, 2000; Thornberry, 1987; Tittle, 1995; Vila, 1994; Vold et al., 1998.

2. *See* Agnew, 1993, 1995a; Brezina, 1998; Farrington, 1993b.

3. *See* Elliott and Menard, 1996; Thornberry, 1987, 1996; Thornberry et al., 1991, 1994; Thornberry et al., 2003a.

4. For selected studies, *see* Akers, 1998; Brame et al., 1999; Elliott, 1994; Elliott et al., 1985; Sampson and Laub, 1993a; Wright et al., 1999b.

5. *See* Bellair and McNulty, 2005; Colvin, 2000; Cullen and Agnew, 2003; Currie, 1998; Felson, 2002; Hagan 1994; LaFree, 1998; Lynch and Stretesky, 2001; Messner and Rosenfeld, 2001; Pratt and Cullen, 2005; Sampson and Wilson, 1995.

6. *See* D'Unger et al., 2002; Lanctot and Le Blanc, 2002; Moffitt et al., 2001; Patterson et al., 1998; Tibbetts and Piquero, 1999.

7. For overviews of the research on gender and crime and selected studies, *see* Agnew, 2008; Bartusch and Matsueda, 1996; Berger, 1989; Bottcher, 2001; Canter, 1982; Cernkovich and Giordano, 1987; Chesney-Lind and Shelden, 2004; Cloward and Piven, 1979; Daly, 1998; Daly and Chesney-Lind, 1988; Giordano, 1978; Giordano et al., 1986; Hagan et al., 1979; Hagan et al., 1996; Heidensohn, 2002; Heimer, 1995, 1996; Heimer et al., 2006; Hubbard and Pratt, 2002; Jensen and Eve, 1976; Lanctot and Le Blanc, 2002; Mears et al., 1998; Moffitt et al., 2001; Morash, 1986; Rowe et al., 1995; Shoemaker, 2000; Simons et al., 1980; Smith and Paternoster, 1987; Steffensmeier and Allan, 1996, 2000; Thornberry et al., 2003b; Wilson and Herrnstein, 1985.

8. *See* Agnew, 2008; Bartol and Bartol, 1986:120; Bennett et al., 2005; Berger, 1989; Broidy and Agnew, 1997; Gilligan and Attanucci, 1988; Hagan et al., 1979; Hagan et al., 1996; Heimer, 1996; Mears et al., 1998; Moffitt et al., 2001; Morash, 1983; Rowe et al., 1995; Rutter et al., 1998; Slaby and Guerra, 1988; Steffensmeier and Allan, 2000; Taylor, 1986; White et al., 1985.

9. *See* Burton et al., 1998; LaGrange and Silverman, 1999; Moffitt et al., 2001.

10. For further information on biological explanations of sex differences in offending, *see* Archer and McDaniel, 1995; Berkowitz, 1993; Blackburn, 1993; Denno, 1990; Fishbein, 2001; Olweus, 1986; Raine, 1993; Rowe, 2002; Rutter et al., 1998; Udry, 2000; Widom and Ames, 1988; Wilson and Herrnstein, 1985.

11. For overviews and selected studies in this area, *see* Agnew, 2008; Akers, 1998; Bartusch and Matsueda, 1996; Berger, 1989; Bottcher, 2001; Canter, 1982; Cernkovich and Giordano, 1987; Chesney-Lind and Shelden, 2004; Cloward and Piven, 1979; Daly, 1998; Daly and Chesney-Lind, 1988; Giordano, 1978; Giordano et al., 1986; Hagan et al., 1979; Hagan et al., 1996; Heidensohn, 2002; Heimer, 1995, 1996; Heimer et al., 2006; Hubbard and Pratt, 2002; Jensen and Eve, 1976;

ENDNOTES (continued)

Lanctot and Le Blanc, 2002; Mears et al., 1998; Moffitt et al., 2001; Morash, 1986; Rowe et al., 1995; Simons et al., 1980; Smith and Paternoster, 1987; Steffensmeier and Allan, 1996, 2000; Thornberry et al., 2003b; Warr, 2002; Wilson and Herrnstein, 1985.

12. *See* especially Agnew, 2008; Akers, 1998; Chappel et al., 2005; Heimer et al., 2006; Lanctot and Le Blanc, 2002; Moffitt et al., 2001; Rowe et al., 1995.

13. *See* note 12 above.

14. *See* Acoca, 1998; Agnew, 2008; Daly, 1992; Gilfus, 1992.

PART 4

The Control and Prevention of Delinquency

Now that we have examined the causes of delinquency (Chapters 6 through 18), we are in a good position to ask what can be done to control or reduce delinquency. At one level, the answer is rather simple. **Society can control delinquency by alleviating or eliminating the causes of delinquency.** For example, we know that family factors like parental rejection and poor parental supervision cause delinquency. Therefore, society can control delinquency by reducing parental rejection and improving parental supervision. We can also control delinquency by doing such things as reducing biological harms like head injury and lead exposure, helping juveniles perform better in school, and preventing juveniles from associating with delinquent peers and gang members. More generally, we can reduce delinquency by reducing strain, reducing the social learning of delinquency, increasing control, and reducing labeling. The key question, however, is: How do we accomplish these goals?

Chapters 19 through 25 examine the efforts of public and private agencies to control delinquency. **The focus is on the juvenile justice system: the police, juvenile courts, and juvenile correctional agencies (which run juvenile institutions and community-based programs).** These government agencies have the primary responsibility for controlling delinquency in our society. Chapter 20 focuses on the police, and Chapter 21 focuses on the juvenile courts and juvenile correctional agencies. I explore what these agencies are doing to control delinquency and how effective they are. Chapter 22 then examines whether these agencies discriminate against certain groups in their efforts to control delinquency. Although we want these agencies to do all they can to control delinquency, we also want them to do so in a way that is fair to everyone in our society.

Chapters 23 and 24 examine **four general strategies for controlling delinquency** that are employed by these agencies and other groups. Chapter 23 focuses on the "get-tough" strategies of deterrence and incapacitation. **Deterrence** tries to scare potential offenders from committing crimes by increasing the certainty and severity of punishment. **Incapacitation** tries to control delinquency by locking up serious offenders so they cannot commit crimes on the street. These strategies have received increased emphasis in recent years. Chapter 24 examines the strategies of rehabilitation and prevention. **Rehabilitation** tries to reform offenders, while **prevention** tries to stop individuals from becoming offenders by attacking the root causes of crime. In Chapter 25, the final chapter of the book, I attempt to synthesize the preceding material by describing what I think society should do to control delinquency.

Most efforts to control delinquency attempt to eliminate or alleviate the causes of delinquency. **Most commonly, they attempt to increase social control, especially direct control** (see Chapter 8). In particular, one of the major functions of the juvenile justice system today is to catch and punish juvenile offenders for their delinquent acts. The police focus on catching suspected juvenile offenders; the juvenile courts determine whether these suspected offenders have committed delinquent acts and, if so, what sanctions they will receive; and juvenile correctional agencies administer many of the sanctions, such as incarceration.

The juvenile justice system and other agencies also attempt to deal with many of the other causes of delinquency. For example, they sometimes attempt to increase other forms of social control, such as the juvenile's stake in conformity and internal control. And they sometimes attempt to reduce strain, labeling, and social learning of crime. In these areas, they often focus on many of the specific causes of delinquency examined in this text, such as those involving individual traits, the family, school, and peer groups. **The juvenile justice system, however, has come to focus on direct control in recent years,** although there are some signs that this is beginning to change.

The central theme in Chapters 20 through 25 is that **this focus on direct control is a mistake;** data suggest that efforts to exercise direct control over juveniles have only a moderate effect on delinquency at best. Efforts to deal with the other causes of delinquency will not eliminate delinquency, but data suggest that properly implemented efforts may result in a substantial reduction in delinquency. I argue that the **best approach to reducing delinquency is one that combines the careful use of direct controls with a serious effort to deal with the other causes of delinquency.**

But before I begin this examination of efforts to control delinquency, I must first address the question of how criminologists determine whether a given program or policy is effective in controlling delinquency.

CHAPTER 19

Policies and Programs

How Is It Determined
if a Policy or Program Is
Effective in Controlling
or Preventing Delinquency?

W e will be examining many programs and policies designed to control delinquency, and the central question we will be asking about these programs and policies is whether they are effective. But how does one go about determining whether a program is effective in controlling delinquency?

Judging effectiveness is an important issue. Politicians and others often claim that some program is or is not effective. They claim, for example, that trying juveniles as adults or placing them in boot camps is an effective way to reduce delinquency. Or they claim that many rehabilitation and prevention programs are ineffective and a waste of taxpayers' money. Much of what you hear, however, is wrong or has little basis in fact. You will be in a much better position to judge the accuracy of the claims you hear if you know the proper way to evaluate the effectiveness of a program. You will also have a more solid foundation on which to construct your own views about what society should and should not do to control delinquency.[1]

The Experimental Model for Determining Program Effectiveness

What is the best way to determine if a program is effective in reducing delinquency? The answer is a *randomized experiment.* As you may recall from Chapter 5, experiments involve doing something to a group of people and then observing the consequences. In evaluating program effectiveness, we place juveniles in a delinquency control or prevention program and observe the consequences. In particular, we observe whether participation in the program leads to a reduction in delinquency. But the experiment must have certain special features if it is to provide accurate information about the program's effectiveness. Let me describe these features and their importance with an example.

A criminologist develops a program designed to improve the school performance of juvenile offenders. A group of offenders then participate in the program. The criminologist measures the delinquency of these juveniles in the year before they enter the program and in the year after they complete the program. The criminologist discovers that these juveniles commit 50 percent fewer delinquent acts in the year after they complete the program. Can we conclude that the program is effective? (I should note that many program evaluations are like this. Researchers do a *before and after study,* examining levels of delinquency before and after juveniles participate in a program. If the juveniles experience a large drop in delinquency, the program is declared a success.)

In fact, we cannot safely claim that the program is effective. While the juvenile offenders may have reduced their delinquent behavior because of the program, they may have reduced their delinquency for other reasons as well. For example, perhaps most of the juveniles in the program were 16 and 17 years old. One of the things that criminologists know about delinquency is that it peaks around 16 and 17 and then declines as juveniles enter adulthood. So the reduction in delinquency detected by the criminologist may not be due to the program. Rather, the reduction may be due to the fact that the juveniles in the program were entering adulthood and maturing out of delinquency. These juveniles would have reduced their level of delinquency even if they had not participated in the program. To give another example, it may be that the police in the city where the program was run instituted a crackdown against local gangs about the time the program ended, so the reduction in delinquency may be due to this police crackdown rather than the program. Thus, simply comparing levels of delinquency before and after a program begins is not a good way to determine if a program is effective.

What should researchers and policy makers do? **How can they determine whether the reduction in delinquency is due to the program or to some other factor?** They can compare the delinquency levels of program participants to the delinquency levels of a roughly identical group of juveniles who did not participate in the program. The juveniles who participate in the program are called the *treatment group,* while the juveniles who do not participate in the program are called the *comparison group or control group.* The two groups of juveniles are roughly identical to one another, except that those in the treatment group participate in the program. If the juveniles in the treatment group experience a greater reduction in delinquency than those in the control group, it can only be because they participated in the program. It cannot be because they are older and more likely to mature out of delinquency, since the juveniles in both the treatment and control groups are roughly identical in terms of age. Nor can it be because the juveniles in the treatment group were subject to a police crackdown while those in the control group were not. Both groups of juveniles were subject to the same treatment by the police. The juveniles in the treatment and control groups differ in only one way: The juveniles in the treatment group participated in the program. So if these juveniles experience a greater reduction in delinquency, it can only be because they participated in the program. One can then say that the program is effective: It caused a reduction in delinquency.

A key question, however, is **how do researchers ensure that the juveniles in the treatment and control groups are roughly identical?** The best way to do this is through a procedure known as *random assignment.* Researchers start out with a single group of juveniles, and they randomly assign each juvenile to either the treatment group or the control group. For example, they flip a coin. If it comes up heads, the juvenile is in the treatment group. If it comes up tails, the juvenile is in the control group. If they are dealing with a fairly large group of juveniles, they can be reasonably confident that the juveniles in the two groups are roughly identical in terms of age, sex, class, race/ethnicity, prior levels of delinquency, and all other variables.

I should note that the juveniles randomly assigned to the control and treatment groups may or may not be a **random sample** of juveniles (see Chapter 5). In most cases, they are not a random sample. For example, they may be a group of juveniles who were referred to a particular juvenile court for serious offenses. The court may then randomly assign certain of these juveniles to participate in a new treatment program and others to go through normal court processing. But these juveniles do not constitute a random sample of all juveniles or even of juveniles in that particular locale. I'll return to this point shortly, because it points to a weakness in many experiments.

You now know the proper way to determine whether a program is effective in reducing delinquency. Let me summarize **the essential elements of a randomized experiment** (these elements are illustrated in Figure 19.1). You begin with a single group of juveniles. You randomly assign each juvenile to either the treatment group or the control group. The juveniles in the treatment group participate in the delinquency control program, while those in the control group do not. You may not do anything to the juveniles in the control group, which would allow you to compare the effectiveness of your program to "doing nothing." Or you may treat the juveniles in the control group the way that such juveniles

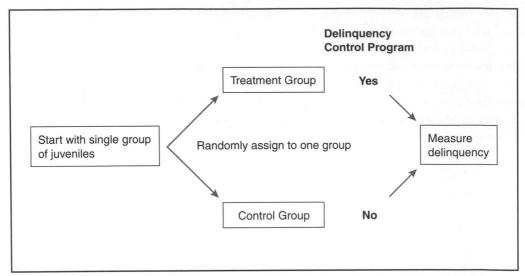

FIGURE 19.1 Essential Elements of Simple Randomized Experiment

are normally treated; for example you might place minor offenders on regular probation. This would allow you to compare the effectiveness of your program to probation. You measure the delinquency of the juveniles in both the treatment group and the control group before and after the program has begun. You then determine if those in the treatment group experienced a larger reduction in delinquency. If they have, you can conclude that the treatment or program was effective. (Since juveniles are randomly assigned to the treatment and control groups, you can assume that they are roughly identical in prior levels of delinquency. Many researchers therefore argue that it is only necessary to compare the delinquency levels of those in the treatment and control groups after the program has ended. If those in the treatment group have lower levels of delinquency than those in the control group, you can conclude that they experienced a larger reduction in delinquency— and that the treatment was effective.)

This model, then, allows criminologists to determine whether the program caused a reduction in delinquency. If you would like a challenging exercise, I invite you to stop reading and **describe how this experimental model meets the four conditions for making causal statements described in Chapter 5: association, association not due to chance, association not due to third variables, and correct causal order** (now is a good time to review the discussion in Chapter 5).

Let me begin with association. If those in the treatment group are lower in delinquency than those in the control group, it has been demonstrated that the treatment is associated with lower delinquency. This association may be due to chance, but a chance association is unlikely if the treatment and control groups are large and the difference between them in delinquency is large. As was the case with survey research, researchers can estimate the probability that the association is due to chance. The association may be due to a third variable, but that is quite unlikely if individuals are randomly assigned to the treatment and control groups. For example, suppose those in the treatment group are found to be lower in delinquency. Someone might claim that this difference is due to the third variable of age: Those in the treatment group are older and so are more likely to have matured out of delinquency. But if the researchers have used random assignment, they know that those in the treatment and control groups are roughly identical in terms of age and all other third variables. Any association they find, therefore, cannot have arisen because those in the treatment and control groups differ in terms of some third variable that causes delinquency. Finally, the experimental model is set up in such a way that researchers administer the treatment or program and then examine subsequent levels of delinquency, so causal order is not a problem: The treatment precedes any change in delinquency that might occur.

The Importance of Doing Randomized Experiments

Let me provide a real-life illustration of the importance of doing randomized experiments. Many communities place juvenile offenders in "Scared Straight" programs. The offenders usually visit a prison and hear a presentation by inmates about the horrors of prison life. They are often told that they will probably end up in prison if they continue their current behavior and that there is a good chance they will be raped and assaulted once in prison. Such programs try to deter or scare juvenile offenders from committing further crimes by making them aware of the severe sanctions that await them. These programs were popularized by the *Scared Straight* video that first aired in 1979, and they remain in wide use today. But are these programs effective at reducing delinquency?

Several studies tried to evaluate the effectiveness of these programs by determining whether the juvenile offenders who participated in them reduced their levels of offending. These before and after studies found that the offenders experienced substantial reductions in delinquency after the program had ended. In one study, offenders experienced a 52 percent reduction in delinquency. Based on these results, many people might conclude that Scared Straight programs are quite effective. Several researchers, however, evaluated Scared Straight programs using randomized experiments. And they found that the offenders in the control group—who did not participate in the Scared Straight programs—experienced reductions in delinquency that were as large as or larger than the program participants'. So the randomized experiments indicate that Scared Straight programs are **not** effective at reducing delinquency. In fact, some of these experiments suggest that offenders in Scared Straight programs are more likely to engage in subsequent delinquency than those in the control group (for overviews, see Finckenauer and Gavin, 1999; Petrosino et al., 2000). (Among other things, it has been argued that the offenders in the Scared Straight programs may have felt a need to engage in delinquent acts to demonstrate that they were not scared by the program.)

So it is important to properly evaluate programs; the failure to do so can lead to very misleading conclusions about the effectiveness of programs. The reason why the before and after evaluations of the Scared Straight programs showed reductions in delinquency is unclear, but researchers speculate that many of the Scared Straight participants were at an age where they were starting to mature out of delinquency. A before and after study is unable to take account of this alternative explanation for the reduction in offending. A randomized experiment, however, can take account of this alternative since the offenders in the experimental and control groups are of roughly the same age—making them equally likely to mature out of delinquency.

Given the results of the randomized experiments on Scared Straight programs, you might ask why such programs are still in wide use. **Unfortunately, program evaluations often have little effect on the extent to which a program is used** (see the discussion of Project DARE in Chapter 20 for another prominent example). Sometimes policy makers and people in the general public are not aware of the results of program evaluations. And in this area, criminologists need to do a better job of disseminating the results of their evaluations. But program evaluations often have little impact even when the results of the evaluations are known. There are a variety of reasons for this. Among other things, the effectiveness of certain programs seems self-evident to many people (e.g., if you threaten people with severe punishments, of course they are going to reduce their offending). So the program evaluations showing no effect are ignored or said to be flawed. And certain programs are supported by powerful groups—including the groups that sponsor the programs—making politicians reluctant to take action (for further discussion, see Weiss, 1998).

Problems in Doing Randomized Experiments

Criminologists often encounter difficulties when they attempt to conduct randomized experiments. Some of the more common difficulties are described in the paragraphs that follow.

The people responsible for randomly assigning juveniles to the treatment and control groups are often workers in the juvenile justice system, such as police, probation officers, and judges. **Sometimes these individuals violate the random assignment procedure.** A judge, for example, may refuse to assign someone to the control group because she feels that the juvenile is in desperate need of the treatment. As a consequence, criminologists cannot be sure that the juveniles in the treatment and control groups are roughly identical.

Many of the juveniles randomly assigned to the treatment and control groups may not complete the experiment. Some of the juveniles may drop out of or fail to successfully complete the treatment program. Or the researchers may not be able to locate many of the juveniles when they are collecting follow-up data on delinquency. As a result, the researchers cannot be sure that the juveniles who remain in the treatment and control groups are roughly identical. For example, many treatment programs are very demanding, and individuals with little motivation to change their behavior often drop out of them. The individuals who successfully complete such programs, then, may be those most motivated to change. If these individuals experience a greater reduction in delinquency than those in the control group, we do not know if it is because of the treatment or because they were more motivated to change to begin with.

Another problem involves the **measurement of delinquency. Delinquency is often measured in terms of arrest rates.** Program evaluations, for example, often report that those in the treatment group were less likely to be arrested during the follow-up period after the treatment ended. Arrest data, however, are not a very accurate measure of delinquency. It may be that those in the treatment group are less likely to be arrested, even though there is no difference in the true rates of delinquency between the treatment and control groups. For example, the police may be more likely to give juveniles in the treatment group a break because they run the program and have a vested interest in its success. On the other hand, those in the treatment group are sometimes more likely to be arrested, even though they are not more delinquent. For example, many delinquency control programs call for the close supervision of juveniles and include features like frequent home visits and random drug tests. Such features increase the likelihood that delinquent acts will be detected and juveniles will be arrested.

Yet another problem with randomized experiments was briefly mentioned above and involves **the issue of** *generalizability.* Researchers who evaluate a program almost never begin with a random sample of juveniles or juvenile offenders. Rather, they typically begin with a nonrepresentative group of juveniles in a single location. They might, for example, examine all minor offenders who are referred to a particular juvenile court. They might then find that the program they are evaluating is effective in reducing delinquency among these juveniles, but that is no guarantee that this program will be effective for other juveniles. It may not be effective for more serious offenders or for minor offenders in other locations. One cannot, then, necessarily generalize the results of a program evaluation to other juveniles or to other settings.

Other problems in running randomized experiments can be listed, but this short list is enough to let you know that evaluating a program is not as straightforward as it might seem. **Researchers sometimes take steps to deal with these problems.** For example, they try to ensure that random assignment proceeds as planned; they go to great lengths to prevent juveniles from leaving the experiment; they measure delinquency using self-report data and other methods such as drug testing; and they evaluate the same program with different groups of juveniles in different locations. Many researchers, however, do not take these sorts of steps; also, these steps are not always effective. For example, the juveniles in the treatment program may not be truthful when they are providing self-reports on their delinquency. As a result of these problems, it is often difficult to state with a high degree of certainty that a program is generally effective at reducing delinquency. Rather, researchers must state that a program is "promising" or that it shows "signs of success." **Some programs, however, have been the subject of a number of fairly rigorous evaluations, and criminologists are more confident about their effectiveness (or lack of effectiveness).**

What if One Is Not Able to Do a Randomized Experiment?

While randomized experiments are often difficult to carry out, they are the best way to determine whether a program is effective. However, it is not always possible to do a randomized experiment. Sometimes **ethical problems** present themselves. To illustrate, researchers have developed a number of programs that are designed to provide alternatives to imprisonment or incarceration. Intensive probation programs, which provide close supervision of juveniles in the community, are an example. Juvenile court judges, however, may feel that it is unethical to randomly send some juveniles to institutions and place others on intensive probation (see Weisburd, 2000). Sometimes the **problems are more practical in nature.** To illustrate, lawmakers may implement a particular policy that affects everyone in the community, such as a new law that increases the penalties for certain crimes. Random assignment is obviously not possible in this case. One cannot use random assignment procedures to decide that some people in the community are subject to the law and others are not.

Researchers usually deal with these situations by employing **nonrandomized experiments** of various types. For example, researchers may employ *nonequivalent control* *group designs.* Since they cannot randomly assign individuals to the treatment and control groups, they may attempt to deliberately create a control group that is similar to the treatment group. To illustrate, imagine a situation where a judge is unwilling to randomly assign people to prison or intensive probation. The researcher can examine the characteristics of the juveniles sent to prison and then attempt to find a similar group of juveniles who were placed on intensive probation. The researcher ideally attempts to **match** the two groups on all relevant variables that may affect subsequent delinquency, such as age and prior delinquency. The researcher can then compare the subsequent delinquency of the two groups. To give another illustration, imagine that a state passes a law increasing the penalties for certain crimes. The researcher may attempt to find a similar state that does not have such a law. The researcher can then compare trends in subsequent delinquency in the two states. This strategy, however, is often difficult to carry out in practice, and **one can never be sure that the treatment and control groups are roughly identical.** Perhaps they differ on some crucial variable that the researcher did not consider.

Another type of nonrandomized experiment is the *time series design.* The researcher periodically measures delinquency before the program or policy takes effect and then after the program or policy takes effect (so this is a type of before and after study). For example, monthly levels of delinquency in a community are measured before a new law takes effect and then after the new law takes effect. If there is a noticeable decrease in delinquency after the new law takes effect, that suggests the new law may be effective. However, **it is possible that the decrease in delinquency was due to factors that coincided with the introduction of the new law.** For example, perhaps the economy started to improve around the time the new law was introduced.

There are still other types of nonrandomized experiments. None of them are as good as randomized experiments, but they do provide us with some information about program effectiveness.

Why Are Some Programs Ineffective at Reducing Delinquency?

There are **two general reasons why researchers find some programs ineffective.** The first is that **the program does not work.** (In the chapters that follow, I mention several programs for controlling delinquency that do not appear to work, including some programs that are popular now.) The second reason is that **the program is not properly implemented.** It is often the case that programs are not carried out as planned. The program may not be delivered to the appropriate group of juveniles. It may be intended for serious offenders but instead be delivered to minor offenders. The services that should be provided by the program may not be provided. The juveniles in the program, for example, may receive less counseling or less supervision than they were supposed to receive. The staff may not be properly trained or committed to the program, so they do not render services in an appropriate manner. As a result of such possibilities, many researchers now do what are known as *implementation or process evaluations.* These evaluations are not designed to determine whether a program is effective in reducing delinquency. Rather, they are designed **to determine whether the program was properly implemented.** It is sometimes found that programs are not properly implemented, which may help explain why they are not effective in reducing delinquency.

An example illustrating the importance of implementation evaluations is found in Krisberg and Schumann (2000:153). They describe a randomized experiment conducted in the Salt Lake City juvenile court:

> For approximately two years, every youth the judges placed on probation was randomized into three groups. The first group was called "notification," which meant that the youths were told the rules of probation but never saw a probation officer again. They received nothing more than the admonition "Go forth and sin no more." The second group received essentially supervision services. They came in once a week and met with the probation officer who did whatever probation officers do. The last group got far more intensive supervision and treatment services. This was supposed to include all the things of which probation staff said, "If only we could do this with every kid, we would get wonderful results."

An evaluation revealed that there were no differences in subsequent delinquency between the groups. This finding was quite shocking to the court staff, because it suggested that just sending kids home and doing nothing yielded about the same results as treatment.

An implementation evaluation, however, helped make sense of these findings. The evaluation revealed that youths in the second and third groups did not receive much in the way of supervision or treatment. In particular, treatment services were limited to informal counseling and/or recreational programs, like camping trips. No educational, vocational, or drug and alcohol addiction services were provided. These findings led the juvenile court to develop better supervision and treatment programs and more carefully monitor the work of probation officers. Implementation evaluations, then, often suggest that programs may be ineffective because they were not delivered as intended.

Summary

You now know the proper way to determine whether a program or policy is effective in reducing delinquency. In actual practice, few program evaluations live up to the ideal model I have presented. Researchers conducting randomized experiments often encounter one or more of the problems I've mentioned. And many researchers find that it is not possible for them to do randomized experiments. Good program evaluations are nevertheless occasionally done, and there has been increased pressure in recent years to do such evaluations. A few programs have been the subject of several evaluations. These evaluations involve different types of juveniles in different locations, and they often complement one another in terms of their strengths and weaknesses. For example, some of the evaluations measure delinquency using arrest data, but others use self-report data or teacher and parental reports. If these evaluations are in general agreement with one another, one can safely conclude that the program is generally effective (or ineffective).

Teaching Aids

Some Challenges

The three challenges that follow are designed to cultivate your ability to apply the materials in this chapter and, in doing so, enable you to better evaluate the claims you hear about the effectiveness (or ineffectiveness) of programs and policies. (Answers to the challenges are given after the Key Terms.)

1. Your college likely has an individual or group that administers sanctions to students convicted of cheating or honor code violations. **Ideally,** how would you go about determining whether these sanctions reduce further cheating among the sanctioned students? **Realistically,** do you think it would be possible to carry out your ideal evaluation? If not, why not? Describe an alternative way of evaluating the effectiveness of the sanctions, a way that has a better chance of being adopted. Describe the disadvantages of this alternative (compared to a randomized experiment).

2. Ten thousand juveniles are arrested in City X. A random sample of 1,000 juveniles is drawn from this group and placed in a rehabilitation program. A series of follow-up studies indicate that only 30 percent of the juveniles in the rehabilitation program commit new offenses over the next several years. Can we conclude that the rehabilitation program is effective in reducing delinquency? If not, why not?

3. A researcher collects data from all juvenile courts in the United States. She finds that 30 percent of the juveniles placed on probation are arrested in the year after their probation ends, while 60 percent of the juveniles sent to institutions are arrested in the year after their release. Can we conclude that probation is more effective at reducing delinquency than placing juveniles in institutions? If not, why not?

TEST YOUR KNOWLEDGE OF THIS CHAPTER

1. What is an experiment?
2. Describe a before and after study or evaluation. Describe the major problem with such studies in determining program effectiveness.
3. Describe the essential features of a randomized experiment. Explain why it is important to randomly assign individuals to the treatment and control groups.
4. How does "random assignment" differ from selecting a "random sample"?
5. Why is it that program evaluations often have little effect on the extent to which programs are used?
6. List the major problems in doing randomized experiments.
7. What do I mean when I state that the results of an experiment may not be "generalizable"?
8. Why is it sometimes not possible to do randomized experiments when evaluating programs?
9. Describe the two major types of nonrandomized experiments (the "nonequivalent control group" design and the "time series" design). Describe the disadvantages of these designs (compared to randomized experiments).
10. What are the two major reasons that some programs are ineffective at reducing delinquency?
11. What is an "implementation" or "process" evaluation? Why is it important to do such evaluations?

THOUGHT AND DISCUSSION QUESTIONS

1. You are asked to evaluate the effectiveness of a new, after-school recreational program in preventing delinquency. Describe the ideal way to conduct such an evalua-

tion, listing the major steps you would take. Describe how you would evaluate this program using one of the alternatives to randomized experiments.

2. What can be done to increase the impact of program evaluations on policy makers?

KEY TERMS

- Randomized experiment
- Before and after study or evaluation
- Treatment group

- Control group or comparison group
- Random assignment
- Generalizability

- Nonequivalent control group design
- Time series design
- Implementation or process evaluation

Answers to Challenges

1. Ideally, we would evaluate the effectiveness of the sanctions by doing a randomized experiment. For example, we might ask the group that administers sanctions to flip a coin whenever someone is convicted of cheating. If the coin comes up heads, that person would be sanctioned in the traditional manner. If the coin comes up tails, that person would escape sanction. We could then determine if the sanctioned individuals are less likely to cheat in the following year (so we would have to exclude seniors from the experiment). Cheating would ideally be measured in several ways, including formal accusations of cheating by others and self-report data. Realistically, however, for ethical reasons it is unlikely that this experiment could be carried out. A more realistic alternative might involve an experiment employing the nonequivalent control group design. We could collect data on the characteristics of those students sanctioned for cheating, especially those characteristics that we think might influence their likelihood of subsequent cheating. The theories and research on the causes of delinquency can help us here, so we might collect data on their sex, GPA, prior history of cheating, career goals, beliefs regarding cheating, whether their friends cheat, and so on. We could then sample a large group of students at our college, asking them whether they had recently cheated and, if so, whether they had been sanctioned for it (the large majority of cheaters escape sanction). We would also collect data on the characteristics of these students. We could then try to match each sanctioned cheater to a nonsanctioned cheater. For example, suppose one of the sanctioned cheaters was a male, had a 2.5 GPA, had no prior history of cheating, and so on. We would try to find a nonsanctioned cheater with the same or similar characteristics. We could then determine whether the sanctioned cheaters were more or less likely to cheat in the future than the nonsanctioned cheaters (see Gold and Williams, 1969, for an example of a similar study). This design, however, has an important disadvantage. It would be difficult to match sanctioned and nonsanctioned cheaters on more than a few variables. Even if we could match them on all of the variables we thought caused cheating, there is still the chance that the sanctioned cheaters differ from the nonsanctioned cheaters in ways that influence the likelihood of future cheating.

2. We cannot conclude that the rehabilitation program is effective. This is an example of a before and after study. All of the 1,000 juveniles had committed offenses before participating in the rehabilitation program, but only 30 percent offended after participating in the program. The problem with this study is that there was no control group or group that did not participate in the rehabilitation program. (The term "random sample" may have thrown you off—remember that selecting a random sample is different than "random

assignment" to a treatment and control group.) As a consequence, it is impossible to determine whether the reduction in delinquency is due to the rehabilitation program or to some other factor. To properly evaluate this program, we should randomly assign some of the arrested juveniles to the rehabilitation program and randomly assign others to be treated in the traditional manner (e.g., placed on regular probation). We should then compare the rates of re-offending in the two groups. We may find that only 30 percent of the juveniles treated in the traditional manner commit new offenses over the next several years, suggesting that the rehabilitation program is not effective. Perhaps the juveniles in both groups reduced their levels of offending because they were maturing out of delinquency as they aged.

3. We cannot safely conclude that probation is more effective than placing juveniles in institutions. We do have a treatment group (those on probation) and a control or comparison group (those sent to institutions). But juveniles were not randomly assigned to each group. The juveniles in each group may differ from one another in ways that affect the likelihood of future offending. In particular, the juveniles placed on probation are probably less serious offenders than those sent to institutions, and this may be why they are less likely to be rearrested.

ENDNOTE

1. For a fuller discussion of evaluation research in the delinquency field, *see* Farrington and Welsh, 2007; Gartin, 1995; Kempf-Leonard, 1990; Krisberg and Schumann, 2000; MacKenzie, 2006; Sechrest and Rosenblatt, 1987; Sherman et al., 2002; Weisburd, 2000.

CHAPTER 20

The Police

What Do the Police Do to Control Delinquency?

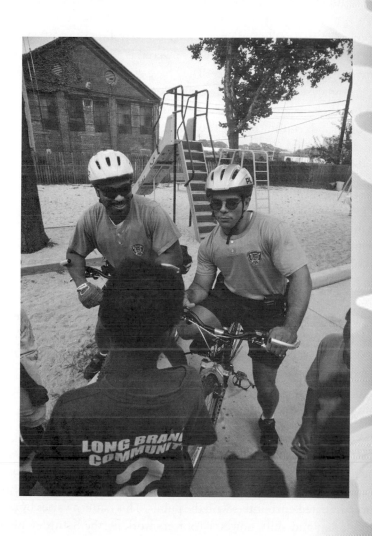

I begin this chapter with a discussion of how the police operate—that is, how they attempt to control delinquency. I then ask how effective the police are in controlling delinquency. Finally, I examine three strategies for improving police effectiveness. The first is hiring more police. The second two strategies call for changing what the police do to control delinquency. One strategy calls for an increased use of "police crackdowns," and the other calls for a greater emphasis on "community policing."[1]

How Do the Police Operate?

What image comes to mind when you think of the police? If you are like most people, your image of the police has been heavily influenced by the mass media and you think of the police as **crime fighters.** They spend most of their time dealing with crime, often serious crime. They cruise around in a patrol car, responding to calls for service and discovering crime on their own. They usually end up catching and arresting most offenders.

This image of the police as crime fighters, however, is partly mistaken. Criminologists have spent much time studying the police. They have ridden with the police, interviewed police officers, and analyzed police records such as logbooks. Some criminologists were police officers before they became criminologists. And a few criminologists have served as police officers for periods of time in order to better understand the police (see Skogan and Frydl, 2004, for an overview). The following points about how the police operate are based on such studies.

Preventive Patrol Is the Major Type of Policing

In *preventive patrol,* a uniformed police officer cruises an assigned beat in a marked patrol car. When the officer is not answering calls or engaged in other activities, he or she usually patrols the beat. It is felt that this patrol prevents crime, since potential offenders never know when a police car might appear. (Most police departments assign just one officer per car. This practice allows them to put more cars on the street, and studies suggest that one-person cars are about as safe and productive as two-person cars.)

Most juveniles who encounter the police deal with officers on preventive patrol. Most police departments, however, also have juvenile officers or divisions (Gaines, 2003; Reaves and Hickman, 2002b; Snyder and Sickmund, 2006). They conduct follow-up investigations on cases referred by patrol officers. They handle special youth problems—like gangs and school crime. And they may run prevention programs, like DARE (Drug Abuse Resistance Education) and police athletic leagues.

The Police Spend Only a Small Amount of Their Time Dealing with Crime

The police spend most of their shift cruising their beat, performing administrative tasks like filling out paperwork, and taking breaks. Less than half their time is spent answering calls or on officer-initiated encounters with the public. This pattern varies by police department, police beat, day, and shift, however (officers working the Saturday night shift in a high-crime beat in a major city may spend most of their time answering calls). Further, most calls to the police involve noncriminal matters, such as traffic accidents, medical emergencies, barking dogs, and disputes between neighbors. Finally, most of the calls they do get about criminal matters involve minor crimes. Several studies have found that, on average, **the police spend less than 20 percent of their time on crime-related matters.** Police often complain about this; many enter the job expecting to be crime fighters but find that most of their time is taken up with noncriminal matters. They often feel as if they function more as social workers than as "crime fighters."

The Police Are Primarily Reactive in Nature

The police usually do not discover crimes on their own. In fact, it is quite rare for a police officer to encounter a serious crime in progress. Rather, someone else calls the police and lets them know that a crime has occurred. Usually it is the victim who calls. The police, however, sometimes make special efforts to discover crime on their own, especially for certain "victimless" crimes such as drug crimes and prostitution. The police, for example, may put certain areas under surveillance or employ undercover agents to catch drug offenders or prostitutes. For the most part, however, the police are largely reactive in nature.

When the Police Do Discover or Hear About a Crime, They Usually Do Not Catch the Offender

As you may recall, only about 20 percent of all crimes known to the police result in arrest. This percentage varies by type of crime. The police are more likely to make an arrest for violent crimes than for property crimes. For example, 54 percent of all aggravated assaults and 41 percent of all rapes known to the police were cleared by arrest in 2006, while only 13 percent of all burglaries and 17 percent of all larcenies were cleared by arrest.

When the police do make an arrest, it is usually because they catch the offender at the scene or there is someone who can identify or help identify the offender. Violent crimes are more likely to result in arrest because the victims of violence almost always see the offender and often can identify him or her (most violence is committed by relatives, friends, and acquaintances). The victims of property crimes like burglary and larceny, however, rarely see the offender. Contrary to mass media accounts and popular views, diligent detective work plays no role or only a minor role in solving the large majority of crimes (Chaiken et al., 1977). If the police do not catch the offender at the scene or there is no one who can identify the offender, the crime will probably go unsolved.

The police recognize this problem, and they have tried to increase their speed in responding to crimes—particularly crimes in progress—with the hope of catching the offender at the scene. Unfortunately, such efforts have had only a small effect on arrest rates. The large majority of crime victims do not call the police until well after the crime is over, so response time makes little difference. The victim usually does not discover the crime until after it has occurred (e.g., you arrive home and discover your house has been burglarized). And in almost half the cases where the victim confronts the offender, the victim waits five minutes or longer after the crime is over before calling the police.

If the Police Do Catch the Offender, They Usually Do Not Arrest the Person

The police do not arrest all suspected offenders they encounter. In fact, only a **minority** of police encounters with suspected juvenile offenders result in arrest—even if the police have adequate legal grounds for making an arrest. Most suspected offenders are handled informally. The police, for example, may lecture the juvenile, call the juvenile's parents, and/or ask the juvenile to make restitution to the victim. But an arrest is not made. In some cases, the police may refer the juvenile to a social service agency or a diversion program (see Chapter 21). When the police do make an arrest, the juvenile is referred to juvenile court about 70 percent of the time (Snyder and Sickmund, 2006).

The *police* exercise much *discretion* in deciding whether to arrest suspected offenders. **The decision to arrest depends on several factors,** including the seriousness of the offense, whether the offender has a prior record, whether the complainant presses for arrest, the offender's demeanor or attitude, whether the offender's parents seem willing and able to help solve the problem, and the norms of the police department and community. Some police departments are more likely to handle matters informally than others (see Eitle et al., 2005; Skogan and Frydl, 2004; Wilson, 1976; also see Chappell et al., 2006), and communities differ in their views about how the police should respond to juvenile offenders. There is also some evidence that the age, race, class, and gender of suspected offenders influence the likelihood of arrest (see Chapter 22).

There are **several reasons why the police do not arrest all suspected offenders** (see Anderson and Newman, 1998, for a fuller discussion). The police and courts would soon be overwhelmed if all suspected offenders were arrested. The police often have a low opinion of the juvenile court, feeling that most offenders only get a "slap on the wrist"; they may therefore feel that arrest and referral would be useless and perhaps even waste their time with paperwork. Further, the police often feel that many offenders are best dealt with in an informal manner. They might encounter a juvenile who has committed a minor offense but otherwise seems like a "good kid." Rather than stigmatizing this juvenile with an arrest record, they handle the matter informally.

How Effective Is Preventive Patrol?

Most criminologists acknowledge that **the police are somewhat effective in controlling crime and delinquency.** In particular, they agree that the crime rate would increase if there were no police. Limited data support this conclusion. For example, when the police went on strike in Montreal in 1969, the hourly burglary rate rose by 13,000 percent and the hourly bank robbery rate rose by 50,000 percent (Sherman, 1995:331; Sherman and Eck, 2002). At the same time, criminologists believe that **preventive patrol is not the best policing strategy.** This belief stems from a series of studies evaluating preventive patrol (for excellent overviews, see Eck and Maguire, 2006; Skogan and Frydl, 2004). Most notably, studies suggest that assigning **more police** to preventive patrol has little or no effect on crime rates (see later discussion). Also, studies indicate that preventive patrol is less effective than many alternative policing strategies in reducing crime (discussed later).

How Can the Police Increase Their Effectiveness?

Several suggestions for increasing the effectiveness of the police have been offered. Some of these suggestions are designed to increase the ability of the police to catch offenders, thereby increasing direct control. Other suggestions are designed to increase the ability of the police to deal with other causes of crime (e.g., reducing strain or the social learning of crime, altering those situations conducive to crime).

Will Hiring More Police Reduce Delinquency?

One obvious suggestion for increasing police effectiveness is to hire more police. And a key provision of the 1994 Violent Crime Control and Law Enforcement Act provided funds to hire about 100,000 additional police, most of whom are now on the street (Worrall and Kovandzic, 2007). (Note: There are about 20,000 federal, state, and local law enforcement agencies in the United States, with about 15,000 of these at the local level. These local agencies employ about 450,000 police officers. Most of these officers are assigned to the patrol bureau, where they typically patrol a beat in a marked patrol car [see Skogan and Frydl, 2004].)

The effect on crime of hiring more police, however, has been very difficult to determine. You might think that all researchers would need to do is determine whether communities with more police per capita have lower crime rates. However, it is much more complicated than that. Researchers need to take account of "third variables" that may affect both the number of police and crime rates (see Chapter 5 for a discussion of third variables). Also, researchers have to take account of the fact that the number of police and crime rates may have **reciprocal effects** on one another. On the one hand, an increase in the number of police may reduce crime rates. On the other hand, an increase in crime rates may cause communities to hire more police. This latter causal effect probably explains why cities with more police per capita tend to have higher crime rates. Researchers, then, need to estimate these reciprocal effects. This is not easily done, even with longitudinal or over-time data (see Eck and Maguire, 2006:208–217, for an excellent discussion of this issue). A few studies, however, have made decent attempts to estimate these effects. The results of these studies are mixed, with most finding that increasing the number of police has little or no effect on crime rates (see Eck and Maguire, 2006, for an overview).[2]

At present, then, we must conclude that there is **no good evidence that increasing the number of police will reduce crime rates.** Researchers, however, argue that while increasing the number of police may not reduce crime, changing what the police do when they are on the street may make a difference. And two major proposals have been made in this area.

Will *Police Crackdowns* Reduce Delinquency?

Police resources are usually spread thin, even in the best of circumstances. As a consequence, many offenders may feel that they can commit crimes with little chance of police detection. Some police departments, however, have tried to increase the likelihood that they will detect crimes by focusing their resources on certain areas, or "hot spots," where crime is common and on certain types of crime. That is, **they "crack down" on the hot spots of crime or on selected types of crime.**[3]

Cracking down on the hot spots of crime. Many police departments try to put the most police where there is the most crime. They may assign more patrol cars to beats with the highest crime rates, or they may have more police working on Friday and Saturday nights, when crime is most likely. Such efforts at focused patrol, however, are somewhat crude because there is much variation in crime even within a high-crime area. Some sections of a high-crime area have little or no crime, while other sections—called *hot spots*—have much crime. Less than 3 percent of the addresses in a city produce more than half of all calls to the police (Sherman, 1995; Sherman and Weisburd, 1995). Some of these addresses may produce several hundred calls to the police each year. Further, crime is more likely to occur on certain days and certain times of the day at these addresses.

There have been several recent efforts to aggressively target these hot spots for crime.[4] Special computer programs have been developed to generate maps showing the location of these hot spots—as well as the days and times of the day when calls for service are most common in these areas. And the police have dramatically increased their presence at these hot spots. In some cases, they have saturated a particular area, doing such things as establishing mini-precincts, increasing patrols, setting up roadblocks, and mounting undercover operations. In 2002, for example, the Philadelphia Police Department stationed officers at 214 of the highest drug activity locations in the city, with an officer at each location 24 hours a day, seven days a week (Lawton et al., 2005). These police crackdowns attempt to increase the certainty and sometimes the severity of punishment. **Crackdowns, then, attempt to deter criminals from committing crime by increasing direct control.**

Data suggest that **such crackdowns are often effective at reducing crime,** although their effect is sometimes modest and short-lived.[5] After the crackdown has ended, crime gradually returns to its former level. One solution to this problem is for the police to crack down on all hot spots on a permanent basis, but they do not have the resources to do this. However, Sherman and his associates (Sherman, 1995; Sherman and Weisburd, 1995) have proposed another, more realistic solution to this problem. **The police should rotate their crackdowns in an unpredictable manner:** The police might crack down on one hot spot of crime for a period of time and then move on to another. But they return to the first hot spot before crime has returned to its former level. This rotating series of crackdowns allows the police to reduce crime in a large number of hot spots.

The Minneapolis Hot Spots Patrol Experiment tested this idea (Sherman and Weisburd, 1995). Researchers randomly selected 55 of 110 hot spots for this rotating series of crackdowns. Each hot spot was a small area that had generated a large number of police calls. The typical hot spot consisted of a group of attached buildings clustered around a street corner, with a few businesses like bars, restaurants, and convenience stores. On average, each hot spot generated 355 calls for service in the year before the experiment began, with most calls coming between 7 p.m. and 3 a.m. The hot spots that were part of the rotating crackdown were supposed to receive three hours of police presence per day, while the other hot spots were to be patrolled in the usual manner. This allocation did not always happen, but the police presence in the "crackdown" hot spots was generally much greater than in the other hot spots, usually by a factor of two or more. The police would visit the hot spots that were part of the crackdown several times each day, remaining for a few minutes to an hour or more each time. Sometimes they would just sit in their car; at other times they would get out and walk around. The increased police presence was associated with a modest reduction in crime, as measured by calls to the police and observer ratings of disorders like fights, drug sales, solicitation for prostitution, and playing loud music. Further, the reduction occurred not only when the police were present, but also when they were absent. This finding suggests that the police do not have to have a permanent presence in an area to reduce crime. **Periodic visits or crackdowns by the police may be an effective strategy for reducing crime.**

Do crackdowns displace crime from one area to another?

Some have argued that while crackdowns may reduce crime in particular locations, they do not reduce overall levels of crime. Rather, they simply displace crime from one location to another. For example, if the police increase their presence at a particular intersection, the drug dealers at that intersection may move to another intersection, and the overall level of drug dealing remains the same. There have been several efforts to determine if this argument is true. Researchers measure changes in the level of crime not only in the areas where crackdowns occur, but in surrounding areas as well. Such studies usually find no evidence that crime is displaced (Weisburd and Eck, 2004; Weisburd et al., 2006). There are several possible reasons for this. For example, some offenders state that it would take too much time and effort to reestablish their criminal activities at another location. Also, some state that they might get into conflicts with other offenders if they moved to another location. There is little evidence, then, that crackdowns result in the displacement of crime. In fact, some studies find that crackdowns in one area led to **declines** in crime in surrounding areas—even though there had been no crackdowns in these areas. One explanation for this is that many offenders **mistakenly** believe that the crackdowns include surrounding areas.

Cracking down on selected crimes.

In addition to focusing on hot spots of crime, the police will sometimes target particular crimes. For example, they may focus on drug crimes, drunken driving, prostitution, or juvenile gun violence. The police will intensify patrols and other police activities in the areas where these crimes are most likely to occur, and they will make a special effort to sanction or control individuals who commit these crimes, often but not always through arrest. Such crackdowns are often accompanied by media coverage, to help convey the message that the certainty and perhaps severity of punishment have increased.

One example of this strategy is the **crackdown on gun violence by youth gangs in Boston.**[6] Research indicated that a substantial number of the youth homicides in Boston were the result of gang members killing one another. Most of these gangs and gang members were well-known to the police and community organizations. The police delivered a clear message to these gangs and gang members: Stop the violence or face intensive police scrutiny. The police said they would saturate the areas in which the gangs congregated and did business, which would disrupt their drug markets, among other things. Severe restrictions would be placed on gang members on probation and parole, including bed checks and room searches. Also, gang members engaged in illegal activities, including disorderly acts like drinking in public, would be severely punished. The police backed up this promise on several occasions; a number of gang members were sentenced to long prison terms. The police did not have the resources to crack down on all gangs at once, but "like an old-West sheriff facing down a band of desperadoes with one bullet in his gun, direct communication with gangs allowed the [police] to say, 'We're ready, we're watching, we're waiting: Who wants to be next?'" (Kennedy, 1998:6). Data suggest that **the crackdown resulted in a substantial reduction in youth homicides in Boston** (Braga et al., 2001). Further, other cities have employed this strategy with success (McGarrell et al., 2006).

Another example of a police crackdown on selected types of crime has attracted much attention throughout the country. Kelling and his associates have argued that the police should **crack down on visible signs of "disorder" in a neighborhood,** such as aggressive panhandling, public drinking, rowdy teenagers hanging out on the street corner, and prostitution.[7] This disorderly behavior, although not serious in nature, inspires much fear in community residents. If this behavior goes unchecked, community residents become less likely to use public spaces like streets and parks. They interact less with one another and play a less active role in their community. Among other things, they become less likely to sanction deviance. Such signs of disorder, then, may lead to a breakdown in direct control at the community level. Further, these signs of disorder may encourage more serious crime by criminals. Criminals may assume that it is easier to get away with serious crime in communities that cannot keep minor crimes under control.

The police, then, are encouraged to crack down on minor signs of disorder. This approach is sometimes referred to as *zero-tolerance policing,* since even minor acts of crime are sanctioned. Kelling suggests several strategies for cracking down on minor crimes. Among other things, he says that it is easier to crack down on such crimes when the police are on foot patrol, which puts them in closer contact with minor offenders and allows them to develop a closer relationship with the noncriminal segment of the community. Several cities have followed Kelling's approach, most notably New York. Police were assigned to foot patrol in high-crime areas and told to crack down on all offenses, however minor. And the large reduction in crime that New York has experienced has been attributed by police officials to this crackdown, although others have offered alternative explanations.[8] Limited evidence, however, suggests that **this strategy may have a modest effect on crime— especially if focused on high-crime areas or hot spots.**[9]

It is important to note, however, that such crackdowns may lead to increases in abusive police behavior and strained relations with community residents unless carefully managed.[10] The likelihood of this occurring appears to be especially high in disadvantaged communities, where the relations between the police and community residents are already problematic. The police in New York and other cities are taking steps to deal with this problem. Such steps usually involve efforts to improve communication between the police and community residents, train the police to be more respectful, better monitor police behavior, and sanction the police for misbehavior (see Sherman, 2002). For example, the New York City Police Department recently launched an effort to reduce rude behavior among its members. A *New York Times* article titled "To Serve and Protect, but Politely" notes that the number of allegations of police misconduct increased 91 percent in the five-year period ending in 2006 (Lueck, 2007). The most common allegation claims that the police used curse words or rude gestures when addressing citizens. Other allegations are more serious, including the use of ethnic, racial, religious, or sexual slurs. The article goes on to state:

> The [New York City Police] department has started a new effort to make sure officers are, quite simply, more polite. It includes role playing—at one recent session, cadets had to deal with actors playing out an interracial dispute, and a transgender robbery victim who was becoming hysterical—and one new but simple tactic: officers are going to have to start introducing themselves to people on the street. (Leuck, 2007)

Such steps are important not only because they may prevent abuses of police power, but also because data suggest that people are more likely to obey the law when they believe the police are fair and treat others in a respectful manner (Carr et al., 2007; Kane, 2005; Sherman, 2002; Skogan and Frydl, 2004).

There is some evidence, then, that **police crackdowns focusing on hot spots or on particular types of crime may be effective in reducing crime,** although the effect is sometimes modest in size. However, not all crackdowns are effective.[11] Limited data suggest that crackdowns are most likely to be effective when the police are able to do the following: (1) identify the individuals or high-crime areas to be targeted; (2) clearly communicate to these individuals or the people in these areas that some or all illegal acts will not be tolerated; (3) adequately monitor the behavior of these individuals or the people in these areas; and (4) consistently punish illegal acts, with punishments being reasonably swift and meaningful.[12] The police, in short, need to do what effective parents do: state clear rules for behavior, adequately monitor behavior, and consistently sanction rule violations in an appropriate manner. These actions are certainly possible in many cases. Most cities have hot spots of crime and neighborhoods plagued by disorder. Further, the police in some cities can identify and monitor the individuals most likely to commit certain types of crime, such as homicide. But delinquency is less concentrated in some communities than others, making it more difficult to adequately monitor and sanction behavior. And certain types of delinquency—like drug use—are spread widely throughout the community, making crackdowns especially difficult. Nevertheless, properly implemented police crackdowns are a promising strategy for reducing at least some delinquency.

Will Community Policing Reduce Delinquency?

There is another major effort under way to transform the nature of policing, and this effort promises to fundamentally alter the nature of police work in the United States. Many researchers and policy makers are arguing that the police should move away from preventive patrol and employ a strategy known as *community policing.*[13] As an example, the 1994 Violent Crime Control and Law Enforcement Act mandated that all of the 100,000 new police hired be used for community policing. And the United States Department of Justice created a new agency—the Office of Community Oriented Policing Services (COPS)—to assist police departments in the move to community policing (see Zhao et al., 2002; http://www.cops.usdoj.gov). Data suggest that all police departments in large cities now employ community policing methods to varying degrees, although many departments only make limited efforts in this area.[14] As you will see, community policing is different from police crackdowns, although police crackdowns may sometimes emerge from community policing efforts.

What is community policing? The best way to answer this question is to review some of the problems of preventive patrol, because community policing was developed in response to these problems.

Problems of preventive patrol. Preventive patrol has been criticized for several reasons, including the following. First, preventive patrol **isolates the police from the communities they patrol.** Police officers spend much time in a patrol car cruising a large area. In some areas, they are rotated between beats on a regular basis. Rotation is done to prevent corruption; some departments feel that you can reduce corruption by preventing officers from developing close ties to the people they police. As a result, the officers are isolated from community residents. In fact, police officers often become suspicious of people in the larger community. And in some cases, particularly in minority communities, there may be tension or outright hostility between the police and many community residents. This tension is unfortunate, since residents are more likely to call the police if they know and trust them (see Kessler, 1999). As discussed in Chapter 2, only about 40 percent of all crimes are reported to the police. The police cannot do anything to solve crimes they do not know about. Residents can also function as good information sources, helping the police solve crimes and better understand the community problems that contribute to crime. Further, as indicated earlier, some evidence suggests that community residents are more likely to obey the law if they respect and are well treated by the police (Kane, 2005; Sherman, 1998, 2002; Sherman and Eck, 2002).

Second, preventive patrol **does not deal with the underlying causes of crime.** Officers on preventive patrol respond to one crime incident after another, with their typical mode of response being arrest or the threat of arrest (when they catch the offender). They rarely examine the underlying causes of those incidents and ask how such causes might be addressed. That is to say, they deal with the symptoms of the problem but not the underlying problem. For example, over the course of a few months, an officer might get several calls regarding burglaries at an apartment complex. The officer responds to each call in turn, and then resumes patrol. The officer never steps back and asks why this apartment complex has so many burglaries and what can be done about it.

Finally, preventive patrol **does not fully involve community residents in crime control efforts.** Community residents might be asked for information about specific crimes, but the police stress that the fight against crime should be left to the police. The police, however, have limited resources, and criminologists argue that any successful crime control program needs to involve community residents.

What is community policing? Community policing was designed to deal with the problems of preventive patrol. Community policing does not refer to one specific strategy or approach, such as the use of foot patrols. Rather, it encompasses a number of related approaches. At the most general level, community policing tries to do three things (or achieve three goals).

First, it tries to **foster closer ties between the police and community residents.** As indicated earlier, there are a number of advantages to such ties (although efforts must also be made to control police corruption). The police have tried to foster such ties in several ways. Most efforts involve: (1) assigning officers to the same community for long periods, so they identify with and become an integral part of the community; and (2) getting officers to spend less time in patrol cars and more time interacting with community residents. The officers may walk a beat,

especially in downtown areas or other densely packed locations. They may spend time on bicycles or motor scooters, where interaction with the public is easier. They may open storefront police stations in the community, where they are more accessible. They may visit community residents in their homes, going door-to-door. They may serve as substitute teachers in the school system. They may attend community meetings and get involved in community organizations, like the YMCA and Boys and Girls Clubs. They may set up their own community programs, like PAL, the Police Athletic League.

Second, community policing **attempts to solve the underlying problems that led to crime.** In some cases, special police officers or police units are charged with the task of dealing with the underlying causes of crime. The advocates of community policing, however, argue that regular officers should also be involved in this process. The officer who is assigned to a community on a day-to-day basis has a special advantage when it comes to understanding that community's problems and developing solutions to them. Most police officers usually have some time when they are not responding to calls or engaged in other tasks. They are encouraged to use this time to deal with the underlying causes of crime on their beat. In particular, they are often urged to engage in what is known as problem-oriented policing—discussed later—which provides a model for how one goes about dealing with the underlying causes of crime. The solutions they develop to these problems often involve efforts to increase direct control, but they sometimes involve efforts to increase other forms of social control, reduce the social learning of crime, reduce strain, or alter situations conducive to crime. The police, then, do not simply rely on arrest or the threat of arrest to control crime—they also explore other options for controlling crime.

Third, community policing attempts to **actively involve community residents in the fight against crime.** Such involvement might take the form of neighborhood watch programs, where community residents watch out for one another's homes and report suspicious activity to the police. It might also include participation in a range of crime prevention and control programs, such as recreational and mentoring programs. In one city, the police encouraged homeowners, apartment superintendents, landlords, and business owners in a number of crime hot spots to assume a greater role in crime control. In particular, the police provided these individuals with advice on what they could do to reduce crime in their immediate area, and they provided assistance when necessary. Among other things, individuals in these areas organized citizen patrols, participated in antidrug rallies, held community cleanup campaigns, and formed community groups to deal with various problems. The police assisted in a variety of ways; for example, they arranged for city inspectors to examine problem locations and enforce housing, fire, and safety codes. And they worked with legal authorities to bring suit against the owners of properties with drug problems. This increased citizen involvement in crime control led to a reduction in several types of crime (Mazerolle et al., 1998).

The proper implementation of community policing is not easy. Community policing generally requires more police, since the police are asked to do more. They not only respond to crime incidents, they also try to foster ties with community residents and attempt to deal with the underlying causes of crime. Many police have the time for such extra activities, but some do not (see Famega et al., 2005). Community policing also represents a major change in the police role, and many police are resistant to this change. Community police officers are sometimes referred to as the "grin and wave" squad, and they are often viewed more as social workers than as police. Further, many police administrators are resistant to community policing, since it means giving more responsibility to regular officers and community residents. Officers and residents play a central role in identifying and responding to community problems.

Nevertheless, community policing is becoming increasingly popular. Let me provide a few brief **examples.**

Problem-oriented policing (POP).

Problem-oriented policing (POP). Many police departments now employ problem-oriented policing (POP), which can be classified as a type of community policing. POP is designed to **deal with the underlying causes of crime,** and it encourages police officers to work with community residents and organizations in doing so. POP proceeds in four steps:

1. **Scanning:** The police are encouraged to identify problems in their community or across the entire city. These problems are groups of related crime incidents, and they might include such things as car thefts in a certain neighborhood, drug sales in an apartment complex, the robbery of tourists, or juveniles who repeatedly run away from home.

2. **Analysis:** The police analyze the problem, in the hope of understanding its causes and developing possible solutions. They collect information from a wide range of sources, including community residents, arrested offenders, and organizations that deal with the problem (e.g., social welfare agencies, the local housing authority, and religious institutions).

3. **Response:** The police decide on a solution to the problem and then implement it. The solution may or may not involve a police response. For example, they may decide to launch a police crackdown on drug sales in a particular community, or they may decide to set up a drug education program in the schools. The police often work with community residents, community organizations, and other government agencies in implementing the solution.

4. **Assessment:** The police evaluate the effectiveness of the solution. If it is not effective, they try other solutions.

As an illustration of POP, the residents of a quiet neighborhood in Newport News, Virginia, began to complain about groups of rowdy teenagers in their community on Friday and Saturday nights. While the teenagers were not violent, they played loud music and occasionally engaged in acts of vandalism. The police responded to a number of incidents involving these teenagers, but the problem persisted. Relations between the police, the teenagers, and community residents were deteriorating. The beat officer was asked to examine the underlying causes of this problem and propose a solution. He discovered that a roller-skating rink in the area was trying to increase business by offering lower rates and free bus service to the rink on Friday and Saturday nights. This offer attracted many teenagers to the rink from outside the community. Conversations with these teenagers revealed that there were not enough buses to take them home after the rink closed. As a consequence, the teenagers would walk home through the neighborhood, creating problems. The rink owner was informed of the problem, and he agreed to lease more buses to take the teenagers home. This action effectively ended the problem (see Trojanowicz et al., 1998:174).

Numerous other examples of POP are available, and most—though not all—have been effective in reducing crime.[15] I should note here that the Office of Community Oriented Policing Services (COPS) collects information about the problem-solving efforts of police departments across the country, as well as the results of such efforts. COPS then disseminates information on successful (and not so successful) efforts to deal with a range of problems. You can examine the guides that COPS provides to the police by going to their website (http://www.cops.usdoj.gov), clicking on Community Policing Topics, then Solving Crime Problems, then POP Guides (or just type "POP Guides" into the website search engine). These guides deal with various problems; titles include *Acquaintance Rape of College Students, Assaults in and Around Bars, Bullying in Schools, Loud Car Stereos,* and *Robbery at Automated Teller Machines (ATMs).* And for an excellent manual describing how to do problem-oriented policing, see *Crime Analysis for Problem Solvers in 60 Small Steps* by Clarke and Eck (2005), also available at the COPS website.

Drug Abuse Resistance Education (DARE) **program.** Another example of community policing is the Drug Abuse Resistance Education program (DARE). DARE did not emerge out of problem-oriented policing, but it does represent another effort of the police to work with the community in dealing with the underlying causes of crime (see Carter, 1995). The program was developed by the Los Angeles Police Department but has been adopted by police departments all over the country. In fact, police officers run this program in over half the school districts in the United States. The DARE program is presented to schoolchildren by a uniformed police officer and focuses on preventing drug abuse, violence, and gang affiliation. The full DARE program begins in kindergarten and continues through high school. The program tries to prevent delinquency in a number of ways. Among other things, it tries to build positive relations with the police, foster antidrug values, and teach kids to resist negative peer pressure. But despite these noble aims, evaluation studies suggest that the DARE program is not effective in reducing drug use (see Chapter 24).

Youth organizations. In yet another example of community policing, the police in many communities have become actively involved in youth organizations that try to prevent delinquency, such as the YMCA, Boys and Girls Clubs, and the Boy and Girl Scouts. Such organizations provide youths with supervised recreational opportunities and other services, like tutoring and mentoring. The police serve as advisers to these organizations; they participate in a variety of program activities; they help provide security in and around the youth centers; and they help recruit high-risk youth to participate in these organizations. In many cases, the police have started their own youth programs—such as PAL, the Police Athletic League. Data suggest that certain of these youth organizations may be effective at reducing delinquency (see Chaiken, 1998; Chapter 24).

Chicago Alternative Policing Strategy (CAPS). The entire patrol division in the city of Chicago moved toward a community policing model in 1995. This model is known as the Chicago Alternative Policing Strategy (CAPS). CAPS draws on several aspects of community policing. Patrol officers are organized into beats corresponding to local communities, with 9 or 10 officers and a sergeant permanently assigned to each beat. Officers are encouraged to interact with community residents and get to know their beat. Among other things, steps are taken to reduce the time that the beat officers spend responding to 911 calls, especially calls from outside their beat (many such calls are answered by free-roving rapid response units). And meetings are sometimes held between the police in each beat and community residents. Further, the police in each beat are trained in problem-oriented policing and encouraged to make use of this method. Committees composed of the police and prominent community citizens are sometimes formed to help identify problems in the beats and devise plans to address them, including plans that make use of citizens and community organizations. Also, the police are encouraged to call on other city agencies to address community problems, like cleaning up graffiti, razing abandoned buildings, and repairing broken streetlights. There have been some problems in implementing certain of these initiatives, but limited evaluation data suggest that the CAPS program has improved perceptions of the police and reduced certain types of crime (Skogan et al., 2002).

Still other examples of community policing could be provided (see the references in note 12). I encourage you to find out what your hometown police department is doing to implement community policing (you can probably do this by going to the website of your hometown police department).

Overall evaluation of community policing.

Does community policing work? Is it effective in reducing crime and delinquency? Many claims for its success have been made. Unfortunately, most community policing efforts have not yet been subject to rigorous evaluation. The limited data that now exist suggest that most community policing efforts are effective in reducing the fear of crime and in improving police-community relations, but not all efforts reduce crime and delinquency rates. Some do and some do not. As indicated earlier, for example, evaluations suggest that the DARE program does not reduce drug use (see Chapter 24). Likewise, neighborhood watch programs are generally not effective in reducing crime. Problem-oriented policing, however, appears to reduce crime in at least some circumstances. Certain efforts to establish closer ties to community residents—like door-to-door visits by the police—show some success at reducing crime. Certain of the youth organizations with which the police are affiliated show some success at reducing crime. Taken as a whole, there is reason to believe that **the community policing movement holds some promise for reducing crime.**[16] However, we need additional and more rigorous evaluations of community policing efforts. Such evaluations will shed further light on those types of community policing efforts that are and are not effective in reducing crime and delinquency.

Summary

Data suggest that society might lower delinquency rates somewhat by **changing what the police do when they are on the street.** In particular, police crackdowns focusing on hot spots and selected types of crime are often effective. Such crackdowns reduce crime by improving the ability of the police to monitor situations and individuals prone to crime and to sanction crime when it occurs. That is, these crackdowns increase direct control by the police. Likewise, certain community policing efforts are sometimes effective at reducing crime. At the most general level, community policing involves efforts to establish closer ties between the police and the community, to deal with the underlying causes of crime, and to better involve the community in crime control efforts. Community policing sometimes involves efforts to increase direct control (e.g., neighborhood watch programs) and sometimes involves efforts to address the other causes of crime (e.g., DARE). Criminologists are still in the process of determining which of the many specific types of community policing are most effective, although data are beginning to point to those community policing programs that do and do not work. Problem-oriented policing, in particular, appears to hold much promise as a crime control strategy.

Drawing on the previously cited research, certain researchers have recently argued that the most successful policing efforts do two things (Clark and Eck, 2005; Eck and Maguire, 2006; Weisburd and Eck, 2004). First, they **focus on a clearly identifiable crime problem,** such as crime at certain hot spots or a particular type of crime in a community. Second, they **employ a range of strategies to address this problem.** They do not rely solely on a single approach, such as arrest. Rather, they may also attempt to address certain of the underlying causes of the problem, such as strain or social learning, and to alter those situations conducive to crime.

Teaching Aids

Controversial Issue

Police crackdowns that target signs of disorder or minor street crimes have become popular in many cities, in large part because of the alleged success of such crackdowns in New York City. William Bratton, former New York City police chief who championed the use of such crackdowns, describes the reasoning behind them as follows:

> Reduce disorder and you WILL reduce crime. The strategy is sending a strong message to those who commit minor crimes that they will be held responsible for their acts. The message goes like this: behave in public spaces, or the police will take action. Police will also check you out to make sure you are not creating chronic problems or wanted for some other serious offense. Police will also question you about what you know about other neighborhood crime. (Quoted in Greene, 2000:317)

Some criminologists, however, argue that while zero-tolerance policing **may** reduce crime in the short term, it has a number of undesirable effects which **may** increase crime over the long term. Zero-tolerance policing may alienate community residents and reduce their respect for the police (thus reducing internal control). Zero-tolerance policing is often associated with aggressive police behavior, which may antagonize community residents (thus increasing strain), and zero-tolerance policing may discourage community residents from taking an active role in crime control (thus reducing direct control).

To illustrate, Jack R. Greene, a prominent police scholar, says the following about zero-tolerance policing:

> Under the zero-tolerance approach, the demand for order may result in a deterioration of law, particularly the lawfulness of the police. Moreover, there are concerns that the normative legitimacy of the police, particularly in minority neighborhoods, will be undermined when the police are seen primarily as a punitive force in society.
>
> Recent events in New York City involving police assaults on minority groups members and the torture of a Haitian immigrant have cast doubt on the efficacy of zero-tolerance policing, particularly the policing of minority communities. These events have been witnessed in several American cities, and in most instances they occur through aggressive police street tactics, not unlike the precipitous events of the urban riots documented by the Kerner Commission in the 1960s. . . .
>
> Zero-tolerance policing, while satisfying short-term interests in gaining order, may actually return the police and the community to a conflictual relationship. Just as important, zero-tolerance policing may be returning the community to a passive role in crime and order maintenance in favor of a more aggressive and active role on behalf of the police. (Greene, 2000:319–320)

Other criminologists acknowledge the potential problems with zero-tolerance policing, but claim that it may be of value if carefully implemented. Among other things, they argue, it should be focused on high-crime areas, and the police should take steps to treat suspected offenders and others in a fair and respectful manner (see Sherman, 2002, for further discussion).

Do you think that the police should employ zero-tolerance policing in high-crime communities? If so, what steps should they take to minimize the possible negative consequences described here?

TEST YOUR KNOWLEDGE OF THIS CHAPTER

1. List the major points made about how the police operate.
2. What is preventive patrol?
3. How do the police spend most of their time?
4. What do I mean when I say that the police are primarily "reactive" in nature?
5. Under what circumstances are the police most likely to catch offenders? Why is it that efforts to improve police response time have had little effect on the likelihood of catching offenders?
6. List any three of the factors that influence the likelihood that police will arrest the suspected offenders they catch.
7. What is one of the reasons why the police end up releasing (without arrest) most of the suspected offenders they catch?
8. Why do criminologists feel that the police are **somewhat** effective at controlling crime?
9. What major challenge have researchers faced when trying to determine whether hiring more police will reduce crime? What does the most recent evidence in this area indicate?
10. Describe the strategy of "police crackdowns." Indicate what it is that the police crack down on. What causes of crime do police crackdowns address?

11. It is difficult for the police to permanently crack down on all "hot spots" for crime. What alternative strategy do Sherman and associates suggest that the police pursue?

12. Describe the police crackdown in Boston, focusing on gun violence.

13. Police crackdowns do not appear to displace crime from one area to another. Why might this be the case?

14. Describe zero-tolerance policing.

15. What steps are the police taking to reduce abusive police behavior?

16. Under what conditions are police crackdowns most likely to be effective?

17. Community policing was developed to overcome the problems of preventive patrol. List the three major problems of preventive patrol.

18. List the three major goals of community policing (or the three things that community policing tries to do in order to overcome the problems of preventive patrol). Provide an example of how police departments have tried to achieve each of these goals (e.g., how police departments have tried to foster closer ties between the police and community residents).

19. What is problem-oriented policing (POP)? Describe the four steps in POP.

20. Describe any two community-policing initiatives other than POP (initiatives like DARE, CAPS, and youth organizations). Indicate why these initiatives are said to be examples of community policing.

21. Describe the evaluation research on community policing.

THOUGHT AND DISCUSSION QUESTIONS

1. How do you think an advocate of community policing would feel about the strategy of police crackdowns? (Ask yourself how police crackdowns relate to the three goals of community policing and whether community policing initiatives might result in police crackdowns.)

2. Most police departments have made efforts to implement community policing, but research suggests that such efforts often have only a minimal impact on police practices (that is, community policing is implemented in little more than name only). Why do you think many police departments resist moving toward the community-policing model?

3. Can you think of any other suggestions beyond those in this chapter for improving police effectiveness?

KEY TERMS

- Preventive patrol
- Police discretion in making arrests
- Police crackdowns
- Hot spots
- Zero-tolerance policing
- Community policing
- Problem-oriented policing (POP)
- Drug Abuse Resistance Education (DARE)
- Chicago Alternative Policing Strategy (CAPS)

ENDNOTES

1. For overviews and selected studies on the police, *see* Anderson and Newman, 1998; Brandl and Barlow, 1996; Chaiken, 1998; Cox and Conrad, 1996; Eck and Maguire, 2000, 2006; Eck and Spelman, 1987; Gaines and Cordner, 1999; Greene, 2000; Kappeler et al., 1996; Kelling, n.d., 1988; Kelling and Coles, 1996; MacDonald, 2002; Mastrofski, 2000; Messner et al., 2007; Moore et al., 1988; Muraskin, 1998; Petersilia, 1989; Rosenfeld et al., 2007; Sherman, 1998, 2002; Sherman and Eck, 2002; Skogan and Frydl, 2004; Trojanowicz et al., 1998; Walker, 1998; Weisburd and Eck, 2004; Worrall and Kovandzic, 2007; Zimring, 2007.

2. For overviews and selected studies, *see* Eck and Maguire, 2000, 2006; Greenberg et al., 1983; Kelling et al., 1974; Sherman and Eck, 2002; Skogan and Frydl, 2004; Weisburd and Eck, 2004; Worrall and Kovandzic, 2007; Zimring, 2007.

3. For overviews, *see* Braga et al., 1999; Cohen et al., 2003; Decker, 2003; Eck and Frydl, 2004; Eck and Maguire, 2000, 2006; Lawton et al., 2005; McGarrell et al., 2006; Scott, 2003; Sherman, 2002; Sherman and Eck, 2002; Weisburd and Eck, 2004; Weisburd et al., 2006; Willis et al., 2004.

4. For overviews and examples, *see* Braga et al., 1999; Cohen et al., 2003; Eck and Frydl, 2004; Eck and Maguire, 2006; Erez, 1995; Katz et al., 2001; Sherman, 1990, 2002; Sherman and Eck, 2002; Sherman and Weisburd, 1995; Weisburd and Eck, 2004; Weisburd et al., 2003; Weisburd et al., 2006.

5. *See* note 4 above.

6. *See* Braga et al., 2001; Kennedy, 1997, 1998; Kleiman, 1999; McGarrell et al., 2006; *also see* Decker, 2003, for similar crackdowns in other cities.

7. *See* Eck and Maguire, 2006; Greene, 2000; Katz et al., 2001; Kelling, 1988; Kelling and Coles, 1996; MacDonald, 2000; Messner et al., 2007; Rosenfeld et al., 2007; Skogan and Frydl, 2004; Taylor, 2001b; Wilson and Kelling, 1982.

8. *See* Eck and Maguire, 2000, 2006; Kelling and Coles, 1996; Messner et al., 2007; Rosenfeld et al., 2007; Sherman et al., 1998; Skogan and Frydl, 2004; Walker 1998:82.

9. *See* Braga et al., 1999; Eck and Maguire, 2006; Fritsch et al., 1999; Katz et al., 2001; MacDonald, 2002; Messner et al., 2007; Rosenfeld et al., 2007; Smith, 2001; Xu et al., 2005.

10. *See* Eck and Maguire, 2000, 2006; Greene, 2000; Kane, 2005; Scott, 2003; Sherman, 1998, 2002; Sherman and Eck, 2002; Stoutland, 2001.

11. *See* Cohen et al., 2003; Decker, 2003; Scott, 2003; Sherman and Eck, 2002.

12. *See* Cohen et al., 2003; Eck and Maguire, 2000; Kennedy, 1998; Kleiman, 1999; McGarrell et al., 2006; Sherman, 2002; Skogan and Frydl, 2004.

13. For overviews and selected studies on community policing, *see* Alpert and Piquero, 1998; Braga et al., 1999; Brown, 1989; Cordner, 1999; Eck and Frydl, 2004; Eck and Maguire, 2000, 2006; Eck and Spelman, 1987; Greene, 2000; Kelling and Coles, 1996; MacDonald, 2002; McEwen, 1994; Moore et al., 1988; National Institute of Justice, 1992; Sherman and Eck, 2002; Skogan, 2004; Spelman and Eck, 1987; Trojanowicz et al., 1998; Weisburd and Eck, 2004; Worrall and Kovandzic, 2007.

14. *See* Eck and Maguire, 2000, 2006; Engel and Worden, 2003; Famega et al., 2005; He et al., 2005; MacDonald, 2002; Pelfrey, 2004; Reaves and Hickman, 2002b; Skogan, 2004; Zhao et al., 2003.

15. *See* Braga et al., 1999; Clarke and Eck, 2005; Eck and Maguire, 2000, 2006; Eck and Spelman, 1987; Skogan, 2004; Skogan and Frydl, 2004; Spelman and Eck, 1987; Trojanowicz et al., 1998; Weisburd and Eck, 2004.

16. For overviews and examples of the evaluations of community policing, *see* Eck and Frydl, 2004; Eck and Maguire, 2000; Greene, 2000; MacDonald, 2002; Sherman and Eck, 2002; Skogan, 2004; Weisburd and Eck, 2004; Worrall and Kovandzic, 2007; Xu et al., 2005; Zhao et al., 2002.

CHAPTER 21

Juvenile Court and Corrections

What Do the Juvenile Court and Juvenile Correctional Agencies Do to Control Delinquency?

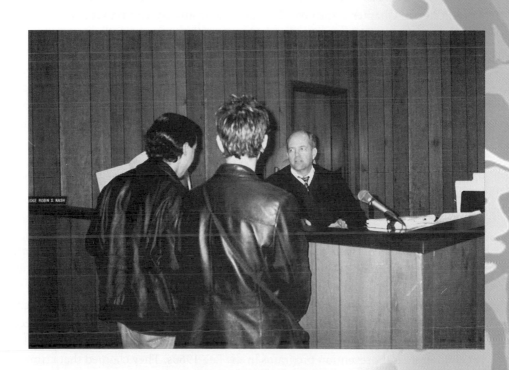

In this chapter, I first examine what happens when juveniles are sent to juvenile court. Next, I examine the ways in which the juvenile correctional system sanctions and attempts to reform juvenile offenders.[1] I also comment briefly on the effectiveness of these sanctioning and reform efforts. Chapters 22–25 also deal with the effectiveness of the juvenile court and correctional system—as well as efforts to increase the effectiveness of these agencies.

What Happens When Juveniles Are Sent to Juvenile Court?

This section examines the goals of the juvenile court; the number and types of cases handled by the juvenile court; and the major stages in the juvenile court process, beginning with the referral to juvenile court and finishing with the "disposition" or sentence that is given out by the juvenile court. Not all juvenile courts operate in the same manner, but this discussion should give you a general sense of what happens in juvenile court.

What Are the Major Goals of Juvenile Court?

As indicated in Chapter 1, the juvenile court was **originally set up to rehabilitate juveniles rather than to punish them.** It was felt that juveniles were not fully responsible for their behavior, including their delinquent behavior, so the court was set up to provide them with the guidance and assistance they needed to lead conventional lives. The court often failed to live up to this lofty goal in actual practice, but the major goal of the juvenile court was nevertheless rehabilitation rather than punishment. And rehabilitation was to be achieved by addressing many of the causes of delinquency examined earlier, such as family and school problems.

Rehabilitation is still an important goal of the juvenile court, but juvenile courts have also come to place an **increased emphasis on holding juveniles accountable for their offenses and punishing them.** Juvenile offenders, particularly serious offenders, are now more likely to be severely sanctioned for their offenses. The juvenile court, then, has started to place more emphasis on direct control, at least for serious offenders.

There are several reasons for this **shift in focus from rehabilitation to accountability and punishment.** First, a series of studies in the 1970s raised serious doubts about society's ability to rehabilitate delinquents (see Chapter 24 for more information). Second, doubts about the effectiveness of rehabilitation were also raised by the rapid increase in delinquency rates during the 1960s and early 1970s—as well as by the more recent increase in violent delinquency. Third, conservative politicians began to aggressively attack rehabilitation and prevention programs in the late 1960s. They claimed that crime and serious delinquency were not caused by social problems like poverty but rather were the result of deliberate choices by bad people. It was said that such people deserved punishment and that punishment was the most effective way to stop their crime. The criminal and juvenile justice systems were portrayed as "too lenient," and there were calls to "crack down" or "get tough" on crime. The conservative call to crack down on crime was aided by the extensive and often biased coverage of crime in the news media and entertainment industry (for excellent discussions of these issues, see Beckett and Sasson, 2000, and Garland, 2001).

How Many and What Types of Cases Are Handled by Juvenile Court?

There were about 1.7 million **delinquency** cases handled by juvenile courts in 2004—or 5.3 cases for every 100 juveniles age 10 and older who were eligible for juvenile court referral. This does not mean that 1.7 million different juveniles were handled by juvenile court. Many juveniles pass through the juvenile court more than once in a given year, and each visit is counted as a separate case (see Stahl et al., 2007, for statistics on juvenile court).

Almost 36 percent of the court cases were for **property crimes** like larceny-theft, burglary, vandalism, and motor vehicle theft. **Public order offenses** like disorderly conduct, weapons offenses, and obstruction of justice accounted for 28 percent of all cases. **Violent crimes** like homicide, rape, and assault accounted for 24 percent of all cases (more than half of these violent crimes involved simple assaults). And **drug offenses,** including sales and use, accounted for 12 percent of all cases. If we focus on specific offenses, the two most common crimes handled by juvenile courts are simple assault and larceny-theft—each accounting for about 17 percent of court cases.

About 73 percent of the delinquency cases were **males.** I should note, however, that the number of females handled by the juvenile court has increased 104 percent since 1985, compared to an increase of 30 percent for males. In 1985, females accounted for 19 percent of all delinquency cases handled by juvenile court, versus 27 percent in 2004. **Older juveniles** were much more likely to be processed by the court than younger juveniles, with 16- and 17-year-old juveniles having the highest rates of court processing. For example, 16- and 17-year-old juveniles had rates of court processing more than 25 times higher than 10-year-olds. **African Americans** had rates of court processing about 2.2 times higher than that of whites (3.0 times higher for violent crimes).

Juvenile courts *formally processed* about 159,000 *status offense* cases in 2004. It is estimated that only about one out of five status offense referrals is formally processed, so the number of status offense cases handled by the court is much higher. Most of these cases are handled informally or dismissed. Good data exist only for those status offense cases that were formally processed, however. These formally processed cases were for truancy (35 percent), underage liquor law violations (19 percent), ungovernability (being beyond the control of one's parents) (14 percent), running away (13 percent), curfew violations (10 percent), and other violations (9 percent). Males were involved in 56 percent of the status offense cases (versus 73 percent of the delinquency cases). Males accounted for about twice as many curfew and liquor law violations as females, and for slightly more than half of the truancy and ungovernability cases. Females, however, accounted for more than 6 out of 10 runaway cases. I will comment on the greater involvement of females in runaway cases in Chapter 22, when I discuss discrimination by the juvenile justice system.

What Are the Major Stages in the Juvenile Court Process?

Referral **to juvenile court.** The first step in the juvenile court process is referral to the juvenile court. Most youths are referred to the juvenile court by the police. In 2004, 81 percent of all **delinquency** cases handled by the court came from the police. (Only 50 percent of formally processed status offense cases were referred by the police, with schools and family members referring most of the rest.) Usually the arresting officer physically takes the juvenile to juvenile court or a juvenile detention center. The officer provides the court staff with a *complaint,* which describes the offense(s) the juvenile has committed.

The remaining 19 percent of the delinquency cases handled by the court were referred by parents, victims, school officials, probation officers, and others. For example, it is not uncommon for parents to go to juvenile court, claim that they cannot do anything to control their child, and fill out a complaint describing the offense(s) the child has committed. Also, probation officers will often file complaints against juveniles under their supervision, claiming that these juveniles have committed new offenses or have otherwise violated the conditions of their probation.

Intake screening.
Juveniles referred to juvenile court are screened by an *intake officer,* who is usually a probation officer associated with the court. The intake screening typically includes an interview with the juvenile and his or her parent(s) or guardians, although the police, victims, and others are sometimes interviewed as well. The main purpose of the intake screening is to gather information about the case and decide what to do with the juvenile. Should the case be dismissed, handled informally, or formally processed by the juvenile court? And if the case is to be formally processed, should the juvenile be released or held by the court while awaiting trial? The decision of the intake officer is often reviewed by a prosecuting attorney in the court.

The intake officer considers a number of factors about the case. How strong is the evidence against the juvenile; specifically, is there "probable cause" to believe that the juvenile committed the offense? How serious is the offense? Does the juvenile admit to the offense? Does the juvenile have a prior record? How old is the juvenile? Does the juvenile have a good or bad attitude? How is the juvenile doing in school? How strongly is the complainant pressing for action? How concerned are the parents, and what action have they taken or do they plan to take? In reaching a decision about what to do with the juvenile, the intake officer considers not only what the juvenile may have done (the offense) but also what the juvenile is like (the offender).

About 43 percent of the delinquency cases referred to juvenile courts were dismissed or handled informally in 2004, although this percentage varied greatly from court to court. Cases involving minor offenses are especially likely to be dismissed or handled informally, particularly if the juvenile does not have a prior record. And data suggest that the large majority of status offense cases are dismissed or handled informally. Cases are dismissed for a variety of reasons. For example, the evidence against the juvenile may be poor; the offense may be trivial; or the intake officer may feel that the situation is best dealt with by another agency, such as a social service agency. Usually, before a case is informally processed, the juvenile must admit to the offense. There is strong pressure to do so, since a failure to admit to the offense may result in formal processing, with the possibility of an official record and more severe sanctions.

Informal processing (or diversion).
Informally processed cases are dealt with in a number of ways. Most commonly, the juvenile is placed on **informal probation** for a brief period of time, say, ninety days. The juvenile is supervised in the community by a probation officer. The officer may provide some counseling to the juvenile, and the officer may require the juvenile to do such things as attend school on a regular basis, abide by a curfew, attend a drug treatment program, participate in family counseling, or make resti-

tution to the victim. Some informally processed offenders are not placed on informal probation but are nevertheless required to do things like apologize and make monetary restitution to the victim of their crime. If the juvenile successfully completes informal probation or meets the requirements of the court, the case is usually dismissed.

Many juvenile courts have set up *diversion programs* for informally processed offenders. Such programs offer services like individual and family counseling, mentoring, tutoring, drug treatment, and employment counseling (Lundman, 2001). These programs may be run by the court, community organizations, and/or volunteers in the community (with court supervision). The Office of Juvenile Justice and Delinquency Prevention is encouraging communities to create a single point of entry or Community Assessment Center where juveniles and their families can gain access to these programs. The Community Assessment Center would function as a "one-stop shop." Diverted youth would be sent to the center, where they would be evaluated and placed in those programs they need (see Dembo et al., 2004; Oldenettel and Wordes, 1999).

The purpose of diversion programs is to divert youth away from formal processing by the court so that they will not be stigmatized with a delinquent label. Diversion programs, then, partly derive from labeling theory. Such programs are also designed to save money, since it is usually cheaper to divert youth from the court than it is to formally process them. Further, diversion programs are said to free court staff to focus on more serious cases. Many of the youth diverted into these programs, however, would have been released by the court in the past rather than formally processed. So diversion programs often do not save as much money or staff time as expected.

Two examples of diversion programs are presented next:

Teen courts are becoming increasingly popular, with at least several hundred now in existence throughout the United States. Such courts are affiliated with juvenile courts, police departments, schools, and private agencies like the YMCA. Teen courts usually receive referrals from intake officers at juvenile courts, although they may also receive referrals from the police and school officials. Referred youth are typically first-time offenders charged with minor offenses like shoplifting, minor assault (fighting), disorderly conduct, and possession of alcohol. And these youth have usually admitted to their offenses. Teen courts, then, usually do not determine whether youth are guilty or innocent of the charged offense. Rather, teen courts hear the facts surrounding the offense and determine the disposition or sentence the youth will receive. Teen courts are run in a variety of ways, but in most cases an adult supervises courtroom activities and oversees the court. Teenagers, however, serve as lawyers and jurors. In particular, teenagers question the youth about the offense and teenagers on the jury determine the youth's disposition. Community service is the most common disposition, followed by victim apology, essays related to the offense, teen court jury duty, drug/alcohol classes, and monetary restitution. Part of the appeal of teen courts is the belief that many youth are more strongly influenced by their peers than by adult authority figures. Also, teen courts encourage youth to become more involved in crime control. Teen courts have not yet been well evaluated.[2]

YES (Youth Enhancement Services) is composed of a coalition of organizations in Harrisburg, Pennsylvania. YES was set up to reduce minority over-representation in the juvenile justice system, with the idea that many minority offenders would be diverted from formal court processing into the YES program. Participants in the YES program, then, are almost entirely minority group members; they are also predominantly male, and most have at least one prior arrest. They are referred to the YES program by intake officers, police officers, school officials, and parents. The YES program targets the known causes of delinquency, like individual, family, school, and peer problems. All participants in the program receive a variety of core services, including instruction in problem-solving skills and antiviolence training (partly designed to increase self-control), drug and alcohol prevention, assistance with schoolwork, and supervised recreational activities. They may also receive other services, like family counseling, the assignment of a mentor, and vocational training. Further, they may be required to participate in community service activities. Limited data (a nonequivalent control group design) suggest that participation in the program reduces subsequent offending. (see Lundman, 2001; Welsh, Jenkins, and Harris, 1999)

Overall, the evaluations of diversion programs have produced mixed results. Certain diversion programs do not appear to reduce subsequent offending. Other programs appear to reduce subsequent offending more than the alternatives of releasing or formally processing juveniles. The more effective programs seem to make a concerted effort to address the known causes of delinquency. However, it is important to note that many diversion programs—like teen courts—have not yet been properly evaluated.

Detention hearing. If the case is to be formally processed, the intake officer must also decide whether to release the juvenile to his or her parents or guardians or detain the juvenile while he or she is awaiting trial. If the intake officer decides to detain the juvenile, there must be a detention hearing within a short period of time (one to three days in most states). This hearing is held before a juvenile court judge and is designed to determine whether the juvenile should continue to be held in detention.

The judge considers whether there is probable cause to believe that the juvenile committed the offense and whether there is good reason to detain him or her. In particular, the judge asks whether the juvenile poses a threat to the community, whether the juvenile might flee if released, and whether the juvenile would be in any danger if released. (Note: The Supreme Court has ruled that juveniles do not have the right to be released on bail, although certain individual states grant juveniles that right.)

Detention facilities. If the judge decides that detention is warranted, the juvenile may be detained in a secure facility or detention center, which is like an adult jail. For example, juveniles are typically held in locked cells with bars on the windows. The conditions in these detention centers are often quite bad: Many centers are overcrowded; many have inadequate educational programs, health services, and/or treatment services; and many are plagued by violence (see Abt Associates, 1994; Acoca, 1998). A newspaper article reported the following about the detention centers in my home state of Georgia:

> A report issued last week by an independent monitor . . . examined the state's 32 juvenile detention facilities, which housed 33,888 inmates . . . and found that more than half the 105 citations the state agreed to fix two years ago are still incomplete. . . . The facilities lack necessary educational and mental health services and were severely overcrowded—some almost double their capacity; 7,864 incidents in juvenile facilities that could harm juvenile inmates, including the use of force by guards and youth-on-youth assaults, were reported in the first six months of this year . . . state records show that there are hundreds of suicide attempts inside the state's detention facilities each year. . . . The report shows that there are problems everywhere, but nowhere are the problems more severe than in Metro [in the Atlanta area], the largest short-term facility in the state with 217 youths. "You have to watch your back

at Metro, because there are boys in there that'll kill you over Oreo cookies," said [a detainee] . . . many of the children incarcerated at detention facilities—particularly at Metro—suffer serious physical and mental trauma inside. (Dyer, 2000:A10)

Some towns or cities lack juvenile detention centers, so juveniles may be detained in adult jails. Federal regulations require that such juveniles have no sight or sound contact with the adults in these jails.

Some juveniles may be detained in less secure facilities, such as group homes and foster homes, and some juveniles may be placed on home detention. They are required to remain at home, except for school, work, or emergencies. They are regularly visited by court staff, and they may be subject to electronic monitoring. That is, they may be fitted with an electronic wrist or ankle bracelet, which alerts authorities if they leave home. Given the problems that often exist at traditional detention centers, there has been some effort to foster the use of these alternatives and to reduce the use of detention.

Twenty-one percent of all delinquency cases referred to the court in 2004 resulted in detention. About 19 percent of whites and 25 percent of African Americans were detained. (I will discuss possible reasons for this difference shortly.) And about 22 percent of males and 17 percent of females were detained. A total of 341,300 juveniles were detained for delinquent offenses in 2004. And there were about 26,300 juveniles in detention on October 22, 2003—the date that the Office of Juvenile Justice and Delinquency Prevention conducted a census of juveniles in residential placement.

Status offense cases are much less likely to result in detention than delinquent cases, although some formally processed status offenders are detained. In 2004, 7 percent of formally processed status offense cases resulted in detention. Federal regulations strongly discourage the detention of status offenders, and there has been a dramatic decrease since the 1970s in the number of status offenders who are detained (although see the later discussion of status offenders and out-of-home placements).

Petition. If the case is going to be formally processed, the intake officer or prosecutor will prepare a formal petition. The *petition* describes the offense or offenses that brought the youth to juvenile court. The juvenile is often brought into court, read the charges in the formal petition, and told of his or her rights, such as the right to have an attorney. Most juveniles end up admitting to the charges in the petition, either at this initial hearing or at a later date.

Waiver. Some juvenile offenders have their cases waived or sent to adult criminal court. This is especially true of older juveniles who commit serious violent crimes and/or have long prior records. Waiver to adult court can occur in three major ways:

Judicial waiver. In 45 states, juvenile court judges can waive cases that meet certain criteria to adult court. The judge must hold a waiver hearing, with this hearing usually taking place after intake and petition. Guidelines usually limit waivers to juveniles above a certain age who are accused of certain offenses—like felonies or serious crimes. When deciding to waive a case, judges and prosecutors usually ask whether there is probable cause to believe that the juvenile has committed the offense and whether the juvenile is "amenable to treatment" by the juvenile court. That is, can the juvenile court help the juvenile? Among other things, they consider the juvenile's offense, prior record, prior dispositions or sentences, age, and the resources available to the juvenile court. They may conclude that the juvenile is not amenable to treatment if he or she has committed a number of previous offenses and has not responded to the previous treatment efforts of the court. Almost 10,000 cases, or about 1 percent of all formally processed cases, were judicially waived to adult court in 2004.

Prosecutor discretion (also known as concurrent jurisdiction and direct file). In 15 states, prosecutors are allowed to determine whether cases that meet certain criteria will be tried in juvenile or adult court. Typically, the cases involve older juveniles who commit certain serious crimes. Prosecutors decide where to try such cases at intake or shortly thereafter. No special hearing is required when prosecutor discretion is employed. We do not know how many cases are waived to adult court by prosecutors, although the number is believed to greatly exceed the number of judicial waivers in those states where prosecutor discretion exists.[3]

Statutory waiver. The state legislatures in 38 states have passed laws stating that certain juvenile offenders will automatically be sent to adult court. Typically, such laws state that the juveniles be above a certain age and be accused of certain serious offenses, usually violent offenses. In my home state of Georgia, for example, juveniles age 13 and above who commit one of the "seven deadly sins" are automatically sent to adult court. The seven deadly sins are murder, voluntary manslaughter, rape, aggravated sodomy, aggravated child molestation, aggravated sexual battery, and armed robbery committed with a firearm. Juveniles who commit one of these offenses are taken directly to the adult system by the police. Once more, it is not known how many cases are waived to adult court through statutory waiver. In certain states, however, the number of cases waived through statutory waiver far exceeds the number that are judicially waived.[4]

The most extreme form of statutory waiver requires that all "juveniles" of a certain age be tried in adult court. Wisconsin and New Hampshire, for example, passed laws in 1996 requiring that all 17-year-old offenders be tried in adult court (they had formerly been under the jurisdiction of the juvenile court). Ten other states exclude 17-year-olds from juvenile court jurisdiction, and two of these states also exclude 16-year-olds (New York and North Carolina). It is estimated that well over 100,000 16- and 17- year old offenders in these states have their cases tried in adult court each year.[5]

As will be discussed in Chapter 23, data suggest that trying juveniles in adult court does not deter them from further offending. In fact, data suggest that juveniles tried as adults are somewhat more likely to re-offend than comparable juveniles tried in juvenile court.[6]

Adjudication. Adjudication is the juvenile equivalent of an adult trial. It is a hearing before the juvenile court judge to determine whether the juvenile committed the offense(s) described in the petition. Most juveniles admit to the offense(s), so a full hearing is not necessary. Juveniles sometimes admit to the offense(s) as part of a plea bargain; that is, they admit to the offense in exchange for a reduction in sentence (e.g., probation instead of incarceration) and/or a reduction in charges (e.g., simple assault instead of aggravated assault). If it is determined that the juvenile committed the offense, the juvenile is **"adjudicated delinquent."** The juvenile is not found "guilty" of a specific offense. For example, juveniles are not found guilty of robbery or assault. Guilt implies that one is responsible for the offense and deserves punishment. Rather, juveniles are adjudicated delinquent. (States use the term "delinquent" for juveniles who have committed offenses that would be crimes if committed by adults. Juveniles who commit status offenses are usually referred to by such other terms as "Persons in Need of Supervision" or "Children in Need of Supervision.")

As discussed in Chapter 1, juvenile court hearings used to be relatively informal—very different from those held in adult court. In particular, juveniles had few *due process rights,* such as the right to an attorney and to present and cross-examine witnesses. Also, the standard of proof was lower in juvenile court than in adult court. Rather than "proof beyond a reasonable doubt," the juvenile court required only a "preponderance of evidence." The rationale behind these differences was that the juvenile court was set up to assist rather than punish the juvenile. Therefore, the legal protections available in adult court were not necessary.

These informal practices changed somewhat during the 1960s and 1970s, when a series of Supreme Court decisions extended several due process rights to juveniles, particularly at the adjudicatory stage. The Supreme Court essentially said that the juvenile court often does punish juveniles; for example, it often confines them in institutions that offer little in the way of treatment. Juveniles therefore should receive many of the same due process protections as adults. The most influential of these decisions was the *Gault decision* in 1967.

> Gerald Gault was a 15-year-old boy living in Arizona. In 1964, he and a friend called his neighbor, Ms. Cook, and asked her: "Do you give any?" "Are your cherries ripe today?" and "Do you have big bombers?" Gerald was arrested and tried in juvenile court. Among other things, Gerald never received notice of the charges against him, was not advised of his right to counsel, was not advised of his right to remain silent, and did not have the opportunity to confront and cross-examine Ms. Cook. The juvenile court judge adjudicated Gerald a delinquent and committed him to the State Industrial School for a period up to six years. If Gerald had been tried as an adult, the maximum penalty would have been a small fine and two months imprisonment. The Supreme Court considered Gerald's case and decided that he had been unjustly denied certain due process rights. In particular, the Supreme Court ruled that in adjudicatory hearings that might result in commitment to an institution, juveniles have (1) the right to notification of the charges against them, (2) the right to an attorney—with the state providing an attorney if the juvenile's family cannot afford one, (3) the right to confront and cross-examine witnesses, and (4) the right against self-incrimination (i.e., the right to remain silent).

Juveniles have been extended other due process rights by the Supreme Court, like the right to proof "beyond a reasonable doubt" (see Bernard, 1992, and Siegel et al., 2003, for overviews of the Supreme Court decisions affecting juveniles). Juvenile court hearings have become more formal, more like those in adult courts, as a result of these Supreme Court decisions.

Juveniles, however, still do not have all the due process rights available to adults. Most notably, they lack the right to a trial **by jury** (although certain individual states grant this right to juveniles). The Supreme Court recognized that there is still some difference between the goals of juvenile courts and those of adult courts, with the juvenile court focusing more on the rehabilitation of the child. It was felt that "juries would be highly disruptive of the informal, cooperative atmosphere in which everyone tried to find the child's best interests, and would tend to create an adversarial atmosphere in which each side attempted to win the case" (Bernard, 1992:125).

Furthermore, research suggests that some juvenile courts fail to provide juveniles with certain of the rights that have been granted to them; that juveniles often elect not to exercise their rights, often with the encouragement of court officials; and that the quality of legal representation for juveniles is often poor. An editorial in the *New York Times* stated:

> The American Bar Foundation, in new studies, has found that juvenile defendants have woefully inadequate representation. . . . Young defendants often lack lawyers at key stages, or meet them for the first time in court. The lawyers often have excessive caseloads and inadequate investigative resources. And many of the lawyers are not trained about alternatives to incarceration for their juvenile clients. (*New York Times*, 2003d)

In addition, while juvenile court proceedings have become more formal in recent years, they still remain less formal than criminal court proceedings. This point was made by Kupchik (2006), who observed several juvenile and adult criminal courts in the Northeast. Kupchik found that the lawyers and judges in juvenile court spend much less time on "legal housekeeping" matters, such as filing formal motions about the admissibility of evidence. Instead, they spend more time simply talking with one another about the juvenile, the juvenile's offense, and possible dispositions (sentences). And in talking with one another, they employ "a far more relaxed conversational style than in criminal court and recognize fewer formalized status distinctions between judge, prosecutor, and defense" (Kupchik, 2006:55). The juvenile court judge also encourages the juvenile and his or her parents to play an active role in the proceedings. The judge, for example, may ask the parents how the child behaves at home, may ask the child about problems at home and school, and may ask the juvenile and parents what they want to happen as a result of the case. So while the juvenile court has become more formal in recent years and juveniles have more due process rights, the juvenile court is still less formal than adult court and places less emphasis on due process rights.

About 67 percent of the cases that are formally processed result in an adjudication of delinquency. The remaining cases are dismissed or dealt with informally. For example, the judge will sometimes withhold adjudication and place a juvenile on informal probation or require that the juvenile make restitution to the victim. If the juvenile successfully completes probation or makes restitution, the judge does not adjudicate the juvenile a delinquent.

Social history or predisposition report. Once a juvenile is adjudicated delinquent, a probation officer will complete a social history or predisposition report on the juvenile. The report is designed to provide a detailed picture of the juvenile and his or her problems, and to suggest a supervision and treatment plan. The judge uses the report to decide what sentence or "disposition" to give the juvenile. The disposition is not simply designed to punish the juvenile for the offense that was committed. Rather, the disposition is also designed to deal with the problems that caused the juvenile to get into trouble with the law. The probation officer writing the social history will explore such things as the juvenile's family environment, school environment, peer relations, neighborhood, and prior history with the court. The juvenile may also undergo a psychological examination.

Risk and needs assessments. Increasingly, juvenile court staff are making use of risk and needs assessment instruments when deciding how to respond to adjudicated offenders. *Risk assessment instruments* attempt to predict which juveniles are most likely to commit offenses in the future. These instruments measure the juveniles' standing on a number of factors found to predict future offending in that particular court or in a sample of juvenile courts. Some of the factors commonly found to predict future offending include the following:

- prior court referral or adjudication at a young age
- prior record of offenses
- parental or sibling criminality
- victim of child abuse or neglect
- substance abuse
- prior out-of-home placements
- poor family relations and parental supervision
- running away
- school problems (low grades, poor attendance, behavioral problems)
- association with delinquent peers

(Note: The seriousness of the juvenile's offense is usually **not** a good predictor of future offending.)

Limited data suggest that there may be some differences in the predictors of offending between males and females, with abuse and running away having a stronger effect on female offending (Funk, 1999).

Based on their score on the risk assessment instrument, juveniles are said to be at low risk, medium risk, or high risk for future offending. The high-risk juveniles are then subject to greater supervision. For example, they may be required to meet with their probation officer twice a week—while the low-risk juveniles may be required to meet with their probation officer only once a month. The predictions made with risk assessment instruments are far from perfect, but they are more accurate than the predictions made by probation officers.[7]

Needs assessments instruments list those factors known to cause delinquency, like individual, family, school, and peer problems. Such instruments help the court staff develop a treatment plan for the juvenile by identifying those areas where the juvenile is most in need of assistance. There is, of course, some overlap between risk and needs assessment instruments—but there are some differences as well. Some of the predictors of future offending, like age at first court referral, are not major causes of delinquency (although they are associated with major causes of delinquency, like low self-control).

Risk and needs assessment instruments are said to improve the decisions made by the court staff, since the instruments take explicit account of the research on the causes and prediction of delinquency. Also, these instruments are said to increase the likelihood that juvenile offenders will be treated fairly. For example, risk assessment instruments increase the likelihood that the juvenile's level of supervision will be based on those factors known to predict future offending—and not on the personal feelings and possibly the prejudices of the court staff. Such instruments, however, do not eliminate input from the court staff—staff are typically given the option of modifying or overriding the recommendations derived from these instruments if they can make a compelling case for doing so. Given the advantages of such instruments, it is not surprising that they are starting to be employed at other stages of the court process. For example, these instruments (or variations of them) are sometimes used by intake officials to help determine whether juveniles should be formally or informally processed or whether they should be detained (see Mears and Kelly, 1999).

I have now described the major stages in the juvenile court process up to the preparation of the social history or predisposition report. The final stage is the disposition or sentence given to the juvenile, and that brings us to a consideration of the juvenile justice system.

Juvenile Corrections: What Happens to Juveniles Who Receive a Disposition or Sentence from the Court?

The judge has a number of sentencing or disposition options, ranging from a verbal reprimand of the juvenile to incarceration. In 2004, 63 percent of adjudicated delinquents were placed on probation, 22 percent were placed in out-of-home facilities, and 15 percent were subject to other sanctions, such as fines, community service, or treatment and counseling of various types (but no probation).

Regular Probation

The most commonly used sentencing option is formal *probation,* which involves the supervision and treatment of the juvenile in the community by a probation officer. More than three-fifths of all adjudicated delinquents were placed on formal probation in 2004. As indicated earlier, a large number of juveniles were also placed on informal probation. In particular, many of the juvenile offenders not formally processed by the court are placed on informal probation.

Juveniles placed on probation are asked to satisfy certain conditions. Such conditions may include reporting to their probation officer at regular intervals, attending school regularly, being home at a certain hour every day, and not associating with certain people. The juvenile may also be required to participate in certain treatment programs, such as counseling programs, drug treatment, and after-school programs that provide a range of services. The conditions of probation must be reasonable and relevant to the juvenile's offense.

Juveniles on probation meet with their probation officer anywhere from several times a week to once a month or less. The probation officers have two major functions or tasks (see Steiner et al., 2003, for information on the functions of probation officers). The first is to supervise the juveniles in their charge, making sure these juveniles do not commit new offenses or violate the conditions of their probation. If offenses or violations are detected, probation may be revoked and the juveniles may face more severe sanctions, such as being sent to an institution. The second function of probation officers is to assist the juveniles in their charge, helping them overcome the problems that contributed to their delinquency. Not surprisingly, many probation officers experience problems reconciling these two functions. On the one hand, they are expected to play the role of law enforcer, supervising juveniles and sanctioning them if they misbehave. On the other hand, they are expected to play the role of social worker, helping juveniles in need. Some probation officers deal with the tension between these roles by emphasizing one function over the other. So some probation officers act more like "tough cops," while others act more like "caring social workers."

Although probation is supposed to provide supervision and assistance in the community, probation officers often have heavy caseloads, and they frequently provide little supervision of or assistance to the juveniles in their charge. In many juvenile courts, regular probation often involves little more than doing nothing to the juvenile. It is therefore not surprising that regular probation does little to lower rates of re-offending (Lipsey, 1992; also see Kurlychek et al., 1999).

Intermediate Sanctions

Most juvenile courts have developed a range of *intermediate sanctions.* These sanctions are designed to provide more control and punishment than juveniles receive on regular probation, but they are less extreme and costly than confinement in an institution. These sanctions include restitution and fines, Scared Straight programs, and intensive supervision programs—often combined with home confinement, day treatment centers, and boot camps. Sometimes these sanctions are used along with probation, so juveniles will be placed on probation **and** subject to certain of these sanctions. Sometimes these sanctions are used in place of probation; for example, juveniles might simply be required to make restitution to their victims.

Restitution may be made directly to the crime victim, in the form of a monetary payment or—less commonly—work. Also, restitution may be made to the community, usually in the form of community service; for example, juveniles may clean up a public park or work in a nursing home. Restitution holds juveniles accountable for their offense(s) and allows them to pay back the victim or community for the harm they have caused.

Scared Straight programs typically involve a tour of an adult prison and a meeting with prison inmates. The inmates describe the horrors of prison life, including such things as homosexual rape and suicide. The students are told that they will eventually end up in prison if they continue on their current path, and they are urged to "go straight."

Intensive supervision programs (ISPs) are run by probation officers with small caseloads. Juveniles in ISPs are subject to frequent home visits and, in many programs, random drug tests. In some cases, juveniles may be confined to their homes except for school, emergencies, and possibly work. This confinement may be enforced through electronic monitoring. A tamper-proof strap with a transmitting device may be attached to the juvenile's wrist or ankle. The device signals a receiver if the juvenile leaves his or her home.

Day treatment centers are after-school facilities that provide educational, recreational, and treatment services. Juveniles report to the center after school and may receive tutoring, counseling, drug treatment, and other services.

Boot camp is perhaps the most extreme of the intermediate sanctions. Juveniles are usually sent to military-style boot camps for three to six months. The guards at such camps are like drill sergeants. They demand strict obedience from the juveniles under them. They secure such obedience by screaming at and otherwise intimidating these juveniles and by frequently imposing punishments like push-ups on them. The juveniles have their heads shaved, are given military-style fatigues, and are treated like military recruits. In particular, there is much emphasis on discipline, close order drill, physical exercise, and hard labor.

Although certain of these intermediate sanctions provide treatment to juveniles, most focus on control and punishment. These sanctions have proved reasonably popular. On the one hand, they satisfy the demand for the control and punishment of juvenile offenders, especially serious offenders. On the other, they are much cheaper than incarceration. It now costs about $40,000 a year, on average, to confine a juvenile offender. Intermediate sanctions cost only a fraction of that. Certain of these sanctions, in fact, were explicitly developed as alternatives to institutions, with the idea that they would save money and reduce overcrowding in institutions. So rather than sending an offender to an institution, a judge might place the offender in an intensive supervision program or in a boot camp. These sanctions, however, have not saved as much money as anticipated because they are frequently used for juveniles who otherwise would have been placed on regular probation.

Evaluations of these intermediate sanctions generally have not produced promising results. Some data suggest that fines and restitution do lower future offending, but only by a small amount. Scared Straight programs do not reduce future offending, and some data suggest that they may even increase offending (see Chapter 19). Most data suggest that intensive supervision programs have little effect on rates of re-offending. There are no good data on the effectiveness of day treatment programs. And data indicate that boot camps do not reduce future offending. My home state of Georgia, in fact, recently abandoned the use of boot camps for juveniles because of such evidence. Other states, however, continue to use boot camps.

At a general level, evaluation data suggest that programs that focus on punishing juveniles, scaring them, or controlling them are not effective at reducing offending. When these programs are combined with efforts to treat or rehabilitate juveniles, they do sometimes work. But simply getting tough is no more effective than traditional methods at reducing future rates of offending.[8] Chapter 23 discusses some of the reasons why such get-tough programs are not effective in reducing re-offending.

Out-of-Home Placements

In 2004, about 22 percent of adjudicated delinquents were placed out of their homes in residential facilities (see Sickmund, 2006; Stahl et al., 2007); that amounts to about 140,700 delinquents. These juveniles were placed in a range of public and private residential facilities, including group homes, wilderness programs, and training schools.

A census of juveniles in correctional facilities found that 70,300 delinquents and status offenders were serving sentences in juvenile correctional facilities on October 22, 2003. The census surveyed 1,170 public, 1,682 private, and 9 tribal facilities. Although there are more private than public facilities, most of the confined juveniles were in public facilities (which are larger, on average, than private facilities). The median length of time that juveniles had been in these institutions on the day of the census was between 3 1/2 and 4 months (half the juveniles had been in longer, and half shorter).

As indicated earlier, about 26,300 juveniles were being **detained** in juvenile facilities on October 22, 2003. So about 96,600 juveniles were serving sentences or being detained in juvenile correctional facilities on October 22, 2003. That amounts to about 3.1 juveniles for every 1,000 juveniles in the population (less than half the confinement rate for adults).

What offenses are juveniles confined for? According to the 2003 census, about 95 percent of juveniles serving sentences in correctional facilities were there for delinquent offenses. The remaining 5 percent were there for status offenses. About 23 percent of the juveniles were confined for serious violent crimes (homicide, sexual assault, robbery, aggravated assault). Juveniles were also confined for simple assault (8 percent), property crimes (28 percent), drug offenses (8 percent), public order offenses such as weapons and alcohol violations (8 percent), and violations of probation, parole, and court orders (15 percent). Contrary to the impression that many people hold, most confined juveniles are not being held for violent crimes.

The confinement of status offenders. Federal guidelines strongly discourage the confinement of status offenders. While these guidelines have been reasonably successful, some status offenders are nevertheless still confined (see Snyder and Sickmund, 2006:178). Further, juvenile courts will sometimes charge status offenders with minor criminal offenses, which allow confinement. For example, ungovernable children might be charged with simple assault if they threatened their parents at some point. Also, status offenders who violate the conditions of their probation can be charged with violation of probation, which allows confinement. For example, a truant may be placed on probation, with the requirement that he or she attend school on a regular basis. If the truant fails to attend school, he or she can then be charged with violation of probation and sent to an institution (see Bernard, 1992). In addition, many nonadjudicated delinquents and status offenders are placed out of home. The juveniles' parents, for example, may agree to voluntarily place them out of home in private facilities, including mental health facilities. In exchange, the court does not formally process the case, or it withholds adjudication. Many criminologists feel that such "voluntary" placements are becoming increasingly common—especially for females and status offenders (see Chesney-Lind and Shelden, 2004).

What are the demographic characteristics of confined juveniles? About 85 percent of all confined juveniles were male (see Sickmund, 2006). About 38 percent were African American, 38 percent were non-Hispanic whites, 19 percent were

Latino, 2 percent were Asian, and 2 percent were Native American. If we consider custody rates, we find that 7.5 African Americans are confined for every 1,000 African American juveniles, 5.0 Native Americans for every 1,000 Native American juveniles, 3.5 Latinos for every 1,000 Latino juveniles, 1.9 whites for every 1,000 white juveniles, and 1.1 Asians for every 1,000 Asian juveniles. African Americans, then, have the highest rate of confinement, more than twice that of Latinos and almost four times that of whites. Also, African Americans and Hispanics were more likely than whites to be confined in public facilities. Public facilities tend to be larger, more secure, more crowded, and less oriented to treatment than private facilities.

What are juvenile correctional facilities like? Juvenile correctional facilities tend to differ from adult prisons in several important ways (see Caeti et al., 2003; Kupchik, 2007; Snyder and Sickmund, 2006). Most notably, juvenile facilities place more emphasis on treatment and less on punishment and control. Juvenile facilities are also typically smaller than adult prisons and have lower staff-to-inmate ratios. It is important to emphasize, however, that juvenile facilities are not all alike; they differ from one another along a number of dimensions. Some are small, housing as few as 10 to 20 juveniles; others house several hundred juveniles. Some provide a moderate amount of freedom, with juveniles attending school in the community and having much freedom to move around the facility. Others are like adult prisons: they are surrounded by a fence, juveniles are held in secure cells, and the juvenile's movement about the institution is closely controlled. Some institutions place much emphasis on treatment, while others focus on the control and punishment of juveniles. Some are well run, while others suffer from a host of problems, such as overcrowding, violence, and inadequate educational, health, recreational, and treatment services. Unfortunately, data suggest that a large percentage of offenders are confined in overcrowded institutions that suffer from a range of problems.[9] For example, data from a 2002 census of juvenile facilities estimated that 36 percent of all confined juveniles were in overcrowded facilities (Snyder and Sickmund, 2006).

One type of juvenile facility is the *group home or halfway house.* These are usually nonsecure facilities that house a small number of juveniles. Group homes and halfway houses are quite similar to one another, except that juveniles are typically sent to a group home instead of a more secure institution, and they are sent to a halfway house after serving time in an institution. Their stay in the halfway house is designed to ease their transition back into the community. Juveniles live in the group home or halfway house, receiving counseling and other services. But they usually attend school in the community. The small size of the house often allows juveniles to build a close relationship with the staff. About 35 percent of the juvenile offenders who receive out-of-home placements are sent to group homes.

Wilderness or outdoor programs provide juveniles with physically challenging activities, such as rock climbing and ocean sailing. The juveniles are usually part of a small group; they learn to work together, follow directions, and overcome challenges that are designed to increase their coping skills and self-esteem (see Roberts, 1998, for an overview). Some wilderness programs last only a week or so, while others last more than a year, often involving outdoor work like maintaining and restoring wilderness areas. About 6 percent of those juveniles who receive out-of-home placements are sent to wilderness programs.

Training schools are most like adult prisons. (Training schools are called by different names in different states; in your state they may be called youth development centers, youth centers, reformatories, or the like.) Many are large, focus on security, do not offer sufficient treatment, and suffer from a host of other problems—including staff-on-inmate violence and inmate-on-inmate violence. The juveniles in such institutions often develop a subculture that discourages cooperation with the staff, encourages the exploitation of weaker inmates, and rewards toughness. Further, as indicated earlier, such institutions are expensive.

A recent study by Inderbitzin (2005) of a maximum security training school provides a rough sense of what many such institutions are like. According to Inderbitzin:

> The institution in this study is very much a juvenile prison. The perimeter of the campus is clearly defined by a tall fence with razor wire coiled around the top. Specialized security staff monitors the double-gated entrance and all movement within the walls. At the time of this study there were about 200 boys sentenced to this training school. . . . Based on his offense, each youth was assigned to a "cottage" living unit, which would be his home during his incarceration. The boys would attend school, work a job somewhere within the institution, go to recreation for one hour a day at the central gym, and eat their meals in the institution's main cafeteria, but each night they would return to their cottage. Cottages generally consisted of a common living room area where the boys would watch television and hold group meetings and counseling sessions; a small kitchen area where they could fix snacks; a game room which held a pool table and a video game; a small laundry room; a bathroom; and a hallway of sixteen locked rooms. While there was some freedom of movement within the common areas of cottages at designated times, the outside doors of the cottages were locked at all times and windows in the rooms had bars on them. (Inderbitzin, 2005:5)

Occasionally, the problems in certain training schools come to public light. A recent article in the *New York Times*, for example, focused on the problems in Mississippi's two training schools:

> [T]he schools are supposed to rehabilitate and treat children charged with misdeeds ranging from mischief to homicide. . . . [But] a 48-page report made public recently by investigators from the United State's Justice Department's civil rights division [paints] a bleak picture of the schools as debilitating dumping grounds for troubled children. Woefully underfinanced, understaffed and ill-equipped, the schools and their poorly trained workers dole out a volatile mix of physical and verbal abuse and mandatory Bible study, but withhold basic medical care and a decent education—all in violation of state and federal laws. . . . Boys and girls were routinely hogtied, shackled to poles or locked in restraint chairs for hours for minor infractions like talking in the cafeteria. . . . Boys and girls were choked, slapped, beaten and attacked with pepper spray. . . . Girls at Columbia [one of the training schools] who misbehaved or were on suicide watch were stripped naked and left in a windowless, stifling cinder-block cell, with nothing but the concrete floor to sleep on and a hole in the floor for a toilet. . . . Experts say that what is happening in Mississippi is by no means rare. Arizona, Arkansas, California, Georgia, Louisiana, Maryland, and South Dakota, among other states, have all had scandals in recent years over the abuse or deaths of children in juvenile lockups. (Halbfinger, 2003:A11)

About 44 percent of those juveniles who receive out-of-home placements are sent to training schools.

How do the institutional experiences of males and females compare? Most confined juveniles are male, and these males tend to be confined for somewhat different offenses than females. Males are much more likely than females to be confined for serious violent crimes: 25 percent of the institutionalized males are confined for such crimes versus 14 percent of the females. Females, on the other hand, are much more likely than males to be confined for status offenses: 14 percent of the institutionalized females are confined for such offenses versus 3 percent of the males. Females are also more likely to be confined for violations of probation or parole. As indicated earlier, probation violations are sometimes used as a device for confining status offenders (also see Chesney-Lind and Sheldon, 2004). These offense differences partly reflect the fact that males are much more likely than females to commit serious violent crimes, while males and females have similar rates of status offending. But, as discussed in Chapter 22, these differences may also reflect discriminatory treatment by criminal justice officials, with males being treated more seriously for violent offenses and females for certain status offenses.

Institutionalized males and females suffer from many of the same problems, although data suggest that the **females are more likely to have been the victims of abuse and to have run away from home.** This reflects one of the key points made about gender and delinquency in Chapter 18: Data suggest that abuse and running away from home play an especially important role in the generation of female delinquency, particularly serious delinquency. Females are more likely than males to be sexually abused and to run away from home to escape such abuse. Once on the street, female runaways experience further abuse and must often engage in income-generating crimes to survive (since they are too young to work and are wanted by the police). Unfortunately, confined females usually receive little help for these problems. In fact, they often experience further abuse when institutionalized (see Chesney-Lind and Shelden, 2004; also see Gaarder et al., 2004).

More generally, **treatment programs are less available in female than male institutions.** And many of the training programs available in female institutions tend to be "limited to traditional feminine options like cosmetology, home economics, and 'business education' (generally simple secretarial training)" (Chesney-Lind and Shelden, 2004). At

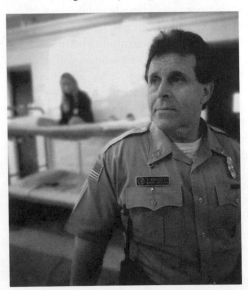

the same time, confined females face more restrictions on their behavior than do confined males, and staff make a greater effort to influence the sexual practices and peer associations of confined females. These differences reflect a greater desire to regulate the sexual behavior of females.

There is also some evidence that **males and females cope differently with confinement,** although the studies in this area are somewhat dated (see Chesney-Lind and Shelden, 2004). Females are more likely to form pseudo-family units whose members support one another. The members of these units may be involved in homosexual relationships with one another, although many are not. Confined males, however, are more likely to form gangs or cliques, whose primary functions are protection from others and the exploitation of others. Males are more likely to develop an *inmate subculture* or system of values that emphasizes the exploitation of weaker inmates and noncooperation with the staff. For example, one study reported that male inmates frequently subscribed to such values as "exploit whomever you can" and "don't play up to staff" (Bartollas et al., 1976). These differences may partly reflect differences in gender roles, with males placing more emphasis on toughness and females on caring for others. They may also reflect the fact that female inmates are more likely to come from families where they have been abused, which may create a stronger need for close bonds to others (see Chesney-Lind and Sheldon, 2004).

Female offenders, then, may have somewhat different problems than male offenders, but these problems are often neglected by correctional officials. Given these facts, **some criminologists argue that it is important to develop programs specifically geared toward the special needs and problems of females.** Several such programs have been developed, although most focus on at-risk females or females on probation (see Krisberg, 2005, for an overview). And the Office of Juvenile Justice and Delinquency Prevention recently formed the "Girls Study Group," made up of scholars and juvenile justice workers with special expertise in the area of female delinquency. This group is charged with identifying and promoting programs that will more effectively respond to female delinquency (their website is http://girlsstudygroup.rti.org).

How effective are juvenile facilities in reducing re-offending?

It should come as no surprise that evaluations suggest that sending juveniles to training schools is no more effective at reducing offending than many community-based alternatives. Some data, in fact, suggest that it may be easier to reduce re-offending in community-based programs than in institutions. Reflecting these data, juveniles released from training schools have re-offending rates ranging from 55 percent to 90 percent (Howell, 2003a:135; Snyder and Sickmund, 2006:234–235). The data on group homes are mixed; they reduce offending in some studies but not in others. Likewise, the data on wilderness programs are mixed. There is, however, some suggestion that those wilderness programs and group homes with a strong treatment component may be effective in reducing re-offending (Howell, 2003a; MacKenzie, 2006).

A number of individuals and groups have recommended that the justice system reduce or eliminate the use of training schools for juveniles (see Greenwood, 2002). They point to the problems and expense associated with such schools, and they argue that the juveniles in these schools can be better handled in other types of facilities or in the community. One study of 14 states found that 31 percent of the juveniles confined in secure facilities scored low on a risk assessment scale, designed to assess the test takers' likelihood of committing more delinquent acts (Krisberg and Howell, 1998). As a consequence, several states have moved away from the use of large, secure training schools. They have placed most of their confined offenders in smaller, more treatment-oriented facilities in the community. Massachusetts adopted such an approach in the 1970s, and states such as Pennsylvania, Vermont, Utah, Maryland, and Florida have followed suit. Most states, however, continue to confine substantial percentages of their adjudicated offenders in large, secure training schools.

Aftercare Services

Once juveniles are released from an institution, they sometimes receive "aftercare" services to ease their transition back into the community. *Aftercare* is similar to probation: The juvenile is supervised by someone associated with the juvenile justice system. The juvenile may also receive counseling and participate in special treatment programs. Aftercare services, however, are generally viewed as poor. The few evaluations of aftercare programs have produced mixed results, with some data suggesting that aftercare programs that combine supervision with treatment may reduce re-offending (Howell, 2003a; MacKenzie, 2002).

The Office of Juvenile Justice and Delinquency Prevention has helped develop and implement a model aftercare program in several jurisdictions, known as the Intensive Aftercare Program. This aftercare program has several components.[10]

1. It targets juveniles with a high risk for further offending (as determined by risk assessment instruments).

2. It develops an individual treatment plan for each juvenile, based on a careful evaluation of the juvenile's needs. This plan focuses on the known causes of offending, like individual, family, school, and peer factors. For example, depending on the juvenile's needs, the juvenile and his or her family may receive such things as anger management training, parent training, educational and vocational skills training, and substance abuse treatment (see Chapter 24 for further information). The treatment begins while the juvenile is still in the institution and continues after the juvenile's release into the community. The treatment program, then, draws on the resources of the correctional institution and a range of community agencies.

3. It closely supervises juveniles when they are released from institutions into the community. Initially, released juveniles may live in group homes, participate in day treatment programs, or be confined to their own homes except for school and emergencies. The level of supervision is gradually reduced if the juveniles abide by program requirements. For example, the juveniles may be released from home confinement after a period of time but may still be required to meet with parole officers on a regular basis and submit to random drug tests.

4. It sanctions inappropriate behavior and rewards progress in the program. Sanctions may include more restrictive curfews, community service, home confinement, and (in extreme cases) the revocation of parole and return to an institution. Rewards may include passes to movies and sporting events, gift certificates, and reductions in the level of supervision.

This aftercare program was implemented in three communities, and its effectiveness was recently evaluated (Wiebush et al., 2005). In particular, researchers randomly assigned juvenile offenders to either the Intensive Aftercare Program or a control group where traditional aftercare services were provided. The juveniles in the Intensive Aftercare Program did **not** have lower rates of re-offending. The researchers, however, point out that there were some problems in fully implementing the Intensive Aftercare Program, and so it should not be dismissed as ineffective. Rather, there should be additional efforts to refine, properly implement, and evaluate the program. The evaluators provide several suggestions in these areas.

An Overview of the Juvenile Justice Process

Figure 21.1 provides an overview of the juvenile justice process (Stahl et al., 2007:57). Looking at the process as a whole, one finds that for every 1,000 delinquency cases referred to juvenile court, 566 are formally processed (have a petition filed). Many of the nonpetitioned cases, however, are placed on informal probation or receive other sanctions. Of the 566 formally processed cases, 379 are adjudicated delinquent, and of these, 237 are placed on probation, 85 are placed out of home, and 57 receive other sanctions (but no probation). Some of the juveniles on probation and some who receive "other sanctions" are subject to the intermediate sanctions listed earlier. If you do the appropriate math, you will find that about 9 percent of the delinquency cases referred to juvenile court are placed out of home. Another 29 percent receive other formal sanctions or treatment, including probation, fines, and/or restitution. Many others are informally sanctioned and/or treated.

I briefly commented on the effectiveness of the juvenile court and correctional agencies in controlling delinquency. In particular, I noted that a number of sanctions do not seem to reduce re-offending; such sanctions include waiving juveniles to adult court; regular probation; intermediate sanctions that focus on punishing, controlling, or scaring juveniles; and placing juveniles in large, secure training schools. The evidence on the effectiveness of other sanctions is mixed or lacking. Studies, however, suggest that sanctions with a strong treatment component are effective in reducing re-offending. I elaborate on these points in the following chapters and ask what the juvenile court and juvenile correctional agencies can do to more effectively control delinquency.

Chapter 23 examines the argument that the juvenile court and correctional system need to "get tough" with offenders, especially serious juvenile offenders. That is, the justice

FIGURE 21.1 Overview of the Juvenile Justice Process
SOURCE: Stahl et al., 2007.

system needs to start punishing more offenders and start punishing them more severely. Chapter 24 examines the argument that the juvenile justice system needs to place more emphasis on the rehabilitation of offenders and the prevention of delinquency. One of the central themes in these chapters is the ongoing debate between those who favor getting tougher with juvenile offenders (i.e., increasing direct control by the justice system) and those who favor placing more emphasis on rehabilitation and prevention (i.e., addressing the varied causes of delinquency described in Chapters 6 through 18). Thomas Bernard (1992) points out in *The Cycle of Juvenile Justice* that the juvenile justice system cycles back and forth between an emphasis on punishing juveniles and an emphasis on rehabilitating them. The focus right now is punishing juveniles more severely, but there are signs that this is beginning to change. Chapter 25, the concluding chapter of the book, argues for a middle ground, one that emphasizes the **smart** use of sanctions, especially for serious offenders, **and** an emphasis on those prevention and rehabilitation programs that **have shown themselves to be effective.**

Before I address these topics, I need to address the critical issue of whether the juvenile justice system treats the juveniles who come before it in a fair manner. In particular, does the juvenile justice system discriminate against certain groups, and, if so, what can be done to reduce such discrimination? Chapter 22 focuses on these questions.

Teaching Aids

Controversial Issue

The central issue facing the juvenile justice system today is whether to respond to delinquency through tougher punishments, through an increased emphasis on rehabilitation and prevention, or through some combination of the two. In recent years, the justice system has focused on getting tough with offenders.

The position one adopts depends, in part, on how one views offenders. Consider the following quotes from former presidents Ronald Reagan and Bill Clinton. The sentiments in the Reagan quote helped propel the crackdown on crime and delinquency that began in the 1970s, while Clinton's quote suggests a different approach to controlling crime. To what extent do you agree with each quote? Justify your response. (I will consider the different approaches to controlling crime and delinquency in some detail in Chapters 23 through 25.)

> Choosing a career in crime is not the result of poverty or an unhappy childhood or of a misunderstood adolescence; it is the result of a conscious, willful choice made by some who consider themselves above the law, who seek to exploit the hard work and, sometimes, the very lives of their fellow citizens. . . . The crime epidemic threat is [not] some inevitable sociological phenomenon. . . . It is, instead, a cumulative result of too much emphasis on the protection of the rights of the accused and too little concern for our government's responsibility to protect the lives, homes, and rights of our law-abiding citizens. . . . [T]he criminal element now calculates that crime really does pay. (Former president **Reagan,** quoted in Beckett and Sasson, 2000:61–62)

> We have to rebuild families and communities in this country. We've got to take more responsibility for these little kids before they grow up and start shooting each other. I know the budget is tight, but I'm telling you, we have got to deal with family, community and education, and find jobs for members of society's underclass to bring structure to their lives. (Former president **Clinton,** quoted in Beckett and Sasson, 2000:70)

TEST YOUR KNOWLEDGE OF THIS CHAPTER

1. Describe the major goals of juvenile court. Indicate how these goals have changed over time and why.

2. Provide a brief overview of the number and types of cases (e.g., property crime, violent crime) handled by juvenile court. Describe the sociodemographic characteristics of those individuals who have the highest rates of court referral.

3. List and briefly describe the major stages in the juvenile court process, from referral to disposition.

4. What are the major purposes of intake screening?

5. How are informally processed cases dealt with? What are diversion programs and the alleged advantages of such programs? Why is it that diversion programs do not save as much money or staff time as expected?

6. Describe how a typical teen court works, from the referral of cases to sentencing. What do you think are the advantages and disadvantages of teen courts (e.g., do you think teen courts reduce labeling, increase control, and so on)?

7. Describe the evaluation data on diversion programs.

8. What is a petition?

9. Describe the three major ways of waiving cases to adult courts and their relative frequency of use.

10. What is the purpose of adjudicatory hearings?

11. What major due process rights were granted in the *Gault* decision?

12. Why has the Supreme Court **not** granted juveniles the right to **jury** trials?

13. What is a social history or predisposition report?

14. What do risk and needs assessment instruments try to do? What are their advantages?

15. List and briefly describe the major dispositions or sentences received by adjudicated delinquents and their relative frequency of use.

16. What happens to juveniles placed on probation? What are the two major functions of probation officers? What does the evaluation data say about the effectiveness of probation?

17. What are intermediate sanctions? List and briefly describe the major intermediate sanctions. What do the evaluation data say about the effectiveness of intermediate sanctions?

18. For what types of offenses are juveniles confined? Describe the sociodemographic characteristics of juveniles with high rates of confinement.

19. How is it that many status offenders are still confined?

20. List and briefly describe the major types of juvenile correctional facilities.

21. How do the institutional experiences of females differ from those of males?

22. Describe the evaluation data on the effectiveness of juvenile correctional facilities.

23. What is juvenile aftercare? Briefly describe the model aftercare program developed by the Office of Juvenile Justice and Delinquency Prevention.

THOUGHT AND DISCUSSION QUESTIONS

1. Do you think that offenders in juvenile court should have the same due process rights as those in adult court, including the right to trial by jury? Justify your response.

2. Why do you think that large, secure training schools fail to reduce offending (compared to the alternatives like community treatment)?

3. More generally, why do you think attempts to control or punish juveniles are not very effective at reducing offending? (This issue is discussed further in Chapter 23.)

4. What criteria or standards should be used in determining whether to employ a particular sanction or treatment program? (One obvious criteria is the effectiveness of the program, but also consider other criteria, like the relative cost of the program.)

KEY TERMS

- Referral
- Complaint
- Intake screening
- Intake officer
- Informal processing
- Diversion programs
- Teen courts
- Detention hearing
- Petition
- Judicial waiver
- Prosecutor discretion
- Statutory waiver

- Adjudication
- Due process rights
- *Gault* decision
- Social history or predisposition report
- Risk and needs assessments
- Risk and needs assessment instruments
- Probation
- Intermediate sanctions
- Restitution

- Intensive supervision probation (ISP)
- Day treatment centers
- Boot camp
- Group home or halfway house
- Wilderness or outdoor programs
- Training schools
- Inmate subculture
- Aftercare

ENDNOTES

1. For overviews of the juvenile court and correctional system, *see* Altschuler, 1998; Bernard, 1992; Champion, 1998; Chesney-Lind and Shelden, 2004; Clement, 1997; Cox and Conrad, 1996; Feld, 1998, 1999; Future of Children, 1996; Howell, 1997a; Inderbitzin, 2005; Kupchik, 2006; Krisburg, 2005; Kurlychek et al., 1999; Lundman, 2001; Petersilia, 1997; Puzzanchera et al., 2003; Roberts, 1998, 2004; Rubin, 1998; Sherman et al., 1998; Sickmund, 2002; Snyder and Sickmund, 2006; Stahl et al., 2007.

2. For overviews of teen courts, *see* Butts and Buck, 2000; Harrison et al., 2001; Rosmussen, 2004.

3. For further information on waivers to adult court, *see* Bishop and Frazier, 2000; Butts and Mitchell, 2000; Fagan and Zimring, 2000; Hortney, 2006; Howell, 2003a; Kupchik, 2006; Myers, 2003; Rainville et al., 2003.

4. *See* note 3 above.

5. *See* Butts and Mitchell, 2000; Hortney, 2006; Howell, 2003a; Kupchik, 2006; Myers, 2003; Snyder et al., 2000; Torbet et al., 2000.

6. *See* Bishop and Frazier, 2000; Butts and Mitchell, 2000; Myers, 2003; Howell, 2003a; Steiner et al., 2006; Steiner and Wright, 2006.

7. For overviews, *see* Andrews and Bonta, 2006; Clear, 1988; Funk, 1999; Howell, 2003a:266–271; Le Blanc, 1998; OJJDP, 2000b; Wiebush et al., 1995.

8. For overviews of the evaluation research, *see* Altschuler, 1998; Andrews et al., 1990; Bishop et al., 1996; Cullen and Applegate, 1997; Cullen, Wright, and Applegate, 1996; Fagan, 1995; Greenwood, 2002; Greenwood et al., 1996; Howell, 1997a, 2003a; Howell et al., 1995; Krisberg and Howell, 1998; Krisberg et al., 1995; Lipsey, 1992; Lipsey and Cullen, 2008; Lipsey and Wilson, 1998; Lundman, 2001; MacKenzie, 2002, 2006; Schneider, 1990; Sherman et al., 2002.

9. *See* Abt Associates, 1994; Acoca, 1998; Roberts, 2004; Smith, 1998; Snyder and Sickmund, 1999.

10. For discussions of the problems with aftercare and an overview of the model aftercare program, *see* Armstrong and Altschuler, 1998; Altschuler et al., 1999; Gies, 2003; Wiebush et al., 2000.

CHAPTER 22

The Juvenile Justice System

Does the Juvenile Justice System Discriminate Against Certain Groups in Its Efforts to Control Delinquency?

The juvenile justice system is not simply supposed to control delinquency; it is supposed to control delinquency in a **fair or just manner.** Among other things, that means that the system is supposed to treat similar offenders in similar ways. It is commonly charged, however, that the system discriminates against certain groups of people. This charge is perhaps most often made with respect to certain race and ethnic groups, but discrimination based on class and gender are also alleged.

This discrimination is sometimes explained in terms of conflict and labeling theories, which argue that powerful groups in our society view minority groups and poor people as a threat to their economic and cultural interests. With respect to race, whites are said to be concerned that minority group members will challenge their privileged position. Some argue that this concern is greatest in communities with large minority populations, high levels of crime, and high levels of racial inequality (i.e., where whites are much wealthier on average than minority group members). Whites respond to this perceived threat by exercising greater social control over minority group members. In particular, the police are more likely to patrol minority communities and arrest minority group members, and the juvenile justice system is more likely to severely sanction minority group members. Lacking power, minority group members are unable to resist these efforts at control. A similar argument is made with respect to poor people.[1]

Labeling theory also explains discrimination in another, related way. It is argued that the general public and justice officials hold certain stereotypes regarding particular groups, with these stereotypes being derived from the media and other sources. Most notably, it is argued that poor people and certain minority group members are more likely to be seen as dangerous or threatening. This view increases the likelihood that they will be arrested and severely sanctioned by the courts. The situation with respect to gender is more complex. Males are generally seen as more dangerous than females, leading to the prediction that males who commit **delinquent offenses** will be treated more severely than females who commit such offenses. But females who engage in sexual behavior or acts believed to increase the likelihood of sexual behavior are viewed more seriously than males who engage in the same behaviors. This, of course, reflects the double standard many people hold regarding the sexual behavior of females and males. As a consequence of this double standard, females who engage in **certain status offenses**—like running away and incorrigibility—should be sanctioned more severely than males who commit the same offenses.

This section examines the evidence on discrimination by the juvenile justice system, focusing on whether the system discriminates against minorities and, to a lesser extent, certain class and gender groups.[2]

Does the Juvenile Justice System Discriminate Against African Americans?

Most of the research on discrimination has focused on racial and ethnic discrimination, particularly discrimination against African Americans. There has been much less research on discrimination against other racial and ethnic groups (but that is starting to change). As a consequence, the discussion that follows focuses on African Americans. Limited data, however, suggest that Latinos and Native Americans face discrimination as well, although not quite to the extent as African Americans.

As discussed in previous chapters, **African Americans are over-represented in all aspects of the juvenile justice system.** While African Americans made up 16 percent of the juvenile population, in 2004 they accounted for 28 percent of all juvenile arrests, 31 percent of all delinquency cases handled by the juvenile court, 35 of all cases formally processed by the court, 37 percent of all juveniles in detention, 36 percent of all adjudicated offenders placed out-of-home, and 41 percent of all cases judicially waived to adult courts (see Snyder et al., 2007).

These data, however, do not prove that **discrimination** exists. That is, they do not prove that African Americans are treated more severely than whites who commit similar offenses and have similar records. Perhaps the reason that African Americans are over-represented in the juvenile justice system is that they commit more delinquent acts and more serious delinquent acts than other groups. As indicated in Chapter 4, evidence suggests that African Americans are involved in more serious delinquency than whites, especially serious violence. A number of studies have tried to determine whether African Americans are over-represented in the juvenile justice system because they are more likely to engage in delinquency, are discriminated against, or some combination of the two.

The typical study focuses on a state or one or more counties within a state. And it examines one or more decision points in the juvenile justice process, such as the decision to arrest a juvenile, to refer the juvenile to juvenile court, to formally process the juvenile, to detain the juvenile, or to place the juvenile in an institution. It is important to note that discrimination can occur at any one of these points in the process. The criminologist conducting the study will attempt to determine whether the race of the juvenile influences the decision that is made after other relevant factors have been taken into account. Most studies, for example, take account of the seriousness of the juvenile's offense and the juvenile's prior record. So the criminologist will ask whether African Americans are treated more severely than whites who have committed similar offenses and have similar records. For example, are African Americans more likely to be arrested or detained or institutionalized than similar whites?

Almost all studies find that **the most important determinants of how juveniles are treated in the justice system are the seriousness of their offense and their prior record.** At the same time, many studies find that the over-representation of African Americans in the juvenile justice system cannot be fully explained in terms of race differences in the extent and seriousness of delinquency. Rather, these studies suggest that this **over-representation is partly due to discrimination against African Americans.** Let me provide two examples of such studies. One study examined the impact of race and ethnicity on arrest and referral to the juvenile court. The researchers focused on three cities: Rochester, New York; Pittsburgh, Pennsylvania; and Seattle, Washington (Huizinga et al., 2007). They collected extensive data from a sample of juveniles in each city, including information on their self-reported delinquency, their standing on many of the causes of delinquency (e.g., socioeconomic status, gang membership), and whether they had been arrested and referred to juvenile court. The researchers found that African Americans were more likely to be arrested and referred to juvenile court in two of the three cities, even after they took account of prior self-reported delinquency and the causes of delinquency. That is to say, the higher arrest and court referral rates of African Americans could *not* be explained by their higher rates of offending or race-related differences in the causes of delinquency (i.e., African Americans were more likely to live in poor families).

In a second study, Leiber and Fox (2005) examined the impact of race on the decisions made at various stages in the juvenile court process, including the decisions to detain juveniles, to formally process them, to send them to diversion programs, to adjudicate them delinquent, and to place them out-of-home. The researchers found that African Americans were more likely to be treated severely at certain stages; in particular, African Americans were more likely to be placed in detention, less likely to be diverted, and more likely to be adjudicated delinquent. This was true even after they took account of a range of third variables, such as the severity of the offense, prior record, school problems, and family status (single- or two-parent household). They also found that processing at earlier stages of the court process affected what happened at later stages. In particular, juveniles who were placed in detention were more likely to be treated severely at later states, even after taking account of other factors. This, of course, works to the disadvantage of African Americans, since they were more likely to be placed in detention (see the discussion on indirect discrimination later in this chapter).

The discrimination against African Americans may be explained by a number of factors (see Bishop, 2005). Among other things, it may occur because the police are more likely to patrol African American communities, complainants are more likely to press for arrest if the offender is African American, and African Americans are less able to afford private attorneys. Recent data, however, suggest that one reason for this discrimination is that juvenile justice officials in certain areas hold negative stereotypes of African Americans. Among other things, these officials believe that African American juveniles are more likely than white juveniles to be dangerous, disrespectful, and to engage in crime because of negative personality traits and bad attitudes—as opposed to negative environmental factors.[3]

If one looks at the data as a whole, there are several general conclusions that can be drawn about discrimination against African Americans.

The Extent of Discrimination Varies Across Police Departments and Juvenile Courts

Some police departments and juvenile courts discriminate against African Americans, while others do not seem to engage in direct or overt discrimination. This conclusion should not be too surprising. Police departments and juvenile courts differ from one another in many ways and exist in different community environments. It is reasonable to expect some differences in the extent of discrimination. This conclusion helps explain why studies examining discrimination produce contradictory results. While many studies find evidence of racial discrimination, many do not. The studies on discrimination usually examine different police departments and juvenile courts at different points in time, so we would expect some difference in results.

Criminologists have begun to investigate those factors that influence whether police and juvenile justice officials discriminate against African Americans and certain other race and ethnic groups. As indicated earlier, the leading argument in this area is that discrimination is most likely in those communities where minority group members are more likely to be viewed as a threat to whites. Most studies tend to support this argument, suggesting that discrimination is greater in communities with high percentages of African American and Latino residents, high levels of crime, and high levels of racial inequality—even after taking a range of other factors into account.[4]

The Extent of Discrimination May Vary by Type of Crime

There is also some evidence that discrimination may be greater for less serious crimes, where the police and court officials have more discretion over how to handle the cases.

There is little question about whether to make an arrest when someone has committed a homicide or armed robbery (although there may be race differences in the punishments imposed by the courts), but much discretion can be exercised when someone is caught using drugs or shoplifting. There is much evidence, in fact, for the existence of discrimination in the enforcement of drug laws. African Americans, in particular, have been especially hard hit by the war on drugs during the 1980s and 1990s. African Americans and whites use drugs at about the same rate overall, but African American juveniles are several times more likely to be arrested for drug abuse violations than white juveniles (see Bishop, 2005; Donziger, 1996; Tonry, 1995). This dramatic difference has occurred partly because the war on drugs has a special focus on crack cocaine. Crack is used more by African Americans than whites. Powdered cocaine, however, is used more by whites.

Further, there is some evidence that discrimination may be more likely when African Americans commit crimes against whites (Poe and Snyder, 2003). It is said that the police and others are more likely to ignore or informally deal with crimes committed against members of minority groups, since they have less sympathy for minority victims. Since most crime is *intraracial* (e.g., African American on African American, white on white), this may help explain why some studies fail to find evidence of discrimination. Most studies, in particular, fail to take account of the race of the victim.

Small Amounts of Discrimination at Different Points in the Juvenile Justice Process Can Have a Large Overall Effect

Many studies find evidence for small to moderate amounts of discrimination at several points in the juvenile justice process. For example, it may be that African Americans are moderately more likely to be arrested than whites, slightly more likely to be referred to juvenile court when arrested, slightly more likely to be detained, slightly more likely to have their cases formally processed, and slightly more likely to be sent to institutions. These small to moderate amounts of discrimination add up, however, so that in the end we find that a much larger proportion of African Americans than whites are confined in institutions (see especially McCord et al., 2001:254–258).

The fact that there may be small to moderate amounts of discrimination at several points in the justice process means that it is important for researchers to examine all major decision points in the process. Some researchers fail to do this. They focus on just one decision point, such as the adjudicatory hearing. They may find little or no evidence of discrimination at this point and conclude that discrimination is not a problem. But discrimination may have occurred at several other points in the process.

Racial Discrimination May Be Direct or Indirect

Researchers examining discrimination usually try to determine whether African Americans are treated more severely than similar whites. So a researcher may compare African Americans and whites who are similar in terms of such variables as the seriousness of their offense, their prior record, their social class, their family status, and so on. The researcher usually includes a range of variables that influence arrest and treatment by the court. **If African Americans are treated more severely than similar whites, that is evidence for** *direct,* **or overt,** *discrimination.* It suggests that the police or court officials may be racist, treating African Americans more harshly solely because of their race. But what if the researcher finds that there is no difference in the way African Americans and whites are treated. Does that mean that discrimination does not exist?

The answer is no. The researcher is comparing African Americans and whites who are similar to one another on a range of variables that influence arrest and court processing. But in the real world, African Americans and whites are **not** similar on many of these variables. Take family status as an example. African American juveniles are more likely to reside in single-parent homes than white juveniles, and some evidence suggests that juveniles from single-parent homes are more likely to be arrested and treated severely by the court. As a consequence, African Americans are treated more severely than whites. This more severe treatment may not stem from direct or overt racial discrimination; African Americans and whites who are similar in terms of family status may be treated the same. Rather, the discrimination occurs because race is associated with a variable that influences treatment by the police and courts—family status in this case. This is *indirect discrimination.* African Americans are treated more severely than whites not because of direct discrimination based on race but because **race is associated with other variables that influence treatment by the police and court.**

Let me give another example of indirect discrimination. While most African Americans are not poor, African Americans are more likely to be poor and to live in poor communities than whites. Some evidence suggests that individuals are more likely to be arrested and treated severely by the court if they are poor or live in poor communities. Among other things, the police may be more likely to patrol poor communities and to stop and question the people there, and the police and court officials may be more likely to discriminate against the poor juveniles they encounter. As a consequence of this association between race and poverty, African Americans are more likely to be arrested and treated severely by the court. The more severe treatment in this case is not due directly to race but rather is due to the indirect effect of race. Race is associated with social class, which in turn affects treatment by the police and courts. Discrimination, then, may be direct or indirect. But the effect is the same in both cases: the over-representation of African Americans in the juvenile justice system.

What Can Be Done to Address the Over-Representation of Minorities in the Juvenile Justice System?

The research described in the previous section led the federal government to take steps to reduce the over-representation of minorities in the juvenile justice system. In 1994, the federal government required each state to determine whether minorities were over-represented in detention and correctional facilities. And in 2002, the federal government broadened this mandate and required each state to determine whether minorities were over-represented at all major points in the juvenile justice process. If minorities were over-represented, the state then had to determine the reason(s) for the over-representation, develop and implement programs to reduce the over-representation, and evaluate the effectiveness of these programs. The federal government said that states that failed to meet these requirements would lose some of their federal funding for delinquency programs. There is some evidence that the federal government has not strictly enforced these requirements, but most states have nevertheless made some effort to meet them (see Leiber, 2002, 2006).

Almost all states have now estimated the extent to which minorities are over-represented in their juvenile justice systems. African Americans are over-represented at one or more points in the juvenile justice process in every state where estimates have been made. Latinos are also over-represented, although not to the extent of African Americans. Most states have also determined the reasons for the over-representation they found. Limited data suggest that this over-representation is partly due to the fact that African Americans have higher offending rates and are more involved in serious crimes than whites. But most states report that this over-representation is also due to discrimination against African Americans (see Leiber, 2002; Pope and Leiber, 2005).

Most states are now implementing programs to reduce minority over-representation, and a small number of states have reached the point where they are evaluating the effectiveness of the programs they have implemented. As indicated, minority over-representation is partly due to the fact that minorities are more involved in delinquency, especially serious delinquency. Programs are being developed to reduce crime by minorities; many of these programs are similar to the prevention and rehabilitation programs discussed in Chapter 24 (see Welsh, Jenkins, and Harris, 1999, for an example of one promising program). And evidence suggests that minority over-representation is also due to direct and indirect discrimination against minorities. Programs are being developed to reduce such discrimination. Such programs include sensitivity training for police and court workers; developing more explicit guidelines for making decisions, including the increased use of risk assessment instruments; closer monitoring of police and court decisions for fairness; developing alternatives to secure detention and confinement; and increasing the representation of minorities in the police and court systems.[5]

It is too early to tell how effective these efforts will be. Nevertheless, there are some signs of success, with preliminary evaluations indicating that a number of programs throughout the country have been able to substantially reduce the over-representation of minorities in the juvenile justice system. For example, a juvenile court in Oregon found that African American and Latino youth were almost twice as likely to be placed in detention as white youth. They developed a racially and ethnically neutral risk assessment instrument and, within a few years, race and ethnic differences in detention were largely eliminated (Cabaniss et al., 2007:395). In the words of Cabaniss et al. (2007:397–398), race-neutral risk assessment instruments do the following:

> Assess a youth's probation status, history of appearing in court, prior record, and the seriousness of the charge, without giving undue weight to social factors that increase the likelihood that minority youth will be detained more often than white youth. For example, instead of asking if a youth resides with both parents, a situation that is less common among African American youth, a race-neutral instrument might ask if two adults capable of supervising a youth live in the home. Based on their responses to intake questions, youth are assigned low, moderate, or high risk scores which suggest their likelihood of reoffending or failing to appear in court.

Other successful efforts to address the over-representation of minorities in the juvenile justice system are described in a report from Building Blocks for Youth (2007) and on the Disproportionate Minority Contact website (http://ojjdp.ncjrs.gov/dmc/). However, it is clearly the case that we still have a long way to go in our efforts to reduce minority over-representation (see Leiber, 2002, 2006).

Does the Juvenile Justice System Discriminate Against the Poor and Against Males or Females?

There has been less research on class- and gender-based discrimination, and the research that has been done in these areas has produced somewhat contradictory results. Nevertheless, there are a few tentative conclusions one can draw.

Although the evidence is somewhat mixed, the data suggest that there is **discrimination against lower-class juveniles in at least certain communities** (e.g., Sampson, 1986b; Sealock and Simpson, 1998). Both the individual's social class and the economic status of the neighborhood in which the individual lives may influence treatment by justice officials. In particular, the economic status of the neighborhood may have an important effect on the likelihood of arrest. The police may be more likely to patrol low-income neighborhoods, stop and question people in such neighborhoods, and arrest people from such neighborhoods. Also, juveniles in many lower-class neighborhoods are more likely to congregate on the street, where they are more visible to the police. The individual's social class, however, may have a larger effect on how juveniles are treated once they have been referred to juvenile court.

Data on gender suggest that males may be somewhat more likely to be arrested and treated severely for **delinquent offenses** than similar females who engage in such crimes. Among other things, it is argued that males are more likely to be seen as a threat than females. Some data, however, suggest that this attitude may be changing: female delinquents have been treated more like male delinquents in recent years. This new equality of treatment is especially true for females who do not conform to gender stereotypes (e.g., do not act submissive when confronted by the police). This change may partly account for the fact that female arrests for violence are increasing faster than male arrests. However, in some jurisdictions females are more likely to be arrested and treated severely for many **status offenses** than similar males. This is especially true for offenses like running away from home and being incorrigible. It is argued that the police and court officials often associate these status offenses with sexual behavior or the possibility of sexual behavior on the part of females, and that they feel that it is necessary to more closely regulate the sexual behavior and "moral life" of females than males (see Chesney-Lind and Shelden, 2004, and Feld, 2008, for excellent discussions).

Summary

This chapter examined race, class, and gender discrimination by the juvenile justice system and concluded that there is some evidence for such discrimination. The variables of race, class, and gender, however, were examined in isolation from one another. A few recent studies indicate that researchers must consider these variables in combination with one another if we are to fully understand discrimination. For example, some data suggest that African American females are treated more severely than white females by the court system (see Chesney-Lind and Shelden, 2004; Leiber and Mack, 2003). Also, some data suggest that the group most likely to experience discrimination is older juveniles who are male and African American (Steffensmeier et al., 1998). Future research will likely focus on the joint effects of race, class, sex, and age, as well as attempts to reduce discrimination in the juvenile justice system.

Teaching Aids

Controversial Issue

There is, of course, no doubt that direct discrimination by the juvenile justice system is wrong. The issue of indirect discrimination, however, is sometimes more controversial. Consider the following: The police often concentrate their patrols in lower-income communities, claiming that such communities have higher crime rates and that it makes sense to put the most police where there is the most crime. This policy means that the lower-class individuals come under greater police scrutiny than middle-class individuals. The police may therefore be more likely to detect a criminal act by a lower-class person than by a middle-class person. It also means that African Americans come under more police scrutiny than whites, since African Americans are more likely to live in lower-class communities (although most African Americans do not live in such communities).

Do you think the police are justified in concentrating their patrols in lower-class communities (which tend to have higher crime rates), even though this practice indirectly discriminates against lower-class individuals and African Americans? Justify your response. Are there any negative consequences that might result from this policy? (Hint: Draw on the delinquency theories.) Is there anything that can be done to reduce these negative consequences? (See the discussion of discrimination in Sherman, 2002.)

Race and Experiences with the Police

The discussion of discrimination in this chapter is rather abstract. I state, for example, that many studies show that the police are more likely to arrest African Americans than similar whites. This statement, however, does not capture the personal experiences that some individuals have with the police. A recent editorial in the *New York Times* attempted to describe such experiences (Herbert, 2007:A25). The editorial began:

> No one is paying much attention, but parts of New York City are like a police state for young men, women and children who happen to be black or Hispanic. They are routinely stopped, searched, harassed, intimidated, humiliated and, in many cases, arrested for no good reason. . . . Last Monday in the Bushwick section of Brooklyn, about three dozen grieving young people on their way to a wake for a teenage friend who had been murdered were surrounded by police, cursed at, handcuffed and ordered into paddy wagons. They were taken to the 83rd precinct stationhouse where several were thrown into jail.

The editorial writer goes on to state that the police said these young people were on a rampage, yelling and blocking traffic, but that "every account [he] was able to find described a large group of youngsters, very sad and downcast about the loss of their friend, walking peacefully toward the station."

Recently, a criminologist interviewed 40 African American adolescent males in a disadvantaged urban community to learn more about their interactions with the police. The author of the study found that

> 83% of respondents reported having experienced harassment themselves, and more than nine out of ten reported that someone they knew had been harassed or mistreated. . . . [R]espondents consistently identified frequent pedestrian and vehicle stops as the bedrock of neighborhood policing efforts. . . . [I]t was not simply that young men objected to being routinely stopped, but they took particular exception to the way officers spoke to them during these encounters. . . . [S]everal study partici-

pants expressed grave concern about being ordered to sit or lie on the pavement while enduring physically intrusive searches. . . . [A]pproximately two-thirds of the young men said the police are almost never polite, and slightly under half reported that the police often harass and mistreat people in the neighborhood. (Brunson, 2007:81)

These quotes are not meant to imply that all police harass African Americans or that all African Americans have negative views of the police. Nevertheless, young African Americans in disadvantaged communities are much more likely than others to report negative experiences with the police, experiences stemming from the aggressive police tactics that are more often used in such communities. And these negative experiences have a range of unfortunate consequences. As indicated earlier, negative treatment by the police may increase the likelihood of crime (see Kane, 2005). And you may have heard about the "Stop Snitching" campaigns in many communities, where songs, websites, and T-shirts urge people to stop cooperating with the police.

What do you think can be done to improve relations between the police and African Americans, particularly young African American males in disadvantaged communities (see the February 2007 issue of *Criminology and Public Policy* for further information and a discussion of possible approaches).

TEST YOUR KNOWLEDGE OF THIS CHAPTER

1. How do conflict and labeling theories explain discrimination against minority groups and the lower class?

2. Why do some criminologists predict that males are more likely than females to be severely punished for serious delinquent acts, while females are more likely to be severely punished for many status offenses?

3. Why did I state that the over-representation of African Americans at various points in the juvenile justice process does not by itself prove that discrimination exists?

4. How do researchers try to determine if juvenile justice officials discriminate against minority group members?

5. What are the two most important determinants of how juveniles are treated in the juvenile justice system?

6. Many studies find evidence of discrimination against African Americans. Describe the stereotypes of African American juveniles that contribute to this discrimination.

7. List a major factor said to influence whether the police and juvenile courts in certain areas discriminate against African Americans. Briefly describe what the research says about this factor.

8. Is discrimination by the police and courts more likely for certain types of crime? Describe the research in this area.

9. Why is it important for researchers studying discrimination to examine all of the major points in the juvenile justice process?

10. What is meant by direct and indirect discrimination? Give a clear-cut example of direct discrimination. Give two clear-cut examples of indirect discrimination.

11. Describe federal efforts to reduce minority over-representation in the juvenile justice system. What have the states found regarding the extent and causes of minority over-representation in their juvenile justice systems?

12. List three programs or strategies being used to reduce discrimination against minorities by juvenile justice officials.

13. Describe the evidence on class-based discrimination by juvenile justice officials.

14. Describe the evidence on gender-based discrimination by justice officials.

THOUGHT AND DISCUSSION QUESTIONS

1. What steps would you recommend for reducing discrimination by the juvenile justice system?

2. To what extent do you think the causes of race/ethnic, class, and gender discrimination are similar and different?

3. To what extent do you think race/ethnic, class, and gender discrimination can be addressed with the same types of programs? If you think different programs are required to address these types of discrimination, describe the differences you have in mind.

4. This chapter examined race/ethnic, class, and gender discrimination in isolation from one another. Do you think it is important for researchers to consider particular race/ethnic, class, and gender combinations when examining discrimination? For example, do you think African American females face special problems in their treatment by the juvenile justice system (problems not faced by white females or African American males)?

KEY TERMS

- Direct discrimination
- Indirect discrimination

ENDNOTES

1. If you have a good memory, you will recall that this argument is very similar to one of the arguments used to explain the invention of juvenile delinquency (see Chapter 1). In particular, it was argued that upper-class people felt threatened by the large concentration of poor people and immigrants in the city, so they created the juvenile court and juvenile correctional institutions in an effort to exercise more control over the children of the poor and immigrants. For a fuller discussion of the conflict and labeling explanations of discrimination, *see* Armstrong and Rodriquez, 2005; Bishop, 2005; Engen et al., 2002; Kent and Jacobs, 2005; Leiber, 2003; Leiber and Fox; Parker et al., 2005.

2. For overviews and selected studies in this area, *see* Armstrong and Rodriguez, 2005; Austin, 1995; Bishop, 2005; Bortner et al., 2000; Bridges and Steen, 1998; Building Blocks For Youth, 2000; Chesney-Lind and Shelden, 2004; Dannefer and Schutt, 1982; DeJong and Jackson, 1998; Donziger, 1996; Engen et al., 2002; Feld, 1995, 2008; Frazier and Bishop, 1995; Hsia and Hamparian, 1998; Huizinga and Elliott, 1987; Huizinga et al., 2007; Kempf-Leonard, 2007; Krisberg, 2005; Lauritsen and Sampson, 1998; Leiber, 2002, 2003; Leiber and Fox, 2005; Leiber and Stairs, 1999; Leonard and Sontheimer, 1995; Leonard et al., 1995; MacDonald and Chesney-Lind, 2001; McCord et al., 2001; Miller, 1996; National Council on Crime and Delinquency, 2007; Penn, 2006; Piliavin and Briar, 1964; Pope and Feyerherm, 1993; Pope and Leiber, 2005; Pope and Snyder, 2003; Reiman, 1995; Sampson, 1986b; Sealock and Simpson, 1998; Short and

Sharp, 2005; Snyder and Sickmund, 1999; Steffensmeier et al., 1998; Tonry, 1995; Tracy, 2005; Walker et al., 2004; Zatz, 1987; Zimring, 2005.

3. For example, *see* Bishop, 2005; Bridges et al., 1995; Leiber, 2003, 2006; Leiber and Stairs, 1999; Sampson and Laub, 1993b.

4. *See* note 1 above.

5. For further information, *see* Bell, 2005; Bishop, 2005; Building Blocks for Youth, 2007; Cabaniss et al., 2007; Feyerherm, 1995; Hsia and Hamparian, 1998; Krisberg, 2005; Leiber, 2002, 2003, 2006; Leonard et al., 1995; Pope and Leiber, 2005; Short and Sharp, 2005.

CHAPTER 23

The Strategies of Deterrence and Incapacitation

Is It Possible to Control Delinquency by Punishing More Offenders and Punishing Them More Severely?

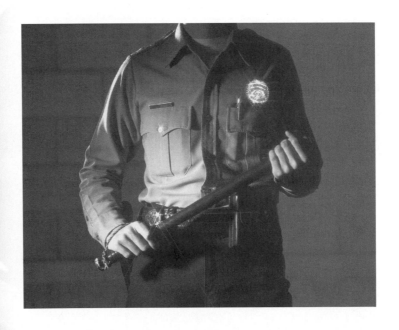

Perhaps the most common criticism of the juvenile court and correctional system is that they are not tough enough, especially in dealing with serious offenders. This criticism is often voiced by politicians and the media. It is shared by many in the juvenile justice system. Many police, for example, complain that the offenders they send to juvenile court usually receive little more than a "slap on the wrist." Court workers often note that unless juveniles commit a very serious offense, they must appear in court several times before they receive a meaningful sanction (see Stone, 1998). Further, most people in the general public believe that the juvenile justice system is not tough enough in dealing with serious offenders, although they *also* believe that the system does not place enough emphasis on rehabilitation and prevention (Bishop, 2006; Meors et al., 2007; Nagin et al., 2006).

As a consequence, it is often argued that **the juvenile justice system needs to get tough with offenders, especially serious offenders.** That is, the justice system needs to start punishing more offenders and start punishing them more severely. In fact, the juvenile justice system has made a concerted effort to do just that in recent years.[1] Certain of these efforts were mentioned in Chapter 21. For example, a new range of intermediate sanctions have been developed, partly with the idea that such sanctions would allow the courts to inflict more punishment and impose more supervision than is the case with regular probation. Also, more offenders are being waived to adult court, where they are often sentenced to long periods of incarceration. Still other efforts to get tough are described in this chapter. All of these efforts, of course, aim to increase the level of **direct control** exercised by the justice system.

Many people feel that these efforts will reduce delinquency. Three arguments are generally made in this area. First, getting tough will deter those juveniles who are punished from committing further delinquency. Second, getting tough will deter juveniles in the general population, including those who were not punished, from committing delinquent acts. Juveniles in the general population will come to realize that the certainty and severity of punishment have increased, and this will increase their fear of engaging in delinquency. And third, getting tough will result in more juvenile offenders being locked up, which will stop them from committing crimes on the street. These arguments make much common sense, and they also appeal to the desire of many people to punish individuals who commit serious crimes.

This chapter has three parts. First, I examine the charge that the juvenile court and correctional system are not tough enough in dealing with offenders, especially serious offenders. Second, I describe the efforts of the juvenile court and correctional system to get tough with offenders. Third, I discuss the effectiveness of these get-tough efforts and what can be done to make them more effective. In particular, I ask whether these efforts deter those specific others who were punished from committing further crime (called *specific deterrence*); whether they deter those in the general population from engaging in crime (called *general deterrence*); and whether they reduce crime by locking up or incapacitating offenders, so they cannot commit crimes on the street (called *incapacitation*).

Are the Juvenile Court and Correctional System Tough Enough in Dealing with Offenders, Especially Serious Offenders?

As I pointed out in Chapter 21, the large majority of juveniles who are referred to juvenile court have their cases dismissed, are handled informally, or are placed on probation. While probation may call for the close supervision of the juvenile and the imposition of meaningful sanctions, it usually does not. In most cases, juvenile offenders have little contact with their probation officers and are subject to only minimal sanctions. Based on these facts, one might conclude that the juvenile court and correctional system is not tough enough in dealing with offenders.

We must keep in mind, however, that most juveniles are referred to juvenile court for minor offenses. It may be that serious offenders are treated differently. Data do, in fact, indicate that serious offenders are more likely to receive severe sanctions. It is still the case, however, that most serious offenders do not receive sanctions beyond probation. Consider two relatively serious violent crimes: aggravated assault and robbery. Data from 2004 indicate that 76 percent of the aggravated assault cases referred to juvenile courts were formally processed. Of these, 65 percent were adjudicated delinquent, and 3 percent were judicially waived to adult court. The rest of the cases were dismissed or informally processed. Of those adjudicated delinquent, 27 percent were placed out-of-home. The rest were placed on probation or, in a small number of cases, sanctioned in some other way or released. If we do the appropriate math, we find that 14 percent of the aggravated assault cases referred to juvenile courts were placed out-of-home and 2 percent were waived to adult courts. The numbers for robbery are as follows: 86 percent of the robbery cases referred to juvenile courts were formally processed. Of these, 64 percent were adjudicated delinquent and 8 percent were judicially waived to adult courts. Of those adjudicated delinquent, 44 percent were placed out-of-home. Overall, 24 percent of the robbery cases referred to juvenile court were placed out-of-home and 7 percent were waived to adult court (Puzzanchera et al., 2003). **Most serious offenders referred to juvenile court, then, do not receive severe sanctions.** (It should be noted, however, that aggravated assault and robbery cases vary in their level of seriousness; while some aggravated assaults involve serious injury, others involve *threats* to injure someone with a weapon like a bat; and while some robberies involve major thefts at gunpoint, others involve taking a fellow student's lunch money under threat of violence.)

Further, data suggest that **adult courts are generally more likely to incarcerate serious juvenile offenders and to incarcerate them for longer periods of time than juvenile courts,** especially when the offenders are charged with violent crimes.[2] One recent study examined how juveniles charged with felonies were dealt with in the *adult* criminal courts of 40 of the nation's largest urban counties. The study found that about two-thirds of these juveniles were convicted of felonies and that about 43 percent of those convicted were sentenced to prison, receiving an average sentence of seven and one-half years. Another 20 percent of the convicted juveniles were sentenced to serve much shorter terms of confinement in jails (Rainville and Smith, 2003). Data such as these have led many people to conclude that juvenile court is not tough enough.

There are several reasons why the juvenile court often fails to impose severe sanctions, some of which are difficult to address. For example, juvenile courts cannot be expected to sanction a juvenile when they lack good evidence that the juvenile committed an offense. But other reasons can be addressed. Juvenile courts and correctional staffs are often limited, which makes it difficult to formally process and impose meaningful sanctions on most juvenile offenders. Although politicians have devoted enormous sums of money to the control of adult crime, they have been reluctant to make substantial investments in the juvenile justice system. Also, most juvenile courts are still at least partly guided by a philosophy that emphasizes rehabilitation over punishment. This philosophy, in particular, tends to view juvenile offenders as not fully responsible for their behavior and in need of assistance rather than punishment.

However, many people argue that the juvenile court and correctional system needs to place more emphasis on punishment or on "getting tough" with offenders, especially serious offenders.

Efforts to Get Tough with Serious Offenders

The federal government has been a leading advocate of taking a tougher stance toward juvenile offenders. In particular, the U.S. Office of Juvenile Justice and Delinquency Prevention (OJJDP) recently developed a comprehensive strategy for responding to delinquency, particularly serious delinquency. One of the cornerstones of this strategy is the proposition that juvenile offenders need to be held accountable for their offenses and subject to meaningful sanctions. Specifically, the OJJDP has stated:

> [Y]oung people who violate the law should be held accountable for their offenses through the swift, consistent application of sanctions that are proportionate to the offenses—both as a matter of basic justice and as a way to combat delinquency and improve the quality of life in the nation's communities. (Andrews and Marble, 2003:1; also see Beyer, 2003)

Further, the OJJDP has recommended that juvenile courts hold offenders accountable by developing a system of *graduated sanctions* that involves:

> immediate sanctions in the community for first-time, nonviolent offenders; intermediate sanctions in the community for more serious offenders; and secure care programs for the most violent offenders. Youths should move between different levels of the continuum through a well-structured system of phases. At each level of the continuum, offenders should understand that they will be subject to more severe sanctions if they reoffend. (Krisberg et al., 1995:143; also see Howell, 2003a)

The OJJDP is now helping juvenile courts and correctional agencies hold offenders accountable for their behavior. Each year the OJJDP gives out several hundred million dollars in grants so that states can do such things as hire additional court workers, set up graduated sanctioning systems, and build or expand juvenile correctional facilities (Andrews and Marble, 2003; Beyer, 2003). (As discussed later, the OJJDP is also encouraging states to combine sanctions with rehabilitation and prevention programs.)

Most states have also come to place an increased emphasis on getting tough with juvenile offenders. For example, many states have recently altered the mission statements for their juvenile court systems, and the new statements explicitly state that the major purposes of juvenile court include holding offenders accountable for their behavior, punishing offenders, and/or protecting the community from offenders. That is not to say that these states have abandoned the goal of rehabilitation, but rather that they now emphasize accountability and punishment along with rehabilitation. This increased emphasis on accountability and punishment is reflected in the efforts that juvenile courts and correctional agencies have made to get tough with offenders, especially serious offenders. These get-tough efforts are described next, and they constitute the major trend in juvenile justice in recent years.[3]

Get-Tough Efforts

Many juvenile courts are attempting to make more efficient use of their limited court staff so they can better concentrate on serious offenders. One of the reasons that diversion programs were developed is that they allow court staff to divert less serious cases out of the court system and focus on more serious cases. Also, many juvenile courts are now **trying to better identify serious offenders so they can concentrate their resources on these individuals.** For example, many courts now use risk assessment instruments to identify those juveniles at greatest risk for future offending (see Chapter 21 for more information).

Juvenile courts are also imposing more severe sanctions on offenders, especially serious offenders. The desire for more severe sanctions is one of the reasons for the development of the **intermediate sanctions** described in Chapter 21; these sanctions include restitution, intensive supervision, home confinement, and boot camps. Beyond that, states have taken a number of steps to increase the certainty and especially the severity of sanctions given out by the juvenile court. The most notable of these steps are as follows:

1. *Mandatory minimum sentences and sentencing guidelines.* Almost half of the states have adopted mandatory minimum sentences or sentencing guidelines in their juvenile courts. Mandatory minimum sentences require judges to confine certain offenders, usually older juveniles who commit serious crimes and/or have prior records, for a predetermined amount of time. For example, Delaware requires that juvenile court judges "sentence any youth convicted of a second felony within one year to a minimum term of six months' confinement" (Feld, 1999:258). Sentencing guidelines are less common, but a few states provide guidelines for judges to follow when sentencing juveniles. The guidelines typically classify juvenile offenders into categories based on the seriousness of their offense, the extent of their prior record, and their age. The guidelines then specify the minimum and maximum sentences for juveniles in each category. For example, the guidelines in Washington State specify that juveniles classified as "serious" offenders receive sentences ranging from 125 weeks to 3 years' confinement (Feld, 1999:255). Judges are strongly encouraged to select a sentence within this range, taking account of certain aggravating and mitigating factors associated with each case.

Mandatory minimum sentences and sentencing guidelines were designed to limit the discretion of judges, and they were created with the goal of increasing the severity of court sanctions. They represent a significant departure from the original mission of the juvenile court, which was to determine the problems that caused juveniles to offend and devise individualized treatment plans to address these problems. That is, the court was supposed to focus on *helping offenders* rather than *punishing offenders for their offenses* (see Chapter 1 and Feld, 1999).

2. *Blended sentences.* Juvenile courts used to be quite limited in the punishments they could inflict. Juvenile courts, in particular, were able to confine offenders in juvenile institutions for only short periods of time—usually until the offenders reached adulthood or shortly thereafter. But in recent years, almost half of all states have passed laws that allow their juvenile courts to sentence certain serious offenders to long periods of confinement in adult correctional institutions. In some states, the sentenced offenders begin

serving their time in juvenile correctional institutions and, upon reaching adulthood, are transferred to adult institutions. In other states, juvenile court judges have the option of sending juvenile offenders directly to adult correctional institutions. And in still other states, juveniles are sentenced to both juvenile and adult correctional facilities, but if they successfully complete the juvenile portion of their sentence and do not re-offend, the adult portion of their sentence is suspended. These sentences are called blended sentences because they often blend sentences in the juvenile correctional system with sentences in the adult system. Such sentences are obviously designed to increase the severity of sanctions administered by the juvenile courts (see Butts and Mitchell, 2000; Redding and Howell, 2000).

3. **Waiver to adult court.** Almost all states have recently passed legislation making it easier to try certain juvenile cases in adult court, where the sanctions are generally more severe. Certain of these laws expand the range of cases that judges can waive to juvenile court; for example, they lower the age limit for waiver or make additional offenses eligible for waiver. Other laws mandate or strongly encourage judges to waive certain types of cases to adult court. Still other laws give prosecutors the power to decide whether cases meeting certain criteria should be tried in adult or juvenile courts. Finally, certain laws state that cases that meet certain criteria will automatically be tried in adult court. These laws tend to focus on cases involving older juveniles who commit certain serious crimes and/or have prior records (see Chapter 21 for further information).

The get-tough approach to juvenile offenders has also been reflected in other ways. As indicated in Chapter 1, most juvenile courts **have reduced the confidentiality of juvenile court proceedings.** Juvenile court hearings used to be closed to the public, the names of juvenile offenders were not revealed to the public or media, court records were rarely shared with agencies outside the juvenile court, and court records were often expunged or destroyed if the juvenile remained crime free for a period of time. The rationale for such actions derived from labeling theory: Juvenile offenders were to be protected from the stigma of a delinquent label. There is now less concern with protecting juvenile offenders and more concern with protecting society *from* juvenile offenders. All states now (1) require or permit open court hearings for juveniles accused of certain serious crimes, (2) allow the names of juveniles convicted of certain serious offenses to be released to the public, (3) allow greater access to juvenile court records, and/or (4) make it more difficult for juveniles to expunge or destroy their court records. To give an example, virtually all states now allow adult criminal courts access to juvenile court records. Such records are often taken into account when adults convicted of crimes are being sentenced, and adults with serious juvenile records receive more severe sentences.

These get-tough policies have had a significant effect on the way that juvenile offenders are treated, especially serious and high-rate offenders. The adoption of get-tough policies peaked during the 1980s and 1990s, partly as a response to the large increase in serious juvenile violence from the mid-1980s to early 1990s (see Chapter 3) And these policies resulted in major changes in the way that juvenile offenders, particularly serious and chronic offenders, were treated. There was a substantial increase in the rate at which juvenile offenders were incarcerated, with this rate peaking in 1997 with 368 juveniles per 100,000 held in juvenile facilities. There was a dramatic increase in the number of juveniles transferred to adult court during the 1980s and 1990s. Reflecting this fact, the number of juveniles serving time in adult jails increased sixfold from the mid-1980s to 1997—when it peaked at 9,105. The number of juveniles admitted to adult prisons more than doubled from 1985 to 1997, when it peaked at 7,400 admissions (Austin et al., 2000). (Note: Individuals serving sentences of more than a year are sent to prisons, while those serving sentences of a year or less are sent to jails.) However, as discussed in Chapter 24, there has been some reaction against these get-tough policies in recent years. Partly as a result, there have been declines in the juvenile incarceration rate, the number of juveniles transferred to adult court, and the number of juveniles in adult prisons and jails since the late 1990s. Even so, these get-tough policies remain in effect in most places and continue to shape the reaction to juvenile crime.[4]

How Effective Are These Get-Tough Measures, and What Can Be Done to Increase Their Effectiveness?

Has this get-tough movement worked? Is it effective? It is difficult to give a definitive answer because not all of the get-tough efforts have been carefully evaluated, and the evaluations do not always produce consistent results. There are, however, enough evaluation data to draw some tentative conclusions about the effectiveness of these get-tough efforts.

I first examine whether these get-tough strategies have a deterrent effect; that is: Do they deter juveniles from engaging in crime? I then examine whether these get-tough strategies have an incapacitation effect; that is: Do they prevent crime by locking people up so they cannot commit crimes on the street? I also discuss what can be done to increase the effectiveness of these get-tough strategies.

Deterrence

Punishing more offenders or punishing them more severely is said to deter juveniles from committing crime.[5] *Deterrence* is based on *the fear of punishment.* If society increases the *certainty and/or severity of punishment,* it increases the fear of punishment among both those who are punished and those in the general population. It is this fear that deters juveniles from committing delinquent acts.

This argument is compatible with control and social learning theories. If you recall, one of the major types of control is direct control. Direct control refers to the probability that one's criminal acts will be detected and punished by others. The strategy of deterrence tries to increase one type of direct control—direct control by the juvenile justice system. People who advocate deterrence want to increase the likelihood that juvenile offenders will be caught by the police and will receive meaningful sanctions by the juvenile courts. Advocates of deterrence usually pay less attention to direct control exercised by family members, friends, school officials, and others. They also pay less attention to other forms of social control, such as one's stake in conformity and internal control.

Social learning theorists also argue that delinquency is less likely if it is punished. Again, advocates of deterrence focus on one type of punishment—punishment by the juvenile justice system. They pay less attention to the punishments administered by family members, friends, and others. Also, they do not focus on the other causes of crime outlined in social learning theory, such as the reinforcements for crime, beliefs conducive to crime, and exposure to delinquent models.

I next examine whether the get-tough efforts described earlier—which focus primarily on increasing the severity of punishment—deter those specific others who are punished from further offending (specific deterrence). I then examine whether these strategies deter people in the general population, including those who were not punished, from further offending (general deterrence).

Specific Deterrence

Do punishments by the juvenile justice system reduce the likelihood of delinquency among those who are punished?

A number of studies have tried to determine whether increasing the severity of punishment reduces delinquency. These studies compare the subsequent delinquency of juveniles who receive more severe and less severe punishments. For example, juveniles on intensive supervision programs are compared to similar juveniles on regular probation. Juveniles tried in adult courts are compared to similar juveniles tried in juvenile courts. The evaluations try to determine whether the get-tough approach reduces the likelihood of future delinquency, with future delinquency most often measured in terms of arrests or court referrals.

One general conclusion that is emerging from the evaluations is that the **get-tough approaches have little or no effect on future offending.** In certain cases, they may actually increase future offending. The major get-tough initiatives include intermediate sanctions (for those who otherwise would have been placed on regular probation), sending juveniles to institutions or sending them there for longer periods, and trying juveniles as adults, which often results in confinement in adult institutions. As indicated in Chapter 21, evaluations suggest that most intermediate sanctions have little or no effect on future offending. Sending juveniles to institutions is no more effective at reducing offending than many community-based alternatives. Some data, in fact, suggest that it may be easier to reduce re-offending in community-based programs than in institutions. Sending juveniles to institutions for longer periods also does not reduce offending; in fact, some data suggest that longer periods of confinement increase the likelihood of subsequent offending. Finally, data suggest that trying juveniles as adults does not reduce re-offending. In fact, trying juveniles as adults may increase their rate of future offending.[6] Subjecting juveniles to more severe punishments, then, does not seem to deter them from further offending.

Are punished offenders less likely to commit delinquent acts than similar offenders who have not been punished by the juvenile justice system? While most studies have compared more severely to less severely punished offenders, a few studies have compared punished offenders to offenders who have not been punished. These later studies are somewhat problematic. The ideal way to compare punished to unpunished offenders is to do a randomized experiment. For example, we might ask the police to flip a coin whenever they catch a juvenile offender. If the coin comes up heads, they release the offender. If it comes up tails, they arrest the offender and refer that person to juvenile court for punishment. We could then determine whether punished offenders have lower rates of subsequent delinquency than released offenders. If the punished offenders do have lower rates, that suggests that punishment does deter those who are punished. But as you might imagine, a study of this type has never been done.

A few studies, however, have compared arrested or convicted offenders to *comparable* offenders who have not been arrested or convicted. The two groups are usually comparable in terms of the offenses they have committed and sociodemographic characteristics like age, sex, race, and class. Since random assignment is not used, however, it may be that the two groups differ in important ways that we are not aware of. The results of these studies are mixed, but they tend to suggest that the arrested and convicted offenders do not have lower rates of subsequent delinquency. Some studies, in fact, find that the arrested offenders have higher rates of subsequent delinquency.[7] Overall, then, one may tentatively conclude that **formally punishing offenders does not reduce their subsequent delinquency.**

Why doesn't punishing offenders deter them from delinquency? There are at least four possible reasons why punishing offenders may not deter them from committing delinquent acts.

First, **the juvenile justice system does not punish in an effective way.** In order to be effective, punishments must be reasonably certain, among other things (see Chapter 8; Andrews and Bonta, 2003). But the certainty or likelihood of punishment is usually very low (see Chapters 3 and 21). As a consequence, punished offenders may feel that they can get away with crime in the future. In fact, some data suggest that punished offenders do not increase their estimates of the certainty of future punishment and may even reduce them.[8]

Second, **many juveniles are not very responsive to punishment.** Some have a low stake in conformity, or little to lose by engaging in delinquency, so they are not very threatened by the prospect of punishment. Some are not very rational; that is, they do not give much thought to the possible costs of their delinquent acts. Rather, they are impulsive and often act without thinking about the consequences of their behavior (see Chapter 13). Furthermore, many juveniles commit their offenses under the influence of drugs or alcohol or delinquent peers, which also reduces their concern for the costs of crime (see Chapters 16 and 17; also Carmichael and Piquero, 2004; Nagin and Pogarsky, 2004; Wright et al., 2004).

Third, there are **several major causes for an individual's delinquency.** Punishing a person for his or her delinquency does little to address these causes. For example, it usually does not reduce the strain that the offender may be experiencing or reduce the extent to which he or she learns crime from others. While punishment does increase one form of direct control, it usually does not increase all the other forms of control.

Fourth, **punishments may sometimes backfire and increase the likelihood of subsequent crime.** This issue was discussed in some detail in Chapter 9, which described labeling theory. As stated in that chapter, punishments may increase strain. Punishments that are excessive, overly harsh, or applied in a discriminatory manner may themselves create strain. For example, institutionalized offenders sometimes state that their imprisonment turned them into angry, vengeful individuals. Furthermore, punishment may make it more difficult for individuals to achieve their goals and may increase the likelihood of negative treatment by others. Punishment may also reduce many types of social control and increase the social learning of crime. If you are confined in an institution, you are physically isolated from conventional others and forced to associate with other delinquents, who teach you to be a better delinquent. It is for this reason that institutions are sometimes referred to as "schools for crime." In addition, individuals who have been labeled delinquent through punishment often find that conventional others are reluctant to associate with them. Partly as a consequence, they often end up associating with other delinquents. There is reason to believe that these negative effects are especially likely when juveniles are punished in the adult system and confined in adult institutions (Bishop and Frazier, 2000).

Can we punish in an effective way? A number of criminologists argue that the effect of punishment on delinquency depends on the nature of the punishment and who is being punished. While punished offenders as a whole may not reduce their subsequent delinquency, it may be that some punished offenders reduce their delinquency, while others increase their delinquency. A few studies, conducted mostly with adults, provide some support for this argument.

Limited data suggest that punishment is likely to deter offenders from committing additional crimes under the following circumstances: (1) the likelihood of meaningful punishment is reasonably high (certain studies on police crackdowns, for example, demonstrate that it is possible to deter offenders from further crime when the probability of meaningful punishments is high); (2) the individuals who are punished have some concern for the costs of crimes (for example, they have a stake in conformity, such as a decent job or close ties to their family members); (3) punishment is combined with rehabilitation, so that some of the other causes of delinquency are addressed; and (4) steps are taken to minimize or counteract the negative effects of punishment (for example, efforts are made to punish in a fair, respectful manner and to reintegrate punished offenders back into conventional society).[9]

Combining punishment with rehabilitation. Some criminologists have drawn on these arguments and proposed that punishment be combined with rehabilitation, with rehabilitation addressing the other causes of crime. In particular, it has been argued that the punishment process often provides an opportunity to rehabilitate offenders. Offenders in intensive supervision programs or in institutions, for example, can be required to participate in rehabilitation programs. These rehabilitation programs can then address many of the other factors that caused the offenders to engage in crime. We now have some knowledge of the types of rehabilitation programs that are effective (see Chapter 24). Further, data suggest that such programs are effective even if offenders are forced to participate in them. Such programs are effective in both community and institutional settings, although they are perhaps somewhat more effective in community settings (e.g., used with offenders on intensive probation supervision). The evaluation research supports these arguments, with data indicating that punishments are effective in reducing subsequent offending when they are combined with carefully selected rehabilitation programs.[10] The OJJDP is now encouraging juvenile courts and correctional agencies to combine punishment with rehabilitation (Beyer, 2003; Kurlychek et al., 1999).

Restorative justice. Some criminologists and policy makers are also proposing that we adopt an alternative style of punishment, known as the restorative justice approach, which is designed to address certain of the problems of punishment described earlier.[11] (This approach was discussed briefly in Chapter 9.) Restorative justice has a range of objectives, but one of its central objectives is to sanction offenders in a more effective manner. Advocates of restorative justice argue that it is important to hold delinquents accountable for their offenses and to impose meaningful sanctions on them. At the same time, they argue that such sanctions should not be excessive and should not isolate offenders from conventional society. Rather, such sanctions should allow offenders to repair the harm they have done, restore their ties with conventional others, and address at least some of the causes of their delinquency.

These ideas have been implemented in different ways (see Bazemore and Umbreit, 2001). Nevertheless, most restorative justice programs share certain features. After the offender has admitted his or her guilt, the offender and victim are usually asked whether they are willing to participate in the restorative justice program. If they agree, a *conference* is scheduled. The conference usually includes the offender, the offender's family, perhaps a few supporters of the offender, the victim, a few supporters of the victim, representatives from the community, and possibly the police officer who was involved. The conference may be held at the local juvenile court or another site, like a school or community center. The conference is typically run by a facilitator or coordinator, who may or may not be on the staff of the local juvenile court.

The conference usually begins with the victim describing the harm that the crime caused. Supporters of the victim may also discuss the harm experienced by the victim. Further, community representatives might talk about the impact of the crime on the local neighborhood. The offender and the offender's supporters may then talk about the crime, the reasons behind the crime, and how the crime has affected them. The victim may then have the opportunity to question the offender. This process helps the offender appreciate how much harm he or she has caused and, perhaps, empathize or identify with the victim. It also helps the victim and others better understand the offender and his or her problems, so that they are less likely to reject or hate the offender. Participants in the conference—including both the victim and offender—then discuss how the harm caused by the crime might be repaired. Typically, the offender apologizes to the victim, makes restitution to the victim to cover the cost of damaged property, medical expenses, and so on, and performs community service. The community service is a way to make restitution to the larger neighborhood and perhaps establish positive ties with conventional others. Community representatives at the conference may also try to establish positive ties with the offender, as well as deal with certain of the problems that motivated the delinquent act.

The restorative justice approach attempts to sanction offenders in a way that does not increase the likelihood of further crime. The sanctions applied are not overly harsh, they do not for the most part involve confinement in an institution, and they do not cut offenders off from conventional others and foster association with delinquent peers. Further, the restorative justice approach **tries to address at least certain of the causes of crime beyond direct control.** Offenders are made aware of the harm caused by their crime, which may increase their internal control. They establish close ties to conventional others and become involved in positive community activities, which may increase their stake in conformity. And efforts may be made to address still other of the causes of crime.

Bazemore (2000:251) provides the following example of how the restorative justice approach often operates. A 14-year-old boy got into an altercation with his teacher, injuring the teacher and breaking his glasses. After the boy admitted to the offense, a conference was held in the local school. The conference was directed by a trained facilitator, and conference participants included the offender, his mother, his grandfather, two of the offender's teachers, the local police officer who made the arrest, the victim, two friends of the victim, and a small group of citizens from the community. The victim, the offender, his mother, his grandfather, and the police officer spoke about the offense and its impact on them. Likewise, citizens from the community had an opportunity to comment on the impact of the crime. Then the facilitator asked the victim and others—including the offender—how the harm caused by the crime could be repaired. A discussion ensued, and it was decided that the offender should pay the victim for his medical expenses and the cost of new glasses. Further, the offender should perform community service work on the school grounds.

The OJJDP is promoting a restorative justice approach to sanctioning. Several hundred communities in the United States have implemented this approach to varying degrees. The approach is usually employed with less serious crimes, although it has been used with more serious crimes in certain areas. The effectiveness of the approach is still being evaluated. Data suggest that both victims and offenders much prefer the restorative justice approach to traditional court processing, and some data suggest that the approach may reduce subsequent rates of offending for at least certain types of offenders.[12]

Summary. For now, we can draw the following tentative conclusion: Overall, punishing juveniles or punishing them more severely does not reduce their subsequent delinquency. But there is reason to believe that punishments may reduce delinquency if administered properly. In particular, punishments need to be made more certain, to address at least some of the other causes of crime, and to be administered in ways that do not increase the likelihood of further crime. These goals can be at least partly accomplished by combining punishments with rehabilitation and, perhaps, through the use of the restorative justice approach.

General Deterrence

Studies on specific deterrence ask whether punishment deters delinquency among those who are punished. Studies on general deterrence ask whether punishment deters delinquency among juveniles in the general population, including those who were not punished. For example, suppose five students are caught cheating and are punished. Their punishment may deter other students in the class from cheating, even though these other students were not punished. The unpunished students may come to fear that they too might be caught and punished if they cheat.

Numerous studies have tried to determine whether there is a general deterrent effect; that is, whether increasing the certainty and/or severity of punishment reduces crime in the general population. Some studies compare geographic areas that differ in terms of the certainty and/or severity of punishment. Usually states are compared, but sometimes cities or counties are compared. Certainty of punishment is usually measured in terms of the arrest rate, that is, the number of offenses known to the police that result in arrest. Severity is often measured in terms of the average length of prison sentence served for various crimes. These studies try to determine whether areas with a higher certainty and/or severity of punishment have lower crime rates.

Such studies, however, are only able to determine whether there is an association between the certainty and severity of punishment and crime rates. They cannot determine whether the certainty and severity of punishment have a causal effect on crime rates. For example, many of these studies find that areas with a high certainty of punishment have lower crime rates. But the association between certainty and crime rates may be due to third variables, like poverty. High levels of poverty may cause crime, on the one hand, and may lead to a low certainty of punishment on the other. Areas high in poverty, for example, may have less money to spend on their police and so may have less efficient police forces. Also, the association between the certainty of punishment and crime rates may be due to the fact that crime rates affect the level of certainty. High rates of crime may overwhelm the police, reducing their ability to catch offenders and thereby lowering the certainty of punishment.

Researchers have tried to overcome these problems by taking account of third variables and doing longitudinal studies. In particular, researchers try to take account of third variables that may influence both the certainty and/or severity of punishment and crime rates. For example, they may examine the relationship between the certainty of punishment and crime rates in areas that have similar levels of poverty. Also, researchers do longitudinal studies that examine whether changes in the certainty and/or severity of punishment affect crime rates at a subsequent point in time. For example, Singer and McDowall (1988) examined a New York law that lowered the age at which juveniles charged with certain crimes could be tried in adult courts. They examined the arrest rates for juveniles affected by this law before and after the law was enacted and did not find any evidence that the law resulted in a significant reduction in arrest rates. They also compared the arrest rates for juveniles affected by the law to the arrest rates for juveniles of the same age in a nearby jurisdiction not affected by the law, and they again did not find any evidence that the law significantly reduced arrest rates.

These studies, however, have also been criticized. Criminologists argue that the studies assume that people are aware of the certainty and severity of punishment in the area where they live. Data, however, suggest that this assumption is often wrong (see Klock et al., 2005). Many people have little idea of the true certainty and severity of punishment. (Do you know the certainty and severity of punishment for marijuana use in your hometown or state?) In particular, people who are law-abiding often greatly overestimate the certainty and severity of punishment. (Officials in my home state of Georgia tried to counter this ignorance of sanctions by making a video describing changes in the law that increased the severity of punishments for certain crimes. This video was then shown to students throughout the state in a deliberate attempt to deter them from committing delinquent acts.)

Some criminologists argue, therefore, that the best way to determine whether people are deterred by the threat of punishment is to ask them to estimate the certainty and severity of punishment—in particular, to ask them to estimate the likelihood that they will be punished if they commit a particular offense and what their punishment will be. If people are deterred by the threat of punishment, their estimate of the certainty and severity of punishment should have an effect on their level of crime. So people who state that they will be caught and severely punished if they engage in crime should be less likely to engage in crime.

A number of studies have been done in this area. For example, students are asked to estimate the likelihood that they will be caught by the police if they use marijuana, and they are asked what punishment they would probably receive if caught. The responses to these questions allow researchers to measure the students' perceptions about the certainty and severity of punishment. The researchers then determine whether these perceptions are related to delinquency. The more recent and better studies are longitudinal in nature and take into account third variables. So researchers compare the subsequent offending of similar juveniles who differ in terms of their perceived certainty and severity of punishment. If deterrence works, the juveniles who believe they will definitely receive severe punishments should have lower levels of subsequent delinquency.

Thus, a range of studies have tried to determine whether the certainty and severity of punishment are related to crime in the general population. These studies do not always agree with one another, but the more recent and best research offers tentative support for the following conclusions.[13]

Most notably, **increasing the certainty of punishment may reduce crime by a moderate amount in some circumstances.** The certainty of punishment, however, is only one of many factors influencing the level of crime. The certainty of punishment is less important than other factors, such as the individual's beliefs regarding delinquency and the threat of informal punishment from family members and others. The severity of punishment is less important than the certainty of punishment. Most studies suggest that **changes in the severity of punishment have little or no effect on delinquency.** The Singer and McDowall (1988) study described earlier, for example, did not find any evidence that increasing the severity of punishment by making it easier to try juveniles as adults reduced offending in the general population (also see Bishop and Frazier, 2000; Steiner et al., 2006). Certain studies, however, suggest that increasing the severity of punishment may reduce delinquency *if the certainty of punishment is high.*

As indicated, the certainty of punishment reduces delinquency in some circumstances. Limited research suggests that the effect of punishment is short-lived and is confined to the specific geographic area in which the punishment is administered. Punishments administered a year earlier, therefore, have little or no effect on current levels of delinquency. (Likewise, individuals' perception of the certainty of punishment a year earlier often has little effect on their current delinquency.) Also, punishments administered outside one's community appear to have little deterrent effect. This makes sense. People are most responsive to recent punishments administered in their communities. Finally, some data suggest that punishments must be reasonably certain if potential offenders are to be deterred. A few studies estimate that the probability of punishment needs to be above 30 to 40 percent if potential offenders are to be deterred, although more research is needed in this area.

Increasing the certainty of punishment, then, may cause a moderate reduction in delinquency in the general population, although this effect tends to be short-lived and confined to the immediate area where the certainty is increased. And it may be that society has to substantially increase the certainty of punishment before we can observe an effect on crime. This is something that is not easily done. It involves hiring more police and changing the way that they function (see Chapter 18). It also involves hiring more juvenile court staff. Increasing the severity of punishment appears to have little or no impact on delinquency, unless, perhaps, the certainty of punishment is high.

Unfortunately, most of the get-tough approaches described earlier **focus on increasing the severity of punishment.** It is easy to understand why this is the case. It is a simple matter for politicians to increase severity; they simply pass a law that raises the penalties for certain crimes. Such laws make them appear tough on crime and may win them votes. But, as just discussed, it is doubtful whether such laws have a deterrent effect. It is possible, however, to **increase the certainty of punishment and perhaps have something of an effect on delinquency rates.** The discussion of police crackdowns in Chapter 20 describes how this may be done. As you may recall, the evidence suggests that police crackdowns do result in a moderate reduction in crime in the immediate area where they are instituted. The effect of the crackdowns is typically short-lived, and crime returns to its former level soon after the crackdowns end. But a strategy of "rotating crackdowns" (discussed in Chapter 20) has the potential for reducing crime over the long term (also see the discussion in Kleiman, 1999). Also, community policing has some potential for increasing the certainty of punishment, since it establishes closer ties between the police and community and better involves community residents in crime control efforts. Finally, we might increase certainty by providing more resources to juvenile courts and correctional agencies, so that they can impose meaningful sanctions on a higher percentage of juvenile offenders.

Summary. Increasing the certainty of punishment may reduce delinquency by a moderate amount in the general population; increasing the severity of punishment has little or no effect on delinquency in the general population unless, perhaps, the certainty of punishment is high. Most of the get-tough approaches described focus on increasing the severity of punishment; as such, there is good reason to believe that they do little to reduce offending in the general population. Unfortunately, it is much more difficult to increase the certainty of punishment than the severity of punishment.

Incapacitation: Will Locking Up Delinquents Reduce Delinquency?

Deterrence is based on the fear of punishment. Increasing the certainty and severity of punishment is supposed to increase the fear of punishment and thereby deter people from committing crime. However, it is often difficult to deter juveniles from committing crimes—both juveniles who have been punished and those in the general population. Partly as a consequence, many people have come to recommend another get-tough approach to controlling delinquency. They argue that we should lock up serious offenders for long periods. This strategy, they claim, will substantially reduce crime. The reason is simple: If you lock up offenders, they cannot commit crimes on the street. Crime is therefore reduced even if no one is deterred from committing crime. This delinquency control strategy is known as incapacitation.[14]

Incapacitation has become the major strategy in the United States for controlling adult crime. The number of adults held in prisons in the United States increased from 200,000 in 1971 to over 1,560,000 in 2006, and the *rate* of incarceration increased about fivefold during this time. The United States is sending many more adults to prison and confining them for longer periods. The average length of confinement for a violent crime, for example, has more than tripled since 1975. The primary reason for this dramatic increase in incarceration rates is the belief that it will reduce crime. Again, locking up criminals prevents them from committing crimes on the streets.

Incapacitation is not the major strategy for controlling juvenile delinquency, but it is an important strategy. As discussed earlier, there has been a movement to increase the number of serious juvenile offenders sent to institutions and to increase the length of time they stay in such institutions. Although this movement is partly designed to deter delinquency, it is also motivated by a desire to protect society by getting serious offenders off the street.

How can one determine how much crime is prevented by incapacitation? The strategy of incapacitation makes much common sense: If you lock people up, you prevent crime on the streets. But how do criminologists go about determining just how much crime is prevented? On the face of it, it seems as if it should be easy to calculate the amount of crime prevented through incapacitation. One simply estimates how many crimes incarcerated offenders commit each year when they are free. This estimation can be done by surveying such offenders or examining their arrest records, although

there are, of course, concerns about the accuracy of such estimates (see Zimring and Hawkins, 1997). Such estimates, then, can be used to determine how many crimes are prevented by locking up criminals.

For example, suppose researchers find that the average juvenile in a training school commits 10 crimes per year when free. And suppose that 100,000 juveniles are in training schools. Incarceration, then, prevents 1 million offenses per year (10 multiplied by 100,000). If society incarcerates an additional 50,000 offenders, it might prevent another 500,000 crimes. Estimates of this sort were offered during the 1970s, when incapacitation was becoming a popular crime control strategy. Several researchers claimed that incapacitating offenders prevents a large amount of crime and that incapacitating additional offenders will prevent much more crime.

It turns out that such claims were exaggerated. Assume that researchers obtain accurate estimates of the number of crimes incarcerated offenders commit each year when free. For example, suppose they determine that the average incarcerated offender commits 10 crimes per year when free. One might then conclude that locking an offender up prevents 10 crimes per year. But this conclusion is not necessarily correct.

First, it may be that when society locks up one offender, another criminal takes that offender's place. So if we lock up someone for selling drugs on a street corner, someone else may start selling drugs on the same corner the next day. As a result, no crime is prevented. This phenomenon is known as a *substitution effect.* It is difficult to estimate how much substitution occurs; it may be high for certain crimes like drug selling but low for other crimes like robbery.

Second, we know that most juvenile offenses are committed in groups. Locking up one juvenile in the group may have little or no effect on the amount of crime committed by the group. Once again, there is no reduction in crime. This is known as a *group effect.* Again, it is difficult to estimate the size of this effect.

Third, many juvenile offenders substantially reduce their level of offending toward the end of adolescence. This phenomenon, sometimes referred to as "maturing out" of delinquency, occurs as juveniles leave their delinquent peers, get jobs or enter college, and form families of their own. Imprisoning such juveniles for long periods would not prevent a large amount of crime, since these juveniles would have stopped committing crimes on their own.

Fourth, estimates about the effect of locking up *additional* offenders may be exaggerated, because these additional offenders may not commit as much crime as the offenders who are already locked up. That is, the offenders who are already locked up may commit more crimes per year when free than those who are not locked up; high-rate offenders are probably more likely to be in prison than low-rate offenders. As a result, locking up additional offenders may not prevent as many crimes as one would estimate, since these additional offenders commit crimes at a lower rate.

It is therefore difficult to estimate the amount of crime that is prevented through incapacitation and the amount of crime that will be prevented by incapacitating additional juveniles. Nevertheless, there have been several efforts to estimate the effectiveness of incapacitation as a crime control strategy. Some of these estimates are based on studies that attempt to determine the number of crimes that offenders commit each year when free. Such estimates are then used to calculate the amount of crime prevented by incapacitation. As indicated, however, there are serious problems with this strategy: It likely exaggerates the size of the incapacitation effect. As a consequence, some researchers have employed alternative strategies.

In particular, some researchers compare states or other areas that have different rates of incarceration. The objective is to determine whether areas with higher rates of incarceration have lower crime rates. However, one must take account of all the other factors that affect crime rates—something that is not easy to do. Also, it is possible that any association between incarceration rates and crime rates is due to the effect of crime rates on incarceration rates. For example, high rates of crime may overwhelm the criminal justice system and lead to low rates of incarceration.

Other researchers examine incarceration rates and crime rates in the same area over time. The objective is to determine whether changes in the incarceration rate are associated with changes in the crime rate. For example, what impact has the massive increase in incarceration rates in recent decades had on crime rates? Such studies, however, must also take account of the other factors that might affect the crime rate. Also, such studies are not able to distinguish **incapacitation** effects from **deterrence** effects. That is, they are not able to determine whether an increase in incarceration rates reduces crime because incarcerated offenders cannot commit crimes on the street (an incapacitation effect) or because potential offenders are deterred from committing crimes.

What is the impact of incapacitation on crime rates? So none of the types of studies just discussed is problem-free. Taken together, however, they give us a **rough** sense of the effectiveness of incapacitation as a crime control strategy. Most studies have focused on adults and have examined the massive increase in incarceration since the 1970s. The best studies suggest that this increase in incarceration has had a moderate effect on crime rates. In particular, the best studies in this area suggest that a 10 percent increase in the incarceration rate is associated with a 2 to 4 percent lower crime rate (see Stemen, 2007:5). However, as the incarceration rate increases, the reduction in crime resulting from further increases is reduced (because more lower-rate offenders are imprisoned). It is estimated that about one-quarter of the crime drop during the 1990s was due to the rapidly increasing rates of incarceration the United States experienced during the 1980s and 1990s.[15]

These studies are based largely on adults. It is not clear to what extent incapacitation prevents crime among juveniles. While we have become more likely to confine serious juvenile offenders, the juvenile incarceration rate has not increased as fast as the adult rate. As indicated earlier, the rate at which juveniles are confined is less than half the adult rate.

Also, juveniles are more likely than adults to offend in groups, so incapacitation may have a smaller effect on juvenile crime rates. Further, most incarcerated juveniles will be released from confinement when they are still relatively young. If incarceration increases their level of subsequent offending, the benefits of incarceration may be lost (see Chapter 9, Vieraitis et al., 2007). Some data suggest that this is the case with trying juveniles as adults. We prevent some crime by confining these juveniles in adult prisons, but these juveniles offend at higher rates when released, which more than wipes out the benefits of confinement. Given these considerations, we may very tentatively conclude that **the strategy of incapacitation has resulted in only a modest reduction in rates of juvenile offending.**

What if we confine more juveniles, especially high-rate offenders? We can, of course, achieve a larger incapacitation effect if we confine more juveniles, especially those who offend at high rates. In particular, we might try to better distinguish between juveniles likely to offend at high rates in the future and those likely to offend at low rates. Once such a distinction is made, we might then confine those predicted to be high-rate offenders for long periods. This approach is sometimes referred to as *selective incapacitation,* since there is an attempt to selectively confine high-rate offenders.

It is difficult, however, for juvenile justice officials to accurately distinguish high-rate from low-rate offenders. You might think that high-rate offenders are simply the juveniles with the longest arrest records. But many juveniles with extensive arrest records are not high-rate offenders. They are simply inept offenders. They do not commit that many crimes; they just get caught a lot. Further, most high-rate offenders do not have extensive arrest records. Dunford and Elliott (1984), for example, found that only 19 percent of the juveniles who self-reported over 200 offenses during a two-year period had been arrested.

Several efforts have been made to develop techniques for distinguishing high-rate from low-rate offenders. These techniques improve our ability to distinguish between offenders by a modest amount, and additional research may result in further improvements. Currently, however, we make a lot of mistakes when attempting to distinguish between offenders (see Auerhahn, 1999; Gottfredson and Gottfredson, 1994). Many of the individuals predicted to be high-rate offenders turn out to be low-rate offenders. And some of the individuals predicted to be low-rate offenders turn out to be high-rate offenders.

Also, there are ethical issues to consider. For example, an individual predicted to be a high-rate offender might be confined for a much longer period than another individual predicted to be a low-rate offender, even though both committed the same offense. Do you think it is appropriate to base a juvenile's punishment on the number of crimes he or she *might* commit in the future rather than simply on the crimes the juvenile has already committed?

Summary. Overall, we can very tentatively conclude that the strategy of incapacitating serious juvenile offenders prevents a modest amount of crime. Efforts to confine additional juvenile offenders, especially high-rate offenders, may prevent more crime. But the amount of additional crime prevented is likely to be modest as well, for reasons indicated in this section.

Furthermore, incapacitation carries a heavy price tag. It is expensive to maintain the juvenile institutions that we now have, and it will be expensive to build and maintain additional institutions. Some argue that incapacitation more than pays for itself in terms of the crime it prevents, although there is much debate here (e.g., Fass and Pi, 2002). Also, some data suggest that alternatives to incapacitation, such as prevention and rehabilitation programs, may be more cost-effective than incapacitation (see Chapter 24).

In addition, many commentators have pointed to the devastating effect that incapacitation has had on both the people who are locked up and the larger community (see Stemen, 2007; Tonry, 1995). In particular, large numbers of people are exposed to the harsh conditions of confinement and are labeled "ex-convicts" upon their release, with this label having a negative effect on their future life prospects. The strategy of incapacitation is said to have an especially negative effect on African American communities, since African Americans are much more likely to be confined than other groups. One study estimates that about one in six African American men has been incarcerated and that, if current trends continue, one in three African American males born today will spend time in prison (Mauer and King, 2007).

This is not to dismiss incapacitation. No one would deny that there are dangerous offenders who need confinement. Such confinement protects society by preventing such individuals from committing crimes on the street. But incapacitation should not be our major strategy for responding to delinquency. To the extent possible, incapacitation should be limited to serious and high-rate offenders, efforts should be made to improve the conditions of confinement, and some attempt should be made to rehabilitate those juveniles who are confined.

Summary

The juvenile court and correctional system have focused on getting tough with serious offenders in recent years. Their get-tough efforts include the increased use of intermediate sanctions (versus regular probation), the increased use of confinement, and making it easier to try serious offenders in adult courts.

Overall, data suggest that these efforts do not deter those juveniles who are punished from further offending. These efforts probably do not deter juveniles in the general population from offending, largely because they focus on increasing the severity rather than the certainty of punishment. These efforts, however, may prevent a modest amount of crime by confining offenders in institutions so that they cannot commit crimes on the street.

Several strategies for increasing the effectiveness of these get-tough efforts were discussed, including strategies designed to increase their specific deterrent effect, general deterrent effect, and incapacitation effect. Such strategies include increasing the certainty of punishment, which involves hiring more police, changing police practices, and devoting more resources to juvenile courts and correctional agencies. They include combining punishment with rehabilitation programs that address the other causes of crime. They include employing the restorative justice approach, which minimizes the negative consequences of punishment and attempts to address certain of the other causes of crime. And they include efforts to improve the conditions of confinement, and, to the extent possible, reserve confinement for serious, high-rate offenders.

As suggested earlier, however, the ultimate effectiveness of get-tough efforts is limited, because they focus on just one of the many causes of crime: low direct control. Any effort to substantially reduce juvenile crime needs to focus on all of the major causes of such crime. While it may be appropriate and sometimes useful to sanction juvenile offenders, we also want to make an effort to rehabilitate such offenders, employing programs that address the other causes of delinquency. And we also want to try to stop delinquency from occurring in the first place by employing prevention programs that address the many causes of delinquency. The strategies of rehabilitation and prevention are discussed in Chapter 24.

Teaching Aids

Controversial Issue: Abolish the Juvenile Court?

As indicated in this chapter and in Chapter 21, juvenile courts are becoming more like adult courts. Many of the due process rights available to adults have been extended to juveniles (e.g., the right to confront and cross-examine witnesses, and to be represented by an attorney). As a consequence, juvenile court hearings have become more formal. (Juveniles, however, do not have all of the due process rights available to adults—for example, the right to a jury trial. Also, many juvenile courts do not extend certain rights to juveniles, and/or they encourage juveniles not to exercise certain rights [see Feld, 1999].) In addition, juvenile courts have come to focus more on punishing juveniles for the offenses they commit as opposed to helping juveniles address their problems. Further, large numbers of juvenile offenders are now being tried in adult courts.

Given these changes, it is not surprising that some criminologists and policy makers have started to wonder about the future of the juvenile court (see Butts and Mitchell, 2000). At one extreme, some argue that the juvenile court should return to its original mission, acting in the best interests of troubled juveniles. In particular, they argue that the juvenile court should have authority over both status offenders and delinquents, that there should be less emphasis on due process rights, and that there should be more emphasis on rehabilitation and prevention. At the other extreme, some argue that the juvenile court should be abolished and that all juveniles who commit criminal acts should come under the jurisdiction of the criminal court (juveniles who commit status offenses should be dealt with by social service agencies).

Perhaps the leading advocate for the abolition of the juvenile court is Feld (1999). Among other things, Feld argues that juvenile courts often subject juveniles to severe sanctions without granting them the due process protections available to adults.

> [Juvenile court has become] a scaled-down, second-class criminal court for young people. . . . [Juvenile courts] use courtroom procedures under which no adult would consent to be tried if she faced the prospect of confinement and then incarcerate youths in prisonlike settings for substantial terms. . . . [Y]ouths whom judges remove from home or incarcerate in institutions for terms of months or years receive substantially fewer procedural safeguards than do adults convicted of comparable crimes. (Feld, 1999:287, 288)

Feld further argues that it is not possible for the juvenile court to successfully address the problems of children. It is difficult to both exercise control over juvenile offenders and address their needs, and juvenile courts come to focus on controlling offenders given their criminal behavior (although concerns with rehabilitation often lead to mild sanctions). Society does not provide juvenile courts with the resources to adequately address the needs of children, partly because there is little compassion for the types of juveniles most often handled by juvenile courts. Addressing the needs of children should not be the province of a judicial agency but, rather, a broadly shared social responsibility.

> Combining social welfare and penal social control functions only ensures that the court performs both functions badly. Providing for child welfare is a social responsibility, not a judicial one, and the polity declines to provide those necessary resources because juvenile court's clients are poor, disproportionately minorities, and criminal offenders. (Feld, 1999:294)

Abolishing the juvenile court and trying all juveniles in criminal court would have several advantages, according to Feld. Most notably, it would ensure that juveniles receive the same due process protections as adults. But Feld does not argue that juvenile offenders should necessarily receive the same sanctions as adults. Rather, he states:

> [Criminal courts should] formally recognize youthfulness as a mitigating factor in criminal sentencing to accommodate the reduced culpability of younger offenders. Young people differ from adults in their breadth of experience, temporal perspective, willingness to take risks, maturity of judgement, and susceptibility to peer influences. . . . I propose an age-based "youth discount" of sentences—a sliding scale of developmental and criminal responsibility—to implement the lesser culpability of young offenders in the legal system. (Feld, 1999:289–290)

What is your reaction to Feld's arguments? Do you feel that the juvenile court should be abolished? Justify your response. If you do **not** feel that the juvenile court system should be abolished, do you feel that it should be altered? If so, how (e.g., more emphasis on rehabilitation, more informal proceedings)?

Controversial Issue: Life Without Parole for Juvenile Offenders?

The United States now prohibits the execution of individuals who committed their crimes while juveniles (see Chapter 1). However, juveniles may be sentenced to life imprisonment without the possibility of parole in certain circumstances. About 2,200 individuals are now serving terms of life without parole for crimes they committed when they were 17 or younger. Some of these individuals were as young as 13 or 14 when they committed their crimes, as indicated in this excerpt from a *New York Times* article:

> In December [2006], the United Nations took up a resolution calling for the abolition of life imprisonment without the possibility of parole for children and young teenagers. The vote was 185 to 1, with the United States the lone dissenter. Indeed, the United States stands alone in the world in convicting young adolescents as adults and sentencing them to live out their lives in prison. According to a new report, there are 73 Americans serving such sentences for crimes they committed at 13 or 14. . . . [One such American] was 14 when she helped her boyfriend kill her grandfather and aunt . . . by stabbing and shooting them and then setting them on fire. [She] also tried to kill her 10 year-old sister. . . . Prosecutors and victims' rights groups say there are crimes so terrible and people so dangerous that only life sentences without the possibility of release are a fit moral and practical response. (Liptak, 2007:A1, A24)

Do you think it is appropriate to sentence certain juveniles to life without parole? In formulating your response, consider the arguments made in this chapter about deterrence (specific and general) and incapacitation, as well as the arguments made for the abolition of the juvenile death penalty in Chapter 1.

TEST YOUR KNOWLEDGE OF THIS CHAPTER

1. Many argue that increasing the certainty and severity of punishment will reduce delinquency in three ways (or for three reasons). What are these ways?

2. Many argue that the juvenile court is not tough enough in dealing with serious offenders. What do the data say in this area? (Describe data on the punishments received by serious offenders in juvenile court and on the punishments given out in juvenile versus adult court.)

3. Why doesn't the juvenile court system give out more severe sanctions?

4. The OJJDP advocates a system of "graduated sanctions." Describe this system.

5. Briefly describe the major ways in which juvenile courts have tried to get tough with offenders in recent years. What does the evidence say about the effect of these get-tough measures on how juvenile offenders are treated by the justice system?

6. Briefly describe mandatory minimum sentences, sentencing guidelines, and blended sentences.

7. List three ways in which states have tried to increase the number of juvenile offenders waived to adult courts.

8. List two ways in which the confidentiality of juvenile court hearings has been reduced.

9. What is meant by "deterrence"? How is deterrence related to control and social learning theories?

10. What is "specific deterrence"?

11. How have researchers tried to determine if punishments have a specific deterrent effect?

12. Why doesn't punishing offenders deter them from further delinquency?

13. How can we punish in a more effective manner?

14. What is the restorative justice approach? Describe the goals of restorative justice, how the approach is implemented (e.g., the conference), and how the approach tries to sanction in a more effective manner.

15. What does the evaluation research say about the restorative justice approach?

16. What is "general deterrence"?

17. How have researchers tried to determine if punishments have a general deterrent effect? Summarize the major research findings regarding general deterrence.

18. How might we go about increasing the certainty of punishment?

19. What is meant by an "incapacitation effect"?

20. How have researchers tried to determine the size of the incapacitation effect? Why do researchers sometimes overestimate the size of the incapacitation effect?

21. Why do I suggest that efforts to incapacitate juvenile offenders have only a modest effect on the level of juvenile crime?

22. What is "selective incapacitation"?

23. What are the disadvantages of incapacitation as a crime control strategy?

THOUGHT AND DISCUSSION QUESTIONS

1. Give an example of a crime control strategy that has an incapacitation effect but little or no deterrent effect. Give an example of a strategy that has a deterrent effect but no incapacitation effect.

2. Many high schools and colleges are experiencing high levels of cheating, with a majority of their students having cheated in many cases. Drawing on the materials in this chapter, design a sanctioning system to reduce levels of school cheating.

3. One college sanctions cheaters by giving them a failing grade for their first offense and expelling them for their second offense. How would you go about evaluating the effectiveness of this strategy (consider specific deterrence, general deterrence, and the possible incapacitation effect achieved through expulsion—expelled students can no longer cheat on campus)?

4. Suppose the governor of your home state seeks your advice about how to control juvenile violence. The governor states that she is thinking of mandating that all juveniles convicted of minor violent crimes serve at least 30 days in a boot camp and that all juveniles charged with serious violent crimes be tried in an adult court. Would you try to discourage the governor from taking these actions? If so, why? What alternative actions would you recommend?

5. One of the major get-tough strategies employed by states involves making it easier to try juvenile offenders in adult courts, where they are often sanctioned with periods of confinement in prison. Do you think a strain theorist would approve of this strategy? Justify your response. What about a control theorist, a social learning theorist, and a labeling theorist?

KEY TERMS

- Specific deterrence
- General deterrence
- Incapacitation
- Graduated sanctions
- Mandatory minimum sentences
- Sentencing guidelines

- Blended sentences
- Deterrence
- Certainty and severity of punishment
- Restorative justice
- Restorative justice conference

- Substitution effect (regarding incapacitation)
- Group effect
- Selective incapacitation

ENDNOTES

1. For overviews of such efforts, *see* Butts and Mitchell, 2000; Campaign for Youth and Justice, 2007; Feld, 1999; Greenwood, 2002, 2006; Howell, 2003a; Krisberg, 2005; Kupchik, 2006; McCord et al., 2001; Roberts, 2004; Snyder and Sickmund, 2006; Zimring, 2005.

2. *See* Bishop and Frazier, 2000; Butts and Mitchell, 2000; Kupchik, 2006; Kurlychek and Johnson, 2004; McCord et al., 2001; Steiner et al., 2006.

3. *See* Butts and Mitchell, 2000; Campaign for Youth and Justice, 2007; Feld, 1999; Greenwood, 2002; Howell, 2003a; Krisberg, 2005; McCord et al., 2001; Snyder and Sickmund, 2006; Steiner et al., 2006; Torbet and Szymanski, 1998.

4. *See* Bishop, 2006; Bishop and Frazier, 2000; Butts and Mitchell, 2000; Howell, 2003a; Puzzanchera et al., 2003.

5. For overviews of the deterrence literature, *see* Akers and Sellers, 2004; Andrews and Bonta, 2003, 2006; Krohn, 2000; Lipsey and Cullen, 2008; MacKenzie, 2006; Nagin, 1998a, 1998b;

Paternoster, 1987; Piquero and Pogarsky, 2002; Rutter et al., 1998; Schneider, 1990; Sherman et al., 1998; Williams and Hawkins, 1986; Wright, R., 1994.

6. *See* Andrews and Bonta, 2003, 2006; Bernburg et al., 2007; Bishop and Frazier, 2000; Bottcher and Ezell, 2005; Bazemore et al., 2004; Butts and Mitchell, 2000; Greenwood, 2002; Howell, 2003a; Johnson et al., 2004; Lin, 2006; Lipsey and Cullen, 2008; MacKenzie, 2002, 2006; Matarazzo et al., 2001; McCord et al., 2001; Parent, 2003; Peters et al., 1997; Petrosino et al., 2000; Pratt and Cullen, 2005; Redding and Howell, 2000; Steiner et al., 2006.

7. *See* Bernburg et al., 2007; Browning and Huizinga, 1999; Farrington, 1977; Farrington et al., 1978; Gold and Williams, 1969; Huizinga et al., 2003; Johnson et al., 2004; Palamara et al., 1986; Paternoster and Iovanni, 1989; Paternoster and Piquero, 1995; Piquero and Pogarsky, 2002; Pogarsky and Piquero, 2003; Schneider, 1990; Sherman, 1993; Sherman et al., 1998; Stewart, Simons, Conger, and Scaramella, 2002; Wolfgang et al., 1972.

8. *See* Bridges and Stone, 1986; Paternoster and Piquero, 1995; Piquero and Paternoster, 1998; Piquero and Pogarsky, 2002; Pogarsky and Piquero, 2003; Pogarsky et al., 2004; Schneider, 1990.

9. For fuller discussions, *see* Andrews and Bonta, 2006; Braithwaite, 1989; Nagin and Paternoster, 1994; Sherman, 1993, 2000; Sherman et al., 1992; Sherman et al., 1998; Wooldredge and Thistlethwaite, 2002.

10. *See* note 6 above.

11. For fuller discussions of the philosophy and practice of restorative justice, *see* Andrews and Bonta, 2003, 2006; Bazemore, 2000; Bazemore and Umbreit, 2001, 2004; Bonta et al., 2006; Braithwaite, 2002, 2005; Levrant et al., 1999; McGarrell and Hipple, 2007; Office of Juvenile Justice and Delinquency Prevention, 1998a; Rodriguez, 2007.

12. *See* note 11 above.

13. *See* Carmichael and Piquero, 2004; Chamlin, 1991; Chamlin et al., 1992; Foglia, 1997; Grasmick and Bursik, 1990; Klepper and Nagin, 1989; Levitt, 2002; Lipsey and Cullen, 2008; MacKenzie, 2006; Matsueda et al., 2006; Nagin and Paternoster, 1991, 1993, 1994; Paternoster and Piquero, 1995; Piquero and Pogarsky, 2002; Pratt and Cullen, 2005; Sherman et al., 1992; Steiner et al., 2006; Yu and Liska, 1993; Wright et al., 2004.

14. For overviews, *see* Andrews and Bonta, 2006; Auerhahn, 1999; Blumstein, 1998; Conklin, 2003; Currie, 1998; MacKenzie, 2006; Nagin, 1998b; Pratt and Cullen, 2005; Sherman et al., 1998; Spelman, 2000, 2006; Stemen, 2007; Visher, 2000; Walker, 1998; Wright, R., 1994; Zimring and Hawkins, 1995.

15. *Also see* Andrews and Bonta, 2006; Conklin, 2003; MacKenzie, 2002, 2006; Pratt and Cullen, 2005; Rosenfeld, 2000; Spelman, 2000; Spelman, 2006; Stemen, 2007; Zimring, 2007.

CHAPTER 24

The Strategies of Prevention and Rehabilitation

Is It Possible to Prevent Delinquency and to Rehabilitate Delinquents?

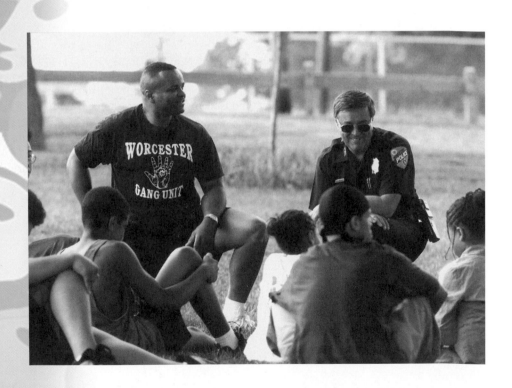

Many criminologists argue that **the juvenile justice system places too much emphasis on get-tough approaches.** They point out that such approaches have no effect or only a modest effect on delinquency. While we can increase the effectiveness of such approaches, their ultimate effect on delinquency is limited, since they address only one of the many causes of offending: low direct control. Further, such approaches are frequently expensive, and they expose many juveniles to the often brutal conditions of juvenile institutions. The Georgia Alliance for Children, a child advocacy group, ran an advertisement that showed a young juvenile curled up on a concrete floor, with the caption: "You're in an 8 × 10 cell with four thugs twice your size. You would scream, but the underwear your grandmother sent is stuffed in your mouth" (McDevitt, 2000).

It is argued that, rather than simply getting tough, **the justice system should place more emphasis on rehabilitating juvenile offenders and preventing juveniles from becoming delinquent in the first place.** Although the juvenile justice system places much emphasis on rehabilitation in theory, juvenile offenders often do not receive effective rehabilitation programs **in practice.** And, with certain exceptions, only limited efforts are made to prevent delinquency.

Prevention and rehabilitation programs do not try to reduce delinquency by increasing direct control by the juvenile justice system. Rather, they try to **reduce delinquency by focusing on the other causes of delinquency.** At the most general level, the more effective prevention and rehabilitation programs attempt to increase the other types of control, reduce strain or the tendency to respond to strain with crime, reduce the social learning of crime, and/or reduce negative labeling. At a more specific level, they try to do such things as alter the individual traits that contribute to crime, increase family bonding, improve parental supervision and discipline, reduce family conflict and abuse, increase school attachment and performance, and reduce association with delinquent peers and gangs.

Prevention programs are distinguished from rehabilitation programs in the following way. Prevention programs try to prevent juveniles from becoming delinquent in the first place; rehabilitation programs try to reduce the delinquency of juveniles who already are delinquent. Some prevention programs focus on all or most juveniles. For example, the federal government is now sponsoring a major advertising campaign to reduce drug use among juveniles. You may have seen or heard some of these ads or ads from earlier campaigns ("Just say no," "Life can be hard . . . sometimes I need to be harder"; see the Ad Gallery at http://www.mediacampaign.org). Other prevention programs target juveniles believed to be at risk for engaging in delinquency. For example, they may target low-birthweight infants, juveniles in high-crime communities, or juveniles whose teachers or parents say they are at risk for delinquency. Prevention and rehabilitation programs are sometimes discussed separately, but I discuss them together because many of the same programs are used for both prevention and rehabilitation purposes.

This chapter has five parts. First, I provide a brief history of prevention and rehabilitation programs. Second, I discuss the effectiveness of prevention and rehabilitation programs and describe the general features of the most successful programs. Third, I describe the characteristics of successful prevention and rehabilitation programs that focus on the early family environment, parent training, the school, individual traits, and delinquent peer groups and gangs. Most prevention and rehabilitation programs focus on these areas. Fourth, I briefly describe prevention and rehabilitation programs in several other areas. Finally, I discuss the crucial role of larger social forces in preventing delinquency. As you will see, the most successful prevention and rehabilitation programs address many of the causes of delinquency described in Chapters 6 through 18.[1]

A Brief History of Prevention and Rehabilitation

Prevention programs have never played a major role in delinquency control efforts, except for a brief period in the 1960s and early 1970s during the heyday of the War on Poverty (see Empey et al., 1999). The *War on Poverty* was initiated by President Kennedy in the early 1960s and largely implemented by his successor, President Johnson. One of the purposes of the War on Poverty was to reduce crime and delinquency by increasing the opportunities for people to achieve success through legitimate channels. Some of the programs that made up the War on Poverty provided educational assistance and job training to juveniles in disadvantaged communities. The War on Poverty, then, was partly based on strain theory, which views the failure to achieve monetary success as a major cause of crime. Most of the programs that were part of the War on Poverty have since been dismantled, but a few remain, like Project Head Start and Job Corps.

You might wonder why prevention does not play a greater role in society's efforts to control delinquency. Prevention seems to make a lot of sense; it seems better to prevent delinquency from developing in the first place than to react to delinquency after it occurs. But several objections have been raised to prevention programs: They are said to interfere in the private affairs of individuals and families (e.g., "It is none of the government's business how parents raise their children"—unless the parents or children engage in illegal behavior). They are said to be costly and ineffective. Conservatives often point to the fact that crime and delinquency rates increased dramatically during the 1960s and early 1970s, at the very time that the War on Poverty was being mounted (data on the effectiveness of the War on Poverty are mixed; see Empey et al., 1999). Finally, prevention programs are at odds with the current get-tough approach to controlling delinquency, which claims that offenders are responsible for their behavior and deserve punishment. Politicians who advocate prevention programs expose themselves to charges of being soft on crime.

Although prevention has played only a small role in delinquency control in the United States, **rehabilitation was the guiding philosophy of the juvenile justice system from its inception in the 1800s until the 1970s.** That does not mean that the juvenile justice system made a serious effort at rehabilitation; there was often a large gap between philosophy and practice. But the major goal of the juvenile justice system was said to be the rehabilitation of delinquents. And rehabilitation is still part of the guiding philosophy of the juvenile justice system, although get-tough approaches have become increasingly popular.

Rehabilitation fell out of favor during the 1970s for several reasons. Rising crime rates during the 1960s and early 1970s caused many to question its effectiveness. These doubts about rehabilitation were reinforced by several studies in the 1970s and 1980s that claimed rehabilitation was largely ineffective. The best known of these studies, the "Martinson Report," examined a wide range of rehabilitation programs employed from 1945 to 1967. The report came to the conclusion that "with few and isolated exceptions the rehabilitative efforts that have been reported so far have had no appreciable effect on recidivism" (Martinson, 1974:25). Finally, the political climate of the country became more conservative. Criminals, including older delinquents, were said to be responsible for their behavior. And politicians and others argued that such individuals deserved punishment and that punishment was the best way to reduce crime and delinquency. In particular, punishment would reduce crime through deterrence and incapacitation.[2]

The past few years, however, have seen **a renewed interest in prevention and rehabilitation,** especially on the part of many criminologists and, increasingly, on the part of the federal government and certain states. The federal strategy for controlling delinquency now emphasizes both punishment (as described in Chapter 23) **and** prevention and rehabilitation. The federal government has done much to publicize the prevention and rehabilitation programs that show promise. The website for the Office of Juvenile Justice and Delinquency Prevention (OJJDP) contains much information on prevention and rehabilitation programs, including a number of publications that you can download (http://ojjdp.ncjrs .org). One federal publication is titled simply *Delinquency Prevention Works* (Office of Juvenile Justice and Delinquency Prevention, 1995). Further, other federal agencies, like the Centers for Disease Control and Prevention (CDC), are promoting prevention programs as well (see Thornton et al., 2002; U.S. Department of Health and Human Services, 2001).

This renewed interest in prevention and rehabilitation partly stems from the research suggesting that get-tough approaches have no effect or only a modest effect on delinquency. It also stems from the high financial and social costs of many get-tough approaches (see Currie, 1998; Stemen, 2007; Tonry, 1995). Many states, in fact, are doing away with certain of the get-tough approaches they adopted because they can no longer afford to fund them (von Zielbauer, 2003). But perhaps most important of all, the renewed interest in prevention and rehabilitation programs stems from recent research suggesting that certain of these programs are effective at reducing delinquency.

Reflecting this renewed interest, several states are now making deliberate efforts to reduce the number of juveniles they incarcerate and/or refer to the adult court system. The state of Connecticut, in fact, recently raised the age at which juvenile offenders are treated as adults from 16 to 18 (*New York Times,* 2007c). More generally, the rate at which juveniles are incarcerated and transferred to adult court has been declining since the late 1990s. Many states are instead placing an increased emphasis on the rehabilitation of offenders and the prevention of delinquency (Paulson, 2006). I next discuss the effectiveness of these strategies.

How Effective Are Prevention and Rehabilitation Programs?

Several researchers have recently reviewed the evaluations of prevention and rehabilitation programs. In one case, 443 evaluations were reviewed (Lipsey, 1992). All of these reviewers faced a major problem: Most prevention and rehabilitation programs had not been properly evaluated. That is, researchers did not employ the procedures for evaluation research described in Chapter 19. Most commonly, they did not randomly assign juveniles to the treatment and control groups. The evaluations also frequently suffer from other problems, such as high dropout rates from the treatment group, a failure to conduct long-term follow-ups, and a failure to examine how well the program was implemented. Further, many of the decent evaluations that have been done are in need of replication. As noted in Chapter 19, programs should be evaluated across different settings and populations. A program that works well in one setting or with one group of juveniles may not work well in another setting or with another group. As a result of these problems, criminologists know much less about the effectiveness of prevention and rehabilitation programs than they would like. Virtually every review of prevention and rehabilitation programs stresses the need for more and better evaluation research.

At the same time, there have been enough moderately well-done evaluations to allow us to draw some conclusions about the effectiveness of prevention and rehabilitation programs. The reviews suggest that well-designed and well-implemented prevention and rehabilitation programs can reduce rates of delinquency anywhere from 20 percent to 50 percent.[3] These estimates vary because different reviews look at different programs and employ different definitions of "well-designed" programs. But the evidence is sufficient to suggest that **prevention and rehabilitation programs have an important role to play in efforts to control delinquency.** As criminologists learn more about the characteristics of effective programs and how to best implement them, the role of prevention and rehabilitation will likely increase. This is not to say that prevention and rehabilitation programs will solve the delinquency problem in the immediate future. But it is to say that society should make greater use of such programs—along with well-designed efforts to deter delinquency and incapacitate serious offenders. This strategy is precisely the one that the federal government is now advocating.

General Characteristics of Effective Prevention and Rehabilitation Programs

It is important to emphasize that the reviews of prevention and rehabilitation programs find that only some programs are effective at reducing delinquency; other programs have little effect on delinquency or actually increase delinquency. For example, some evaluations suggest that group discussions involving delinquent and conventional juveniles are counterproductive. The conventional juveniles are supposed to influence the delinquents in positive ways, but often the reverse occurs.

Criminologists now have a rough idea of what characteristics distinguish effective from ineffective programs. Such information, of course, is vital if society is to effectively control delinquency. Many individuals and groups are unaware of this information, and they continue to invest resources in programs that are likely to have little effect on delinquency. Drawing on several reviews, we can tentatively state that the most effective prevention and rehabilitation programs have the following characteristics:

1. **Focus on the major causes of delinquency in the group being treated.** This may sound obvious, but many prevention and rehabilitation programs focus on factors that are not causes, or at least not important causes, of delinquency. For example, they try to increase the juvenile's level of self-esteem. Other programs have no clear focus. Many programs, for example, employ unstructured counseling sessions. Counselors frequently hold "rap sessions" with juveniles where they discuss a wide range of issues. These types of programs have little effect on delinquency. In order for a program to be effective, it must address the causes of delinquency described in earlier chapters, such as individual traits, family and school problems, and association with delinquent peers.

Further, programs should attempt to target the causes of delinquency that are most relevant to the group being treated. For example, it makes little sense to target gang membership in a group where the rate of gang membership is low. Programs should also attempt to target all or most of the major causes of delinquency in a group. Delinquency is usually caused by several factors. Programs that focus only on one factor, even if it is an important cause of delinquency, will be less effective. An example of a very effective program that targets several causes is multisystematic therapy, or MST (see Blueprints for Violence Prevention; Gottfredson, 2006). MST draws on elements from several of the more focused programs described later.

2. **Are intensive.** The most effective programs usually last a long time and employ several techniques to influence the juvenile or group. One cannot change a juvenile's traits or alter a juvenile's social environment in a short period of time with minimal effort. For example, you cannot change the juvenile's level of irritability in a single counseling session. Likewise, you cannot change the way that family members relate to one another by simply giving parents a pamphlet to read over the weekend. Individual traits and interactional patterns have developed over many years, and they can be resistant to change. The most effective programs, then, tend to be the most intensive.

Many programs that try to change the behavior of individuals employ the following strategy, sometimes referred to as the *cognitive-behavioral approach.* First, instructors describe what they want the juvenile (or parent, etc.) to do. For example, they might tell the juvenile that he or she should employ a particular anger management technique when mad at others. The technique and its use are described in detail. The juvenile may also be given reading material on the technique. Second, the instructors display or model what it is that they want the juvenile to do; they may stage several situations in which someone gets angry and then uses the technique. Third, they get the juvenile to practice the technique, so juveniles may participate in a number of role-playing situations: Someone pretends to anger the juvenile, and the juvenile then employs the anger management technique. The instructors provide the juvenile with feedback, taking special care to reinforce successful performances. Fourth, the juvenile begins to apply the technique to situations in the real world. The juvenile might be asked to use the anger management technique the next time someone makes him or her angry. After reporting on the real world application and receiving feedback, the juvenile applies the technique to additional real world situations. Still more feedback and reinforcement are provided. Fifth, the juvenile reaches a point where regular instruction is no longer necessary. But the instructors are available for consultation if necessary, and the juvenile may periodically participate in refresher or booster courses. Influencing individuals and groups, then, is not an easy process. You should be suspicious if you hear someone claim that a program can reduce delinquency in a short period of time with minimal effort.

The fact that the most successful programs are intensive poses some problems for policy makers. It raises the cost of such programs, although most good programs are cost-effective, saving more money than they cost over the long run. (Aos et al., 2001; Greenwood, 2006). Also, the intensive nature of many prevention and rehabilitation programs makes it difficult to implement them on a large scale. Most programs have been implemented in small groups, where it is easier to ensure that they are properly run. It is more difficult to ensure that programs are properly run if they are implemented at many sites with many thousands of juveniles. The large-scale implementation of good prevention and rehabilitation programs, in fact, is perhaps the major challenge facing policy makers (beyond securing support for such programs). Not surprisingly, studies suggest that programs are much less successful when they are poorly implemented (Wilson et al., 2003).

3. **Focus on juveniles at high risk for subsequent delinquency.** Juveniles at high risk for delinquency are the ones who can benefit the most from prevention and rehabilitation programs, and programs focusing on such juveniles achieve the greatest reductions in subsequent delinquency. It makes little sense to provide programs to juveniles at low risk for delinquency; such juveniles will likely refrain from delinquency whether they participate in prevention and rehabilitation programs or not.

4. **Are run in the community.** Some data suggest that programs may be slightly more effective when they are run in the community rather than in juvenile institutions. It is easy to think of reasons why this might be the case. Juveniles confined in institutions are cut off from the larger community, including family, school, peer group, and neighborhood. As a result, it is more difficult for rehabilitation programs to address the family, school, and other problems that cause delinquency. Further, juveniles confined in institutions are exposed to other delinquents on a regular and intimate basis. These other delinquents often encourage delinquency and discourage cooperation with the staff. The staff, in fact, are often defined as the "enemy." Rehabilitation is obviously difficult under such circumstances. Finally, juveniles in institutions are often preoccupied with the stresses of confinement, including the threat of physical and sexual assault from others. These circumstances also make rehabilitation difficult. It is possible to help juveniles in institutions, but it may be somewhat more difficult to do so.

5. **Have a warm but firm relationship between counselors and juveniles.** Some evidence suggests that programs are more effective when counselors establish a warm or close relationship with the juveniles, and when they strongly discourage deviant behavior while encouraging conventional behavior. A close bond between counselors and juveniles reduces strain. Also, the juveniles are more likely to model the counselors' behavior, accept their beliefs, and respond to their sanctions. At the same time, it is important that the counselors clearly promote conventional behavior and condemn deviance. The counselors cannot be lax or let the juveniles take advantage of them. I should note that the importance of being warm but firm was also emphasized in the context of the family and school.

What Are the Characteristics of Successful Prevention/Rehabilitation Programs in Different Areas?

Many programs have shown some success at preventing delinquency and rehabilitating delinquents. It is impossible to describe all these programs in this book, but this section describes the key features of programs in several areas: programs focusing on the early family environment, parent training, the school, individual traits, and delinquent peers and gangs. These programs all address one or more of the causes of delinquency described in earlier chapters.

A few words of caution are in order, however, before I present the program descriptions. First, many different programs have been employed in each of the areas cited. Rather than describing these individual programs, I describe what I believe are the key features of successful programs in an area. Many of the individual programs contain only some of these key features. Second, while the evaluation research provides reason to believe that these programs can reduce delinquency, more and better research is needed. In certain cases, my conclusions are based on a small number of less-than-ideal evaluations. Third, while I describe the programs in each area separately from one another, these programs are sometimes combined in the real world. As indicated earlier, the most effective way to prevent delinquency or rehabilitate delinquents is to combine several programs so as to address the multiple causes of delinquency. Fourth, these programs—alone or in combination with one another—should not be viewed as the definitive solution to the delinquency problem. These programs can reduce delinquency in at least some circumstances, but it is unlikely that they will eliminate delinquency.

There are several reasons why these programs are unlikely to eliminate delinquency. They are often difficult to properly implement, especially on a large scale (see Gottfredson and Gottfredson, 2002). It is often difficult to ensure that everyone who needs these programs participates in them. In fact, the people who need these programs the most are often the least likely to participate in them—especially prevention programs, where participation is often voluntary. Furthermore, even if these programs are properly administered to the people who need them the most, they are still able to help only some of the program participants.

Programs Focusing on the Early Family Environment

As you know, the family has a major impact on delinquency. The family affects the juvenile's level of control, strain, labeling, and the social learning of crime. Some parents, for example, fail to develop a strong emotional bond with their children, fail to properly supervise their children, and abuse and neglect their children. These (in)actions directly increase the likelihood of delinquency. Also, they indirectly increase the likelihood of delinquency through their effect on such things as individual traits, school experiences, and association with delinquent peers and gangs (see Chapter 14 and the other chapters on the causes of delinquency for a full discussion). Juveniles in certain types of families, for example, more often experience biological harms like head injuries, birth complications, and exposure to toxic substances. They are therefore more likely to develop traits conducive to delinquency.

Several early family intervention programs have been developed in an effort to **reduce the likelihood that families produce delinquent children.** These programs typically target disadvantaged families or families at risk for certain problems, such as child abuse. For example, these programs might target single parents, adolescent mothers, the parents of premature or low-birth-weight babies, and/or families where there is a history of drug abuse or family violence. Some programs begin before the birth of the child, while others begin at or shortly after birth. In the most effective programs, the parents are visited weekly by a nurse, social worker, or trained paraprofessional. When necessary, these home visitors can turn to physicians, psychologists, or teachers for further assistance. These programs last anywhere from a few months to several years, with the longer programs being more successful.[4] Programs focusing on the early family environment address the causes of delinquency in three major ways.

First, they attempt to **reduce the child's exposure to biological harms by providing medical care to the child and mother and by providing health and safety training to the parents.** Expectant mothers may be given prenatal care and advice. Among other things, they are encouraged to avoid smoking, alcohol use, and drug use during pregnancy. If necessary, the mother will be provided with counseling and drug treatment. Such activities help prevent problems like low birth weight and birth complications. After birth, the child receives regular medical care and the parents receive assistance in caring for the child. The child in particular receives regular pediatric exams, and steps are taken to address any developmental or other problems that arise. The parents are also given information on child development and how to best care for their child. Such information and assistance can prevent a range of harmful biological events, such as head injuries and exposure to toxic substances such as lead.

Second, these programs also **attempt to foster good parenting practices by reducing parental stress and providing information on good parenting.** As you may recall from Chapter 14, two of the major determinants of poor parenting are stress and lack of knowledge. It is difficult to be a good parent if you do not have decent housing or a job, you struggle to put food on the table, you are involved in an abusive relationship, and the like. One of the first things these programs attempt to do is help parents address some of the basic problems they face. In particular, they may do such things as help the parents find decent housing, get a job, obtain food, secure medical care, arrange transportation, and end spouse abuse. Sometimes the home visitor provides this assistance. Home visitors often function as counselors to the family, discussing problems, offering advice and assistance, and providing emotional support. The home visitors also refer family members to various social service and treatment programs when necessary. The assistance of the home visitor not only makes it easier for the parents to engage in good parenting, but it also helps foster a bond between the home visitor and the parents.

It is also difficult to be a good parent if you were never exposed to good parenting, so the home visitors attempt to teach good parenting skills. They provide information on child development, offer advice on parenting, model parenting skills, and assist parents when necessary. They also monitor the progress of the child and intervene when necessary. For example, they may provide special assistance if it appears that the parents are not forming an emotional bond with their baby. In some cases, the parents may take special parent training classes or participate in parent-support groups. Also, male home visitors may make a special effort to work with the father if the father is present.

It is important to emphasize that these home visitors do not attempt to coerce or "talk down" to the parents. Rather, they try to function as friends and allies to the parents. For example, the home visitor in the Hawaii Healthy Start program introduces herself to the parents by saying something like the following:

> I work with the Healthy Start program. I have new information about babies that I didn't know when I was raising my kids. It can make being a mother easier, but not easy! Also, you can look at me as your information center about this community. I live here, too, and I didn't know about WIC [Special Supplemental Food Program for Women, Infants, and Children] or the well baby clinic before I started this job. I hope you learn to think of me as your "special" friend, someone here completely for you and the baby. I am here to talk when you need to share something that concerns you. I know that it is hard to start with a new baby and to have so much on your mind. (Earle, 1995:6)

Third, these programs **often provide educational child care.** Such care better prepares the child for school. Also, it reduces the stress on the parents by providing them with a break from constant child care and by making it easier for them to obtain employment. In addition, the parents are taught how to provide a stimulating environment to their child so as to foster the child's cognitive development. Related to this, a toy- and book-lending library is often made available to the parents.

Programs focusing on the early family environment, then, **address several of the most important causes of delinquency. They reduce the likelihood of biological harm,** which in turn reduces the likelihood that juveniles will develop traits conducive to crime. They **address several family factors that are related to delinquency,** including the emotional bond between the parents and child, the level of parental supervision, and child abuse and neglect. (For a discussion of programs focusing specifically on child abuse, see Barlow et al., 2006; Cronin et al., 2006.) They also supplement the socialization efforts of parents by placing the child in a well-designed preschool program. These effects, in turn, have an impact on other causes of delinquency, such as poor school performance and association with delinquent peers. It is not surprising, then, that early intervention programs have shown some success at preventing delinquency. Such programs are becoming more common, with a few states implementing them on a large scale.

Parent Training Programs

One of the most widely used programs to deal with delinquency is parent training.[5] Parent training programs are sometimes used alone, and they are sometimes used in combination with other programs—such as programs focusing on the early family environment, school-based programs, and programs focusing on individual traits.

Given the central role that the family plays in delinquency, it is not surprising that parent training is so widely used. As indicated, a variety of family factors affect delinquency, including weak emotional bonds between the parent(s) and child, poor supervision, abuse and neglect, and family conflict. These factors are important in and of themselves, and they are important because they affect certain of the other causes of delinquency, such as individual traits, school performance and attachment, and association with delinquent peers. Programs that can change the way parents relate to their children have much potential for controlling delinquency.

Parent training programs usually target the families of delinquents or juveniles at risk for delinquency. They also target families that are at risk for poor parenting, such as adolescent mothers or families where there is evidence of family violence. These programs are offered in the home, in clinics, or in other settings like schools. Sometimes they are provided to individual families, and sometimes they are provided to several families at once.

Parent training programs **typically have several components.** Most notably, they **teach parents how to more effectively discipline their children.** Poor discipline is not only a major cause of delinquency, but it also undermines the emotional bond between the parent and child and contributes to family conflict. Parents are taught how to set clear rules, better monitor their child's behavior, recognize both deviant and prosocial behavior, and properly sanction deviant behavior and reinforce prosocial behavior. Parents are encouraged to make more use of positive reinforcers, such as praise, rewards, privileges, and attention; and to make less use of punishers, such as criticism, yelling, and hitting. The preferred strategies of punishment involve time out (for children), loss of privileges, imposition of chores, clear expressions of disapproval, and reasoning. (If you would like to get a better sense of the skills that parent training programs try to teach, see the book *Living with*

Children by Patterson and Gullion, 1977, which is used as a manual in one major parent training program.)

Parent training programs also **frequently teach family members how to better resolve conflicts with one another.** While proper disciplinary techniques reduce family conflict, they do not eliminate it. The parents and juvenile, for example, may still disagree over the rules that parents try to enforce or the punishments that parents administer. A common strategy for resolving such conflicts involves the negotiation of a behavioral contract between the parents and the juvenile, particularly adolescents. The contract clearly specifies the rules that juveniles must follow and the consequences for following and breaking rules. For example, adolescents may agree to go to school every day during the week in exchange for the privilege of staying out until midnight on Friday and Saturday nights. The adolescent typically plays a major role in developing such contracts. Parents and juveniles are taught how to negotiate such contracts, and they may also call on a therapist for assistance. By reducing conflict, such negotiation also helps strengthen family bonds.

Parent training programs may also do such things as **teach family members better communication skills, alter the expectations that parents have for their children** (the unrealistic expectations of parents sometimes contribute to abuse and other problems), and **encourage family members to spend more time together in pleasurable activities.** Parents are taught such skills and practices through a variety of strategies: They receive reading materials and/or direct instruction, they are exposed to models who display these practices, they rehearse these practices themselves and receive feedback, and they receive continued guidance when they apply these practices in their homes.

Parent training programs have shown much promise in reducing delinquency, although they are not effective with all families. There are difficulties in inducing families to participate, especially the families that need it most (Kazdin, 1994). Also, parent training is often difficult to successfully implement when families face multiple stressors—poverty, poor housing, work problems, and family violence. Efforts, however, are being made to deal with these problems, including efforts to reduce family stressors and improve the ability of parents to cope with stressors. Also, there are efforts to provide financial and other incentives to participate in these programs.

The effectiveness of these programs is undoubtedly the result of a number of factors. As indicated, they **strengthen the bond between parent and child, improve parental discipline,** and **reduce family conflict and abuse.** At a more general level, they reduce strain. Adolescents are subject to less negative treatment and receive more positive stimuli from parents. In particular, there is a reduction in family conflict, abuse, and the use of harsh disciplinary techniques. These programs also **promote the social learning of conventional behavior.** Parents clearly state rules that condemn deviance; parents function as conventional role models, avoiding the use of violent disciplinary techniques; conventional behavior is consistently reinforced; and deviant behavior is consistently punished. Further, such programs clearly result in an **increase in control.** Direct control is obviously increased; also, the adolescent's emotional bond to parents is increased, and the adolescent is more likely to internalize beliefs condemning deviance and develop a high level of self-control. Finally, such programs **reduce negative labeling,** since parents are less likely to verbally (as well as physically) abuse their children.

Several researchers have suggested that society make parent training programs generally available, incorporating them into the high school curriculum or offering them to the parents of all newborn children. This would reduce the stigma of participating in such programs and might make it easier to secure funding for such programs (since they would no longer be seen as special programs for the poor or disadvantaged). Many European countries have moved in this direction, but only a few schools and areas in the United States have done so (see Sherman et al., 2002, for more information).

Programs Focusing on School Factors

As you know, delinquency is also related to a range of negative school experiences, including poor school performance, low attachment to school, low school involvement, low educational goals, and poor relations with teachers. Delinquency is also more common in certain types of schools, including schools that are large, have poor discipline, provide few opportunities for student success, have low expectations for students, have unpleasant working conditions for students, have poor cooperation between teachers and administrators, and have low community involvement (see Chapter 15 for more information).

Several programs try to address these factors. Some programs focus on the individual, with most such programs attempting to boost school performance. It is felt that individuals who perform well in school will come to like school, get involved in school activities, develop high educational goals, and get along well with teachers. Other programs focus on the larger school environment—including the classroom and entire school—and attempt to change this environment in ways that will reduce delinquency.[6]

Preschool programs. Evidence suggests that good preschool programs can both improve school performance and reduce delinquency. Most such programs focus on preschool children in disadvantaged areas, and they attempt to promote the social and intellectual development of these children as well as increase their parents' involvement in the educational process. The best preschool programs begin early in life, last two years or more, have low student-to-teacher ratios, and employ carefully designed curriculums. In addition, the teachers meet regularly with the parents to discuss ways that the parents can foster their child's social and intellectual development. The success of preschool programs is further enhanced if the children continue to receive assistance once they have begun school. Many of the *Head Start* programs throughout the country meet these criteria, with these programs providing preschool to almost 1 million disadvantaged children—or about three out of five eligible children.

In-school programs. A range of in-school programs attempt to improve the school performance of individual students and address other school experiences related to delinquency. These programs tend to focus on students doing poorly in school, students rated as disruptive by teachers and others, and delinquents. The most straightforward of these programs provide tutoring to students, with the tutoring being done by other students, community volunteers, trained paraprofessionals, and teachers. Such programs are effective at boosting school performance, but it is not yet known whether they reduce delinquency.

Other programs are more elaborate, and several have been found to affect both school experiences and delinquency. In certain programs, for example, juveniles sign a contract with school officials. The juveniles agree to do such things as attend school on a regular basis, do their schoolwork, and behave properly in class. Program staff members provide needed services to the juveniles, such as tutoring and counseling. The program staff also train teachers and sometimes parents to monitor the juveniles' performance and provide assistance when necessary. The juveniles receive regular feedback about their performance from program staff. Staff members discuss ways in which the juveniles might improve when they receive negative reports, and they reinforce the juveniles when the juveniles meet the terms of their contracts. For example, they praise the juveniles and provide them with points that can be traded in for things like CDs and school trips.

Altering the classroom environment. Other programs attempt to alter the classroom environment in ways that improve classroom performance, increase school attachment and involvement, improve relations with teachers and classmates, and improve discipline.

For example, researchers have attempted to reduce delinquency through the strategies of interactive teaching, proactive classroom management, and cooperative learning groups. Interactive teaching provides students with specific objectives they must master, provides frequent feedback, provides help when necessary, employs objective grading, and bases grades on mastery of material and improvement over past performance—not on comparisons with other students. Such teaching increases the opportunities for the students to succeed, and the grading methods increase perceptions of fairness and decrease competition with other students. Teachers using proactive classroom management are taught to clearly state rules for classroom behavior, recognize and reward attempts to cooperate, make frequent use of encouragement and praise, and minimize the impact of disruptions. Cooperative learning groups consist of small, heterogeneous groups of students who help one another master classroom materials and who receive recognition as a team for their accomplishments. These groups serve to reduce alienation, reinforce cooperation, and promote attachment among students.

Another example of a successful program focusing primarily on the classroom environment is an antibullying program that is modeled on the program developed by Olweus (1991) in Norway. Bullying is an important form of delinquency in itself, and it may contribute to further delinquency, partly for reasons related to strain theory. According to Olweus (1991:413), "a person is being bullied when he or she is exposed, repeatedly and over time, to negative actions on the part of one or more other persons" (also see Chapter 15). Negative actions are defined as intentional actions that inflict or attempt to inflict injury or discomfort upon another. A successful antibullying program has several key features. A school-based team is formed to address bullying, with team members including administrators, teachers, counselors, parents, and students. A questionnaire is administered in the school to determine the nature and extent of bullying. The results from this questionnaire are publicized to make everyone aware of the problem. Clear rules against bullying are established, and these rules are widely publicized. Teachers and others closely monitor student activities; students are taught to report bullying and help victims; and anonymous reporting procedures are established. Instances of bullying are quickly sanctioned in a nonhostile manner. And the victims of bullying are provided support and taught skills to reduce the likelihood of further bullying (see Whitted and Dupper, 2005, for more information).

Changing the school environment. A number of programs have tried to change the school environment as a whole. These programs usually employ several strategies, and it is often difficult to determine which of these strategies has the greatest impact on delinquency. Most programs try to change schools in ways that improve student performance, increase school attachment and involvement, improve school discipline, and generally make the school environment more satisfying.

These programs often begin by creating teams that include school administrators, teachers, parents, students, and others. These teams evaluate the school and then help plan and implement school improvements. Such improvements often include the following: Teachers are taught innovative teaching and classroom management techniques. Students help develop school disciplinary rules. Steps are taken to make sure that these rules are clearly stated; widely publicized through devices like newsletters, posters, and ceremonies; and enforced in a consistent and fair manner. There is an effort to make greater use of positive reinforcers, like praise and privileges, for conventional behavior. There is better communication with parents about the positive and negative behaviors of their children. An effort is made to involve parents more actively in the school. For example, volunteer opportunities are created for parents, and parental input is solicited on important issues. An effort is made to reduce student "downtime," so that students have less unsupervised and unstructured time. There is increased monitoring of the lunchroom, rest rooms, and school grounds. An effort is made to increase the involvement and success experiences of high-risk students, usually through an expansion of extracurricular activities and through special academic and counseling programs such as career exploration programs and job-seeking skills programs. A variety of programs addressing individual traits conducive to delinquency are developed. These include social skills training, anger management, and programs designed to instill conventional beliefs. Students, teachers and others launch school pride campaigns, which include things like pep rallies and school cleanup programs. The problems associated with large schools are addressed by creating "schools within schools." That is, small groups of students are assigned to the same homeroom and many of the same classes.

Taken together, such programs can have a substantial impact on those school factors associated with delinquency. They **reduce strain.** Students are better able to achieve their educational goals, they are treated more fairly by school officials, they find school more interesting and pleasant, and they get along better with teachers and fellow students. These programs also **increase control.** Students are better supervised at school; they develop a stronger bond to teachers and fellow students. They develop a greater investment in conventional activities—through their higher school performance and educational goals—and they are exposed to conventional beliefs and taught to exercise self-control. Further, these programs **foster the social learning of conventional behavior.** Students are more likely to form close associations with conventional role models, be exposed to conventional beliefs, and be consistently reinforced for conventional behavior and punished for deviance. Finally, these programs **reduce negative labeling** by school officials.

Programs Focusing on Individual Traits

As indicated in Chapter 13, the super-traits of low self-control and irritability contribute to delinquency. These super-traits encompass several more specific traits, including the following:

- impulsivity (the tendency to act without thinking)
- risk seeking
- amoral beliefs or beliefs favorable to delinquency
- a tendency to become easily upset or angry

- a tendency to blame one's problems on others
- little concern for the feelings or rights of others
- an aggressive or antagonistic interactional style

Many of the programs described earlier have an impact on these traits. As you may recall, these traits are often a function of biological factors and the early family environment. Many of the family programs I described attempt to reduce biological harms and improve the family environment, so they should affect these traits. Many school-based programs also affect individual traits, including such traits as impulsivity and beliefs regarding delinquency.

The programs described in this section, however, focus directly on individual traits. These programs are offered in both preschool and regular school. They may be offered to all juveniles or to juveniles at risk for delinquency. Also, these programs are frequently used to rehabilitate juvenile delinquents who are in community treatment programs or institutions. There are several common programs, each focusing on a somewhat different set of traits. These programs go under a variety of names, including social and interpersonal skills training, problem-solving training, anger management, conflict resolution, and violence prevention curriculums.[7]

Officials sometimes employ several programs or elements from several programs. They target a range of individual traits and often do the following: They teach juveniles the skills necessary for effective interaction with others. (These include such basic social skills as maintaining eye contact when talking with someone. They also include more advanced skills, such as recognizing and showing sensitivity to the feelings of others.) The programs teach juveniles how to respond to problems without engaging in delinquency. In particular, they teach juveniles how to be assertive (rather than aggressive), how to negotiate with others, how to manage their anger, and how to respond to a range of problems, including teasing from peers and criticism from teachers. Related to this, they teach basic problem-solving skills. In particular, juveniles are taught to stop and think before they act rather than responding in an impulsive manner. The programs also teach juveniles beliefs that favor conventional behavior and condemn delinquency. This is done by providing information about the negative consequences of delinquency, letting students know that various forms of delinquency are less common among their peers than they might think, and getting students and classes to take public stands against various types of delinquency, such as drug use and violence. Peer leaders often assist in this process, since students may be more likely to trust and identify with them.

These programs, then, target a range of individual traits conducive to delinquency, including impulsivity, risk seeking, beliefs favorable to delinquency, anger, lack of concern for others, and aggressive interactional styles. In some cases, officials may also treat certain traits with medication. Most notably, hyperactivity is often treated with drugs like Ritalin. Such drugs have shown some success in reducing delinquency, although certain evidence suggests that drugs are most effective when combined with programs of the type described here (see Wasserman and Miller, 1998).

Targeting individual traits may reduce strain, reduce negative labeling, increase control, and foster the social learning of conventional behavior. In particular, juveniles will be in a better position to achieve their goals, will be treated in a more positive manner by others, and will be less likely to respond to strain with delinquency. They will be less likely to be negatively labeled by others. They will be higher in control—particularly self-control and beliefs condemning delinquency. And they will be better able to resist the influence of delinquent peers and act in conventional ways that result in reinforcement.

In order to give you a better sense of what these programs are like, let me describe the basic components of problem-solving training and anger management programs.

Problem-solving training. Dodge (1986) lists the following five steps in effective problem-solving: (1) search for cues in the environment; (2) interpret these cues; (3) generate possible responses to the situation; (4) consider the possible consequences of the responses; and (5) enact the chosen response. Data suggest that delinquents have problems at each of these steps. They attend to fewer environmental cues; they tend to focus on aggressive cues; they often attribute hostile intent when there is none; they generate fewer alternate solutions; they generate more aggressive responses; they fail to recognize the negative consequences of delinquent behavior; and they often lack the social skills to enact prosocial responses (see Kazdin, 1994). Problem-solving training teaches juveniles to carefully perform each of the steps necessary for effective problem solving and to avoid the mistakes just listed. The instructor describes and models the steps in effective problem solving. The child is then asked to apply these steps to an imaginary problem, often making statements to himself or herself which call attention to the mental tasks that are to be performed. In the Think Aloud program, for example, children are taught to ask themselves a series of four questions: "What is my problem?" "What is my plan?" "Am I using my plan?" and "How did I do?" (Hollin, 1990a:66). The WISER way teaches youth to Wait, Identify the problem, generate Solutions, Evaluate the consequences, and self-Reinforce (Hollin, 1990b:485). The instructor prompts the youth when necessary and provides feedback and reinforcement. Eventually, the youths apply the steps to real-life problems. Such training addresses several of the specific traits listed earlier, including impulsivity, risk seeking, and aggressive interactional styles.

Anger management. Anger management programs teach juveniles how to limit or control their anger, with the goal of promoting more adaptive behavior. Most programs have several features in common. First, juveniles explore the causes and consequences of their anger. They may do this by keeping a diary or log of events that made them angry and their reaction to these events. The causes of anger include not only external events but also the internal statements made about those events. Aggressive individuals, for example, are more likely to interpret the ambiguous acts of others as hostile in intent, so the stare of a stranger may be interpreted as a deliberate challenge. The diary may help identify such self-statements. It may also help identify the early warning signs of anger, such as tensed muscles or flushing. Second, the juveniles learn techniques for more effectively controlling their anger—counting backward, imagining a peaceful scene, deep breathing, muscle relaxation, and self-statements like "calm down" and "cool off." Some programs also attempt to increase the juvenile's level of self-efficacy in an attempt to further increase self-control. In addition to teaching juveniles to reduce or more effectively control their anger, these programs often teach social and problem-solving skills that allow for a more adaptive response to situations. Finally, juveniles receive much practice applying the preceding techniques, first in response to imaginary provocations and eventually in real-life settings. And they receive much feedback and reinforcement as they apply these techniques (see Blackburn, 1993; Hollin, 1990a).

The most effective programs focusing on individual traits employ similar training techniques. These techniques include direct instruction; modeling of the desired behaviors by the trainer or others; role playing by the youth, with feedback from the trainer and others; reinforcement for appropriate behavior; and homework assignments that require using the newly acquired traits or skills in real-life settings. Certain programs make special efforts to ensure that these skills will be used in the outside world, such as making the training as similar to real life as possible and attempting to ensure that the new skills are reinforced in real-life settings. Many of the parent training and other programs described earlier use similar training techniques. Such techniques are part of the cognitive-behavioral approach described earlier.

Programs Focusing on Delinquent Peers and Gangs

As you know, associating with delinquent peers and gang members is a major cause of delinquency. Such association creates much strain, since delinquent peers and gang members frequently get into conflicts with one another and others. Such association reduces control, since it draws juveniles away from parents, school, and other conventional groups. Such association contributes to the social learning of crime, since juveniles are exposed to delinquent models, taught beliefs favorable to delinquency, and reinforced for delinquency. And such association increases the likelihood of negative labeling by others.

The **family, school, and individual-trait programs** described in the preceding sections **all have an impact on peer relations.** They reduce the likelihood that juveniles will get involved with delinquent peers and gangs; they reduce the negative influence of peers on the juvenile; and they reduce the likelihood that peers will treat one another badly. For example, parent training programs teach parents how to better supervise their children. Well-supervised juveniles are less likely to join delinquent peer groups, are less likely to succumb to negative peer pressures, and are less likely to get into serious disputes with peers. In fact, one might argue that the best way to counter the effect of delinquent peers on delinquency is to strengthen individual traits and the family, school, and community. Delinquent peers and gangs often flourish when these agencies are weak.

This section, however, focuses on programs that directly target delinquent peer groups and gangs—with most such programs targeting gangs. Such programs usually focus on adolescents, since peer influence is greatest at this time. Some programs focus on adolescents in general; others focus on at-risk adolescents, such as adolescents in schools with gang problems; and still others focus on adolescents who belong to delinquent peer groups or gangs. The most common response to delinquent peer groups and gangs involves efforts by the justice system to suppress illegal activities in these groups. Many communities, however, have made an attempt to supplement suppression with crisis intervention programs, rehabilitation programs, and prevention programs.[8]

Suppression programs by the police and courts. The police often target gangs in certain areas. They gather information on these gangs, increase patrols in areas where the gangs hang out (gang "hot spots"), and closely monitor gang members. They may also do such things as aggressively enforce curfew and truancy laws and conduct "street sweeps," rounding up and searching suspected gang members. And they attempt to severely sanction gang members for their crimes. The police are often supported by prosecutors and probation officers who focus on gang cases. These prosecutors seek serious penalties for gang-related crimes. In this connection, many states have passed laws increasing the penalties for gang-related crimes. Probation officers closely supervise gang members, strictly enforcing the conditions of their probation.

These suppression techniques have met with mixed success, although they are sometimes able to reduce gang activity if carefully implemented (see the discussion of police crackdowns in Chapter 20 and Braga et al., 2002). One example of a successful suppression program was provided in Chapter 20: the crackdown on gun violence by youth gangs in Boston. Most gang researchers, however, argue that suppression techniques will be more effective if they are combined with other efforts to address gang problems—including efforts involving crisis intervention, rehabilitation, and prevention.

Crisis intervention programs try to prevent disputes from escalating into violence. Much gang crime involves disputes between gangs or gang members. In some communities, mediators make an active effort to learn about disputes or conflicts that might erupt into violence. They patrol the streets in gang areas and encourage gang members and community residents to call them when problems arise. They attempt to reduce gang conflict in several ways: They challenge the rumors that sometimes fuel conflict. They attempt to discourage gang members from resorting to violence, sometimes enlisting the aid of the families of gang members and others close to the gang. And they mediate disputes between gangs and between gang members. In some cases, they may hold "gang summits" and try to negotiate truces between different gangs. Evidence on the effectiveness of such programs is somewhat encouraging, although these programs are in need of further evaluation.

Rehabilitation programs are directed at the members of delinquent peer groups and gangs. Such individuals may be offered a range of rehabilitation services, including counseling, mentoring, programs focusing on family problems, help with school problems, vocational training, and assistance finding a job. The House of Umoja in Philadelphia, for example, provides a sanctuary for gang members and offers such members educational assistance, counseling, and job training and placement. Efforts to rehabilitate gang members have not been well evaluated, although some carefully constructed programs show signs of success.

I should note, however, that not all efforts to rehabilitate gang members are successful. For example, some programs attempt to place gang members or delinquents in conventional peer groups, with the thought that they will be exposed to conventional role models, taught conventional beliefs, reinforced for conventional behavior, and punished for delinquency. Such programs, however, have shown mixed results. Putting delinquent and conventional juveniles together in the same group can often increase the delinquency of the conventional juveniles—especially when there are more than a few delinquents in the group.[9]

Prevention programs attempt to discourage juveniles from joining gangs and to teach them the skills to resist gang and peer influence. For example, a number of educational programs provide information about gang violence and drug use, the negative consequences of gang membership, how gangs recruit individuals, and methods of resisting recruitment. Other programs attempt to counter peer pressure to use drugs by providing juveniles with information about the negative consequences of drug use, letting them know that drug use is less common than they think, teaching them to recognize and resist peer pressure to use drugs, and getting them to make a public commitment against drug use.

One of the most popular antigang education programs in the country is GREAT, or Gang Resistance Education and Training (Esbensen et al., 2004). This program is run in many school systems and involves a series of nine lessons given by a uniformed police officer—with the lessons focusing on topics such as conflict resolution, goal setting, and resisting peer pressure. (The GREAT program, however, is in the process of being revised in an effort to increase its limited effectiveness.) The most effective education programs tend to have certain traits in common. They make use of the cognitive-behavioral strategies described earlier—as opposed to simply lecturing juveniles or holding discussions with them. They employ individuals with whom the juveniles can identify, often making use of peer instructors. They not only focus on the negative consequences of gang membership or delinquency, but they also teach juveniles the skills they need to recognize and resist influence attempts. And they often try to establish a norm against gang membership or delinquency. For example, they may let juveniles know that most kids their age do not use drugs, or they may try to get class members to take a public stand against drug use.

Summary. As you can see, there have been a number of efforts to deal with delinquent peer groups and gangs. Many have failed, although some show promise. The federal government has encouraged communities to form coalitions to combat gang crime, with these coalitions involving representatives from the police, other government agencies, and community organizations. These coalitions are supposed to engage in tasks like collecting information on the extent and nature of the gang problem in their community, designing police suppression programs, developing rehabilitation and prevention programs, and coordinating the delivery of these programs. A number of such coalitions have been formed, although some have been more successful than others at completing these tasks. We lack good evaluation data on the effectiveness of most of these coalitions, but some show evidence of success in reducing gang crime. And most gang researchers feel that a coordinated strategy involving the suppression of gang activities and the use of carefully selected rehabilitation and prevention programs is our best hope for reducing gang activity.

Selected Other Prevention and Rehabilitation Programs

A variety of other prevention and rehabilitation programs have shown promise. Many of these are run in the community, with some attempting to change the nature of the community in ways that reduce delinquency. Brief overviews of selected programs are provided next.[10]

Mentoring. Mentoring programs match at-risk or delinquent juveniles with nonprofessional volunteers, such as college students, community residents, and businesspeople. Ideally, the mentors form a close relationship with the juveniles. They function as conventional role models, offer guidance, and help the juveniles deal with a range of problems, including family, school, and peer problems. Mentors, then, have the potential to reduce strain, increase control, and foster the social learning of conventional behavior. Evidence on the effectiveness of mentoring programs is mixed, but data suggest that mentoring programs may reduce delinquency if they are intensive, carefully train volunteers, and ensure that volunteers reinforce prosocial behavior and sanction deviant behavior.[11]

Supervised recreational opportunities. A number of programs provide supervised recreational activities for juveniles, especially after school, when rates of delinquency peak. Such programs attempt to monitor youth who might otherwise be unsupervised (and so increase direct control). They may also attempt to establish a relationship between the conventional adults who run the program and the youths. Evidence on the effectiveness of these programs is also mixed, but data suggest that carefully constructed recreational programs may reduce delinquency. Such programs provide structured activities, are well supervised, are small in size, and make an effort to aggressively recruit and retain youth in the community.[12]

Vocational training and employment programs. These programs teach job skills and help juveniles find employment. In doing so, they most obviously reduce strain and create a stake in conformity. Vocational programs typically focus on delinquents and at-risk juveniles, like high school dropouts or juveniles doing poorly in school. Some vocational programs are based in the community, and some are incorporated into the school system. Once again, evidence on the effectiveness of these programs is mixed. Many vocational programs do not appear to reduce delinquency, but certain well-designed programs show much promise for reducing delinquency. Such programs are intensive and long-term, they help juveniles deal with other problems they may be facing, and they provide incentives for participation. The *Jobs Corps* program of the federal government is an example.[13]

Situational crime prevention. As indicated in Chapter 11, crime is a function of both the juvenile's predisposition for delinquency and the situations that the juvenile encounters. Predisposed juveniles are more likely to engage in delinquency when they are in situations where they are provoked by others, drugs and alcohol are present, the benefits of delinquency are seen as high, and the costs of delinquency are seen as low. A variety of strategies have been developed to reduce the likelihood that individuals will encounter such situations. Certain of these strategies were briefly described in Chapter 11, such as placing theft-proof change boxes on buses and placing attendants in parking lots. Clarke (1992, 1995) describes 12 general techniques of situational crime prevention, including "deflecting [potential] offenders" (e.g., separating rival fans at sporting events); "target hardening" (e.g., putting steering locks on cars); "target removal" (e.g., removable car radios); and "formal surveillance" (e.g., cameras to detect speeding). Clarke (1995), Clarke and Eck (2005), Eck (2002), and Felson (2002) also provide examples of situational prevention approaches that appear to be successful. These approaches reduce the likelihood that individuals will encounter others who provoke them, reduce the availability of drugs and alcohol, reduce the perceived benefits of crime, or increase the perceived costs of crime.

Drug and gun programs. Most of the family, school, individual, peer, and other types of programs described in the previous sections have been employed to reduce drug use as well as delinquency, and they have shown some effect on levels of drug use. In addition, a number of programs focus specifically on drugs (for overviews, see Brochu, 2006; National Institute on Drug Abuse, 2006; Winters, 2007; and the National Drug Control Strategy at http://www.whitehousedrugpolicy.gov).[14] As mentioned earlier, the National Youth Anti-Drug Media Campaign is designed to affect certain of the factors known to cause drug use. For example, the campaign tries to convince juveniles that drug use has a number of negative consequences. A recent evaluation, however, suggests that this campaign is not effective in reducing drug use (Orwin et al., 2004). A more promising approach involves the use of *drug courts.* In those areas where drug courts exist, court personnel attempt to identify and refer individuals with drug problems to the court. The drug court develops a treatment program for these individuals, closely monitors their behavior to ensure compliance with the plan—with frequent drug tests being employed—and rewards individuals for compliance and punishes them for noncompliance. Drug courts are used extensively with adults, and evidence suggests that they are effective in reducing drug use (Gottfredson, M., 2006). Such courts are becoming more common with juveniles, with juvenile drug courts not only providing drug treatment but also addressing other problems—such as family, school, and peer problems. Preliminary evidence suggests that such courts are effective in reducing juvenile drug use (e.g., Rodriguez and Webb, 2004).

A number of programs have also tried to reduce the prevalence of guns among juveniles, or at least reduce the likelihood that juveniles will use guns. Most such programs have not been well evaluated, or the evidence on the effectiveness of these programs is mixed. However, there is good evidence that a few programs, like gun buybacks, do not work. Certain programs appear promising, especially carefully planned police crackdowns that target individuals who may be illegally carrying or using guns. Such crackdowns are usually instituted in areas with high rates of gun crime ("gun hot spots"). These programs increase the **certainty** of punishment and, sometimes, the severity of punishment as well.[15]

Community crime prevention. Some programs attempt to reduce delinquency by attacking the community problems that contribute to delinquency.[16] As indicated in Chapter 12, economic deprivation and other factors increase community crime rates through their effect on strain, control, and the social learning of crime.

The most common community crime prevention program is Neighborhood Watch. As you may recall, one reason that some communities have higher crime rates is that neighborhood residents fail to effectively monitor their communities and sanction deviance. That is, some communities are low in direct control. Neighborhood Watch programs try to address this problem by gathering neighborhood residents together, encouraging them to more closely monitor their community, and encouraging them to re-

port suspicious activity to the police. Such programs, however, are difficult to implement in the high-crime communities that need them the most. Further, evidence suggests that they have little or no effect on crime rates in the communities where they are implemented. There are a number of possible reasons for this lack of effectiveness, one of which is the low involvement of program participants (see Hope, 1995).

Other community crime prevention programs are more ambitious and attempt to address a range of community problems that contribute to crime. Although these programs are often initiated by people outside the community, an attempt is usually made to actively involve community residents in the program. Some community programs attempt to provide social services to juveniles and others in the community; such services include mentoring, tutoring and other educational programs, vocational programs, counseling, health programs, and recreational programs. Few such programs have been properly evaluated, although some show signs of success. These programs are discussed further in Chapter 25.

Still other programs attempt to stimulate economic development in the community. This has been done by providing tax breaks and other financial incentives to attract businesses to disadvantaged communities. Also, grants have been provided to local governments; these grants are used to do such things as improve housing and public services in disadvantaged communities (see Bushway and Reuter, 2002; DePledge, 2002). The impact of these programs on economic development has not been well evaluated, although some evidence suggests that these programs have had **limited** success in certain communities.

The Critical Role of Larger Social Forces in Preventing Delinquency

Most of the prevention and rehabilitation programs described in the foregoing pages focus on the individual and the individual's immediate social environment—family, school, peer group, and local community. The nature of one's immediate environment, however, is strongly influenced by larger social forces. These forces play a major role in generating problems such as dysfunctional families, school failure, gangs, and neighborhoods plagued by crime and other problems. Further, these forces influence the success or failure of prevention and rehabilitation programs, since they shape the context in which these programs operate. It is difficult for parent training programs to be successful, for example, when parents are unemployed and struggling to survive.

Of all the social forces that I might discuss, **economic forces are the most important.** A range of economic forces in the United States have contributed to a high overall level of prosperity, but this prosperity has not been shared by all. Consider the following:

- The United States is the third most prosperous country in the world—based on per capita income in 2004 dollars (Norway and Japan are the most prosperous nations; see Dreier, 2007).
- This prosperity has not been shared by a large portion of the population. Among the affluent countries of the world, the United States ranks second in the percentage of wealth owned by the richest 10 percent of the population. In particular, about 70 percent of the wealth is owned by this group.
- The United States also has the highest child poverty rate among affluent countries (the poverty line being set at one-half of each country's median income level; see Dreier, 2007; UNICEF, 2007).
- About 17 percent of all children in the United States (roughly 13 million children) lived below the poverty line in 2006, which was $20,500 for a family of four (U.S. Census Bureau; also see Federal Interagency Forum on Child and Family Statistics, 2007).
- Further, the United States ranks next to last among affluent countries in economic resources devoted to government social programs, such as family assistance and health (Dreier, 2007). Related to this, Americans pay lower taxes than people in all other affluent countries except Japan (taxes calculated as the percentage of gross domestic product; see Dreier, 2007).

- There are several reasons for the high rate of poverty in the United States, in addition to low government spending on social programs. These reasons include a major loss of manufacturing jobs in recent decades, an increase in service sector jobs that pay poorly and carry few benefits, and an increase in single-parent families (which are more likely to live in poverty).[17]

This poverty contributes to a range of problems conducive to crime and delinquency, including poor health care; family problems, like broken homes, poor parenting, and abuse; school problems; and a range of neighborhood problems.[18] The prevention and rehabilitation programs described earlier have shown some success in reducing the negative effects of this poverty and, in some cases, helping individuals escape from poverty. But these programs deal largely with the symptoms of the widespread poverty in the United States. Any serious approach to reducing delinquency must devote greater attention to reducing poverty throughout the United States—both individual poverty and the concentration of poverty in certain communities.

A range of programs have been suggested in this area. Some argue that society should do more to attract jobs to inner-city areas plagued by crime and to induce employers to hire people from such areas. Some argue that we should increase the pay and benefits associated with jobs so that all work pays a living wage. Many full-time workers now earn less than the poverty level. In fact, about 20 percent of full-time working men and 30 percent of working women are in jobs that do not pay enough to raise a family out of poverty (Herbert, 2007). And many workers do not receive and cannot afford health care. Some argue that we should make jobs located in suburban areas more accessible to inner-city residents through improved transportation and new housing policies. Some argue that we should create new jobs in the public sector, particularly in inner-city communities. Such jobs might be in areas like child care, health care, public safety, and child protection. Some argue that we should provide increased tax benefits and other financial assistance to families with children, and we should do more to help families collect child support. Some argue that we should increase social services, including job training, educational programs, health care, child care, preschool programs like Head Start and Early Head Start, food programs, housing assistance, and a range of pro-family policies like flexible work schedules and stronger family leave policies.[19]

I do not mean to end this chapter on a pessimistic note, but the United States is at a critical point in its efforts to reduce delinquency. We now have a reasonably good idea how to go about reducing delinquency, but it is not at all clear whether we will take the necessary steps.

Summary

A number of rehabilitation and prevention programs have been reviewed. Not all programs work, but criminologists now have a reasonably good idea of the characteristics that distinguish the most successful programs from the least successful ones. The key feature of the most successful programs is that they address the causes of delinquency, identified in earlier chapters. Further, these programs are cost-effective. Data indicate that they more than pay for themselves in terms of the crime and other problems they prevent, such as dropping out of school and going on welfare.[20] One study estimated that several rehabilitation programs for juvenile offenders save $5 to $10 dollars for each dollar of taxpayer cost (Aos et al., 1999). In addition, data suggest that many prevention and rehabilitation programs are more cost-effective than get-tough strategies like incapacitation. On average, it costs about $40,000 a year to confine a juvenile offender. While confining juveniles does stop some crime, many prevention and rehabilitation programs can stop crime at a much lower cost.[21] Finally, these programs have wide popular support. Even though the public wants to get tough with juvenile offenders, especially serious offenders, polls indicate that most people *also* support an increased emphasis on rehabilitation and prevention.[22]

Rehabilitation and prevention programs will not solve the delinquency problem. As indicated, they reduce but do not eliminate delinquency. And as indicated, we are likely to encounter problems if we try to implement these programs on a large scale. It will be difficult to ensure that these programs are run as designed. And it will be difficult to ensure that the people who need these programs the most participate in them. But it is nevertheless clear that prevention and rehabilitation should be a central part of any serious effort to control delinquency.

Teaching Aids

Exercise: Extend Your Knowledge of Rehabilitation and Prevention Programs

I've described a number of prevention and rehabilitation programs in this chapter, but most were described in general terms (e.g., parent training programs and anger management programs). Also, space limitations prevented me from describing many other programs. I would like you to add to this chapter by doing the following: Select a **specific** prevention or rehabilitation program, either an example of one of the general programs described in this chapter (e.g., a specific parent training program) or a program not described in this chapter. To make this exercise more interesting, you might select a program that is used in your home community (call your local juvenile court or go to their website for information). Then attempt to answer the following questions about the program (this will be easier for some programs than others, but do the best you can):

1. What happens in the program; that is, what does the program do to rehabilitate offenders and/or prevent delinquency? Does the program possess the five general characteristics of effective rehabilitation and prevention programs described at the start of this chapter?

2. What causes of delinquency does the program address?

3. What groups does the program target (e.g., serious juvenile offenders, high school students, teenage mothers)? To what extent is the program being used (e.g., is it used in only one location or throughout the United States)?

4. Has the program been evaluated? How good are the evaluations? What do the evaluations say about the effectiveness of the program in reducing delinquency?

5. Are there any other advantages or disadvantages of the program that people should be aware of (e.g., the program reduces the fear of crime, but is quite expensive)?

You may obtain this information from a variety of sources, including books, newspapers and magazines, academic journals, government publications, technical reports issued by research organizations, and websites. Do not limit your search to the book index at your library. I suggest you look at the following sources:

- Relevant references in this text (and the references in these references); for example, the CDC volume titled *Best Practices of Youth Violence Prevention* contains information on many specific programs (go to http://www.cdc.gov/ncipc/dvp/ bestpractices.htm).
- Indexes to academic journal articles, like *Sociological Abstracts, PsycINFO, Criminal Justice Abstracts,* and the *National Criminal Justice Reference Service Abstracts Database* (http://www.ncjrs.gov/abstractdb/search.asp).
- Indexes to newspaper articles, like the *New York Times Index* and *Lexis/Nexis.*
- The websites for the Office of Juvenile Justice and Delinquency Prevention (OJJDP) and the National Criminal Justice Reference Service (NCJRS). Be sure to look at the OJJDP Model Programs Guide. Also look at the websites for Blueprints for Violence Prevention and the Campbell Crime and Justice Group.
- The website for the program you are interested in (if it has a website) and/or literature produced by the program sponsors.
- Other relevant websites, including those that focus on the prevention of delinquency and rehabilitation of delinquents. The best place to look for such websites is on the Criminal Justice Links website maintained by Cecil Greek for the Florida State University School of Criminology and Criminal Justice (http://www.criminology.fsu .edu/cjlinks).

Do not overwhelm yourself. Try to focus on recent reports that provide a summary or overview of your program—look at a few such reports if possible. Pay attention to the source of the report. Ask yourself whether the organization producing the report might have a reason to be overly optimistic or overly pessimistic about the program you are examining. If you do not have much success finding information on your program, switch to another program.

TEST YOUR KNOWLEDGE OF THIS CHAPTER

1. Why do many criminologists believe that the United States places too much emphasis on get-tough approaches?
2. How do prevention and rehabilitation programs differ from get-tough approaches? How does prevention differ from rehabilitation?
3. Why haven't prevention programs played a greater role in efforts to reduce delinquency in the United States?
4. Why did rehabilitation programs fall out of favor in the 1970s?
5. How might we explain the renewed interest in prevention and rehabilitation programs in the last few years?
6. What are the general characteristics of successful prevention and rehabilitation programs? Describe the cognitive-behavioral approach.
7. Why are prevention and rehabilitation programs unlikely to eliminate delinquency?
8. I provided moderately detailed descriptions of prevention and rehabilitation programs in five areas: the early family environment, parent training, school factors,

individual traits, and delinquent peers and gangs. **For each area,** describe what is done to prevent delinquency and rehabilitate delinquents, describe the effectiveness of such efforts, and describe the causes of delinquency that the prevention or rehabilitation programs address.

9. Briefly describe the other prevention and rehabilitation programs that were mentioned (e.g., mentoring, supervised recreational opportunities) and the evidence on their effectiveness.

10. Why do I state that "larger social forces" play a crucial role in the prevention of delinquency? What larger social force do I highlight, and why?

11. List any three proposals that have been made to reduce poverty and/or the concentration of poverty in the United States.

THOUGHT AND DISCUSSION QUESTIONS

1. Can you think of any prevention and/or rehabilitation programs that were **not** discussed in this chapter—programs you've read or heard about or programs of your own design? What causes of crime do these programs address?

2. As indicated in Chapter 23, many high schools and colleges are experiencing high levels of cheating. Drawing on the materials in this chapter, describe how you would go about preventing school cheating and rehabilitating cheaters.

3. Most people favor placing more emphasis on prevention and rehabilitation programs. Nevertheless, current programs to reduce delinquency place much more emphasis on getting tough than they do on rehabilitation and prevention. And politicians who stress rehabilitation and prevention programs are often attacked as being soft on crime. Why do you think there is this disjuncture between public policies and the desire of the general public for more emphasis on prevention and rehabilitation?

4. Even though we now have a reasonably good idea about which programs are and are **not** effective in controlling delinquency, the United States still invests large sums of money in ineffective programs, including get-tough programs (e.g., Scared Straight, trying juveniles as adults) and rehabilitation and prevention programs (DARE, programs designed to increase self-esteem). Why do you think this is the case? What can be done to change this?

KEY TERMS

- Rehabilitation programs
- Prevention programs
- War on Poverty
- Cognitive-behavioral approach
- Parent training programs
- Head Start
- Problem-solving training
- Crisis intervention programs (for gangs)
- Job Corps
- Situational crime prevention
- Drug courts

ENDNOTES

1. For overviews of rehabilitation and prevention, *see* Andrews and Bonta, 2006; Aos et al., 1999; Barlow, 1995; Blueprints for Violence Prevention at www.colorado.edu/cspv/blueprints/; Burns et al., 2003; Campbell Crime and Justice Group at www.campbellcollaboration.org/CCJG/;

ENDNOTES (continued)

Coordinating Council on Juvenile Justice and Delinquency Prevention, 1996; Cullen, 2002, 2008; Cullen and Applegate, 1997; Cullen and Gendreau, 2000; Currie, 1998; Farrington, 1996a, 1996b, 2002b; Farrington and Welsh, 2007; Greenwood, 1995, 2002, 2006; Guerra et al., 1994; Hawkins, Catalano, and Brewer, 1995; Heyman and Slep, 2007; Howell, 2003a, 2003b; Howell and Hawkins, 1998; Kazdin, 1994; Kellermann et al., 1998; Kumpfer and Alvarado, 1998; Lipsey and Wilson, 1998; Loeber et al., 2003; Losel, 2007; MacKenzie, 2006; McCord et al., 2001; McGuire, 1995; Morley et al., 2000; Muller and Mihalic, 1999; Office of Juvenile Justice and Delinquency Prevention, 1995; Rutter et al., 1998; Sawhill, 2003; Sherman et al., 2002; Thornton et al., 2002; Tremblay and Craig, 1995; U.S. Department of Health and Human Services, 2001; Wasserman and Miller, 1998; Weissbourd, 1996; Wilson et al., 2003.

2. For discussions of the decline of rehabilitation, *see* Andrews and Bonta, 2006; Beckett and Sasson, 2000; Cullen 2002; Cullen and Gendreau, 2000; Feld, 2003; Garland, 2001 Greenwood, 2006; Zimring, 2005.

3. *See* Andrews and Bonta, 2006; Andrews et al., 1990; Brewer et al., 1995; Catalano et al., 1998; Cullen, 2002; Cullen and Gendrea, 2000; Currie, 1998; Farrington, 1996a, 1996b; Farrington and Welsh, 2007; Gottfredson, 2001; Greenwood, 2006; Guerra, 1997; Guerra et al. 1994; Hawkins et al., 1995; Howell, 2003a, 2003b; Kazdin, 1994; Krisberg et al., 1995; Lipsey, 1992; Lipsey and Wilson, 1998; Losel, 1995; MacKenzie, 2006; McCord et al., 2001; McGuire, 1995; Sherman et al., 2002; Thornton et al., 2002; Tremblay and Craig, 1995; Wasserman and Miller, 1998; Wilson et al., 2001; Yoshikawa, 1994.

4. For overviews of programs focusing on the early family environment, *see* Bilukha et al., 2005; Currie, 1998; Earle, 1995; Farrington, 1996a, 1996b; Farrington and Welsh, 2002, 2007; Greenwood, 2006; Guerra, 1997; Hawkins et al., 1995; Howell, 2003a; Howell and Hawkins, 1998; Kazdin, 1994; Kumpfer and Alvarado, 1998; McCord et al., 2001; Olds et al., 1998; Sherman et al., 2002; Thornton et al., 2002; Tremblay and Craig, 1995; Wasserman and Miller, 1998; Yoshikawa, 1994; Zigler et al., 1992.

5. For overviews of parent training programs, *see* Andrews and Bonta, 2003; Brewer et al., 1995; Farrington, 1996a, 1996b; Farrington and Welsh, 2002, 2007; Greenwood, 2006; Guerra, 1997; Hollin, 1992; Howell, 2003a; Kazdin, 1994; Kumpfer and Tait, 2000; McCord et al., 2001; McDonald and Frey, 1999; Patterson, 1982; Petrucci and Roberts, 2004; Rankin and Wells, 1987; Sherman et al., 2002; Thornton et al., 2002; Tremblay and Craig, 1995; Wasserman and Miller, 1998.

6. For overviews of school programs, *see* Arnette and Walsleben, 1998; Brewer et al., 1995; Catalano et al., 1998; Elliott et al., 1998; Farrington and Welsh, 2007; Gottfredson, 2001; Gottfredson and Gottfredson, 2002; Gottfredson et al., 2002a, 2002b; Greenwood, 2006; Hawkins and Lishner, 1987; Hawkins et al., 1995; Hawkins et al., 1998; Howell, 2003a; Maguin and Loeber, 1996; McCord et al., 2001; Samples and Aber, 1998; Sherman et al., 2002; Tremblay and Craig, 1995; Wasserman and Miller, 1998; Wilson et al., 2001; Wilson et al., 2003.

7. For overviews of programs focusing on individual traits, *see* Blackburn, 1993; Brewer et al., 1995; Farrington, 1996a, 1996b; Farrington and Welsh, 2007; Gottfredson, 2001; Gottfredson et al., 2002a, 2002b; Guerra, 1997; Guerra et al., 1994; Hawkins, Catalano, and Brewer, 1995; Hawkins et al., 1998; Howell, 2003a; Kazdin, 1994; Kellermann et al., 1998; Losel and Beelmann, 2003; Pearson et al., 2002; Samples and Aber, 1998; Sherman et al., 2002; Thornton et al., 2002; Wasserman and Miller, 1998.

8. For overviews and selected examples of peer programs, *see* Braga et al., 2002; Brewer et al., 1995; Burch and Kane, 1999; Catalano et al., 1998; Decker and Curry, 2000; Esbensen and Osgood, 1999; Farrington, 1996a, 1996b; Farrington and Welsh, 2007; Fearn et al., 2001; Fritsch et al., 1999; Gifford-Smith et al., 2005; Gorman and White, 1995; Guerra, 1997; Hawkins et al., 1995; Howell, 1997b, 1998b, 1999, 2003a; Huff, 2002; Klein, 1998; Klein and Maxson, 2006; McCord et al., 2001; Morley et al., 2000; Maxson, 2004; Office of Juvenile Justice and Delinquency Prevention, 2007; Shelden et al., 2001; Sherman et al., 2002; Spergel, 1995; Thornberry et al., 2003; Welsh and Hoshi, 2002.

9. *See* Farrington, 1996a, 1996b; Gifford-Smith et al., 2005; Gorman and White, 1995; Howell, 2003a; McCord et al., 2001.

10. *Also see* Brewer et al., 1995; Catalano et al., 1998; Kellermann et al., 1998; Sampson, 2002; Sherman et al., 2002.

11. *See* Catalano et al., 1998; Farrington and Welsh, 2007; Grossman and Garry, 1997; Howell, 2003a; McCord et al., 2001; Morley et al., 2000; Office of Juvenile Justice and Delinquency Prevention, 1998b; Thornton et al., 2002; Welsh and Hoshi, 2002.

12. *See* Farrington and Welsh, 2007; Gottfredson et al., 2002a,b; Gottfredson et al., 2007; McCord et al., 2001; Morley et al., 2000; Welsh and Hoshi, 2002.

13. *See* Brewer et al., 1995; Bushway and Reuter, 2002; Currie, 1998; and Lipsey, 1992; *also see* Hamilton and McKinney, 1999.

14. *Also see* Boyum and Kleiman, 2002; MacCoun and Reuter, 1998; Office of National Drug Control Policy, 1999; Orwin et al., 2006; National Institute on Drug Abuse, 2006; Vander Waal et al., 2001.

15. *See* Brewer et al., 1995; Catalano et al., 1998; Cook and Ludwig, 2000; Cook et al., 2002; Hahn et al., 2005; Harcourt, 2003; Kellermann et al., 1998; Kleck, 1997; Kovandzic and Marvell, 2003; Ludwig and Cook, 2003; McGarrell et al., 2002; Office of Juvenile Justice and Delinquency Prevention, 1996; Sherman, 2001; Sherman and Eck, 2002; Welsh and Hoshi, 2002; Wintemute, 2006; Zimring, 2005, 2007.

16. *See* Bushway and Reuter, 2002; Hope, 1995; McCord et al., 2001; Sampson, 2002; Sherman et al., 2002; and Welsh and Hoshi, 2002, for excellent overviews of community crime prevention programs.

17. *See* Currie, 1998; Hagan, 1994; Lewit et al., 1997; Sampson and Wilson, 1995; Wilson, 1987, 1996.

18. *See* Brooks-Gunn and Duncan, 1997; Currie, 1998; Hagan, 1994; Sampson, 1997; Sampson and Wilson, 1995; Wilson, W., 1987, 1996.

19. For fuller discussions of these issues, *see* Center for American Progress Task Force on Poverty, 2007; Currie, 1998; Lewit et al., 1997; Messner and Rosenfeld, 2001; Plotnick, 1997; Stemen, 2007; Wilson, 1987, 1996.

20. *See* Aos et al., 1999; Burns et al., 2003; Caldwell et al., 2006; Farrington and Welsh, 2007; Greenwood, 2002; McCord et al., 2001; Welsh et al., 2001.

21. *See* Greenwood, 1998, 1999, 2006; Greenwood et al., 1996; *also see* Fass and Pi, 2002.

22. *See* Martin and Glantz as cited in Greenwood, 1998; *also see* Beckett and Sasson, 2000; Bishop, 2006; Cullen, 2006, 2008; Cullen and Applegate, 1997; Cullen et al., 1998; Flanagan and Longmire, 1996; Moon et al., 2000; Nagin et al., 2006; Roberts and Stalans, 1998.

CHAPTER 25

What Should We Do to Reduce Delinquency?

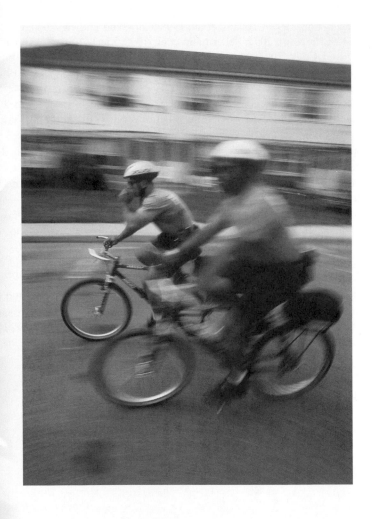

I f you tell someone that you have just read a book on delinquency or taken a course in the area, they may well ask you a question like: "So what should we do to reduce delinquency?" How would you respond?

If you are like many of the students in my classes, your initial response will be one of silence. You have been exposed to a great deal of material. Some of this material may have challenged your beliefs about the causes of delinquency and the best ways to control it. There is a lot to reflect on and pull together.

I want to help you in this process by presenting what I think is a reasonable strategy for reducing delinquency—a strategy that I think takes account of the research on the causes and control of delinquency, that is just or fair, that is within our means, and that is acceptable to most people in this country. This strategy reflects, in large measure, the strategy that is now being advocated by the federal government.[1] First, I believe that society should place much more emphasis on prevention and rehabilitation. And second, I believe that we should hold juveniles accountable for their behavior and protect the community from dangerous juveniles—but we should do so in a more effective and just manner than is now the case.

We Should Place More Emphasis on Prevention and Rehabilitation

I think we need to place much more emphasis on prevention and rehabilitation programs of the type described in Chapter 24. It makes more sense to prevent individuals from becoming delinquent in the first place rather than respond to their delinquency after the fact. And it makes much sense to attempt to reform or rehabilitate the individuals who do become delinquent. The vast majority of these individuals are returned to the community after being processed by the juvenile justice system, sometimes immediately and sometimes after an out-of-home placement. We want to do all that we can to ensure that they cease or at least reduce their offending.

Most of the prevention and rehabilitation programs described in Chapter 24 work or at least show much promise for success. The best of these programs are able to reduce offending rates upwards of 50 percent, and there is reason to believe that criminologists will be able to design even more effective programs as additional program evaluations are completed and our knowledge of the causes of delinquency increases. **Such programs also represent a fair or just response to delinquency.** Data suggest that delinquency is partly due to forces beyond the individual's control—forces like genetic inheritance, biological harms, the early family environment, the school one attends, the peers one is exposed to, and the community in which one lives. That is not to say that juveniles have no responsibility for their behavior. But it is to say that delinquency is not simply a matter of free choice. Delinquents are to some extent victims of their environment, and they both need and deserve our assistance. Further, **most prevention and rehabilitation programs are cost-effective,** as indicated in Chapter 24. In particular, these programs typically save much more money than they cost, and they frequently prevent delinquency at a lower cost than the get-tough approaches that are so popular today. Finally, there is **strong public support for prevention and rehabilitation programs,** as well as for get-tough approaches to controlling delinquency.

But **how should we go about putting such prevention and rehabilitation programs into place?** The federal government, many states, and a lot of communities have come to place an increased emphasis on prevention and rehabilitation in recent years (although get-tough approaches still dominate). One model for implementing prevention and reha- bilitation programs has shown some promise. This model is reflected to varying degrees in several programs sponsored by the National Institute of Justice and other agencies, programs like the Comprehensive Strategy for Serious, Violent, and Chronic Juvenile Of- fenders; SafeFutures; the Communities that Care model; Weed and Seed; the Strategic Ap- proaches to Community Safety Initiative; Project PACT (Pulling America's Communities Together); the Comprehensive Communities Program; the Comprehensive Anti-Gang Initiative; Project Safe Neighborhoods; and Empowerment Zones/Enterprise Communi- ties.[2] Some of these programs focus specifically on crime and delinquency, while others focus on a broad range of social problems, including crime. These programs are typically run in high-crime communities, sometimes in neighborhoods and sometimes in larger units, including entire cities and counties. And several states are attempting to implement these programs in communities statewide.

The programs employ a similar strategy. First, community leaders are told about the program, and an effort is made to enlist their support. These community leaders may in- clude the mayor, police chief, judges, school superintendent, leaders from the business, civic, and religious communities, and sometimes representatives from state and federal agencies. **Second,** if these community leaders are supportive, they can put together a team of people responsible for implementing and running the program. This broad-based team may include representatives from the police and courts, social welfare agencies, school sys- tem, health system, business and religious communities, and community organizations. **Third,** after receiving some training, this team proceeds to identify community problems that contribute to delinquency and community resources that might be used to deal with these problems. Among other things, the team collects information from community resi- dents, including juveniles, and from experts in the area. **Fourth,** the team takes responsi- bility for designing a comprehensive approach for addressing the community problems they have identified. The team may be provided with a menu of promising programs from which they can choose. And they may appoint task forces in different areas. One task force, for example, may focus on the development of programs to address family problems.

Fifth, the team helps develop mechanisms to coordinate the delivery of services to at- risk and delinquent juveniles, so that each juvenile receives the full range of services he or she needs. They also attempt to ensure that cases are carefully managed, such that officials keep close track of the juvenile's progress and adjust services accordingly. One device for accomplishing these goals is the Community Assessment Center, briefly described in Chap- ter 21. The Community Assessment Center links together all of the agencies providing ser- vices to at-risk and/or delinquent youth. Youth are sent to the center for assessment, linked with the agencies that provide the services that they (and their families) need, and tracked over time to make sure they get the services they need. **Sixth,** the team assumes responsi- bility for evaluating the approach they have developed and revising it if necessary. Given the range of prevention and rehabilitation programs provided, it is quite likely that prob- lems will arise: Some programs may not be offered to the youths who need them, some programs may not be properly implemented, some programs may not be effective, and so on. The ongoing evaluation of the approach is critical.

The federal government and other organizations assist communities in this effort. The federal government, for example, provides technical assistance on a range of topics, such as promising programs, program implementation, and program evaluation. The federal government also provides information on funding sources, often provides some funding, and facilitates communication with other teams across the country. (The following websites are examples of federally supported programs designed to spread information about promising programs, funding opportunities, and issues like program implementation and evaluation. Blueprints for Violence Prevention: http://www.colorado.edu/cspv/blueprints/ and Pave II—Pathways to Advance Virtual Education: http://www.pavenet.org. Also see the *Targeted Community Action Planning Toolkit,* developed by the Office of Juvenile Justice and Delinquency Prevention [Flores, 2003].) Many communities, in addition, may develop a group of local experts to assist in the process.

The comprehensive approach that is mounted differs somewhat from community to community, since different communities have different problems and resources. For example, one community may have a serious gang problem and so may mount a variety of gang intervention programs. Another community may have little or no problem with gangs. At the same time, there are **certain common features in the comprehensive approaches that are developed.** Prevention programs are typically developed in a range of different areas, since delinquency is caused by a range of problems. These programs involve broad segments of the community, including the juvenile justice system, the schools, social service agencies, community organizations, the business community, and religious organizations. These programs usually target juveniles at high risk for delinquency. Efforts are sometimes made to encourage family members and school officials to identify such juveniles (e.g., family members are encouraged to seek help if they are having problems with their children). Likewise, a number of rehabilitation programs are usually developed. The local juvenile court develops a procedure to carefully screen all referred youths so that they can be provided with the rehabilitation services they need. A special effort is made to target serious, high-rate, and chronic offenders for treatment, since they account for such a large share of the delinquency problem.

Most efforts to implement this strategy have not yet been formally evaluated. But the few evaluations that have been done suggest that communities often have problems carrying out certain of the six tasks described earlier. For example, this strategy requires that a range of different government and community organizations work together in order to develop needed services and ensure that juveniles receive the services they need, but it can be difficult to get these organizations to coordinate with one another (steps 4 and 5). The evaluations, however, provide advice on how to better implement the strategy.[3] Those few communities that have been able to carry out the tasks to some degree appear to have had some success at reducing delinquency, although more and better evaluations need to be done (see Howell 2003a, 2003b).

We Should Hold Juveniles Accountable for Their Behavior and Protect the Community

I also believe that juveniles should be sanctioned for their delinquent acts and that the community should be protected from dangerous offenders. Data indicate that one of the reasons that juveniles engage in delinquency is low direct control. That is, they are not consistently sanctioned for their delinquent acts. Further, most people believe that juveniles, especially older juveniles, have at least some responsibility for their behavior. This issue is the subject of much debate in the social and behavioral sciences and philosophy (see Agnew, 1995c; Wright and Brezina, 2001; Zimring, 1998). It is commonly argued that human behavior is not fully determined by outside forces, so sanctioning juveniles for their behavior may prevent some delinquency and may be viewed as a just approach in some cases. Further, this strategy has much political and public support.

The **juvenile justice system**, of course, now **places much emphasis on sanctioning juveniles, but it does not sanction them in an efficient manner.** We pass laws that increase the severity of punishment, especially for serious offenders. The passage of such laws is easily done and is politically popular. Data, however, indicate that the certainty of punishment is much more important than the severity. Unfortunately, it is not so easy to **increase the certainty of punishment.** But among other things, we might do the following: We should teach parents, teachers, and others how to better exercise direct control, for they are in the best position to detect and sanction delinquent acts. The juvenile justice system should also make a better effort to detect and sanction delinquency. As indicated in Chapter 20, communities can improve strategies of policing in ways that increase the ability of the police to catch offenders. In particular, data suggest that focused police crackdowns and certain types of community policing are effective in this area. And society can provide more resources to the juvenile court and juvenile corrections system so that they can better sanction offenders. In particular, the juvenile justice system should employ a system of "graduated sanctions," such that all offenders receive meaningful sanctions and that these sanctions increase in severity if offending continues.

We not only need to increase the certainty of punishment, but we also need to **change how we punish.** The punishments now employed often have a number of negative effects: They increase strain, isolate juveniles from conventional society, and foster the social learning of crime. The system should punish in ways that minimize these negative effects. Community-based sanctions should be employed to the extent possible, since these sanctions avoid the sometimes negative effects of institutions. As indicated in Chapter 21, a range of new community-based sanctions have been developed, and these sanctions are more cost-effective than institutionalization. We should punish in a way that rebuilds the ties between offenders and the larger community, perhaps employing some of the initiatives associated with the restorative justice movement (see Chapter 23). Our efforts to punish should be combined with efforts to rehabilitate. In particular, data indicate that sanctions are most effective when combined with efforts that address the other causes of delinquency. Finally, we should work to eliminate discrimination in the justice system.

It is also important, of course, to **protect the community from dangerous offenders.** This protection is now often accomplished by institutionalizing juveniles in large facilities that place little emphasis on rehabilitation. Data, however, suggest that the system institutionalizes more juveniles than is necessary. And data suggest that it is **better to confine juveniles in small-scale institutions that place a strong emphasis on treatment.** Such juveniles are less likely to be harmed by their institutional confinement and are more likely to be rehabilitated, which, of course, contributes to the protection of the community. Adjudicated delinquents can be screened for their risk of future offending, particularly serious offending. Juveniles who pose some risk to the community can be placed under close supervision or confined in institutions, if warranted. Close supervision and institutional confinement may prevent some delinquency through their "incapacitation effect," as discussed in Chapter 23.

These strategies are described in detail in the publications listed in notes 1 and 2. I also encourage you to examine the websites of the National Institute of Justice (NIJ) and many of the agencies that are part of the NIJ, such as the Office of Juvenile Justice and Delinquency Prevention (see http://www.ojp.usdoj.gov/nij). Also, call 800-WE-PREVENT to receive a booklet that describes what you can do to reduce delinquency (or visit www.weprevent.org). I hope that your examination of delinquency does not end with this book. Rather, I hope that this book represents the beginning of a serious commitment to work toward the reduction of delinquency in our society.

Teaching Aids

Exercise

In the exercise for Chapter 18, I asked you to imagine that a family member or friend asked you: "What causes delinquency?" For this exercise, imagine that a family member or friend asks you: "What should we do to reduce delinquency?" Outline a 5- to 10-minute response to this question—one that draws on the materials in this text and will be meaningful to the family member or friend. With your instructor's permission, several of the people in your class should share their responses with the class and solicit feedback.

TEST YOUR KNOWLEDGE OF THIS CHAPTER

1. What criteria do I employ to evaluate the suitability of delinquency control measures (e.g., cost, public acceptance)?
2. Why do I argue that we need to place more emphasis on prevention and rehabilitation?
3. Describe the strategy that I suggest (and the federal government recommends) for putting prevention and rehabilitation programs into place.
4. Describe the limited evaluation research on the strategy that I suggest.
5. Why do I argue that we need to hold juveniles accountable for their delinquency?
6. Why do I argue that we do not sanction juveniles in an efficient or effective manner? What do we need to do to more effectively sanction juveniles?
7. How do I suggest that we go about protecting the community from dangerous offenders?

THOUGHT AND DISCUSSION QUESTIONS

1. Can you think of any criteria beyond those that I have listed that should be used to evaluate the suitability of delinquency control programs?
2. To what extent do you agree and/or disagree with the recommendations that I make for controlling delinquency? How would you alter these recommendations?
3. The exercise for this chapter asks you to develop your own set of recommendations for controlling delinquency. What might you do to help implement these recommendations, both in your local community and beyond?

ENDNOTES

1. *See* Bilchik, 1998; Caliber Associates, 2006; Coolbough and Monsel, 2000; Coordinating Council on Juvenile Justice and Delinquency Prevention, 1996; Department of Justice, 2007; Flores, 2003; Howell, 1997a, 2003a, 2003b; Krisberg et al., 2004; Kurlychek et al., 1999; Morley et al., 2000; Office of Juvenile Justice and Delinquency Prevention, 2006.

2. *See* Caliber Associates, 2006; Coleman et al., 1999; Coolbough and Hansel, 2000; Coordinating Council on Juvenile Justice and Delinquency Prevention, 1996; Department of Justice, 2007; Dunworth and Mills, 1999; Flores, 2003; Howell, 1997a, 2003a, 2003b; Howell and Hawkins, 1998; Kelling et al., 1998; Krisberg et al., 2004; Morley et al., 2000; National Institute of Justice, 1996; Office of Juvenile Justice and Delinquency Prevention, 1999b, 2006; Office of Justice Programs, 1999; Robinson, 1996; Sherman et al., 2002; the Weed and Seed Data Center at http://www.weedandseeddatacenter.org.

3. For example, *see* Caliber Associates, 2006; Coolbaugh and Monsel, 2000; Howell, 2003a; Krisberg et al., 2004; Morley et al., 2000.

References

Abt Associates

1994 Conditions of Confinement: Juvenile Detention and Corrections Facilities. Washington, DC: Office of Juvenile Justice and Delinquency Prevention.

Acoca, Leslie

1998 "Outside/inside: The violation of American girls at home, on the streets, and in the juvenile justice system." Crime and Delinquency 44:561–589.

Adams, Mike S., and T. David Evans

1996 "Teacher disapproval, delinquent peers, and self-reported delinquency: A longitudinal test of labeling theory." Urban Review 28:199–211.

Adams, Mike S., James D. Johnson, and T. David Evans

1998 "Racial differences in informal labeling effects." Deviant Behavior 19:157–171.

Adams, Mike S., Craig T. Robertson, Phyllis Gray-Ray, and Melvin C. Ray

2003 "Labeling and delinquency." Adolescence 38:171–186.

Agnew, Robert

1983 "Physical punishment and delinquency." Youth and Society 15:225–236.

1984 "Autonomy and delinquency." Sociological Perspectives 27:219–240.

1985a "A revised strain theory of delinquency." Social Forces 64:151–167.

1985b "Social control theory and delinquency: A longitudinal test." Criminology 23:47–62.

1986 "Work and delinquency among juveniles attending school." Journal of Crime and Justice 9:19–41.

1990a "The origins of delinquent events: An examination of offender accounts." Journal of Research in Crime and Delinquency 27:267–294.

1990b "Adolescent resources and delinquency." Criminology 28:535–566.

1991a "A longitudinal test of social control theory and delinquency." Journal of Research on Crime and Delinquency 28:126–156.

1991b "The interactive effect of peer variables on delinquency." Criminology 29:47–72.

1992 "Foundation for a general strain theory of crime and delinquency." Criminology 30:47–87.

1993 "Why do they do it? An examination of the intervening mechanisms between 'social control' variables and delinquency." Journal of Research in Crime and Delinquency 30:245–266.

1994a "Delinquency and the desire for money." Justice Quarterly 11:411–427.

1994b "The techniques of neutralization and violence." Criminology 32:555–580.

1995a "Testing the leading crime theories: An alternative strategy focusing on motivational processes." Journal of Research in Crime and Delinquency 32:363–398.

1995b "Strain and subcultural theories of criminality." Pp. 305–327 in Joseph F. Sheley, ed., Criminology: A Contemporary Handbook. Belmont, CA: Wadsworth.

1995c "Determinism, indeterminism, and crime: An empirical exploration." Criminology 33:83–109.

1997 "Stability and change in crime over the life course: A strain theory explanation." Pp. 101–132 in Terence P. Thornberry, ed., Developmental Theories of Crime and Delinquency: Advances in Criminological Theory, Volume 7. New Brunswick, NJ: Transaction.

1999 "A general strain theory of community differences in crime rates." Journal of Research in Crime and Delinquency 36:123–155.

2001a "An overview of general strain theory." Pp. 161–174 in Ray Paternoster and Ronet Bachman, eds., Explaining Criminals and Crime. Los Angeles: Roxbury.

2001b "Building on the foundation of general strain theory: Specifying the types of strain most likely to lead to crime and delinquency." Journal of Research in Crime and Delinquency 38:319–361.

2002 "Experienced, vicarious, and anticipated strain." Justice Quarterly 19:603–632.

2003a "An integrated theory of the adolescent peak in offending." Youth and Society 34:263–299.

2003b "The interactive effects of social control variables on delinquency." In Chester Britt and Michael R. Gottfredson, eds., Control Theories of Crime and Delinquency, Advances in Criminological Theory, Volume 12. New Brunswick, NJ: Transaction.

2005 Why Do Criminals Offend: A General Theory of Crime and Delinquency. Los Angeles: Roxbury.

2006a Pressured Into Crime. New York: Oxford University Press.

2006b "General strain theory: Current status and directions for further research." Pp.101–123 in Francis T. Cullen, John Paul Wright, and Kristie R. Blevins, eds., Taking Stock: The Status of Criminological Theory. New Brunswick, NJ: Transaction.

2006c "Storylines as a neglected cause of crime." Journal of Research in Crime and Delinquency 43:119–147.

2008 "The contribution of 'mainstream' theories to the explanation of crime and delinquency." In Margaret Zahn, ed., Delinquent Girls: Findings from the Girls' Study Group. Philadelphia: Temple University Press.

Agnew, Robert, and Timothy Brezina
1997 "Relational problems with peers, gender and delinquency." Youth and Society 29:84–111.

Agnew, Robert, Timothy Brezina, John Paul Wright, and Francis T. Cullen
2002 "Strain, personality traits, and delinquency: Extending general strain theory." Criminology 40:43–72.

Agnew, Robert, Francis T. Cullen, Velmer S. Burton, Jr., T. David Evans, and R. Gregory Dunaway
1996 "A new test of classic strain theory." Justice Quarterly 13:681–704.

Agnew, Robert, and Ardith A. R. Peters
1985 "The techniques of neutralization: An analysis of predisposing and situational factors." Criminal Justice and Behavior 13:81–97.

Agnew, Robert, and David M. Petersen
1989 "Leisure and delinquency." Social Problems 36:332–350.

Agnew, Robert, and Helene Raskin White
1992 "An empirical test of general strain theory." Criminology 30:475–499.

Aguilar, Benjamin, L. Alan Sroufe, Byron Egeland, and Elizabeth Carlson
2000 "Distinguishing the early-onset/persistent and adolescent-onset antisocial behavior types: From birth to 16 years." Development and Psychopathology 12:109–132.

Akers, Ronald L.
1985 Deviant Behavior: A Social Learning Approach. Belmont, CA: Wadsworth.

1990 "Rational choice, deterrence, and social learning theory in criminology: The path not taken." Journal of Criminal Law and Criminology 81:653–676.

1992 Drugs, Alcohol, and Society. Belmont, CA: Wadsworth.

1998 Social Learning and Social Structure: A General Theory of Crime and Deviance. Boston: Northeastern University Press.

1999 "Social learning and social structure: Reply to Sampson, Morash, and Krohn." Theoretical Criminology 3:477–493.

Akers, Ronald L., and Gary F. Jensen
2003 Social Learning Theory and the Explanation of Crime, Advances in Criminological Theory, Volume 11. New Brunswick, NJ: Transaction.

Akers, Ronald L., Marvin D. Krohn, Lonn Lanza-Kaduce, and Marcia Radosevich
1979 "Social learning and deviant behavior: A specific test of a general theory." American Sociological Review 44:635–655.

Akers, Ronald L., James Massey, William Clarke, and Ronald M. Lauer
1983 "Are self-reports of adolescent deviance valid? Biochemical measures, randomized response, and the bogus pipeline in smoking behavior." Social Forces 62:234–251.

Akers, Ronald L., and Christine S. Sellers
2004 Criminological Theories. Los Angeles: Roxbury.

Alexander, Karl L.
1997 "Public schools and the public good." Social Forces 76:1–30.

Allan, Emile Andersen, and Darrell J. Steffensmeier
1989 "Youth, underemployment, and property crime: Differential effects of job availability and job quality on juvenile and young adult arrest rates." American Sociological Review 54:107–123.

Alpert, Geoffrey P., and Alex Piquero
1998 Community Policing. Prospect Heights, IL: Waveland Press.

Altschuler, David M.
1998 "Intermediate sanctions and community treatment for serious and violent juvenile offenders." Pp. 367–388 in Rolf Loeber and David P. Farrington, eds., Serious and Violent Juvenile Offenders. Thousand Oaks, CA: Sage.

Altschuler, David M., Troy L. Armstrong, and Doris Layton MacKenzie
1999 Reintegration, Supervised Release, and Intensive Aftercare. Washington, DC: Office of Juvenile Justice and Delinquency Prevention.

Altschuler, David M., and Paul J. Brounstein
1991 "Patterns of drug use, drug trafficking, and other delinquency among inner-city adolescent males in Washington, DC." Criminology 29:589–622.

Ambert, Anne-Marie
1997 Parents, Children, and Adolescents. New York: Haworth.

Anderson, Craig A.
2004 "An update of the effects of playing violent video games." Journal of Adolescence 27:113–122.

Anderson, Craig A., Leonard Berkowitz, Edward Donnerstein, L. Rowell Huesmann, James D. Johnson, Daniel Linz, Neil M. Malamuth, and Ellen Wortella
2003 "The influence of media violence on youth." Psychological Science in the Public Interest 4:81–110.

Anderson, Craig A., and Brad J. Bushman
2001a "Media violence and the American public: Scientific facts versus media misinformation." American Psychologist 56:477–489.
2001b "Effects of violent video games on aggressive behavior, aggressive cognition, aggressive affect, physiological arousal, and prosocial behavior: A meta-analytic review of the scientific literature." Psychological Science 12:353–359.
2002 "The effects of media violence on society." Science 295:2377–2378.

Anderson, Craig A., Nicholas L. Carnagey, and Janie Eubanks
2003 "Exposure to violent media: The effect of songs with violent lyrics on aggressive thoughts and feelings." Journal of Personality and Social Psychology 84:960–971.

Anderson, Craig A., Douglas A. Gentile, and Katherine E. Buckley
2007 Violent Video Game Effects on Children and Adolescents. New York: Oxford University Press.

Anderson, David C.
1998 "Curriculum, culture, and community: The challenge of school violence." Pp. 317–363 in Michael Tonry and Mark H. Moore, eds., Crime and Justice: A Review of Research, Volume 24. Chicago: University of Chicago Press.

Anderson, Elijah
1990 Streetwise: Race, Class and Change in an Urban Community. Chicago: University of Chicago Press.
1994 "The code of the streets." Atlantic Monthly 273(May):81–94.
1997 "Violence and the inner-city street code." Pp. 1–30 in Joan McCord, ed., Violence and Childhood in the Inner City. Cambridge, England: Cambridge University Press.
1999 Code of the Street. New York: W. W. Norton.

Anderson, Patrick R., and Donald J. Newman
1998 Introduction to Criminal Justice. Boston: McGraw-Hill.

Andrews, Chyrl, and Lynn Marble
2003 Changes to OJJDP's Juvenile Accountability Program. Washington, DC: Office of Juvenile Justice and Delinquency Prevention.

Andrews, D. A., and James Bonta
2006 The Psychology of Criminal Conduct. LexisNexis.

Andrews, D. A., Ivan Zinger, Robert D. Hoge, James Bonta, Paul Gendreau, and Francis T. Cullen
1990 "Does correctional treatment work? A clinically relevant and psychologically informed meta-analysis." Criminology 28:369–404.

Aos, Steve, Polly Phipps, Robert Barnoski, and Roxanne Lieb
2001 The Comparative Costs and Benefits of Programs to Reduce Crime. Olympia, WA: Washington State Institute for Public Policy.

Apel, Robert, Shawn Bushway, Robert Brame, Amelia M. Haviland, Daniel S. Nagin, and Ray Paternoster
2007 "Unpacking the relationship between adolescent employment and antisocial behavior." Criminology 45:67–98.

Apel, Robert, Raymond Paternoster, Shawn D. Bushway, and Robert Brame
2006 "A job isn't just a job: The differential impact of formal versus informal work on adolescent problem behavior." Crime and Deliquency 52:333–369.

Applegate, Brandon K., Francis T. Cullen, and Bonnie S. Fisher
1997 "Public support for correctional treatment: The continuing appeal of the rehabilitative ideal." Prison Journal 77:237–258.

Archer, Dane, and Patricia McDaniel
1995 "Violence and gender: Differences and similarities across societies." Pp. 63–88 in R. Barry Ruback and Neil Alan Weiner, eds., Interpersonal Violent Behaviors. New York: Springer.

Aries, Philippe
1962 Centuries of Childhood. New York: Vintage Books.

Armstrong, Gaylene S., and Nancy Rodriquez
2005 "Effects of individual and contextual characteristics on preadjudication detention of juvenile deliquents." Justice Quarterly 22:521–539.

Armstrong, Troy L., and David M. Altschuler
1998 "Recent developments in juvenile aftercare: Assessment, findings, and promising programs." Pp. 448–472 in Albert K. Roberts, ed., Juvenile Justice. Chicago: Nelson-Hall.

Arneklev, Bruce J., Harold G. Grasmick, and Robert J. Bursik, Jr.
1999 "Evaluating the dimensionality and invariance of low self-control." Journal of Quantitative Criminology 15:1999.

Arnett, Jeffrey J
1997 "Young people's conceptions of the transition to adulthood." Youth and Society 29:3–23.

Arnette, June L., and Marjorie C. Walsleben
1998 Combating Fear and Restoring Safety in Schools. Washington, DC: Office of Juvenile Justice and Delinquency Prevention.

Arthur, Raymond
2005 "Punishing parents for the crimes of their children." Harvard Journal of Criminal Justice 44:233–253.

Aseltine, Robert H., Jr.
1995 "A reconsideration of the effect of parental and peer influences on deviance." Journal of Health and Social Behavior 36:103–121.

Aseltine, Robert H., Jr., Susan Gore, and Jennifer Gordon
2000 "Life stress, anger and anxiety, and delinquency: An empirical test of general strain theory." Journal of Health and Social Behavior 41:256–275.

Assaad, Jean-Marc, and M. Lyn Exum
2002 "Understanding intoxicated violence from a rational choice perspective." Pp. 65–84 in Alex R. Piquero and Stephen G. Tibbetts, eds., Rational Choice and Criminal Behavior. New York: Routledge.

Athens, Lonnie
2005 "Violent encounters." Journal of Contemporary Ethnography 34:1–48.

Atkin, Ross
2003 "Public housing at a crossroads." Christian Science Monitor, March 12, 11.

Atlanta Constitution
2003 "Hope VI program is worth keeping." July 25, A14.

Auerhahn, Kathleen
1999 "Selective incapacitation and the problem of prediction." Criminology 37:703–734.

Austin, James
1995 "The overrepresentation of minority youths in the California juvenile justice system." Pp. 153–178 in Kimberly Kempf Leonard, Carl E. Pope, and William H. Feyerherm, eds., Minorities in Juvenile Justice. Thousand Oaks, CA: Sage.

Austin, James, Kelly Dedel Johnson, and Maria Gregoriou
2000 Juveniles in Adult Prisons and Jails. Washington, DC: Bureau of Justice Assistance.

Babbie, Earl
2006 The Practice of Social Research. Belmont, CA: Wadsworth.

Baier, Colin J., and Bradley R. E. Wright
2001 " 'If you love me, keep my commandments': A meta-analysis of the effect of religion on crime." Journal of Research in Crime and Delinquency 38:3–21.

Baker, Laura A., Serena Bezdjian, and Adrian Raine
2006 "Behavioral genetics: The science of antisocial behavior." Law and Contemporary Problems 69: 7–46.

Baldwin, John D., and Janice I. Baldwin
1981 Behavior Principles in Everyday Life. Englewood Cliffs, NJ: Prentice-Hall.

Balkwell, James W.
1990 "Ethnic inequality and the rate of homicide." Social Forces 69:53–70.

Bandura, Albert
1973 Aggression: A Social Learning Approach. Englewood Cliffs, NJ: Prentice-Hall.
1986 Social Foundations of Thought and Action: A Social Cognitive Theory. Englewood Cliffs, NJ: Prentice-Hall.
1990 "Selective activation and disengagement of moral control." Journal of Social Issues 46:27–46.

Barlow, Hugh D.
1995 Crime and Public Policy. Boulder, CO: Westview.

Barlow, Jane, Doug Simkiss, and Sarah Stewart-Brown
2006 "Interventions to prevent or ameliorate child physical abuse and neglect." Journal of Children's Services 3:6–28.

Barnes, Grace M., Joseph H. Hoffman, John W. Welte, Michael Farrell, and Barbara A. Dintcheff
2006 "Effects of parental monitoring and peer deviance on substance use and deliquency." Journal of Marriage and the Family 68:1084–1104.

Baron, Robert A., and Deborah R. Richardson
1994 Human Aggression. New York: Plenum.

Baron, Stephen W.
2003 "Self-control, social consequences, and criminal behavior." Journal of Research in Crime and Delinquency 40:403–425.

Baron, Stephen W.
2004 "General strain, street youth and crime: A test of Agnew's revised theory." Criminology 42:457–483.
2007 "Street youth, gender, financial strain, and crime." Deviant Behavior 28:273–302.

Baron, Stephen W., and Timothy F. Hartnagel
1997 "Attributions, affect, and crime: Street youth's reactions to unemployment." Criminology 35:409–434.
2002 "Street youth and labor market strain." Journal of Criminal Justice 30:519–533.

Bartol, Curt R., and Anne M. Bartol
1986 Criminal Behavior: A Psychosocial Approach. Englewood Cliffs, NJ: Prentice-Hall.

Bartollas, Clemens, Stuart J. Miller, and Simon Dinitz
1976 Juvenile Victimization: The Institutional Paradox. New York: Halsted Press.

Bartusch, Dawn R. Jeglum, Donald R. Lynam, Terrie E. Moffitt, and Phil A. Silva
1997 "Is age important? Testing a general versus a developmental theory of antisocial behavior." Criminology 35:13–48.

Bartusch, Dawn R. Jeglum, and Ross L. Matsueda
1996 "Gender, reflected appraisals, and labeling: A cross-group test of an interactionist theory of delinquency." Social Forces 75:145–177.

Battin, Sara R., Karl G. Hill, Robert D. Abbott, Richard F. Catalano, and J. David Hawkins
1998 "The contribution of gang membership to delinquency beyond delinquent friends." Criminology 36: 93–115.

Bazemore, Gordon
2000 "Community justice and a vision of collective efficacy: The case of restorative conferencing." Pp. 225–297 in Julie Horney, ed., Policies, Processes, and Decisions of the Criminal Justice System; Criminal Justice 2000, Volume 3. Washington, DC: Office of Justice Programs.

Bazemore, Gordon, Jeanne B. Stinchcomb, and Leslie A. Leip
2004 "Scared smart or bored straight?" Justice Quarterly 21:269–300.

Bazemore, Gordon, and Mark S. Umbreit
1994 Balanced and Restorative Justice: Program Summary. Washington, DC: Office of Juvenile Justice and Delinquency Prevention.
2001 A Comparison of Four Restorative Conferencing Models. Washington, DC: Office of Juvenile Justice and Delinquency Prevention.

Bazemore, Gordon, and Mark Umbreit
2004 "Balanced and restorative justice." Pp. 467–510 in Albert R. Roberts, ed., Juvenile Justice Sourcebook. New York: Oxford University Press.

Becker, Howard S.
1953 "Becoming a marihuana user." American Journal of Sociology 59:235–242.
1963 Outsiders: Studies in the Sociology of Deviance. New York: Free Press.

Beckett, Katherine, and Theodore Sasson
2000 The Politics of Injustice. Thousand Oaks, CA: Pine Forge.

Bell, James
2005 "A solvable problem: Reducing the disproportionality of youths of color in juvenile detention facilities." Corrections Today 67:80–83.

Bellair, Paul E.
1997 "Social interaction and community crime: Examining the importance of neighborhood networks." Criminology 35:677–704.
2000 "Informal surveillance and street crime: A complex relationship." Criminology 38:137–170.

Bellair, Paul E. and Thomas L. McNulty
2005 "Beyond the bell curve: Community disadvantage and the explanation of black-white differences in adolescent violence." Criminology 43:1135–1168.

Bellair, Paul E., and Vincent J. Roscigno
2000 "Local labor-market opportunity and adolescent delinquency." Social Forces 78:1509–38.

Bellair, Paul E., Vincent J. Roscigno, and Thomas L. McNulty
2003 "Linking local labor market opportunity to violent adolescent delinquency." Journal of Research in Crime and Delinquency 40:6–33.

Belsky, Joy, Deborah Lowe Vandell, Margaret Burchinal, K. Alison Clarke-Stewart, Kathleen McCartney, and Margaret Tresch Owen
2007 "Are there long-term effects of early child care?" Child Development 78:681–701.

Bennett, Sarah, David P. Farrington, and L. Rowell Huesmann
2005 "Explaining gender differences in crime and violence: The importance of social cognitive skills." Aggression and Violent Behavior 10:263–288.

Bennett, Trevor, and Richard Wright
1984 Burglars on Burglary. Aldershot, England: Gower.

Bennett, William J., John J. DiIulio, Jr., and John P. Walters
1996 Body Count: Moral Poverty and How to Win America's War Against Crime and Drugs. New York: Simon and Schuster.

Bensley, Lillian, and Juliet Van Eenwyk
2001 "Video games and real-life aggression: Review of the literature." Journal of Adolescent Health 29:244–257.

Benson, Michael
2002 Crime and the Life Course. Los Angeles: Roxbury.

Berger, Kathleen Stassen
2007 "Update on bullying at school: Science forgotten?" Developmental Review 27:90 126.

Berger, Ronald J.
1989 "Female delinquency in the emancipation era: A review of the literature." Sex Roles 21:375–399.

Berkowitz, Leonard
1993 Aggression: Its Causes, Consequences, and Control. New York: McGraw-Hill.
1994 "Guns and youth." Pp. 251–279 in Leonard D. Eron, Jacquelyn H. Gentry, and Peggy Schlegel, eds., Reason to Hope. Washington, DC: American Psychological Association.

Berman, Mitchell E., Richard J. Kavoussi, and Emil F. Coccaro
1997 "Neurotransmitter correlates of human aggression." Pp. 305–313 in David M. Stoff, James Breiling, and Jack D. Maser, eds., Handbook of Antisocial Behavior. New York: Wiley.

Bernard, Thomas J.
1984 "Control criticisms of strain theories: An assessment of theoretical and empirical adequacy." Journal of Research in Crime and Delinquency 21:353–372.
1990 "Angry aggression among the 'truly disadvantaged.'" Criminology 28:73–96.
1992 The Cycle of Juvenile Justice. New York: Oxford University Press.
1999 "Juvenile crime and the transformation of juvenile justice: Is there a juvenile crime wave?" Justice Quarterly 16:337–356.

Bernard, Thomas J., and Jeffrey B. Snipes
1996 "Theoretical integration in criminology." Pp. 301–348 in Michael Tonry, ed., Crime and Justice, Volume 20. Chicago: University of Chicago Press.

Bernburg, Jon Gunnar, and Marvin Krohn
2003 "Labeling, life chances, and adult crime." Criminology 41:1287–1318.

Bernburg, Jon Gunnar, Marvin D. Krohn, and Craig J. Rivera
2006 "Official labeling, criminal embeddedness, and subsequent delinquency." Journal of Research in Crime and Delinquency 43:67–88.

Beyer, Marty
2003 Best Practices in Juvenile Accountability: Overview. Washington, DC: Office of Juvenile Justice and Delinquency Prevention.

Bilchik, Shay
1998 A Juvenile Justice System for the 21st Century. Washington, DC: Office of Juvenile Justice and Delinquency Prevention.

Bilukha, Oleg, Robert A. Hahn, Alex Crosby, Mindy T. Fullilove, Akiva Liberman, Eve Moscicki, Susan Snyder, Farris Tuma, Phaedra Corso, Amanda Schofield, and Peter A. Briss
2005 "The effectiveness of early childhood home visitation in preventing violence." American Journal of Preventive Medicine 28:11–39.

Binder, Arnold, Gilbert Geis, and Dickson D. Bruce, Jr.
1997 Juvenile Delinquency. Cincinnati: Anderson.

Birkbeck, Christopher, and Gary LaFree
1993 "The situational analysis of crime and deviance." Annual Review of Sociology 19:113–137.

Bishop, Donna

2005 "The role of race and ethnicity in juvenile justice processing." Pp. 23–82 in Darnell F. Hawkins and Kimberly Kemp-Leonard, eds., Our Children, Their Children. Chicago: University of Chicago Press.

Bishop, Donna M.

2006 "Public opinion and juvenile justice policy: Myths and misconceptions." Criminology and Public Policy 4:653–664.

Bishop, Donna M., and Charles Frazier

2000 "Consequences of transfer." Pp. 227–276 in Jeffrey Fagan and Franklin E. Zimring, eds., The Changing Borders of Juvenile Justice. Chicago: University of Chicago Press.

Bishop, Donna M., Charles E. Frazier, Lonn Lanza-Kaduce, and Lawrence Winner

1996 "The transfer of juveniles to criminal court: Does it make a difference?" Crime and Delinquency 42: 171–191.

Bjerk, David

2007 "Measuring the relationship between youth criminal participation and household economic resources." Journal of Quantitative Criminology 23:23–39.

Bjerregaard, Beth, and Alan J. Lizotte

1995 "Gun ownership and gang membership." Journal of Criminal Law and Criminology 86:37–58.

Bjerregaard, Beth, and Carolyn Smith

1993 "Gender differences in gang participation, delinquency, and substance use." Journal of Quantitative Criminology 4:329–355.

Blackburn, Ronald

1993 The Psychology of Criminal Conduct. Chichester, England: John Wiley and Sons.

Blazak, Randy

1999 "Hate in the suburbs: The rise of the skinhead counterculture." Pp. 49–56 in Lisa J. McIntyre, ed., The Practical Skeptic: Readings in Sociology. Mountain View, CA: Mayfield.

Bloom, Richard W.

2002 "On media violence: Whose facts? Whose misinformation?" American Psychologist 57:447–448.

Blueprints for Violence Prevention

http://www.colorado.edu/cspv/blueprints/

Blumstein, Alfred

1995 "Youth violence, guns, and the illicit-drug industry." Journal of Criminal Law and Criminology 86: 10–36.

1998 "U.S. criminal justice conundrum: Rising prison populations and stable crime rates." Crime and Delinquency 44:127–135.

2000 "Disaggregating the violence trends." Pp. 13–44 in Alfred Blumstein and Joel Wallman. eds., The Crime Drop in America. Cambridge, England: Cambridge University Press.

2002 "Why is crime falling—or is it?" Pp. 1–34 in National Institute of Justice, ed., Perspectives on Crime and Justice: 2000–2001 Lecture Series. Washington, DC: National Institute of Justice.

Blumstein, Alfred, and Richard Rosenfeld

1998 "Exploring recent trends in U.S. homicide rates." Journal of Criminal Law and Criminology 88:1175–1216.

Blumstein, Alfred, and Joel Wallman

2006 The Crime Drop in America. Cambridge, England: Cambridge University Press.

Bohm, Robert M.

2003 "Death penalty." Pp. 109–114 in Marilyn D. McShane and Frank P. Williams III, eds., Encyclopedia of Juvenile Justice. Thousand Oaks, CA: Sage.

Bonta, James, Rebecca Jesseman, Tanya Rugge, and Robert Cormier

2006 "Restorative justice and recidivism." Pp. 108–120 in D. Sullivan and L. Tifft, eds., Handbook of Restorative Justice. New York: Routledge.

Bortner, M. A., Marjorie S. Zatz, and Darnell F. Hawkins

2000 "Race and transfer: Empirical research and social context." Pp. 277–320 in Jeffrey Fagan and Franklin E. Zimring, eds., The Changing Borders of Juvenile Justice. Chicago: University of Chicago Press.

Bottcher, Jean
2001 "Social practices of gender: How gender relates to delinquency in the everyday lives of high-risk youth." Criminology 39:893–932.

Bottcher, Jean, and Michael E. Ezell
2005 "Examining the effectiveness of boot camps." Journal of Research in Crime and Delinquency 42:309–332.

Bottoms, Anthony E., and Paul Wiles
2002 "Environmental criminology." Pp. 620–656 in Mike Maguire, Rod Morgan, and Robert Reiner, eds., The Oxford Handbook of Criminology, 3rd edition. Oxford: Oxford University Press.

Bourgois, Philippe
2003 In Search of Respect. New York: Cambridge University Press.

Bowker, Lee H., and Malcolm W. Klein
1983 "The etiology of female juvenile delinquency and gang membership: A test of psychological and social structural explanations." Adolescence 18:739–751.

Boyum, David, and Mark A. R. Kleiman
2002 "Substance abuse policy from a crime-control perspective." Pp. 331–382 in James Q. Wilson and Joan Petersilia, eds., Crime. Oakland, CA: ICS Press.

Braga, Anthony
2003 "Serious youth gun offenders and the epidemic of youth violence in Boston." Journal of Quantitative Criminology 19:33–54.

Braga, Anthony A., David M. Kennedy, and George E. Tita
2002 "New approaches to the strategic prevention of gang and group-involved violence." Pp. 271–286 in C. Ronald Huff, ed., Gangs in America III. Thousand Oaks, CA: Sage.

Braga, Anthony A., David M. Kennedy, Elin J. Waring, and Anne Morrison Piehl
2001 "Problem-oriented policing, deterrence, and youth violence: An evaluation of Boston's Operation Ceasefire." Journal of Research in Crime and Delinquency 38:195–225.

Braga, Anthony A., David L. Weisburd, Elin J. Waring, Lorraine Green Mazerolle, William Spelman, and Francis Gajewski
1999 "Problem-oriented policing in violent crime places: A randomized controlled experiment." Criminology 37:541–580.

Braithwaite, John
1981 "The myth of social class and criminality reconsidered." American Sociological Review 46:36–57.
1989 Crime, Shame and Reintegration. Cambridge, England: Cambridge University Press.
2002 Restorative Justice and Responsive Regulation. Oxford: Oxford University Press.

Braithwaite, John
2005 "Between proportionality and impunity." Criminology 43:283–306.

Braithwaite, John, Eliza Ahmed, and Valerie Braithwaite
2006 "Shame, restorative justice, and crime." Pp. 397–418 in Francis T. Cullen, John Paul Wright, and Kristie R. Blevins, eds., Taking Stock: The Status of Criminological Theory. New Brunswick, NJ: Transaction.

Brame, Robert, Shawn Bushway, and Raymond Paternoster
1999 "On the use of panel research designs and random effects models to investigate static and dynamic theories of criminal offending." Criminology 37:599–642.

Brame, Robert, and Alex R. Piquero
2003 "Selective attribution and the age-crime relationship." Journal of Quantitative Criminology 19:107–127.

Brandl, Steven G., and David E. Barlow
1996 Classics in Policing. Cincinnati, OH: Anderson.

Brank, Eve M., Stephanie A. Hays, and Victoria Weisz
2006 "All parents are to blame (except this one)." Journal of Applied Social Psychology 36:2670–2684.

Brantingham, Paul, and Patricia Brantingham
1984 Patterns in Crime. New York: Macmillan.

Brennan, Patricia A., Sarnoff A. Mednick, and Jan Volavka
1995 "Biomedical factors in crime." Pp. 65–90 in James Q. Wilson and Joan Petersilia, eds., Crime. San Francisco: ICS Press.

Brennan, Patricia A., and Adrian Raine
1997 "Biosocial bases of antisocial behavior: Psychophysiological, neurological and cognitive factors." Clinical Psychology Review.

Brewer, Devon D., J. David Hawkins, Richard F. Catalano, and Holly J. Neckerman
1995 "Preventing serious, violent, and chronic juvenile offending: A review of evaluations of selected strategies in childhood, adolescence, and the community." Pp. 61–141 in James C. Howell, Barry Krisberg, J. David Hawkins, and John J. Wilson, eds., A Sourcebook: Serious, Violent, and Chronic Juvenile Offenders. Thousand Oaks, CA: Sage.

Brezina, Timothy
1998 "Adolescent maltreatment and delinquency: The question of intervening processes." Journal of Research in Crime and Delinquency 35:71–99.
2000 "Delinquent problem-solving: An interpretative framework for criminology theory and research." Journal of Research in Crime and Delinquency 37:3–30.

Brezina, Timothy, Robert Agnew, Francis T. Cullen, and John Paul Wright
2004 "The code of the street." Youth Violence and Juvenile Justice 2:303–328.

Brezina, Timothy, and Alex R. Piquero
2003 "Exploring the relationship between social and non-social reinforcement in the context of social learning theory." Pp. 265–288 in Ronald L. Akers and Gary F. Jensen, eds., Social Learning Theory and the Explanation of Crime, Advances in Criminological Theory, Volume 11. New Brunswick, NJ: Transaction.

Briar, Scott, and Irving Piliavin
1965 "Delinquency, situational inducements, and commitment to conformity." Social Problems 13:35–45.

Bridges, George S., Darlene J. Conley, Rodney L. Engen, and Townsand Price-Spratlen
1995 "Racial disparities in the confinement of juveniles: Effects of crime and community structure on punishment." Pp. 128–152 in Kimberly Kempf Leonard, Carl E. Pope, and William H. Feyerherm, eds., Minorities in Juvenile Justice. Thousand Oaks, CA: Sage.

Bridges, George S., and Sara Steen
1998 "Racial disparities in official assessments of juvenile offenders: Attributional stereotypes as mediating mechanisms." American Sociological Review 63:554–570.

Bridges, George S., and James A. Stone
1986 "Effects of criminal punishment on perceived threat of punishment: Toward an understanding of specific deterrence." Journal of Research on Crime and Delinquency 23:207–239.

Britt, Chester L., and Michael R. Gottfredson
2003 Control Theories of Crime and Delinquency. New Brunswick, NJ: Transaction.

Brochu, Serge
2006 "Evidence-based drug policies." Journal of Scandinavian Studies in Criminology and Crime Prevention 7:36–45.

Broidy, Lisa M.
2001 "A test of general strain theory." Criminology 39:9–33.

Broidy, Lisa M., and Robert Agnew
1997 "Gender and crime: A general strain theory perspective." Journal of Research in Crime and Delinquency 34:275–306.

Broidy, Lisa M., Daniel S. Nagin, Richard E. Tremblay, John E. Bates, Bobby Baume, Kenneth A. Dodge, David Fergusson, John L. Horwood, Rolf Loeber, Robert Laird, Donald R. Lynam, Terrie E. Moffitt, Gregory S. Pettit, and Frank Vitaro
2003 "Developmental trajectories of childhood disruptive behaviors and adolescent delinquency." Developmental Psychology 39:222–245.

Brooks-Gunn, Jeanne, and Greg J. Duncan
1997 "The effects of poverty on children." Future of Children 7:55–71.

Brown, Lee P.
1989 "Community policing: A practical guide for police officials." Washington, DC: National Institute of Justice.

Browne, Kevin D., and Catherine Hamilton-Giachritsis
2005 "The influence of violent media on children and adolescents." Lancet 365:702–710.

Brownfield, David
1986 "Social class and violent behavior." Criminology 24:421–438.

Brownfield, David, Ann Marie Sorenson, and Kevin M. Thompson
2001 "Gang membership, race, and social class." Deviant Behavior 22:73–89.

Brownfield, David, Kevin M. Thompson, and Ann Marie Sorenson
1997 "Correlates of gang membership: A test of strain, social learning, and social control theories." Journal of Gang Research 4:11–22.

Browning, Katharine, and David Huizinga
1999 Highlights of Findings from the Denver Youth Survey. Washington, DC: Office of Juvenile Justice and Delinquency Prevention.

Bruce, Marino A., Vincent J. Roscigno, and Patricia L. McCall
1998 "Structure, context, and agency in the reproduction of black-on-black violence." Theoretical Criminology 2:29–55.

Brunson, Rod K.
2007 "Police don't like black people: African-American young men's accumulated police experiences." Criminology and Public Policy 6:71–102.

Buikhuisen, W.
1988 "Chronic juvenile delinquency: A theory." Pp. 27–47 in W. Buikhuisen and Sarnoff A. Mednick, eds., Explaining Criminal Behavior. New York: E. J. Brill.

Building Blocks for Youth
2000 And Justice for Some. Available at http://www.buildingblocksforyouth.org.
2007 No Turning Back. Available at http://www.buildingblocksforyouth.org.

Burch, Jim, and Candice Kane
1999 Implementing the OJJDP Comprehensive Gang Model. Washington, DC: Office of Juvenile Justice and Delinquency Prevention.

Bureau of Justice Statistics
1992 Drugs, Crime, and the Justice System. Washington, DC: Bureau of Justice Statistics.

Burkett, Steven R., and Bruce O. Warren
1987 "Religiosity, peer associations, and adolescent marijuana use: A panel study of underlying causal structures." Criminology 25:109–131.

Burns, Barbara J., James C. Howell, Janet K. Wiig, Leena K. Augimeri, Brendan C. Welsh, Rolf Loeber, and David Petchuck
2003 Treatment, Services, and Intervention Programs for Child Delinquents. Washington, D.C.: Office of Juvenile Justice and Delinquency Prevention.

Bursik, Robert J., Jr.
1986 "Delinquency rates as sources of ecological change." Pp. 63–74 in James M. Byrne and Robert J. Sampson, eds., The Social Ecology of Crime. New York: Springer-Verlag.
1988 "Social disorganization and theories of crime and delinquency: Problems and prospects." Criminology 26:519–551.

Bursik, Robert J., Jr., and Harold G. Grasmick
1993 Neighborhoods and Crime. New York: Lexington.
1995 "Neighborhood-based networks and the control of crime and delinquency." Pp. 107–130 in Hugh Barlow, ed., Crime and Public Policy. Boulder, CO: Westview.
1996 "The use of contextual analysis in models of criminal behavior." Pp. 236–267 in J. David Hawkins, ed., Delinquency and Crime. Cambridge, England: Cambridge University Press.

Burt, Callie Harbin, Ronald L. Simons, and Leslie G. Simons
2006 "A longitudinal test of the effects of parenting and the stability of self-control." Criminology 44:353–396.

Burton, Velmer S., Jr., and Francis T. Cullen
1992 "The empirical status of strain theory." Journal of Crime and Justice 15:1–30.

Burton, Velmer S., Jr., Francis T. Cullen, T. David Evans, Leanne Fiftal Alarid, and R. Gregory Dunaway
1998 "Gender, self-control, and crime." Journal of Research in Crime and Delinquency 35:123–147.

Burton, Velmer S., Jr., Francis T. Cullen, T. David Evans, R. Gregory Dunaway, Sesha R. Kethineni, and Gary L. Payne
1995 "The impact of parental controls on delinquency." Journal of Criminal Justice 23:111–126.

Burton, Velmer S., Jr., and R. Gregory Dunaway
1994 "Strain, relative deprivation, and middle-class delinquency." Pp. 79–95 in Greg Barak, ed., Varieties of Criminology: Readings from a Dynamic Discipline. New York: Praeger.

Bushway, Shawn D., and Peter Reuter
2002 "Labor markets and crime risk factors." Pp. 198–240 in Lawrence W. Sherman, David P. Farrington, Brandon C. Welsh, and Doris Layton MacKenzie, eds., Evidence-Based Crime Prevention. London: Routledge.

Bushway, Shawn D., Terence P. Thornberry, and Marvin D. Krohn
2003 "Desistance as a developmental process: A comparison of static and dynamic approaches." Journal of Quantitative Criminology 19:129–153.

Butts, Jeffrey A., and Janeen Buck
2000 Teen Courts: A Focus on Research. Washington, DC: Office of Juvenile Justice and Delinquency Prevention.

Butts, Jeffrey A., and Ojmarrh Mitchell
2000 "Brick by brick: Dismantling the border between juvenile and adult justice." Pp. 167–213 in Charles M. Friel, ed., Criminal Justice 2000, Volume 2, Boundary Changes in Criminal Justice Organizations. Washington, DC: National Institute of Justice.

Butts, Jeffrey A., and Howard N. Snyder
2006 Too Soon to Tell: Deciphering Recent Trends in Youth Violence. Chicago: Chapin Hall Center for Children, University of Chicago.

Byrne, James M., and Robert J. Sampson
1986 "Key issues in the social ecology of crime." Pp. 1–22 in James M. Byrne and Robert J. Sampson, eds., The Social Ecology of Crime. New York: Springer-Verlag.

Cabaniss, Emily R., James M. Frabutt, Mary H. Kendrick, and Margaret B. Arbuckle
2007 "Reducing disproportionate minority contact in the juvenile justice system." Aggression and Violent Behavior 12:393–401.

Caeti, Tory J., Craig Hemmens, Francis T. Cullen, and Velmer S. Burton Jr.
2003 "Management of juvenile correctional facilities." Prison Journal 83:383–405.

Caldwell, Michael F., Michael Vitacco, and Gregory J. Van Rybroek
2006 "Are violent delinquents worth treating?" Journal of Research in Crime and Delinquency 43:148–168.

Caliber Associates
2006 National Evaluation of the Title V Community Prevention Grants Program. Washington, DC: Office of Juvenile Justice and Delinquency Prevention.

Campaign for Youth and Justice
2007 The Consequences Aren't Minor. Available at www.campaignforyouthjustice.org.

Campbell, Anne
1984 The Girls in the Gang. New York: Basil Blackwell.
1990 "Female participation in gangs." Pp. 163–182 in C. Ronald Huff, ed., Gangs in America. Newbury Park, CA: Sage.

Campbell Crime and Justice Group
http://www.campbellcollaboration.org/CCJG/

Canada, Geoffrey
1995 Fist Stick Knife Gun. Boston: Beacon Press.

Canter, Rachelle J.
1982 "Family correlates of male and female delinquency." Criminology 20:149–167.

Cantor, David, and James P. Lynch
2000 "Self-report surveys as measures of crime and criminal victimization." Pp. 85–138 in David Duffee, ed., Criminal Justice 2000, Volume 4, Measurement and Analysis of Crime and Justice. Washington, DC: National Institute of Justice.

Cao, Ligun, Anthony Adams, and Vickie J. Jenson
1997 "A test of the block subculture of violence thesis: A research note." Criminology 35:367–379.

Capowich, George P., Paul Mazerolle, and Alex R. Piquero
2001 "General strain theory, situational anger, and social networks: An assessment of conditional influences." Journal of Criminal Justice 29:445–461.

Carey, Gregory, and David Goldman
1997 "The genetics of antisocial behavior." Pp. 243–254 in David M. Stoff, James Breiling, and Jack D. Maser, eds., Handbook of Antisocial Behavior. New York: Wiley.

Carmichael, Stephanie, and Alex R. Piquero
2004 "Sanctions, perceived anger, and criminal offending." Journal of Quantitative Criminology 20:371–393.

Carr, Patrick J., Laura Napolitano, and Jessica Keating
2007 "We never call the cops and here is why." Criminology 45:445–480.

Carter, David L.
1995 "Community policing and D.A.R.E.: A Practitioner's Perspective." Washington, DC: Bureau of Justice Statistics Bulletin.

Caspi, Avshalom
1998 "Personality development across the life course." Pp. 311–388 in Nancy Eisenberg, ed., Handbook of Child Psychology, Volume 3. New York: Wiley.

Caspi, Avshalom, Daryl J. Bem, and Glen H. Elder, Jr.
1989 "Continuities and consequences of interactional styles across the life course." Journal of Personality 57:375–406.

Caspi, Avshalom, and Terrie E. Moffitt
1995 "The continuity of maladaptive behavior: From description to understanding in the study of antisocial behavior." Pp. 472–511 in Dante Cicchetti and Donald J. Cohen, eds., Developmental Psychopathology, Volume 2: Risk, Disorder, and Adaptation. New York: Wiley.

Caspi, Avshalom, Terrie E. Moffitt, Phil A. Silva, Magda Stouthamer-Loeber, Robert F. Krueger, and Pamela S. Schmutte
1994 "Are some people crime-prone? Replications of the personality-crime relationship across countries, genders, races, and methods." Criminology 32:163–195.

Caspi, Avshalom, Brent W. Roberts, and Rebecca L. Shiner
2005 "Personality development: Stability and change." Annual Review of Psychology 56:453–484

Catalano, Richard F., Michael W. Arthur, J. David Hawkins, Lisa Berglund, and Jeffrey J. Olson
1998 "Comprehensive community- and school-based interventions to prevent antisocial behavior." Pp. 248–283 in Rolf Loeber and David P. Farrington, eds., Serious and Violent Juvenile Offenders. Thousand Oaks, CA: Sage.

Catalano, Richard F., and J. David Hawkins
1996 "The social development model: A theory of antisocial behavior." Pp. 149–197 in J. David Hawkins, ed., Delinquency and Crime. Cambridge, England: Cambridge University Press.

Cauffman, Elizabeth, Laurence Steinberg, and Alex R. Piquero
2005 "Psychological, neuropsychological and physiological correlates of serious antisocial behavior in adolescence: The role of self-control." Criminology 43:133–176.

Center for American Progress Task Force in Poverty
2007 From Poverty to Prosperity: A National Strategy to Cut Poverty in Half. Available at www.americanprogress.org.

Cernkovich, Stephen A., and Peggy C. Giordano
1987 "Family relationships and delinquency." Criminology 25:295–321.
1992 "School bonding, race, and delinquency." Criminology 30:261–291.
2001 "Stability and change in antisocial behavior: The transition from adolescence to early adulthood." Criminology 39:371–410.

Cernkovich, Stephen A., Peggy C. Giordano, and Meredith D. Pugh
1985 "Chronic offenders: The missing cases in self-report delinquency research." Journal of Criminal Law and Criminology 76:705–732.

Chaiken, Jan M., Peter W. Greenwood, and Joan Petersilia
1977 "The criminal investigation process: A summary report." Policy Analysis 3:187–217.

Chaiken, Marcia R.
1998 Kids, COPS, and Communities. Washington, DC: National Institute of Justice.

Chambliss, William J.
1973 "The saints and the roughnecks." Society 11(1):24–31.

Chamlin, Mitchell B.
1991 "A longitudinal analysis of the arrest-crime relationship: A further examination of the tipping effect." Justice Quarterly 8:187–199.

Chamlin, Mitchell B., Harold G. Grasmick, Robert J. Bursik, Jr., and John K. Cochran
1992 "Time aggregation and time lag in macro-level deterrence research." Criminology 30:377–395.

Champion, Dean J.
1998 The Juvenile Justice System. Upper Saddle River, NJ: Prentice-Hall.
2005 Research Methods for Criminal Justice and Criminology. Upper Saddle River, NJ: Prentice-Hall.

Chappell, Allison, John M. MacDonald, and Patrick W. Manz
2006 "The organizational determinants of police arrest decisions." Crime and Delinquency 52:287–306.

Chapple, Constance
2005 "Self-control, peer relations, and delinquency." Justice Quarterly 22:89–106.

Chapple, Constance L., Julia A. McQuillan, and Terceira A. Berdahl
2005 "Gender, social bonds, and delinquency: A comparison of boys' and girls' models." Social Science Research 34:357–383.

Chapple, Constance L., Kimberly A. Tyler, and Bianca E. Bersani
2005 "Child neglect and adolescent violence." Violence and Victims 20:39–53.

Chesney-Lind, Meda
1989 "Girls' crime and woman's place: Toward a feminist model of female delinquency." Crime and Delinquency 35:5–29.
2001 "Girls, violence, and delinquency." Pp. 135–158 in Susan O. White, ed., Handbook of Youth and Justice. New York: Kluwer Academic.

Chesney-Lind, Meda, and Randall G. Shelden
2004 Girls, Delinquency, and Juvenile Justice. Belmont, CA: Thomson/Wadsworth.

Chesney-Lind, Meda, Randall G. Shelden, and Karen A. Joe
1996 "Girls, delinquency, and gang membership." Pp. 185–204 in C. Ronald Huff, ed., Gangs in America. Thousand Oaks, CA: Sage.

Child Trends
2002 "The unfinished business of welfare reform: Improving prospects for poor children and youth." LexisNexis Database (Current Issues Universe, R219-11), available at http://www.lexisnexis.com/ciuniv.

Chitwood, Dale E., James E. Rivers, and James A. Inciardi
1996 The American Pipe Dream: Crack Cocaine and the Inner City. Fort Worth: Harcourt Brace.

Christensen, P. Niels, and Wendy Wood
2007 "Effects of media violence on viewers' aggression in unconstrained social interaction." Pp. 145–168 in Raymond W. Preiss, Barbara Mae Gayle, Nancy Burrell, Mike Allen, and Jennings Bryant, eds., Mass Media Effects Research. Mahwah, NJ: Lawrence Erlbaum.

Chung, Ick-Joong, Karl G. Hill, J. David Hawkins, Lewayne D. Gilchrist, and Daniel S. Nagin
2002 "Childhood predictors of offense trajectories." Journal of Research in Crime and Delinquency 39: 60–90.

Cintron, Myrna
2006 "Latino delinquency: Defining and counting the problem." Pp. 27–46 in Everette B. Penn, Helen Taylor Greene, and Shaun L. Gabbidon, eds., Race and Juvenile Justice. Durham, NC: Carolina Academic Press.

Clark, Carol
2007 "Teen brain and mental illness focus of book edited by Emory Expert." Emory Report, June 11.

Clark, John, and Larry Tift
1966 "Polygraph and interview validation of self-reported deviant behavior." American Sociological Review 31:516–523.

Clarke, Ronald V.
1992 Situational Crime Prevention. New York: Harrow and Heston.
1995 "Situational crime prevention." Pp. 91–150 in Michael Tonry and David F. Farrington, eds., Crime and Justice: A Review of Research, Volume 19. Chicago: University of Chicago Press.

Clarke, Ronald V., and Derek B. Cornish
1985 "Modeling offenders' decisions: A framework for research and policy." Pp. 147–183 in Michael Tonry and Norval Morris, eds., Crime and Justice: An Annual Review of Research, Volume 6. Chicago: University of Chicago Press.

Clarke, Ronald V., and John E. Eck
2005 Crime Analysis for Problem Solvers. Washington, DC: Office of Community Policing Services, U.S. Department of Justice.

Clear, Todd
1988 "Statistical prediction in correction." Research in Correction 1:1–39.

Clement, Mary
1997 The Juvenile Justice System. Boston: Butterworth-Heinemann.

Clemetson, Lynette
2003 "More Americans in poverty in 2002, census study says." New York Times, September 27, A1,10.

Cloninger, C. Robert
1987 "A systematic method for clinical description and classification of personality variants." Archives of General Psychiatry 44:573–588.

Cloward, Richard A., and Lloyd E. Ohlin
1960 Delinquency and Opportunity. New York: Free Press.

Cloward, Richard A., and Frances Fox Piven
1979 "Hidden protest: The channeling of female innovation and resistance." Signs 4:651–669.

Cochran, John K., Peter B. Wood, and Bruce J. Arneklev
1994 "Is the religiosity-delinquency relationship spurious? A test of arousal and social control theories." Journal of Research in Crime and Delinquency 31:92–123.

Cohen, Albert K.
1955 Delinquent Boys. New York: Free Press.

Cohen, Jacqueline, Wilpen Gorr, and Piyusha Singh
2003 "Estimating intervention effects in varying risk settings: Do police raids reduce illegal drug dealing at nuisance bars?" Criminology 41:257–292.

Cohen, Lawrence E., and Marcus Felson
1979 "Social change and crime rate trends: A routine activity approach." American Sociological Review 44: 588–608.

Cohen, Lawrence E., James R. Kluegel, and Kenneth C. Land
1981 "Social inequality and predatory criminal victimization: An exposition and test of a formal theory." American Sociological Review 46:505–524.

Cohen, Lawrence E., and Bryan J. Vila
1996 "Self-control and social control: An exposition of the Gottfredson-Hirschi/Sampson-Laub debate." Studies on Crime and Crime Prevention 5:125–150.

Cohen, Mark
1998 "The monetary value of saving a high-risk youth." Journal of Quantitative Criminology 14:5–31.

Colder, Craig R., and Eric Stice
1998 "A longitudinal study of the interactive effects of impulsivity and anger on adolescent problem behavior." Journal of Youth and Adolescence 27:255–274.

Coleman, James S., Thomas Hoffer, and Sally Kilgore
1982 High School Achievement. New York: Basic Books.

Coleman, Veronica, Walter C. Holton, Jr., Kristine Olson, Stephen C. Robinson, and Judith Stewart
1999 "Using knowledge and teamwork to reduce crime." National Institute of Justice Journal (October): 17–23.

Colvin, Mark
2000 Crime and Coercion. New York: St. Martin's Press.

Compas, Bruce E.
1987 "Stress and life events during childhood and adolescence." Clinical Psychology Review 7:275–302.

Conger, Rand D.
1976 "Social control and social learning models of delinquent behavior." Criminology 14:17–54.

Conger, Rand D., Katherine J. Conger, Glen H. Elder, Jr., Frederick O. Lorenz, Ronald L. Simons, and Les B. Whitbeck
1992 "A family process model of economic hardship and adjustment of early adolescent boys." Child Development 63:526–541.

Conger, Rand D., Xiaojia Ge, Glen H. Elder, Jr., Frederick O. Lorenz, and Ronald L. Simons
1994 "Economic stress, coercive family process, and developmental problems of adolescents." Child Development 65:541–561.

Conger, Rand D., Gerald R. Patterson, and Xiaojia Ge
1995 "It takes two to replicate: A mediational model for the impact of parents' stress on adolescent adjustment." Child Development 66:80–97.

Conklin, John E.
1992 Criminology. New York: Macmillan.
2003 Why Crime Rates Fell. Boston: Allyn and Bacon.

Cook, Philip J.
1991 "The technology of personal violence." Pp. 1–71 in Michael Tonry, ed., Crime and Justice: A Review of Research, Volume 14. Chicago: University of Chicago Press.

Cook, Philip J., and John H. Laub
1998 "The unprecedented epidemic in youth violence." Pp. 27–64 in Michael Tonry and Mark H. Moore, eds., Crime and Justice: A Review of Research, Volume 24. Chicago: University of Chicago Press.

Cook, Philip J., and Jens Ludwig
1997 "Guns in America: National Survey on Private Ownership and Use of Firearms." Washington, DC: National Institute of Justice.
1998 "Defensive gun uses: New evidence from a national survey." Journal of Quantitative Criminology 14: 111–130.
2000 Gun Violence: The Real Costs. New York: Oxford University Press.
2004 "Does gun prevalence affect teen gun carrying after all?" Criminology 42:27–54.

Cook, Philip J., Mark H. Moore, and Anthony A. Braga
2002 "Gun control." Pp. 291–329 in James Q. Wilson and Joan Petersilia, eds., Crime. Oakland, CA: ICS Press.

Coolbough, Kathleen, and Cynthia J. Monsel
2000 The Comprehensive Strategy: Lessons Learned From the Pilot Sites. Washington, DC: Office of Juvenile Justice and Delinquency Prevention.

Coordinating Council on Juvenile Justice and Delinquency Prevention

1996 Combating Violence and Delinquency: The National Juvenile Justice Action Plan. Washington, DC: U.S. Department of Justice.

Cordner, Gary W.

1999 "Elements of community policing." Pp. 137–149 in Larry K. Gaines and Gary W. Cordner, eds., Policing Perspectives. Los Angeles: Roxbury.

Cork, Daniel

1999 "Examining space-time interaction in city-level homicide data: Crack markets and the diffusion of guns among youth." Journal of Quantitative Criminology 15:379–406.

Cornish, Derek B., and Ronald V. Clarke

1986 The Reasoning Criminal. New York: Springer-Verlag.

Costello, Barbara J., and Paul R. Vowell

1999 "Testing control theory and differential association: A reanalysis of the Richmond youth project." Criminology 37:815–842.

Cothern, Lynn

2000 Juveniles and the Death Penalty. Washington, DC: Office of Juvenile Justice and Delinquency Prevention.

Cox, Steven M., and John J. Conrad

1996 Juvenile Justice. Madison, WI: Brown and Benchmark.

Cromwell, Paul, Lee Parker, and Shawna Mobley

1999 "The five-finger discount: An analysis of motivations for shoplifting." Pp. 57–70 in Paul Cromwell, ed., In Their Own Words: Criminals on Crime. Los Angeles: Roxbury.

Cronin, Roberta, Francis Gragg, Dana Schultz, and Karlu Eisen

2006 Lessons Learned from Safe Kids/Safe Streets. Washington, DC: Office of Juvenile Justice and Delinquency Prevention.

Crowe, Ann H.

1998 Drug Identification and Testing in the Juvenile Justice System. Washington, DC: Office of Juvenile Justice and Delinquency Prevention.

Crutchfield, Robert D., Ross L. Matsueda, and Kevin Drakulich

2006 "Race, labor markets, and neighborhood violence." Pp. 199–220 in Ruth D. Peterson, Lauren J. Krivo, and John Hagan, eds., The Many Colors of Crime. New York: New York University Press.

Cullen, Francis T.

1984 Rethinking Crime and Deviance Theory. Totowa, NJ: Rowman and Allanheld.

1994 "Social support as an organizing concept for criminology." Justice Quarterly 11:527–559.

2002 "Rehabilitation and Treatment Programs." Pp. 253–289 in James Q. Wilson and Joan Petersilia, eds., Crime. Oakland, CA: ICS Press.

Cullen, Francis T.

2006 "It's time to reaffirm rehabilitation." Criminology and Public Policy 4:665–672.

2008 "Reaffirm rehabilitation as corrections' guiding paradigm." Criminology and Public Policy.

Cullen, Francis T., and Robert Agnew

2006 Criminological Theory: Past to Present. Los Angeles: Roxbury.

Cullen, Francis T., and Brandon K. Applegate

1997 Offender Rehabilitation. Dartmouth, England: Ashgate.

Cullen, Francis T., and Paul Gendreau

2000 "Assessing correctional rehabilitation: Policy, practice, and prospects." Pp. 109–176 in Julie Horney, ed., Policies, Processes, and Decisions of the Criminal Justice System: Criminal Justice 2000, Volume 3. Washington, DC: National Institute of Justice.

Cullen, Frances T., Martha Todd Larson, and Richard A. Mothers

1985 "Having money and delinquent involvement: The neglect of power in delinquent theory." Criminal Justice and Behavior 12:171–192.

Cullen, Francis T., James D. Unnever, John Paul Wright, and Kevin M. Beaver

2008 "Parenting and self-control." In Erich Goode, ed., Out of Control? Assessing the General Theory of Crime. Palo Alto, CA: Stanford University Press.

Cullen, Francis T., Nicolas Williams, and John Paul Wright

1997 "Work conditions and juvenile delinquency: Is youth employment criminogenic?" Criminal Justice Policy and Research 8:119–143.

Cullen, Francis T., and John Paul Wright

1996 "Social support as the basis of social control." Paper presented at the annual meeting of the American Society of Criminology, Chicago.

Cullen, Francis T., John Paul Wright, and Brandon K. Applegate

1996 "Control in the community: The limits of reform?" Pp. 69–116 in Alan T. Harland, ed., Choosing Correctional Options That Work. Thousand Oaks, CA: Sage.

Cullen, Francis T., John Paul Wright, and Kristie R. Blevins

2006 Taking Stock: The Status of Criminological Theory. New Brunswick, NJ: Transaction.

Cullen, Francis T., John Paul Wright, Shayna Brown, Melissa M. Moon, Michael B. Blankenship, and Brandon K. Applegate

1998 "Public support for early intervention programs: Implications for a progressive policy agenda." Crime and Delinquency 44:187–204.

Currie, Elliott

1998 Crime and Punishment in America. New York: Owl Books.

Curry, G. David

1998 "Female gang involvement." Journal of Research in Crime and Delinquency 35:100–118.

Curry, G. David, Richard A. Ball, and Scott H. Decker

1996 Update on Gang Crime and Law Enforcement Record Keeping. Washington, DC: U.S. Department of Justice.

Curry, G. David, and Scott H. Decker

2003 Confronting Gangs. Los Angeles: Roxbury.

Curtis, Lynn A.

1974 Criminal Violence: National Patterns and Behavior. Lexington, MA: Lexington Books.

Daly, Kathleen

1992 "Women's pathways to felony court: Feminist theories of lawbreaking and problems of representation." Review of Law and Women's Studies 2:11–52.

1998 "Gender, crime, and criminology." Pp. 85–108 in Michael Tonry, ed., The Handbook of Crime and Punishment. New York: Oxford University Press.

Daly, Kathleen, and Meda Chesney-Lind

1988 "Feminism and criminology." Justice Quarterly 5:497–538.

Dannefer, Dale, and Russell K. Schutt

1982 "Race and juvenile justice processing in court and police agencies." American Journal of Sociology 87:1113–1132.

Deane, Glenn, David P. Armstrong, and Richard Felson

2005 "An examination of offense specialization using marginal logit models." Criminology 43:955–988.

Decker, Scott H.

2003 Policing Gangs and Youth Violence. Belmont, CA: Wadsworth.

Decker, Scott H., and G. David Curry

2000 "Responding to gangs: Does the dose match the problem?" Pp. 561–575 in Joseph F. Sheley, ed., Criminology: A Contemporary Handbook. Belmont, CA: Wadsworth.

Decker, Scott H., and Janet L. Lauritsen

1996 "Breaking the bonds of membership: Leaving the gang." Pp. 103–136 in C. Ronald Huff, ed., Gangs in America. Thousand Oaks, CA: Sage.

Decker, Scott H., Susan Pennell, and Ami Caldwell

1997 "Illegal firearms: Access and use by arrestees." Washington, DC: National Institute of Justice.

Decker, Scott H., and Barrik Van Winkle

1996 Life in the Gang. Cambridge, England: Cambridge University Press.

DeComo, Robert E.
1998 "Estimating the prevalence of juvenile custody by race and gender." Crime and Delinquency 44:489–506.

DeCoster, Stacy, and Lisa Kort-Butler
2006 "How general is general strain theory." Journal of Research in Crime and Delinquency 43:297–325.

DeJong, Christina, and Kenneth C. Jackson
1998 "Putting race into context: Race, juvenile justice processing, and urbanization." Justice Quarterly 15:487–504.

De Li, Spencer
1999 "Legal sanctions and youths' status achievement: A longitudinal study." Justice Quarterly 16:377–401.
2004 "The impacts of self-control and social bonds on juvenile deliquency in a national sample of adolescents." Deviant Behavior 25:351–373.

DeMause, Lloyd
1974 The History of Childhood. New York: Harper Books.

Dembo, Richard, James Schmeidler, and Wansley Waters
2004 "Juvenile assessment centers." Pp. 511–536 in Albert R. Roberts, ed., Juvenile Justice Sourcebook. New York: Oxford University Press.

Denno, Deborah W.
1990 Biology and Violence. Cambridge, England: Cambridge University Press.

DePledge, Derrick
2002 "Plan to stop urban zone grants not based on data." Gannett News Service, May 29, from LexisNexis Database.

Demuth, Stephen and Susan L. Brown
2004 "Family structure, family process, and adolescent delinquency." Journal of Research in Crime and Delinquency 41:58–81.

Department of Justice
2006 Fact Sheet: Department of Justice Initiative to Combat Gangs. Washington, DC: Department of Justice.

Department of Justice
2007 Fact Sheet: Project Safe Neighborhoods. Washington, DC: Department of Justice.

De Waal, Frans B. M.
2003 "Morality and the social instincts: Continuity with the other primates." The Tanner Lecture on Human Values, Princeton University. Available at www.tannerlectures.utah.edu/lectures/documents/volume25/deWaal_2005.pdf.

Dill, Karen E., and Jody C. Dill
1998 "Video game violence: A review of the empirical evidence." Aggression and Violent Behavior 3:407–428.

Dodge, Kenneth
1986 Social Competence in Children. Chicago: University of Chicago Press.

Dodge, Kenneth A., and D. Schwartz
1997 "Social information processing mechanisms in aggressive behavior." Pp. 171–180 in David M. Stoff, James Breiling, and Jack D. Maser, eds., Handbook of Antisocial Behavior. New York: Wiley.

Donohue, John, J., III, and Steven D. Levitt
2000 "Legalized abortion and crime." John M. Olin Program in Law and Economics Working Paper N. 177. Palo Alto, CA: Stanford Law School. Available at http://repositories.cdlib.org/blewp/10.

Donnerstein, Edward, and Daniel Linz
1995 "The media." Pp. 237–264 in James Q. Wilson and Joan Petersilia, eds., Crime. San Francisco: ICS Press.

Donnerstein, Edward, Ronald G. Sloby, and Leonard D. Eron
1994 "The mass media and youth aggression." Pp. 219–250 in Leonard D. Eron, Jacquelyn H. Gentry, and Peggy Schlegel, eds., Reason to Hope. Washington, DC: American Psychological Association.

Donziger, Steven R.
1996 The Real War on Crime. New York: HarperCollins.

Dreier, Peter
2007 "The United States in comparative perspective." Contexts 6:38–46.

Dubow, Eric F., and Graham J. Reid
1994 "Risk and resource variables in children's aggressive behavior." Pp. 187–211 in L. Rowell Huesmann, ed., Aggressive Behavior: Current Perspectives. New York: Plenum.

Duggan, Mark
2001 "More guns, more crime." Journal of Political Economy 109:1086–1114.

Dunford, Franklyn W., and Delbert S. Elliott
1984 "Identifying career offenders using self-report data." Journal of Research in Crime and Delinquency 21:57–86.

D'Unger, Amy V., Kenneth C. Land, and Patricia L. McCall
2002 "Sex differences in age patterns of delinquent/criminal careers: Results from Poisson latent class analyses of the Philadelphia cohort study." Journal of Quantitative Criminology 18:349–375.

D'Unger, Amy V., Kenneth C. Land, Patricia L. McCall, and Daniel S. Nagin
1998 "How many latent classes of delinquent/criminal careers? Results from mixed Poisson regression analysis." American Journal of Sociology 103:1593–1630.

Dunworth, Terence, and Gregory Mills
1999 National Evaluation of Weed and Seed. Washington, DC: National Institute of Justice.

Durkin, Keith F., Timothy W. Wolfe, and Gregory A. Clark
2005 "College students and binge drinking: An evaluation of social learning theory." Sociological Spectrum 25:255–272.

Dyer, Jim
2000 "Georgia's youngest inmates often at risk in detention." Atlanta Constitution, August 13, A1, 10.

Earle, Ralph B.
1995 "Helping to prevent child abuse—and future criminal consequences." Washington, DC: National Institute of Justice.

Earleywine, Mitchell
2002 Understanding Marijuana: A New Look at the Scientific Evidence. Oxford: Oxford University Press.

Earls, Felton, and Jacqueline Barnes
1997 "Understanding and preventing child abuse in urban settings." Pp. 207–255 in Joan McCord, ed., Violence and Childhood in the Inner City. Cambridge, England: Cambridge University Press.

Early Child Care Research Network
2003 "Does amount of time in child care predict socioemotional adjustment during the transition to kindergarten?" Child Development 74:976–1005.

Eck, John E.
2002 "Preventing crime at places." Pp. 241–294 in Lawrence W. Sherman, David P. Farrington, Brandon C. Welsh, and Doris Layton MacKenzie, eds., Evidence-Based Crime Prevention. London: Routledge.

Eck, John E., and Edward R. Maguire
2006 "Have changes in policing reduced violent crime? An assessment of the evidence." Pp. 207–265 in Alfred Blumstein and Joel Wallman, eds., The Crime Drop in America. Cambridge, England: Cambridge University Press.

Eck, John E., and William Spelman
1987 Problem Solving. Washington, DC: National Institute of Justice.

Egan, Timothy
2002 "Pastoral Poverty: The seeds of decline." New York Times, December 8, A.3.

Egley, Arlen, Jr., and Christina E. Ritz
2006 "Highlights of the 2004 National Youth Gang survey." Washington, DC: Office of Juvenile Justice and Delinquency Prevention.

Eisenbraun, Kristin D.

2007 "Violence in schools: Prevalence, prediction, and prevention." Aggression and Violent Behavior 12: 459–469.

Eitle, David J.

2002 "Exploring a source of deviance-producing strain for females: Perceived discrimination and general strain theory." Journal of Criminal Justice 30:429–442.

2005 "Parental gender, single-parent families, and delinquency." Social Science Research 35:727–748.

Eitle, David J., and R. Jay Turner

2002 "Exposure to community violence and young adult crime: The effects of witnessing violence, traumatic victimization, and other stressful life events." Journal of Research in Crime and Delinquency 39:214–237.

Eitle, David, Lisa Stolzenberg, and Stewart J. D'Alessio

2005 "Police organization factors, the racial composition of the police, and the probability of arrest." Justice Quarterly 22:30–57.

Elifson, Kirk W., David M. Petersen, and C. Kirk Hadaway

1983 "Religiosity and delinquency." Criminology 21:505–527.

Elliott, Delbert S.

1982 "Measuring delinquency (a review essay)." Criminology 20:527–538.

1994 "Serious violent offenders: Onset, developmental course, and termination." Criminology 32:1–21.

1995 "Lies, damn lies and arrest statistics." Paper presented at the annual meeting of the American Society of Criminology, Boston.

Elliott, Delbert S., and Suzanne S. Ageton

1980 "Reconciling race and class differences in self-reported and official estimates of delinquency." American Sociological Review 45:95–110.

Elliott, Delbert S., Suzanne Ageton, and Rachel Canter

1979 "An integrated theoretical perspective on delinquent behavior." Journal of Research in Crime and Delinquency 16:3–27.

Elliott, Delbert S., Beatrix A. Hamburg, and Kirk R. Williams

1998 Violence in American Schools. Cambridge, England: Cambridge University Press.

Elliott, Delbert S., and David Huizinga

1983 "Social class and delinquent behavior in a national youth panel: 1976–1980." Criminology 21:149–177.

Elliott, Delbert S., David Huizinga, and Suzanne S. Ageton

1985 Explaining Delinquency and Drug Use. Beverly Hills, CA: Sage.

Elliott, Delbert S., David Huizinga, and Scott Menard

1989 Multiple Problem Youth. New York: Springer-Verlag.

Elliott, Delbert S., and Scott Menard

1996 "Delinquent friends and delinquent behavior: Temporal and developmental patterns." Pp. 28–67 in J. David Hawkins, ed., Delinquency and Crime: Current Theories. Cambridge, England: Cambridge University Press.

Elliott, Delbert S., William Julius Wilson, David Huizinga, Robert J. Sampson, Amanda Elliott, and Bruce Rankin

1996 "The effects of neighborhood disadvantage on adolescent development." Journal of Research in Crime and Delinquency 33:389–426.

Ellis, Lee, and Anthony Walsh

1997 "Gene-based evolutionary theories in criminology." Criminology 35:229–276.

1999 "Criminologists' opinions about causes and theories of crime and delinquency." Criminologist 24:1, 4–5.

Empey, LaMar T., Mark C. Stafford, and Carter H. Hay

1999 American Delinquency. Belmont, CA: Wadsworth.

Engel, Robin Shepard and Robert E. Worden

2003 "Police officers' attitudes, behaviors and supervisory influences." Criminology 41:131–166.

Engen, Rodney L., Sara Steen, and George S. Bridges
2002 "Racial disparities in the punishment of youth: A theoretical and empirical assessment of the literature." Social Problems 49:194–220.

England, Ralph W.
1960 "A theory of middle class juvenile delinquency." Journal of Criminal Law, Criminology, and Police Science 50:535–540.

English, Diana J.
1998 "The extent and consequences of child maltreatment." Future of Children 8:39–53.

Erez, Edna, editor
1995 Justice Quarterly 12(4).

Ericson, Nels
2001 Addressing the Problem of Juvenile Bullying. Washington, DC: Office of Juvenile Justice and Delinquency Prevention.

Esbensen, Finn-Aage
2001 "The national evaluation of the Gang Resistance Education and Training (G.R.E.A.T.) Program." Pp. 289–302 in Jody Miller, Cheryl L. Maxson, and Malcolm W. Klein, eds., The Modern Gang Reader. Los Angeles: Roxbury.

Esbensen, Finn-Aage, and Elizabeth Piper Deschenes
1998 "A multisite examination of youth gang membership: Does gender matter?" Criminology 36:799–828.

Esbensen, Finn-Aage, Elizabeth Piper Deschenes, and L. Thomas Winfree, Jr.
1999 "Differences between gang girls and gang boys." Youth and Society 31:27–53.

Esbensen, Finn-Aage, and David Huizinga
1993 "Gangs, drugs, and delinquency in a survey of urban youth." Criminology 31:565–589.

Esbensen, Finn-Aage, David Huizinga, and Anne W. Weiher
1993 "Gang and non-gang youth: Differences in explanatory factors." Journal of Contemporary Criminal Justice 9:94–116.

Esbensen, Finn-Aage, and D. Wayne Osgood
1997 Research in Brief: National Evaluation of G.R.E.A.T. Washington, DC: Office of Juvenile Justice and Delinquency Prevention.
1999 "Gang resistance education and training (GREAT): Results from the national evaluation." Journal of Research in Crime and Delinquency 36:194–225.

Esbensen, Finn-Aage, Dana Peterson, Terrance J. Taylor, Adrienne Freng, and D. Wayne Osgood
2004 "Gang prevention." Pp. 351–374 in Finn-Aage Esbensen, Stephen G. Tibbetts, and Larry Gaines, eds., American Youth Gangs at the Millennium. Long Grove, IL: Waveland Press.

Esbensen, Finn-Aage, Stephen G. Tibbetts, and Larry Gaines
2004 American Youth Gangs at the Millennium. Long Grove, IL: Waveland Press.

Esbensen, Finn-Aage, L. Thomas Winfree, Jr., Ni He, and Terrance J. Taylor
2001 "Youth gangs and definitional issues: When is a gang a gang, and why does it matter?" Crime and Delinquency 47:105–130.

Evans, T. David, Francis T. Cullen, Velmer S. Burton, Jr., and Michael L. Benson
1997 "The social consequences of self-control: Testing the general theory of crime." Criminology 35:475–504.

Evans, T. David, Francis T. Cullen, Velmer S. Burton, Jr., R. Gregory Dunaway, Gary L. Payne, and Sesha R. Kethineni
1996 "Religion, social bonds, and delinquency." Deviant Behavior 17:43–70.

Evans, T. David, Francis T. Cullen, R. Gregory Dunaway, and Velmer S. Burton, Jr.
1995 "Religion and crime reexamined: The impact of religion, secular controls, and social ecology on adult criminality." Criminology 33:195–224.

Eysenck, Hans J.
1977 Crime and Personality. London: Routledge and Kegan Paul.

Fagan, Jeffrey

1989 "The social organization of drug use and drug dealing among urban gangs." Criminology 27:633–669.

1990 "Social processes of delinquency and drug use among urban gangs." Pp. 183–219 in C. Ronald Huff, ed., Gangs in America. Thousand Oaks, CA: Sage.

1995 "Separating the men from the boys: The comparative advantage of juvenile versus criminal court sanctions on recidivism among adolescent felony offenders." Pp. 238–260 in James C. Howell, Barry Krisberg, J. David Hawkins, and John J. Wilson, eds., A Sourcebook: Serious, Violent, and Chronic Juvenile Offenders. Thousand Oaks, CA: Sage.

1996 "Gangs, drugs, and neighborhood change." Pp. 39–74 in C. Ronald Huff, ed., Gangs in America. Thousand Oaks, CA: Sage.

1998 Adolescent Violence: A View From the Street. Washington, DC: National Institute of Justice.

Fagan, Jeffrey, and Franklin E. Zimring

2000 The Changing Borders of Juvenile Justice. Chicago: University of Chicago Press.

Famega, Christine N., James Frank, and Lorraine Mazerolle

2005 "Managing police patrol time." Justice Quarterly 22:540–559.

Farber, Henry, and Leon Stafford

1999 "Parents mystified as to what set off son." Atlanta Constitution, August 11, E1, 3.

Farnworth, Margaret, Terence P. Thornberry, Marvin D. Krohn, and Alan J. Lizotte

1994 "Measurement in the study of class and delinquency: Integrating theory and research." Journal of Research in Crime and Delinquency 31:32–61.

Farrington, David P.

1977 "The effects of public labeling." British Journal of Criminology 17:112–125.

1986 "Age and crime." Crime and Justice 7:189–250.

1993a "Have any individual, family or neighborhood influences on offending been demonstrated conclusively?" Pp. 7–37 in David P. Farrington, Robert J. Sampson, and Per-Olof Wikstrom, eds., Integrating Individual and Ecological Aspects of Crime. Stockholm: National Council for Crime Prevention, Sweden.

1993b "Motivations for conduct disorder and delinquency." Development and Psychopathology 5:225–241.

1994 "Human development and criminal careers." Pp. 511–584 in Mike Maguire, Rod Morgan, and Robert Reiner, eds., The Oxford Handbook of Criminology. New York: Oxford University Press.

1995 "The development of offending and antisocial behaviour from childhood: Key findings from the Cambridge study in delinquent development." Journal of Child Psychology and Psychiatry 360:929–964.

1996a "The explanation and prevention of youthful offending." Pp. 68–148 in J. David Hawkins, ed., Delinquency and Crime: Current Theories. Cambridge, England: Cambridge University Press.

1996b "Criminological psychology: Individual and family factors in the explanation and prevention of offending." Pp. 3–39 in Clive R. Hollin, ed., Working with Offenders. Chichester, England: John Wiley and Sons.

1998 "Individual differences and offending." Pp. 241–268 in Michael Tonry, ed., The Handbook of Crime and Punishment. New York: Oxford.

2002a "Families and crime." Pp. 129–148 in James Q. Wilson and Joan Petersilia, eds., Crime. Oakland, CA: ICS Press.

2002b "Developmental criminology and risk-focused prevention." Pp. 657–701 in Mike Maguire, Rod Morgan, and Robert Reiner, eds., The Oxford Handbook of Criminology, 3rd edition. Oxford: Oxford University Press.

2005 "Introduction to integrated developmental and life-course theories of offending." Pp. 1–14 in David Farrington, ed., Integrated Developmental and Life-Course Theories of Offending. New Brunswick, NJ: Transaction.

2006 "Building developmental and life-course theories of offending." Pp. 335–364 in Francis T. Cullen, John Paul Wright, and Kristie R. Blevins, eds., Taking Stock: The Status of Criminological Theory. New Brunswick, NJ: Transactions.

Farrington, David P., Darrick Jolliffe, Rolf Loeber, and D. Lynn Homish
2007 "How many offenses are really committed per juvenile court offender?" Victims and Offenders 2: 227–249.

Farrington, David P., Rolf Loeber, and Magda Stouthamer-Loeber
2003 "How can the relationship between race and violence be explained?" Pp. 213–237 in Darnell F. Hawkins, ed., Violent Crime: Addressing Race and Ethnic Differences. Cambridge, England: Cambridge University Press.

Farrington, David P., Rolf Loeber, Magda Stouthamer-Loeber, Welmoet B. Van Kammen, and Laura Schmidt
1996 "Self-reported delinquency and a combined delinquency seriousness scale based on boys, mothers, and teachers: Concurrent and predictive validity for African-Americans and Caucasians." Criminology 34:493–517.

Farrington, David, Howard Snyder, and Terence Finnegan
1988 "Specialization in juvenile court careers." Criminology 26:461–485.

Farrington, David P., S. G. Soborn, and D. J. West
1978 "The persistence of labeling effects." British Journal of Criminology 18:277–284.

Farrington, David P., and Brandon C. Welsh
2002 Family-based crime prevention. Pp. 22–55 in Lawrence W. Sherman, David P. Farrington, Brandon C. Welsh, and Doris Layton MacKenzie, eds., Evidence-Based Crime Prevention. New York: Routledge.
2007 Saving Children from a Life of Crime. New York: Oxford University Press.

Fass, Simon M., and Chung-Ron Pi
2002 "Getting tough on juvenile crime: An analysis of costs and benefits." Journal of Research in Crime and Delinquency 39:363–399.

Fearn, Noelle E., Scott H. Decker, and G. David Curry
2001 "Public policy responses to gangs: Evaluating the outcomes." Pp. 330–344 in Jody Miller, Cheryl L. Maxson, and Malcolm W. Klein, eds., The Modern Gang Reader. Los Angeles: Roxbury.

Federal Bureau of Investigation
2003 Crime in the United States, 2002. Washington, DC: U.S. Government Printing Office.

Federal Interagency Forum on Child and Family Statistics
2007 America's Children: Key National Indicators of Well-Being 2007. Washington, DC: U.S. Government Printing Office.

Feindler, Eva L., and Judith V. Becker
1994 "Interventions in family violence involving children and adolescents." Pp. 405–430 in Leonard D. Eron, Jacquelyn H. Gentry, and Peggy Schlegel, eds., Reason to Hope. Washington, DC: American Psychological Association.

Feld, Barry C.
1993 "Juvenile (in)justice and the criminal court alternative." Crime and Delinquency 39:403–424.
1995 "The social construction of juvenile justice administration: Racial disparities in an urban juvenile court." Pp. 66–97 in Kimberly Kempf Leonard, Carl E. Pope, and William H. Feyerherm, eds., Minorities in Juvenile Justice. Thousand Oaks, CA: Sage
1998 "The juvenile court." Pp. 509–541 in Michael Tonry, ed., The Handbook of Crime and Punishment. New York: Oxford University Press.
1999 Bad Kids. New York: Oxford University Press.
2003 "The politics of race and juvenile justice: The 'due process revolution' and the conservative reaction." Justice Quarterly 20:765–800.

Feld, Barry C.
2008 "Girls in the juvenile justice system." In Margaret Zahn, ed., Delinquent Girls: Findings from the Girls' Study Group. Philadelphia: Temple University Press.

Felson, Marcus
1987 "Routine activities and crime prevention in the developing metropolis." Criminology 25:911–931.

1994 Crime and Everyday Life. Thousand Oaks, CA: Pine Forge.

2002 Crime and Everyday Life, 3rd edition. Thousand Oaks, CA: Pine Forge.

2006 Crime and Nature. Thousand Oaks, CA: Sage.

Felson, Marcus, and Michael Gottfredson

1984 "Adolescent activities near peers and parents." Journal of Marriage and the Family 46:709–714.

Felson, Richard B.

1993 "Predatory and dispute-related violence: A social interactionist approach." Pp. 103–125 in Ronald V. Clarke and Marcus Felson, eds., Routine Activity and Rational Choice; Advances in Criminological Theory, Volume 5. New Brunswick, NJ: Transaction.

1996 "Big people hit little people: Sex differences in physical power and interpersonal violence." Criminology 34:433–452.

1997 "Routine activities and involvement in violence as actor, witness, or target." Violence and Victims 12: 209–221.

Felson, Richard B., and Keri B. Burchfield

2004 "Alcohol and the risk of physical and sexual assault victimization." Criminology 42:837–860.

Felson, Richard B., and Jeremy Staff

2006 "Explaining the academic performance-delinquency relationship." Criminology 44:299–320.

Felson, Richard B., and Henry J. Steadman

1983 "Situations and processes leading to criminal violence." Criminology 21:59–74.

Fergusson, David M., L. John Horwood, and Daniel S. Nagin

2000 "Offending trajectories in a New Zealand birth cohort." Criminology 38:525–552.

Feyerherm, William H.

1995 "The DMC initiative." Pp. 1–15 in Kimberly Kempf Leonard, Carl E. Pope, and William H. Feyerherm, eds., Minorities in Juvenile Justice. Thousand Oaks, CA: Sage.

Finckenauer, James O., and P. W. Gavin

1999 Scared Straight: The Panacea Phenomenon Revisited. Prospect Heights, IL: Waveland Press.

Finestone, Harold

1976 Victims of Change: Juvenile Delinquents in American Society. Westport, CT: Greenwood.

Finkelhor, David, and Nancy J. Asdigian

1996 "Risk factors for youth victimization: Beyond a lifestyle/routine activities approach." Violence and Victims 11:3–19.

Finkelhor, David, and Patricia Y. Hashima

2001 "The victimization of children and youth: A comprehensive overview." Pp. 49–78 in Susan O. White, ed., Handbook of Youth and Justice. New York: Kluwer Academic.

Finkelhor, David, and Richard Ormond

1999 Reporting Crimes Against Juveniles. Washington, DC: Office of Juvenile Justice and Delinquency Prevention.

Finkelhor, David, Richard Ormrod, Heather Turner, and Sherry L. Hamby

2005 "The victimization of children and youth: A comprehensive national survey." Child Maltreatment 10: 5–25.

Fischer, Donald G.

1984 "Family size and delinquency." Perceptual and Motor Skills 58:527–534.

Fishbein, Diana

2001 Biobehavioral Perspectives in Criminology. Belmont, CA: Wadsworth.

Fisher, Bonnie S., and Francis T. Cullen

2000 "Measuring the sexual victimization of women: Evolution, current controversies, and future research." Pp. 317–390 in David Duffee, ed., Measurement and Analysis of Crime and Justice, Criminal Justice 2000, Volume 4. Washington, DC: National Institute of Justice.

Fisher, Bonnie S., John J. Sloan, Francis T. Cullen, and Chunmeng Lu

1998 "Crime in the ivory tower: The level and sources of student victimization." Criminology 36:671–710.

Fishman, Laura T.
1995 "The vice queens: An ethnographic study of black female gang behavior." Pp. 83–92 in Malcolm Klein, Cheryl L. Maxson, and Jody Miller, eds., The Modern Gang Reader. Los Angeles: Roxbury.

Flanagan, Timothy, and Dennis Longmire
1996 Americans View Crime and Justice. Thousand Oaks, CA: Sage.

Flores, J. Robert
2003 Targeted Community Action Planning Kit. Washington, DC: Office of Juvenile Justice and Delinquency Prevention.

Foglia, Wanda D.
1997 "Perceptual deterrence and the mediating effect of internalized norms among inner-city teenagers." Journal of Research in Crime and Delinquency 34:414–442.

Fonseca, A. C., and W. Yule
1995 "Personality and antisocial behavior in children and adolescents: An enquiry into Eysenck's and Gray's theories." Journal of Abnormal Child Psychology 23:767–781.

Foshee, V., and K. E. Bauman
1992 "Parental and peer characteristics as modifiers of the bond-behavior relationship: An elaboration of control theory." Journal of Health and Social Behavior 33:66–76.

Fox, Greer Litton, and Michael L. Benson
2000 Families, Crime and Criminal Justice. New York: JAI.

Fox, James Alan, and Marianne W. Zawitz
1999 Homicide Trends in the United States. Washington, DC: Bureau of Justice Statistics.

Frazier, Charles E., and Donna M. Bishop
1995 "Reflections on race effects in juvenile justice." Pp. 16–46 in Kimberly Kempf Leonard, Carl E. Pope, and William H. Feyerherm, eds., Minorities in Juvenile Justice. Thousand Oaks, CA: Sage.

Freedman, Jonathan L.
1984 "Effect of television violence on aggressiveness." Psychological Bulletin 96:227–246.
2002 Media Violence and Its Effects on Aggression. Toronto: University of Toronto Press.

French, Lawrence Armand
2006 "Native American youth and delinquency." Pp. 77–94 in Everette B. Penn, Helen Taylor Greene, and Shaun L. Gabbidon, eds., Race and Juvenile Justice. Durham, NC: Carolina Academic Press.

Freng, Adrienne, and L. Thomas Winfree, Jr.
2004 "Exploring race and ethnic differences in a sample of middle school gang members." Pp. 142–143 in Finn-Aage Esbensen, Stephen G. Tibbetts, and Larry Gaines, eds., American Youth Gangs at the Millennium. Long Grove, IL: Waveland Press.

Fritsch, Eric J., Tory J. Caeti, and Robert W. Taylor
1999 "Gang suppression through saturation patrol, aggressive curfew and truancy enforcement: A quasi-experimental test of the Dallas anti-gang initiative." Crime and Delinquency 45:122–139.

Funk, Stephanie J.
1999 "Risk assessment for juveniles on probation: A focus on gender." Criminal Justice and Behavior 26: 44–68.

Furstenberg, Frank F., Jr., J. Brooks-Gunn, and S. P. Morgan
1987 Adolescent Mothers in Later Life. Cambridge, England: Cambridge University Press.

Future of Children, The
1996 The Juvenile Court, Volume 6, Number 3. Los Altos, CA: Center for the Future of Children.

Gaarder, Emily, Nancy Rodriguez, and Marjorie S. Zatz
2004 "Criers, liars, and manipulators: Probation officers' views of girls." Justice Quarterly 21:547–578.

Gaines, Larry K.
2003 "Police responses to delinquency." Pp. 286–290 in Marilyn D. McShane and Frank Williams III, eds., Encyclopedia of Juvenile Justice. Thousand Oaks, CA: Sage.

Gaines, Larry K., and Gary W. Cordner
1999 Policing Perspectives. Los Angeles: Roxbury.

Gallagher, Catherine A.
1999 Juvenile Offenders in Residential Placement, 1997. Washington, DC: Office of Juvenile Justice and Delinquency Prevention.

Garland, David
2001 The Culture of Control. Chicago: University of Chicago Press.

Garofalo, James, Leslie Siegel, and John Laub
1987 "School-related victimizations among adolescents: An analysis of national crime survey (NCS) narratives." Journal of Quantitative Criminology 3:321–338.

Gartin, Patrick R.
1995 "Dealing with design failures in randomized field experiments: Analytic issues regarding the evaluation of treatment effects." Journal of Research in Crime and Delinquency 32:425–445.

Gatti, Uberto, Richard E. Tremblay, Frank Vitaro, and Pierre McDuff
2005 "Youth gangs, delinquency, and drug use." Journal of Child Psychology and Psychiatry 46:1178–1190.

Geason, Susan and Paul R. Wilson
1989 Designing Out Crime. Canberra: Australian Institute of Criminology.

Gentry, Cynthia
1995 "Crime control through drug control." Pp. 477–493 in Joseph F. Sheley, ed., Criminology. Belmont, CA: Wadsworth.

Gerber, J., and S. Engelhardt-Greer
1996 "Just and painful: Attitudes toward sentencing criminals." Pp. 62–74 in T. Flanagan and D. Longmire, eds., Americans View Crime and Justice. Thousand Oaks, CA: Sage.

Gies, Steve V.
2003 Aftercare Services. Washington, DC: Office of Juvenile Justice and Delinquency Prevention.

Gifford-Smith, Mary, Kenneth A. Dodge, Thomas J. Dishion, and Joan McCord
2005 "Peer influence in children and adolescents." Journal of Abnormal Child Psychology 33:255–265.

Gilbert, Susan
2003 "Two studies link child care to behavior problems." New York Times, July 16, A12.

Gilfus, Mary E.
1992 "From victims to survivors to offenders: Women's routes of entry and immersion into street crime." Women and Criminal Justice 4:63–89.

Gilligan, Carol, and Jane Attanucci
1988 "Two moral orientations: Gender differences and similarities." Merrill-Palmer Quarterly 34:223–237.

Giordano, Peggy C.
1978 "Girls, guys, and gangs: The changing social context of female delinquency." Journal of Criminal Law and Criminology 69:126–132.

Giordano, Peggy C., Stephen A. Cernkovich, and M. D. Pugh
1986 "Friendships and delinquency." American Journal of Sociology 91:1170–1202.

Giordano, Peggy C., Stephen A. Cernovich, and Jennifer L. Rudolph
2002 "Gender, crime, and desistance: Toward a theory of cognitive transformation." American Journal of Sociology 107:990–1064.

Glueck, Sheldon, and Eleanor Glueck
1950 Unraveling Juvenile Delinquency. New York: Commonwealth Fund.

Gold, Martin
1966 "Undetected delinquent behavior." Journal of Research in Crime and Delinquency 3:27–46.

Gold, Martin, and Jay R. Williams
1969 "The effect of getting caught: Apprehension of a juvenile offender as a cause of subsequent delinquencies." Prospectus 3:1–12.

Goldsmid, Charles A., and Everett K. Wilson
1980 Passing on Sociology. Washington, DC: American Sociological Association.

Goldstein, Paul J.
1985 "The drugs/violence nexus: A tripartite conceptual framework." Journal of Drug Issues 15:493–506.

Goode, Erich
2008 Drugs in American Society. New York: McGraw-Hill.

Goode, Erich
2008 "Out of control? Introduction to the general theory of crime." In Erich Goode, ed., Out of Control? Assessing the General Theory of Crime. Palo Alto, CA: Stanford University Press.

Gordon, Rachel A., Benjamin B. Lahey, Eriko Kawai, Rolf Loeber, Magda Stouthamer-Loeber, and David Farrington
2004 "Antisocial behavior and gang membership: Selection and socialization." Criminology 42:55–87.

Gorman, D. M., and Helene Raskin White
1995 "You can choose your friends, but do they choose your crime? Implications of differential association theories for crime prevention policy." Pp. 131–155 in Hugh Barlow, ed., Crime and Public Policy. Boulder, CO: Westview.

Gottfredson, Denise C.
2001 Schools and Delinquency. Cambridge, England: Cambridge University Press.

Gottfredson, Denise C., Amanda Cross, and David A. Soule
2007 "Distinguishing characteristics of effective and ineffective after-school programs." Criminology and Public Policy 6:289–318.

Gottfredson, Denise C., and Gary D. Gottfredson
2002 "Quality of school-based prevention programs: Results from a national survey." Journal of Research in Crime and Delinquency 39:3–35.

Gottfredson, Denise C., and David A. Soule
2005 "The timing of property crime, violent crime, and substance use among juveniles." Journal of Research in Crime and Delinquency 42:110–120.

Gottfredson, Denise C., David B. Wilson, and Stacy Skroban Najaka
2002a "School-based crime prevention." Pp. 56–164 in Lawrence W. Sherman, David P. Farrington, Brandon C. Welsh, and Doris Layton MacKenzie, eds., Evidence-Based Crime Prevention. London: Routledge.
2002b "The Schools." Pp. 149–190 in James Q. Wilson and Joan Petersilia, eds., Crime. Oakland, CA: ICS Press.

Gottfredson, Gary D., and Denise C. Gottfredson
1985 Victimization in Schools. New York: Plenum.

Gottfredson, Gary D., Denise C. Gottfredson, Allison Ann Payne, and Nisha C. Gottfredson
2005 "School climate predictors of school disorder." Journal of Research in Crime and Delinquency 42: 412–444.

Gottfredson, Michael R.
2006 "The empirical status of control theory in criminology." Pp. 77–100 in Francis T. Cullen, John Paul Wright, and Kristie R. Blevins, eds., Taking Stock: The Status of Criminological Theory. New Brunswick, NJ: Transaction.

Gottfredson, Michael R., and Travis Hirschi
1990 A General Theory of Crime. Stanford, CA: Stanford University Press.

Gottfredson, Stephen D., and Don M. Gottfredson
1994 "Behavioral prediction and the problem of incapacitation." Criminology 32:441–474.

Gove, Walter R., and Robert D. Crutchfield
1982 "The family and juvenile delinquency." Sociological Quarterly 23:301–319.

Gove, Walter R., Michael Hughes, and Omer R. Galle
1979 "Overcrowding in the home: An empirical investigation of its possible pathological consequences." American Sociological Review 44:59–80.

Gove, Walter R., Michael Hughes, and Michael Geerken
1985 "Are uniform crime reports a valid indicator of the index crimes? An affirmative answer with minor qualifications." Criminology 23:451–502.

Grasmick, Harold G., and Robert J. Bursik, Jr.
1990 "Conscience, significant others, and rational choice: Extending the deterrence model." Law and Society Review 24:837–861.

Grasmick, Harold G., Charles R. Tittle, Robert J. Bursik, and Bruce J. Arneklev
1993 "Testing the core empirical implications of Gottfredson and Hirschi's general theory of crime." Journal of Research in Crime and Delinquency 30:5–29.

Greenbaum, Stuart
1997 "Kids and guns: From playgrounds to battlegrounds." Juvenile Justice 3:3–10.

Greenberg, David F.
1977 "Delinquency and the age structure of society." Contemporary Crises 1:189–223.
1985 "Age, crime, and social explanation." American Journal of Sociology 91:1–27.

Greenberg, David F., Ronald C. Kessler, and Colin Loftin
1983 "The effect of police employment on crime." Criminology 21:375–394.

Greene, Jack R.
2000 "Community policing in America: Changing the nature, structure, and function of the police." Pp. 299–370 in Julie Horney, ed., Policies, Processes, and Decisions of the Criminal Justice System; Criminal Justice 2000, Volume 3. Washington, DC: National Institute of Justice.

Greenfeld, Lawrence A.
1998 Alcohol and Crime. Washington, DC: Bureau of Justice Statistics.

Greenhouse, Linda
2005 "Supreme Court, 5–4, forbids execution in juvenile crime." New York Times, March 2, A1, 14.

Greenwood, Peter W.
1995 "What works with juvenile offenders: A synthesis of the literature and experience." Federal Probation 58:63–67.
1998 "Investing in prisons or prevention: The state policy makers' dilemma." Crime and Delinquency 44: 136–142.
1999 Costs and Benefits of Early Childhood Intervention. Washington, DC: Office of Juvenile Justice and Delinquency Prevention.
2002 "Juvenile crime and juvenile justice." Pp. 75–108 in James Q. Wilson and Joan Petersilia, eds., Crime. Oakland, CA: ICS Press.
2006 Changing Lives: Delinquency Prevention as Crime-Control Policy. Chicago: University of Chicago Press.

Greenwood, Peter W., Karyn E. Model, C. Peter Rydell, and James Chiesa
1996 Diverting Children from a Life of Crime: Measuring Costs and Benefits. Santa Monica, CA: RAND.

Griffiths, Mark
1999 "Violent video games and aggression: A review of the literature." Aggression and Violent Behavior 4: 203–212.

Grogger, Jeffrey
1997 "Incarceration-related costs of early childbearing." Pp. 231–255 in Rebecca A. Maynard, ed., Kids Having Kids. Washington, DC: Urban Institute Press.
2006 "An economic model of recent trends in violence." Pp. 266–287 in Alfred Blumstein and Joel Wallman, eds., The Crime Drop in America. Cambridge, England: Cambridge University Press.

Grossman, Jean Baldwin, and Eileen M. Garry
1997 Mentoring: A Proven Delinquency Prevention Strategy. Washington, DC: Office of Juvenile Justice and Delinquency Prevention.

Gruber, Staci A., and Deborah A. Yurgelun-Todd
2005 "Neurobiology and the law: A role in juvenile justice?" Ohio State Journal of Criminal Law 3:321–340.

Guerra, Nancy G.
1997 "Intervening to prevent childhood aggression in the inner city." Pp. 256–312 in Joan McCord, ed., Violence and Childhood in the Inner City. Cambridge, England: Cambridge University Press.

Guerra, Nancy G., Patrick H. Tolan, and W. Rodney Hammond
1994 "Prevention and treatment of adolescent violence." Pp. 383–403 in Leonard D. Eron, Jacquelyn H. Gentry, and Peggy Schlegel, eds., Reason to Hope. Washington, DC: American Psychological Association.

Hagan, John
1989 Structural Criminology. New Brunswick, NJ: Rutgers University Press.
1991 "Destiny and drift: Subcultural preferences, status attainments, and the risks and rewards of youth." American Sociological Review 56:567–581.
1992 "The poverty of a classless criminology." Criminology 30:1–19.
1994 Crime and Disrepute. Thousand Oaks, CA: Pine Forge Press.

Hagan, John, A. R. Gillis, and David Brownfield
1996 Criminological Controversies. Boulder, CO: Westview.

Hagan, John, and Bill McCarthy
1997a Mean Streets. Cambridge, England: Cambridge University Press.
1997b "Anomie, social capital, and street criminology." Pp. 124–141 in Nikos Passas and Robert Agnew, eds., The Future of Anomie Theory. Boston: Northeastern University Press.

Hagan, John, and Ruth D. Peterson
1995 "Criminal inequality in America: Patterns and consequences." Pp. 14–36 in John Hagan and Ruth D. Peterson, eds., Crime and Inequality. Stanford, CA: Stanford University Press.

Hagan, John, John H. Simpson, and A. R. Gillis
1979 "The sexual stratification of social control: A gender-based perspective on crime and delinquency." British Journal of Sociology 30:25–38.

Hagedorn, John
1988 People and Folks: Gangs, Crime and the Underclass in a Rustbelt City. Chicago: Lake View Press.

Hahn, Robert A., Oleg Bilukha, Alex Crosby, Mindy T. Fullilove, Akivo Liberman, Eve Moscicki, Susan Snyder, Farris Tuma, and Peter A. Briss
2005 "Firearms laws and the reduction of violence." American Journal of Preventive Medicine 28: 40–71.

Halbfinger, David M.
2003 "Care of juvenile offenders in Mississippi is faulted." New York Times, September 1, A11.

Hamilton, Robin, and Kay McKinney
1999 Job Training for Juveniles: Project CRAFT. Washington, DC: Office of Juvenile Justice and Delinquency Prevention.

Hansen, Jane O.
2001 "Selling Atlanta's Children." Atlanta Journal-Constitution, January 7, A1, 8, 9.

Harcourt, Bernard E.
2003 Guns, Crime, and Punishment in America. New York: New York University Press.

Harris, Anthony R., and James A. W. Shaw
2000 "Looking for patterns: Race, class, and crime." Pp. 128–163 in Joseph F. Sheley, ed., Criminology: A Contemporary Handbook. Belmont, CA: Wadsworth.

Harrison, Paige, James R. Maupin, and G. Larry Mays
2001 "Teen court: An examination of processes and outcomes." Crime and Delinquency 47:243–264.

Hart, Timothy C.
2003 National Crime Victimization Survey, 1995–2000: Violent Victimization of College Students. Washington, DC: Bureau of Justice Statistics.

Hartney, Christopher
2006 Youth under 18 in the Adult Criminal Justice System. Oakland, CA: National Council on Crime and Delinquency.

Hawkins, Darnell F.
2003 Violent Crime: Assessing Race and Ethnic Differences. Cambridge, England: Cambridge University Press.

Hawkins, Darnell F., John H. Laub, and Janet L. Lauritsen
1998 Race, Ethnicity, and Serious and Violent Juvenile Offending. Pp. 30–46 in Rolf Loeber and David P. Farrington, eds., Serious and Violent Juvenile Offenders. Thousand Oaks, CA: Sage.

Hawkins, J. David, Michael W. Arthur, and Richard F. Catalano
1995 "Preventing substance abuse." Pp. 343–347 in Michael Tonry and David P. Farrington, eds., Crime and Justice: A Review of Research, Volume 19. Chicago: University of Chicago Press.

Hawkins, J. David, Richard F. Catalano, and Devon D. Brewer
1995 "Preventing serious, violent, and chronic juvenile offending: Effective strategies from conception to age 6." Pp. 47–60 in James C. Howell, Barry Krisberg, J. David Hawkins, and John J. Wilson, eds., A Sourcebook: Serious, Violent, and Chronic Juvenile Offenders. Thousand Oaks, CA: Sage.

Hawkins, J. David, David P. Farrington, and Richard F. Catalano
1998 "Reducing violence through the schools." Pp. 188–216 in Delbert S. Elliott, Beatrix A. Hamburg, and Kirk R. Williams, eds., Violence in American Schools. Cambridge, England: Cambridge University Press.

Hawkins, J. David, Todd Herrenkohl, David P. Farrington, Devon Brewer, Richard F. Catalano, and Tracy W. Harachi
1998 "A review of predictors of youth violence." Pp. 106–146 in Rolf Loeber and David P. Farrington, eds., Serious and Violent Juvenile Offenders. Thousand Oaks, CA: Sage.

Hawkins, J. David, and Denise M. Lishner
1987 "Schooling and delinquency." Pp. 179–221 in Elmer H. Johnson, ed., Handbook on Crime and Delinquency Prevention. New York: Greenwood Press.

Hay, Carter
2001a "Parenting, self control, and delinquency: A test of self-control theory." Criminology 39:707–736.
2001b "An exploratory test of Braithwaite's reintegrative shaming theory." Journal of Research in Crime and Delinquency 38:132–153.
2003 "Family strain, gender, and delinquency." Sociological Perspectives 46:107–136.

Hay, Carter, and Michelle M. Evans
2006 "Violent victimization and involvement in delinquency: Examining predictions from general strain theory." Journal of Criminal Justice 34:261–274.

Hay, Carter, and Walter Forrest
2006 "The development of self-control: Examining self-control theory's stability thesis." Criminology 44:739–774.

Hay, Carter, Edward N. Fortson, Dusten R. Hollist, Irshad Altheimer, and Lonnie M. Schaible
2006 "The impact of community disadvantage on the relationship between the family and juvenile crime." Journal of Research in Crime and Delinquency 43:326–356.

Hayes, Hennessey, and Kathleen Daly
2003 "Youth justice conferencing and reoffending." Justice Quarterly 20:725–764.

Haynie, Dana L.
2001 "Delinquent peers revisited: Does network structure matter?" American Journal of Sociology 106:1013–57.
2002 "Friendship networks and delinquency: The relative nature of peer delinquency." Journal of Quantitative Criminology 18:99–134.

Haynie, Dana L., Peggy C. Giordano, Wendy P. Manning, and Monica Longmore
2005 "Adolescent romantic relationships and delinquency involvement." Criminology 43:177–210.

Haynie, Dana L., and Suzanne McHugh
2003 "Sibling deviance: In the shadows of mutual and unique friendship effects." Criminology 41:355–392.

Haynie, Dana L., and D. Wayne Osgood
2005 "Reconsidering peers and delinquency: How do peers matter?" Social Forces 84:1109–1130.

Haynie, Dana L., and Danielle C. Payne
2006 "Race, friendship networks, and violent delinquency." Criminology 44:775–806.

Haynie, Dana L., Eric Silver, and Brent Teasdale
2006 "Neighborhood characteristics, peer networks, and adolescent violence." Journal of Quantitative Criminology 22:147–169.

He, Ai (Phil), Jihong (Solomon) Zhao, and Nicholas P. Lovrich
2005 "Community policing." Crime and Delinquency 51:295–317.

Heidensohn, Frances
2002 "Gender and crime." Pp. 491–530 in Mike Maguire, Rod Morgan, and Robert Reiner, eds., The Oxford Handbook of Criminology, 3rd edition. Oxford: Oxford University Press.

Heimer, Karen
1995 "Gender, race, and the pathways to delinquency." Pp. 140–173 in John Hagan and Ruth D. Peterson, eds., Crime and Inequality. Stanford, CA: Stanford University Press.
1996 "Gender, interaction, and delinquency: Testing a theory of differential social control." Social Psychology Quarterly 59:36–61.
1997 "Socioeconomic status, subcultural definitions, and violent delinquency." Social Forces 75:799–833.

Heimer, Karen, Stacy De Coster, and Haline Unal
2006 "Opening the black box: The social psychology of gender and delinquency." Pp. 109–136 in Mathieu Deflem, ed., Sociological Theory and Criminological Research. Boston: Elsevier.

Heimer, Karen, and Ross L. Matsueda
1994 "Role-taking, role commitment, and delinquency: A theory of differential social control." American Sociological Review 59:365–390.

Hellman, Daryl A., and Susan Beaton
1986 "The pattern of violence in urban public schools: The influence of school and community." Journal of Research in Crime and Delinquency 23:102–127.

Hemenway, David, and Matthew Miller
2004 "Gun threats against and self-defense gun use by California adolescents." Archives of Pediatrics and Adolescent Medicine 158:395–400.

Henggeler, Scott W.
1989 Delinquency in Adolescence. Newbury Park, CA: Sage.

Herbert, Bob
2007a "Arrested while grieving." New York Times, May 26, A25.
2007b "The millions left out." New York Times, May 12, A25.

Heyman, Richard E., and Amy M. Smith Slep
2007 "Therapeutic treatment approaches to violent behavior." Pp. 602–617 in Daniel J. Flannery, Alexander T. Vazsonyi, and Irwin D. Waldman, eds., The Cambridge Handbook of Violent Behavior and Aggression. New York: Cambridge.

Hill, Karl G., James C. Howell, J. David Hawkins, and Sara R. Battin-Pearson
1999 "Childhood risk factors for adolescent gang membership: Results from the Seattle social development project." Journal of Research in Crime and Delinquency 36:300–322.

Hill, Karl G., Christina Lui, and J. David Hawkins
2004 "Early precursors of gang membership." Pp. 191–199 in Finn-Aage Esbensen, Stephen G. Tibbitts, and Larry Gaines, eds., American Youth Gangs at the Millennium. Long Grove, IL: Waveland Press.

Hindelang, Michael J.
1978 "Race and involvement in common law personal crimes." American Sociological Review 43:93–109.
1981 "Variations in age-race-sex-specific incidence rates of offending." American Sociological Review 46:461–474.

Hindelang, Michael J., Michael Gottfredson, and James Garofalo
1978 Victims of Personal Crime. Cambridge, MA: Ballinger.

Hindelang, Michael J., Travis Hirschi, and Joseph G. Weis
1979 "Correlates of delinquency: The illusion of discrepancy between self-report and official measures." American Sociological Review 44:99–101.
1981 Measuring Delinquency. Beverly Hills, CA: Sage.

Hirschi, Travis
1969 Causes of Delinquency. Berkeley: University of California Press.
1977 "Causes and prevention of juvenile delinquency." Sociological Inquiry 47:322–341.
1995 "The family." Pp. 121–140 in James Q. Wilson and Joan Petersilia, eds., Crime. Oakland, CA: ICS Press.
2004 "Self-control and crime." Pp. 537–552 in R. F. Baumeister and K. D. Vohs, eds., Handbook of Self-Regulation. New York: Guilford Press.

Hirschi, Travis, and Michael Gottfredson
1983 "Age and the explanation of crime." American Journal of Sociology 89:552–584.

Hirschi, Travis, and Michael J. Hindelang
1977 "Intelligence and delinquency: A revisionist review." American Sociological Review 42:571–587.

Hirschi, Travis, and Hanan C. Selvin
1967 Delinquency Research: An Appraisal of Analytic Methods. New York: Free Press.

Hoffmann, John P.
2003 "A contextual analysis of differential association, social control, and strain theories of delinquency." Social Forces 81:753–786.

Hoffmann, John P., and Felicia Gray Cerbone
1999 "Stressful life events and delinquency escalation in early adolescence." Criminology 37:343–374.

Hoffmann, John P., and Alan S. Miller
1998 "A latent variable analysis of strain theory." Journal of Quantitative Criminology 14:83–110.

Hoffmann, John P., and S. Susan Su
1997 "The conditional effects of stress on delinquency and drug use: A strain theory assessment of sex differences." Journal of Research in Crime and Delinquency 34:46–78.

Hollin, Clive R.
1990a Cognitive-Behavioral Interventions with Young Offenders. New York: Pergamon.
1990b "Social skills training with delinquents: A look at the evidence and some recommendations for practice." British Journal of Social Work 20:483–493.
1992 Criminal Behaviour: A Psychological Approach to Explanation and Prevention. London: Falmer Press.
2002 "Criminal Psychology." Pp. 144–174 in Mike Maguire, Rod Morgan, and Robert Reiner, eds., The Oxford Handbook of Criminology, 3rd edition. Oxford: Oxford University Press.

Honohan, Michael
2001 "Shootings will continue until bullies are corralled." Atlanta Constitution, March 13.

Hope, Tim
1995 "Community crime prevention." Crime and Justice 19:21–89.

Howell, James C.
1995 "Gangs and youth violence: Recent research." Pp. 261–274 in James C. Howell, Barry Krisberg, J. David Hawkins, and John J. Wilson, eds., A Sourcebook: Serious Violence and Chronic Juvenile Offenders. Thousand Oaks, CA: Sage.
1997a Juvenile Justice and Youth Violence. Thousand Oaks, CA: Sage.
1997b "Youth Gangs." Washington, DC: Office of Juvenile Justice and Delinquency Prevention.
1998a Youth Gangs: An Overview. Washington, DC: Office of Juvenile Justice and Delinquency Prevention.
1998b "Promising programs for youth gang violence prevention and intervention." Pp. 284–312 in Rolf Loeber and David P. Farrington, eds., Serious and Violent Juvenile Offenders. Thousand Oaks, CA: Sage.
1999 "Youth gang homicides: A literature review." Crime and Delinquency 45:208–241.
2003a Preventing and Reducing Juvenile Delinquency. Thousand Oaks, CA: Sage.
2003b "Diffusing research into practice using the comprehensive strategy for serious, violent, and chronic juvenile offenders." Youth Violence and Juvenile Justice 1:219–245.
2004 "Youth gangs: An overview." Pp. 16–51 in Finn-Aage Esbensen, Stephen G. Tibbitts, and Larry Gaines, eds., American Youth Gangs at the Millennium. Long Grove, IL: Waveland Press.

Howell, James C., Arlen Egley, Jr., and Debra K. Gleason
2002 Modern Day Youth Gangs. Washington, DC: Office of Juvenile Justice and Delinquency Prevention.

Howell, James C., and Debra K. Gleason
1999 Youth Gang Drug Trafficking. Washington, DC: Office of Juvenile Justice and Delinquency Prevention.

Howell, James C., and J. David Hawkins
1998 "Prevention of youth violence." Pp. 263–315 in Michael Tonry and Mark H. Moore, eds., Crime and Justice, Volume 24. Chicago: University of Chicago Press.

Howell, James C., Barry Krisberg, J. David Hawkins, and John J. Wilson
1995 A Sourcebook: Serious, Violent, and Chronic Juvenile Offenders. Thousand Oaks, CA: Sage.

Howell, James C., Barry Krisberg, and Michael Jones
1995 "Trends in juvenile crime and youth violence." Pp. 1–35 in James C. Howell, Barry Krisberg, J. David Hawkins, and John J. Wilson, eds., A Sourcebook: Serious, Violent, and Chronic Juvenile Offenders. Thousand Oaks, CA: Sage.

Hoyt, Dan R., Kimberly D. Ryan, and Ana Mari Cauce
1999 "Personal victimization in a high-risk environment: Homeless and runaway adolescents." Journal of Research in Crime and Delinquency 36:371–392.

Hsia, Heidi, and Donna Hamparian
1998 Disproportionate Minority Confinement: 1997 Update. Washington, DC: Office of Juvenile Justice and Delinquency Prevention.

Huang, Bu, Helene R. White, Rick Kosterman, Richard F. Catalano, and J. David Hawkins
2001 "Developmental associations between alcohol and interpersonal aggression during adolescence." Journal of Research in Crime and Delinquency 38:64–83.

Hubbard, Dana Jones, and Travis C. Pratt
2002 "A meta-analysis of the predictors of delinquency among girls." Journal of Offender Rehabilitation 34:1–13.

Huesmann, L. Rowell, and Lucyna Kirwil
2007 "Why observing violence increases the risk of violent behavior by the observer." Pp. 545–571 in Daniel J. Flannery, Alexander T. Vazsonyi, and Irwin D. Waldman, eds., The Cambridge Handbook of Violent Behavior and Aggression. Cambridge: Cambridge University Press.

Huff, C. Ronald
1998 Comparing the Criminal Behavior of Youth Gangs and At-Risk Youth. Washington, DC: National Institute of Justice.
2002 Gangs in America III. Thousand Oaks, CA: Sage.

Huff, C. Ronald
2004 "Comparing the criminal behavior of youth gangs and at-risk youths." Pp. 77–89 in Finn-Aage Esbensen, Stephen G. Tibbitts, and Larry Gaines, eds., American Youth Gangs at the Millennium. Long Grove, IL: Waveland Press.

Hughes, Lorine A., and James F. Short Jr.
2005 "Disputes involving youth street gang members: Micro-social contexts." Criminology 43:43–76.

Hughes, Michael, and Melvin E. Thomas
1998 "The continuing significance of race revisited: A study of race, class, and quality of life in America, 1972 to 1996." American Sociological Review 63:785–795.

Huizinga, David
1995 "Developmental sequences in delinquency: Dynamic typologies." Pp. 15–34 in Lisa J. Crockett and Ann C. Crouter, eds., Pathways Through Adolescence. Mahwah, NJ: Lawrence Erlbaum.
1996 The Influence of Delinquent Peers, Gangs, and Co-offending on Violence. Washington, DC: Office of Juvenile Justice and Delinquency Prevention.

Huizinga, David, and Delbert S. Elliott
1986 "Reassessing the reliability and validity of self-report delinquency measures." Journal of Quantitative Criminology 2:293–327.
1987 "Juvenile offenders: Prevalence, offender incidence, and arrest rates by race." Crime and Delinquency 33:206–223.

Huizinga, David, Finn-Aage Esbensen, and Anne Wylie Weiher
1991 "Are there multiple paths to delinquency?" Journal of Criminal Law and Criminology 82:83–118.

Huizinga, David H., Scott Menard, and Delbert S. Elliott
1989 "Delinquency and drug use: Temporal and developmental patterns." Justice Quarterly 6:419–455.

Huizinga, David, Terence Thornberry, Kelly Knight, and Peter Lovegrove
2007 Disproportionate Minority Contact in the Juvenile Justice System. Washington, DC: National Criminal Justice Reference Service.

Huizinga, David, Anne Wylie Weiher, Rachele Espiritu, and Finn-Aage Esbensen
2003 "Delinquency and crime: Some highlights from the Denver youth survey." Pp. 47–91 in Terence P. Thornberry and Marvin D. Krohn, eds., Taking Stock of Delinquency. New York: Kluwer.

Hundleby, John D.
1987 "Adolescent drug use in a behavioral matrix: A conformation and comparison of the sexes." Addictive Behaviors 12:103–112.

Hutchinson, Asa
2002 "Drug Legalization Doesn't Work." Washington Post, October 9, A31.

Inciardi, James A., Rith Horowitz, and Anne E. Pottieger
1993 Street Kids, Street Drugs, Street Crime. Belmont, CA: Wadsworth.

Inciardi, James A., and Karen McElrath
1998 The American Drug Scene. Los Angeles: Roxbury.

Inderbitzen, Michele
2005 "Growing up behind bars." Journal of Offender Rehabilitation 42:1–22.

Ingersoll, Sarah
1999 Investing in Youth for a Safer Future. Washington, DC: Office of Juvenile Justice and Delinquency Prevention.

Ireland, Timothy O., Carolyn A. Smith, and Terence P. Thornberry
2002 "Developmental issues in the impact of child maltreatment on later delinquency and drug use." Criminology 40:359–400.

Jackson, Mary S., and Paul Knepper
2003 Delinquency and Justice. Boston: Allyn and Bacon.

Jackson, Pamela Irving
1991 "Crime, youth gangs, and urban transition: The social dislocations of postindustrial economic development." Justice Quarterly 8:379–397.

Jackson, Patrick G.
1990 "Sources of data." Pp. 21–50 in Kimberly L. Kempf, ed., Measurement Issues in Criminology. New York: Springer-Verlag.

Jang, Sung Joon
1999 "Age-varying effects of family, school, and peers on delinquency: A multilevel modeling test of interactional theory." Criminology 37:643–686.
2002 "Race, ethnicity, and deviance: A study of Asian and non-Asian adolescents in America." Sociological Forum 17:647–680.

Jang, Sung Joon, and Byron R. Johnson
2001 "Neighborhood disorder, individual religiosity, and adolescent use of illicit drugs: A test of multilevel hypotheses." Criminology 39:109–144.
2003 "Strain, negative emotions, and deviant coping among African Americans: A test of general strain theory." Journal of Quantitative Criminology 19:79–105.

Jang, Sung Joon, and Carolyn A. Smith
1997 "A test of reciprocal causal relationships among parental supervision, affective ties, and delinquency." Journal of Research in Crime and Delinquency 34:307–336.

Jang, Sung Joon, and Terence P. Thornberry
1998 "Self-esteem, delinquent peers, and delinquency: A test of the self enhancement thesis." American Sociological Review 63:586–598.

Jankowski, Martin Sanchez
1995 "Ethnography, inequality, and crime in the low-income community." Pp. 80–94 in John Hagan and Ruth D. Peterson, eds., Crime and Inequality. Stanford, CA: Stanford University Press.

Jargowsky, Paul A.
2003 Stunning Progress, Hidden Problems: The Dramatic Decline of Concentrated Poverty in the 1990s. Washington, DC: Brookings Institution.

Jarjoura, G. Roger
1993 "Does dropping out of school enhance delinquent involvement? Results from a large-scale national probability sample." Criminology 31:149–172.
1996 "The conditional effect of social class on the dropout-delinquency relationship." Journal of Research in Crime and Delinquency 33:232–255.

Jarjoura, G. Roger, and Ruth A. Triplett
1997 "Delinquency and class: A test of the proximity principle." Justice Quarterly 14:763–792.

Jarjoura, G. Roger, Ruth A. Triplett, and Gregory P. Brinker
2002 "Growing up poor: Examining the link between persistent childhood poverty and delinquency." Journal of Quantitative Criminology 18:159–187.

Jenkins, Patricia H.
1997 "School delinquency and the school social bond." Journal of Research in Crime and Delinquency 34: 337–367.

Jennings, William S., Robert Kilkenny, and Lawrence Kohlberg
1983 "Moral-development theory and practice for youthful and adult offenders." Pp. 281–355 in William S. Laufer and James M. Day, eds., Personality Theory, Moral Development, and Criminal Behavior. Lexington, MA: Lexington.

Jensen, Gary F.
1972 "Parents, peers, and delinquent action: A test of the differential association perspective." American Journal of Sociology 78:562–575.
1998 "Television and violence: The rest of the story." Paper presented at the annual meeting of the Academy of Criminal Justice Sciences, Albuquerque.

Jensen, Gary F., and David Brownfield
1983 "Parents and drugs: Specifying the consequences of attachment." Criminology 21:543–554.
1986 "Gender, lifestyles, and victimization: Beyond routine activity." Violence and Victims 1:85–99.

Jensen, Gary F., and Raymond Eve
1976 "Sex differences in delinquency." Criminology 13:427–448.

Jensen, Gary F., and Dean G. Rojek
1998 Delinquency and Youth Crime. Prospect Heights, IL: Waveland Press.

Johnson, Byron R., Sung Joon Jang, David B. Larson, and Spencer De Li
2000 "Escaping from the crime of inner cities: Church attendance and religious salience among disadvantaged youth." Justice Quarterly 17:377–391.
2001 "Does adolescent religious commitment matter? A reexamination of the effects of religiosity on delinquency." Journal of Research in Crime and Delinquency 38:22–44.

Johnson, Byron R., Spencer De Li, David B. Larson, and Michael McCullough
2000 "A systematic review of the religiosity and delinquency literature: A research note." Journal of Contemporary Criminal Justice 16:32–52.

Johnson, Calvin C., and Chanchalat Chanhatasilpa
2003 "The race/ethnicity and poverty nexus of violent crime: Reconciling differences in Chicago's community area homicide rates." Pp. 89–113 in Darnell F. Hawkins, ed., Violent Crime: Assessing Race and Ethnic Differences. Cambridge, England: Cambridge University Press.

Johnson, Lee Michael, Ronald L. Simons, and Rand D. Conger
2004 "Criminal justice system involvement and continuity of youth crime." Youth and Society 36:3–29.

Johnson, Matthew C., and Glen A. Kercher
2007 "ADHD, strain, and criminal behavior." Deviant Behavior 28:131–152.

Johnson, Richard E.
1979 Juvenile Delinquency and Its Origins. Cambridge, England: Cambridge University Press.
1986 "Family structure and delinquency: General patterns and gender differences." Criminology 24:65–84.

Johnson, Richard E., Anastasios C. Marcos, and Stephen Bahr
1987 "The role of peers in the complex etiology of adolescent drug use." Criminology 25:323–340.

Kane, Robert J.
2005 "Compromised police legitimacy as a predictor of violent crime in structurally disadvantaged communities." Criminology 43:469–498.

Kappeler, Victor E., Mark Blumberg, and Gary W. Potter
1996 The Mythology of Crime and Criminal Justice. Prospect Heights, IL: Waveland Press.

Katz, Charles M., Vincent J. Webb, and David R. Schaffer
2001 "An assessment of the impact of quality-of-life policing on crime and disorder." Justice Quarterly 18:
825–876.

Katz, Jack
1988 Seductions of Crime. New York: Basic Books.

Katz, Rebecca S.
2000 "Explaining girls' and women's crime and desistance in the context of their victimization experiences." Violence Against Women 6:633–660.

Kaufman, Joanne M.
2005 "Explaining the race/ethnicity-violence relationship." Justice Quarterly 22:224–251.

Kaufman, Philip, Xianglei Chen, Susan P. Choy, Sally A. Ruddy, Amanda K. Miller, Christopher D. Chapman, Kathryn A. Chandler, Michael R. Rand, and Patty Klaus
1999 Indicators of School Crime and Safety, 1999. Washington, DC: U.S. Department of Education and U.S. Department of Justice.

Kazdin, Alan E.
1994 "Interventions for aggressive and antisocial children." Pp. 341–382 in Leonard D. Eron, Jacquelin H. Gentry, and Peggy Schlegel, eds., Reason to Hope. Washington, DC: American Psychological Association.

Kellermann, Arthur L., Dawna S. Fuqua-Whitley, Frederick P. Rivara, and James Mercy
1998 "Preventing youth violence: What works." Annual Review of Public Health 19:271–292.

Kelley, Barbara Tatem, Rolf Loeber, Kate Keenan, and Mary DeLamatre
1997 Developmental Pathways in Boys' Disruptive and Delinquent Behavior. Washington, DC: Office of Juvenile Justice and Delinquency Prevention.

Kelling, George L.
n.d. What Works—Research and the Police. Washington, DC: National Institute of Justice.
1988 Police and Communities: The Quiet Revolution. Washington, DC: National Institute of Justice.

Kelling, George L., and Catherine M. Coles
1996 Fixing Broken Windows. New York: Martin Kessler Books.

Kelling, George L., Mona R. Hochberg, Sandra Lee Kaminska, Ann Marie Rocheleau, Dennis P. Rosenbaum, Jeffrey A. Roth, and Wesley G. Skogan
1998 The Bureau of Justice Assistance Comprehensive Communities Program: A Preliminary Report. Washington, DC: Office of Justice Programs.

Kelling, George L., Tony Plate, Duane Dieckman, and Charles E. Brown
1974 The Kansas City Preventive Patrol Experiment: A Summary Report. Washington, DC: Police Foundation.

Kempf-Leonard, Kimberly
1990 Measurement Issues in Criminology. New York: Springer-Verlag.
1993 "The empirical status of Hirschi's control theory." Pp. 143–185 in Freda Adler and William S. Laufer, eds., New Directions in Criminological Theory; Advances in Criminological Theory, Volume 4. New Brunswick, NJ: Transaction.
2007 "Minority youths and juvenile justice." Youth Violence and Juvenile Justice 5:71–87.

Kennedy, David M.
1997 Juvenile Gun Violence and Gun Markets in Boston. Washington, DC: National Institute of Justice.
1998 "Pulling levers: Getting deterrence right." National Institute of Justice Journal 236:2–8.

Kennedy, Leslie W., and Stephen W. Baron
1993 "Routine activities and a subculture of violence: A study of violence on the street." Journal of Research in Crime and Delinquency 30:88–112.

Kennedy, Leslie W., and David R. Forde
1990 "Routine activities and crime: An analysis of victimization in Canada." Criminology 28:137–152.
1996 "Pathways to aggression: A factorial survey of 'routine conflict.'" Journal of Quantitative Criminology 12:417–438.
1999 When Push Comes to Shove. Albany: State University of New York Press.

Kent, Stephanie L., and David Jacobs
2005 "Minority threat and police strength from 1980 to 2000." Criminology 43:731–760.

Kessler, David A.
1999 "The effects of community policing on complaints against officers." Journal of Quantitative Criminology 15:333–372.

Kirsh, Steven J.
2006 Children, Adolescents, and Media Violence. Thousand Oaks, CA: Sage.

Klaus, Patsy, and Callie Marie Rennison
2002 Age Patterns in Violent Victimization, 1976–2000. Washington, DC: Bureau of Justice Statistics.

Kleck, Gary
1997 Targeting Guns: Firearms and Their Control. New York: Aldine de Gruyter.

Kleck, Gary, and Marc Gertz
1995 "Armed resistance to crime: The prevalence and nature of self-defense with a gun." Journal of Criminal Law and Criminology 86:150–187.

Kleck, Gary, Brian Sever, Spencer Li, and Marc Gertz
2005 "The missing link in general deterrence research." Criminology 43:623–660.

Kleiman, Mark A. R.
1999 "Getting deterrence right: Applying tipping models and behavioral economics to the problems of crime control." Pp. 1–29 in National Institute of Justice (ed.), Perspectives on Crime and Justice: 1998–1999 Lecture Series. Washington, DC: National Institute of Justice.

Klein, Malcolm W.
1971 Street Gangs and Street Workers. Englewood Cliffs, NJ: Prentice-Hall.
1995 The American Street Gang. New York: Oxford University Press.
1998 "Street gangs." Pp. 111–132 in Michael Tonry, ed., The Handbook of Crime and Punishment. New York: Oxford University Press.

Klein, Malcolm W., and Cheryl L. Maxson
2006 Street Gang Patterns and Policies. New York: Oxford University Press.

Klein, Malcolm W., Cheryl L. Maxson, and Jody Miller
1995 The Modern Gang Reader. Los Angeles: Roxbury.

Kleinfield, N. R.
2003 "Reputation for trouble fills portrait of boy 10, accused of murder." New York Times, March 30, A18.

Klepper, Steven, and Daniel Nagin
1989 "The deterrent effect of perceived certainty and severity of punishment revisited." Criminology 27:721–746.

Klinkenborg, Verlyn
2002 "Living under the virtual volcano of video games this holiday season." New York Times, December 16, A30.

Knox, George W.
2000 An Introduction to Gangs. Peotone, IL: New Chicago School Press.

Kocieniewski, David
2003 "A teenage loner, an arsenal and, to the police, a close call." New York Times, July 8, A21.

Kohlberg, Lawrence
1976 "Moral stages and moralization: The cognitive-developmental approach." Pp. 31–53 in T. Lickona, ed., Moral Development and Behavior. New York: Holt, Rinehart and Winston.

Kohn, Paul M., and Jill A. Milrose
1993 "The inventory of high-school students' recent life experiences: A decontaminated measure of adolescents' hassles." Journal of Youth and Adolescence 22:43–55.

Kopka, Deborah L.
1997 School Violence. Santa Barbara, CA: ABC-CLIO.

Kornhauser, Ruth Rosner
1978 Social Sources of Delinquency. Chicago: University of Chicago Press.

Kovandzic, Tomislav V., and Thomas B. Marvell
2003 "Right-to-carry concealed handguns and violent crime: Crime control through gun decontrol." Criminology and Public Policy 2:363–396.

Kretschmar, Jeff M., and Daniel J. Flannery
2007 "Substance use and violent behavior." Pp. 647–663 in Daniel J. Flannery, Alexander T. Vazsonyi, and Irwin D. Waldman, eds., The Cambridge Handbook of Violent Behavior and Aggression. Cambridge: Cambridge University Press.

Krisberg, Barry
2005 Juvenile Justice. Thousand Oaks, CA: Sage.

Krisberg, Barry, Giselle Barry, and Emily Sharrock
2004 Reforming Juvenile Justice Through Comprehensive Community Planning. Oakland, CA: National Council on Criminal Delinquency.

Krisberg, Barry, Elliott Currie, David Onek, and Richard G. Wiebush
1995 "Graduated sanctions for serious, violent, and chronic juvenile offenders." Pp. 142–170 in James C. Howell, Barry Krisberg, J. David Hawkins, and John J. Wilson, eds., A Sourcebook: Serious, Violent, and Chronic Juvenile Offenders. Thousand Oaks, CA: Sage.

Krisberg, Barry, and James C. Howell
1998 "The impact of the juvenile justice system and prospects for graduated sanctions in a comprehensive strategy." Pp. 346–366 in Rolf Loeber and David P. Farrington, eds., Serious and Violent Juvenile Offenders. Thousand Oaks, CA: Sage.

Krisberg, Barry, and Karl F. Schumann
2000 Crime and Delinquency 46 (April).

Krivo, Lauren J., and Ruth D. Peterson
1996 "Extremely disadvantaged neighborhoods and urban crime." Social Forces 75:619–650.

Krohn, Marvin D.
1999 "Social learning theory: The continuing development of a perspective." Theoretical Criminology 3: 462–476.
2000 "Sources of criminality: Control and deterrence theories." Pp. 373–403 in Joseph F. Sheley, ed., Criminology. Belmont, CA: Wadsworth.

Krohn, Marvin D., William F. Skinner, James L. Massey, and Ronald L. Akers
1985 "Social learning theory and adolescent cigarette smoking: A longitudinal study." Social Problems 32: 455–473.

Krohn, Marvin D., Terence P. Thornberry, Lori Collins-Hall, and Alan J. Lizotte
1995 "School dropout, delinquent behavior, and drug use." Pp. 163–183 in Howard B. Kaplan, ed., Drugs, Crime, and Other Deviant Adaptations. New York: Plenum.

Kubrin, Charis E., and Ronald Weitzer
2003a "New directions in social disorganization theory." Journal of Research in Crime and Delinquency 40:374–402.
2003b "Retaliatory violence: Concentrated disadvantage and neighborhood culture." Social Problems 50: 157–180.

Kumpfer, Karol L., and Rose Alvarado
1998 Effective Family Strengthening Interventions. Washington, DC: Office of Juvenile Justice and Delinquency Prevention.

Kumpfer, Karol L., and Connie M. Tait.
2000 Family Skills Training for Parents and Children. Washington, DC: Office of Juvenile Justice and Delinquency Prevention.

Kupchik, Aaron
2006 Judging Juveniles. New York: New York University Press.
2007 "The correctional experiences of youth in adult and juvenile prisons." Justice Quarterly 24:247–270.

Kurlychek, Megan, and Brian D. Johnson
2004 "The juvenile penalty." Criminology 42:485–517.

Kurlychek, Megan, Patricia Torbet, and Melanie Bozynski
1999 Focus on Accountability: Best Practices for Juvenile Court and Probation. Washington, DC: Office of Juvenile Justice and Delinquency Prevention.

LaFree, Gary
1998 Losing Legitimacy. Boulder, CO: Westview.
1999 "Declining violent crime rates in the 1990s: Predicting crime booms and busts." Annual Review of Sociology 25:145–68.

LaGrange, Teresa, and Robert A. Silverman
1999 "Low self-control and opportunity: Testing the general theory of crime as an explanation for gender differences in delinquency." Criminology 37:41–72.

Lahey, Benjamin B., and Irwin D. Waldman
2005 "A developmental model of the propensity to offend during childhood and adolescence." Pp. 15–50 in David F. Farrington, ed., Integrated Developmental and Life-Course Theories of Offending. New Brunswick, NJ: Transaction.

Lanctot, Nadine, and Marc Le Blanc
2002 "Explaining deviance by adolescent females." Crime and Justice: A Review of Research 29:113–202.

Land, Kenneth C., Patricia L. McCall, and Lawrence E. Cohen
1990 "Structural covariates of homicide rates: Are there any invariances across time and social space?" American Journal of Sociology 95:922–963.

Landau, Simha F.
1998 "Crime, subjective social stress and support indicators, and ethnic origin: The Israeli experience." Justice Quarterly 15:243–272.

Larson, Reed W., Maryse H. Richards, Giovanni Moneta, Grayson Holmbeck, and Elena Duckett
1996 "Changes in adolescents' daily interactions with their families from ages 10 to 18: Disengagement and transformation." Developmental Psychology 32:744–754.

Larzelere, Robert E., and Gerald R. Patterson
1990 "Parental management: Mediator of the effect of socioeconomic status on early delinquency." Criminology 28:301–324.

Laub, John H., and Robert J. Sampson
2001 "Understanding desistance from crime." Crime and Justice: A Review of Research 28:1–70.

Laub, John H., Robert J. Sampson, and Gary A. Sweeten
2006 "Assessing Sampson and Laub's life-course theory of crime." Pp. 313–334 in Francis T. Cullen, John Paul Wright, and Kristie R. Blevins, eds., Taking Stock: The Status of Criminological Theory. New Brunswick, NJ: Transaction.

Lauritsen, Janet L.
2005 "Racial and ethnic differences in offending." Pp. 83–104 in Darnell F. Hawkins and Kimberly Kempf-Leonard, eds., Our Children, Their Children. Chicago: University of Chicago Press.

Lauritsen, Janet L., and Robert J. Sampson
1998 "Minorities, crime, and criminal justice." Pp. 58–84 in Michael Tonry, ed., The Handbook of Crime and Punishment. New York: Oxford University Press.

Lawrence, Richard
1998 School Crime and Juvenile Justice. New York: Oxford University Press.

Lawton, Brian A., Ralph B. Taylor, and Anthony J. Luongo
2005 "Police officers on drug corners in Philadelphia, drug crime, and violent crime." Justice Quarterly 22: 427–451.

Le Blanc, Marc
1993 "Late adolescence deceleration of criminal activity and development of self- and social control." Studies on Crime and Crime Prevention 2:51–68.
1998 "Screening of serious and violent juvenile offenders: Identification, classification, and prediction." Pp. 167–193 in Rolf Loeber and David P. Farrington, eds., Serious and Violent Juvenile Offenders. Thousand Oaks, CA: Sage.

Le Blanc, Marc, and Rolf Loeber
1998 "Developmental criminology updated." Crime and Justice 23:115–198.

Lee, Matthew R.
2000 "Community cohesion and violent predatory victimization: A theoretical extension and cross-national test of opportunity theory." Social Forces 79:683–706.

Leiber, Michael J.
2002 "Disproportionate minority confinement (DMC) of youth: An analysis of state and federal efforts to address the issue." Crime and Delinquency 48:3–45.
2003 The Contexts of Juvenile Justice Decision Making: When Race Matters. Albany: State University of New York Press.
2006 "Disproportionate minority confinement (DMC) of youth." Pp. 141–186 in Everette B. Penn, Helen Taylor Greene, and Shaun L. Gabbidon, eds., Race and Juvenile Justice. Durham, NC: Carolina Academic Press.

Leiber, Michael J., and Kristan C. Fox
2005 "Race and the impact of detention on juvenile justice decision making." Crime and Delinquency 51: 470–497.

Leiber, Michael J., and Kristin Y. Mack
2003 "The individual and joint effects of race, gender, and family status on juvenile justice decision-making." Journal of Research in Crime and Delinquency 40:34–70.

Leiber, Michael J., and Jayne M. Stairs
1999 "Race, contexts, and the use of intake diversion." Journal of Research in Crime and Delinquency 36: 56–86.

Lemert, Edwin M.
1951 Social Pathology. New York: McGraw-Hill.
1972 Human Deviance, Social Problems, and Social Control. Englewood Cliffs, NJ: Prentice-Hall.

Leonard, Eileen B.
1982 Women, Crime and Society: A Critique of Theoretical Criminology. New York: Longman.

Leonard, Kimberly Kempf, Carl E. Pope, and William H. Feyerherm
1995 Minorities in Juvenile Justice. Thousand Oaks, CA: Sage.

Leonard, Kimberly Kempf, and Henry Sontheimer
1995 "The role of race in juvenile justice in Pennsylvania." Pp. 98–127 in Kimberly Kempf Leonard, Carl E. Pope, and William H. Feyerherm, eds., Minorities in Juvenile Justice. Thousand Oaks, CA: Sage.

Leuck, Thomas J.
2007 "To serve and protect, but politely." New York Times, July 29, A21.

Levine, Madeline
1996 Viewing Violence. New York: Doubleday.

Levitt, Steven D.
2002 "Deterrence." Pp. 435–450 in James Q. Wilson and Joan Petersilia, eds., Crime. Oakland, CA: ICS Press.

Levrant, Sharon, Francis T. Cullen, Betsy Fulton, and John F. Wozniak
1999 "Reconsidering restorative justice: The corruption of benevolence revisited?" Crime and Delinquency, 45:3–27.

Lewin, Tamar
2003 "1 in 5 teenagers has sex before 15, study finds." New York Times, May 20, A18.

Lewit, Eugene M., Donna L. Terman, and Richard E. Behrman
1997 "Children and poverty: Analysis and recommendations." Future of Children 7:4–24.

Liberman, Akiva
2007 Adolescents, Neighborhoods, and Violence. Washington, DC: Office of Justice Programs.

Lilly, J. Robert, Francis T. Cullen, and Richard Ball
2002 Criminological Theory. Thousand Oaks, CA: Sage.

Lin, Jeffrey
2006 Exploring the Impact of Institutional Placement on the Recidivism of Delinquent Youth. Washington, DC: National Institute of Justice.

Lipsey, Mark W.
1992 "Juvenile delinquency treatment: A meta-analytic inquiry into the variability of effects." Pp. 83–208 in Thomas D. Cook, Harris Cooper, David S. Cordray, Heidi Hartmann, Larry V. Hedges, Richard J. Light, Thomas A. Louis, and Frederick Mosteller, eds., Meta-Analysis for Explanation. New York: Russell Sage.

Lipsey, Mark W., and Francis T. Cullen
2008 "The effectiveness of correctional rehabilitation." Annual Review of Law and Social Science 3 (December).

Lipsey, Mark W., and David B. Wilson
1998 "Effective intervention for serious juvenile offenders." Pp. 313–345 in Rolf Loeber and David P. Farrington, eds., Serious and Violent Juvenile Offenders. Thousand Oaks, CA: Sage.

Liptak, Adam
2007 "Lifers as teenagers, now seeking a second chance." New York Times, October 17, A1, A24.

Liska, Allen E., John R. Logan, and Paul E. Bellair
1998 "Race and violent crime in the suburbs." American Sociological Review 63:27–39.

Liska, Allen E., and Barbara D. Warner
1991 "Functions of crime: A paradoxical process." American Journal of Sociology 96:1441–1463.

Little,, Michelle, and Laurence Steinberg
2006 "Psychosocial correlates of adolescent drug dealing in the inner city." Journal of Research in Crime and Delinquency 43:357–386.

Lizotte, Alan J., Trudy J. Bonsell, David McDowall, Marvin D. Krohn, and Terence P. Thornberry
2002 "Carrying guns and involvement in crime." Pp. 153–167 in Robert A. Silverman, Terence P. Thornberry, Bernard Cohen, and Barry Krisberg, eds., Crime and Justice at the Millennium; Essays by and in Honor of Marvin E. Wolfgang. Boston: Kluwer Academic Publishers.

Lizotte, Alan J., and David Sheppard
2001 "Gun Use by Male Juveniles: Research and Prevention." Washington, DC: Office of Juvenile Justice and Delinquency Prevention.

Lizotte, Alan J., James M. Tesoriero, Terence P. Thornberry, and Marvin Krohn
1994 "Patterns of adolescent firearms ownership and use." Justice Quarterly 11:51–74.

Lockwood, Daniel
1997 "Violence among middle school and high school students: Analysis and implications for prevention." Washington, DC: National Institute of Justice.

Loeber, Rolf, David P. Farrington, and David Petechuk
2003 Child Delinquency: Early Intervention and Prevention. Washington, DC: Office of Juvenile Justice and Delinquency Prevention.

Loeber, Rolf, David P. Farrington, Magda Stouthamer-Loeber, and Welmoet B. Van Kammen
1998 Antisocial Behavior and Mental Health Problems. Mahwah, NJ: Lawrence Erlbaum.

Loeber, Rolf, David P. Farrington, Magda Stouthamer-Loeber, Terrie E. Moffitt, and Avshalom Caspi
1998 "The development of male offending: Key findings from the first decade of the Pittsburgh youth study." Studies on Crime and Crime Prevention 7:141–171.

Loeber, Rolf, David P. Farrington, Magda Stouthamer-Loeber, Terrie E. Moffitt, Avshalom Caspi, Helene Raskin White, Evelyn H. Wei, and Jennifer M. Beyers
2003 "The development of male offending: Key findings from fourteen years of the Pittsburgh youth study." Pp. 93–136 in Terence P. Thornberry and Marvin D. Krohn, eds., Taking Stock of Delinquency. New York: Kluwer Academic.

Loeber, Rolf, David P. Farrington, and Daniel A. Waschbusch
1998 "Serious and violent juvenile offenders." Pp. 13–29 in Rolf Loeber and David P. Farrington, eds., Serious and Violent Juvenile Offenders. Thousand Oaks, CA: Sage.

Loeber, Rolf, and Magda Stouthamer-Loeber
1986 "Family factors as correlates and predictors of juvenile conduct problems and delinquency." Pp. 29–149 in Michael Tonry and Norval Morris, eds., Crime and Justice, Volume 7. Chicago: University of Chicago Press.

Loeber, Rolf, Magda Stouthamer-Loeber, Welmoet Van Kammen, and David P. Farrington
1991 "Initiation, escalation and desistance in juvenile offending and their correlates." Journal of Criminal Law and Criminology 82:36–82.

Lofland, John, and Lyn H. Lofland
1995 Analyzing Social Settings. Belmont, CA: Wadsworth.

Lombroso, Cesare
1911 Criminal Man. New York: G.P. Putnam.

Longa, Lyda
1998 "A bad way to die." Atlanta Journal-Constitution, March 3, B3.

Longshore, Douglas A.
1998 "Self-control and criminal opportunity: A prospective test of the general theory of crime." Social Problems 45:102–113.

Longshore, Douglas, Eunice Chang, and Nena Messina
2005 "Self-control and social bonds: A combined control perspective on juvenile offending." Journal of Quantitative Criminology 21:419–437.

Longshore, Douglas A., Susan Turner Rand, and Judith A. Stein
1996 "Self-control in a criminal sample: An examination of construct validity." Criminology 34:209–228.

Losel, Friedrich
1995 "The efficacy of correctional treatment: A review and synthesis of meta-evaluations." Pp. 79–111 in James McGuire, ed., What Works: Reducing Reoffending. Chichester, England: Wiley.
2007 "It's never too early and never too late: Towards an integrated science of developmental intervention in criminology." Criminologist 32:1, 3–9.

Losel, Friedrich, and Andreas Beelmann
2003 "Effects of child skills training in preventing antisocial behavior." Annals of the American Academy of Political and Social Science 587:84–109.

Lott, John R.
1998 More Guns, Less Crime. Chicago: University of Chicago Press.

Lotz, Roy, and Leona Lee
1999 "Sociability, school experience, and delinquency." Youth and Society 31:199–223.

Lowenkamp, Christopher T., Francis T. Cullen, and Travis C. Pratt
2003 "Replicating Sampson and Grove's test of social disorganization theory: Revisiting a criminological classic." Journal of Research in Crime and Delinquency.

Luckenbill, David F.
1977 "Criminal homicide as a situated transaction." Social Problems 25:176–186.

Ludwig, Jens, and Philip J. Cook
2003 Evaluating Gun Policy. Washington, DC: Brookings Institution Press.

Lundman, Richard J.
2001 Prevention and Control of Juvenile Delinquency. New York: Oxford University Press.

Lykken, David T.
1995 The Antisocial Personalities. Hillsdale, NJ: Lawrence Erlbaum.
1996 "Psychopathy, sociopathy, and crime." Society 34(1):29–38.

Lynam, Donald R. and Joshua D. Miller
2004 "Personality pathways to impulsive behavior and their relations to deviance." Journal of Quantitative Criminology 20:319–341.

Lynch, James P.
2002 Trends in Juvenile Violent Offending: An Analysis of Victim Survey Data. Washington, DC: Office of Juvenile Justice and Delinquency Prevention.

Lynch, Michael J., and Paul B. Steretesky
2001 "Radical criminology." Pp. 267–286 in Raymond Paternoster and Ronet Bachman, eds., Explaining Criminals and Crime. Los Angeles: Roxbury.

MacCoun, Robert, and Peter Reuter
1998 "Drug control." Pp. 207–238 in Michael Tonry, ed., The Handbook of Crime and Punishment. New York: Oxford University Press.

MacDonald, John M.
2002 "The effectiveness of community policing in reducing urban violence." Crime and Delinquency 48: 592–618.

MacDonald, John M., and Meda Chesney-Lind
2001 "Gender bias and juvenile justice revisited: A multiyear analysis." Crime and Delinquency 47:173–195.

MacKenzie, Doris Layton
2002 "Reducing the criminal activities of known offenders and delinquents." Pp. 330–404 in Lawrence W. Sherman, David P. Farrington, Brandon C. Welsh, and Doris Layton MacKenzie, eds., Evidence-Based Crime Prevention. London: Routledge.
2006 What Works in Corrections. New York: Cambridge University Press.

MacKenzie, Lynn Ryan
1999 Residential Placement of Adjudicated Youth, 1987–1996. Washington, DC: Office of Juvenile Justice and Delinquency Prevention.

MacLeod, Jay
1995 Ain't No Makin' It. Boulder, CO: Westview Press.

Maguin, Eugene, and Rolf Loeber
1996 "Academic performance and delinquency." Pp. 145–264 in Michael Tonry, ed., Crime and Justice: A Review of Research, Volume 20. Chicago: University of Chicago Press.

Maguire, Kathleen, and Ann L. Pastore
2003 Sourcebook of Criminal Justice Statistics. Available at http://www.albany.edu/sourcebook/.

Majors, Richard, and Janet Mancini Billson
1992 Cool Pose. New York: Lexington Books.

Markowitz, Fred E., and Richard B. Felson
1998 "Socio-demographic differences in attitudes and violence." Criminology, 36:117–138.

Martinez, Ramiro, Jr., and Matthew T. Lee
2000 "On immigration and crime." Pp. 485–524 in Gary LaFree, ed., Criminal Justice 2000, Volume 1: The Nature of Crime: Continuity and Change. Washington, DC: National Institute of Justice.

Martinez, Ramiro, Jr., and Amie L. Nielsen
2006 "Extending ethnicity and violence research in a multiethnic city." Pp. 108–137 in Ruth Peterson, Lauren J. Krivo, and John Hagan, eds., The Many Colors of Crime. New York: New York University Press.

Martinson, Robert
1974 "What works? Questions and answers about prison reform." Public Interest 35:22–54.

Martz, Ron
1999 "Crime stats: Questions linger after Atlanta audit." Atlanta Journal-Constitution, January 28, C1, 4.

Maruna, Shadd, and Heith Copes

2005 "What have we learned from five decades of neutralization research." Crime and Justice 32:221–320.

Marvell, Thomas B., and Carlisle E. Moody

1996 "Specification problems, police levels, and crime rates." Criminology 34:609–646.

Massey, James L., Marvin D. Krohn, and Lisa M. Bonati

1989 "Property crime and the routine activities of individuals." Journal of Research in Crime and Delinquency 26:378–400.

Mastrofski, Stephen D.

2000 "The police in America." Pp. 405–445 in Joseph F. Sheley, ed., Criminology: A Contemporary Handbook. Belmont, CA: Wadsworth.

Matarazzo, Anthony, Peter J. Carrington, and Robert D. Hiscott

2001 "The effect of prior youth court dispositions on current dispositions: An application of societal-reaction theory." Journal of Quantitative Criminology 17:169–200.

Matsueda, Ross L.

1988 "The current state of differential association theory." Crime and Delinquency 34:277–306.

1992 "Reflected appraisals, parental labeling, and delinquency: Specifying a symbolic interactionist theory." American Journal of Sociology 97:1577–1611.

2001. "Labeling theory." Pp. 223–241 in Raymond Paternoster and Ronet Bachman, eds., Explaining Criminals and Crime. Los Angeles, CA: Roxbury.

Matsueda, Ross L., and Kathleen Anderson

1998 "The dynamics of delinquent peers and delinquent behavior." Criminology 36:269–308.

Matsueda, Ross L., and Karen Heimer

1987 "Race, family structure, and delinquency: A test of differential association and social control theories." American Sociological Review 52:826–840.'

Matsueda, Ross L., Derek A Kreager, and David Huizinga

2006 "Deterring delinquents: A rational choice model of theft and violence." American Sociological Review 71:95–122.

Matza, David

1964 Delinquency and Drift. New York: Wiley.

1969 Becoming Deviant. Englewood Cliffs, NJ: Prentice-Hall.

Matza, David, and Gresham Sykes

1961 "Juvenile delinquency and subterranean beliefs." American Sociological Review 26:713–719.

Mauer, Marc, and Ryan S. King

2007 Uneven Justice. The Sentencing Project, available at www.sentencingproject.org.

Maxfield, Michael G.

1999 "The national incident-based reporting system: Research and policy implications." Journal of Quantitative Criminology 15:119–149.

Maxson, Cheryl L.

1995 "Research in brief: Street gangs and drug sales in two suburban cities." Pp. 228–235 in Malcolm W. Klein, Cherly L. Maxson, and Jody Miller, eds., The Modern Gang Reader. Los Angeles: Roxbury.

Maxson, Cheryl L.

2004 "Civil gang injunctions." Pp. 375–389 in Finn-Aage Esbensen, Stephen G. Tibbitts, and Larry Gaines, eds., American Youth Gangs of the Millennium. Long Grove, IL: Waveland Press.

Maxson, Cheryl L., and Malcolm W. Klein

1990 "Street gang violence: Twice as great, or half as great?" Pp. 71–100 in C. Ronald Huff, ed., Gangs in America. Newbury Park, CA: Sage.

1996 "Defining gang homicide: An updated look at member and motive approaches." Pp. 3–20 in C. Ronald Huff, ed., Gangs in America. Thousand Oaks, CA: Sage.

Maxson, Cheryl L., and Monica L. Whitlock

2002 Joining the gang: Gender differences in risk factors for GANF membership. Pp. 19–36 in C. Ronald Huff, ed., Gangs in America III. Thousand Oaks, CA: Sage.

Maynard, Rebecca A.
1997 Kids Having Kids. Washington, DC: Urban Institute Press.

Maynard, Rebecca A., and Eileen M. Garry
1997 Adolescent Motherhood: Implications for the Juvenile Justice System. Washington, DC: Office of Juvenile Justice and Delinquency Prevention.

Mazerolle, Lorraine Green, Collen Kadleck, and Jan Roehl
1998 "Controlling drug and disorder problems: The role of place managers." Criminology 36:371–404.

Mazerolle, Paul
1998 "Gender, general strain, and delinquency: An empirical examination." Justice Quarterly 15:65–91.

Mazerolle, Paul, and Jeff Maahs
2000 "General strain and delinquency: An alternative examination of conditioning influences." Justice Quarterly 17:753–778.

Mazerolle, Paul, and Alex Piquero
1997 "Violent responses to strain: An examination of conditioning influences." Violence and Victims 12: 323–343.
1998 "Linking exposure to strain with anger: An investigation of deviant adaptations." Journal of Criminal Justice 26:195–211.

Mazerolle, Paul, Alex Piquero, and George E. Capowich
2003 "Examining the links between strain, situational and dispositional anger, and crime." Youth and Society 35:131–157.

McBride, Duane C., and Clyde B. McCoy
1993 "The drugs-crime relationship: An analytical framework." Prison Journal 73:257–278.

McCabe, Donald L.
1992 "The influence of situational ethics on cheating among college students." Sociological Inquiry 62: 365–374.

McCarthy, Bill
1995 "Not just 'for the thrill of it': An instrumentalist elaboration of Katz's explanation of sneaky thrill property crimes." Criminology 33:519–538.

McCarthy, Bill, Diane Felmlee, and John Hagan
2004 "Girl friends are better: Gender, friends, and crime among school and street youth." Criminology 42: 805–836.

McClelland, Gary H., and Charles M. Judd
1993 "Statistical difficulties of detecting interactions and moderator effects." Psychological Bulletin 114: 376–390.

McCluskey, Cynthia Perez
2002 Understanding Latino Delinquency. New York: LFB Scholarly Publishing.

McCord, Joan
1991 "Family relationships, juvenile delinquency, and adult criminality." Criminology 29:397–417.
2001 "Forging criminals in the family." Pp. 223–236 in Susan O. White, Handbook of Youth and Justice. New York: Kluwer Academic.

McCord, Joan, and Margaret E. Ensminger
2003 "Racial discrimination and violence: A longitudinal perspective." Pp. 319–330 in Darnell F. Hawkins, ed., Violent Crime: Addressing Race and Ethnic Differences. Cambridge, England: Cambridge University Press.

McCord, Joan, Cathy Spatz Widom, and Nancy A. Crowell
2001 Juvenile Crime, Juvenile Justice. Washington, DC: National Academy Press.

McDermott, Joan
1993 "Crime in the school and in the community: Offenders, victims, and fearful youths." Crime and Delinquency 29:270–282.

McDevitt, Rick
2000 "Juvenile 'reform' only hurts." Atlanta Journal-Constitution, May 28, Q5.

McDonald, Lynn, and Heather E. Frey

1999 Families and Schools Together: Building Relationships. Washington, DC: Office of Juvenile Justice and Delinquency Prevention.

McDowall, David, Alan J. Lizotte, and Brian Wiersema

1991 "General deterrence through civilian gun ownership: An evaluation of the quasi-experimental evidence." Criminology 29:541–559.

McDowall, David, Colin Loftin, and Stanley Presser

2000 "Measuring civilian defensive firearm use: A methodological experiment." Journal of Quantitative Criminology 16:1–19.

McDowall, David, and Brian Wiersema

1994 "The incidence of defensive firearm use by U.S. crime victims, 1987 through 1990." American Journal of Public Health 84:1982–1984.

McEwen, T.

1994 National Assessment Program: 1994 Survey Results. Washington, DC: National Institute of Justice.

McGarrell, Edmund F., Steven M. Chermak, and Alexander Weiss

2002 Reducing Gun Violence: An Evaluation of the Indianapolis Police Department's Directed Patrol Project. Washington, DC: Office of Justice Programs.

McGarrell, Edmund F., Steven Chermak, Jeremy M. Wilson, and Nicholas Corsaro

2006 "Reducing homicide through a 'lever-pulling' strategy." Justice Quarterly 23:188–213.

McGarrell, Edmund F., and Natalie Kroovand Hipple

2007 "Family group conferencing and re-offending among first-time juvenile offenders." Justice Quarterly 24:221–246.

McGloin, Jean Marie, Travis C. Pratt, and Jeff Maaks

2004 "Rethinking the IQ-delinquency relationship." Justice Quarterly 21:603–635.

McGloin, Jean Marie, Travis C. Pratt, and Alex R. Piquero

2006 "A life-course analysis of the criminogenic effects of maternal cigarette smoking during pregnancy." Journal of Research in Crime and Delinquency 43:412–426.

McGuire, James

1995 What Works: Reducing Offending. Chichester, England: Wiley.

McHugh, Donald J.

2003 "Parental guidance required." New York Times, July 12, A23.

McNulty, Thomas L., and Paul E. Bellair

2003 "Explaining racial and ethnic differences in serious adolescent violent behavior." Criminology 41: 709–748.

McNulty, Thomas L., and Steven R. Holloway

2000 "Race, crime, and public housing in Atlanta: Testing a conditional effect hypothesis." Social Forces 79:707–729.

Mears, Daniel P., and Avinash S. Bhati

2006 "No community is an island: The effects of resource deprivation on urban violence in spatially and socially proximate communities." Criminology 44:509–548.

Mears, Daniel P., Carter Hay, Marc Gertz, and Christina Mancini

2007 "Public opinion and the foundation of the juvenile court." Criminology 45:223–258.

Mears, Daniel P., and William R. Kelly

1999 "Assessments and intake processes in juvenile justice processing: Emerging policy considerations." Crime and Delinquency 45:508–529.

Mears, Daniel P., Matthew Ploeger, and Mark Warr

1998 "Explaining the gender gap in delinquency: Peer influence and moral evaluations of behavior." Journal of Research in Crime and Delinquency 35:251–266.

Meich, Richard A., Avshalom Caspi, Terrie E. Moffitt, Bradley R. Entner Wright, and Phil A. Silva

1999 "Socioeconomic status and mental disorders: A longitudinal study of selection and causation during young adulthood." American Journal of Sociology 104:1096–1131.

Meier, Robert F., Steven R. Burkett, and Carol A. Hickman
1984 "Sanctions, peers, and deviance: Preliminary models of a social control process." Sociological Quarterly 25:76–82.

Meier, Robert F., and Gilbert Geis
1997 Victimless Crime? Los Angeles: Roxbury.

Merton, Robert K.
1938 "Social structure and anomie." American Sociological Review 3:672–682.
1968 Social Theory and Social Structure. New York: Free Press.

Messerschmidt, James W.
1993 Masculinities and Crime. Lanham, MD: Rowman and Littlefield.

Messner, Steven F., Glenn D. Deane, Luc Anselin, and Benjamin Pearson-Nelson
2005 "Locating the vanguard in rising and falling homicide rates across U.S. cities." Criminology 43:661–696.

Messner, Steven F., Sandra Galea, Kenneth J. Tardiff, Melissa Tracy, Angela Bucciarelli, Tinka Markham Piper, Victoria Frye, and David Vlahov
2007 "Policing, drugs, and the homicide decline in New York City in the 1970s." Criminology 45:385–414.

Messner, Steven F., and Reid M. Golden
1992 "Racial inequality and racially disaggregated homicide rates: An assessment of alternative theoretical explanations." Criminology 30:421–447.

Messner, Steven F., Marvin D. Krohn, and Allen E. Liska
1989 Theoretical Integration in the Study of Deviance and Crime: Problems and Prospects. Albany: State University of New York Press.

Messner, Steven F., and Richard Rosenfeld
2001 Crime and the American Dream. Belmont, CA: Wadsworth.

Miethe, Terance D., and Richard McCorkle
2001 Crime Profiles. Los Angeles, CA: Roxbury.

Miethe, Terance D., and Robert F. Meier
1990 "Opportunity, choice, and criminal victimization: A test of a theoretical model." Journal of Research in Crime and Delinquency 27:243–266.
1994 Crime and Its Social Context. Albany: State University of New York Press.

Miller, Jerome
1996 Search and Destroy. Cambridge, England: Cambridge University Press.

Miller, Jody
2001 One of the Guys: Girls, Gangs, and Gender. New York: Oxford University Press.

Miller, Jody, and Rod K. Brunson
2004 "Gender dynamics in youth gangs." Pp. 163–190 in Finn-Aage Esbensen, Stephen G. Tibbetts, and Larry Gaines, eds., American Youth Gangs of the Millennium. Long Grove, IL: Waveland Press.

Miller, Jody, Cheryl L. Maxson, and Malcolm W. Klein
2001 The Modern Gang Reader. Los Angeles: Roxbury.

Miller, Joshua D., and Donald Lynam
2001 "Structural models of personality and their relation to antisocial behavior: A meta-analytic review." Criminology 39:765–798.

Miller, Walter B.
1958 "Lower class culture as a generating milieu of gang delinquency." Journal of Social Issues 14:5–19.
1982 Crime by Youth Gangs and Groups in the United States. Washington, DC: U.S. Department of Justice.
2001 The Growth of Youth Gang Problems in the United States: 1970–98. Washington, DC: Office of Juvenile Justice and Delinquency Prevention.

Minor, William W.

1981 "Techniques of neutralization: A reconceptualization and empirical examination." Journal of Research in Crime and Delinquency 18:295–318.

Moffitt, Terrie E.

1990 "The neuropsychology of juvenile delinquency: A critical review." Pp. 99–169 in Michael Tonry and Norval Morris, eds., Crime and Justice, Volume 12. Chicago: University of Chicago Press.

1993 " 'Life-course persistent' and 'adolescent-limited' antisocial behavior: A developmental taxonomy." Psychological Review 100:674–701.

1997 "Adolescent-limited and life-course persistent offending: A complementary pair of developmental theories." Pp. 11–54 in Terence P. Thornberry, ed., Developmental Theories of Crime and Delinquency: Advances in Criminological Theory, Volume 7. New Brunswick, NJ: Transaction.

2006 "A review of research on the taxonomy of life-course persistent versus adolescence-limited antisocial behavior." Pp. 277–312 in Francis T. Cullen, John Paul Wright, and Kristie R. Blevins, eds., Taking Stock: The Status of Criminological Theory. New Brunswick, NJ: Transaction.

Moffitt, Terrie E., Avshalom Caspi, Paul Fawcett, Gary L. Brammer, Michael Raleigh, Arthur Yuwiler, and Phil Silva

1997 "Whole blood serotonin and family background relate to male violence." Pp. 231–249 in Adrian Raine, Patricia A. Brennan, David P. Farrington, and Sarnoff A. Mednick, eds., Biosocial Bases of Violence. New York: Plenum.

Moffitt, Terrie E., Avshalom Cuspi, Michael Rutter, and Phil A. Silva

2001 Sex Differences in Antisocial Behaviour. Cambridge, England: Cambridge University Press.

Moffitt, Terrie E., and Hona Lee Harrington

1996 "Delinquency: The natural history of antisocial behaviour." Pp. 163–185 in Phil A. Silva and Warren R. Stanton, eds., From Child to Adult. Oxford: Oxford University Press.

Moffitt, Terrie E., and Bill Henry

1989 "Neuropsychological assessment of executive functions in self-reported delinquents." Development and Psychopathology 1:105–118.

Moffitt, Terrie E., Donald R. Lynam, and Phil A. Silva

1994 "Neuropsychological tests predicting persistent male delinquency." Criminology 32:277–300.

Moon, Melissa M., Jody L. Sundt, Francis T. Cullen, and John Paul Wright

2000 "Is child saving dead? Public support for juvenile rehabilitation." Crime and Delinquency 46:38–60.

Moore, Joan

1991 Going Down to the Barrio: Homeboys and Homegirls in Change. Philadelphia: Temple University Press.

Moore, Joan, and John M. Hagedorn

1996 "What happens to girls in the gang?" Pp. 205–218 in C. Ronald Huff, ed., Gangs in America. Thousand Oaks, CA: Sage.

2001 Female Gangs: A Focus on Research. Washington, DC: Office of Juvenile Justice and Delinquency Prevention.

Moore, John P., and Ivan L. Cook

1999 Highlights of the 1998 National Youth Gang Survey. Washington, DC: Office of Juvenile Justice and Delinquency Prevention.

Moore, Kristin Anderson, Donna Ruane Morrison, and Angela Dungee Greene

1997 "Effects on the children born to adolescent mothers." Pp. 145–180 in Rebecca A. Maynard, ed., Kids Having Kids. Washington, DC: Urban Institute Press.

Moore, Mark H., Robert C. Trojanowicz, and George L. Kelling

1988 Crime and Policing. Washington, DC: National Institute of Justice.

Morash, Merry

1983 "An explanation of juvenile delinquency: The integration of moral reasoning theory and sociological knowledge." Pp. 385–409 in William S. Laufer and James M. Day, eds., Personality Theory, Moral Development, and Criminal Behavior. Lexington, MA: Lexington.

1986 "Gender, peer group experiences, and seriousness of delinquency." Journal of Research in Crime and Delinquency 23:43–67.

Morenoff, Jeffery D.
2005 "Racial and ethnic disparities in crime and delinquency in the United States." Pp. 139–173 in Michael Rutter and Morta Tienda, eds., Ethnicity and Causal Mechanisms. Cambridge: Cambridge University Press.

Morenoff, Jeffrey D., and Robert J. Sampson
1997 "Violent crime and the spatial dynamics of neighborhood transition: Chicago, 1970–1990." Social Forces 76:31–64.

Morley, Elaine, Shelli B. Rossman, Mary Kopczynski, Janeen Buck, and Caterina Gouvis
2000 Comprehensive Responses to Youth at Risk: Interim Findings from the SafeFutures Initiative. Washington, DC: Office of Juvenile Justice and Delinquency Prevention.

Morris, Gregory D., Peter B. Wood, and R. Gregory Dunaway
2006 "Self-control, native traditionalism, and native american substance use." Crime and Deliquency 52: 572–598.

Mosher, Clayton J., Terance D. Miethe, and Dretha M. Philips
2002 The mismeasure of Crime. Thousand Oaks, CA: Sage.

Muller, Janice, and Sharon Mihalic
1999 Blueprints: A Violence Prevention Initiative. Washington, DC: Office of Juvenile Justice and Delinquency Prevention.

Muraskin, Roslyn
1998 "Police work with juveniles." Pp. 151–164 in Albert R. Roberts, ed., Juvenile Justice. Chicago: Nelson-Hall.

Murphy, Kim, and Melissa Healy
1999 "Lawsuits now putting onus of youth crime on parents." Atlanta Constitution, May 2, A15.

Mustaine, Elizabeth Ehrhardt, and Richard Tewksbury
1998a "Predicting risks of larceny theft victimization: A routine activity analysis using refined lifestyle measures." Criminology 36:829–857.
1998b "Specifying the role of alcohol in predatory victimization." Deviant Behavior 19:173–200.

Myers, David L.
2003 "Waiver to adult court." Pp. 387–394 in Marilyn D. McShane and Frank P. Williams III, eds., Encyclopedia of Juvenile Justice. Thousand Oaks, CA: Sage.

Nagin, Daniel S.
1998a "Criminal deterrence research at the outset of the twenty-first century." Pp. 1–42 in Michael Tonry, ed., Crime and Justice: A Review of Research, Volume 23. Chicago: University of Chicago Press.
1998b "Deterrence and incapacitation." Pp. 345–368 in Michael Tonry, ed., The Handbook of Crime and Punishment. New York: Oxford University Press.

Nagin, Daniel S., and Raymond Paternoster
1991 "The preventive effects of the perceived risk of arrest: Testing an expanded conception of deterrence." Criminology 29:561–587.
1993 "Enduring individual differences and rational choice theories of crime." Law and Society Review 27: 467–496.
1994 "Personal capital and social control: The deterrence implications of a theory of individual differences in criminal offending." Criminology 32:581–606.

Nagin, Daniel S., Alex R. Piquero, Elizabeth S. Scott, and Laurence Steinberg
2006 "Public preferences for rehabilitation versus incarceration of juvenile offenders." Criminology and Public Policy 5:627–652.

Nagin, Daniel S., and Greg Pogorsky
2004 "Time and punishment: Delayed consequences and criminal behavior." Journal of Quantitative Criminology 20:295–317.

Nagin, Daniel S., and Richard E. Tremblay
2005a "What has been learned from group-based trajectory modeling?" ANNALS of the American Academy of Political and Social Science 602:82–117.
2005b "Developmental trajectory groups: Fact or useful fiction." Criminology 43:873–904.

National Council on Crime and Deliquency
2007 And Justice for Some. Available at www.nccd-crc.org/nccd/.

National Institute on Drug Abuse
2006 Principles of Drug Abuse Treatment for Criminal Justice Populations. Washington, DC: National Institute on Drug Abuse.

National Institute of Justice
1992 National Institute of Justice Journal, Community Policing, No. 225.
1996 National Institute of Justice Journal, August, No. 231.
1998a National Institute of Justice Journal, October, No. 237.
1998b 1997 Drug Use Forecasting. Washington, DC: National Institute of Justice.
2003 2000 Arrestee Drug Abuse Monitoring: Annual Report. Washington, DC: National Institute of Justice.

National Television Violence Study
1997 National Television Violence Study, Volume 1. Thousand Oaks, CA: Sage.
1998 National Television Violence Study, Volume 2. Thousand Oaks, CA: Sage.

National Youth Gang Center
2003 "Frequently asked questions regarding gangs." Available at http:// www.iir.com/nygc/faq.htm.
2007 National Youth Gang Center Survey Analysis. Available at http://www.iir.com/nygc/nygsa/.

Neff, Joan L., and Dennis E. Waite
2007 "Male versus female substance abuse patterns among incarcerated juvenile offenders." Justice Quarterly 24:106–132.

New York Times
2003a "Department of justice." February 4, A22.
2003b "Married households rise again among blacks, census finds." April 26, A13.
2003c "Smoke and mirrors on Head Start." July 11, A18.
2003d "Lawyers for juveniles." November 3, A18.
2007a "Positive trends recorded in U.S. data on teenagers." July 13, A17.
2007b "3 Teenagers sought after homeless man is set on fire." October 6, B3.
2007c "Back where they belong." July 5, A12.

Nielsen, Amie L., Matthew T. Lee, and Ramiro Martinez, Jr.
2005 "Integrating race, place, and motive in social disorganization theory." Criminology 43:837–872.

NSDUH Report
2006 Youth Violence and Illicit Drug Use. Washington, DC: Substance Abuse and Mental Health Services Administration.

Nye, Ivan F.
1958 Family Relationships and Delinquent Behavior. New York: Wiley.

O'Brien, Robert M.
2000 "Crime facts: Victim and offender data." Pp. 59–83 in Joseph F. Sheley, ed., Criminology. Belmont, CA: Wadsworth.

Office of Justice Programs
1999 Weed and Seed Best Practices. Washington, DC: Office of Justice Programs.

Office of Juvenile Justice and Delinquency Prevention
1995 Delinquency Prevention Works. Washington, DC: Office of Juvenile Justice and Delinquency Prevention.
1996 Reducing Youth Gun Violence. Washington, DC: Office of Juvenile Justice and Delinquency Prevention.
1998a Guide for Implementing the Balanced and Restorative Justice Model. Washington, DC: Office of Juvenile Justice and Delinquency Prevention.
1998b Juvenile Mentoring Program: 1998 Report to Congress. Washington, DC: Office of Juvenile Justice and Delinquency Prevention.
1999a Report to Congress on Juvenile Violence Research. Washington, DC: Office of Juvenile Justice and Delinquency Prevention.
1999b Title V Incentive Grants for Local Delinquency Prevention Programs: 1998 Report to Congress. Washington, DC: Office of Juvenile Justice and Delinquency Prevention.
2000a Kids and Guns. Washington, DC: Office of Juvenile Justice and Delinquency Prevention.

2000b Jurisdictional Technical Assistance Package for Juvenile Court. Washington, DC: Office of Juvenile Justice and Delinquency Prevention.

2003 OJJDP Statistical Briefing Book. Available at http://ojjdp.ncjrs.org/ojstatbb.

2006 Attorney General's Comprehensive Anti-gang Initiative. Washington, DC: Office of Juvenile Justice and Delinquency Prevention.

Office of National Drug Control Policy

1999 The National Drug Control Strategy, 1999. Washington, DC: Office of National Drug Control Policy.

2003 Juveniles and Drugs. Washington, DC: Office of National Drug Control Policy.

2007 The President's National Drug Control Strategy. Washington, DC: Office of National Drug Control Policy.

Oldenettel, Debra, and Madeline Wordes

1999 Community Assessment Centers. Washington, DC: Office of Juvenile Justice and Delinquency Prevention.

Olds, David, Peggy Hill, and Elissa Rumsey

1998 Prenatal and Early Childhood Nurse Home Visitation. Washington, DC: Office of Juvenile Justice and Delinquency Prevention.

Oliver, William

1994 The Violent Social World of Black Men. New York: Lexington.

Olweus, Dan

1986 "Aggression and hormones: Behavioral relationship with testosterone and adrenaline." Pp. 51–72 in Dan Olweus, Jack Block, and Marian Radke-Yarrow, eds., Development of Antisocial and Prosocial Behavior. Orlando, FL: Academic Press.

1991 "Bully/victim problems among schoolchildren: Basic facts and effects of a school-based intervention program." Pp. 411–448 in Debra J. Pepler and Kenneth H. Rubin, eds., The Development and Treatment of Childhood Aggression. Hillsdale, NJ: Lawrence Erlbaum.

Orwin, Robert, Diane Cadell, Adam Chu, Graham Kalton, David Maklan, Carol Morin, Andrea Piesse, Sanjeev Sridharan, Diane Steele, Kristie Taylor, and Elena Tracy

2004 Evaluation of the National Youth Anti-Drug Media Campaign: 2004 Report of Findings. Rockville, MD: Westat.

Osgood, D. Wayne, and Amy L. Anderson

2004 "Unstructured socializing and rates of delinquency." Criminology 42:519–550.

Osgood, D. Wayne, and Jeff M. Chambers

2000 "Social disorganization outside the metropolis: An analysis of rural youth violence." Criminology 38:81–116.

Osgood, D. Wayne, Patrick M. O'Malley, Jerald G. Bachman, and Lloyd D. Johnston

1989 "Time trends and age trends in arrests and self-reported illegal behavior." Criminology 27:389–417.

Osgood, D. Wayne, and Christopher J. Schreck

2007 "A new method for studying the extent, stability, and predictors of individual specialization in violence." Criminology 45:273–312.

Osgood, D. Wayne, Janet K. Wilson, Patrick M. O'Malley, Jerald G. Bachman, and Lloyd D. Johnston

1996 "Routine activities and individual deviant behavior." American Sociological Review 61:635–655.

Ousey, Graham C., and Michelle Campbell Augustine

2001 "Young guns: Examining alternative explanations of juvenile firearm homicide rates." Criminology 39:933–968.

Ousey, Graham C., and Matthew R. Lee

2004 "Investigating the connections between race, illicit drug markets, and lethal violence, 1984–1997." Journal of Research in Crime and Delinquency 41:352–383.

2007 "Homicide trends and illicit drug markets." Justice Quarterly 24:48–79.

Ousey, Graham C., and Pamela Wilcox

2007 "The interaction of antisocial propensity and life-course varying predictors of delinquent behavior." Criminology 45:313–354.

Padilla, Felix
1992 The Gang as an American Enterprise. New Brunswick, NJ: Rutgers University Press.

Palamara, Frances, Francis T. Cullen, and Joanne C. Gersten
1986 "The effect of police and mental health intervention on juvenile deviance: Specifying contingencies in the impact of formal evaluation." Journal of Health and Social Behavior 27:90–105.

Parent, Dale G.
2003 Correctional Boot Camps: Lessons from a Decade of Research. Washington, DC: Office of Justice Programs.

Parker, Karen F., Brian J. Stults, and Stephen K. Rice
2005 "Racial threat, concentrated disadvantage and social control." Criminology 43:1111–1134.

Paschall, Mallie J., Miriam L. Ornstein, and Robert L. Flewelling
2001 "African American male adolescents' involvement in the criminal justice system: The criterion validity of self-report measures in a prospective study." Journal of Research in Crime and Delinquency 38: 174–187.

Pastore, Ann L., and Kathleen Maguire
2003 Sourcebook of Criminal Justice Statistics. Available at http://www.albany.edu/sourcebook/.

Paternoster, Raymond
1987 "The deterrent effect of the perceived certainty and severity of punishment: A review of the evidence and issues." Justice Quarterly 4:173–217.

Paternoster, Raymond, and Ronet Bachman
2001 Explaining Criminals and Crime. Los Angeles: Roxbury.

Paternoster, Raymond, Robert Brame, Ronet Bachman, and Lawrence W. Sherman
1997 "Do fair procedures matter? The effect of procedural justice on spouse assault." Law and Society Review 57.163–204.

Paternoster, Raymond, Shawn Bushway, Robert Brame, and Robert Apel
2003 "The effect of teenage employment on delinquency and problem behaviors." Social Forces 82:297–335.

Paternoster, Raymond, and Leeann Iovanni
1989 "The labeling perspective and delinquency: An elaboration of the theory and an assessment of the evidence." Justice Quarterly 6:359–394.

Paternoster, Raymond, and Paul Mazerolle
1994 "General strain theory and delinquency: A replication and extension." Journal of Research in Crime and Delinquency 31:235–263.

Paternoster, Raymond, and Alex Piquero
1995 "Reconceptualizing deterrence: An empirical test of personal and vicarious experiences." Journal of Research in Crime and Delinquency 32:251–286.

Patterson, Gerald R.
1982 Coercive Family Process. Eugene, OR: Castalia.
1986 "Performance models for antisocial boys." American Psychologist 41:432–444.

Patterson, Gerald R., Barbara D. DeBaryshe, and Elizabeth Ramsey
1989 "A developmental perspective on antisocial behavior." American Psychologist 44:329–335.

Patterson, Gerald R., and Thomas J. Dishion
1985 "Contributions of families and peers to delinquency." Criminology 23:63–79.

Patterson, Gerald R., Marion S. Forgatch, Karen L. Yoerger, and Mike Stoolmiller
1998 "Variables that initiate and maintain an early-onset trajectory for juvenile offending." Development and Psychopathology 10:531–547.

Patterson, Gerald R., and M. Elizabeth Gullion
1977 Living with Children. Champaign, IL: Research Press Company.

Patterson, Gerald R., John B. Reid, and Thomas J. Dishion
1992 Antisocial Boys. Eugene, OR: Castalia.

Paulson, Amanda
2006 "New tack on teen justice: A push away from prisons." Christian Science Monitor, December 8, 2.

Payne, Allison Ann, Denise C. Gottfredson, and Gary D. Gottfredson
2003 "Schools as communities." Criminolgy 41:749–778.

Pearce, Lisa D., and Dana L. Haynie
2004 "Intergenerational religious dynamics and adolescent delinquency." Social Forces 82:1553–1572.

Pearson, Frank S., Douglas S. Lipton, Charles M. Cleland, and Dorline S. Lee
2002 "The effects of behavioral/cognitive-behavioral programs on recidivism." Crime and Delinquency 48:476–496.

Pearson, Frank S., and Neil Alan Weiner
1985 "Toward an integration of criminological theories." Journal of Criminal Law and Criminology 76: 116–150.

Peeples, Faith, and Rolf Loeber
1994 "Do individual factors and neighborhood context explain ethnic differences in juvenile delinquency?" Journal of Quantitative Criminology 10:141–157.

Pelfrey, Jr., William V.
2004 "The inchoate nature of community policing." Justice Quarterly 21:579–602.

Penn, Everette B.
2006 "Black youth: Disproportionality and delinquency." Pp. 47–64 in Everette B. Penn, Helen Taylor Greene, and Shaun L. Gabbidon, eds., Race and Juvenile Justice. Durham, NC: Carolina Academic Press.

Pepler, Debra J., and Ronald G. Slaby
1994 "Theoretical and developmental perspectives on youth and violence." Pp. 27–58 in Leonard D. Eron, Jacquelyn H. Gentry, and Peggy Schlegel, eds., Reason to Hope. Washington, DC: American Psychological Association.

Perkins, Craig A.
1997 Age Patterns of Victims of Serious Violent Crime. Washington, DC: Bureau of Justice Statistics.

Peters, Michael, David Thomas, Christopher Zamberlan, and Caliber Associates
1997 Boot Camps for Juvenile Offenders. Washington, DC: Office of Juvenile Justice and Delinquency Prevention.

Petersilia, Joan
1989 "The influence of research on policing." Pp. 230–247 in Roger G. Dunham and Geoffrey P. Alpert, eds., Critical Issues in Policing. Prospect Heights, IL.: Waveland Press.
1997 "Probation in the United States." Pp. 149–200 in Michael Tonry, ed., Crime and Justice: A Review of Research, Volume 22. Chicago: University of Chicago Press.

Peterson, Dana, Jody Miller, and Finn-Aage Esbensen
2001 "The impact of sex composition on gangs and gang member delinquency." Criminology 39:411–440.

Peterson, Dana, Terrance J. Taylor, and Finn-Aage Esbensen
2004 "Gang membership and violent victimization." Justice Quarterly 21:793–816.

Peterson, Ruth D., Lauren J. Krivo, and Mark A. Harris
2000 "Disadvantage and neighborhood violent crime: Do local institutions matter?" Journal of Research in Crime and Delinquency 37:31–63.

Petrosino, Anthony, Carolyn Turpin-Petrosino, and James O. Finkenauer
2000 "Well-meaning programs can have harmful effects! Lessons from experiments of programs such as Scared Straight." Crime and Delinquency 46:354–379.

Petrucci, Carrie J., and Albert R. Roberts
2004 "Principles and evidence on the effectiveness of family treatment." Pp. 339–364 in Albert R. Roberts ed., Juvenile Justice Sourcebook. New York: Oxford University Press.

Piliavin, Irving, and Scott Briar
1964 "Police encounters with juveniles." American Journal of Sociology 51:101–119.

Piquero, Alex
2000 "Frequency, specialization, and violence in offending careers." Journal of Research in Crime and Delinquency 37:392–418.

2008 "Measuring self-control." In Erich Goode, ed., Out of Control? Assessing the General Theory of Crime. Palo Alto, CA: Stanford University Press.

Piquero, Alex R., and Jeff A. Bouffard
2007 "Something old, something new: A preliminary investigation of Hirschi's redefined self-control." Justice Quarterly 24:1–27.

Piquero, Alex R., and Timothy Brezina
2001 "Testing Moffitt's account of adolescent-limited delinquency." Criminology 39:353–370.

Piquero, Alex R., Timothy Brezina, and Michael G. Turner
2005 "Testing Moffitt's theory of delinquency abstention." Journal of Research in Crime and Delinquency 42:27–54.

Piquero, Alex R., David P. Farrington, and Alfred Blumstein
2003 "The criminal career paradigm." Crime and Justice 30:359–506.

Piquero, Alex, and Paul Mazerolle
2001 Life-Course Criminology. Belmont, CA: Wadsworth.

Piquero, Alex, and Raymond Paternoster
1998 "An application of Stafford and Warr's reconceptualization of deterrence to drinking and driving." Journal of Research in Crime and Delinquency 35:3–39.

Piquero, Alex, Raymond Paternoster, Paul Mazerolle, Robert Brame, and Charles W. Dean
1999 "Onset age and offense specialization." Journal of Research in Crime and Delinquency 36:275–299.

Piquero, Alex R., and Greg Pogarsky
2002 "Beyond Stafford and Warr's reconceptualization of deterrence: Personal and vicarious experiences, impulsivity, and offending behavior." Journal of Research in Crime and Delinquency 39:153–186.

Piquero, Alex, and Stephen G. Tibbetts
1996 "Specifying the direct and indirect effects of low self-control and situational factors in an offender's decision making: Toward a more complete model of rational offending." Justice Quarterly 13:481–510.

Piquero, Alex R., Valerie West, Jeffrey Fagan, and Jan Holland
2006 "Neighborhood, race, and the economic consequences of incarceration in New York City, 1985–1996." Pp. 256–273 in Ruth D. Peterson, Lauren J. Krivo, and John Hagan, eds., The Many Colors of Crime. New York: New York University Press.

Piquero, Nicole Leeper, Angela R. Gover, John M. MacDonald, and Alex R. Piquero
2005 "The influence of delinquent peers on delinquency: Does gender matter?" Youth and Society 36:251–275.

Piquero, Nicole Leeper, and Miriam D. Sealock
2000 "Generalizing general strain theory: An examination of an offending population." Justice Quarterly 17:449–484.
2004 "Gender and general strain theory: A preliminary test of Broidy and Agnew's gender/gst hypotheses." Justice Quarterly 21:125–157.

Platt, Anthony M.
1969 The Child Savers. Chicago: University of Chicago Press.

Ploeger, Matthew
1997 "Youth unemployment and delinquency: Reconsidering a problematic relationship." Criminology 35:659–675.

Plomin, Robert, and Stephen A. Petrill
1997 "Genetics and intelligence: What's new?" Intelligence 24:53–77.

Plotnick, Robert D.
1997 "Child poverty can be reduced." Future of Children 7:72–87.

Poe-Yamagata, Eileen, and Jeffrey A. Butts
1996 Female Offenders in the Juvenile Justice System. Washington, DC: Office of Juvenile Justice and Delinquency Prevention.

Pogarsky, Greg, Alan J. Lizotte, and Terence P. Thornberry
2003 "The delinquency of children born to young mothers." Criminology 41:1249–1286.

Pogarsky, Greg, and Alex R. Piquero
2003 "Can punishment encourage offending? Investigating the 'resetting' effect." Journal of Research in Crime and Delinquency 40:95–120.

Pogarsky, Greg, Alex R. Piquero, and Ray Paternoster
2004 "Modeling change in perceptions about sanction threats." Journal of Quantitative Criminology 20: 343–369.

Polakowski, Michael
1994 "Linking self- and social control with deviance: Illuminating the structure underlying a general theory of crime and its relation to deviant activity." Journal of Quantitative Criminology 10:41–78.

Pope, Carl E., and William Feyerherm
1993 Minorities and the Juvenile Justice System. Washington, DC: Office of Juvenile Justice and Delinquency Prevention.

Pope, Carl E., and Michael J. Leiber
2005 "Disproportionate minority confinement/contact (DMC): The federal initiative. Pp. 351–389 in Darnell F. Hawkins and Kimberly Kempf-Leonard, eds., Our Children, Their Children. Chicago: University of Chicago Press.

Pope, Carl E., and Howard N. Snyder
2003 Race as a Factor in Juvenile Arrests. Washington, DC: Office of Juvenile Justice and Delinquency Prevention.

Pratt, Travis C., and Francis T. Cullen
2000 "The empirical status of Gottfredson and Hirschi's general theory of crime." Criminology 38:931–964.
2005 "Assessing macro-level predictors and theories of crime: A meta-analysis." Crime and Justice 32:373–450.

Pratt, Travis C., Francis T. Cullen, Kristoe R. Blevins, Leah Daigle, and Jame Unnever
2002 "The relationship of attention deficit hyperactivity disorder to crime and delinquency: A meta-analysis." International Journal of Police Science and Management 4:344–360.

Pratt, Travis C., Michael G. Turner, and Alex Piquero
2004 "Parental socialization and community context: A longitudinal analysis of the structural sources of low self-control." Journal of Research in Crime and Delinquency 41:219–243.

Press, Eyal
2006 "Do immigrants make us safer?" New York Times Magazine, December 3, 20, 22–24.

Pulkkinen, Lea
1986 "The role of impulse control in the development of antisocial and prosocial behavior." Pp. 149–175 in Dan Olweus, Jack Block, and Marian Radke-Yarrow, eds., Development of Antisocial and Prosocial Behavior. Orlando, FL: Academic Press.

Puzzanchera, Charles, Anne L. Stahl, Terrence A. Finnegan, Nancy Tierney, and Howard N. Snyder
2003 Juvenile Court Statistics 1999. Washington, DC: Office of Juvenile Justice and Delinquency Prevention.

Quay, Herbert C.
1983 "Psychological theories." Pp. 330–342 in Sanford H. Kadish, ed., Encyclopedia of Crime and Justice. New York: Free Press.

Quillian, Lincoln
1999 "Migration patterns and the growth of high-poverty neighborhoods." American Journal of Sociology 105:1–37.

Quillian, Lincoln, and Devah Pager
2001 "Black neighbors, higher crime? The role of racial stereotypes in evaluations of neighborhood crime." American Journal of Sociology 107:717–767.

Rafter, Nicole Hahn
1997 Creating Born Criminals. Urbana: University of Illinois Press.

Raine, Adrian
1993 The Psychopathology of Crime. San Diego, CA: Academic Press.
2002a "Biosocial studies of antisocial behavior in children and adults: A review." Journal of Abnormal Child Psychology 30:311–326.
2002b "The biological basis of crime." Pp. 43–74 in James Q. Wilson and Joan Petersilia, eds., Crime. Oakland, CA: ICS Press.

Raine, Adrian, Patricia A. Brennan, and David P. Farrington
1997 "Biosocial bases of violence." Pp. 1–20 in Adrian Raine, Patricia A. Brennan, David P. Farrington, and Sarnoff A. Mednick, eds., Biosocial Bases of Violence. New York: Plenum.

Raine, Adrian, Patricia A. Brennan, David P. Farrington, and Sarnoff A. Mednick
1997 Biosocial Bases of Violence. New York: Plenum.

Rainville, Gerald A., and Steven K. Smith
2003 Juvenile Felony Defendants in Criminal Courts: Survey of 40 Counties, 1998. Washington, DC: Bureau of Justice Statistics.

Ramey, Craig T., and Sharon Landesman Ramey
1995 "Successful early interventions for children at high risk for failure in school." Pp. 129–145 in George J. Demko and Michael C. Jackson, eds., Populations at Risk in America. Boulder, CO: Westview.

Rankin, Joseph H.
1983 "The family context of delinquency." Social Problems 30:466–479.

Rankin, Joseph H., and Roger Kern
1994 "Parental attachments and delinquency." Criminology 32:495–515.

Rankin, Joseph H., and L. Edward Wells
1987 "The preventive effects of the family on delinquency." Pp. 257–277 in Elmer H. Johnson, ed., Handbook on Crime and Delinquency Prevention. New York: Greenwood.
1990 "The effect of parental attachments and direct controls on delinquency." Journal of Research in Crime and Delinquency 27:140–165.
1994 "Social control, family structure, and delinquency." Pp. 97–116 in Greg Barak, ed., Varieties of Criminology. Westport, CT: Praeger.

Rashbaum, William K.
2003 "Crime data manipulated in precinct, officials say." New York Times, June 20, A23.

Rasmussen, Andrew
2004 "Teen court referral, sentencing, and subsequent recidivism." Crime and Delinquency 50:615–635.

Reaves, Brian A., and Matthew J. Hickman
2002a Census of State and Local Law Enforcement Agencies, 2000. Washington, DC: Bureau of Justice Statistics.
2002b Police Departments in Large Cities, 1990–2000. Washington, DC: Bureau of Justice Statistics.

Rebellon, Cesar
2002 "Reconsidering the broken homes/delinquency relationship and exploring its mediating mechanisms." Criminology 40:103–136.
2006 "Do adolescents engage in delinquency to attract the social attention of peers?" Journal of Research in Crime and Delinquency 43:387–411.

Rebellon, Cesar J., and Michelle Manasse
2004 "Do 'bad boys' really get the girls? Delinquency as a cause and consequence of dating behavior among adolescents." Justice Quarterly 21:355–389.

Rebellon, Cesar J., and Karen Van Gundy
2005 "Can control theory explain the link between parental physical abuse and delinquency?" Journal of Research in Crime and Delinquency 42:247–274.

Reckless, Walter C.
1961 "A new theory of crime and delinquency." Federal Probation 25:42–46.

Redding, Richard E., and James C. Howell
2000 "Blended sentencing in American juvenile courts." Pp. 145–179 in Jeffrey Fagan and Franklin E. Zimring, eds., The Changing Borders of Juvenile Justice. Chicago: University of Chicago Press.

Reed, Mark D., and Pamela Wilcox Rountree
1997 "Peer pressure and adolescent substance use." Journal of Quantitative Criminology 13:143–180.

Regnerus, Mark
2003 "Moral communities and adolescent delinquency." Sociological Quarterly 44:523–554.

Regnerus, Mark D., and Glen H. Elder
2003 "Religion and vulnerability among low-risk adolescents." Social Science Research 32:633–658.

Regnerus, Mark D., and Christian Smith
2005 "Selection effects in studies of religious influence." Review of Religious Research 47:23–50.

Reiman, Jeffrey
1995 The Rich Get Richer and the Poor Get Prison. Boston: Allyn and Bacon.

Reiss, Albert J., Jr.
1951 "Delinquency as the failure of personal and social controls." American Sociological Review 16:196–207.
1988 "Co-offending and criminal careers." Pp. 117–170 in Michael Tonry and Norval Morris, eds., Crime and Justice: A Review of Research, Volume 10. Chicago: University of Chicago Press.

Reiss, Albert J., Jr., and Jeffrey A. Roth
1993 Understanding and Preventing Violence. Washington, DC: National Academy Press.

Rennison, Callie Marie
2001 Violent Victimization and Race, 1993–98. Washington, DC: Office of Justice Programs.

Rennison, Callie Marie, and Michael R. Rand
2003 Criminal Victimization, 2002. Washington, DC: Bureau of Justice Statistics.

Rhee, Soo Hyun, and Irwin Waldman
2002 "Genetic and environmental influences on anti-social behavior." Psychological Bulletin 128:490–529.

Riedel, Marc
2003 "Homicide in Los Angeles County: A study of Latino victimization." Pp. 44–66 in Darnell F. Hawkins, ed., Violent Crime: Assessing Race and Ethnic Differences. Cambridge, England: Cambridge University Press.

Riley, David
1987 "Time and crime: The link between teenage lifestyle and delinquency." Journal of Quantitative Criminology 3:339–354.

Rivera, Ray
2007 "In a Mexican town lies a key, Bloomberg hopes, to reducing poverty in New York." New York Times, April 25, A28.

Roberts, Albert R.
1998 Juvenile Justice. Chicago: Nelson-Hall.
2004 Juvenile Justice Sourcebook. New York: Oxford University Press.

Roberts, Julian
2004 "Public opinion and youth justice." Crime and Justice 31:495–542.

Roberts, Julian V., and Loretta J. Stalans
1997 Public Opinion, Crime, and Criminal Justice. Boulder, CO: Westview.
1998 "Crime, criminal justice, and public opinion." Pp. 31–57 in Michael Tonry, ed., The Handbook of Crime and Punishment. New York: Oxford University Press.

Robinson, Laurie
1996 "Linking community-based initiatives and community justice: The office of justice programs." National Institute of Justice Journal 231(August):4–7.

Robinson, Matthew B.
2004 Why Crime? Upper Saddle River, NJ: Pearson/Prentice-Hall.

Robinson, Matthew B., and Barbara H. Zaitzow
1999 "Criminologists: Are we what we study? A national self-report study of crime experts." Criminologist 24(2):1, 4, 17.

Rodgers, Joseph Lee, Maurt Buster, and David C. Rowe
2001 "Genetic and environmental influences on delinquency: DF Analysis of NLSY kinship data." Journal of Quantitative Criminology 17:145–168.

Rodriquez, Nancy
2007 "Restorative justice at work." Crime and Delinquency 53:355–379.

Rodriquez, Nancy, and Vincent J. Webb
2004 "Multiple measures of juvenile drug court effectiveness." Crime and Delinquency 50:292–314.

Rogers, Joseph W., and M. D. Buffalo
1974 "Fighting back: Nine modes of adaptation to a deviant label." Social Problems 22:101–118.

Rosen, Lawrence
1985 "Family and delinquency: Structure or function?" Criminology 23:553–573.

Rosenfeld, Richard
2000 "Patterns in adult homicide: 1980–1995." Pp. 130–163 in Alfred Blumstein and Joel Wallman, eds., The Crime Drop in America. Cambridge, England: Cambridge University Press.

Rosenfeld, Richard, Timothy M. Bray, and Arlen Egley
1999 "Facilitating violence: A comparison of gang-motivated, gang-affiliated, and nongang youth homicides." Journal of Quantitative Criminology 15:495–516.

Rosenfeld, Richard, Robert Fornango, and Andres F. Rengifo
2007 "The impact of order-maintenance policing on New York City homicide and robbery rates: 1988–2001." Criminology 45:355–384.

Rosenfeld, Richard, Steven F. Messner, and Eric P. Baumer
2001 "Social capital and homicide." Social Forces 80:283–309.

Rosenheim, Margaret K., Frankin E. Zimring, David S. Tanenhaus, and Bernardine Dohrn
2002 A Century of Juvenile Justice. Chicago: University of Chicago Press.

Rountree, Pamela Wilcox, and Barbara D. Warner
1999 "Social ties and crime: Is the relationship gendered?" Criminology 37:789–814.

Rowe, Alan R., and Charles R. Tittle
1977 "Life cycle changes and criminal propensity." Sociological Quarterly 18:223–236.

Rowe, David C.
1995 "Sex differences in crime: Do means and within-sex variation have similar causes?" Journal of Research in Crime and Delinquency 32:84–100.
1996 "An adaptive strategy theory of crime and delinquency." Pp. 268–314 in J. David Hawkins, ed., Delinquency and Crime. New York: Cambridge University Press.
2002 Biology and Crime. Los Angeles: Roxbury.

Rowe, David C., and David P. Farrington
1997 "The familial transmission of criminal convictions." Criminology 35:177–201.

Rowe, David C., and Bill L. Gulley
1992 "Sibling effects on substance use and delinquency." Criminology 30:217–233.

Rowe, David C., Alexander T. Vazsonyi, and Daniel J. Flannery
1995 "Sex differences in crime: Do means and within sex variation have similar causes?" Journal of Research in Crime and Delinquency 32:84–100.

Rubin, H. Ted
1998 "The juvenile court landscape." Pp. 205–230 in Albert R. Roberts, ed., Juvenile Justice. Chicago: Nelson-Hall.

Rusby, Julie C., Kathleen K. Forrester, Anthony Biglan, and Carol W. Metzler
2005 "Relationships between peer harassment and adolescent problem behaviors." Journal of Early Adolescence 25:453–477.

Rutter, Michael
1985 "Family and school influences on behavioural development." Journal of Child Psychology and Psychiatry 26:349–368.
1997 "Nature-Nurture Integration." American Psychologist 52:390–398.

Rutter, Michael, and Henri Giller
1983 Juvenile Delinquency. New York: Guilford Press.

Rutter, Michael, Henri Giller, and Ann Hagell
1998 Antisocial Behavior by Young People. Cambridge, England: Cambridge University Press.

Rutter, Michael, Barbara Maughan, Peter Mortimore, Janet Ouston, and Alan Smith
1979 Fifteen Thousand Hours. Cambridge, MA: Harvard University Press.

Rutter, Michael, Terrie D. Moffitt, and Avshalom Caspi
2006 "Gene-environment interplay and psychopathology." Journal of Child Psychology and Psychiatry 47: 226–261.

Rutter, Michael, and Judy Silberg
2002 "Gene-environment interplay in relation to emotional and behavioral disturbance." Annual Review of Psychology 53:463–490.

Salerno, Anthony W.
1991 "The child saver movement: Altruism or a conspiracy?" Juvenile and Family Court Journal 42: 37–49.

Samples, Faith, and Larry Aber
1998 "Evaluations of school-based violence prevention programs." Pp. 217–252 in Delbert S. Elliott, Beatrix A. Hamburg, and Kirk R. Williams, eds., Violence in American Schools. Cambridge, England: Cambridge University Press.

Sampson, Robert J.
1985 "Neighborhood and crime: The structural determinants of personal victimization." Journal of Research in Crime and Delinquency 22:7–40.
1986a "Neighborhood family structure and the risk of personal victimization." Pp. 25–46 in James M. Byrne and Robert J. Sampson, eds., The Social Ecology of Crime. New York: Springer-Verlag.
1986b "Effects of socioeconomic context on official reaction to juvenile delinquency." American Sociological Review 51:876–885.
1987 "Urban black violence: The effect of male joblessness and family disruption." American Journal of Sociology 93:348–382.
1997 "The embeddedness of child and adolescent development: A community-level perspective on urban violence." Pp. 31–77 in Joan McCord, ed., Violence and Childhood in the Inner City. Cambridge, England: Cambridge University Press.
2002 "The Community." Pp. 225–252 in James Q. Wilson and Joan Petersilia, eds., Crime. Oakland, CA: ICS Press.
2006 "Collective efficacy theory: Lessons learned and directions for future inquiry." Pp. 149–168 in Francis T. Cullen, John Paul Wright, and Kristie R. Blevins, eds., Taking Stock: The Status of Criminological Theory. New Brunswick, NJ: Transaction.

Sampson, Robert J., and Dawn Jeglum Bartusch
1999 Attitudes Toward Crime, Police, and the Law: Individual and Neighborhood Differences. Washington, DC: National Institute of Justice.

Sampson, Robert J., and Lydia Bean
2006 "Cultural mechanisms and killing fields: A revised theory of community-level racial inequality." Pp. 8–38 in Ruth D. Peterson, Lauren J. Krivo, and John Hagan, eds., The Many Colors of Crime. New York: New York University Press.

Sampson, Robert J., and W. Byron Groves
1989 "Community structure and crime: Testing social-disorganization theory." American Journal of Sociology 94:774–802.

Sampson, Robert J., and John H. Laub
1993a Crime in the Making. Cambridge, MA: Harvard University Press.
1993b "Structural variations in juvenile court processing: Inequality, the underclass, and social control." Law and Society Review 27:285–311.
1997 "A life-course theory of cumulative disadvantage and the stability of delinquency." Pp. 133–161 in Terence P. Thornberry, ed., Developmental Theories of Crime and Delinquency, Advances in Criminological Theory, Volume 7. New Brunswick, NJ: Transaction.

Sampson, Robert J., and Janet L. Lauritsen

1993 "Violent victimization and offending: Individual-, situational-, and community-level risk factors." Pp. 1–114 in National Research Council, ed., Understanding and Preventing Violence, Volume 3, Social Influences. Washington, DC: National Research Council.

1997 "Racial and ethnic disparities in crime and criminal justice in the United States." Crime and Justice 21:311–374.

Sampson, Robert J., Jeffrey D. Morenoff, and Stephen Raudenbush

2005 "Social anatomy of racial and ethnic disparities in violence." American Journal of Public Health 95: 224–232.

Sampson, Robert J., and Stephen W. Raudenbush

1999 "Systematic social observation of public spaces: A new look at disorder in urban neighborhoods." American Journal of Sociology 105:603–651.

Sampson, Robert J., Stephen W. Raudenbush, and Felton Earls

1997 "Neighborhoods and violent crime: A multilevel study of collective efficacy." Science 277:918–924.

Sampson, Robert J., and William Julius Wilson

1995 "Toward a theory of race, crime and urban inequality." Pp. 37–54 in John Hagan and Ruth Peterson, eds., Crime and Inequality. Stanford, CA: Stanford University Press.

Sampson, Robert J., and John D. Wooldredge

1987 "Linking the micro- and macro-level dimensions of lifestyle-routine activity and opportunity models of predatory victimization." Journal of Quantitative Criminology 3:371–393.

Saum, Christine A.

1998 "Rohypnol: The date-rape drug?" Pp. 254–261 in James A. Inciardi and Karen McElrath, eds., The American Drug Scene. Los Angeles: Roxbury.

Sawhill, Isabel V.

2003 One Percent for the Kids. Washington, DC: Brookings Institution Press.

Schemo, Jean

2003 "Plan to shift Head Start to states' control worries supporters." New York Times, February 12, A24.

Schlossman, Steven

1977 Love and the American Delinquent. Chicago: University of Chicago Press.

Schneider, Anne L.

1990 Deterrence and Juvenile Crime. New York: Springer-Verlag.

Schroeder, Ryan D., Peggy C. Giordano, and Stephen A. Cernkovich

2007 "Drug use and desistance process." Criminology 45:191–222.

Schur, Edwin M.

1973 Radical Nonintervention: Rethinking the Delinquency Problem. Englewood Cliffs, NJ: Prentice-Hall.

Scott, Elizabeth S.

2002 "The legal construction of childhood." Pp. 113–141 in Margaret K. Rosenheim, Frankin E. Zimring, David S. Tanenhaus, and Bernardine Dohrn, eds., A Century of Juvenile Justice. Chicago: University of Chicago Press.

Scott, Michael S.

2003 The Benefits and Consequences of Police Crackdowns. Washington, DC: Office of Community Oriented Policing Services.

Sealock, Miriam, and Sally S. Simpson

1998 "Unraveling bias in arrest decisions: The role of juvenile offender type-scripts." Justice Quarterly 15: 427–457.

Sechrest, Lee, and Abram Rosenblatt

1987 "Research methods." Pp. 417–450 in Herbert C. Quay, ed., Handbook of Juvenile Delinquency. New York: Wiley.

Sellers, Christine S.

1999 "Self-control and intimate violence: An examination of the scope and specification of the general theory of crime." Criminology 37:375–404.

Sellers, Christine S., John K. Cochran, and L. Thomas Winfree, Jr.
2003 "Social learning theory and courtship violence: An empirical test." Pp. 109–127 in Ronald L. Akers and Gary F. Jensen, eds., Social Learning Theory and the Explanation of Crime, Advances in Criminological Theory, Volume 11. New Brunswick, NJ: Transaction.

Shaffer, Jennifer N., and R. Barry Ruback
2002 Violent Victimization as a Risk Factor for Violent Offending Among Juveniles. Washington, DC: Office of Juvenile Justice and Delinquency Prevention.

Sharp, Susan F., Meghan K. McGhee, Trina L. Hope, and Randall Coyne
2007 "Predictors of support of legislation banning juvenile executions in Oklahoma: An examination of race and sex." Justice Quarterly 24:133–155.

Shaw, Clifford R., and Henry D. McKay
1942 Juvenile Delinquency and Urban Areas. Chicago: University of Chicago Press.

Shelden, Randall G., and Lynn T. Osborne
1989 " 'For their own good': Class interests and the child saving movement in Memphis, Tennessee, 1900–1917." Criminology 27:747–767.

Shelden, Randall G., Sharon K. Tracy, and William B. Brown
2001 Youth Gangs in American Society. Belmont, CA: Wadsworth.

Sheley, Joseph F.
1983 "Critical elements of criminal behavior explanations." Sociological Quarterly 24:509–525.

Sheley, Joseph F., and James D. Wright
1995 In the Line of Fire. New York: Aldine De Gruyter.
1998 High School Youths, Weapons, and Violence: A National Survey. Washington, DC: National Institute of Justice.

Sherman, Lawrence W.
1990 "Police crackdowns." National Institute of Justice Reports 219:2–6.
1993 "Defiance, deterrence, and irrelevance: A theory of the criminal sanction." Journal of Research in Crime and Delinquency 30:445–473.
1995 "The police." Pp. 327–348 in James Q. Wilson and Joan Petersilia, eds., Crime. Oakland, CA: ICS Press.
1998 "American policing." Pp. 429–456 in Michael Tonry, ed., The Handbook of Crime and Punishment. New York: Oxford University Press.
2000 The Defiant Imagination. The Albert M. Greenfield Chair Inaugural Lecture, University of Pennsylvania.
2001 "Reducing gun violence: What works, what doesn't, what's promising." Criminal Justice 1:11–25.
2002 "Fair and effective policing." Pp. 383–412 in James Q. Wilson and Joan Petersilia, eds., Crime. Oakland, CA: ICS Press.

Sherman, Lawrence W., and John E. Eck
2002 "Policing for crime prevention." Pp. 295–329 in Lawrence W. Sherman, David P. Farrington, Brandon C. Welsh, and Doris Layton MacKenzie, eds., Evidence-Based Crime Prevention. London: Routledge.

Sherman, Lawrence W., David P. Farrington, Brandon C. Welsh, and Doris Layton MacKenzie
2002 Evidence-Based Crime Prevention. London: Routledge.

Sherman, Lawrence W., Patrick R. Gartin, and Michael E. Buerger
1989 "Hot spots of predatory crime: Routine activities and the criminology of place." Criminology 27:27–55.

Sherman, Lawrence W., Denise Gottfredson, Doris MacKenzie, John Eck, Peter Reuter, and Shawn Bushway
1998 Preventing Crime: What Works, What Doesn't, What's Promising. Available at http://www.preventingcrime.org/.

Sherman, Lawrence W., Douglas A. Smith, Janell D. Schmidt, and Dennis P. Rogan
1992 "Crime, punishment, and stake in conformity: Legal and informal control of domestic violence." American Sociological Review 57:680–690.

Sherman, Lawrence W., and David Weisburd

1995 "General deterrent effects of police patrol in crime 'hot spots': A randomized, controlled trial." Justice Quarterly 12:625–648.

Sherry, John L.

2001 "The effects of violent video games on aggression: A meta-analysis." Human Communication Research 27:409–431.

2007 "Violent video games and aggression." Pp. 245–262 in Raymond W. Preiss, Barbara Mae Gayle, Nancy Burrell, Mike Allen, and Jennings Bryant, eds., Mass Media Effects Research. Mahwah, NJ: Lawrence Erlbaum.

Shihadeh, Edward S., and Darrell J. Steffensmeier

1994 "Economic inequality, family disruption, and urban black violence: Cities as units of stratification and social control." Social Forces 73:729–751.

Shoemaker, Donald J.

2004 Theories of Delinquency. New York: Oxford University Press.

Short, James F., Jr.

1997 Poverty, Ethnicity, and Violent Crime. Boulder, CO: Westview.

Short, James F., Jr., and F. Ivan Nye

1958 "Extent of unrecorded juvenile delinquency: Tentative conclusions." Journal of Criminal Law, Criminology, and Police Science 49:296–302.

Short, James F., Jr., and Fred L. Strodtbeck

1965 Group Process and Gang Delinquency. Chicago: University of Chicago Press.

Short, Jessica, and Christy Sharp

2005 Disproportionate Minority Contact in the Juvenile Justice System. Washington, DC: Child Welfare League of America.

Shover, Neal

1996 Great Pretenders: Pursuits and Careers of Persistent Thieves. Boulder, CO: Westview.

Sickmund, Melissa

2006 Juvenile Residential Facility Census, 2002: Selected Findings. Washington, DC: Office of Juvenile Justice and Delinquency Prevention.

Sickmund, Melissa, Howard N. Snyder, and Eileen Poe-Yamagata

1997 Juvenile Offenders and Victims: 1997 Update on Violence. Washington, DC: National Center for Juvenile Justice.

Sickmund, Melissa, and Yi-chun Wan

2001 Census of Juveniles in Residential Placement Databook. Available at http://www.ojjdp.ncjrs.org/ojstatbb/cjrp.

Siegel, Jane A., and Linda M. Williams

2002 "The relationship between child sexual abuse and female delinquency and crime: A prospective study." Journal of Research in Crime and Delinquency 40:71–94.

Siegel, Larry J., Brandon C. Welsh, and Joseph J. Senna

2003 Juvenile Delinquency. Belmont, CA: Wadsworth.

Silver, Eric, and Lisa L. Miller

2004 "Sources of informal social control in Chicago neighborhoods." Criminology 42:551–583.

Simons, Ronald L., Jay Beaman, Rand D. Conger, and Wei Chao

1993 "Stress, support, and antisocial behavior trait as determinants of emotional well-being and parenting practices among single mothers." Journal of Marriage and the Family 55:385–398.

Simons, Ronald L., Yi-Fu Chen, Eric A. Stewart, and Gene H. Brody

2003 "Incidents of discrimination and risk for delinquency: A longitudinal test of strain theory with an African American sample." Justice Quarterly 20:827–854.

Simons, Ronald L., Joanne Christine, Jay Beaman, Rand D. Conger, and Les B. Whitbeck

1996 "Parents and peers as mediators of the effect of community structure on adolescent problem behavior." American Journal of Community Psychology 24:145–171.

Simons, Ronald L., Christine Johnson, Rand D. Conger, and Glen Elder, Jr.
1998 "A test of latent trait versus life-course perspectives on the stability of adolescent antisocial behavior." Criminology 36:217–244.

Simons, Ronald L., Martin G. Miller, and Stephen M. Aigner
1980 "Contemporary theories of deviance and female delinquency: An empirical test." Journal of Research in Crime and Delinquency 17:42–53.

Simons, Ronald L., Leslie Gordon Simons, Callie Harbin Burt, Gene H. Brody, and Carolyn Cutrona
2005 "Collective efficacy, authoritative parenting, and delinquency." Criminology 43:989–1030.

Simons, Ronald L., Leslie Gordon Simons, and Lora Ebert Wallace
2007 Families, Delinquency, and Crime. New York: Oxford University Press.

Simons, Ronald L., Eric Stewart, Leslie C. Gordon, Rand D. Conger, and Glen H. Elder, Jr.
2002 "A test of life-course explanations for stability and change in antisocial behavior from adolescence to young adulthood." Criminology 40:401–434.

Simons, Ronald L., Chyi-In Wu, Rand D. Conger, and Frederick O. Lorenz
1994 "Two routes to delinquency: Differences between early and late starters in the impact of parenting and deviant peers." Criminology 32: 247–276.

Singer, Simon I.
2001 "Juvenile court and its systems of juvenile justice." Pp. 349–366 in Susan O. White, ed., Handbook of Youth and Justice. New York: Kluwer.

Singer, Simon I., Murray Levine, and Susan Jou
1993 "Heavy metal music preference, delinquent friends, social control, and delinquency." Journal of Research in Crime and Delinquency 30:317–329.

Singer, Simon I., and David McDowall
1988 "Criminalizing delinquency: The deterrent effects of the New York juvenile offender law." Law and Society Review 22:521–535.

Skogan, Wesley
2004 Community Policing: Can It Work? Belmont, CA: Wadsworth.

Skogan, Wesley, and Kathleen Frydl
2004 Fairness and Effectiveness in Policing. Washington, DC: National Academies Press.

Skogan, Wesley G., Lynn Steiner, Jill DuBois, J. Erik Gudell, and Aimee Fagan
2002 Taking Stock: Community Policing in Chicago. Washington, DC: Office of Justice Programs.

Slaby, Ronald G., and Nancy G. Guerra
1988 "Cognitive mediators of aggression in adolescent offenders: 1. Assessment." Developmental Psychology 24:580–588.

Smith, Bradford
1998 "Children in custody: 20-year trends in juvenile detention, correctional, and shelter facilities." Crime and Delinquency 44:526–543.

Smith, Carolyn, and Marvin D. Krohn
1995 "Delinquency and family life among male adolescents: The role of ethnicity." Journal of Youth and Adolescence 24:69–93.

Smith, Carolyn, and Terence P. Thornberry
1995 "The relationship between childhood maltreatment and adolescent involvement in delinquency." Criminology 33:451–481.

Smith, David A.
1984 "The organizational context of legal control." Criminology 22:19–38.

Smith, David J.
2002 "Crime and the life course." Pp. 702–745 in Mike Maquire, Rod Morgan, and Robert Reiner, eds., The Oxford Handbook of Criminology, 3rd edition. Oxford: Oxford University Press.

Smith, Douglas A., and Robert Brame
1994 "On the initiation and continuation of delinquency." Criminology 32:607–629.

Smith, Douglas A., and Raymond Paternoster
1987 "The gender gap in theories of deviance: Issues and evidence." Journal of Research in Crime and Delinquency 24:140–172.

Smith, Michael R.
2001 "Police-led crackdowns and cleanups: An evaluation of a crime control initiative in Richmond, Virginia." Crime and Delinquency 47:60–83.

Smokowski, Paul R., and Kelly Holland Kopasz
"Bullying in school." Children and Schools 27:101–110.

Snyder, Howard N.
1999 "The overrepresentation of juvenile crime proportions in robbery clearance statistics." Journal of Quantitative Criminology 15:151–161.
2003 Juvenile Arrests 2001. Washington, DC: Office of Juvenile Justice and Delinquency Prevention.

Snyder, Howard N., and Melissa Sickmund
1995 Juvenile Offenders and Victims: A National Report. Pittsburgh, PA.: National Center for Juvenile Justice.
1999 Juvenile Offenders and Victims: 1999 National Report. Pittsburgh, PA.: National Center for Juvenile Justice.
2006 Juvenile Offenders and Victims: 2006 National Report. Pittsburgh, PA: National Center for Juvenile Justice.

Snyder, Howard N., Melissa Sickmund, and Eileen Poe-Yamagata
2000 Juvenile Transfers to Criminal Court in the 1990s: Lessons Learned from Four Studies. Washington, DC: Office of Juvenile Justice and Delinquency Prevention.

Snyder, James, and Gerald R. Patterson
1987 "Family interaction and delinquent behavior." Pp. 216–243 in Herberet C. Quay, ed., Handbook of Juvenile Delinquency. New York: Wiley.

Snyder, H., C. Puzzanchera, and B. Adams
2007 National Disproportionate Minority Contact Databook. Washington, DC: Office of Juvenile Justice and Delinquency Prevention.

Spano, Richard, Craig Rivera, and John Bolland
2006 "The impact of timing of exposure to violence on violent behavior in a high poverty sample of inner city African American youth." Journal of Youth and Adolescence 35:681–692.

Spelman, William
2000 "The limited importance of prison expansion." Pp. 97–129 in Alfred Blumstein and Joel Wallman, eds., The Crime Drop in America. Cambridge, England: Cambridge University Press.

Spelman, William, and John E. Eck
1987 Newport News Tests Problem-Oriented Policing. Washington, DC: National Institute of Justice.

Spergel, Irving A.
1995 The Youth Gang Problem. New York: Oxford University Press.

Stafford, Leon
1999 "Lawyers: Teen shooter needs psychiatric hospital." Atlanta Constitution, August 10, C1, 6.

Stahl, Anne L.
2000 Offenders in Juvenile Court, 1997. Washington, DC: Office of Juvenile Justice and Delinquency Prevention.

Stahl, Anne L., Charles Puzzanchera, Anthony Sladky, Terrence A. Finnegan, Nancy Tierney, and Howard N. Snyder
2007 Juvenile Court Statistics 2003 2004. Washington, DC: National Center for Juvenile Justice.

Starbuck, David, James C. Howell, and Donna J. Lindquist
2004 "Hybrid and other modern gangs." Pp. 200–217 in Finn-Aage Esbensen, Stephen G. Tibbitts, and Larry Gaines, eds., American Youth Gangs at the Millennium. Long Grove, IL: Waveland Press.

Stark, Rodney, and William Sims Bainbridge
1996 Religion, Deviance, and Social Control. New York: Routledge.

Steffensmeier, Darrell
1993 "National trends in female arrests, 1969–1990: Assessment and recommendations for research." Journal of Quantitative Criminology 9:411–441.

Steffensmeier, Darrell, and Emilie Allan
1995 "Age-inequality and property crime: The effects of age-linked stratification and status attainment processes on patterns of criminality across the life course." Pp. 95–115 in John Hagan and Ruth D. Peterson, eds., Crime and Inequality. Stanford, CA: Stanford University Press.
1996 "Gender and crime: Toward a gendered theory of female offending." Annual Review of Sociology 22: 459–487.
2000 "Looking for patterns: Gender, age, and crime." Pp. 85–127 in Joseph F. Sheley, ed., Criminology. Belmont, CA: Wadsworth.

Steffensmeier, Darrell, Emilie Allan, Miles Harer, and Cathy Streifel
1989 "Age and the distribution of crime." American Journal of Sociology 94:803–831.

Steffensmeier, Darrell, and Miles D. Harer
1999 "Making sense of recent U.S. crime trends, 1980 to 1996/1998: Age composition effects and other explanations." Journal of Research in Crime and Delinquency 36:235–274.

Steffensmeier, Darrell, Jennifer Schwartz, Hua Zhong, and Jeff Ackerman
2005 "An assessment of recent trends in girls' violence using diverse longitudinal sources: Is the gender gap closing?" Criminology 43:355–406.

Steffensmeier, Darrell, Jeffrey Ulmer, and John Kramer
1998 "The interaction of race, gender, and age in criminal sentencing: The punishment cost of being young, black, and male." Criminology 36:763–798.

Steinberg, Laurence
1996 Beyond the Classroom. New York: Simon and Schuster.

Steinberg, Laurence, and Elizabeth Cauffman
2000 "A developmental perspective on jurisdictional boundary." Pp. 379–406 in Jeffrey Fagan and Franklin E. Zimring, eds., The Changing Borders of Juvenile Justice. Chicago: University of Chicago Press.

Steiner, Benjamin, Craig Hemmens, and Valerie Bell
2006 "Legislative waiver reconsidered." Justice Quarterly 23:34–59.

Steiner, Benjamin, Elizabeth Roberts, and Craig Hemmens
2006 "Where is juvenile probation today?" Criminal Justice Studies 16:217–281.

Steiner, Benjamin, and Emily Wright
2006 "Assessing the relative effects of state direct file laws on violent juvenile crime." Journal of Criminal Law and Criminology 96:1451–1478.

Stemen, Don
2007 Reconsidering Incarceration. New York: Vera Institute of Justice.

Stewart, Eric A.
2003 "School social bonds, school climate, and school misbehavior: A multilevel analysis." Justice Quarterly 20:575–604.

Stewart, Eric A., and Ronald L. Simons
2006 "Structure and culture in African American adolescent violence: A partial test of the 'code of the streets' thesis." Justice Quarterly 23:1–33.

Stewart, Eric A., Ronald L. Simons, and Rand D. Conger
2000 "The effects of delinquency and legal sanctions on parenting behaviors." Pp. 257–279 in Greer Litton Fox and Michael L. Benson, eds., Families, Crime, and Criminal Justice. New York: JAI.
2002 "Assessing neighborhood and social psychological influences on childhood violence in an African-American sample." Criminology 40:801–830.

Stewart, Eric A., Ronald L. Simons, Rand D. Conger, and Laura V. Scaramella
2002 "Beyond the interactional relationship between delinquency and parenting practices: The contribution of legal sanctions." Journal of Research in Crime and Delinquency 39:36–59.

Stolzenberg, Lisa, and Stewart J. D'Alessio
2000 "Gun availability and violent crime: New evidence from the national incident-based reporting system." Social Forces 78:1461–1482.

Stone, Sandra
1998 "Should the juvenile justice system get tougher on juvenile offenders?" Pp. 199–295 in John R. Fuller and Eric W. Hickey, eds., Controversial Issues in Criminology. Boston: Allyn and Bacon.

Stormshak, Elizabeth A., Colleen A. Comeau, and Stephanie A. Shepard
2004 "The relative contribution of sibling deviance and peer deviance in the prediction of substance use across middle childhood." Journal of Abnormal Child Psychology 32:635–647.

Stoutland, Sara E.
2001 "The multiple dimensions of trust in resident/police relations in Boston." Journal of Research in Crime and Delinquency 38:226–256.

Straus, Murray
1994 Beating the Devil Out of Them. New York: Lexington.

Stretesky, Paul B., Arnie M. Schuck, and Michael J. Hogan
2004 "Space matters: An analysis of poverty, poverty clustering, and violent crime." Justice Quarterly 21: 817–841.

Strom, Kevin J.
2000 Profile of State Prisoners Under Age 18, 1985–1997. Washington, DC: Bureau of Justice Statistics.

Strom, Kevin J., and Steven K. Smith
1998 Juvenile Felony Defendants in Criminal Courts. Washington, DC: Bureau of Justice Statistics.

Sullivan, Christopher J., Jean Marie McGloin, Travis C. Pratt, and Alex R. Piquero
2006 "Rethinking the 'norm' of offender generality: Investigating specialization in the short term." Criminology 44:199–234.

Sullivan, Mercer L.
1989 Getting Paid. Ithaca, NY: Cornell University Press.

Sutherland, Edwin H., Donald R. Cressey, and David F. Luckenbill
1992 Principles of Criminology. Dix Hills, NY: General Hall.

Sutton, John R.
1988 Stubborn Children: Controlling Delinquency in the United States. Berkeley: University of California Press.

Sweeten, Gary
2006 "Who will graduate? Disruption of high school education by arrest and court involvement." Justice Quarterly 23:462–480.

Sykes, Gresham M., and David Matza
1957 "Techniques of neutralization: A theory of delinquency." American Sociological Review 22:664–670.

Tannenbaum, Frank
1938 Crime and the Community. New York: Columbia University Press.

Tark, Jongyeon, and Gary Kleck
2004 "Resisting crime: The effects of victim action on the outcomes of crimes." Criminology 42:861–909.

Turver, Marsha, Steve Walker, and Harvey Wallace
2002 Multicultural Issues in the Criminal Justice System. Boston: Allyn and Bacon.

Taylor, E. A.
1986 "Childhood hyperactivity." British Journal of Psychiatry 149:562–573.

Taylor, Ralph B.
2001a "The ecology of crime, fear, and delinquency." Pp. 124–139 in Raymond Paternoster and Ronet Bachman, eds., Explaining Criminals and Crime. Los Angeles: Roxbury.
2001b Breaking Away from Broken Windows: Baltimore Neighborhoods and the Nationwide Fight Against Crime, Grime, Fear, and Decline. Boulder, CO: Westview.

Tedeschi, James T. and Richard B. Felson
1994 Violence, Aggression, and Coercive Actions. Washington DC: American Psychological Association.

Thaxton, Sherod, and Robert Agnew
2004 "The nonlinear effects of parental control and teacher attachment on delinquency." Justice Quarterly 21:763–792.

Thornberry, Terence P.
1987 "Toward an interactional theory of delinquency." Criminology 25:863–891.
1996 "Empirical support for interactional theory: A review of the literature." Pp. 198–235 in J. David Hawkins, ed., Delinquency and Crime. Cambridge, England: Cambridge University Press.
1997 Developmental Theories of Crime and Delinquency: Advances in Criminological Theory, Volume 7. New Brunswick, NJ: Transaction.
1998 "Membership in youth gangs and involvement in serious and violent offending." Pp. 147–166 in Rolf Loeber and David P. Farrington, eds., Serious and Violent Juvenile Offenders. Thousand Oaks, CA: Sage.

Thornberry, Terence P., and James H. Burch II
1997 Gang Members and Delinquent Behavior. Washington, DC: Office of Juvenile Justice and Delinquency Prevention.

Thornberry, Terence P., and Margaret Farnworth
1982 "Social correlates of criminal involvement: Further evidence on the relationship between social status and criminal behavior." American Sociological Review 47:505–517.

Thornberry, Terence P., Adrienne Freeman-Gallant, Alan J. Lizotte, Marvin D. Krohn, and Carolyn A. Smith
2003c "Linked-lives: The intergenerational transmission of antisocial behavior." Journal of Abnormal Child Psychology 31:171–184.

Thornberry, Terence P., David Huizinga, and Rolf Loeber
1995 "The prevention of serious delinquency and violence: Implications from the program of research on the causes and correlates of delinquency." Pp. 213–237 in James C. Howell, Barry Krisberg, J. David Hawkins, and John J. Wilson, eds., A Sourcebook: Serious, Violent, and Chronic Juvenile Offenders. Thousand Oaks, CA: Sage.

Thornberry, Terence P., and Marvin D. Krohn
2000 "The self-reporting method for measuring delinquency and crime." Pp. 33–83 in David Duffee, ed., Criminal Justice 2000, Volume 4: Measurement and Analysis of Crime and Justice. Washington, DC: National Institute of Justice.
2001 "The development of delinquency." Pp. 289–305 in Susan O. White, ed., Handbook of Youth and Justice. New York: Kluwer Academic/Plenum.
2003 Taking Stock of Delinquency. New York: Kluwer Academic/Plenum.

Thornberry, Terence P., and Marvin D. Krohn
2005 "Applying interactional theory to the explanation of continuity and change in antisocial behavior." Pp. 183–210 in David P. Farrington, ed., Integrated Developmental and Life-Course Theories of Offending. New Brunswich, NJ: Transaction.

Thornberry, Terence P., Marvin D. Krohn, Alan J. Lizotte, and Deborah Chard-Wierschem
1993 "The role of juvenile gangs in facilitating delinquent behavior." Journal of Research in Crime and Delinquency 30:55–87.

Thornberry, Terence P., Marvin D. Krohn, Alan J. Lizotte, Carolyn A. Smith, and Pamela K. Porter
2003 "Causes and consequences of delinquency: Findings from the Rochester youth development study." Pp. 11–46 in Terence P. Thornberry and Marvin D. Krohn, eds., Taking Stock of Delinquency. New York: Kluwer Academic/Plenum.

Thornberry, Terence P., Marvin D. Krohn, Alan J. Lizotte, Carolyn A. Smith, and Kimberly Tobin
2003 Gangs and Delinquency in Developmental Perspective. Cambridge, England: Cambridge University Press.

Thornberry, Terence P., Alan J. Lizotte, Marvin D. Krohn, Margaret Farnworth, and Sung Joon Jang
1991 "Testing interactional theory: An examination of reciprocal causal relationships among family, school, and delinquency." Journal of Criminal Law and Criminology 82:3–35.
1994 "Delinquent peers, beliefs, and delinquent behavior: A longitudinal test of interactional theory." Criminology 32:47–83.

Thornberry, Terence P., Melanie Moore, and R. L. Christenson
1985 "The effect of dropping out of high school on subsequent criminal behavior." Criminology 23: 3–18.

Thornberry, Terence P., Carolyn A. Smith, Craig Rivera, David Huizinga, and Magda Stouthamer-Loeber

1999 Family Disruption and Delinquency. Washington, DC: Office of Juvenile Justice and Delinquency Prevention.

Thornberry, Terence P., Evelyn H. Wei, Magda Stouthamer-Loeber, and Joyce Van Dyke

2000 Teenage Fatherhood and Delinquent Behavior. Washington, DC: Office of Juvenile Justice and Delinquency Prevention.

Thornton, Timothy N., Carole A. Craft, Linda L. Dahlberg, Barbara S. Lynch, and Katie Baer

2002 Best Practices of Youth Violence Prevention: A Sourcebook for Community Action. Atlanta, GA. Centers for Disease Control and Prevention.

Thrasher, Federic M.

1927 The Gang. Chicago: University of Chicago Press.

Tibbetts, Stephen G., and Chris L. Gibson

2002 "Individual propensities and rational decision-making: Recent findings and promising approaches." Pp. 3–24 in Alex R. Piquero and Stephen G. Tibbetts, eds., Rational Choice and Criminal Behavior. New York: Routledge.

Tibbetts, Stephen G., and Alex Piquero

1999 "The influence of gender, low birth weight, and disadvantaged environment in predicting early onset of offending: A test of Moffitt's interactional hypothesis." Criminology 37:843–878.

Tita, George, and Greg Ridgeway

2007 "The impact of gang formation on local patterns of crime." Journal of Research in Crime and Delinquency 44:208–237.

Titterington, Victoria E., and Kelly R. Damphousse

2003 "Economic correlates of racial and ethnic disparity in homicide: Houston, 1945–1994." Pp. 67–88 in Darnell F. Hawkins, ed., Violent Crime: Assessing Race and Ethic Differences. Cambridge, England: Cambridge University Press.

Tittle, Charles R.

1995 Control Balance: Toward a General Theory of Deviance. Boulder, CO: Westview.

2000 "Theoretical developments in criminology." Pp. 51–101 in Gary LaFree, ed., Criminal Justice 2000, Volume 1: The Nature of Crime: Continuity and Change. Washington, DC: National Institute of Justice.

Tittle, Charles R., Marty Jean Burke, and Elton F. Jackson

1986 "Modeling Sutherland's theory of differential association: Toward an empirical classification." Social Forces 65:405–432.

Tittle, Charles R., and Robert F. Meier

1990 "Specifying the sex/delinquency relationship." Criminology 28:271–299.

Tittle, Charles R., Wayne J. Villemez, and Douglas A. Smith

1978 "The myth of social class and criminality: An empirical assessment of the empirical evidence." American Sociological Review 43:643–656.

Tittle, Charles R., David A. Ward, and Harold G. Grosmick

2004 "Capacity for self-control and individuals' interest in exercising control." Journal of Quantitative Criminology 20:143–172.

Tittle, Charles R., and Michael R. Welch

1983 "Religiosity and deviance: Toward a contingency theory of constraining effects." Social Forces 61: 653–682.

Tjaden, Patricia, and Nancy Thoennes

1999 "Prevalence and incidence of violence against women: Findings from the National Violence Against Women survey." Criminologist 24(3):1, 4, 12, 14, 17–19.

Toby, Jackson

1957 "Social disorganization and stake in conformity: Complementary factors in the predatory behavior of hoodlums." Journal of Criminal Law, Criminology, and Police Science 48:12–17.

1995 "The schools." Pp. 141–170 in James Q. Wilson and Joan Petersilia, eds., Crime. Oakland, CA: ICS Press.

Tolan, Patrick
2002 "Crime Prevention: Focus on Youth." Pp. 109–127 in James Q. Wilson and Joan Petersilia, eds., Crime. Oakland, CA: ICS Press.

Tolan, Patrick H., and Deborah Gorman-Smith
1998 "Development of serious and violent offending careers." Pp. 68–85 in Rolf Loeber and David P. Farrington, eds., Serious and Violent Juvenile Offenders. Thousand Oaks, CA: Sage.

Tonry, Michael
1995 Malign Neglect. New York: Oxford University Press.

Topalli, Volkan
2005 "When being good is bad: An expansion of neutralization theory." Criminology 43:797–836.

Torbet, Patricia, Patrick Griffin, Hunter Hurst, Jr., and Lynn Ryan MacKenzie
2000 Juveniles Facing Criminal Sanctions: Three States That Changed the Rules. Washington, DC: Office of Juvenile Justice and Delinquency Prevention.

Torbet, Patricia, and Linda Szymanski
1998 State Legislative Responses to Violent Juvenile Crime: 1996–97 Update. Washington, DC: Office of Juvenile Justice and Delinquency Prevention.

Tracy, Paul E., Jr.
1990 "Prevalence, incidence, rates, and other descriptive measures." Pp. 51–77 in Kimberly Kempf, ed., Measurement Issues in Criminology. New York: Springer-Verlag.
2005 "Race, ethnicity, and juvenile justice." Pp. 300–350 in Darnell F. Hawkins and Kimberly Kempf-Leonard, eds., Our Children, Their Children. Chicago: University of Chicago Press.

Tracy, Paul E., Jr., Marvin E. Wolfgang, and Robert M. Figlio
1990 Delinquency Careers in Two Birth Cohorts. New York: Plenum.

Traver, Marsha, Steve Walker, and Harvey Wallace
2002 Multicultural Issues in the Criminal Justice System. Boston: Allyn and Bacon.

Tremblay, Richard E., and Wendy M. Craig
1995 "Developmental Crime Prevention." Crime and Justice 19:151–236.

Triplett, Ruth A.
1996 "The growing threat: Gangs and juvenile offenders." Pp. 137–150 in Timothy J. Flanagan and Dennis R. Longmire, ed., Americans View Crime and Justice. Thousand Oaks, CA: Sage.

Triplett, Ruth A., and G. Roger Jarjoura
1994 "Theoretical and empirical specification of a model of informal labeling." Journal of Quantitative Criminology 10:241–276.

Trojanowicz, Robert, Victor E. Kappeler, Larry K. Gaines, and Bonnie Bucqueroux
1998 Community Policing: A Contemporary Perspective. Cincinnati, OH: Anderson.

Turner, C. F., L. Ku, S. M. Rogers, L. D. Lindberg, J. H. Pleck, and F. L. Sonenstein
1998 "Adolescent sexual behavior, drug use and violence: Increased reporting with computer survey technology." Science 280:867–873.

Tygart, C. E.
1991 "Juvenile delinquency and number of children in a family." Youth and Society 22:525–536.

Udry, J. Richard
2000 "Biological limits of gender construction." American Sociological Review 65:443–457.

UNICEF
2007 Child Poverty in Perspective. Florence: UNICEF Innocenti Research Center.

Unnever, James D., Francis T. Cullen, and Travis C. Pratt
2003 "Parental management, ADHD, and delinquent involvement: Reassessing Gottfredson and Hirschi's general theory." Justice Quarterly 20:471–500.

Unnithan, N. Prabha
2006 "Asian Americans and juvenile justice." Pp. 65–66 in Everette B. Penn, Helen Taylor Greene, and Shaun L. Gabbidon, eds., Race and Juvenile Justice. Durham, NC: Carolina Academic Press.

U.S. Department of Education and Office of Justice Programs
2006 Indicators of School Crime and Safety 2006. Washington, DC: U.S. Government Printing Office.

U.S. Department of Education and Office of Juvenile Justice and Delinquency Prevention
1996 Creating Safe and Drug-Free Schools: An Action Guide. Washington, DC: U.S. Government Printing Office.

U.S. Department of Health and Human Services
2001 Youth Violence Prevention: A Report of the Surgeon General. Rockville, MD: U.S. Department of Health and Human Services.

Van Voorhis, Patricia, Francis T. Cullen, Richard A. Mathers, and Connie Chenoweth Garner
1988 "The impact of family structure and quality on delinquency: A comparative assessment of structural and functional factors." Criminology 26:235–261.

Vander Ven, Thomas, and Francis T. Cullen
2004 "The impact of maternal employment on serious youth crime." Crime and Delinquency 50:272–291.

Vander Ven, Thomas M., Francis T. Cullen, Mark A. Corrozza, and John Paul Wright
2001 "Home alone: The impact of maternal employment on delinquency." Social Problems 48:236–257.

Vander Waal, Curtis J., Duane C. McBride, Yvonne M. Terry-McElrath, and Holly Van Buren
2001 Breaking the Juvenile Drug-Crime Cycle: A Guide for Practitioners and Policymakers. Washington, DC: Office of Justice Programs.

Vaz, Edmund W.
1967 "Juvenile delinquency in the middle class youth culture." Pp. 131–147 in Edmund W. Vaz, ed., Middle-Class Juvenile Delinquency. New York: Harper and Row.

Vazsonyi, Alexander T., Lloyd E. Pickering, Lara M. Belliston, Dick Hessing, and Marianne Junger
2002 "Routine activities and deviant behaviors: American, Dutch, Hungarian, and Swiss youth." Journal of Quantitative Criminology 18:397–422.

Velez, Maria B.
2001 "The role of public social control in urban neighborhoods: A multi-level analysis of victimization risk." Criminology 39:837–864.
2006 "Toward an understanding of the lower rates of homicide in Latino versus black neighborhoods: A look at Chicago." Pp. 91–107 in Ruth D. Peterson, Lauren J. Krivo, and John Hagan, eds., The Many Colors of Crime. New York: New York University Press.

Velez, Maria B., Lauren J. Krivo, and Ruth D. Peterson
2003 "Structural inequality and homicide." Criminology 41:645–672.

Veysey, Bonita M., and Steven F. Messner
1999 "Further testing of social disorganization theory: An elaboration of Sampson and Grove's 'community structure and crime.'" Journal of Research in Crime and Delinquency 36:156–174.

Vieraitis, Lynne M., Tomislav V. Kovandzic, and Thomas B. Marvell
2007 "The criminogenic effects of imprisonment." Criminology and Public Policy 6:589–624.

Vigil, James Diego, and Steve C. Yun
1996 "Southern California gangs: Comparative ethnicity and social control." Pp. 139–156 in C. Ronald Huff, ed., Gangs in America. Thousand Oaks, CA: Sage.

Vila, Bryan
1994 "A general paradigm for understanding criminal behavior: Extending evolutionary ecological theory." Criminology 32:311–359.

Visher, Christy A.
2000 "Career offenders and crime control." Pp. 601–619 in Joseph H. Sheley, ed., Criminology. Belmont, CA: Wadsworth.

Vold, George B., Thomas J. Bernard, and Jeffrey B. Snipes
2001 Theoretical Criminology. New York: Oxford University Press.

Von Zielbauer, Paul
2003 "The American agenda for fighting crime: More prison time . . . and less." New York Times, September 28, A25.

Wacquant, L. D., and William J. Wilson
1989 "The costs of racial and class exclusion in the inner city." Annals of the American Academy of Political and Social Science 501:8–25.

Wadsworth, Ted
2000 Labor markets, delinquency, and social control theory: An empirical assessment of the mediating processes. Social Forces 78:1041–1066.

Walker, Elaine, and Daniel Romer
2006 Adolescent Psychopathology and the Developing Brain. New York: Oxford University Press.

Walker, Samuel
1998 Sense and Nonsense About Crime and Drugs. Belmont, CA: West/Wadsworth.

Walker, Samuel, Cassia Spohn, and Miriam DeLone
2004 The Color of Justice. Belmont, CA: Wadsworth.

Wallace, Harvey
2005 Family Violence. Boston: Allyn and Bacon.

Wallace, John M., Jr., Ryoka Yamaguchi, Jerald G. Bachman, Patrick M. O'Malley, John E. Schulenberg, and Lloyd D. Johnston
2007 "Religiosity and adolescent substance use." Social Problems 54:308–327.

Wallace, Lisa Hutchinson, Justin W. Patchin, and Jeff D. May
2005 "Reactions of victimized youth: Strain as an explanation of school delinquency." Western Criminology Review 6:104–116.

Walsh, Anthony
2002 Biosocial Criminology. Cincinnati, OH: Anderson.

Wang, C. T., and D. Daro
1998 Current Trends in Child Abuse Reporting and Fatalities: The Results of the 1997 Annual Fifty State Survey. Chicago: Prevent Child Abuse America.

Ward, David A., and Charles R. Tittle
1993 "Deterrence or labeling: The effects of informal sanctions." Deviant Behavior 14:43–64.

Warner, Barbara D.
2003 "The role of attenuated culture in social disorganization theory." Criminology 41:73–98.
2007 "Directly intervene or call the authorities?" Criminology 45:99–130.

Warner, Barbara D., and Shannon K. Fowler
2003 "Strain and violence: Testing a general strain theory model of community violence." Journal of Criminal Justice 31:511–521.

Warr, Mark
1993 "Age, peers, and delinquency." Criminology 31:17–40.
1996 "Organization and instigation in delinquent groups." Criminology 34:11–37.
1998 "Life-course transitions and desistance from crime." Criminology 36:183–216.
2002 Companions in Crime. Cambridge, England: Cambridge University Press.
2005 "Making delinquent friends: Adult supervision and children's affiliations." Criminology 43:77–106.

Warr, Mark, and Mark Stafford
1991 "The influence of delinquent peers: What they think or what they do?" Criminology 29:851–866.

Wasserman, Gail A., and Laurie S. Miller
1998 "The prevention of serious and violent juvenile offending." Pp. 197–247 in Rolf Loeber and David P. Farrington, eds., Serious and Violent Juvenile Offenders. Thousand Oaks, CA: Sage.

Watamura, Sarah E., Bonny Donzella, Jan Alwin, and Megan R. Gunnar
2003 "Morning-to-afternoon increases in cortisol concentrations for infants and toddlers at child care: Age differences and behavioral correlates." Child Development 74:1006–1020.

Watkins, Adam M.
2005 "Examining the disparity between juvenile and adult victims in notifying the police." Journal of Research in Crime and Delinquency 42:333–353.

Weber, Rene, Ute Ritlerfeld, and Anna Kostygina
2006 "Aggression and violence as effects of playing violent video games." Pp. 347–361 in Peter Vorderer and Jennings Bryant, eds., Playing Violent Video Games. Mahwah, NJ: Lawrence Erlbaum.

Weerman, Frank M., and Wilma M. Smeenk
2005 "Peer similarity in delinquency for different types of friends." Criminology 43:499–524.

Weis, Joseph G.

1986 "Issues in the measurement of criminal careers." Pp. 1–51 in Alfred Blumstein, Jacqueline Cohen, Jeffrey A. Roth, and Christy A. Visher, eds., Criminal Careers and Career Criminals, Volume 2. Washington, DC: National Academy Press.

1987 "Social class and crime." Pp. 71–90 in Michael Gottfredson and Travis Hirschi, eds., Positive Criminology. Newbury Park, CA: Sage.

Weisburd, David

2000 "Randomized experiments in criminal justice policy: Prospects and problems." Crime and Delinquency 46:181–193.

Weisburd, David, and John E. Eck

2004 "What can police do to reduce crime, disorder, and fear?" Annals of the American Academy of Political and Social Science 593:42–65.

Weisburd, David, Stephen D. Mastrofski, Ann Marie McNally, Rosann Greenspan, and James J. Willis

2003 "Reforming to preserve: COMPSTAT and strategic problem solving in American policing." Criminology and Public Policy 3:421–456.

Weisburd, David, Laura A. Wyckoff, Justin Ready, John E. Eck, Joshua C. Hinkle, and Frank Gajewski

2006 "Does crime just move around the corner? A controlled study of spatial displacement and diffusion of crime control benefits." Criminology 44:549–592.

Weishew, Nancy L., and Samuel S. Peng

1993 "Variables predicting students' problem behaviors." Journal of Educational Research 87:5–17.

Weiss, C. H.

1998 Evaluation. Englewood Cliffs, NJ: Prentice-Hall.

Weissbourd, Richard

1996 The Vulnerable Child. Reading, MA: Addison-Wesley.

Wells, Edward L., and Joseph H. Rankin

1988 "Direct parental controls and delinquency." Criminology 26:263–284.

1991 "Families and delinquency: A meta-analysis of the impact of broken homes." Social Problems 38: 71–93.

1995 "Juvenile victimization: Convergent validation of alternative measurements." Journal of Research in Crime and Delinquency 32:287–307.

Wells, William, and Julie Horney

2002 "Weapon effects and individual intent to do harm: Influences on the escalation of violence." Criminology 40:265–296.

Welsh, Brandon C., David P. Farrington, and Lawrence W. Sherman

2001 Costs and Benefits of Crime Prevention. Boulder, CO: Westview.

Welsh, Brandon C., and Akemi Hoshi

2002 "Communities and crime prevention." Pp. 165–197 in Lawrence W. Sherman, David P. Farrington, Brandon C. Welsh, and Doris Layton MacKenzie, eds., Evidence-Based Crime Prevention. London: Routledge.

Welsh, Wayne N., Jack R. Greene, and Patricia H. Jenkins

1999 "School disorder: The influence of individual, institutional, and community factors." Criminology 37:73–116.

Welsh, Wayne N., Patricia H. Jenkins, and Philip W. Harris

1999 "Reducing minority overrepresentation in juvenile justice: Results of community-based delinquency prevention in Harrisburg." Journal of Research in Crime and Delinquency 36:87–110.

Welsh, Wayne N., Robert Stokes, and Jack R. Greene

2000 "A macro-level model of school disorder." Journal of Research in Crime and Delinquency 37:243–283.

Welte, John W., Lening Zhang, and William F. Wieczorek

2001 "The effects of substance use on specific types of criminal offending in young men." Journal of Research in Crime and Delinquency 38:416–438.

White, Garland

1999 "Crime and the decline of manufacturing, 1970–1990." Justice Quarterly 16:81–97.

White, Helene Raskin, and D. M. Gorman
2000 "Dynamics of the drug-crime relationship." Pp. 151–218 in Gary LaFree, ed., The Nature of Crime: Continuity and Change, Criminal Justice 2000, Volume 1. Washington, DC: National Institute of Justice.

White, Helene Raskin, and Stephen Hansell
1996 "The moderating effects of gender and hostility on the alcohol-aggression relationship." Journal of Research in Crime and Delinquency 33:450–470.

White, Helene Raskin, and Erich W. Labouvie
1994 "Generality versus specificity of problem behavior: Psychological and functional differences." Journal of Drug Issues 24:55–74.

White, Helene Raskin, Erich W. Labouvie, and Marsha E. Bates
1985 "The relationship between sensation seeking and delinquency: A longitudinal analysis." Journal of Research in Crime and Delinquency 22:197–211.

White, Helene Raskin, Robert J. Pandina, and Randy L. LaGrange
1987 "Longitudinal predictors of serious substance use and delinquency." Criminology 25:715–740.

White, Helene Raskin, Peter C. Tice, Rolf Loeber, and Magda Stouthamer-Loeber
2002 "Illegal acts committed by adolescents under the influence of alcohol and drugs." Journal of Research in Crime and Delinquency 39:131–152.

White, Jennifer L., Terrie E. Moffitt, Avshalom Caspi, Dawn Jeglum Bartusch, Douglas J. Needles, and Magda Stouthamer-Loeber
1994 "Measuring impulsivity and examining its relationship to delinquency." Journal of Abnormal Psychology 103:192–205.

Whitted, Kathryn S., and David R. Dupper
2005 "Best practices for preventing or reducing bullying in schools." Children and Schools 27:167–175.

Wiatrowski, Michael D., and Kristine L. Anderson
1987 "The dimensionality of the social bond." Journal of Quantitative Criminology 3:65–81.

Wiatrowski, Michael D., David B. Griswold, and Mary K. Roberts
1981 "Social control theory and delinquency." American Sociological Review 46:525–541.

Wiatrowski, Michael D., Stephen Hansell, Charles R. Massey, and David L. Wilson
1982 "Curriculum tracking and delinquency." American Sociological Review 47:151–160.

Widom, Cathy Spatz
1989 "Does violence beget violence? A critical examination of the literature." Psychological Bulletin 106: 3–28.
1997 "Child abuse, neglect, and witnessing violence." Pp. 159–170 in D. M. Stoff, J. Breiling, and J. D. Maser, eds., Handbook of Antisocial Behavior. New York: Wiley.
2001 "Child abuse and neglect." Pp. 31–48 in Susan O. White, ed., Handbook of Youth and Justice. New York: Kluwer Academic.

Widom, Cathy Spatz, and Ashley Ames
1988 "Biology and female crime." Pp. 308–331 in Terrie E. Moffitt and Sarnoff A. Mednick (eds.), Biological Contributions to Crime Causation. Dordrecht, The Netherlands: Martinus Nijhoff.

Wiebush, Richard G., Christopher Baird, Barry Krisberg, and David Onek
1995 "Risk assessment and classification for serious, violent, and chronic juvenile offenders." Pp. 171–212 in James C. Howell, Barry Krisberg, J. David Hawkins, and John J. Wilson, eds., A Sourcebook: Serious, Violent, and Chronic Juvenile Offenders. Thousand Oaks, CA: Sage.

Wiebush, Richard G., Betsie McNulty, and Thao Le
2000 Implementation of the Intensive Community-Based Aftercare Program. Washington, DC: Office of Juvenile Justice and Delinquency Prevention.

Wiebush, Richard G., Dennis Wagner, Betsie McNulty, Yanging Wang, and Thao N. Le
2005 Implementation and Outcome Evaluation of the Intensive Aftercare Program. Washington, DC: Office of Juvenile Justice and Delinquency Prevention.

Wiesner, Margit, and Deborah M. Capaldi
2003 "Relations of childhood and adolescent factors to offending trajectories of young men." Journal of Research in Crime and Delinquency 40:231–262.

Wikstrom, Per-Olof H., and Rolf Loeber
2000 "Do disadvantaged neighborhoods cause well-adjusted children to become adolescent delinquents? A study of male juvenile serious offending, individual risk and protective factors, and neighborhood context." Criminology 38:1109–1142.

Wilcox, Pamela, Kenneth C. Land, and Scott A. Hunt
2003 Criminal Circumstance. New York: Aldine de Gruyter.

Wilcox, Pamela, David C. May, and Staci D. Roberts
2006 "Student weapon possession and the 'fear of victimization hypothesis.'" Justice Quarterly 23:502–529.

Wilkinson, Deanna L.
2002 "Decision making in violent events among adolescent males: An examination of sparks and other motivational factors." Pp. 163–196 in Alex R. Piquero and Stephen G. Tibbetts, eds., Rational Choice and Criminal Behavior. New York: Routledge.
2003 Guns, Violence, and Identity Among African American and Latino Youth. New York: LFB Scholarly Publishing.
2007 "Local social ties and willingness to intervene: Textured views among violent urban youth of neighborhood social control dynamics and situations." Justice Quarterly 24:185–220.

Williams, Carolyn L., and Craig Uchiyama
1989 "Assessment of life events during adolescence: The use of self-report inventories." Adolescence 24:95–118.

Williams, Kirk R., and Richard Hawkins
1986 "Perceptual research on general deterrence: A critical review." Law and Society Review 20:545–572.

Williams, Nicolas, Francis T. Cullen, and John Paul Wright
1996 "Labor market participation and youth crime: The neglect of working in delinquency research." Social Pathology 2:195–217.

Willis, James J., Stephen D. Mastrofski, and David Weisburd
2004 "COMPSTAT and bureaucracy." Justice Quarterly 21:463–496.

Wilson, David B., Denise C. Gottfredson, and Stacy S. Najaka
2001 "School-based prevention of problem behaviors: A meta-analysis." Journal of Quantitative Criminology 17:247–272.

Wilson, James Q.
1976 Varieties of Police Behavior. New York: Atheneum.

Wilson, James Q., and Richard Herrnstein
1985 Crime and Human Nature. New York: Simon and Schuster.

Wilson, James Q., and George L. Kelling
1982 "Broken windows: Police and neighborhood safety." Atlantic Monthly 249 (March):29–38.

Wilson, Sandra Jo, Mark W. Lipsey, and James H. Derzon
2003 "The effects of school-based intervention programs on aggressive behavior." Journal of Consulting and Clinical Psychology 71:136–149.

Wilson, William Julius
1987 The Truly Disadvantaged. Chicago: University of Chicago Press.
1996 When Work Disappears. Chicago: University of Chicago Press.

Winfree, L. Thomas, Jr., Terrance J. Taylor, Ni He, and Finn-Aage Eshensen
2006 "Self-control and variability over time: Multivariate results using a 5-year, multisite panel of youths." Crime and Delinquency 52:253–286.

Wintemute, Garen J.
2006 "Guns and gun violence." Pp. 45–96 in Alfred Blumstein and Joel Wallman, eds., The Crime Drop in America. New York: Cambridge University Press.

Winters, Ken C.
2007 Treatment of Adolescents with Substance Abuse Disorders. Rockville, MD: U.S. Department of Health and Human Services.

Wolfgang, Marvin E., and Franco Ferracuti
1982 The Subculture of Violence. Beverly Hills, CA: Sage.

Wolfgang, Marvin E., Robert M. Figlio, and Thorsten Sellin
1972 Delinquency in a Birth Cohort. Chicago: University of Chicago Press.

Wood, Peter B., Walter R. Gove, James A. Wilson, and John K. Cochran
1997 "Nonsocial reinforcement and habitual criminal conduct: An extension of learning theory." Criminology 35:335–366.

Wood, Peter B., Betty Pfefferbaum, and Bruce J. Arneklev
1993 "Risk-taking and self-control: Social psychological correlates of delinquency." Journal of Crime and Justice 16:111–130.

Wooden, Wayne S., and Randy Blazak
2001 Renegade Kids, Suburban Outlaws. Belmont, CA: Wadsworth.

Wooldredge, John, and Amy Thistlethwaite
2002 "Reconsidering domestic violence recidivism: Conditional effects of legal controls by individual and aggregate levels of stake in conformity." Journal of Quantitative Criminology 18:45–70.

Wordes, Madeline, and Timothy S. Bynum
1995 "Policing juveniles: Is there bias against youths of color?" Pp. 47–65 in Kimberly Kempf-Leonard, Carl E. Pope, and William H. Feyerherm, eds., Minorities in Juvenile Justice. Thousand Oaks, CA: Sage.

Worrall, John L., and Tomislav V. Kovandzic
2007 "COPS grants and crime revisited." Criminology 45:159–190.

Wright, Bradley R. Entner, Avshalom Caspi, Terrie E. Moffitt, Richard A. Meich, and Phil A. Silva
1999a "Reconsidering the relationship between sex and delinquency: Causation but not correlation." Criminology 37:175–194.

Wright, Bradley R. E., Avshalom Caspi, Terrie E. Moffitt, and Ray Paternoster
2004 "Does the perceived risk of punishment deter criminally prone individuals?" Journal of Research in Crime and Delinquency 41:180–213.

Wright, Bradley R. Entner, Avshalom Caspi, Terrie E. Moffitt, and Phil A. Silva
1999b "Low self-control, social bonds, and crime: Social causation, social selection, or both?" Criminology 37:479–514.
2001 "The effects of social ties on crime vary by criminal propensity: A life-course model of interdependence." Criminology 39:321–352.

Wright, James D., and Timothy Brezina
2001 "Free will and Deviance." Pp. 102–4 in Clifton Bryant, ed., Encyclopedia of Criminology and Deviant Behavior, Volume 1. Philadelphia, PA: Brunner Routledge.

Wright, James D., Joseph F. Sheley, and M. Dwayne Smith
1992 "Kids, guns, and killing fields." Society 30:84–89.

Wright, James D., and Teri E. Vail
2000 "The guns-crime connection." Pp. 577–599 in Joseph F. Sheley, ed., Criminology: A Contemporary Handbook. Belmont, CA: Wadsworth.

Wright, John Paul, and Kevin M. Beaver
2005 "Do parents matter in creating self-control in their children?" Criminology 43:1169–1202.

Wright, John Paul, and Francis T. Cullen
2000 "Juvenile involvement in occupational delinquency." Criminology 38:863–896.
2001 "Parental efficacy and delinquent behavior: Do control and support matter?" Criminology 39:707–736.

Wright, John Paul, Francis T. Cullen, Robert Agnew, and Timothy Brezina
2001 "The root of all evil: An exploratory study of money and delinquent involvement." Justice Quarterly 18:239–268.

Wright, John Paul, Francis T. Cullen, and Nicolas Williams
1997 "Working while in school and delinquent involvement: Implications for social policy." Crime and Delinquency 43:203–221.

Wright, Kevin N., and Karen E. Wright
1995 Family Life, Delinquency, and Crime: A Policymaker's Guide. Washington, DC: Office of Juvenile Justice and Delinquency Prevention.

Wright, Richard A.
1994 In Defense of Prisons. Westport, CT: Greenwood.

Wright, Richard T., and Scott Decker
1997 Armed Robbers in Action. Boston: Northeastern University Press.

Wu, Ping, and Denise B. Kandel
1995 "The role of mothers and fathers in intergenerational behavioral transmission: The case of smoking and delinquency." Pp. 49–81 in Howard B. Kaplan, ed., Drugs, Crime, and Other Deviant Adaptations. New York: Plenum.

Yoder, Kevin A., Les B. Whitbeck, and Dan R. Hoyt
2003 "Gang involvement and membership among homeless and runaway youth." Youth and Society 34: 441–467.

Xu, Yili, Mora L. Fiedler, and Karl H. Flaming
2005 "Discovering the impact of community policing." Journal of Research in Crime and Delinquency 42: 147–186.

Yoshikawa, Hirokazu
1994 "Prevention as cumulative protection: Effects of early family support and education on chronic delinquency and its risks." Psychological Bulletin 115:28–54.

Yu, Jiang, and Allen E. Liska
1993 "The certainty of punishment: A reference group effect and its functional form." Criminology 31: 447–464.

Zatz, Marjorie S.
1987 "The changing forms of racial/ethnic biases in sentencing." Journal of Research in Crime and Delinquency 24:69–92.

Zawitz, Marianne W.
1995 "Guns used in crime: Firearms, crime, and criminal justice." Washington, DC: Bureau of Justice Statistics.

Zhang, Lening, and Steven F. Messner
2000 "The effects of alternative measures of delinquent peers on self-reported delinquency." Journal of Research in Crime and Delinquency 37:323–337.

Zhang, Lening, William F. Wieczorek, and John W. Welte
1997 "The impact of age of onset of substance use on delinquency." Journal of Research in Crime and Delinquency 34:253–268.

Zhang, Lening, and Sheldon Zhang
2004 "Reintegrative shaming and predatory delinquency." Journal of Research in Crime and Delinquency 41:433–453.

Zhang, Quauwu, Rolf Loeber, and Magda Stouthamer-Loeber
1997 "Developmental trends of delinquent attitudes and behaviors: Replications and synthesis across domains, time, and samples." Journal of Quantitative Criminology 13:181–215.

Zhao, Jihong Solomon, Ni He, and Nicholas P. Lovrich
2003 "Community policing: Did it change the basic functions of policing in the 1990s? A national follow-up study." Justice Quarterly 20:697–724.

Zhao, Jihong Solomon, Matthew C. Scheider, and Quint Thurman
2002 "Funding community policing to reduce crime: Have COPS grants made a difference?" Criminology and Public Policy 2:7–32.

Zigler, Edward, Cara Taussig, and Kathryn Black
1992 "Early childhood intervention: A promising preventative for juvenile delinquency." American Psychologist 47:997–1006.

Zimring, Franklin E.
1998 American Youth Violence. New York: Oxford University Press.

2005 American Juvenile Justice. New York: Oxford University Press.
2007 The Great American Crime Decline. New York: Oxford University Press.

Zimring, Franklin E., and Gordon Hawkins
1995 Incapacitation: Penal Confinement and the Restraint of Crime. New York: Oxford University Press.
1997 Crime Is Not the Problem: Lethal Violence in America. New York: Oxford University Press.

Zingraff, Matthew T., Jeffrey Leiter, Matthew C. Johnsen, and Kristen A. Myers
1994 "The mediating effect of good school performance on the maltreatment-delinquency relationship." Journal of Research in Crime and Delinquency 31:62–91.

Zingraff, Matthew T., Jeffrey Leiter, Kristen A. Meyers, and Matthew C. Johnsen
1993 "Child maltreatment and youthful problem behavior." Criminology 31:173–202.

Photo Credits

Name Index

Subject Index